HIPPOCRENE STANDARD DICTIONARY

PULAAR-ENGLISH/
ENGLISH-PULAAR

T0275309

HIPPOCRENE STANDARD DICTIONARY

PULAAR-ENGLISH/ ENGLISH-PULAAR

Mamadou Niang

HIPPOCRENE BOOKS
New York

For information, address:
HIPPOCRENE BOOKS, INC.
171 Madison Avenue
New York, NY 10016

Library of Congress Cataloging-in-Publication Data
Niang, Mamadou Ousmane.
    Pulaar-English/English-Pulaar / Mamadou Niang.
        p.   cm. -- (Hippocrene standard dictionary)
    Includes bibliographical references.
    ISBN 0-7818-0479-5
    1. Pular dialect--Dictionaries--English.   2. English language-
    -Dictionaries--Pular.   I. Title.   II. Series
    PL8184.Z9P85656   1997
    496'.322--dc21   97-24082
                                                           CIP
Printed in the United States of America.

Dedicated to
my parents, family and friends
with love, respect and gratitude

CONTENTS

ACKNOWLEDGMENTS

I am greatly indebted to a number of people whose contributions and support played a major role in the making of this dictionary. I am grateful to Professor Ladislav Zgusta for his valuable advice and recommendations, Dr. Ba Oumar whose research and feedback were highly valuable to this dictionary, Dean James R. Durig for his support that helped resolve many shortcomings concerning data collection and computer equipment, the Department of Linguistics of Kansas University at Lawrence for their valuable suggestions. I am greatly indebted to my wife, Michelle, for her support, understanding and patience, Hippocrene Books Inc, for editing and publishing this dictionary. Finally, my deepest gratitude goes to my parents, brothers, sisters and friends for their love, their sacrifices and their support.

BACKGROUND NOTES

This Pulaar-English/English-Pulaar Dictionary, a five year-old project, is intended to serve as a tool for the obvious needs of students, teachers, and researchers. It contains over 30,000 entries. The data is fairly extensive and the transcription conforms to the recognized standard. Grammatical features, pronunciation, etymology and usage have been incorporated in this study which aims at addressing inadequacies typical of African language dictionaries.

MOTIVATIONS FOR A PULAAR-ENGLISH/ ENGLISH-PULAAR DICTIONARY

Various reasons may be invoked to motivate the making of a Pulaar-English/English-Pulaar Dictionary. The three major compelling reasons behind the making of this dictionary relate to the importance of Fula and the Pulaar dialect, the lack of an adequate Pulaar-English/English-Pulaar dictionary, and the need for adequate research and teaching tools for researchers, teachers and learners.

Importance of Fula and Pulaar
Pulaar is a dialect of Fula, a major African language both in its geographical distribution and number of speakers. Fula is spoken in Western, Eastern and Central Africa by over 25 million speakers. In addition to Africa, major concentrations of Fula speakers can be found in Europe and America. At the African Language Conference held in 1979 in Michigan, Fula was not only ranked high following the priority criteria utilized (i.e. -number of speakers; -political, cultural and social importance; -importance for US national interests) but it was also included in Group A Languages (Highest Priority).

Lack of Adequate Pulaar dictionaries
I am unaware of the existence of a Pulaar-English/English-Pulaar dictionary. Even though some lexica involving either Pulaar or other dialects of Fula may be found (Arnott 1932, 1955; Ba 1968, 1972, 1980; Gaden 1967, 1969, 1972; Gamble 1958, 1981; Ly 1986; Osborne 1993), these fall short of the expectations. They are very limited as far as content is concerned, and the transcription used in these reference materials is not consistent with the recognized transcription. Many features concerning the pronunciation of lexical items are omitted in these previous works, which may cause misunderstandings. Usage, an important feature in dictionaries, tends to be ignored in these lexica. Despite the wide orientation of the scope of the dictionary, the work is constrained by the very nature of dictionary making itself and space constraints.

Researchers, Learners and Teachers's needs
In addition to being taught in numerous institutions throughout the world, Pulaar has been the subject of research by various scholars and important large scale research is still being conducted. This project provides adequate tools for the obvious needs of these millions of speakers, students, and researchers.

SOURCES

Part of the data came from sources in the USA, Canada, the Bibliotheque Nationale in Paris and Institutes of National Languages in Mauritania, Senegal, Mali, Burkina Faso, and Niger. Additional data came from native speakers' input, and radio and TV broadcast materials. The data collection was drastically complicated by the unavailability or scarcity of sources. In addition to the lack of sources, there is no adequate networking among researchers on Fula. Various research projects are being undertaken here and there but many individuals outside these projects are not aware of their existence. For this reason, related or similar projects are being undertaken without consultation.

DIALECTAL DECISIONS

Fula, like any other language, has various dialects, the number of which cannot easily be ascertained as a systematic study of Fula dialects and their delimitation is yet to be conducted. None of the dialects has been standardized. This dictionary deals with the Pulaar dialect spoken essentially in Mauritania, Senegal, and The Gambia. Even though this project deals with Pulaar, it includes variations from other dialects. The Pulaar dialect is not uniform and variations can be observed in certain areas. Even though these variations are minor in most cases, they are noted in the entries, a strategy motivated by the fact that this dictionary attempts to target all areas where Pulaar is spoken and inform research.

ENTRY STRUCTURE

Entries in this dictionary are not structured around the root system approach. This decision is motivated by considerations pertaining to shortcomings associated with this approach. These shortcomings relate to the difficulty in determining the shape of the root, dialectal variations, the extensive use of coreference, morphological and semantic considerations. Unlike other lexica which attempt to organize the entries around a root format, the organization of entries in this dictionary is conducted on a semantic field basis. Related forms are grouped together without specification of the form of the root itself.

CATEGORIAL CORRESPONDENCE

As suggested in the lexicographic literature (Landau, 1993), a major attempt has been undertaken to consistently translate a category in the source language with the same category in the target language; i.e. a noun to a noun correspondence, a verb to a verb correspondence. Despite this attempt, in a number of instances, this categorial correspondence could not always be observed due to restrictions on the target language. Indeed, even though an adjective in English may be translated as an adjective in Pulaar, in many instances an English adjective must be translated by various adjectival forms. For example, the adjective "big" in English may be translated with the Pulaar adjectives *mawɗo, mawba, mawngu, mawɗe, mawnde, mawndu, mawngal, mawɗi, mawɓe, mawndi, mawnge, mawka, mawki, mawko* depending on the class of the referent. In addition, an English adjective may be translated into a relative clause (i.e. hesitant *mo fellitaani*), a noun (i.e. racial *leñamleñaagu*), a noun and an adverb (i.e. quotidian *ñande kala*).

PRONUNCIATION

The same transcription is used for both Pulaar-English and English-Pulaar sections. In both sections, the transcription is provided for the main entry only. In the Pulaar-English section, in order to avoid repetitions, the transcription of the main entry is provided only when assimilation is involved as in "*fotde*" pronounced [*fodde*]. A gap in the following inventory indicates the absence of the particular sound in the language under consideration.

VOWEL SOUNDS

English	Pulaar	
[iy] as in feet [fiyt]	[ii] as in wiisde	[wiisde]
[i] as in fit [fit]	[i] as in wisde	[wisde]
[ɨ] as in roses [rozɨz]		
[ey] as in wait [weyt]		
[e] as in wet [wet]	[e] as in welde	[welde]
	[ee] as in weelde	[weelde]
	[é] as in céli	[céli]
	[éé] as in cééli	[cééli]
[a] as in fat [fat]	[a] as in amde	[amde]
[ɑ] as in father [fɑðə]	[aa] as in aamde	[aamde]
[ay] as in bite [bayt]		
[aw] as in out [awt]		
[o] as oi sow [sow]	[o] as in towde	[towde]
	[oo] as in toowde	[toowde]
	[ó] as in ɓólél	[ɓólél]
	[óó] as in ɓóólél]	[ɓóólél]
[ow] as in boat [bowt]		
[ɔ] as in bought [bɔt]		
[oy] as in boil [boil]		
[u] as in put [put]	[u] as in	[urde]
[uw] as in boot [buwt]	[uu] as in	[uurde]
[ʌ] as in but [bʌt]		
[ə] as in better [betə]		
[ɚ] as in bird [bɚd]		

CONSONANTAL SOUNDS

English		Pulaar	
[p] as in pen	[pen]	[p] as in paaka	[paaka]
[b] as in bag	[bag]	[b] as in bata	[bata]
		[ɓ] as in ɓalal	[ɓalal]
[t] as in ten	[ten]	[t] as in tata	[tata]
[d] as in do	[du]	[d] as in daga	[daga]
		[ɗ] as in ɗaɗól	[ɗaɗól]
[k] as in kit	[kit	[k] as in kawle	[kawle]

xi

English		Pulaar	
[g] as in go	[gow]	[g] as in gacce	[gacce]
[m] as in meat	[miyt]	[m] as in mata	[mata]
		[ᵐb] as in mbaalu	[ᵐbaalu]
[n] as in no	[now]	[n] as in nay	[nay]
		[ⁿd] as in ndiwri	[ⁿdiwri]
		[ⁿj] as in njawdi	[ⁿjawdi]
		[ŋ] as in ŋari	[ŋari]
[f] as in foot	[fuwt]	[f] as in faɗo	[faɗo]
[v] as in vase	[veyz]		
[Θ] as in thin	[Θin]		
[ð] as in then	[ðen]		
[s] as in sin	[sin]	[s] as in sago	[sago]
[z] as in zone	[zown]		
[ʒ] as in rouge	[ruwʒ]		
[l] as in late	[leyt]	[l] as in leeso	[leeso]
[š] as in show	[šow]		
[č] as in chin	[čin]	[č] as in cakka	[čakka]
[r] as in rim	[rim]	[r] as in raayre	[raayre]
[h] as in hit	[hit]	[h] as in haala	[haala]
[j] as in jot	[jot]	[j] as in jalo	[jalo]
[y] as in yet	[yet]	[y] as in yeeso	[yeeso]
		[ɣ] as in ɣero	[ɣero]
[w] as in wet	[wet]	[w] as in wafdu	[wafdu]
		[ʔ] as in haʔay	[haʔay]

NUMERALS

CARDINAL NUMBERS

	English	Pulaar
1	one	góó
2	two	ɗiɗi
3	three	tati
4	four	nay
5	five	jóy
6	six	jeegom (jóy e goo)
7	seven	jééɗiɗi (jóy e ɗiɗi)
8	eight	jeetati (jóy e tati)
9	nine	jeenay (jóy e nay)
10	ten	Sappo
11	eleven	sappóy góó (sappo e góó)
12	twelve	sappóy ɗiɗi (sappo e ɗiɗi)
13	thirteen	sappóy tati (sappo e tati)
14	fourteen	sappóy nay (sappo e nay)
15	fifteen	sappóy jóy (sappo e jóy)

	English	Pulaar
16	sixteen	sappóy jeegom (sappo e jóy e góó)
17	seventeen	sappóy jéédidi(sappo e jóy e didi)
18	eighteen	sappóy jeetati (sappo e jóy e tati)
19	nineteen	sappóy jeenay (sappo e jóy e nay)
20	twenty	noogaas
30	thirty	capande tati
40	forty	capande nay
50	fifty	capande jóy
60	sixty	capande jeegom
70	seventy	capande jéédidi
80	eighty	capande jeetati
90	ninety	capande jeenay
100	one hundred	teemedere
200	two hundred	teemedde didi
300	three hundred	teemedde tati
400	four hundred	teemedde nay
500	five hundred	teemedde jóy
600	six hundred	teemedde jeegom
700	seven hundred	teemedde jéédidi
800	eight hundred	teemedde jeetati
900	nine hundred	teemedde jeenay
1000	one thousand	ujundere
10000	ten thousand	ujunnaaji sappo
100000	one hundred thousand	ujunnaaji teemedere
1000000	one million	milioŋ
10000000	one billion	milyaar

ORDINAL NUMBERS

	English	Pulaar
1	first	gadano
2	second	didabo
3	third	tatabo
4	fourth	nayabo
5	fifth	joyabo
6	sixth	jeegobo
7	seventh	jéédibo
8	eighth	jeetabo
9	ninth	jeenabo
10	tenth	sappobo
11	eleventh	sappo e goo?abo
12	twelfth	sappo e didabo
13	thirteenth	sappo e tatabo
14	fourteenth	sappo e nayabo
15	fifteenth	sappo e joyabo

xiii

	English	*Pulaar*
16	sixteenth	sappo e jeegoɓo
17	seventeenth	sappo e jééɗiɓo
18	eighteenth	sappo e jeetaɓo
19	nineteenth	sappo e jeenaɓo
20	twentieth	noogaaso
30	thirtieth	capanɗe tataɓo
40	fortieth	capanɗe nayaɓo
50	fiftieth	capanɗe joyaɓo
60	sixtieth	capanɗe jeegoɓo
70	seventieth	capanɗe jééɗiɓo
80	eightieth	capanɗe jeetaɓo
90	ninetieth	capanɗe jeenaɓo
100	one hundredth	battoowo teemedere
200	two hundredth	teemedde ɗiɗaɓo
300	three hundredth	teemdedde tataɓo
400	four hundredth	teemedde nayaɓo
500	five hundredth	teemedde joyaɓo
600	six hundredth	teemedde jeegoɓo
700	seven hundredth	teemedde jééɗiɓo
800	eight hundredth	teemedde jeetaɓo
900	nine hundredth	teemedde jeenaɓo
1000	one thousandth	battoowo ujunere

PUNCTUATION

The semicolon is used to separate words or word groups. The use of the semicolon indicates a different meaning or a slight variation of the meaning in that the additional word (group) further specifies the meaning of the entry or shows a different meaning. The tilda stands for the position of the entry. The comma is used to separate words or phrases in a series. The period is used to separate the meanings from illustrations of usage and to mark the end of a sentence. The slash is used to indicate and separate alternative and equivalent forms. Square brackets indicate pronunciation. Curly brackets signal borrowings. Parentheses mark the presence of an optional element.

ABBREVIATIONS

adj.	adjective	**ord.**	ordinal number
adv.	adverb	**part.**	particle
alt.	alternative form	**pl.**	plural
ar.	Arabic	**poss.**	possessive marker
comp.	comparative	**pref.**	prefix
conj.	conjunction	**prep.**	preposition
dem.	demonstrative marker	**prog.**	progressive marker
det.	determiner	**pron.**	pronoun
emph.	emphatic particle	**prov.**	proverb
eng.	English	**quest.**	question word
excl.	exclamation marker	**sing.**	singular
foc.	focus particle	**son.**	Soninke
fr.	French	**suf.**	suffix
imperf.	imperfective marker	**super.**	superlative
inter.	interrogative particle	**v.**	verb
interj.	interjection	**wol.**	Wolof
let.	letter of the alphabet	/	equivalent forms
n.	noun	{ }	borrowing
num.	numerical number	[ ]	phonetic form

The Pulaar Language

DIALECTOLOGY
FULA DIALECTS

A systematic study and analysis of the dialects of Fula and their delimitations is yet to be conducted. Arnott (1970) distinguishes the following dialects:

1) Fuuta Tooro (Senegal)
2) Fuuta Jaloo (Guinea)
3) Maasina (Mali)
4) Sokoto and Western Niger
5) "Central" Northern Nigeria (roughly Katsina, Kano, Zaria, Plateau, Bauchi, and Bornu Provinces) and Eastern Niger.
6) Adamawa

In the absence of any systematic study, the above classification is necessarily tentative. Like Fula, the Pulaar dialect is not uniform. Ka (1991) distinguishes three subvarieties of Pulaar:

1) Fuutankoore (Mauritania, Northern Senegal)
2) Jeerinkoore (Senegal excluding Northern Senegal)
3) Southern Pulaar (Fuladu-Gaaɓu, South and South East toward Guinea Bissau and Guinea).

WRITING SYSTEM

Various orthographies have been proposed for the writing of Fula. The initial formal attempt to designate a writing system for Fula based on the Latin alphabet occurred at a UNESCO conference held in Bamako, Mali in 1966 from February 28th through March 6th. Below is listed the alphabet that was formally designated and adopted as the official alphabet of Fula in Mali, Senegal and Niger.

a b **b** c d **d** e f g h i j k l m n mb n nd ng ny nj **n** o p r s t u w y y

After this conference, various developments (UNESCO 1971, Baldeh 1981, Noye 1989) of this alphabet have occurred concerning chiefly the representation of the implosives ɓ, Ƴ, ɗ; the prenasalized consonants **ng, nj, nd, mb**; the palatal nasal ñ; the velar nasal ŋ and vowel length. The implosives are represented in various forms of which we note the use of capital letters. The representation of the prenasalized consonants has ranged from sequencing a nasal and the forms that can be prenasalized (i.e. **mb, nd, ng, nj**), raising the nasal preceding the voiced obstruent (i.e. ^{m}b, ^{n}d, ^{n}g, ^{n}j), to duplicating the nasal before the voiced obstruent (i.e. mmb, nnd, nng, nnj). The palatal nasal has been represented as ñ or **ny**. The velar nasal ŋ has been represented by **N**. Vowel length is represented by the duplication of the vowel.

xvi

In this study, the representation of implosives follows their usual representation as ɓ, Ɣ, ɗ. This adoption is motivated by considerations pertaining to conformity to the literature on phonetics. In addition, the palatal nasal is represented as ñ to avoid confusion because the **ny** representation may lead to confusion in a writing system that attempts to show a one to one correspondence between a sound and the symbol used to represent it. The graphemic representation of prenasalized consonants is a sequence of a nasal and the form of the prenasalized consonant (i.e. nj) and the phonetic form is represented with a raised nasal before the obstruent (i.e. ⁿj). This decision is partly motivated by conformity and partly by pedagogical and clarification considerations. The distribution of prenasalized consonants is pervasive. However, the sequence of a nasal and a potential prenasalized form does not always result in prenasalized consonants. For the nonnative speaker of Pulaar it is difficult to determine when to pronounce a potential form as a prenasalized consonant or as a regular sequence of a nasal followed by a voiced obstruent. The provision of the phonetic representation of the prenasalized consonants will facilitate the task of the nonnative speaker of Pulaar. In addition to the discrepancies in the types of alphabets used, various differences exist in the orthographies regarding what morphemes can be attached to roots and the representation of assimilation processes. In this study, in general, bound morphemes are included in the word while free morphemes are excluded from the word except in the case of the negative particle "**ni**". The Pulaar alphabet used in this dictionary is displayed in the following.

a b ɓ c d ɗ e f g h i j k l m mb n nd ng nj ñ ŋ o p r s t u w y Ɣ

RELEVANT PHONETIC AND PHONOLOGICAL NOTES
CONSONANT AND VOWEL INVENTORY

Consonant Assimilation

Consonant assimilation occurs following the juxtaposition of impermissible consonant sequences. The consonantal sequences (tn, dn, ɗn, yn, jn, dt, ɗt, Ɣt, jt, td, ɗd, jd, tɗ, dɗ, Ɣɗ, jd, Ɣd) represent some instances of consonant sequences not permitted in Pulaar. Whenever an impermissible sequence is to result from the juxtaposition of certain elements, consonant assimilation occurs.

Stress Patterns

The primary stress is not marked in the entries as stress is not a distinctive feature in Pulaar. Pulaar stress is accounted for by the following generalizations (Niang, 1995 and 1997). The last syllable of the word is never stressed. The first syllable carries the primary stress if there is no heavy syllable in the word as in (a' du na). The penultimate syllable is stressed if it is the only heavy syllable in the word as in (ma laa' ɗo), (da do'r de). When both first and penult syllables have the same structure CVC, CVV or CVVC, the primary stress falls on the first syllable as in (ta'l lor de), (baa' waa ɗo), (haa'l pu laar ?en). When both first and penult syllables are heavy but with different weight, the primary stress is placed on the heaviest syllable as in (hal kaa' de), (gaa's to too ɗo), (ha'l ku de). CVVC is heavier than CVV which is heavier than CVC which is heavier than CV.

RELEVANT SYNTACTIC AND MORPHOLOGICAL NOTES

Pulaar is an SVO language. In addition, it is a class language in that agreement patterns are marked on the basis of the class of the referent. The number of class markers varies from one dialect to another and, in some cases, within a dialect. The Pulaar dialect under investigation has twenty-one noun classes.

NOUN CLASS MARKERS

Singular
"O" class: includes human referents and loan words
"Ba" class: includes animals
"ɗam" class includes liquids, abstract nouns, mass nouns
"ɗum" class includes borrowed words without a suffix. It is also considered a neuter class.
"Ka" class includes various types of objects; abstract nouns
"Kal" class includes liquids in relatively small quantities
"Ki" class includes body parts, plants, grass, abstract nouns
"Ko" class includes body parts, plants, grass
"Nde" class includes objects with certain shapes
"Ndi" class includes uncountables, male animals and birds, augmentatives
"Ndu" class includes cylindrical and circular objects
"Ngal" class includes body parts, birds, trees and plants and their parts, augmentatives
"Nge" class includes cattle, celestial nouns, abstract nouns
"Ngel" class includes singular diminutives
"Ngo" class includes various objects, animals, abstract nouns
"Ngol" class includes long thin entities, animals, nouns of action
"Ngu" class includes insects, worms, fish, animals, collective and abstract nouns

Plural
"ɓe" class includes human plurals
"ɗe" class includes animals, objects
"ɗi" class includes animals, objects
"Kon/Koñ" class includes plural diminutives

Consonant Alternation

A number of consonants in the initial position of a word undergo alternation. The general features of initial consonant alternation (Sylla, 1982) and examples illustrating this alternation are provided in the following.

sing.	f	s	h	r	w ʔ y
	|	|	|	|	| |/ |
plur.	p	c	k	d	b g j
	|	|	|	|	| | |
plur. dim.	p	c	k	nd	mb ng nj

The following data illustrate the above alternation chart.

Sing.	Plural	Plur. dim.	Gloss	
faɗo	paɗe	paɗon	shoe/s	little shoes
sekko	cekke	cekkon	reed/s	little reeds
haayre	kaaƳe	kaaƳon	stone/s	little stones
raɲalde	daɲaale	ndaɲalon	backside /s	little backsides

Unlike other consonants that show a one-way alternation between singular and plural, /w/ and /y/ may have a two-way alternation between singular and plural as illustrated by the following data.

Singular	Plural	Plural dim.	Gloss
wudere	gude	ngudon	sarong / little sarongs
wowru	boɓi	mboɓon	mortar / little mortars
yertere	gerte	ngerton	peanut / tiny peanuts
yeeso	jeese	njeeson	face / little faces

The consonants ɓ, ɗ, Ƴ, m, n, ŋ, ñ, l and t do not alternate. The consonant alternation may be motivated by number distinctions or distinctions pertaining to diminutive and augmentative considerations. Such data are illustrated in the following.

Singular	Plural	Gloss
yeeso	jeese	face / faces
wudere	gude	sarong / sarongs

Singular	Dim.	Augmen.	Gloss
faɗo	paɗel	paɗal	shoe/ little shoe/ big shoe
hello	kellel	kellal	slap/ little slap/ big slap

GRAMMATICAL CATEGORIES

Nouns
The noun in Pulaar is composed of a root form that is generally followed by the nominal class marker of the particular noun.

Pronouns
All noun class markers may function as pronouns as in "**O** nanii, **ki** yanii, **kal** rufii.

Verbs
The verb in Pulaar is composed of a root form as in "**yar**," "**haal**." The infinitive form of the verb is marked by the addition of the infinitival suffix "**de**" at the end of the root. For instance the infinitive of the verb "**hel**" (break) is "**helde**" (to break). The verb may also be subject to consonant alternation if the initial consonant is the type that undergoes alternation.

Adjectives
The adjective is positioned after the noun that it modifies. The adjective is generally followed by the noun class suffixed to the adjective as illustrated in the following forms.

        sondu (ndu)   "bird (the)"
        sondu mawndu (ndu) "big bird (the)"

Adverbs
The adverb, is an independent free morpheme. Examples of adverbs include "ɗoo" (here), "ɗaa" (there), "toon" (there), "nde" (when).
Adverbs are used as main entries and their presence is indicated by the abbreviation "adv."

Prepositions
The preposition, in general, is an independent free morpheme. Examples of prepositions include "dow" (over, on); "les" (under, underneath, below), "sara" (near).

Determiners
Determiners can be used to signal nouns. All noun class markers may be used as determiners. Determiners follow the noun they refer to. Determiners are used as main entries and their presence is indicated by the abbreviation "det."

ENTRY STRUCTURE
Entries in this dictionary are not structured around the root system approach. Syntactic categories such as nouns, verbs, adjectives, and adverbs are listed as entries. The first entry of related forms is bold face and all other related forms appear bold face and italicized under the first entry item. The choice of this first related form is determined solely by alphabetical ordering. The same consideration is observed for the following related forms which are bolded and italicized. Even though no claim is made concerning the form of the root, the provision of related forms may certainly give an indication of the shape of the root. Every entry reflects the shape of the morpheme or morphemes

prior to the application of certain processes. So the entry "hoɗde" is composed of the morpheme "hoɗ" (live) and the morpheme "de" (infinitival suffix). The pronunciation of the entire word [hodde] is then provided. Pronunciation in the Pulaar-English dictionary is provided only when the actual pronunciation differs from the form of the actual entry. The provision of this pronunciation serves a number of purposes. First, it informs the user (especially the nonnative speaker of Pulaar) of the actual pronunciation. Second, it shows various processes that may be useful to the researcher. The organization of entries is illustrated in the following examples:

> **accande** *v.* forgive; leave for someone. ~ *hakke* forgive. *Mi accanii ma geɗalam* I am giving you my share. *ɓe ngaccanii ma hakke* They forgive you.

> *accirde* *v.* leave for or with someone. *Mi accirii ma ɗum* I leave it with you.

> *accitde* [accidde] *v.* abandon; release. *O accitaama hanki* He has been released. *ɗaccitde alt.*

> *accude* *v.* let go; leave; give up. *Accu dee Ya* Leave it to rest. *ɓe ngaccii simme* They gave up smoking.

Prenasalization
Since a nasal and a voiced obstruent sequence does not always result in prenasalization (i.e. **bonande**), it is important to indicate instances where prenasalization occurs. This feature is indicated only in the pronunciation of the entry word.
    hómbude [hom^mbude] *v.* hem

Advanced Tongue Root
When relevant, the Advanced Tongue Root feature is marked in the entry and the actual pronunciation.
    addóyde *v.* go and bring something; fetch. *Addóy ndiyam* Go and fetch water.

The provision of the Advanced Tongue Root feature is motivated by the fact that the misuse of this feature may affect pronunciation and intelligibility.
Following the pronunciation of the particular entry is the noun class for nominals.
    amdaare (nde) deliberate action. *ɗum ko amdaare* This is a deliberate action.

The nominal class markers are provided because they cannot be easily inferred from the shape of the word. The presence of the nominal class marker signals a nominal category. In this case, the listing of the syntactic category "*n.*" leads to redundancy.

Following the pronunciation and the nominal class (where appropriate) is the syntactic category of the word.

> **amdaade** *v.* do deliberately.

Then follows the origin of the borrowed word when known.

> **amiiru** *(o) {ar.}* chief.

When the source of the word is not provided, the entry may be either a Fula word or a word whose origin is unknown. The source provided attempts to trace the donor language; that is, from what language a particular word entered Pulaar.

Then are listed the meanings of the entry word as illustrated in the following:

> *andinde* [an^{n}dinde] *v.* teach; familiarize someone with; impart; notify; publicize. *So a andii andin* You should teach what you know.

When the meanings are not related, the different meanings are listed under different numbers as illustrated in the following example.

> **baawal** *(ngal)* **1)** bird **2)** fishing instrument **3)** ability. *Yeewen ɗo baawal makko tólnii* Let us see what he is capable of.

Following the meanings, usage is illustrated by means of idioms, phrases, sentences, and proverbs.

Idiom illustration

> **baajól** *(ngól)* strip. ~ *leydi* snake.

Phrase illustration

> **baasal** *(ngal)* poverty. *wondude e* ~ be poor.

Sentence illustration

> **baafal** *(ngal)* door. *uddude* ~ close the door. *udditde* ~ open the door. *buɓɓude* ~ slam the door. *Uddu baafal ngal* Close the door.

Proverb illustration

> **ekkaade** *v.* learn by trial. ~ *yahde* learn the first steps. *prov. Mo ekkaaki waawataa* A person who does not try will not learn.

Where consonant alternation is involved, the singular, plural, nominal or verbal form is provided at the end of the entry.

> **aaludere** *(nde)* kernel; stone. *gaaluuDe (ɗe) pl.*

Where appropriate, an alternative form of the entry is also listed at the end of the entry as illustrated in the following:

> **gacce** *(ɗe)* shame *(pl.* use only). *A dañii gacce* Shame on you. *kersa (o) alt.*

DIALECT NOTES FOR ENGLISH LANGUAGE

The English dialect used in this dictionary is American English, a variety replete with variations.

ORTHOGRAPHY AND PRONUNCIATION
ENGLISH ALPHABET

A, B, C, D, E, F, G, H, I, J, K, L, M, N, O, P, Q, R, S, T, U, V, W, X, Y, Z

PHONEMES OF AMERICAN ENGLISH

Consonantal phonemes

[p] as in pen
[b] as in big
[t] as in ten
[d] as in desk
[k] as in kilt
[g] as in get
[f] as in fit
[v] as in vent
[Ɵ] as in thin
[ð] as in then
[s] as in sip
[z] as in zip
[š] as in shop
[ʒ] as in rouge
[h] as in hit
[č] as in chin
[j] as in jet
[m] as in men
[n] as in no
[l] as in leaf
[r] as in rim
[w] as in win
[y] as in you

Vowel phonemes

[iy] as in feet
[i] as in fit
[ɨ] as in roses
[ey] as in wait
[e] as in wet
[a] as in fat
[ɑ] as in father
[ay] as in bite
[aw] as in about
[o] as in bother
[ow] as in boat
[ɔ] as in bought
[oy] as in boil
[u] as in put
[uw] as in boot
[ʌ] as in but
[ə] as in better
[ɚ] as in bird

Allophones

[ʔ] as in ow
[ŋ] king
[ɾ] as in better

GRAMMATICAL CATEGORIES

Nouns
Nouns are entities used to refer to people, places, events, states, and qualities. They may be abstract or concrete, count or noncount. Nouns may be used with determiners and they may be modified by adjectives. Nouns may be subject to number distinctions, gender distinctions and case marking. The plural morpheme generally used to mark the plural of English nouns is {-s} which is added at the end of the noun. In this section of the dictionary, nouns are entered in their singular forms. The abbreviation "n." signals a nominal entry.

Pronouns
Pronouns are used to replace nouns. Some of the English pronouns listed here may be personal (I, me, you, him, she, her, it, we, us, they, them), reflexive (myself, yourself, himself, herself, itself, ourselves, yourselves, themselves), possessive (mine, yours, his, hers, its, ours, theirs), interrogative (who, which, what, whom, whose), relative (who, whom, which, what, whose, that), indefinite (all, everyone, nobody, someone, one), demonstrative (this, that, these, those), reciprocal (each other, one another).

Adjectives
Adjectives further specify nouns or pronouns. Adjectives, unlike nouns, are not inflected for number distinctions. Adjectives precede nouns they modify, can take comparative and superlative markers and they can be further specified by adverbs. Adjectives are used as main entries. Both comparative and superlative forms are also used as main entries. The presence of the abbreviation "adj." signals an adjectival entry.

Adverbs
Adverbs, in general, are formed by the addition of the suffix -ly to adjectives. Adverbs may further specify adjectives, verbs, and adverbs. Adverbs are used as main entries and they are signaled by the abbreviation "adv."

Prepositions
Prepositions may indicate relationships between a noun, a pronoun and another element in the sentence. The preposition is also used as a main entry, in which case it is signaled by the abbreviation "prep."

HIPPOCRENE STANDARD DICTIONARY

PULAAR-ENGLISH

A

a *pron.* you. **A** *yahii toon* You went there.

aa *interj.* well.

aaɓde *v.* be fortunate; be lucky. *O mo aaɓi* He is fortunate. *Eɓe ngaaɓi* They are fortunate.

aaɓnude *v.* make someone fortunate. *A aaɓnii mo* He became fortunate thanks *to* you.

aaɓru *(ndu)* excavation. ~ *mawndu* big excavation. *gaabi (ɗi) pl.*

aactaade [aaccaade] *v.* ruminate; chew the cud. *aacto* chew the cud. *Eɗin ngaactoo* They are chewing the cud.

aactere *(nde)* rumination; chewing of the cud. *gaacte (ɗe) pl.*

aada *(o)* custom; tradition. ~ *ɓooydo* old tradition. *luutndaade* ~ disobey tradition. *ɗum ko aada men* That is our tradition. *pl. aadaaji (ɗi).*

Aadama *(o)* male first name; Adam. *Baaba men* ~ Adam. *O wiyetee ko Aadama* His name is Aadama.

aadee *(o)* person; being. *innama* ~ human being *pl. aadee?en.*

ahdaade [aadaade] *v.* promise

ahdande [aadande] *v.* promise to someone. *A ahdanii mo* You made him a promise.

ahdi [aadi]*(o)* agreement; promise; deadline. *firtude* ~ break a promise. *Ahdi firtetaake* You must keep a promise. *ahdiiji (ɗi) pl.*

ahdóndirde [aadó"dirde] *v.* agree; accord. *En ngaadondirii* We have agreed upon it.

aafde *v.* place one's hand into a hole.

aaftaade *v.* dig up; remove from a hole. *Aafto ɗum* Take it out. *ɓe ngaaftiima ɗum* They took it out.

aahde *v.* divide food; dish out food.

aalaango *(ngo)* mattress. *wertude* ~ spread a mattress.

aalde *v.* cover with leather.

aalde *(nde)* booty.

aalim *(o)* {*ar.*} scholar. *Ko o aalim dowlu ɗo* He is a well known scholar.

aalnude *v.* shed tears. *Gite makko ngaal ɗii gon ɗi* His eyes are watery.

aaltaade *v.* change direction; select. *O woni ko e aaltaade* He is making a selection. *ɓe ngaaltiima* They have made the selection.

aaludere *(nde)* kernel; stone. *Wukkit aaludere nde* Spit out the stone. *gaaluu ɗe (ɗe) pl.*

aamaare *(nge)* cow.

aamde *v.* be lazy. *Ko aan aami* You are lazy. *Eɓe ngaami* They are lazy.

aamnude *v.* make lazy. *A aamnii kam* You have made me lazy.

aamre *(nde)* laziness. *Mbe ɗe wondi e aamre* I am lazy.

aamiin amen. *Mbiyen aamiin* Let us say amen.

aamtude *v.* smell rotten; smell bad. *Eɗum aamta* It smells bad.

aan *pron.* you *(sing.)* *Ko aan* It is you.

aande *v.* be in a dilemma. *Ko mi gaan ɗo* I have a dilemma. Mbe ɗe aani I have a dilemma. *Eɓe ngaani no feewi* They have a major a dilemma.

aannude *v.* put someone in a dilemma. *A aannii mo* You put him in a dilemma. *ɓe ngaannii mo* They have put him in a dilemma.

aarabaagal *(ngal)* Arab pride.

aarabe *(o)* an Arab. *Ko o Aarabe* S/He is Arab.

aarabeere *(nde)* Arabic. *Aarabeére woni ɗemngal makko* His native language is Arabic.

aarde *v.* open halfway; open. *O woni ko e aaraade* He is opening it halfway.

aarnude *v.* indicate.

aas *(o)* {*fr.*} ace.

aawasaagal *(ngal)* roguishness. *Aawasaagal mo Ɏaani* Roguishness is despised.

aawase *(o)* rogue; thug. *Ko o aawase maw ɗo* He is a big thug. *aawaseeɓe (ɓe) pl.*

aawaseejo *(o)* rogue. *aawaseeɓe (ɓe) pl.*

aawde *v.* sow. *Mi aawii gawri ndi* I sowed the millet. *ɓe ngaawii maaro* They sowed rice.

aawdi *(ndi)* seeds for sowing. *Aawdi fijirtaake* You must not play with sowing seeds.

aawre *(nde)* sowing.

aawru *(ndu)* sowing.

aawtaade v. dig out; scratch around; sow again. *eɓen ngaawtoo ngesa maɓɓe* They are sowing their farm again.

aawtere (nde) something sown again. *Min ngoni ko e aawtere* We are sowing seeds again.

aayaade v. be reduced. *ɗum aayiima* It is reduced. *prov. So goo bonii limmore aayiima* One cannot build upon a bad foundation.

aayaare (nde) reduction. *ɗum ko aayaare mawnde* This is a major loss.

aayandere [aayandere] *(nde)* major reduction.

aaye (o) Koranic verse; "magical" lotion. *Moomo aaye ma* Rub your "magical" lotion on your body. *aayééji (ɗi) pl.*

abaari (o) linen; mater.

ababo (ko) grass.

abada adv. for ever. *haa ~* for ever; never. *Mi jogoraani waɗɗe ɗum haa abada* I will never do it.

abadu (o) {ar.} measurement.

abbaade v. follow; trail. *Abbo mo* Follow him/her.

abbitaade v. follow again; suffer the results of. *Abbito mo* Go after him/her.

abbóndirde v. follow one another; move closer to.

abbo (o) father. *~ Muusa* Muusa's father.

abbere (nde) grain. *~ gawri* millet grain. *ɗum ko abbere* It is a grain. *gabbe (ɗe) pl.*

abiyo], (o) airoplane *abiyoɲaaji (ɗi) pl. jolde e ~* board a plane.

aɓugo (ngo) cheek. *alt. gabgal (ngal) gable (ɗe) pl.*

accande v. forgive; leave for someone. *~ hakke* forgive. *Mi accanii ma geɗalam* I am leaving my share for you. *ɓe ngaccanii ma hakke* They forgive you.

accirde v. leave for or with someone. *Mi accirii ma ɗum* I leave it with you.

accitde [accidde] v. abandon; release. *O ɗaccitaama* He has been released. *alt. ɗaccitde.*

accude v. let; leave; give up *Accu deeYa* Let it rest. *ɓe ngaccii simme* They gave up smoking.

aɗa pers. pron. you are (progressive). *Aɗa yiya* Do you see.

adaadaa {o} race.

adaade v. precede. *Ko aan adii* You preceded us/you came first. *Kamɓe ngadii en* They preceded us.

adan first. *gila ~* since the beginning.

aditaade v. forego; precede; anticipate.

aɗɗaade v. heat oneself.

aɗde [adde] v. steam dry; dry.

addande v. bring for. *Addan mo ndiyam* Bring him water. *Ngaddanee mo laafa makko* Bring him his hat.

addorde v. bring with. *Addor mo* Bring him/her with you. *Ngaddoree mo* Bring him with you.

addóyde v. go and bring; fetch. *Addoy ndiyam* Go and fetch water.

addude v. bring. *Addu mo gaay* Bring him/her here. *ɓe ngaddii ɗum* They brought it.

aɗɗere (nde) stool.

aɗɗitde [aɗɗidde] v. defecate *O woni koy aɗɗitde* He is defecating. *alt. huwde.*

addo (ngo) child gum disease. *O mo wondi e addo* He is suffering from gum disease. *addooji (ɗi) pl.*

aduna (o) world. *adunaaji (ɗi) pl.*

afara (o) barbecued meat. *~ belɗo* tasty barbecued meat *afaraaji (ɗi) pl.*

aflaade v. use as a pillow. *Aflo ɗoo* Use this as a pillow. *Ngaflo ɗee* Rest your head on a pillow.

afo (o) first born. *Hawwaa ko afo makko* Hawwa is her first born.

afal (ngal) useless first born.

Afirik *(o)* Africa. *duunde ~* the African continent.

afiriknaajo (o) African *afriknaaɓe (ɓe) pl.*

aga (o) herdsman.

aggitaade v. fall from; be removed from.

aggitde [aggidde] v. pull; dig up. *O woni ko e aggitde ñiire makko* He is pulling his tooth up. *alt. ɗuggitde.*

aggutere (nde) molar *alt. aggitere (nde). gaggutte (ɗe) pl.*

ahde [aade] v. belch. *O ahii* He belched.

ahre [aare] *(nde)* belching.

ajjaade v. lay on one's back *Ajjo* Lay on your back. *ɓe ngajjiima* They are laying on their backs.

jjinde v. make lay on the back. *Ajjin mo* Make him lay on his back.

ksida *(o) {fr.}* accident; collision. *O wadīi aksida* He had an accident.

laa *(o)* no. *O wii alaa* He said no.

laasara *(o)* late afternoon.

lamaan *(o)* fine; tax; duty. *fawde ~* fine a person. *O yoɓii alamaan (o)* He paid the fine.

lambanaare *(nde)* zebra.

lambe *(ɓe)* Soninke people *galambo (o)* sing.

larba *(o) {ar.}* Wednesday. *Hanki wonnoo alarba* Yesterday was Wednesday.

lɓaade v. eat without chewing; offend. *daccu alɓaade* Chew your food before swallowing it.

lbarka thank you. *Albarka maa* I thank you.

lde v. place animals in a hedged area.

ldinde v. enrich. *ɓe ngaldinii mo* They made him rich.

ldude v. be wealthy. *O aldīi* He has become wealthy.

let *(o)* Sunday. *Hande ko alet* Today is Sunday.

Alfaa *(o)* learned Muslim scholar; chief. *O wiyetee ko Alfaa* His name is Alfaa.

lhaali *(o) {ar.}* matter. *dum wonaa alhaali maa* That is not your concern.

Alhajji *(o)* pilgrim.

alhamdulillaay thanks to god.

aljanna *(o)* paradise; heaven. *naatde ~* go to heaven. *O naatii aljanna* He is in heaven. *aljannaaji (dī) pl.*

aljumaa *(o) {ar.}* Friday. *Hande ko aljumaa* Today is Friday. *aljumaaji (dī) pl.*

alkaali *(o)* judge. *Ko o alkaali* S/he is a judge.

alkabeere *(nde)* stirrup *alkabeeje (de) pl.*

alkamiisa *(o) {ar.}* Thursday.

alkol *(o) {fr.}* alcohol. *yarde ~* drink alcohol.

alkulal *(ngal)* letter of the alphabet. *~ muumal* vowel. *~ tekkinaangal* geminate. *alkule (de) pl.*

Alla Allah; God. *~ meho* free, gratis.

allaade v. stumble.

allaadu *(ndu)* horn. *~ ngaari* the horn of an ox. *gallaadi (dī) pl.*

alluki *(ki)* tree.

alluwal *(ngal)* wooden tablet used for writing. *alluuje (de) pl.*

almaade v. lead.

almaami *(o) {ar.}* imam; chief of Fuuta. *almameeɓe (ɓe) pl.*

almet *(o) {fr.}* box of matches. *almetaaji (dī) pl.*

almuudo *(o)* student; adept; disciple. *~ maa* your student *almuuɓe (ɓe) pl.*

altine *(o) {ar.}* Monday.

alyatiimu *(o) {ar.}* orphan. *Muusaa ko alyatiimu* Muusa is an orphan. *pl. alytimeeɓe (ɓe).*

-am poss. pron. my. *hooram* my head. *ko ~* mine. *hoor~ hoor~* egoism.

ambilaas [am^mbilaas] *{fr.}* ambulance. *ɓe njolnii mo e nder ambilaas* They put him in an ambulance.

ambaasadeer [am^mbasadeer]*(o)* *{fr.}* ambassador.

ambude [am^mbude] v. isolate; prevent; build a dike.

amdaade v. do deliberately. *O amdi* He did it deliberately.

amdaare *(nde)* deliberate action. *dum ko amdaare* This is a deliberate action.

amde v. dance. *O amii* S/he danced. *ɓe ngamii* They danced.

amdude v. dance with. *Amdu e makko* Dance with him/her.

amnude v. make someone dance *Amnu mo* Make him dance. *ɓe ngamnii mawɓe* They made the elderly dance.

amen poss. pron. our (postposed). *maaro ~* our rice.

amiiru *(o)* chief.

amin pers. pron. we are. *Amin njaha* We are leaving.

amminde v. show; delineate. *Amminam hol to kodɗaa* Give me directions to your residence.

amo *(ngo)* flood. *amóóji (dī) pl. Amo sinkant* The flood of 1950.

amre *(nde)* tortoise; turtle.

amumal *(ngal)* chicken pox; rash.

añande v. be jealous of.

añde [añje] *v.* abhor; disdain; loathe; scorn; detest; hate; resent.

añóndirde [añóⁿdirde] *v.* hate one another. **gañóndiral** *(ngal).*

añtude [añcude] *v.* hate forever. *Mi añtii ɗum* I hate it forever.

andaaka [anⁿdaaka] *adj.* unknown; anonymous. *O andaaka* He is unknown.

andande [anⁿdande] *v.* know about someone. *O mo andan maa* He knows about you.

andinde [anⁿdinde] *v.* teach; familiarize someone with; impart; notify; ventilate; publicize. *So a andii andin* You should share what you know.

anditde [anⁿdidde] *v.* recognize.

andude [anⁿdude] *v.* know; learn. *gandal (ngal).*

ande [anⁿde] *(nde)* slice; piece. ~ *liingu* a slice of fish.

ande *v.* cut fish into pieces; slice; be obscure.

andoonde [anⁿdoode] *(nde)* small fish. *Mi jaggii andoonde* I caught a small fish. *gandooɗe (ɗe) pl.*

angale [aŋⁿgale] *(o) {fr.}* English.

angare [aⁿŋgare] *(o) {fr.}* fertilizer.

angere [aⁿŋgere] *(nde)* restlessness due to suffering.

angude [aⁿŋgude] *v.* be restless because of suffering.

angisaade [aⁿgisaade] *v.*

annabi *(o)* prophet. ~ *Iisaa* Jesus Christ. *annabaaɓe (ɓe) pl.* *annabiiji (o) alt.*

annama *(o)* image; concept; like; design.

aññeere *(nde)* grave. *Mi yii aññeere makko* I saw his grave. *gañ̃eeje (ɗe) pl.*

anniya *(o)* intent; intention. ~ *mo ⅄o* good intention.

anniyaade *v.* intend; decide. *Mi anniyiima* I have decided. *anniyaaji (ɗi) pl.*

annoore *(nde)* brightness.

aparante *(o) {fr.}* assistant to a mechanic or a driver

araaraay *(o)* flag. *araaraayuuji (ɗi) pl.*

arande *v.* come for. *Aran mo* Come for him.

arani *(o)* alien; foreigner; immigrant; outsider. *Muusaa ko arani* Muusaa is a foreigner.

ardaade *v.* head; govern; manage; preside; lead; precede. *Ardo njuulen* Lead the prayer. *gardagol (ngol).*

arde *v.* come. *Ar gaay* Come here. *ɓe ngarii* They came. *garaangal (ngal).*

ardinde *v.* place in front of.

arditaade *v.* lead again.

ardude *v.* come with. *Ardu e jom galle maa* Come with your husband.

artirde *v.* return something or someone; repatriate. *Artir defteram* Return my book. *ɓe ngartirii mo* They brought him back. *gartirgól (ngól).*

artude *v.* return; come back. *Artu ɗo njeyaɗaa* Return to where you belong. *gartugól (ngól).*

arɗo *(o)* chief.

ari *interj.* sound used to make a donkey walk.

arkille *(o)* mosquito net. *diilaade* ~ set a mosquito net. *diiltaade* ~ bring a mosquito net down.

armoor *{o}* book shelf.

arsi *(o) {ar.}* Heaven.

arsuku *(o)* fortunate profit *arsukaaji (ɗi) pl.*

arwan first (beginning).

arwude *v.* *{fr.}* be successful; pass. *O arwii* He passed (the exam). *ɓe ngarwii* They passed the exam.

asaade *v.* dig itself; be deep.

asaɓere *(nde)* hole holding water.

asande *v.* dig for someone. *ngaska (ka).*

asde *v.* drill; excavate; dig. *Asanam ngaska* Dig a hole for me. *ngaska (ka).*

asnude *v.* make someone dig.

asaale *(ɗe)* thighs. *asangal (ngal) sing.*

asakal *(ngal)* tithe.

asamaan *(o) {ar.}* sky. ~ *laaɓɗo* clear sky. *asamaanuuji (ɗi) pl.*

asangal [asaⁿgal] *(ngal)* thigh.

aset *(o)* Saturday. *Hande ko aset* Today is Saturday.

askinde *v.* tell the genealogy of someone. *Askin mo* Tell his genealogy.

askitinaade *v.* tell one's own genealogy.

asko *(ngo)* pedigree; lineage; genealogy. *andude* ~ *mum* know one's genealogy.

askude *v.* levy a tithe.

li (o) origin. *Hol ko woni asli maa* What s your origin? *Lasli (o) alt.*

lude v. lend.

pirin (o) {fr.} an aspirin tablet. *spirinaaji (ɗi) pl.*

ri (o) third daily prayer. *Njuulen asri* Let us pray the third daily prayer.

aaye (o) {ar.} tea. *atayuuji (ɗi) pl.*

turu (ndu) dread; dreadlocks.

vde v. fish; trawl. *Omon awa* He is fishing.

vnude v. make someone fish.

vo (ngo) fishing. ~ e ngaynaaka fishing and farming; agriculture.

Yal (ngal) oar; paddle. *Aw Yal maa nani* Here is your paddle.

Yirgal (ngal) paddle *aw Yirɗe (ɗe) pl.*

Yitde [awYidde] v. agitate.

Yoowo (o) person who paddles; paddler.

Yude v. paddle. *Omon awYa* He is paddling.

vlude v. flatter. *Hande mi awlu maa* I will praise you today.

ayaa (o) sound for chasing birds off fields. *O wii ayaa* He made the ayaa sound.

aybanduru [aybaⁿduru](ndu) greediness.

aybinde v. discredit; disrespect; accuse someone of greed. *A aybinii mo* You showed him disrespect.

aybude v. be greedy. *Ko Muusaa aybi* Muusaa is very greedy.

aylude v. take animals to graze.

aynaaynaare (nde) herdmans' share.

ayninde v. make someone herd.

aynóyde v. go herding. *O aynóyii* He went herding.

aynude v. herd; take care of. *Aynu ndeena* Take care of the herd.

ayto (ngo) fever; flu. *Mbeɗe wondi e ayto* I am feverish.

aƳƳere (nde) break; blow.

aƳƳude v. break by pounding.

ayyiiba (o) vice. *Ayyiiba muƳƳaani* Vice is bad. *ayyibaaji (ɗi) pl.*

B

ba *det.* 1) the. *mbabba ba* the donkey 2) last name.

baaba *(o)* father. ~ *maa* your father. ~ *galle* father; head of the household. ~ *mawɗo* old father; grandfather. *baabiraaɗo (o)* father; dad.

baabaade *v.* threaten. *ɗaccu ko mbaaboto ɗaa ko* Stop those threats.

baabagól *(ngól)* threat.

baaɓatti *(ɗi)* locusts *mbaaɓattu (ngu) sing.*

baaɗe *(ɗe)* ant hills. *waande (nde) sing.*

baaɗiraaɗo *(o)* nephew; niece (one's sister's child). *Ko o baaɗam* He is my nephew.

baafal *(ngal)* door. *uddude* ~ close a door. *udditde* ~ open a door. *buɓɓude* ~ slam a door. *aarde* ~ open the door half way. *Uddu baafal ngal* Close the door.

baag *(o) {fr.}* ferry boat. *ɓe taccinirii oto o baag* They used a ferry boat to get the car across the river.

baagal *(ngal)* bucket for drawing water. *jolnude* ~ jiggle a bucket down into a well. *sefde* ~ draw water from a well.

baajól *(ngól)* strip. ~ *leydi* snake. *ɓe kaɓɓiri leɗɗe ɗe baaji* They tied the woods with strips. *baaji (ɗi) pl.*

baalél *(ngél)* little sheep.

baali *(ɗi)* sheep. *mbaalu (ngu) sing.*

baami *(ɗi)* fibers used for false hair.

baamuule *(ɗe)* cemetery. *ɓe nawii mo baamuule* They took him to the cemetery for burial.

baanabaana *(o)* peddler. *Ko o baanabaana* He is a peddler.

baañaaru *(o)* herder.

baañe *(ɗe)* clouds. *Baañe ɗe ndendii* The clouds have gathered.

baape *(ɗe)* leafy bush.

baaról *(ngól)* farm land; field; small excavation. *ɗum ko baarolam* This is my farm.

baasal *(ngal)* poverty. *wondude e* ~ be poor. *Baasal moƳƳaani* Poverty is not good.

baasɗo *adj.* poor. *Ko o baasɗo* He is poor.

baasi *(o) {wol.}* dish made with a ligh peanut butter sause and couscous.

baata *(o)* full moon.

baatarp *adj.* ugly.

baawal *(ngal)* 1) type of bird 2) fishin instrument 3) ability. *Ƴeewen ɗo baawa makko tólnii* Let us see what he is capabl of.

baawɗe *(ɗe)* power.

baawɗo *adj.* able. *alaa* ~ No one can do it.

baayaade *v.* submit.

baayo *(o)* orphan *alt. baaye (o).*

bablaali *(ɗi)* loud and unclear talks.

bablude *v.* speak loudly and unclearly.

bablugól *(ngól)* loud and unclear talk.

bacce *(ɗe)* fish scales. *Ruf bacce ɗe* Throv the fish scales away. *waccere (nde) sing.*

baccude *v.* scale. *O woni ko baccude liing ngu* He is scaling the fish.

baddi *(ki)* tree.

baddo *adj.* young. ~ *kecco* very young.

badɗo *(o)* doer; performer. ~ **bone** ev doer.

baɗoowo *(o)* doer. ~ *jam* a person wh performs good deeds. ~ *bonande/bon* person with evil deeds.

baɗtane [battane] *(ɗe)* end. ~ *moƳƳe.* happy ending.

baɗtano [battano] *adj.* final; ultimate.

baɗtindiiɗo [battiⁿdiiɗo] *(o)* last; latte final. *Ko kanko waɗtindii arde* He arrive last.

baggél *(ngél)* little drum. ~ *ibliis* devil' drum.

baggól *adj.* young.

bagi *(o)* fabric; textile. *Mi sooda nii m bagi o* I bought the fabric for him. *bagi pl.*

bahe *(ɗe)* 1) beards 2) pieces of wood tie together *wahre (nde) sing.*

bajjo *adj.* unique. *gooto* ~ one and only. *K o bajjo* She is their only child. *Petto alt.*

baka *(o)* blue cloth. ~ *rombal* blue dye gown.

bakane *(ɗe)* trunks. *wakande (nde) sing.*

bakañi *(ki)* type of tree.

bakde *v.* dye blue.

kkaat *(o)* sin. *ɗum ko bakkaat* It is a sin.

kkódinde v. sin; transgress *A bakkodini* ʿou committed a sin.

kkódin ɗo *adj.* sinful.

kke *(ɗe)* 1) leftovers 2) snott.

kkiliiɗo *adj.* resolute.

kki *(ɗi)* gowns.

l *(o) {fr.}* balloon; ball. *fettude* ~ kick the ʿall; play soccer. *jaggude* ~ catch the ball. *Werlo bal o* Throw the ball.

la *(o)* fish.

laade v. hoe.

lanji *(ɗi)* xylophone.

lankaar [balaŋkaar] *(o) {fr.}* stretcher. *Vjolnee mo e balankaar o* Place him in ʿhe stretcher.

layse *(ɗe) {fr.}* scales. ~ *kaŋŋe* scales for ʿveighing gold.

lɗe *(ɗe)* days. ~ *juutɗe* a long life. ~ *laɓɓe* short life. *Yo Alla rokku mo balɗe ʿuutɗe* May he live long. *Hande waɗi balɗe nay* It has been four days. *ñalawma ʿo) sing.*

llaade v. reach with the arm. *Ballo koppu o* Reach for the cup.

llotooɗo *(o)* person who reaches.

llal *(ngal)* help; assistance. ~ *mawngal* major help. *Mbeɗe sokli ballal maa* I need your help. *Ballal maa ina soklaa no ʿeewi* Your help is really needed.

lloowo *(o)* helper. *Ko o balloowo no ʿeewi* S/He is very helpful.

llifaagól *(ngól)* writing.

lól *(ngól)* ridge.

ltirgal *(ngal)* drain pipe; gutter. ~ *julngal* a leaking pipe.

alΓoowo *(o)* person who spits.

alΓugól *(ngól)* the act of spitting out.

alΓude v. spit out.

amɗi *(ɗi)* 1) donkeys 2) lice *mbabba (ba)* sing.

amfaro *(o)* shaft; arrow.

ambaaɗo [bamᵐbaaɗo] *(o)* griot. *Ko o bambaaɗo* He belongs to the griot caste.

ambu [bamᵐbu] *(ngu)* cloth used for tying a child on one's back alt. *Mbambu (ngu).*

anaade v. sniff; smell.

anaana *(o) {fr.}* banana. *Bóóltude* ~ peel a banana. *O mo yiɗi banaana* He likes bananas.

banda [banⁿda] *(o) {fr.}* tape. *fawde* ~ play a tape. *Fawanam banda o* Play this tape for me.

bandaas [banⁿdaas] *(o) {fr.}* bandage. *Filtu bandaas o* Remove the bandage.

bandi [banⁿdi] *(o) {fr.}* thug. *Ko o bandi* He is a thug.

bandiraaɗo [banⁿdiraaɗo] *(o)* relative. ~ *debbo* sister. ~ *gorko* brother.

bandiraagal [banⁿdiraagal] *(ngal)* kinship relationship.

banke [baŋke] *(o) {fr.}* bank. *O liggotoo ko e banke* He works in a bank.

bandotooɗo [banⁿdotooɗo] *(o)* fisherman.

bange [baŋŋe] *(o)* flank; side. ~ *goɗɗo* elsewhere. ~ *nano* left side. ~ *ñaamo* the right side.

banna *(o)* male first name.

bannude v. load a gun.

bantaɲ *(ki)* tree.

bantiɲééwi *(ki)* tree.

bantude v. be finished.

baɲbaɲru *(ndu)* tomcat. *ullundu* ~ tomcat.

bappaaño *(o)* step father; uncle.

bara *(o)* grass.

baraaji *(ɗi)* blessings; awards; benediction. *A dañii baraaji* You have gained God's blessings.

baraale *(ɗe)* currents. *waraango (ngo)* sing.

barak *(o) {fr.}* shanty; shack. *O hoɗi ko e barak* He lives in a shack.

baramléfól *(ngól)* tree leaf. *baramlefi (ɗi)* pl.

baras *(o)* leprosy; smallpox. *wondude e* ~ have leprosy.

barigal *(ngal)* tun. ~ *tokosal* keg.

barja *(o)* barter; trade by barter. *haaɗi haaɗa* alt.

barke *(ɗe) {ar.}* blessings. *Yo Alla waɗ e maa barke* May Allah bless you.

barkinde v. be blessed. *O mo barkini* He is blessed.

barkééwi *(ki)* tree.

barki *(ki)* tree.

barmande [barmanⁿde] *(nde)* wound.

barme *(o)* wound.

barminde v. wound seriously.

barmude v. be wounded seriously.

barme *(o)* 1) cooking pot 2) wound. **toggude** ~ start cooking. **dirtude** ~ remove the pot from the fire. *Barme maa sumii* Your food is burning. **barmééji** *(ɗi) pl.*

barooɗe *(ɗe)* fauna. ~ *ladde* wild animals. ~ *ladde* wild animals. *mbaroodi (ndi) sing.*

baroowo *(o)* killer. *Ko o baroowo* He is a killer.

basalle *(ɗe)* onions. *wasalde (nde) sing.*

basawal *(ngal)* lizard.

basél *(ngél)* little bag.

bata *(o)* bag.

batde [badde] *v.* 1) court; surround 2) hold a meeting.

batilo (o) courtier; flatterer.

batirde (nde) meeting place; venue.

batoowo (o) participant in a meeting.

batu (ngu) meeting. *Batu ngu fusi* The meeting is over.

batuuji (ɗi) sing.

batiri *(o)* *{fr.}* battery. *Batiri o gasii* The battery is weak.

batte *(ɗe)* traces. *hay* ~ nothing.

battinde v. leave a trace. *ɗum battinii* It left a trace.

bawɗi *(ɗi)* drums. *fiide* ~ hit the drums; play the music *mbaggu (ngu) sing.*

bawlude *v.* *{ar.}* urinate.

baylagól *(ngól)* mutation; metamorphosis; variation; change.

bayliiɗo adj. changed person. *O wayliima no feewi* He has changed so much.

baylo (o) blacksmith. *Ko o baylo* He belongs to the Smith caste.

bayloowo (o) person who makes changes.

baylugól (ngól) alteration; change.

baylól *(ngól)* bow; musical instrument. *O mo waawi baylol* He is a skilled bow player.

baynóndiral *(ngal)* good-bye; farewell. *Baynondiral ina muusi* It is not easy to say good-bye. *waynaade v.*

bayral (ngal) absence.

beccal *(ngal)* rib.

becce (ɗe) torso; chest; ribs.

beddal *(ngal)* 1) lock 2) jump.

bedek *(o)* *{wol.}* lead.

bédól *(ngól)* umbilical cord.

béélél *(ngél)* small pond; small shade. *béél (ɗi) pl.*

béélól *(ngól)* shade; soul. *ownude* ~ *neɗɗo* make life difficult for someone.

beemɗo *adj.* tomfool; stupid *neɗɗo* ~ stupid person. *Ko o beemɗo* He is stupid.

beembal [bemᵐbal] *(ngal)* large spac reserved for farming.

beere *(o)* *{fr.}* beret. **boornaade** ~ wear beret.

bees *(o)* title.

beetawe *(o)* morning. ~ *jango* tomorrov morning.

belɗo *adj.* pleasant; sweet. ~ *ñiiñan* affable person. *neɗɗo* ~ a pleasan individual.

beltagól (ngól) happiness; satisfaction *al weltaare (nde).*

béltiiɗo adj. happy; fain; glad; merr prolate.

bélgól *(ngól)* muddy area.

bempeᵞᵞe *(ɗe)* waves. *wemfeᵞere (nde sing.*

berɗo adj. tired.

berko *(ngo)* leveling.

bérkude v. flatten; level. *O wóni ko berkude* He is levelling the floor.

béttude *v.* surprise. *O bettu mo* He caugh him by surprise.

béttugól (ngól) surprise.

bewde *v.* be spoiled. *Aɗa bewi* You are spoiled brat.

béwnude v. pamper; spoil. *Ko aan béwn mo* You spoiled him.

bewre (nde) act of being spoiled. *Bewr burtunde moᵞᵞaani* Excessive care i bad.

béy *(ɗi)* goats. *mbeewa (ba) sing.*

beyaat *(o)* second clearance of weeds. *b ngoni ko e beyaat* They are clearing th weeds for the second time.

beytaade v. clear weeds a second tim around.

beytoowo *(o)* singer of religious poems.

béytude v. sing religious poems. *O woni k e beytude* He is singing religious songs.

beytugol (ngól) the singing of religiou songs.

bi *(o)* *{fr.}* goal.

aa *(o)* belief (outside Islam); taboo. *ɪm ko bidaa* It is taboo.

rgal *(ngal)* fan.

aade *v.* snatch. *O bifti ɗum* He atched it away. *alt. diftaade.*

ɪól *(ngól)* diaphragm.

kitaade *v.* free oneself or one's hand ruptly. *Bikkito* Free your hand.

kitde [bikkidde] *v.* free something ddenly.

ɪnka [bilaŋka] *(o)* carrier. *Ko o bilanka* ɛ works as a carrier.

ɪilel *(ngél)* a bat.

le *v.* roof. *ɓe ngoni ko e bilde huɓeere le* They are roofing the house.

ɪgo [bilⁿgo] *(ngo)* roofing.

ɛ *(ɗe)* traps. ~ *mehe* empty traps. ɪfaade ~ lay traps. *wilde (nde) sing.*

ɛejo *(o)* charlatan. *Ko o bileejo* He is a ɪarlatan.

al *(ngal)* big snake. *bille (ɗe) pl.*

ɪbi [bimᵐbi] *(ɗi)* morning.

e *(ɗe)* honey comb.

ɪeegara *(o) {fr.}* vinegar. *ɓeydu heen ɪneegara mbele ina safa* Add vinegar to ake it tasty.

ɪdól [binⁿdól] *(ngól)* notation; writing. ~ ɪoɗngol calligraphy.

ɪdoowo [binⁿdoowo] *(o)* writer. *Ko o ɪndoowo* S/He is a writer.

ɪduɗo [binⁿduɗo] *(o)* author.

ɪpameernoo *(o)* big mosquito.

ɪpude *v.* pull. *Hol to bippu* Do not pull

gude *v.* frisk; frolic; prance; cavort.

ɪó *(o) {fr.}* office. *dawde* ~ go to work at ɪne's office in the morning. *Hol to biro ɪaa woni* Where is your office? *birooji ɗi) pl.*

ɪaade *v.* fish.

ɪimilla *(o) {ar.}* welcome *Bisimilla maa* ɪelcome!

ɪmaade *v. {ar.}* welcome; say God's ame; recite verses for protection. ɪmillaay in the name of Allah.

ɪkalet *(o) {fr.}* bicycle. *waɗɗaade* ~ sit ɪn a bike. *dognude* ~ ride a bike.

ɪkitde [biskidde] *v.* belittle; discredit.

ɪik *(o) {fr.}* store; shop. *bitikaaji (ɗi) pl.*

ɪtól *(ngól)* belly fold.

bittoowo *(o)* researcher. ~ **hanki men** historian.

biwaade *v.* resist; jump around.

biwaango [biwaaⁿgo] *(ngo)* resistance.

biyé *(o) {fr.}* ticket. *Hol to biyé maa woni* Where is your ticket?

biƳƳe *(ɗe)* cotton seeds *wiƳƳere (nde) sing.*

boɓɓaade *v.* fall.

bóɓɓude *v.* make fall.

bóɓóri *(ki)* tree.

boɗeejo *adj.* red. *Ko o boɗeejo* He is light-skinned. *Ina wojji* It is red.

bójél *(ngél)* little rabbit.

bójjude *v.* crush; pound. ~ **tamaate** crush tomatoes.

bókól *(ngól)* neck.

bol *(o)* fish.

bolce *(ɗe)* vomited milk.

bólééru *(ndu)* vestibule; hall; lobby.

bóli *(ɗi)* paths; ways.

bólól *(ngól)* path; way. *rewde* ~ follow the path. *Yah bólól maa* This is not your business.

bóliiru *(ndu)* gourd.

bolle *(ɗe)* speech; talk.

boloɭ *(o)* gourd. *Yuppu ɗam e nder boloŋ o* Pour it in the gourd.

bómpileede *v.* be blinded by a shock; be bewildered. *Ko o bompilaaɗo* He is bewildered.

bonakitangél *(ngél)* insect.

bonande *(nde)* damage; mess; waste; tragedy; havoc; destruction. *ɗum ko bonande* It is a waste.

bonde *v.* be bad. ~ *jikku* misbehave. ~ *mbalndi* be unable to sleep still.

bonɗo *adj.* bad; evil; hostile; nasty; mean. *neɗɗo* ~ a bad person.

bone *(o)* danger; harm *reentaade.* ~ get away from danger; be careful. *bónééji (ɗi) pl.*

bonnanaaɗo *(o)* victim.

bonnande *v.* spoil for someone; mess things up for someone. *A bonnanii mo* You messed things up for him.

bónnitaade *v.* urinate or defecate on one's clothing.

bónnitde *v.* denigrate; vilify; debase; spoil again.

bonnoowo (o) malefactor.

bónnude v. spoil; tarnish; impair; pervert; ravage; spoliate.

boobo *(o)* kid; child. ~ *jam* a good child. ~ *bone* a bad child. *Boobo ina foti heɗaade mawɓe mum* A child should listen to his elders.

bool *(o)* tin bowl.

bóólumbal [bóóluᵐbal] *(ngal)* bird.

boom in fact.

boomaade *v.* be ruined.

boomaare *(nde)* ruin; pogrom; calamity; catastrophe. ~ *mawnde* a major catastrophe.

boomde *v.* decimate; ruin; destroy.

boosde *v.* abort; miscarry. *O boosii* She miscarried.

boosgól *(ngól)* abortion.

boot *(o)* bag; sack.

boowal *(ngal)* exterior; outside; outdoors. *yahde* ~ go outside. *boowe (ɗe) pl.*

borde *v.* dye. *O woni ko e borde comci ɗi* He is dyeing the clothes.

bóru *(ngu)* dye; indigo.

bórdólól *(ngól)* big intestine.

bordooɗe *(ɗe)* lamb or goat waste.

borjoɈ *(o)* rogue.

boroode *(nde) {fr.}* embroidery.

botoboto *(o)* feast organized by children.

bottaari *(ndi)* lunch. *róttude* ~ serve lunch. *defde* ~ cook lunch. *deftude* ~ complete the process of lunch cooking. *Bottaari maa nani* Here is your lunch.

bowte *(ɗe)* rain outside rainy season.

bóy *(o)* jackal.

boyde *v.* escape; catch fire.

boyet *(o) {fr.}* carton; box. *boyetaaji (ɗi) pl.*

bóyli *(ɗi)* wells. *woyndu (ndu) sing.*

bóyngél *(ngél)* little well.

bóyli *(ki)* type of tree.

bubbude *v.* slam. *Hol to bubbu baafe* Do not slam the doors.

buhal *(ngal)* thigh; hip. *buhe (ɗe) pl.*

bujubuju *(o)* fry; young fish.

bukde *v.* tighten.

bulde *v.* color blue. *O woni ko e bul comci ɗi* He is dyeing the clothes blue.

bulo *(o)* blue.

bumangal [bumaⁿgal] *(ngal)* pollen.

bunaa *(o)* dried fish. *ñiiri e* ~ a millet a dried fish dish. *Mi yiɗaa bunaa* I do n like dried fish.

buɈéé *(o)* monkey.

bunna *(o)* anus.

burdaama *(o)* cow.

burli *(ki)* tree.

burlól *(ngól)* chain of pearls.

burwet *(o) (fr.}* wheelbarrow. *yuppude mum* empty one's wheelbarrow.

butél *(o) (fr.}* bottle ~ *sangara* a bottle wine *butelaaji (ɗi) pl.*

butoɈ *(o) (fr.}* button. *nebbude ~a* button up. *nebbitde ~aaji* unbutt *butoɈaaji (ɗi) pl.*

butut *(o)* until.

buubaa *(o)* talking drum. *fiide* ~ play t talking drum. *Omon fiya buubaa* He playing the talking drum.

buubi *(ɗi)* flies. *mbuubu (ngu) sing.*

buuditaade *v.* be overcooked into pieces.

buumde *v.* cover completely.

buunal *(ngal)* bird. ~ *daⲨⲨe* a stupid useless person.

buur *(o) {wol.}* king.

buurnaade *v.* make a fire.

buurtól *(ngól)* ravine.

buuse *(o) (fr.}* butcher. *Ko o buuse* He i butcher.

buutufal *(ngal)* doomsday.

buy *adv.* very yellow. *E ɗum oolɗi buy* is really yellow.

ɓ

.ftude *v.* take a big handful of. *O ɓaaftii ꞥaro ko* He took a big handful of rice.

gaade *v.* insinuate.

raade *v.* lean against; rely on. *ɓaaro e ꞥlal ngal* Lean on the wall.

ragól *(ngól)* leaning against.

ꞥrde *v.* lean against; rely on. *Ko e maa o ꞥarii* He relies on you.

ꞥrgól *(ngól)* leaning against.

ꞥróndirde [ɓaaró"dirde] *v.* lean on each her; assist each other.

ꞥroowo *(o)* person who leans something mewhere.

ꞥrtude *v.* remove from a leaning position.

ꞥarto e ɓalal ngal Stay away from the ꞥll.

ꞥsde *v.* pin.

ꞥtde [ɓaadde] *v.* rub dirt on someone; cuse. *O ɓaati ɗum e makko* He cused him of the offense.

ꞥtgól *(ngól)* rubbing.

ꞥwo *(ngo)* 1) rectum 2) after; back; hind.~ *jango* the day after tomorrow. *'a mi yah toon ɓaawo jango* I will go ere tomorrow. *ɓaawóóji (ɗi) pl.*

ꞥwótél in three days. *haa ~* in three days.

ꞥYde [ɓaajje] *v.* make a discrete sign; gn. *O woni ko e ɓaaYde mo* He is ꞥempting to get his attention.

ꞥbitaade *v.* be detached from.

ꞥbitde [ɓabbitde] *v.* detach from.

ꞥbiteede *v.* be detached.

ꞥbo *(ngo)* bird backside. *O fetti ndu ko e ꞥbbo ngo* He hit the bird on the backside.

ꞥaade *v.* be close *fu ɗnaange ɓadii ɗo ꞥe* Near East. *ɓado* Get close. *Ina ɓadii* is close.

ꞥagól *(ngól)* proximity; closeness.

ꞥdinde *v.* bring close. *ɓadin mo ɗum* ring it close to him.

ꞥdóndiral [ɓadó"diral] *(ngal)* proximity.

ꞥdóndirde [ɓadó"dirde] *v.* be close to one ꞥother. *amin ɓadondiri* We live close to ꞥe another.

ꞥdtaade [ɓattaade] *v.* approach; be close ꞥ; come close. *En ɓattiima wuro ngo* We ꞥe getting close to the town.

ꞥdtiiɗo [ɓattiiɗo] *adj.* proximate.

ɓadtinde [ɓattinde] *v.* bring near.

ɓadtóndirde [ɓattó"dirde] *v.* be near. *E ɗi ɓadtondiri* They are close.

ɓafde *v.* move while sitting.

ɓafgól *(ngól)* movement while sitting.

ɓagde *v.* threaten.

ɓagoore *(nde)* threat.

ɓakkaade *v.* be stuck to.

ɓakkere *(nde)* clay; mire; shale; mud. *jiiɓde ɓakke* mix into mud. *prov. ɓakke mahetee ko gila eɗe ngoni kecce* Strike the hammer while the iron is hot.

ɓakkitde [ɓakkidde] *v.* remove stick. *ɗakkitde alt.*

ɓakkude *v.* stick on; accuse. *O ɓakki ɗum e makko* He blamed it on him.

ɓakólinde *v.* be muddy. *Ina ɓakolini* It is muddy.

ɓalal *(ngal)* wall. *ɓale (ɗe) pl.*

ɓaleejo *adj.* black; negro. *~ kurum* very black. *neɗɗo ~* a person of African decent. *Ko o ɓaleejo* S/He is black.

ɓalééri *(ndi)* black color; type of millet.

ɓaléwól *(ngól)* blackness.

ɓallaade *v.* get/be close *ɓallo* Come closer.

ɓallinde *v.* make close. *ɓallin mo ɗum* Bring it closer to him.

ɓallitaade *v.* get closer. *Ngonmi ko e ɓallitaade* I am getting closer.

ɓalnude *v.* be stout. *O mo ɓalni* He is big.

ɓamaade *v.* be pretty. *Safi ina ɓamii* Safi is pretty.

ɓamde *v.* take *prov. ɓamde ko faala jeyaaka e nguyka* Taking what you need does not mean stealing.

ɓamoowo *(o)* person who takes away.

ɓamtaade *v.* 1) be successful; thrive; progress 2) be raised. *O mo ɓamtii* He is successful.

ɓamtaare *(nde)* success. *ɗum ko ɓamtaare mawnde* That is a major success.

ɓamtii ɗo *adj.* successful person.

ɓamtude *v.* lift; retake. *Mo ɓamti ga ɗa faaburu ne faati ko leydi* If you lift the bottom of the frog it will return the ground (help those who help themselves).

ɓammude *v.* hit.

ɓande [ɓanⁿde] *(nde)* haft. ~ *jambere* the haft of an ax ɓane *(ɗe) pl.*

ɓandu [ɓanⁿdu] *(ndu)* body. ~ **mehru** a naked body. ~ *muusooru* a body that aches. *Wuj ɗum e ɓandu maa* Rub it on your body. *ɓalli (ɗi) pl.*

ɓalnude *v.* be big.

ɓaŋnude *v.* be known.

ɓappaade *v.* fall.

ɓappiɗde [ɓappidde] *v.* be low/flat.

ɓappinaade *v.* subside.

ɓarfinaade *v.* sit flat on one's bottom.

ɓarfinande [ɓarfinanⁿde] *(nde)* the act of sitting flat on one's bottom.

ɓasde *v.* mend; weld; patch. *ɓasanam jamberam nde* Weld my ax for me.

ɓasirgal *(ngal)* tool for mending. *A helii ɓasirgalam* You broke my tool.

ɓasóndirde [ɓasoⁿdirde] *v.* weld; put together.

ɓasoowo *(o)* mender; welder. *Ko o ɓasoowo* He is a welder.

ɓataake *(o)* letter. *~ jam* a letter with good news. *heɓde* ~ receive a letter. *jaaɓtaade* ~ reply to a letter. *neldude* ~ send a letter. *jolnude* ~ mail a letter. *Jolnu ɓataake o* Mail the letter.

ɓawlinaade *v.* blacken oneself.

ɓawlinde *v.* blacken. *~ yeeso* have an angry look. *ɗaccu ɓawlinde yeeso* Do not show an angry face.

ɓawlude *v.* be black; become black. *Ina ɓawli* It is black.

ɓawlugól *(ngól)* blackness ɓalewol *(ngól) alt.*

ɓayde *v.* 1) be attractive 2) be damp. *Ndaw ko ɓayi* People like him.

ɓayre *(nde)* charm for attraction. *O mo wondi e ɓayre* He has a charm for attraction.

ɓayo *(ngo)* moisture; dampness.

ɓayto *(ngo)* dampness; moisture.

ɓaytude *v.* be damp. *Ina ɓayti* It is damp.

ɓayri *conj.* since; as. *Njahen ɓayri o alaa ɗoo* Let us leave since he is not here. *ɓayde alt.*

ɓe *det.* the; they. *yimɓe* ~ the people. *ɓe ngarii* They arrived.

ɓee *det.* these. *~ yimɓe* these people.

ɓeya *det.* those. *yimɓe* ~ those individuals.

ɓeeɓde *v.* be dry. *ɗum ɓeeɓii* It is dryin up.

ɓééɓi *(ɗi)* area that dries last *ɓeeɓiiji (o pl.*

ɓeeɓo *(ngo)* draining.

ɓeeɓre *(nde)* drained area.

ɓéésóó *(o)* fish.

ɓeeynaade *v.* steal.

ɓelle *(ɗe)* fat. ɓellere *(nde)* sing.

ɓellere *(nde)* fat. ɓelle *(ɗe) plur.*

ɓéllinde *v.* fatten; be fat. *O mo ɓellini* He fat.

ɓéllinɗo *adj.* plump; obese; fat.

ɓéndinde [ɓenⁿdinde] *v.* make cook; mak ripe.

ɓéndude [ɓenⁿdude] *v.* be ripe; be cooke maturate. *Maaro ko ɓendii* The rice cooked.

ɓénduɗo *adj.* [ɓenⁿduɗo] 1) cooked mature.

ɓénninde *v.* implement. ~ *dewgal* we marry. *O ɓenninii dewgal* He just g married.

ɓénnitde [ɓénnidde] *v.* pass again.

ɓénnude *v.* pass; elapse; go past. *ɗu ɓennii* It has happened.

ɓénnuɗo *adj.* previous. *jamaanu* ~ in th old days; in the past.

ɓernde [ɓernɗe] *(nde)* heart. *mo ΥΥude.* have a good heart; be kind. *ɓonde* ~ to b mean. *O alaa ɓernde* He has no heart. *mo mo ΥΥi ɓernde* He is kind.

ɓérninde *v.* upset.

ɓérnude *v.* be angry; be upset. *Ko ɓernu ɗo* He is upset.

ɓesɗo *(o)* person who has given birth; a individual with a large family. *Ko o ɓesɗ* She gave birth not long ago.

ɓésngu *(ngu)* family; offspring. *No ɓesng maa waɗi* How is your family?

ɓésnude *v.* give birth.

ɓésnugol *(ngol)* procreation.

ɓetde [ɓedde] *v.* measure.

ɓetgól *(ngól)* measurement.

ɓétirde *v.* measure with.

ɓétirgal *(ngal)* instrument for measurin measurement.

ɓeydaade *v.* be added; be increased. *ɗu ɓeydiima* It has been increased.

ɗydaari (ndi) addition; plus; extra; ncrement; increase.

ɗydude v. add; augment; append; increase; add one's piece of salt. *Ndaw ko waawi ɓeydude* He likes to add his grain of salt.

ɗydugol (ngól) addition; increase.

iɗde [bidde] v. squeeze.

iɗɗo (o) child; baby. ~ *debbo* daughter. ~ *gorko* son. ~ *léydi* citizen. ~ *tekke* doll.

ɗi (o) son; daughter. ~ *moYYo* a child of good parents. ~ *bonɗo* a child of bad parents.

ingal (ngal) big child.

ingél [bingel] (ngél) little child. ~ *leɗɗe* fruit. ~ *haram* child born out of wedlock; bastard.

iicaade v. sound with disapproval.

iicaango (ngo) creak.

iicde [biijje] v. be tight.

iiñaango (ngo) grimace; grin.

iiñde v. make a face; grin. *Hol ko ɓiiñataa* What are you making a face at?

iirtinde v. give away used items. *Mi ɓiirtinii ma wutte o* I am giving you this used gown.

iirtude v. empty a dish with fingers. ~ *haa laaɓa* wipe clean.

iiYde [biijje] v. screw.

iiYtude [biiccude] v. unscrew.

ilde v. place one's leg around another's; insert. ~ *neɗɗo* get a person into trouble. *Ko o ɓiliiɗo* He is in trouble/he is busy.

iltude v. free. *O ɓiltiima* S/he is out of trouble.

inaare (nde) animal.

iraɗam (ɗam) fresh milk. *kosam* ~ fresh milk.

irande v. milk for someone.

irde v. milk. *Omon ɓira nagge nge* He is milking the cow.

irdugal (ngal) calabash for milking.

iroowo (o) person who milks. *ɓiroowo darotaako* It is unusual for a person who milks to be in a standing position.

irtaade v. milk again.

ittaade v. be squeezed tightly.

itteede v. be poor. *O mo ɓittaa* He is poor.

itteende (nde) shortage.

ittude v. squeeze tightly; oppress.

ɓóbbude v. dent. *Ko ɗum boɓɓiɗum* It is dented.

ɓóbbude v. pick up.

ɓóccinde v. lay an egg. *Ngal ɓoccinii* The hen laid an egg.

ɓoccoonde (nde) egg. ~ *harilde* a bad egg.

ɓocokcok bad egg.

ɓóccitaade v. escape. *O ɓoccitiima* He escaped.

ɓóccitél (ngél) diarrhea. *O mo wondi e ɓoccitel* He has diarrhea.

ɓóccitoreede v. 1) fumble 2) make an involuntary mistake. *O ɓoccitora* It was just a mistake.

ɓodde v. lag; creep along.

ɓóɗɗude v. feel by pressing the thumb on.

ɓóftirgél (ngél) dustpan.

ɓóftude v. gather up; pick up. *ɓoftu kurjuru o* Pick up the garbage.

ɓóggól (ngól) rope. ~ *njamndi* wire.

ɓóggude v. pick fruit.

ɓohere (nde) baobab fruit.

ɓokkaade v. 1) fan insects away from oneself 2) detach oneself. *ko o ɓokkiiɗo* He does not want to be involved.

ɓókkirgal (ngal) fan.

ɓókkude v. fan flies away.

ɓokki (ki) baobab tree.

ɓokko (ko) bark. *sirde* ~ remove the bark; strip.

ɓolde v. strip off.

ɓolɗude v. be stripped off. *O mo ɓolɗi* She is not wearing jewelery.

ɓólkude v. make love.

ɓoñde v. shed tears; have watery eyes.

ɓoodde v. be slippery. *Ina ɓoodi* It is slippery.

ɓoodde (nde) 1) lump 2) useless person. ~ *suukara* a lump of sugar. ~ *lacciri* lump of couscous.

ɓóóldu (ndu) big stick. *O fiiri mo ko ɓooldu* He hit him with a big stick.

ɓóóltinaade v. wait. *O woni ko e ɓooltinaade* He is not eating his food now.

ɓóóltude v. skin; peel. *ɓooltu nguru ngu* Remove the skin.

ɓólum adj. empty.

ɓoomde v. change shape.

bóómtude v. regain the normal shape.

booraade v. undress. **booro jóóni** Undress now.

boreede v. be banned; be undressed. **O booraama** He is banned from the Police force.

boorde v. 1) pull off; remove clothing 2) ban.

bóórdude v. chase; remove by way of.

boornaade v. 1) put clothes on 2) undergo circumcision. **boorno cómci maa** Put your clothing on.

boornoowo (o) person who performs circumcision.

bóórnude v. circumcise.

boororde (nde) nightgown; night dress.

boortaade v. undress. **Hol to boorto e hakkunde yimbe** Do not undress in front of people.

bóórtiido adj. naked; nude.

bóórtude v. undress. **bóórtu cómci maa** Undress.

bóórtugol v. removal of one's clothings.

boosaaru (ndu) puppy.

boosde v. massage. **mbede sokli booseede** I need a massage.

bóósgól (ngól) massage.

bootere (nde) grass.

booyde v. be long. **booyaani ko dum wadi** It just happened.

booydo adj. old. **neddo** ~ an old person.

bóóytude v. remain for a long time; be outdated.

booYere (nde) kidney.

boraade v. lose hair or feathers. **hoore bóriinde** a bald head.

borde v. pull up; deplume; pluck.

boro (ngo) small feathers.

borke (de) disease.

bortere (nde) type of grass **bórwude** v. be slippery. **Ina borwi** It is slippery.

bosde v. move a little.

bóslitaade v. move while sleeping. **O bóslitiima** She just moved.

bota (ba) little goat.

bottere (nde) 1) testicule 2) useless/ignorant person.

bóttude v. pinch. **O bótti mo e réédu** He pinched him on the belly.

bóttugól (ngól) pinch.

bówdi (ki) baobab tree.

bowngu (ngu) mosquito pl. **bowdi** (di).

buddu (ngu) worm.

buftaade v. bathe; shower. **Mi buftiima** I have already taken a shower.

buftagol (ngól) bathing; showering. ~ **jaawngol** a quick shower.

bujiri (ndi) castrated bullock.

bulbi (ki) tree.

bulde v. flow. **dum bulii** The water is flowing.

bulél (ngél) little well.

bulnaade v. wait for water to flow. **Ko mi bulniido** I am waiting for the water to flow.

bultaade v. harvest gum.

buñde [buñje] v. have many worms.

bundu [bunⁿdu] (ndu) well. **bulli** (di) pl.

bural (ngal) advantage; preference; superiority. **dum alaa bural** It is not advantageous.

burde v. surpass; predominate; transcend. **Ko aan buri mo darnde** You are taller than him.

burnaade v. act important. **O mo burnii** He likes to act important.

burnaado (o) chosen person.

burnude v. prefer; advocate.

burtaade v. outgrow; surpass. **O burti maama** He has outgrown you.

burtaari (ndi) profit.

burtinde v. 1) overdo 2) lie.

burtude v. exceed; be excessive. **Ina burti** It is excessive.

bursude v. grind peanuts.

burtungal (ngal) veil. **fiilde** ~ wear a veil.

buttidde v. be big; be fat; gain weight. **O butti daani** He did not gain weight.

buttidgól (ngól) stout.

buttidinde v. make big; fatten. **Ina butti dina** It makes a person big/fat.

butto adj. robust; big; fat. **neddo** ~ a big/fat person.

buubde v. be cold; be calm. **Ina buubi** It is cold.

buubnude v. make cold; make fresh; cool.

buuból (ngól) cold; chill.

ɓuɓri *(ndi)* 1) shade 2) bladder infection. **o mo wondi e ɓuuɓri** He has a bladder infection.

ɓuɓtude *v.* be colder.

ucaade *v.* kiss; suck. *O ɓuucii mo* He kissed her.

ucagól *(ngól)* kiss.

ucóndirde [ɓuucóⁿdirde] *v.* kiss each other.

utdi [ɓuuddi] *(ndi)* swelling. *ɓuutɗi ndi aayii* The swelling is gone.

ɓuutaaɗo *(o)* person suffering from overeating. *Ko o ɓuutaaɗo* He is suffering from overeating.

ɓuutde [ɓuudde] *v.* be swollen. *Ko ko ɓuuti* It is swollen.

ɓuuteede *v.* suffer from overeating. *Ko o ɓuutaaDo* He is suffering from excessive food intake.

ɓuutnude [ɓuunnude] *v.* make swell up.

ɓuuƴeede *v.* have the urge to urinate/defecate. *Mbeɗe ɓuuƴaa coofe* I have the urge to urinate.

ɓuƴde [bujje] *v.* bend.

C

ca goat calling word.

caabi *(ɗi)* *{wol.}* keys. ~ **wakande** keys to the trunk. ~ **oto** car keys. ~ **galle** keys to the house. ~ **aduna** keys to the world.

caaɗngól [caanⁿgól] *(ngól)* stream. *saaɗde v.*

caaju *(ngu)* horse.

caakaan *(o)* *{wol.}* triviality.

caakri *(ndi)* dish.

caali *(ki)* roof made with grass and wood. *firtude* ~ undo the roof. *caaleeje (ɗe) pl.*

caamaaba *(ba)* snake.

caangól [caanⁿgól] *(ngól)* stream; creek. *caalɗi (ɗi) pl.*

caaról *(ngól)* diarrhea.

caasɗo *adj.* energetic. *Ndaw ko saasi* He is a hard working individual.

caasgól *(ngól)* energy; strength.

caaygól *(ngól)* fusion.

cabbiiɗo *(o)* a person who is waiting for someone or something.

cafɗo *adj.* sweet; tasty; likeable. *neɗɗo* ~ a likeable person. *safde v.*

cafroowo *(o)* doctor. ~ *gite* eye doctor; ophthalmologist. ~ *koyɗe* orthopedist. *Ko o cafroowo* He is a doctor. *safrude v.*

caggal *(ngal)* rear; posterior; behind; after. ~ *maa* after you left. ~ *léydi* foreign country; abroad. ~ *ɗum* afterward.

cajal *(ngal)* bamboo fence.

cakalo *adj.* outgoing; friendly. *Ko o cakalo* He is friendly. *sakoliɗde v.*

cakka *(ka)* necklace; collar. *ɓoorno cakka ka* Wear the necklace.

cakutal *(ngal)* leg. *cakute (ɗe) pl.*

callalal *(ngal)* chain. *tellinde* ~ anchor. *jolnude* ~ leave. *callale (ɗe) pl.*

calli *(ki)* tree.

calligiiɗo *(o)* a person who has performed his/her ablution ritual. *salligaade v.*

calngél *(ngél)* small fork shaped wooden pillar. ~ *tuggortééngél* a cane.

camalle *(ɗe)* kindling wood.

cami *(ki)* tree.

cañcorgal *(ngal)* instrument for untying/unbraiding hair. **cañctirgal** *(ngal)* alt.

cañgól *(ngól)* weaving.

cañirgal *(ngal)* loom.

cañoowo *(o)* weaver. *Ko o cañoowo* He is a weaver.

cañtirgal [cañcirgal] *(ngal)*

cañtoowo [cañcoowo] *(o)* person who unbraids hair.

cañtugól [cañcugól] *(ngól)* the unbraiding of hair.

cañu *(ngu)* weaving. *O mo waawi cañu* He is a skilled weaver.

candal [candal] *(ngal)* instrument for weaving.

capaato *(o)* Moor. *Ko o capaato* He is a Moor.

capanɗe *(ɗe)* tens. ~ *joyaɓo* fiftieth. ~ *nayaɓo* fortieth. ~ *jeegom* sixty. ~ *nay* forty.

caru *(ngu)* 1) dispersion; separation 2) animosity. *ɗum addata ko caru* This will bring animosity. *sarde v.*

caroowo *(o)* 1) person who scatters 2) person who causes animosity between individuals.

carwoowo *(o)* waiter. *Ko o carwoowo* He is a waiter.

caski *(ki)* tree.

casól *(ngól)* hoed soil. *remde* ~ *mum* take care of one's business.

catal *(ngal)* branch. ~ *lekki* a tree branch. *cate (ɗe) pl.*

catel *(ngél)* little branch.

cawndiiɗo [cawⁿdiiɗo] person who is close to another person.

cawndotooɗo [cawⁿdiiɗo]*(o)* person who gets close to another person.

cawndóndiral [cawⁿdóⁿdiral] *(ngal)* the act of getting close to one another.

cawél *(ngél)* little stick.

cawgal *(ngal)* big skin of a dead animal.

cawgél *(ngél)* little skin of a dead animal.

cawgu *(ngu)* skin of a dead animal. *cawɗi (ɗi) pl.*

cawndiiɗo *(o)* person who is next.

caygal *(ngal)* bird.

ceɓe *(ɗe)* peaks; tops. *seɓre (nde) sing.*

ɓtam (ɗam) peak; pinnacle; ridge; tip; nadir. *O yettiima ceɓtam* He reached the very top.

celle *(ɗe)* first rains.

ɗɗo *(o)* person of the Warrior caste. *Ko o ceɗɗo* He belongs to the Warrior caste.

ɛbɗe *adj.* sharp.

ɛbɗo *adj.* acute; intelligent; sharp. *suka ~* an intelligent child.

ɛɓndam *(ɗam)* sharpness.

ɛede *(ɗe)* cowry shells. *seedere (nde) sing.*

ɛ́diiɗo *(o)* witness. *seedaade v.*

ɛ́ɗu *(ngu)* dry season; summer. *Céédu arii* It is summer.

efe *(ɗe)* herds of cattle.

ɛ́lól *(ngól)* strip of dried meat. *seelde v.*

ɛ́ltól *(ngól)* shred; strip.

ɛ́ltugól *(ngól)* the act of tearing something into strips.

eeltoowo *(o)* person who tears something into strips.

eemeedo *(o)* young woman. *Ko o ceemeedo* She is a young woman.

een *(o) {fr.}* chain. *~ kaɲɲe* gold chain.

eenal *(ngal)* sand *pl. ceene (ɗe).* *~ boɗewal* red sand. *~ danewal* white sand.

eeraaɗo *(o)* divorcée; divorcé.

eerɗo *(o)* a person who divorced.

eergal *(ngal)* divorce.

eerno *(o)* religious teacher. *~ mawɗo* a great religious teacher. *Hol gonɗo ceerno maa* Who is your teacher?

efe *(ɗe)*.

eggannooɗo *(o)* person who used to filter liquids.

eggitoowo *(o)* person who filters liquids again. *seggude v.*

eggoowo *(o)* person who filters liquids.

éggugól *(ngól)* the filtering of liquids.

ɛkɗo *adj.* irate; angry. *Ko o cekɗo* He is angry.

ɛkke *(ɗe)* fences of woven reed. *sekko (ngo) sing.*

ɛ́kkiri *(ndi)* ashes used for making soap.

ɛ́li *(ɗi)* branching roads; cross roads. *laabi ~* branching roads.

ɛ́lól *(ngól)* ramp; branching road.

cellal *(ngal)* health; sanity. *cellal ɓuri ngalu* Health is better than wealth. *Ko cellal ardii* Health comes first.

céllinoowoo *(o)* healer.

céllingól *(ngól)* treatment; healing.

célluɗo *adj.* healthy; sane; vigorous. *gorko ~* a healthy man.

cemte *(ɗe)* lies. *cemtol (ngol) sing. semtude v.*

cemtoowo *(o)* liar.

cemtunooɗo *(o)* person who lied.

ceɲalal *(ngal)* calabash. *~ makka* calabash full of corn ears.

céɲdi *(ndi)* bait.

céɲondiral *(ngal)* linking; joining.

céɲondiroowo *(o)* person who joins elements together.

ceɲle *(ɗe)* pounded grains. *laawde ~* put pounded grains in the pot.

cettal *(ngal)* sharpened piece of wood used for unbraiding hair. *settude v.*

cettoowo *(o)* person who makes sharp wooden objects.

cewɗo *adj.* 1) thin person; slim; slender; lean 2) trashy type of person. *sewde v.*

céwngu *(ngu)* panther.

ciftól *(ngól)* charade; conundrum; puzzle; riddle. *siftude v.*

ciibe *(ɗe)* grass. *siiwre (nde).*

ciifgól *(ngól)* signing of.

ciifól *(ngól)* line. signature.

**ciifi *(ɗi) pl.*

ciifoowo *(o)* person who signs.

ciilal *(ngal)* eagle; falcon.

ciiwgol *(ngol)* the pouring of liquids.

ciiwoowo *(o)* person who pours.

ciññoowo *(o)* a shaking person.

ciññuɗo *(o)* a shivering individual.

ciññugol *(ngol)* shivering; shaking.

ciiwoowo *(o)* person who pours liquids.

cilbi *(ɗi)* fringes.

cilo *(o) {fr.}* kilogram *cilóóji (ɗi).*

ciluki *(ki)* ree.

cingóóli [ciɲⁿgóóli] *(ki)* tree.

cirééwi *(ki)* tree.

cirƳe *(ɗe)* spits.

cirƳoowo (o) person who spits.

cirƳugol (ngol) spitting.

ciyam *(ɗam)* leak. ~ *muusɗam* a bad/major leak.

coccagól *(ngól)* tooth cleaning; cleaning.

coccorgal *(ngal)* toothpick. *ɗum ko coccorgal maa* That is your toothpick.

cóccugól *(ngól)* cleaning; cleansing.

códól *(ngól)* short cut. *laawól* ~ a short cut.

cófél *(ngél)* small baby chicken.

cofal *(ngal)* big baby chicken.

coggal *(ngal)* herd of cattle; herd of animals.

coggoowo *(o)* herder; person who drive cattle to pasture.

cóggu *(ngu)* price. *ɓeydude* ~ increase the price. *ustude* ~ reduce the price. *Hol no coggu mum foti* What is the price?

cókki *(ɗi)* checkers game; chess. *fiide* ~ play a checkers game.

cokoowo *(o)* person who locks; janitor.

cóktirgal *(ngal)* key. ~ *galle* house key. ~ *aduna* key to the world. *coktirɗe (ɗe) pl.*

coktoowo *(o)* person who unlocks.

coktugol *(ngol)* removal of a lock; unlocking.

cóku *(ngu)* dam.

colɗo *adj.* person whose teeth have fallen off. *Ko o colɗo* He has lost many teeth.

coloowo *(o)* person who removes teeth.

coltoowo *(o)* person who removes teeth that came up again.

cólél *(ngél)* sparrow; little bird. *colli (ɗi) pl.*

colla *(ka)* dust.

collaay *(o)* dust.

cómcól *(ngól)* piece of clothing; garment; outfit; raiment; uniform.

coñaandi *(ndi)* produce; yield; harvest.

coñal *(ngal)* harvest.

coñoowo *(o)* harvester.

cóndi [conⁿdi] *(ndi)* flour; powder. ~ *fetel* gunpowder.

coodoowo *(o)* purchaser; buyer. *O wonaa coodoowo* He is not buying.

coofɗo *adj.* ugly.

cooragol *(ngol)* the act of wandering all over the place. *sooraade v.*

cooriiɗo *(o)* person who is wandering all over the place.

coorgal *(ngal)* perch; pole; spar.

cóórumbal [cóóruᵐbal] *(ngal)* flute.

cooyɗo *adj.* spinster. *debbo* ~ a spinster.

cosɗo *(o)* founder.

cottaandi [cottaandi] *(ndi)* millet devoid of bran; shelled millet.

cówól *(ngól)* fold. *cowe (ɗi) pl. sowde v.*

coy very red (used for emphasis). *Ina wójji coy* It is really red.

cuɓagól *(ngól)* choice; alternative; selection.

cuɓaaɗo *(o)* chosen individual.

cuɓoowo *(o)* person who selects.

cuɓotooɗo *(o)* chooser.

cuddaaɗo *(o)* 1) married woman; bride 2) covered person.

cuddiiɗo *(o)* 1) married woman 2) person who covered himself. *Hol to cuddiiɗo maa woni* Where is your wife?

cuddoowo *(o)* groom.

cuddungu *(ngu)* wedding. ~ *Hammat* Hammat's wedding.

cukaagu *(ngu)* infancy; childhood. *Ko cukaagu waɗi ɗum* It is childish behavior.

cukalél *(ngél)* boy; infant; brat. ~ *moYYel* a good boy. ~ *bongel* a bad boy.

cukkiri *(ndi)* thicket. *naatirde e* ~ get angry. *O naatirimi e cukkiri* He got angry at me.

cukko *(o)* next. *Ko kanko woni cukko maa* He comes after you.

cumaram *(ɗam)* scald; burn. ~ *muusɗam* first degree burn.

cumu *(ngu)* fire. *cum ɓerel* heartburn. *Ngaree cumu* fire! fire!

cuuɗiiɗo *adj.* clandestine.

cuuraay *(o)* incense.

cuurél *(ngél)* little room.

cuuron *(kon)* little rooms. *suudu (ndu) sing.*

cuurki *(ki)* steam; reek; smoke.

cuusal *(ngal)* bravery; mettle; prowess. *O mo hééwi cuusal* he is brave.

cuusɗo *adj.* brave. ~ *réédu* brave. ~ *gacce* a shameless person. ~ *bone* quarrelsome.

cuutirgal *(ngal)* instrument for lifting or pulling out.

D

daabaa *(o)* animal for riding such as a donkey.

daaɓaaɗo *(o)* person who has been contaminated.

daaɓoowo *(o)* a person who contaminates others. *raaɓde v.*

daaɓondiral [daaɓóⁿdiral] *(ngal)* mutual contamination.

daagaade *v.* shamble; pace slowly. *O woni ko e daagaade* He is pacing slowly.

daagotooɗo *(o)* a person who paces slowly.

daago *(ngo)* mat. *wertude* ~ spread the mat. *taggude* ~ roll up a mat.

daakaa *(o)* camp; gathering *pl.* **daakaaji** *(ɗi)*.

daakaade *v.* be assembled.

daakande [daakanⁿde] *(nde)* gathering.

daakde *v.* camp.

daalnude *v.* Be reduced; become weak.

daande [daaⁿde] *(nde)* voice; neck. ~ *loornde* a hoarse voice. ~ *welnde* a beautiful voice *pl.* **daaɗe** *(ɗe)*.

daarde *v.* 1) tell a story 2) diminish; subside.

daaról *(ngól)* story; tale. *ɗum wonaa tindol, ko daarol* It is not a story but it is a tale.

daasaade *v.* drag oneself. *Hol ko waɗmaa daasaade* Why are you lagging behind?

daasde *v.* draw; lug; drag along.

daasirde *v.* drag with.

daasnaade *v.* pace slowly.

daasól *(ngól)* track; trace. ~ *ngooroondi* trace left by a snake.

daawnude *v.* inform.

daayde *v.* be calm. *Hendu ndu daayi* The wind has subsided.

daaɾde *v.* stop a baby animal from sucking. *Daaɾ ñale nge* Stop the heifer from sucking.

daaye *(ɗe)* nenuphar plants *sing.* **raayre** *(nde)*.

daayo *(ngo)* exile.

daaɾoowo *(o)* a person who stops a baby animal from sucking.

dabaade *v.* 1) guide 2) perform sorcery.

dabanaade *v.* perform sorcery for someone. *Mbeɗe yiɗi dabaneede* I want someone to perform sorcery for me.

dabare *(ɗe)* sorcery; magic.

dabotooɗo *(o)* person who performs witchcraft.

dabbirde *(nde)* winter camp.

dabbude *v.* spend winter; camp for the winter.

dabbunde [dabbuⁿde] *(nde)* winter.

dabbo *adj.* short; scrimp. *neɗɗo* ~ a short person. *sahaa* ~ a short period.

dabi *(o)* guide *pl.* **dabiiji** *(ɗi)*.

dadaade *v.* tie around the waist; tie one's belt.

dadól *(ngól)* belt. *habbude* ~ tie a belt.

dadnude [dannude] *v.* tie a belt for someone.

dadorde *(nde)* waist. *nadorde* *(nde)* alt.

dadorgal *(ngal)* belt.

daɗɗaade *v.* stretch.

daɗde [dadde] *v.* 1) win a race 2) escape danger; get away. *O daɗi o dandii* The delivery was very successful.

daɗɗo *adj.* safe; winner.

daɗóndirde [daɗóⁿdirde] *v.* race/precede one another.

daɗtaade [dattaade] *v.* outrun; outpace; overtake again; pass. *Mi daɗti maama* I passed you.

daɗɗude *v.* spread a mat. ~ *leeso* spread a mat.

daggude *v.* stagger.

dahaa *(o)* ink. *ku ɗol* ~ a writing pen.

dajde [dajje] *v.* lessen; reduce.

dakkande *v.* make a dish called kodde for someone. *Dakkanam kodde* Make the kodde dish for me.

dakkere *(nde)* dish.

dakkiri *(ndi)* steamed millet.

dakkude *v.* make the kodde dish. *O woni ko e dakkude* He is making the kodde dish.

dakmude *v.* be tasty. *E ɗum dakmi* It is very tasty.

daliilu *(o)* {ar.} reason; proof. *jogaade* ~ have a good reason for doing something. *Mi alanaa ɗum daliilu* I cannot justify it.

dallinde v. prove.

dalirde *(nde)* camp.

dallaade *(nde)* port.

damal *(ngal)* entry; access; gate; door. *uddude* ~ close the door. *udditde* ~ open the door. *buɓɓude* ~ slam a door. *dajjitde* ~ break the door. ~ *suudu* bedroom door. ~ *galle* gate.

dambaade [damᵐbaade] v. wed; undergo the wedding ceremony.

dambitaade [daᵐbitaade] v. complete the wedding ceremony. *O dambitiima* S/he has commpleted the wedding ceremony.

dambórdu [damᵐbórdu] *(ndu)* bridal room. *naatde* ~ enter the bridal room/begin the wedding ceremony.

dambude [damᵐbude] v. participate in a wedding ceremony.

dammuhól *(ngól)* lamb; goat.

dampe *(ɗe)* one-piece type of female clothing.

dampoowo *(o)* kicker.

dampude v. kick. *O dampi mo e reedu* He kicked him in the belly.

dampugól *(ngól)* kicking.

daŋ *(o)* edge.

dañal *(ngal)* gain; fortune; asset. *jom* ~ a wealthy person. *Dañal e baasal ngondi* One may be wealthy today and poor tomorrow.

dañde [dañje] v. gain; acquire. *O dañii ko o yiɗnoo* He got what he wanted.

dandoowo [danⁿdoowo] *(o)* savior. *ko Alla woni dandoowo* Allah is the savior.

dandude [danⁿdude] v. save; secure. *Ko Alla tan waawi dandude* Allah is the only savior.

daneejo adj. white. *neɗɗo* ~ a white person.

danga *(o)* [daŋ]ⁿga] pouch prov. *So wonko hammayaroyel waawi danga baaba mum yooliima* You have the opportunity to show us what you can do.

dankaade [daŋkaade] v. pay attention. *Aɗa foti dankaade ko kaalat mi ko* You should pay attention to what I say.

danki [daŋki] *(ki)* raised platform.

danna *(o)* hunter.

dara *(o)* naught; nothing; zero. *Hay dara mi wiyaani* I said nothing.

daraade v. stand up; stop; cease; halt; stagnate.

daragól *(ngól)* truce.

daraniiɗo *(o)* militant. *Omo daranii leñol no feewi* He is fighting for his ethnic group indeed.

darnde *(nde)* height; stop; standing up. *Hol ɗo darnde maa tolnii*: How tall are you?

darngo *(ngo)* standing up.

darnude v. make stand; erect. *Ko o darnu ɗo* He is hard.

darorde *(nde)* stop.

dartaade v. defend; resist *Darto mo* Stand up to him.

dartagól *(ngól)* pause; defense.

dartinde v. erect again.

dartinde *(nde)* pause; stop.

daraja *(o)* popularity; fame. *heewde* ~ be famous.

darjude v. be popular; be well known. *Omo darji no feewi* He is very popular.

darju ɗo *(o)* famous; popular.

dargeede v. have spots.

datól *(ngól)* path. *pl. dati (ɗi)*.

dawaaɗi *(ɗi)* dogs. *Aan ko a rawaandu* You are a dog. *sing. rawaandu (ndu)*.

dawde v. go to work in the morning. ~ *law* go to work early in the morning.

dawnude v. make work. *Mi dawnii mo hande* I made him work today.

dawól *(ngól)* act of going to work in the morning.

dawlude v. pay part of a debt.

daⅯe *(ɗe)* hard grass roots. *raⅯere (nde)*.

de *suf.* infinitive marker; to *helde* break.

debati gorkati *(o)* gay; homosexual; a male with female mannerisms.

debbo *(o)* woman. ~ *galle* housewife. ~ *dambiiɗo* bride. ~ *reedu* pregnant woman.

dewal *(ngal)* big woman.

dewel *(ngél)* little woman.

débbude v. sink.

deedaaɗo *(o)* bastard; born out of wedlock. *Ko o deedaaɗo* He was born out of wedlock.

deedal *(ngal)* lake; large pond/lake.

deede *(o)* older sibling. *Ko o deede am* S/he is my older sibling.

deelaade *v.* be spilled.

deelde *v.* spill.

déémóóru *(ndu)* chimpanze; ape.

deenoowo *(o)* guard. ~ *neɗɗo* bodyguard; guardian.

deentagól *(ngól)* vigilance; precaution; prudence; caution.

déentiiɗo *adj.* vigilant; careful; cautious. *Ko o neɗɗo deentiiɗo* He is a very cautious person.

déeringi [déériⁿgi] *(o)* big belly.

deeʸde *v.* be calm. *Omo deeʸi no feewi* She is very calm.

deeʸɗo [deeʸʸo] *adj.* calm; quiet; peaceful; still; immobile; stable; serene. *Ko o neɗɗo deeʸɗo* He is a quiet person.

deeʸere *(nde)* calm; silence.

dééʸnude [dééññude] *v.* cool; appease; placate; pacify; soothe; immobilize.

deeʸre *(nde)* calm; hush; quiescence.

defaade *v.* be in charge of. *Miin defii piye maa* I am in charge of your contributions.

defande *v.* cook for someone. *Defanam maaro e teew* Please make the rice and meat dish for me.

defde *v.* cook. ~ *botaari* cook lunch. ~ *hiraande* cook dinner. *O woni ko e defde* He is cooking.

defirde *v.* cook with. *O defirta ko leɗɗe* He is cooking with firewood.

defnude *v.* make someone cook.

defoowo *(o)* cook; chef. *Ko o defoowo* He is a cook.

défrude *v.* cook with.

deftagól *(ngól)* repetition.

deftere *(nde)* book. ~ *Quraana* The Koran. *wilde* ~ sequence the pages of a book in a disorderly fashion. *wiltude* ~ arrange the pages of a book in their proper sequence.

dege *(ɗe)* peanut.

degere *(o) (fr.}* degree.

déggóndiral [deggóⁿdiral] *(ngal)* succession.

délfinde *v.* tie around the waist.

demal *(ngal)* farming.

demoowo *(o)* peasant. *Ko o demoowo* He is a farmer. *remooɓe (ɓe) pl.*

démminaade *v.* camp before the rainy season.

démminaare *(nde)* pre-rainy season.

dempeteŋ pound fresh rice.

dendaangal [denⁿdaaⁿgal] *(ngal)* all. ~ *koreeji* all relatives.

déndingól [denⁿdingól] *(ngól)* combination.

déndinoowo [denⁿdinoowo] *(o)* collector; a person who creates animosity between people.

dental *(ngal)* union; confederation rally. ~ *jongal* quorum. ~ *yimɓe* throng. ~ *mawngal* mob; mass. *Deental waawi ceeral* Better to unite than be divided.

dende [denⁿde] *(nde)* watermelon.

dénɗiraaɗo *(o)* one's mother's brother's child; first cousin.

dénɗiraagal *(ngal)* kinship between cousins and first cousins.

denkaade [deŋkaade] *v.* sit down abruptly.

dénkude [deŋkude] *v.* make someone (or something) sit down abruptly.

deŋloode *(nde)* small quantity of liquids.

deŋŋere *(nde)* harpoon. *yiwde* ~ pierce with a harpoon.

deppaade *v.* fall on one's bottom.

dewal *(ngal)* big woman.

dewel *(ngel)* little woman.

dewɗo *adj.* devout; follower. ~ *jóómiraaɗo* pious. ~ *aduna* person who is after pleasures of life.

dewgal *(ngal)* marriage; matrimony. ~ *moʸʸal* a good marriage. *ɓenninde* ~ wed. *firtude* ~ divorce.

déwóndiral *(ngal)* sequel; order.

dewoowo *(o)* 1) adept; pupil 2) person who owes money.

deʸʸere *(nde)* silence.

déʸʸinde *v.* quieten; silence. *Deʸʸin mo* Keep him quiet.

déʸʸude *v.* be quiet. *Deʸʸu* Be quiet.

déʸʸuɗo *adj.* silent; quiet.

diccaade *v.* 1) kneel 2) urinate. *O woni ko e diccaade* He is urinating.

diccande [diccanⁿde] *(nde)* kneeling.

dicce *(ɗe)* urine.

diftaade *v.* snatch. ~ *debbo* take one's future bride away.

diftagól *(ngól)* snatching.

digaade *v.* thunder.

digaango [digaaⁿgo] *(ngo)* thunder. *digaali (ɗi) pl.*

dihal *(kal)* little quantity of water.

diidde *v.* mark; draw a line; sketch; draw. **~huɓeere** begin the foundation of a building.

diidól *(ngól)* line; mark; trace. **~ hakkunde** diameter. **~ ɲooyre** a fact.

diiñde *v.* put down.

diine *(o) {ar.}* religion; faith. **Hol ko woni diine ma** What is your religion? **diinééji (ɗi) pl.**

diiraali *(ɗi)* loud noises. **ɗiiraango (ngo)** sing.

diirde *v.* make a loud noise such as car noise.

diirgól *(ngól)* loud noise.

diisnaade *v.* consult. **Neɗɗo yo diisnoto mawɓe mum** A person should consult his elders.

diiwaan *(o)* province; county. **~ Calgu** the Calgu county.

dikkaade *v.* give birth for the first time.

dikkuru *(ndu)* first pregnancy.

dille *(ɗe)* thud; noise. **Aɗa heewi dille** You make a lot of noise.

dillere *(nde)* 1) sound; noise; movement 2) ceremony.

dillinde *v.* rattle; wag; wiggle; waggle; shake. **~ hoore** nod.

dillude *v.* move; vibrate; sound; throb. **Hoore makko dillii** He has a mental breakdown.

dimaali *(ɗi)* lies.

dimaas *(o) {fr.}* Sunday. **Haɲki wonnoo dimaas** Yesterday was Sunday. **alet alt.**

dimaro *(o)* infertile; sterile.

dimbaade [dimᵐbaade] *v.* sway; jump in bed.

dimbinde [dimᵐbinde] *v.* shake.

dimle *(ɗe)* loads.

dimndoowo [dimⁿdoowo] *(o)* loader.

dimngal [dimⁿgal] *(ngal)* animal load. **~ mawngal** a heavy/big load.

dimo *adj.* dignified; free; noble. **Ko o dimo** He is a noble person.

dingiral [diⁿgiral] *(ngal)* arena; open space. **O naatii dingiral.** He entered the arena. **pl. dingire (ɗe).**

dipite *(o) {fr.}* deputy.

diraa *(o)* arm's length; measurement. **diraaji (ɗi) pl.**

dirde *v.* 1) move 2) crush peanuts. **~ gerte** grind peanuts into a creamy substance.

dirnude *v.* displace; move.

dirtinde *v.* move something or someone.

dirtude *v.* move over. **Dirtu seeɗa** Move a little.

dirkude *v.* polish.

diwal *(ngal)* jumping; jump. **~ lella e seendu** a big jump *alt.* diwgól *(ngól).*

diwde *v.* 1) hurdle; leap; skip; pulse; jump; fly 2) mature. **~ ina do ɲɲo** jump up and down. **Abiyoɲ o diwii** The plane took off.

diwgól *(ngól)* flight; jump; jumping.

diwnude *v.* 1) make fly 2) breed past maturity; nurture; foster; upbring.

diwlin *(o) {fr.}* cooking oil.

diwo *(o)* divorced lady; a previously married lady; an unmarried lady. **Ko o diwo** She is unmarried.

docotal *(ngal)* burning piece of wood. **docotte (ɗe) pl.**

dogde *v.* run; elope; stampede. **~ ñaawoore** abscond.

dogɗo *adj.* fugitive.

dógdu *(ndu)* race.

dógnirgal *(ngal)* racing instrument.

dognoowo *(o)* racer; driver. **~ puccu** a horse rider. **~ oto** a car driver.

dógnude *v.* drive; make run; operate; maneuvre. **~ oto** drive. **~ puccu** ride a horse.

dogoowo *(o)* runner.

dóggól *(ngól)* 1) cord 2) arrangement; order.

dokkal *(ngal)* gift. **rokkude** *v.*

dokkoowo *(o)* donor. **~ ɲiiɲam** blood donor.

dókkuɗo *(o)* donor.

dókkééru *(ndu)* big stick.

doktoor *(o)* *(fr.}* doctor. **~ gite** ophthalmologist. **~ koyɗe** orthopedist.

dolde *v.* digest. **Mi dolii ɗum** I have already digested it.

dolnude *v.* make digest.

dolokke *(o)* male gown.

dóllundu [dóllunⁿdu] *(ndu)* badger. **dolluɗi (ɗi) pl.**

domdomal *(ngal)* sternum; breast bone. **domdome (ɗe) pl.**

omodaa *(o)* peanut and flower sauce. *O defii domodaa* He cooked the domoda dish.

ónkuɗo [dóɲkuɗo] *(o)* inept; incapable; ill.

ongal [doɲⁿgal] *(ngal)* head load. *~ leɗɗe* wood load.

onɗo *(o)* heir; heiress. *ronde v.*

ɔno *(o)* heir; heiress.

ɔnoowo *(o)* heir.

oɲal *(ngal)* area covered with shrubs and long grass.

ooba *adj.* poor person.

oobal *(ngal)* bird.

óódél *(ngél)* piece of excrement.

óódi *(ndi)* stools of animals; excrements; feces.

ookde *v.* watch over.

óókóyde *v.* go and watch over.

oole *(ɗe)* power; momentum; might; strength; power. *jom ~* a strong person. *O alaa doole* He is not strong.

óólnude *v.* be powerful; be strong. *Omo doolni* He is powerful.

óóliɲɲe *(o)* fishing net with hooks.

óómburu [dóóᵐburu] *(ndu)* mouse *pl. doombi (ɗi).*

oomde *v.* hang around.

oonaade *v.* proceed; continue.

onaaɗo *adj.* shared inheritance.

onondiral *(ngal)* inheritance sharing.

oondotooɗo [dooⁿdotooɗo] *(o)* carrier; porter. *~ ina yoɓee* peddler.

ongal [donⁿgal] *(ngal)* load.

oole *(ɗe)* strength.

óólnude *v.* be powerful.

óólnuɗo *adj.* powerful.

ongal [donⁿgal] *(ngal)*

ooñoo *(o)* chameleon.

óórumaaru *(ndu)* small excavation. *~ luggiɗndu* a deep excavation. *doorumaaji (ɗi).*

oosde *v.* put out a fire.

oppude *v.* put out a fire.

óppude *v.* repel.

órlól *(ngól)* reptile tail.

orwude *v.* be wet; be half clean.

ote *(ɗe)* backside; buttocks. *rotere (nde) sing.*

dóttude *v.* 1) chop 2) summarize; shorten. *~ haala* shorten one's intervention.

dów *adv.* over; top; upon; beyond; above; top of; up. *~ makko* above him.

doygal *(ngal)* post.

doⲅⲅaade *v.* come down heavily. *Diwde ina doⲅⲅo* Jump up and down.

duballééwi *(ki)* tree.

duɓɓi *(ki)* tree.

dubbude *v.* poke. *O dubbi mi e yitere* He poked me in the eye.

dubuuje *(ɗe)* stools (of cows and oxen). *rubundere (nde) sing.*

duddu *(o)* fish.

duflaade *v.* dirty oneself.

duggande *v.* shop for. *Mi dugganii ma liɗɗi* I bought fish for you.

duggóyde *v.* go and shop for groceries. *O duggoyii* He went to do the groceries.

duggude *v.* 1) dig up 2) shop.

duhaade *v.* 1) tie/wear one's pants 2) be circumcised. *O duhiima* He has been circumcised.

duhagól *(ngól)* excision.

duhól *(ngól)* waistline; belt; sash.

duhorde *(nde)* waistline.

duhórgól *(ngól)* waistline.

duhtude [duutude] *v.* untie one's pants.

dujal *(ngal)* an island.

dukde *v.* yell in a dispute. *ɓe ngoni ko e dukde* They are involved in a dispute.

duko *(ngo)* dispute.

dukoowo *(o)* person involved in a dispute.

dukkere *(nde)* bushy area.

dukuduku *(o)* board for tanning leather.

dul *emph.* strike (used for emphasis when postposed).

dulééndu [duleendu] *(ndu)* whirlwind.

duluulól *(ngól)* coil.

dumaade *v.* fume; grumble; mumble. *Omon dumoo* He is grumbling.

dumunna *(o)* period. *oo ~* this period. *oon ~* that period.

duñande *(nde)* [duñanⁿde] a push.

duñde [duñje] *v.* 1) shove; push 2) be pregnant.

duñtude [duñcude] *v.* 1) repel 2) poke. *~ woroɗde* repel a misfortune.

duñtoowo [duñcoowo] *(o)* poker.

dundariyanke [dunⁿdariyaŋke] *(o)* wealthy person.

dundu [dunⁿdu] *(ndu)* thicket.

duppude *v.* burn; set a blaze.

durde *v.* graze. *ɗi ngoni ko e durde* They are grazing.

durirde (nde) pasture; grazing area.

durnude v. make animals graze.

dursitaade *v.* recite.

dursude v. memorize the Koran.

dursu ɗo (o) person who has memorized the Koran.

dus *foc.* used for emphasis when postposed. *Ina luuɓi dus It smells really bad.*

dutal *(ngal)* [dural] vulture. *dute (ɗe) pl.*

duttude *v.* remove grains form stalks.

duuɓi *(ɗi)* age; years:~ *sappo* decade. ~ *teemedere* century. *Hol no duuɓi maa poti* How old are you?

duudeede *v.* desire strongly; be addicted to; have a craving for. *Mbeɗe duudaa ataaye* I have a craving for tea.

duudeeteeɗo adj. addict.

duudo (ngo) strong desire; addiction.

duuki *(ki)* tree.

duukon (kon) islands.

duulaade *v.* weed around.

duulalɗe *(ɗe)* lizards *sing. nduulaldi (ndi).*

duule *(ɗe)* clouds. *ruulde (nde) sing.*

duumaade *v.* last; stay long.

duumde v. remain long; stay long.

duuŋél *(ngél)* island.

duurde *v.* wrestle.

duus *(o) (fr.}* shower room. *Omon nder duus* He is in the shower room.

duusde *v.* see someone out. *O duusii hoɓɓe* He is seeing the guests out.

duwaade *v. {ar.}* pray; pray for someone.

duwaawu (o) {ar.} prayer; condolences.

duwanaade v. bless; pray for. *Mi duwani maama* You have my blessings.

duworaade v. pray in the name of.

duwaañ *(o) (fr.}* customs; customs duty officer. *Ko o duwaañ* He is a customs duty officer.

ɗ

ɗaa *adv.* there; you. ~ *yenne* over there *prov.* **ɗaa woɗɗaani** What you can see is not far from you / What you can see is within reach.

ɗaalde *(nde)* 1) mark left by an insect bite 2) a dummy.

ɗaamól *(ngól)* spleen. *wondude e* ~ have a spleen disease *ɗaami (ɗi) pl.*

ɗaanaade *v.* sleep. ~ *ɗoyngol belngol* sleep well. *leelde* ~ sleep late. *O ɗaaniima* He is asleep.

ɗaankinaade *v.* pretend to sleep. *O woni ko e ɗaankinaade* He is pretending to be asleep.

ɗaanotooɗo *(o)* person who sleeps.

ɗaantaade *v.* go back to sleep.

ɗaantóyaade *v.* go back to sleep. *ɗaantoyo kono hoto weetndor* Go back to sleep but do not oversleep.

ɗanninde *v.* make someone sleep. *O woni ko e ɗanninde mo* He is putting him to sleep.

ɗaatde [ɗaadde] *v.* be soft; be smooth. ~ *haala* be a sweet talker. ~ *juuɗe* have soft hands.

ɗaatnude *v.* soften. *ɗaatnu haala maa* Soften your voice.

ɗaawuuna *(o)* disease.

ɗaayde *v.* be stupid; be foolish. *Kooli ko aan ɗaayi* You are so stupid.

ɗaayɗo *adj.* daft; fool; stupid person. *neɗɗo* ~ a stupid person.

ɗaayre *(nde)* stupidity; foolishness.

ɗabbande *v.* seek for someone.

ɗabboowo *(o)* seeker.

ɗabbóyde *v.* go and seek. ~ *ko alaa* go and seek what one does not have.

ɗabbude *v.* seek; look for. ~ *liggeey* seek a job.

ɗaccande *v.* yield; leave for. ~ *hakke* forgive.

ɗaccitde *v.* abjure; release; abandon *O ɗaccitaama hande* He was released today.

ɗaccude *v.* let go; acquit; quit; leave; abandon. *ɗaccu dee Ya* Leave it alone.

ɗaccere *(nde)* gum. *bultaade* ~ harvest gum. *ɗacce* (ɗe) *pl.*

ɗaccuki *(ki)* pole star.

ɗaɗól *(ngól)* nerve; radix; sinew; root. ~ *lekki* the root of the tree. ~ *neɗɗo* vein.

ɗahde [ɗaade] *v.* convince someone to perform something.

ɗakaañe *(o)* palate; tonsil.

ɗakkaade *v.* be stuck.

ɗakkitde *v.* loosen; remove; unstick.

ɗakkude *v.* patch clothes; stick; glue.

ɗalde *v.* 1) let go 2) boil. *Satalla maa ɗali* Your water is boiling.

ɗam *det.* the (used for liquids). *kosam* ~ the milk *ndiyam* ~ the water.

ɗamaawu *(o)* optimism; hope.

ɗaminaade *v.* hope; anticipate. *Mbeɗe ɗaminii mo YYere* I hope something good will happen.

ɗaminiiɗo *adj.* hopeful. *ɗaminiiɗo ko booraaɗo* One should never rely on hope alone.

ɗamtindaade [ɗamti^ndaade] *v.* lose hope. *Mi ɗamtindiima* I have lost hope.

ɗannaade *v.* travel; take a trip. *Ko o ɗanniiɗo* He has traveled.

ɗannanaade *v.* travel for.

ɗangal [ɗan^ngal] *(ngal)* voyage; trip; journey. ~ *laana* travel by boat. ~ *ndiwoowa* travel by plane.

ɗatde [ɗadde] *v.* tan.

ɗatgól *(ngól)* tan; leather work.

ɗatoowo *(o)* leather worker. *Ko o ɗatoowo* He is a leather worker.

ɗawde *v.* refuse food to someone.

ɗawre *(nde)* refusal to give food to someone.

ɗawsude *v.* be skinny.

ɗe *det.* the; plural class. *defte* ~ the books.

ɗebde *v.* be about to. *O ɗebii yande* He almost fell down.

ɗeɗɗaade *v.* choke.

ɗéɗɗude *v.* throttle; strangle. ~ *haa maaya* strangle to death.

ɗéɗɗugól *(ngól)* strangle.

ɗeeɗaade *v.* cut oneself accidentally.

ɗeeɗagól *(ngól)* a cut.

ɗééɗól *(ngól)* a cut.

ɗehaade v. suck one's belly in. ɗeho Take a deep breath; breathe in.

ɗehagol (ngól) breathing in.

ɗélkude v. be shiny; be shining. hoore ɗelkoore a shining head.

ɗemngal [ɗemⁿgal] (ngal) tongue; language. ~ muynangal mother tongue. ~am my mother tongue. ɗemɗe (ɗe) pl.

ɗéréwól (ngól) sheet of paper.

ɗesde v. just fail to. O ɗesii maayde He was about to die.

ɗi det. the (plural). lampaaji ~ the lamps.

ɗiya det. those. comci ~ those shoes.

ɗiɗabo num. second; secondary.

ɗiɗi num. two; double; couple; pair. duuɓi ~ two years.

ɗiɗo two people. yimɓe ~ two individuals.

ɗimmitde [ɗimmidde] v. do something twice.

ɗimmo (o) second.

ɗiftere (nde) recovery.

ɗiftinde v. revive.

ɗiftude v. feel better; recover from fainting. O ɗiftii He has recovered from fainting.

ɗigginde v. 1) turn into flower 2) know well; master. Mi ɗigginii I have memorized it.

ɗiggude v. be turned into flower; be mastered.

ɗiin det. those. ~ noppi those ears.

ɗimmital (ngal) repetition.

ɗimmitde v. repeat; do again; double. O ɗimmitii ɗum He did it again.

ɗinginde v. be hard.

ɗingude [ɗinⁿgude] v. erect one's penis; be hard.

ɗisde v. stick into a place.

ɗisngo [ɗisⁿgo] (ngo) sticking into a place.

ɗo adv. here. ~ e ndeen in the meantime. Jooɗo ɗo Sit here.

ɗoftaade v. obey. O mo ɗoftii He is compliant.

ɗoftal (ngal) help; help in the field.

ɗóftude v. 1) accompany 2) help with field work.

ɗóftugól (ngól) company.

ɗojjere (nde) cough.

ɗojjo (ngo) cough.

ɗójjude v. cough.

ɗojjugól (ngól) cough.

ɗókkiɗde [ɗókkidde] v. be one-eyed.

ɗokko (o) one-eyed person.

ɗómɗitde [ɗómɗidde] v. quench one's thirst. Mi ɗomɗitii I have quenched my thirst.

ɗómɗude v. be thirsty. Mbeɗe ɗomɗi I am thirsty.

ɗomka (ka) thirst. wondude e ~ be thirsty.

ɗoofde v. pull out; uproot; fallow.

ɗoofoowo (o) person who pull something out.

ɗooftaade v. pull weeds out.

ɗóóki (ki) tree.

ɗoon adv. there. ~ e ɗoon outright; right away.

ɗowde v. lead/guide (a blind person/an animal).

ɗówgól (ngól) the guiding of an animal or a blind person).

ɗowoowo (o) guide prov. Gumɗo jinganta ko ɗowoowo mum A blind person will side with his guide (One will side with one's relative/friend).

ɗowtaade v. abide by; follow; be devoted to; comply with. O ɗowtaaki He is not compliant.

ɗowtaare (nde) obedience; compliance; submission.

ɗowtagól (ngól) devotion; allegiance.

ɗoyngól (ngól) sleep. ɗoyngol jaggi mi I fell asleep.

ɗóyru (ndu) bird.

ɗuggitde v. uproot.

ɗuhaade v. shelter. ɗuho ɗen haa toɓo ngo siilta Let us shelter until the rain stops. ɗuhorde (nde) shelter.

ɗum det. this; that; it. ~ noon therefore.

ɗumininde v. do.

ɗunginaade [ɗuɲⁿginaade] v. pretend not to see.

ɗuuɗal (ngal) abundance.

ɗuuɗde [ɗuudde] v. be abundant.

ɗuulde (nde) swelling of the skin. fiide e ~ hit on the nail.

ɗuulnude v. swell. ɗum ɗuulnii It is swollen.

ɗuurnaade v. show contempt by turning one's head away.

ɗuurtaade v. express contempt by making a face.

ɗuurtagól (ngól) show of contempt by turning one's head away.

E

and; on; in. *miin ~ maa* me and you.

ɔɓere *(nde)* plan.

ɔɓet *interj.* used when something opens/breaks apart. *Lahal ngal wii eɓɓet* The calabash was broken into pieces.

ɓɓitaade *v.* break into pieces.

ɔe *pers. pron.* they. *Eɓe njiya* They see.

ɔcitaade *v.* be split into pieces.

la *(ba)* buffalo.

lda *(o)* widowhood. *Edda makko timmii* She has completed her widowhood retreat. *eddaaji (ɗi) pl.*

ɗen *pers. pron.* we. *Eɗen njaha* Are we going?

eɓde *v.* slice; sliver; slit; cut. *Eeɓ dende nde* Cut the watermelon into slices.

eɓól *(ngól)* fissure; cut.

eɓre *(nde)* slice.

edere *(nde)* tree.

eltaaɗo *adj.* docile.

elto *(ngo)* taming.

eltoowo *(o)* tamer.

eltude *v.* retrain; reeducate; tame; coax. *Ma mi eelte* I will tame you.

eltugól *(ngól)* tameness.

eraade *v.* hail; call with a loud voice.

erɗude *v.* be white.

eri *(ki)* tree.

ewaali *(ɗi)* first cries of a baby.

ewaango *(ngo)* first cry of the baby.

ewnaade *v.* 1) hail 2) call for prayer. *Eewno njuulen* Call for prayer so that we can say our prayers.

ewnaango *(ngo)* loud call; call for prayer.

ewnotooɗo *(o)* person who calls for prayer. *Eewnotooɗo o weetndorii* The person who calls for prayer overslept.

ey *interj.* yes. *O wii eey* He said yes.

gginde *v.* make someone move; evict. *Ndiyam egginii min* We were forced out by the water.

gginoowo *(o)* mover.

ggoowo *(o)* individual who is moving. *Ko kanko woni eggoowo* He is the one moving.

ggude *v.* vacate; move from one place to another. *Mi eggii* I moved.

éggudu *(ndu)* moving from one residence to another.

éggugól *(ngól)* moving places.

ejde *[ejje]* *v.* perceive; have an impression; have a hunch. *Mi ejii ɗum* I had a hunch.

ekkaade *v.* learn by trial. *~ yahde* learn the first steps. *O mon ekkoo yahde* He is learning his first steps. *Mo ekkaaki waawataa* A person who does not try will not learn.

ekkagól *(ngól)* training.

ékkinde *v.* teach someone. *Ar mi ekkin maa* Come I will teach you.

ékkinoowo *(o)* trainer.

ékkitaade *v.* learn again.

ékkitinde *v.* teach again.

ekko *(ngo)* trial; attempt; apprenticeship.

ekkorde *(ndi)* school; place for learning.

ekkotooɗo *(o)* apprentice; trainee. *Ko o ekkotooɗo* He is just a trainee.

elal *(ngal)* big wooden piece.

elde *v.* cut/slice wood.

élél *(ngél)* small wooden piece.

elde *v.* disdain; dislike.

elko *(ngo)* dislike; distaste.

eloowo *(o)* 1) person who disdains 2) person who cuts wood into pieces.

élimaan *(o) {ar.}* 1) imam; person who leads the prayer; a leader 2) male first name.

ella *(o)* vice; excuse; defect; period; menses. *O alaa ella* He is beyond reproach. *ellaaji (ɗi) pl.*

éllééy *part.* like; as if.

elo *(o)* iguana.

en *pron.* 1) we; 2) x-people; x-~place. *galle Hammadi ~* at Hammadi's compound.

enen *us; we. ~fof* all of us.

enɗam *(ɗam)* parenthood. *jokkude ~* reinforce relations. *taYde ~* destroy relations.

eñde *[eñje]* *v.* slice a fish from head to tail.

eño *(ngo)* sliced (dried) fish; hole for sowing.

éndu *[énⁿdu] (ndu)* breast; bosom; pap; womb. *ɗaccude ~* wean. *enɗi (ɗi) pl.*

27

endoowo *(o)* person who tries.

éndude [enⁿdude] *v.* try; attempt; experiment. *Ma mi endu* I will give it a try.

enteede *v.* be weaned.

entere (nde) act of weaning.

éntude v. wean; sever.

enu *(ngu)* fish.

esaas *(o) (fr.}* gas; petrol. *loowde* ~ put gas in the tank.

esde *v.* peel.

esiraaɗo *(o)* in-law. *esiraaɓe (ɓe) pl.*

ésiraagal (ngal) in-law relationship.

ésondirde [ésóⁿdirde] *v.* be related by an in-law relationship.

éskéy *interj.* used to show admiration. ~ *maa* I admire you.

etaade *v.* attempt; essay; try. *Ma mi eto* I will try. *Neɗɗo ina foti etaade* One ought to try.

etagól (ngól) essay; trial; attempt.

ewre *(nde)* calabash.

éyyó *foc. part.* yes

F

faabaade *v.* rescue; help *faabo mo* rescue him.

faabaare *(nde)* rescue salvage; help.

faabóndirde *v.* help one another.

faabóyaade *v.* go and rescue; help.

faaburu *(ndu)* toad; frog *prov. Mo ɓamti gaɗa faaburu ne ko leydi fayi* You can help only those who want to be helped.

faaɗde [faadde] *v.* 1) be narrow 2) be easily upset 3) become deaf. *paaɗgol (ngol).*

faaɗeede *v.* lack space, be poor.

faaɗnude [faannude] *v.* tighten; narrow.

faade *v.* head towards.

faatude *v.* return towards.

faafde *v.* make a mark with a hoe. *paafal (ngal).*

faaleede *v.* want; desire; love. *Mbeɗe faala maa* I fancy you.

faalkisaade *v.* ignore. **faamamuya** *(o)* comprehension.

faamde *v.* comprehend; understand. *A faamii* Do you understand?

faamminde *v.* explain; make someone understand.

faandaade [faaⁿdaade] *v.* 1) be close to 2) intend.

faandaare *(nde)* intent; expectation; hope.

faandu [faaⁿdu] *(ndu)* gourd.

faaro *(ngo)* pride; vanity. *O mo heewi faaro* He acts important.

faasko *(ngo)* pubic hair.

faataade *v.* 1) go past 2) die. *O faatiima* He died.

faawngude [faawⁿgude] *v.* be feverish. *Ko mi paawnguɗo* I am feverish. *faawnude alt.*

faawru *(ndu)* cache; granary; loft.

faayde *v.* be worried. *A faaynii kam* You got me worried.

faayoore *(nde)* worry.

faaynude *v.* get someone worried.

faaytude *v.* fail to recognize. *Mi faaytii mo* I did not recognize him.

fabɓinde *v.* prolong; adjourn; defer; procrastinate; postpone. *Pabɓinen ɗum haa jango* Let us postpone it until tomorrow.

faccirde *v.* decode; elucidate; illustrate.

faccude *v.* flow.

faddaade *v.* close the way to.

fadde *v.* wait for. *Fadam* Wait for me. *Mi fadii haa mi tampii* I am tired of waiting.

faɗɗaade *v.* faint. *Ko o paɗɗiiɗo* He has fainted.

faɗɗeede *v.* be less elegant than; be hit by.

faɗɗude *v.* 1) hit with a stick 2) be better dressed than someone else. *Ko aan faɗɗi mo* You are better dressed than him.

faddinde *v.* protect with a prayer. *Faddin hoore maa hadee maa ɗanaade* Say a prayer for protection before you go to sleep.

faddungo [fadduⁿgo] *(ngo)* prayer.

faɗo *(ngo)* shoe. ~ *ñaamo* right shoe. ~ *nano* left shoe. *ɓoornaade* ~ wear a shoe. *ɓoortude* ~ remove a shoe.

fafaade *v.* move while agonising. *E ngal fafoo* The chicken is agonizing.

faggaade *v.* store food.

faggo *(ngo)* loading or storage of food.

fahɗude [faaɗude] *v.* become deaf.

fajiri *(o)* {*ar.*} early morning; early morning prayer. *Fajiri feerii* The night is over.

fajjo *(ngo)* light rain.

fakitde [fakidde] *v.* be too much; be excessive. *O mo fakiti* He is excessive.

fakkude *v.* be dirty. *Aɗa fakki* You are dirty.

falaade *v.* be across; prevent; be an obstacle to.

falde *v.* place across. ~ *galle* close the gate.

faltaade *v.* put aside; choose; select.

faltude *v.* open the gate. *Faltu damal ngal* Open the gate.

falanteere *(nde)* window. *uddude* ~ close a window. *udditde* ~ open a window.

falkaade *v.* drink.

falo *(ngo)* farm at the bank of a river. ~ *makka* corn farm.

famɗinde *v.* minimize; minify.

famɗitinde *v.* belittle; reduce further; reduce the size of something that was already small.

fam ɗude v. be little. *O mo fam ɗi* He is small.

fanaa *(o)* midday.

fañaade v. cut someone's ear.

fantinde v. exaggerate.

fantude v. be too much.

fannu *(o)* shape; dimension; characteristic.

faram *(o)* halter.

farayse *(o) (fr.)* French. *O mo haala farayse* He speaks French.

farfitde v. stumble against.

farilla *(o)* obligation.

faro *(ngo)* rice.

fasawól *(ngól)* vein.

fasde v. be boiling. *Ndiyam maa fasii* Your water is boiling.

fasnude v. seeth; boil. ~ *ndiyam* boil water.

fasiraaɓe *(ɓe)* people of related social status. *Ko min fasiraaɓe* We have a similar social status.

fasoɭ *(o) (fr.)* mode; model; way; manner.

fatareere *(nde)* piece of clothing.

fatere *(nde)* stain.

fattude v. 1) boil 2) be pretty.

fawaade v. rely; be placed upon; depend upon. *Pawii mi ko e maa* I depend on you.

fawde v. bet; place on. ~ *kuugal* impose a sentence. *Faw mo e keeci ma* Put him on your back.

fawande v. place for someone.

faweede v. be placed upon.

fawóndirde [fawóⁿdirde] v. accumulate; superpose; superimpose; place on top of.

fawre (nde) load.

fayande *(nde)* [fayaⁿde] cooking pot. *payane (ɗe) pl.*

fayde v. be fat.

fayfayru (ndu) pride.

faynude v. fatten; make fat.

feccande v. divide for. *Feccan ɓe kaalis o* Divide the money amongst them.

feccere (nde) semi; half of; share. *Ndaa feccere maa* Here is your share.

fécitinde (nde) subdivision.

féccitaade v. subdivide.

féccude v. share; divide.

fedande [fedaⁿde] *(nde)* sour milk.

fedde v. put together.

fedde *(nde)* age group; organization; team. ~ *dow* older age group. ~ *les* younger age group. *Ko min fedde* We belong to the same age group.

feɗɗeede v. itch.

féɗɗitaade v. be burst.

féɗééndu *(ndu)* finger. ~ *koyngal* toe. ~ *wórdu* thumb.

feecde [feejje] v. crack; craze; split; rive.

feeñde [feeñje] v. appear. *Naange nge feeñii* The sun has appeared.

feer *(o) (fr.)* iron.

feeraade v. 1) be split up 2) swim.

feerde v. appear; rise; be intelligent; be half open. *O mo feeri* She is intelligent *Naange feerii* The sun is up.

feeteeto *(ngo)* pond.

feetere *(nde)* spark.

feewde v. behave; be straight; be good; be right. *Ina feewi* It is good. *peewal (ngal)*.

fééwnitde [fééwnidde] v. repair; amend; renovate; rectify; restore. *ɓe ngoni ko e feewnitde huɓeere nde* They are rebuilding the house.

fééwnude v. make straight; prepare; establish; make; devise.

fééwtinde v. straighten.

fééwtude v. be repaired; be straight again.

féfindaade [féfiⁿdaade] v. 1) fib; lie; speculate 2) take a short cut.

feggere *(nde)* ring. ~ *jungo* a finger ring. ~ *koyngal* a toe ring.

fehre *(nde)* 1) incense burner 2) plan; way; strategy; method; procedure. ~ *wonde* an alternative.

fekkorde v. lose consciousness.

fekkoreede v. be about to lose consciousness.

felde v. reproach; blame. *A ɗa felnii* You are to blame.

feloore *(nde)* reproach; blame. *Feloore alaa e maa* You are beyond reproach.

féllitde [féllidde] v. decide. *Mi fellitii* I have decided.

féllitere (nde) decision.

féllude v. shoot; execute; fire. ~ *diine* go to a holy war. *O felli mo e koyngal* He shot his leg.

felmaade v. stumble against; run into accidentally.

elo *(ngo)* foot track.

élsitere *(nde)* half of a cola nut.

elso *(ngo)* half of a cola nut.

élsude *v.* open into halves (e.g. cola nut).

embaade [fem^mbaade] *v.* get shaved; shave onself.

émbude [fém^mbude] *v.* shave. *O woni ko e fembude wahre makko* He is shaving his beard.

enaande [fenaa^nde] *(nde)* wrong; lie. *ɗum ko fenaande* It is a lie.

ende *v.* lie; distort. *A fenii* You lied.

énnude *v.* discredit someone; contradict.

eŋde *v.* plant; choke; nail; spike.

eŋeede *v.* be planted.

eññaange *(nge)* east. *huccitde* ~ face the east.

énñinde *v.* make appear; divulge; disclose.

endaade [fen^ndaade] *v.* coagulate; clot.

endude [fen^ndude] *v.* set milk; condense; concentrate; freeze.

eraade *v.* meet accidentally; stumble against. *Ko oto ferii mo* He was hit by a car.

erde *v.* 1) migrate; exile 2) pave. *Ko mi perɗo* I have migrated.

ergitaade *v.* 1) stumble against 2) bear out of wedlock.

ergo *(ngo)* exodus; migration.

érlude *v.* migrate.

fereŋ *(o)* *(fr.}* brake *fereŋaaji (ɗi) pl.*

ferlo *(ngo)* hill.

fesaade *v.* 1) be intelligent; 2) be vaccinated. *O mo fesii* S/he is very intelligent. *O fesaaki* He is stupid.

fesande [fesan^nde] *(nde)* vaccination mark.

fesde *v.* vaccinate; mark a person's face; inoculate.

fesoode *(nde)* cicatrix; a vaccination mark.

fétél *(o)* *(fr.}* gun; rifle. *fellude* ~ shoot. *loowde* ~ load a gun.

feto *(ngo)* rainwater.

fettaade *v.* move while agonizing.

féttude *v.* 1) burst open 2) kick; aim at. ~ *bal* kick the ball.

féttuuwo *(ngo)* sandal. *faɗo* ~ a sandal.

fewde *v.* start pregnancy.

fewjande *v.* 1) make food for someone; 2) conspire; plot. *Ɓe ngoni ko e fewjande mo* They are plotting against him.

féwjude *v.* plan.

fewre *(nde)* early pregnancy stage.

feɤde [fejje] *v.* decorticate; shell. ~ *gerte* shell the peanut.

feɤɤere *(nde)* chopped branches and trees.

féɤɤirde *v.* cut with.

féɤɤude *v.* chop trees and branches; hack.

fiɓde *v.* 1) make a knot; twist into a string 2) intend.

fiɓre *(nde)* knot; intent *piɓol (ngól) alt.*

fiɓtude *v.* untie.

ficcande *v.* shake for someone.

ficcude *v.* shake away. ~ *jungo* shake the hand away.

fiɗande [fiɗan^nde] *(nde)* sting.

fiɗde [fidde] *v.* 1) sting 2) hit a target.

fiɗo *(ngo)* gonorrhea. *O mo wondi e fiɗo* He has gonorrhea.

fiɗɗitde [fiɗɗidde] *v.* 1) shake off again; 2) deplete. *Mi fiɗɗitii* I am sold out.

fiɗɗude *v.* 1) shake off; brush off 2) deplete.

fii *(o)* 1) matter; business 2) vagina.

fiide *v.* 1) strike; hit 2) contribute. ~ *womre* punch. ~ *cukalel e dote* spank. *O fiyii buuɗi sappo* He contributed ten monetary units.

fiindirde [fii^ndirde] *v.* clash; hit each other.

fiitaade *v.* strike back. *Fii to* Hit him back.

fiyande [fiyan^nde] *(nde)* a gunshot. *ɗum ko fiyande fetel* It is a gunshot.

fiifaade *v.* blow one's nose.

fiifiire *(nde)* hunting of crocodiles; poaching.

fiifoonde [fiifoo^nde] *(nde)* insect.

fiilaade *v.* 1) have a period 2) tie a head scarf.

fiilayru *(ndu)* period.

fiilde *v.* 1) tie around a head; 2) appoint a chief.

fiileede *v.* be sworn in; accede. *O fiilaama* He has been appointed a chief.

fiiltude *v.* dethrone; impeach; topple; untie.

fiimde *v.* *(fr.}* smoke.

fiimlude *v.* desire something strongly.

fiire *(nde)* wound; disease.

fijde [fijje] *v.* play. *O woni ko e fijde* He is playing.

fijirde *(nde)* game. ~ *sukaaɓe* a boy's game.

fijirde *v.* play with something.

fijiróyde *v.* go and play with.

fijóyde *v.* go and play. *O fijoyii* he went to play.

fijjude *v.* play with one another.

filñitaade *v.* show anger.

filsideer *(o) (fr.)* refrigerator.

filtinde *v.* deflect; reject; refute. ~ *haala* interrupt; trivialize someone's point of view.

filtude *v.* be deflected.

finaade *v.* tatoo.

fino *(ngo)* tatoo.

finde *v.* wake up. ~ *law* wake up early. *A finii* Are you awake?.

finde [fin^nde] *(nde)* remembrance.

findinde *v.* wake up; rouse *Findin mo* Wake him up.

finirde *v.* wake up with.

finnude *v.* be angry n. pinnugol *(ngól)*. *Ko o pinnu ɗo* He is angry.

firde *v.* construe; translate. ~ *haala* translate.

firo *(ngo)* translation; change.

firtaade *v.* be dispersed; be undone; be changed. *Ahdi men firtiima* Our agreement is off.

firtude *v.* abrogate; cancel; rescind; change; loosen.

firlaade *v.* revolve; tumble.

firlude *v.* surround with.

firlitde [firlidde] *v.* sell one's belongings. *Mi firlitii ɗum ko ɓooyi* I sold it a long time ago.

firlorde *(nde)* restroom. *O yahii firlorde* He went to the restroom.

fitaade *v.* agonize; move.

fittaandu [fittaa^ndu] *(ndu)* soul. *O alaa fittaandu* he has no soul.

fitina *(o) (ar.)* quarrel; fight.

fittude *v.* sweep; scavenge. *Fittu haa laaɓa* Sweep it clean.

fitturu *(ndu)* fishing with hands.

foɓɓande *v.* acclaim.

fóɓɓude *v.* clap; applaud.

focco *(ngo)* bird's waste / excrement.

fóccude *v.* 1) discharge excrement 2) lie.

fodde *(nde)* duty; right.

foddore *(nde)* predicament.

foɗɗere *(nde)* 1) pill; tablet 2) pip; stone; seed. *yarde* ~ take a pill.

fóf *part.* whole; total.

foflaade *v.* clean one's bottom by rubbing it on the sand.

fogde *v.* build (a shelter).

fokaade *v.* wash by hand; handwash. *O woni ko e fokaade* He is washing by hand.

fókkitde [fókkidde] *v.* 1) leave 2) remove from its normal place. *ɓe pokkitii* They just left.

folde *v.* jump around.

follere *(nde)* sorrel.

foloŋ *(o)* elbow.

foloŋtóŋru *(ndu)* elbow.

fómpude *v.* wipe.

fóndude [fon^ndude] *v.* compare; equate; size up; measure.

fondaade [fon^ndaade] *v.* try on. *Fondo tuuba ba* Try the pants on.

fongo [foŋ^ngo] *(ngo)* bank of a river. ~ *maayo* bank of the river.

fongude [fon^ngude] *v.* remember and say something during a meal.

fooɓnaade *v.* lift a person up while wrestling.

foobre *(nde)* tree trunk.

fooctaade *v.* be straight.

fóóctude [fóóccude] *v.* straighten out.

fooɗde [foodde] *v.* draw; tug; pull.

féɣɣdóndirde [fóóɗó^ndirde] *v.* pull on ends.

foofaango [foofaa^ngo] *(ngo)* breath; breathing. **naatnude** ~ breathe in. *yaltinde* ~ breathe out. *foofaandu (ndu) alt.*

foofde *v.* 1) breathe; yank 2) rest. *ɗaccam mi foofa* Let me have some peace.

fóófirde *v.* breathe with.

fóófirde *(nde)* 1) comma 2) nose.

fooftaade *v.* rest. *Foofto* Take a rest. *Ngonmi ko e fooftaade* I am taking a rest.

fooftere *(nde)* a rest.

fóóftude *v.* be rested; be worry free.

foolde *v.* dominate; defeat; subjugate; subdue; triumph; win.

ooleede v. be defeated.

oonde [foonde] (nde) higher ground; bush.

óóndu [fóóndu] (ndu) pigeon; dove.

oorde v. (fr.} be strong; be intelligent.

ooɣde [foojje] v. be skinny. O mo foo ɲi s/he is skinny.

óóynude v. brighten.

ooyre (nde) light; aura.

oppaade v. oil one's body ~ nebam rub oil on one's body.

óppude v. mop; wipe; clean. Fóppu haa laaɓa Wipe it clean.

orlaade v. return.

orñere (nde) sprain; twist. O wondi ko e forñere He twisted his ankle.

órñinde v. sprain someone's ankle.

órñude v. sprain/twist one's ankle.

orso (o) (fr.} force.

órsude v. (fr.} force.

ortaade v. lay straight. ɗum fortaaki It is not straight.

órtude v. extend; stretch out. Fórtu koyɗe maa Stretch your legs.

óruuje (ɗe) golden earrings.

ósin (o) student from Coranic school; student.

otande [fotande] (nde) interval.

otde [fodde] v. 1) fit; be equal; should 2) amount to; cost 3) take a picture. Kamɓe poti They are equal.

otde [fodde] (nde) duty; obligation. waɗde ~ do one's duty.

oto (ngo) picture.

óttude v. meet; encounter n. pottal (ngal). Min pottii hande We met today.

ówru (ndu) hyena.

fuccitaade v. explode; burst.

fuccitde [fuccidde] v. burst a pimple.

fuɗaade v. wear perfume.

fuɗande [fuɗande] (nde) shoot.

fuɗɗaade v. start; begin; commence. Mi fuɗɗiima liggaade I have started working.

fuɗde [fudde] v. germinate; arise; come up.

fuɗɗitaade v. start over fuɗɗito start all over again.

fuɗɗoode (nde) beginning; outset; onset; prelude. Fuɗɗoro fuɗɗoode Start from the beginning. fuɗɗorde (nde) alt.

fuɗɗude v. initiate; innovate; create; invent. Ko kanko fuɗɗi ɗum He invented it.

fuɗnaange [funnaange] (nde) east.

fuɗnanke [funnaŋke] (o) easterner.

fuɗtinde v. stare; open wide.

fuɗtude [futtude] v. come up again.

fugu (o) (fr.} soccer.

fukaade v. give a child his first bath; wash.

fukeede v. get one's first bath.

fukkaade v. fall on the ground; be wealthy.

fukkude v. make fall on the ground. Fukku mo e leydi Throw him on the ground.

fulɓe (ɓe) Fulani people. ~ jeeri nomadic Fulani. ~ waalo sedentary Fulani.

fulfulde (nde) Fulfulde; Fula language.

fullinaade v. herd for someone.

fulfitde [fulfidde] v. come out.

fulkuru (ndu) stomach.

fulla (o) 1) respect; honor 2) hammer. O alaa fulla He has no self respect.

fullude v. scatter.

fulñitde [fulñidde] v. gaze; stare; open eyes widely.

fulsinde v. do with haste.

fumminde v. lead a holiday prayer.

fummorde (nde) area where the two major holiday prayers are held.

fummude v. pray a major holiday prayer. Min pummii We completed the holiday prayer.

funaade v. give birth to twins. O funiima She gave birth to twins.

funeere (nde) twin brother or sister. funeeɓe (ɓe) pl.

fundu [fundu] (ndu) dust. heewde ~ be dusty.

furaade v. chide; nag; scold; snarl; yell.

furɓaade v. eat watery substance.

furde v. fade (color).

furɗude v. be covered with dust; be grey.

furset(o) {fr.} fork. ñaamrude ~ eat with a fork.

furtaade v. dash; escape; run away.

furtude v. lay an egg.

fusande [fusande] (nde) burst.

fusde v. 1) make a hole; burst; break; puncture 2) end, finish.

fuseede v. 1) be broken into pieces; 2) be finished.

futtere *(nde)* nothing. *puttere (nde) alt.*

futtinde *v.* stare. *gite puttiniide* wide open eyes.

futuro *(o)* 1) dusk; gloaming; twilight; 2) sunset prayer. *Futoro yonii* It is time for the sunset prayer.

fuudaade *v.* henna; lay henna on one's palms or feet.

fuudde [fuudde] *v.* lay henna on someone's palms or feet.

fuufde *v.* blow; spray.

fuujaade *v.* make a speech mistake. *A fuujiima* You made a speech mistake.

fuujoore *(nde)* mistake; speech mistake.

fuunde *v.* rust; rot.

fuuñéé *(o)* albinos.

fuunti *(o)* lure.

fuuntude *(o)* delude; mislead; deceive. *O fuuntu mo* He deceived him.

fuupde *v.* hiss.

fuurna *(o) (fr.}* stove.

Fuuta (o) Fuuta region.

fuutanke [fuutaŋke] *(o)* native of Futa; person from Fuuta.

fuuybe *(ɓe)* fools; foolish persons. *puuydo* sing.

fuuyde *v.* be foolish; be stupid. *Ada fuuyi* You are acting stupid.

fuuynude *v.* trivialize; make foolish. *Fuuynu dum* Do not pay attention to it.

fuybaade *v.* splash around; jump into water.

fuYde [fujje] *v.* kill lice.

fuYere *(nde)* pimple

G

gaa *adv.* here. *Ar gaa* Come here. *gaay*; *gaayenne* alt.

gaaci *(ɗi)* music.

gaajaade *v.* joke; kid around. *Ó woni ko e gaajaade* He is just kidding. *gaajaare (nde)* farce; trifle. *Mi alaa e gaajaare* I am not joking. *gaajóndiral* [gaajóⁿdiral] *(ngal)* joke.

gaalɗi *(ɗi)* façade. *gaalgól (ngó) sing.*

gaali *(ki)* iron container.

gaamɗo *adj.* slug; lazy person. *Ko a gaamɗo* You are lazy.

gaañaade *v.* be hurt.

gaañande [gaañanⁿde] *(nde)* injury; wound. ~ *muusnde* a serious wound.

gaañde [gaañje] *v.* hurt; wound. *A gaañii mo* You hurt him.

gaañeteeɗo *(o)* vulnerable.

gaaraas *(o) (fr.)* car parking. *naatnude oto e ~* park a car (in the garage).

gaarawól *(ngól)* string; thread.

gaarnól *(ngól)* indirect.

gaas *(o) {fr.}* gaz.

gaawal *(ngal)* spear.

gaawól *(ngól)* pipeage; tube; canal. *asde ~* dig a canal.

gaay *adv.* here. *Ar gaay* Come here.

gaaye *(ɗe)* scabies.

gaayeede *v.* have scabies.

gaayiiɗo *adj.* reduced; damaged; spoiled.

gabbél *(ngél)* small seed. ~ *gawri* little millet seed.

gacce *(ɗe)* shame; scandal. *A dañii gacce* Shame on you.

gaccungól [gaccuⁿgól] *(ngól)* net for carrying millet ears or luggage.

gaɗa *(o)* behind; bottom. *Neɗɗo ko huli ko fof gaɗa mum ko caggal heedata* One cannot change a person's nature.

gadano *adj.* first; primitive. ~ *o* the first.

gadiiɗo *adj.* former; fore; predecessor. *mawɗo ~* a forefather.

gafakke *(o)* nosebag.

gaggitte *(ɗe)* molar teeth. *aggutere (nde) sing. gaggutte (ɗe) alt.*

gajawal *(ngal)* bird.

gajjal *(ngal)* fish.

gakkande *(nde)* stain.

gakkinde *v.* stain.

gakkude *v.* speckle; stain; be stained.

gallaaɗi *(ɗi)* horns. *allaadu (ndu) sing.*

galle *(o)* compound; home; house; façade; enclosure for animals. *jom ~* husband. ~ *jawdi* park.

gallu *(o)* district.

gallude *v.* be small.

galól *(ngól)* string of waist beads. *Galol maa ta ƴii* Your string of beads is broken.

gamból [gamᵐból] *(ngól)* dam.

gañaaɗo *(o)* hated person.

gaño *(o)* enemy. *O alaa gaño* Everyone likes him.

gandaaɗo [ganⁿdaaɗo] *adj.* renown.

gandal [ganⁿdal] *(ngal)* knowledge; science; loot; competence. *keewɗo ~* knowledgeable.

gando [ganⁿdo] *(o)* philosopher; lettered. *Ko o gando* He very knowledgeable.

gane *(ɗe)* secret language; coded language.

garanke [garaɲke] *(o)* leather worker. *Ko o garanke* He is a leather worker.

garba *(o)* prostitute.

garbaade *v.* prostitute.

garbotooɗo *(o)* prostitute; whore.

garci *(ɗi)* camps.

garcinaade *v.* camp.

garde *(o) (fr.}* guard.

gardiiɗo *(o)* leader; chief; manager. ~ *peewɗo* a good leader.

garɗo *(o)* newcomer; person who just arrived.

gargulle *(ɗe)* ravines.

gasde *v.* be finished. *ɗum gasii* It is finished.

gasnude *v.* conclude; exhaust; deplete; finish; complete.

gasnuɗo *adj.* person who finished his/her action; dead person.

gattoñ (kon) small braids. *atturu (du) sing.*

gawdi *(ki)* tree.

gawe *(ɗe)* millets.

gawri *(ndi)* millet.

gawlo *(o)* griot. *Ko o gawlo* He belongs to the griot caste.

gawoowo *(o)* fisherman.

gawƴal *(ngal)* millet stalk gawƴe *(ɗe) pl.*

gay *(ɗi)* bulls. *ngaari (ndi) sing.*

gaybuɗo *adv.* greedy; voracious. *Aan ko a gaybuɗo* You are greedy.

gaynaako *(o)* shepherd; herdsman; swain.

gaynude *v.* finish. *Mi gaynii* I have finished. *gasnude alt.*

geɗal *(ngal)* portion; share. ~ *kala* a piece. ~ *maa* your share. ~ *makko* his/her.

géddu *(o)* enclosure/park for animals. *gedduuji (ɗi) pl.*

géddude *v.* refuse food. *Ko o gedduɗo* He refused to eat.

gééc *(o) {wol.}* ocean; sea. *nder* ~ in the ocean. *liingu* ~ sea fish.

gééjól *(ngól)* crest; tuft.

géénól *(ngól)* neck; nape of the neck. *juutde* ~ have a long neck. **O** mo *juuti geenol* He has a long neck.

geese *n.* cotton thread. ~ *njamala* cobweb.

geewaade *v.* jump. **O** mo *waawi geewaade* He is a skilled acrobat.

geewotooɗo (o) acrobat.

gélóóki *(ki)* tree.

gennewalla *(o) {wol.}* half of.

génsu *(ngu)* undershirt; vest.

gerde *v.* court; flirt; philander. *Ó woni ko e gerde* He is flirting.

gerlal *(ngal)* partridge; bush fowl.

gerngal [gerⁿgal] *(ngal)* place for gathering crops.

gérnude *v.* gather millet ears in a crop gathering area.

gerte *(ɗe)* ground peanuts *sing. yertere (nde)*.

gertogal *(ngal)* hen. *gertooɗe (ɗe) pl.*

géwól *(ngól)* crack. *gewi (ɗi) pl.*

geworgal *(ngal)* big calabash.

gidaade *v.* frighten.

gideede v. be frightened. *Ko o gidaaɗo* He cannot not rise up because of fear.

giddude *v.* threaten; rise up abruptly.

gideede v. be caught by fear. *Ko o gidaaɗo* He could not rise up because of fear.

giɗél *(ngél)* darling.~*lam* my darling.

giɗo (o) darling; friend.

giile *(ɗe)* vision. *Giile makko moƴƴaani* He does not see well.

gite *(ɗe)* eyes. ~ *mawɗe* big eyes. *yitere (nde) sing.*

gijaade *v.* threaten.

gijili *(ki)* tree.

gila since; ever since. ~ *ndeen* since then. *Mi yiyaani mo gila ndeen* I have not seen her since then.

gilɗi *(ɗi)* worms *sing. ngilngu (ngu)*.

gilli *(ɗi)* love; feelings. *Gilli ina muusi* Love is not easy.

ginal *(ngal)* pelican.

ginól *(ngól)* leash; cord for guiding a camel/an ox.

gisde *v.* predict.

giyal *(ngal)* thorn.

giƴiraaɗo *(o)* person of one's age group; age-mate.

góƀƀude *v.* slog; punch.

góɗɗi *(ɗi)* other ones.

goɗɗo (o) another person; other. *neɗɗo* ~ another person.

góɗɗum (ɗum) another thing; something else.

góddól *(ngól)* pharynx; throat.

góddude v. desire strongly. *Mbeɗe goddi heen* I really would like to have some.

godoroŋ *(o) (fr.}* tar.

gókkude *v.* waste.

golgolal *(ngal)* jaw bone *pl. golgole (ɗe)*.

gollaade *v.* perform; work. *Ó woni ko e gollaade* S/He is working.

gollal *(ngal)* activity; deed; task; work; service; profession. *liggeey (o) alt. pl. golle (ɗe)*.

gollanaade v. work for. *Ngollanii mi ko hoore am* I am working for myself.

gollande v. work for.

gollinde v. employ someone; make someone work.

gollirde (nde) work place.

golloowo (o) a worker.

gollorde (nde) work place.

gollorgal (ngal) tool used for a particular work.

gollotooɗo (o) person who works; person who is employed.

gollude v. work.

golo *(ngo)* horse.

gombal [gom^mbal] *(ngal)* empty corn cob; leafless stalk.

góndi *(ɗi)* tears. ~ *kecci* unreal tears.

góngól [gón^ngól] *(ngól)* 1) tear 2) another time.

góndiiɗo *(o)* partner; mate; fellow. *Ko min wondiiɓe* We are together / we are roommates.

gonɗo *adj.* factual; present.

góó *num.* one. *Wii goo* Say one.

gooto *adj.* single; alone; sole; one. *hay* ~ nobody. *aan* ~ you alone.

góótól *(ngól)* once. *laawol* ~ one time; once.

goobde *v.* dye.

gooboowo *(o)* dyer.

góóbu *(ngu)* dye.

góóɓél *(ngél)* small drink; little mouthful.

gooɗɗo [gooɗɗo] *adj.* actual.

gool *(o)* small calf.

góólóóli *(ɗi)* red ants; ants *goololol (ngól) sing.*

goomgal *(ngal)* threshold goomle *(ɗe) pl.*

goonga [goonga] *(o)* truth. *haalde* ~ tell the truth. *ɗum ko goonga* It is true.

goongante [goo^ngante] *adj.* truthful; trustworthy. *Ko o goongante* He is trustworthy.

góóngɗinde [góó^ngɗinde] *v.* trust; believe. *Mbeɗe gooŋɗini Alla* I believe in God.

góóngɗinɗo [góóŋɗinɗo] *adj.* devout.

góóngɗingól [góóŋɗingól] *(ngól)* belief.

góóngɗude [góóŋɗude] *v.* be truthful; be trustworthy.

góóski *(ki)* stretcher.

goowɗo *adj.* familiar.

góóƳól *(ngól)* dead bean plant for animal consumption.

góppu *(o)* spade.

goram *interj.* used to express amazement or sympathy. *haa goram!* it is amazing!

gorgal *(ngal)* west.

gorbal *(ngal)* strong heavy person/animal.

górbél *(ngél)* little man; little male animal.

górgilaaɗo *(o)* paternal aunt.

górgól *(o)* paternal aunt.

gorko *(o)* male person; man *biɗɗo* ~ a son.

goro *(ko)* kola nut *alt. woroore (nde).*

góról *(ngól)* line. *Ngol gorol fortaaki* This line is not straight.

gósi *(o)* porridge.

góstóndiral [góstó^ndiral] *(ngal)* trade; exchange; interchange.

gowe *(ɗe)* strings of beads.

gowlaali *(ɗi)* screams *sing. wowlaango (ngo). wulaango (ngo) alt.*

gówól *(ngól)* string of beads.

goyoowo *(o)* a crying individual.

goytagól *(ngól)* complaint.

góytiiɗo *(o)* plaintiff. *Mi woytiima haa mi tampii* I am tired of complaining.

gufi *(ɗi)* peels; pods.

gujjittooɗo *(o)* furtive.

gujjo *(o)* burglar; robber; thief. ~ *bey* a goat thief. *Ko o gujjo* He is a thief.

gukkude *v.* reject.

gulaali *(ɗi)* cries. *wulaango (ngo) sing.*

gullitaagól *(ngól)* complaint.

gullitiiɗo *(o)* plaintiff. *Ko aan woni gullitiiɗo o* You are the plaintiff.

gulwulti *(ɗi)* confrontation. *Wulwulti (o) sing.*

gullól *(ngól)* umbilical cord.

gulucce *(ɗe)* variety of milk.

gulumból *(ngól)* [gulum^mból] dry stream bed.

gumbalaa [gu^mbalaa] *(o)* caste specilizing in woodwork.

gumɗo *adj.* blind; eyeless. *Gumɗo jinganta ko ɗowoowo mum* A blind person will side with his guide.

gumgummééwi *(ki)* plant.

gundo [gu^ndo] *(o)* lizard.

gunɗo *adj.* secret.

guppól *(ngól)* laundry. *Guppol maa laaɓaani* Your laundry is not clean.

guppoowo *(o)* launderer.

gure *(ɗe)* towns. *wuro (ngo) sing.*

gurél *(ngél)* village; little skin; small town.

guri *(ɗi)* skins. *nguru (ngu) sing.* ~ *gerte* peanut shells.

guttere *(nde)* cloud.

guttu *(o)* water holder.

guube *(ɗe)* tree.

guumi *(ki)* tree.

guurti *(ɗi)* recess; vacation. *wonde e* ~ be on vacation.

guurtingól *(ngól)* revival.

H

ha *interj.* yes; used to express joy and approval.

haa *adv.* till; until. ~ *ngaraa* until you come.

haaɓde *v.* be fed up. *Mi haaɓii ɗum* I cannot take it any more.

haaɓnaade *v.* be annoying.

haaɓnude *v.* upset; frustrate; annoy. *A ɗa haaɓnii* You are annoying.

haaɓre *(nde)* annoyance; frustration.

haacande [haacanⁿde] *(nde)* scream.

haacde [haajje] *v.* vociferate; cry aloud; scream.

haaɗde [haadde] *v.* be bitter. ~ *lamɗam* be very salty. ~ *suukaara* be very sweet. *Ina haaɗi* It is bitter.

haaɗnude [haannude] *v.* confine; make bitter; limit; stop. ~ *e keerol* stop at the boundary. *Haaɗnu ɗum ɗoo* Stop it here.

haaɗirde [haattirde] *(nde)* limit. *En njettiima e haaɗirde* We have reached the limit.

haaɗude [haattude] *v.* stop.

haajde [haajje] *v.* decide; need. *So Alla haajii* If Alla is willing.

haaju *(o)* need; problem; affair; business; concern.

mo alaa ~ vagabond. *ɗum wonaa haaju maa* It is not your business. *Haalanam haaju maa* Tell me what you need.

haakde *v.* scrape.

haakeede *v.* have a cold.

haaktaade *v.* clear one's throat. *O haaktii e makko* He spat on him.

haako *(ko)* leaves; type of dish.

haala *(ka)* speech. ~ *nokku* dialect. ~ *njaawka* fast speech. ~ *maayka* useless speech.

haalande *v.* tell; inform.

Haalan mo feere men Inform him of our decision.

haalde *v.* say; state; speak; chat. ~ *dow* speak up. ~ *les* be soft spoken.

haaldeede *v.* negotiate; transact. *Min kaaldii ha min nanondirii* We have negotiated and agreed on a price.

haaldude *v.* talk to each other; negotiate; transact.

haalnude *v.* make someone speak.

haaltude *v.* disclose.

haameede *v.* regret.

haame *(o)* regret.

haande *v.* be right. *Ina haani wonde* It should be.

haandinde *v.* make someone deserve something. Make someone worthy of something.

haandude *v.* deserve; merit. *O mo haandi heen* she deserves it.

haange [haaⁿge] *(nge)* cow.

haangeede [haaⁿgeede] *v.* be mad. *O haangaama* He lost his mind. *kaaɗi (ɗi).*

haaranduru [haaraⁿduru] *(ndu)* plentiness.

haarde *v.* be satiated; be full. ~ *ndiyam* have enough water. ~ *Yii Yam* recognize.

haarnude *v.* satiate; sate.

haare *(nde)* defense.

haasidaade *v.* envy.

haasidaagal *(ngal)* envy; jealousy; egoism.

haaside *(o)* jealous person.

haatande [haataⁿde] *(nde)* stones on which the cooking pot rests.

haatumeere *(nde)* magical symbol.

haawde *v.* fascinate; stupefy; be puzzling.

haaweede *v.* be astonished; be puzzled. *Mbeɗe haawaa* I am puzzled.

haawnaade *v.* be puzzling. *E ɗum haawnii* It is puzzling.

haawngo [haawngo] *(ngo)* puzzle; surprise.

haawniinde [haawniiⁿde] *(nde)* mystery; puzzle.

haawnude *v.* amaze.

haayde *v.* urinate. (Usage is restricted to animals).

haaYde [haajje] *v.* twist.

haayre *(nde)* rock; flint; stone. ~ *jamaa* diamond. *kaaYel manaango* thunderbolt.

haaytude *v.* give up; rescind; cancel. *Be kaaytii yahde* They cancelled the trip.

habbitaade *v.* 1) tie again. 2) untie.

habbitde [habbidde] *v.* untie. *Habbit juuɗe makko* Untie his hands.

habbondirde *v.* tie together; make a united front.

habbude *v.* tie; pack; attach.

bde v. fight. *be ngoni ko e habde* They are fighting.

beede v. fight; combat.

birde *(nde)* instrument for fighting.

btaade v. fight back. *Habto* Fight back.

brude v. disseminate; inform. ~ *kabaaru bondo* give bad news. *Habru mo sankaare taane* Inform him of your grandparent's death.

daade v. abstain.

ode [hadde] *(nde)* obstacle.

ode [hadde] v. veto; ban; disallow; deter; hinder; impede; interdict. *Ko ko hadaa* It is forbidden.

diinde [hadii"de] *(nde)* dam.

dtaade [hattaade] v. miss. *Mi hadtiima tuuba ba* I am missing a pair of pants.

addaade v. 1) tie/wear one's sarong/skirt 2) be circumcised.

addaare *(nde)* sarong. *habbude* ~ *mum* tie one's sarong. *tellinde* ~ *mum* untie one's sarong.

addinaade v. be circumcised.

addinde v. circumcise.

addude v. tie a sarong for someone.

adee before. ~ *maa yahde* before you go.

afeere *(nde) (fr.}* affair; business. *dum ko hafeere maa* That is your business.

aftaade v. rise up suddenly. *Hafto* Get up.

aggude v. be stopped.

ajaade v. forbid; prevent.

ajjóyde v. go on a pilgrimage to Mecca. *O hajjóyii* He went on a pilgrimage to Mecca.

ajju *(o)* pilgrimage to Mecca.

ajjude v. pilgrimage to Mecca.

akde v. contest while wrong. *A hakii mo* You cheated him.

akeede v. be denied.

akindaare [haki"daare] *(nde)* moderation.

akke *(o)* right. *dum ko hakke maa* That is your right.

akkilante *(o)* intelligent person.

akkilde v. have a brain; make sense; be thoughtful. *O hakkilaani* He has no sense. *hakkille (o)* brain; sense; mind. *Hakkille makko ko ko ustii* He is senile. *O alaa hakkille* He has no sense.

akkitde [hakkidde] v. help; save. *Kakkitee kam* help! help!

hakkunde [hakku"de] *(nde)* center; mid; average; amid; mean; medium; semi. *fedde* ~ *leydeele* an international organization.

hakkundeejo [hakku"deejo] *adj.* neutral; medial; adiaphorous.

halal *(ngal)* belonging; possession; property. *O rendotaako halal* He is greedy.

halde v. be pregnant.

halfinaabe *(be)* delegation; entrusted people. *kalfinaado (o) sing.*

halfinde v. empower; entrust. ~ *Allah* leave in the hands of Allah. *Mi halfinii ma besngu am* My family is in your hands. *halfineede* v. be entrusted with.

halfude v. be a master; own.

haljeende *(nde)* dilemma.

haljinde v. disturb; pester; perturb.

haljude v. be busy. *Mbede halji* I am busy.

halkaade v. perish; be destroyed. *O halkii ma* He perished.

halkaare *(nde)* peril.

halkude v. destroy.

hallere *(nde)* penis.

hamdaat *(o)* measurement.

hamde v. wring out clothing.

hamYude v. squeeze **hammayéróyél** *(ngél)* kingfisher.

hammu *(o)* concern. *O alaa haaju o alaa hammu* He has no concern.

hanawere *(nde)* profile; one side of the face.

handaade v. lock up.

hande v. bray.

hande [han"de] *(o)* today.

hañde [hañje] v. ejaculate.

hanki [haI)ki] *(o)* yesterday. ~ *men* past; history. ~ *jammad* last night. *Mi yii mo haI)ki* I saw him yesterday.

hanti *part.* then.

happaade v. claim someone's belongings.

happu *(o)* term; limit. *Kó jógii* ~ finite. *ko alaa* ~ infinite.

haraam *(o)* sin; taboo. *dum ko haraam* It is forbidden.

harminde v. forbid. ~ *sangara* quit drinking forever.

harmube *(be)* cursed people *karmudo sing.*

harmude v. be forbidden. *Ina harmi* It is forbidden.

haraango [haraaⁿgo] *(ngo)* snoring. *karaali (ɗi) pl.*

harde v. snore. *O woni ko e harde* He is snoring.

hare (nde) fight; conflict; affray; struggle; strife; warfare; combat.

harfeere (nde) letter of the alphabet.

harlude v. twist round. *Harlu Yo Ya* Make it stick.

harsude v. make a slip-knot.

hartaade v. chide; express disapproval.

hartaango [hartaaⁿgo] *(ngo)* thunder noise.

hartude v. 1) chase birds away 2) be very salty.

hasbude v. judge.

hasde v. initiate.

hasnude v. shroud. *O hasnaama* He is ready for burial.

hattande v. be able to; be capable of. *Mi hattanaani ɗum* I am not able to do it.

hawde v. 1) charge with the head 2) prevail; win; defeat.

hawngo [hawⁿgo] *(ngo)* edge of a boat.

hawjude v. be foolish.

hawrinde v. join.

hawritde [hawridde] v. meet again; coincide.

hawróyde v. go and meet. *Kawroyen toon* Let us meet there.

hawrude v. encounter; agree; converge; concur; coincide. *Mi hawrii e makko* I met with him.

hay conj. even; not even. *~ huunde* nothing.

hayde v. float. *ɗal haya* Let it float.

hayngo [hayⁿgo] *(ngo)* floating; current.

haynude v. make float.

hayyó part. welcome. *Hayyoo maa* It is so good to see you.

hebaade v. get ready. *O woni ko e hebaade* He is getting ready.

hebɓaade v. catch while in the air.

hébɓitaade v. interrupt; intervene.

hebɗe v. obtain; gain; achieve; receive; acquire; attain. *Mi heɓii ɓataake maa* I received your letter.

héɓirde v. get with.

héɓóyde v. go and reach/get.

héɓtinde v. recognize. *A hebtinii mo* Do you recognize him?

héɓtude v. regain; recapture; repossess. *hakkille neɗɗo* convince someone. *keɓtii galle makko* They repossessed his compound.

hebbere (nde) thorn.

hébbinde v. fill up. *Mi hebbinii maaro* have gathered plenty of rice.

heblaade v. get ready for prayer. *M hebliima* I am ready for the prayer.

héccidde v. 1) be wet 2) be unripe.

héccude v. be older than. *Ko kanko hecc maa* He is older than you.

heɗaade v. listen.

heɗtaade [hettaade] v. listen carefully; hark *Heɗto paamaa* Listen carefully so that yoi understand.

heddaade v. remain; be left over; remain maintain. *~ e* uphold.

héddude v. leave over.

heɗɗaawo (ngo) barrier.

hedde adv. around; near; towards. *~ tooi* around that area.

heɗɗere (nde) clot.

héé interj. calling word (used to attrac someone's attention).

heedande v. advocate; side with.

heedde v. be situated; be located. *Hol ti ɗum heedi* Where is it located?

héédnude [héénnude] v. place something ii a particular position.

héédtinde [hééttinde] v. place in anothe place. *Héédtin ɗum gaa* Place it ove here.

héédtude [hééttude] v. change places.

heeɗelde (nde) broken piece of a wate holder.

heefande [heefanⁿde] *(nde)* scraped ou area.

heefde v. scrape out.

hééforidde [hééforidde] v. sin.

heege v. starvation; dearth; famine; hunge *wondude e ~* be hungry.

heegeede v. be starving; be famished *Mbeɗe heegaa* I am famished.

heen adv. in. *nder ~* in it.

heeñere (nde) liver.

heeraade v. select; delimit.

heertaade v. delimit.

wbe *adj.* several; various. *yimbe* ~ many ople.

vde *v.* be plenty. *dum heewii* It is full.

re *(nde)* isolated area.

inde *v.* make someone go early in the orning.

ude *v.* go very early.

inde [helan^{n}de] *(nde)* break; fracture.

le *v.* break; cut; shatter; smash. ~ *hoore* come senile.

aade *v.* break again; break into pieces.

inde [héltin^{n}de] *(nde)* piece of.

ude *v.* break off.

ande *v.* acclaim.

o *(ngo)* clap; slap; smack *fiide* ~ *e kkille* slap in the face.

ude *v.* clap; applaud.

ere *(nde)* fruit.

ifeede *v.* become adult; maturate; be ature. *Ko a mawdo kellifaado* You are mature person.

nere *(nde)* word.

aade *v.* be in a hurry; rush; hurry.

aare *(nde)* hurry; rush; haste.

du [hén^{n}du] *(ndu)* wind. *dum ko hendu* is not true.

dude [hén^{n}dude] *v.* be open; clean.

tude *v.* remove and set aside.

pere *(nde)* impatience. *keppugol (ngol)* t.

pude *v.* be impatient. *Mbede heppi ko o ata* I can't wait for his arrival; I can't ait to see him.

de *v.* 1) crow 2) be solid 3) laugh.

kitde *v.* [herkidde] laugh.

sinde *v.* scandalize; humiliate; shame.

sude *v.* be ashamed. *Mi hersii* I am hamed.

Tude *v.* feel sand grains while chewing.

ande [hesan^{n}de] *(nde)* tuft of trimmed ass.

de *v.* trim; cut; mow; shear. *O woni ko e sde hudo* He is trimming the grass.

ditinde *v.* renew. ~ *sallige mum* renew le's ablution.

dude *v.* be new. *Ina hesdi* It is new.

de [hedde] *v.* clot; coagulate.

tere *(nde)* piece; clot. ~ *tééw* steak. ~ ii *Yam* a clot. ~ *leydi* a piece of land.

hettande *v.* buy new clothing for. *O hettanii kam wutte* He bought me a new gown.

héttude *v.* buy new clothing.

heYde [hejje] *v.* fit in. *dum heYii e maa* Does it fit you?

héydude *v.* be hungry. *Mbede heydi* I am hungry.

heytaade *v.* be careful.

hibbude *v.* close.

hiidaade *v.* oppress.

hiiddude *v.* be old. *cómci kiiddi* old clothing.

hiinnitaade *v.* be selfish.

hiirde *v.* be night. *Jamma o hiirii* The night is late/ young.

hiisa *(o)* measurement; estimate.

hiisaade *v.* assess; estimate; gauge; measure.

hiiteede *v.* be unfortunate.

hijaago *(ngo)* neigh.

hijde [hijje] *v.* neigh.

hijjude *v.* spell; read syllable by syllable. *O woni ko e hijjude* He is learning to read syllables.

hikka this year. *So wonaani hikka wona mo wuuri* If it is not this year it will be next year.

hikkitde [hikkidde] *v.* cry.

hilleede *v.* be interested.

hiltude *v.* found.

himmude *v.* be a hard and consciencious working person; be consciencious. **O mo** *himmi* He is very consciencious.

himYude *v.* squeeze.

hiñaade *v.* remove grains from the ear.

hindirbe [hi^{n}dirbe] *(be)* people of similar ethnic group/caste.

hinde [hin^{n}de] *(nde)* tribe; caste.

hinere *(nde)* nose. *Ko faati e* ~ nasal. *wuddere* ~ a nostril. *O mo juuti hinere* He has a long nose.

hinnaade *v.* take good care of.

hinnude *v.* greet.

hippaade *v.* lay on one's stomach. *Hippo* Lay on your stomach.

hippitde [hippidde] *v.* Open; uncover.

hippoode *(nde)* cover; lid; hood.

hippude v. 1) cover 2) wear inside out. ~ *wutte mum* wear one's gown inside out.

hiraande [hiraa^{n}de] *(nde)* supper. *deftude* ~ finish cooking supper. *sagginde* ~ begin cooking supper.

hirɓude v. catch; apply pressure; close on.

hirde v. 1) be jealous 2) be cooked improperly. *Ko o kirɗo* He is jealous.

hirke *(o)* saddle.

hirnaange [hirnaa^{n}ge] *(nge)* west. *huccitde* ~ face the west. *gorgal (ngal).*

hirnanke [hirnaŋke] *(o)* westerner.

hirndude [hir^{n}dude] v. leave in the afternoon.

hirsude v. 1) slaughter; cut the throat 2) overcharge. *O hirsumo* He overcharged him.

hirtaade v. eat supper; dine. ~ *law* eat dinner early. *leelde* ~ eat dinner late. *Mi hirtiima* I have eaten dinner.

hisde v. be well. *A hisii* Are you well?

hitaande [hitaa^{n}de] *(nde)* year. ~ *kala* annual.

hiwaade v. be bent. *O mo hiwii* He can not not stand straight.

hiwde v. chase birds off fields.

hoɓaade v. remove grains from the ear.

hoɓɓitde [hoɓɓidde] shell.

hoɓde v. shell.

hoɓre (nde) shell; cover.

hóɓtude v. shell.

hóccude v. pick up. ~ *kaalis* find money on the ground.

hócde [hojje] v. be thorny.

hoɗaade v. be a host.

hoɗande [hoɗan^{n}de] *(nde)* inhabited area.

hoɗande v. play the guitar for someone.

hoɗde v. 1) populate; reside; live; settle; inhabit 2) play the guitar. *Ko toon o hoɗi* He lives there.

hóɗdude [hóddude] v. live with; be a neighbor. *Kamɓe koɗdi* They are neighbors.

hóɗnude [hónnude] v. accommodate.

hoɗorde (nde) house; accommodation; habitat. ~ *laamɗo* palace; castle.

hóɗdu [hóddu] *(ndu)* guitar *piyoowo* ~ guitar player. *fiide* ~ play the guitar.

hoddere *(nde)* dish.

hóddiro *(ngo)* destiny.

hodoore *(nde)* shell.

hofaade v. sit on one's crossed legs; bent.

hofde v. bend. ~ *jungo* fold one's arm.

hófnude v. visit.

hófru (ndu) knee. *tumbude* ~ kneecap.

hogaade v. be crooked.

hogde v. make a hook.

hoggo (ngo) tusk; nib.

hogolde (nde) fruit.

hojom *(o)* minute.

hokde v. close tightly.

hokkere *(nde)* drought; shortage. *An ngondi e hokkere* We are experiencin shortage of rain.

hókkude v. lack rain. *Nokku o ina ho no feewi* This region needs rain.

hókkitde [hókkidde] v. separate; loose grip.

hókkóndirde v. give each other.

hókkude v. give; offer. ~ *yéru* exempl give an example.

hókóndirde [hókó^{n}dirde] v. cure by b contact.

hol *pron.* which; who; what. ~ *toon* wh ~ *oon* who. *Hol to paaɗaa* Where are going?.

hólɓundu [hólɓu^{n}du] *(ndu)* ankle.

holde v. lack clothing. *Mbeɗe holi* I l clothing.

hóltinde v. buy clothing for someone.

hóltude v. have clothing.

holfere *(nde)* shout.

holfo *(ngo)* wooden spoon.

hollalde *(nde)* hard ground near the river

hóllinde v. show; show oneself.

hóllirde v. expose. *O woni ko holli miijo makko* He is just giving his opini

hóllitde v. show.

hóllóndirde [hólló^{n}dirde] v. introdu acquaint.

hóllude v. show; present. ~ *miijo m* suggest. ~ *laawól* show the way. ~ *m* make a suggestion.

holñaade v. cut nails.

holsere *(nde)* 1) foot (of and animal); h 2) a cow or an ox.

hómbitande [hóm^{m}bitan^{n}de] removal hem.

nbitde [hóm^mbitde] *v.* remove the hem.

nbude [hóm^mbude] *v.* hem. *Hombanam uba ba* Can you hem the pants for me?

1de *v.* raid; plunder; foray; ransack.

1gude [hóɲⁿgude] *v.* knock; sound. *ongu hadee maa naatde* Knock before ɔu enter.

ɔdere *(nde)* star. ~ *siirtotoonde* a **ɪooting** star.

ɔlaade *v.* trust; rely. *Mbeɗe hooli maa* I ɪust you.

ɔlaare *(nde)* trust.

ɔleede *v.* be trusted; be trustworthy.

ólkisaade *v.* distrust.

ɔltaade *v.* peel; skin; carve. ~ *cegeneeji* ɪt nails.

óltude *v.* peel; carve.

ɔmto *(ngo)* unwariness.

ómtude *v.* make someone unwary.

oñde *v.* be overcooked. *Maaro maa ooñii* Your rice has been overcooked.

óñóldu *(ndu)* snail.

óntinde *v.* milk.

óntude *v.* suck before the cow is milked. *ɪge hoontii* The heifer has sucked the ɔw before it was milked.

oram hooram *(o)* egoism.

ore *(nde)* head. ~ *muusoore* headache. ~ *ala* apiece. ~ *haala* the beginning of the ɪlk.

orde *v.* fast. *Kó mi koorɗo* I am fasting.

ornaade *v.* fake fasting.

orngo [hoorⁿgo] *(ngo)* fasting.

órtude *v.* break fasting.

osde *v.* plunder; win all opponent's ɔssessions.

otde [hoodde] *v.* return home. ~ *to jeyaa* ɪeturn to one's home *Ó hóóti* he returned ɔome.

otonde [hootonⁿde] *(nde)* earring.

owde *v.* copulate.

oweede *v.* be made love to.

owoyre *(nde)* insect.

oɤeede *v.* be hungry. *Mbeɗe hooɤaa* I m hungry.

oynaade *v.* look up. *Hooynaade ko ɪeɓataa ko hebbinde gite mum loji* One ɪould have realistic expectations.

horaade *v.* fail. *Mi horiima yiide mo* I failed to see him; I could not see him.

horde *v.* 1) be tired 2) be empty. *ɓunndu ndu horii* The well's dried up.

horde *(nde)* calabash.

hórééru *(ndu)* relative.

hórfinaade *v.* sit on one's knees.

hórkitde [hórkidde] *v.* dig; irritate.

hórlinde *v.* open up.

hormere *(nde)* shelled corn ear.

horndolde [horⁿdolde] *(nde)* ant hill.

horoore *(nde)* shell.

hórsinde *v.* cherish; pamper. *Mbeɗe horsini mo* I cherish him.

hórsineede *v.* be cherished.

hórsude *v.* be cherished.

hortaade *v.* be very tired; be worn out. *Kó mi kortiiɗo* I am worn out.

hórtinde *v.* finish pounding. *Mi hortinii* I finished pounding.

hórtude *v.* pound grain into flower. *ɗiggude alt.*

horwaade *v.* wind into balls.

howde *v.* seclude; barricade; enclose; hedge; gird. *Ó hówii galle o* He built a fence for the house.

hóybinde *v.* alleviate.

hoyde *v.* be light. ~ *e leydi* be agile. **O mo hoyi** He is light.

hóyfiɗde [hóyfidde] *v.* be light.

hoyde *v.* be ashamed. *A hoyii* shᵃʳ.. on you.

hóynude *v.* shame. *A hoynii mo* You made him ashamed.

hoɤde [hojje] *v.* give water to drink.

hóyɗitaade *v.* ejaculate while dreaming.

hóyɗude *v.* dream. ~ *neɗɗo* dream about someone.

hóɤɤudu *(ndu)* neck; back of the neck; scruff. ~ *juutndu* a long neck.

huɓɓude *v.* light; ablaze; kindle; stoke; ignite; glow. ~ *oto* start a car. ~ *jeyngol* start a fire.

hubde *v.* chase; bleat.

huɓeere *(nde)* building. ~ *ɓakke* a mud building.

huccaango [huccaaⁿgo] *(ngo)* direction toward.

huccinde v. direct toward. ~ *fudnaange* direct East.

huccitde [huccidde] v. face.

huccude v. head for. ~ *laakara* go to hell. *Hol to kuccu daa* Where are you headed?.

hudde [hudde] v. curse.

hudeede v. be cursed.

huddu *(ndu)* enclosure.

hudo *(ko)* grass. ~ *siiwre* turf.

hudusuru *(ndu)* leather gourd.

huftude v. shell.

hujja *(o)* right. *jogaade* ~ have a right.

hulbinde v. scare; daunt; terrorize; startle; terrify. *A hulbinii mo* You scared him.

hulde v. be afraid of; dread. ~ *reedu* be afraid of. *Alaa ko o huli* He is not afraid of anything.

hulnde [hul^nde] *(nde)* bell. *Hulnde nde siɲlii* The bell rang.

hulquum *(o)* pharynx.

humam binne *(o)* ignorant person; illiterate. *Ko a humam binne* You are ignorant.

humande v. wed. *Mi humanii* I have gotten engaged.

humaneede v. be wed; be engaged.

humde v. tie to. ~ *dewgal* tie the knot.

humtude v. 1) untie 2) remove a spell. *Humtu nagge nge* Untie the cow.

humbaldu [hu^mbaldu] *(ndu)* musical instrument.

humbude [hum^mbude] v. float.

humpeede v. ignore; be unaware; be without news of. *Mbede humpaa mo* I have no news concerning him.

humpitaade v. be informed.

humpitde v. inform. *Humpitam* Keep me informed.

humpude v. be unknown.

huñaade v. memorize; recite.

huñde [huñje] v. lift or to roll clothing up.

hundude [hun^dude] v. roof. ~ *suudu* roof a house with woven reeds.

hunuko *(ko)* mouth. *ko faati e* ~ oral. *mubbude* ~ shut up.

hurbaango [hurbaa^ngo] *(ngo)* roar.

hurbude v. roar.

hurgo *(ngo)* woven reed fence.

hurkaƳere *(nde)* laterite stone.

hurmude v. be black.

hurjo *(ngo)* holidays. *yahde* ~ go o vacation.

hurtaade v. move to the husband compound. *O hurtiima* She moved to h husband's compound.

hurtinde v. bring the wife to one compound.

husde v. sew.

husere *(nde)* piece of meat. ~ *teew* a pie of meat.

hutaade v. despise. *Mbede hutii mo* despise him.

huttóóru *(ndu)* iguana.

huttude v. skin.

huudaade v. leave early morning. *huudiima* He left early in the morning.

huufde v. hold in arms resting on one legs.

huufnude v. place in front of someone.

huunaade v. boast.

huunaango [huunaa^ngo] *(ngo)* bellov lowing.

huunde v. moo; bellow.

huunde [huu^nde] *(nde)* thing; object. *hay* nothing; nought; none; zero. ~ *ka* everything.

huuñdude [huuñƳude] v. be greedy; voracious.

huurde v. cover; surround with wove reed. *lewru huurndu* the whole month.

huureede v. be covered.

huusde v. remove hair.

huutoraade v. utilize; exploit.

huuwde v. work.

huwde v. 1) defecate 2) lie.

huywere *(nde)* vagrant; useless person. *o huywere* He is useless.

huywinde v. cause someone to be useless vagrant.

huywineede v. be considered useless vagrant.

huywude v. wander.

I

iis *(o) {ar.}* satan; devil. **baggel** ~ devil's drum. **golle** ~ devil's work. **reentaade** ~ stay away from devilish deeds.

citaade *v.* cry.

aade *v.* be first. **Idaade ɓuri wattindaade** t is better to be first than last. **Ko kanko dii** He arrived first. **adaade** *alt.*

oraade *v.* start with. **Idoro toon** Start from there.

aade *v.* cry.

de *v.* sneeze.

ɗude *v.* be dark; be stormy. **Asamaan o irɗii** It is stormy.

taade *v.* 1) be angry 2) be painful.

tóndirde [iirtó^{n}dirde] *v.* be mixed.

tude *v.* dig out; stir up. ~ **barme** stir the ɔot. ~ **hakkille nedɗo** render a person nsane/senile.

tugól *(ngól)* stirring up.

kaade *v.* go aside.

kinde *v.* put aside.

um *(ɗam)* flood. ~ **keewɗam** a major flood.

de *v.* flow; spread over. **Ilam ilii** The river s high.

ól *(ngól)* stream.

wól *(ngól)* excavation; thalweg.

ude *v.* shine; flash.

kinaade *v.* scream.

aa *part.* except. ~ **aan** except you.

maade *v.* rise. ~ **law** rise early. **Immo dow** Get up. **ummade** *alt.*

minde *v.* make rise; make stand. **umminde** *alt.*

sinaade *v.* repent.

sinaango *(ngo)* repentance.

suf. causative suffix. **MoYYin ɗum** Do it well.

inna *(o)* mother.

innama *(o)* being. ~ **aadee** human being.

inde [in^{n}de] *(nde)* 1) name 2) naming cermony. ~ **deftere** chosen name; first name. **Ko ɗum wóni inde maa** That is your first name.

inniraaɗo *(o)* namesake.

iinnirde *v.* name after. **Mi innirii ma Muusaa** I name you after Muusaa.

innitaade *v.* say one's. genealogy. **Innito** Tell me your genealogy.

innitde [innidde] *v.* rename.

innitoore *(nde)* genealogy.

innude *v.* baptize; dub.

-ir *suf.* instrumental suffix; by means of. **helirde jungo** break with the hand.

iraade *v.* be covered with sand; be buried; bury oneself.

irde *v.* cover with sand; bury.

ittindirde [itti^{n}dirde] *v.* separate.

ittirde *v.* remove with. **Ittir ɗum peel** remove it with a shovel.

ittude *v.* 1) abolish; subtract; remove; deduct 2) be plenty.

ittugól *(ngól)* ablation; removal.

ittital *(ngal)* type of soil.

iwde *v.* 1) originate from; come from; be from 2) stop.

iwdi *(ndi)* origin; source. **Hol iwdi maa** What is your origin?

iwrude *v.* come by way of. **Iwru gaa** Come this way.

iwtude *v.* return from; leave. **Mi iwtii toon gila ko ɓooyi** I left that place a long time ago.

iwlaade *v.* warm oneself at the fire.

J

jaabaade *v.* answer. *Jaabo mo* Reply to him.

jaabawól *(ngól)* reply; answer. *Lamndal naamnii ko jaabawol* A question requires an answer.

jaabtaade *v.* reply. ~ *bataake* reply to a letter.

jaabondirde *v.* answer one another.

jaabe *(de)* fruit from a jaabi tree. *yaabre (nde) sing.*

jaabi *(ki)* jujube tree. *lekki* ~ jujube tree.

jaadde [jaadde] *v.* be numb. *Jungo am ina jaadi* My arm is numb.

jaddinde *v.* stiffen; harden.

jaddude *v.* 1) be stiff; be hard 2) be numb.

jaafiido *adj.* person who gave forgiveness.

jaafotoodo *adj.* merciful. *Alla ko jaafotoodo* God is merciful.

jaajdo [jaaŕŕo] *adj.* vast; wide; patient. *Ko o neddo jaajdo* He is patient.

jaaje type of grass.

jaajude *v.* be executed.

jaakde *v.* be troubled; be puzzled; have a dilemma. *Mbede jaaki* I do not know where to turn to.

jaaklude *v.* be troubled; be puzzled.

jaakre *(nde)* wonder; dilemma.

jaalaade *v.* show grief.

jaalal *(ngal)* pillar; stake.

jaaltaabe *(o)* fisherman's title.

jaande [jaanᵈde] *(nde)* grass for cattle. *O addoyii jaande* He went to get grass for animal consumption.

jaandere [jaanᵈdere] cattle food; grass for animal consumption.

jaandu [jaanᵈdu] *(ndu)* private land.

jaañe *(de)* excrement; feces; cow dung.

jaangde [jaaⁿgde] *v.* be cold. *Ina jaangi* it is cold.

jaangeede [jaaⁿgeede] *v.* be cold. *Mbede jaangaa* I am cold.

jaangól [jaaⁿgol] *(ngól)* cold; cold weather. ~ *cadtungol* a bitter cold.

jaandu [jaanᵈdu] *(ndu)* type of bird.

jaaraama thanks; well done. *Alla* ~ thanks be to Allah. *A jaaraama* I thank you.

jaarde *v.* commend; eulogize; thank. *ɓ ngoni ko e jaarde nelaado* They ar praising the Prophet.

jaareejo *(o)* griot.

jaarnude *v.* give thanks to.

jaaroowo *(o)* praise singer.

jaarga *(o)* head; chief.

jaasde *v.* be useless; be stupid. *O mo jaaⁱ* He is useless.

jaasdo *adj.* useless person.

jaasre *(nde)* uselessness.

jaasi *(ki)* matchet; saber.

jaawando [jaawanᵈdo] *(o)* type of griot.

jaawdo *adj.* prompt; fast; swift; rapiᵉ *neddo* ~ a fast person.

jaawngal [jaawⁿgal] *(ngal)* guinea fow *jaawle (de) pl.*

jaawnaade *v.* be intelligent.

jaawre *(nde)* antilope.

jaaŕaade *v.* return safely. *A jaa ŕiima* Di you arrive safely.

jaa ŕtagól *(ngól)* 1) safe arrival/journey 2 speeding; acceleration.

jaaynde [jaayⁿde] *(nde)* announcement.

jaaynirgal *(ngal)* publicity device.

jaaynude *v.* publicize; announce; mak public. *O woni ko e jaaynude* He i making a public announcement.

jaayngal [jaayⁿgal] *(ngal)* announcement.

jaayre *(nde)* planet.

jabande *v.* allow; grant. ~ *ngantu* accep someone's excuse.

jabde *v.* agree; admit; nod; adopt; approvᵉ concede. *Mi jabii* I accept.

jabgól *(ngól)* adhesion; acceptance.

jabbaade *v.* welcome. ~ *kodo* welcome guest.

jabbaaru *(o)* God.

jabbe *(de)* tamarind trees; tamarind fruit.

jabbi *(ki)* tamarind tree.

jabbere *(nde)* holes for sowing. *reende mum* be careful.

jabbirgal *(ngal)* farming tool used fᵉ making holes for sowing.

jabbitaade *v.* dig holes for sowing a secon time.

bude v. make holes for sowing. *O woni e jabbude* He is making holes for wing.

gitaade v. Hold tight; grab tightly.

goowo (o) holder.

gude v. 1) grasp; record; 2) arrest; hold. *o hande Ɓe njaggi mo* They arrested m today.

gugól (ngól) grip.

diiɗo (o) companion. ~ *bonɗo* a bad mpanion. ~ *moYYo* a good companion.

re (nde) hollow.

hokoore (nde) small white shell.

ɔoowo adj. shiny.

bude v. radiate; twinkle; shine. *Ina jalbi* is shining.

buɗo adj. shining.

bugol (ngol) shine.

de v. laugh; sneer. ~ *neɗɗo* laugh at meone.

eɗe (ɗe) laughter; laughs.

kitde [jalkidde] v. deride; fleer; gibe; fout; off; laugh at.

eede v. be laughed at.

niiɗo adj. funny. *Ndaw ko jalnii* He is so nny.

noowo (o) comedian. *Ko o jalnoowo* He a comedian.

nude v. make someone laugh. *Ko kanko Jni mi* He made me laugh.

e (ɗe) hoes; hoe blades **jalo** (ngo) sing.

ɔ (ngo) hoe; hoe blade.

la fishing net.

li griot.

n (o) peace. ~ *tan* peace only. *Yo Alla ɔkku jam* Get well.

njam adv slowly; gently. *waarude* ~ do ɔmething slowly.

naa (o) {ar.} daily prayer place. *O Juloyii jamaa* He went to say his prayers t the daily prayer place.

naanu (o) {ar.} era; world today. ~ *booyɗo bénnuɗo* antiquity. ~ *hande o* ne world today; nowadays.

nba [jam^mba] rice seedlings.

nbere [jam^mbere] (nde) ax; tomahawk.

niroowo (o) chief; individual who gives rders.

nma (o) night. ~ *hande* tonight. ~ *Jutɗo* a long night.

jamminde v. be night. *ɗum jamminii* The night has come / The night is well advanced.

jananaaɗo (o) certain; sure *aɗa yananaa* Are you sure?.

janano someone else's. *debbo* ~ someone else's wife.

jangde [ja^ngde] (nde) education; instruction; literacy. ~ *terɗe* anatomy. *ko faati e* ~ pedagogical. ~ *terɗe* anatomy.

janginde [ja^nginde] v. educate; instruct; lecture; teach.

janginoowo [jaŋ^nginoowo] (o) lecturer; instructor; educator. ~ *hanki men* a history teacher.

jangirde [jaŋ^girde] (nde) school.

jangoowo [jaŋ^goowo] (o) learner; reader; student. *Ko o jangoowo* He is a student.

jangude [jaŋ^gude] v. read; decipher; study; learn.

janguɗo [jaŋ^guɗo] adj. literate.

jandere [jan^dere] (nde) type of fish.

janfa (o) treason; betrayal.

janfaade v. betray; traduce. *A janfiima koreeji maa* You betrayed your relatives.

janfotooɗo (o) traitor. *Ko o janfotooɗo* He is a traitor. *janfanke* (o) alt.

jango [jaŋ^go] (o) tomorrow. *haa* ~ until tomorrow.

jankiniiɗo adj. modest; chaste. *ko o neɗɗo jankiniiɗo* he is a modest person.

jaŋtaade v. testify; narrate; relate; report; relay; explain.

jaŋtagól (ngól) narration; narrative; report.

jaŋtotooɗo (o) narrator; reporter.

jantóndiral (ngal) coalition; alliance.

jantuɗo (o) participant.

jappeere (nde) saddle; pad.

jappude v. lay; saddle.

jarabi (o) temptation.

jarribaade v. test; tempt. *Ngonmi ko e jarribaade mo* I am tempting him.

jarde v. be worth; amount to. *Ina jari ɗum* It is worth it / It is not expensive.

jarnude v. be sold out. *Mi jarnii* I am sold out.

jardugal (ngal) pipe for smoking.

jarlal adj. female animal; hen.

jaroowo (o) drinker. ~ *sangara* a person who drinks alcohol.

jatde [jadde] *v.* stretch.

jattinaade *v.* resist; revolt.

jattiniiɗo (o) obstinate.

jawdi *(ndi)* 1) cattle; animals 2) possessions. *golle ~* savage. *~ maa* your belongings.

jawdiyanke (o) wealthy person.

jawél *(ngél)* small bracelet.

jawo (ngo) bracelet. *~ jungo* a wrist bracelet. *~ koyngal* an ankle bracelet.

jawwinde *v.* smoke; light a fire. *O mo jawwina* he smokes.

jawwude v. glow; catch fire. *ɗum jawwii* It caught fire.

jayde *v.* swing.

jaylaade *v.* walk hurriedly; pick hurriedly.

jébbilaade *v.* renounce; give up; accept; be submissive. *Mi jebbiliima* I give up.

jebe (nge) cow.

jeeɓoowo *(o)* spectator.

jééɗiɓo *(o)* seventh.

jééɗiɗi seven. *balɗe ~* seven days. *laabi ~* seven times.

jééfulɓe Arɗo's first wife.

jeegom *num.* six. *sappo e ~* sixteen.

jeemaayo *(o)* fisherman's first wife.

jeenaɓo *num.* the ninth.

jeenay num. nine.

jeenayo num. the ninth person in rank.

jeere *(nde)* mart; market. *O yahii jeere* He went to the market.

jééri *(ndi)* higher grounds.

jeertaade *v.* have a hunch; notice. *Mi jeerti* I had a hunch.

jeertagól (ngól) hunch.

jéértinde v. profess; warn; deliver a message.

jeertinoowo (o) messenger.

jeerto (ngo) hunch; warning.

jéértoyaade v. patrol.

jéértungo [jéértuⁿgo] *(ngo)* hunch.

jeetaɓal *num.* the eighth.

jeetati um. eight.

jeewal *(ngal)* big first wife.

jééwél (ngél) little first wife.

jeewo (o) first wife. *Ko kanko woni jeewo maa* She is your first wife.

jeewaaɗo *adj.* lonely. *Ko mi jeewaaɗo* am lonely.

jééwnuɗo adj. nostalgic.

jééwru *(ndu)* cabin; room.

jeeƳere *(nde)* panic.

jeeƳude v. panic.

jeeyoowo *(o)* salesperson; vendor; tradeᵣ *Ko o jeeyoowo* He is a salesperson.

jéjji *(ɗi)* oblivion. *jejjitgol (ngól) sing.*

jéjjitoowo (o) forgetful. *Ko o jejjitoowo* H is forgetful.

jelde *v.* mark. *O woni ko e jelde nay ɗi* H is putting marks on the cows.

jeloode (nde) mark.

jelotooɗo (o) beggar. *sakkaade ~* givᵣ charity to the beggar.

jéngude [jéŋgude] *v.* be late. *Jammᵣ jengii* The night is late.

jennooje *(ɗe)* disparaging remarks *njennoor (o) sing.*

jennoowo *(o)* person who makeᵣ disparaging remarks. *yennude v.*

jérɓugól *(ngól)* earthquake; shaking. *léydi* seism; cataclysm.

jettagól *(ngól)* arrival.

jewde *v.* exist.

jeyaaɗo *(o)* slave.

jeyal (ngal) ownership.

jeyde v. own; possess; pertain. *Ko miin jeᵣ ɗum* It is mine.

jeyeede v. belong; pertain. *Mbeɗe yiᵣ jeyeede e fedde mon* I would like to bᵣ part of your age group.

jeyba *(ka)* pocket. *nder ~* in the pocket.

jéyngól [jeyⁿgól] *(ngól)* fire. *~ jahannamᵣ* hell.

jéysi *(o)* type of dance; fantasia.

jéysude v. dance.

-ji plural suffix. *tuubaaji (ɗi)* the pants.

jibidineede *v.* be born with.

jibinande *(nde)* offsprings

jibinde *v.* yield; engender; teem; give birth *~ ɓiɗɗo debbo* give birth to a daughter.

jibingól (ngól) birth.

jibinoowo *adj.* fecund; fertile.

jiɗgól (ngól) affection; liking.

jiggoore *(nde)* caravan.

jihaadi *(o) {ar.}* holy war.

jihe *(ɗe)* squirrels. *jihre (nde) sing.*

jiiba *(o)* carcass; kelt; carrion.

jiibde *v.* die and rot.

jiibaade *v.* be confused. *Ko o jiibiido* He is confused.

jiibde *v.* mix; confuse.

jiibre *(nde)* mixture of mud, water and animal waste.

jiibru *(ndu)* confusion.

jiidal *(ngal)* sight. *Jiidal* See you later.

jiyoowo *(o)* person who sees. *yiide v.*

jiidde *v.* copulate with the bride.

jiidgól *(ngól)* defloration; copulation.

jiidigal *(ngal)* act of being related; relation; kinship.

jiidude *v.* be related.

jiilagól *(ngól)* 1) adventure; search 2) turning around; swirling motion.

jiilotoodo *(o)* searcher; seeker.

jiimde *v.* 1) bend one's head forward; 2) be above; administer. *Ko kanko jiim maa* He is above you.

jiimdo *(o)* patron; manager; head; ruler; colonizer.

jiimoowo *(o)* head; ruler.

jiiraade *v.* eat fast.

jikde *v.* tangle.

jikóndirde [jikóndirde] *v.* entangle.

jikkaade *v.* hope.

jikkande [jikkan^nde] *(nde)* grabbing; handful.

jikkande *v.* grab for.

jikkude *v.* 1) grab; grab a handful of 2) to have a hunch.

jikke *(o)* 1) reputation 2) hope.

jikkóndirde [jikkón^dirde] *v.* suspect each other.

jikku *(o)* habit; custom; character; behavior. *bonde* ~ have a bad behavior. *jikkuuji (di)* pl.

jilankoonde [jilaŋkoo^nde] *(nde)* drum.

jilbere *(nde)* confusion; mixture. *addude* ~ bring confusion.

jilbude *v.* be mixed up; be confused.

jillande [jillan^nde] *(nde)* mixture.

jillóndirde [jilló^ndirde] *v.* be mixed.

jillude *v.* mix; be mixed. *Ina jilli* It is not pure.

jilludo *(o)* mongrel; mixed.

jimbaŋ [jim^mbaan] *(o)* verandah.

jimól *(ngól)* song. ~ *belngol* a good song. ~ *mettungol* a bad song.

jimoowo *(o)* singer. *Ko o jimoowo* She is a singer.

jinaa *(o)* adultery.

jinde *v.* commit adultery. *Ko o jindo* He committed adultery.

jinoowo *(o)* adulterer; person who commits adultery.

jinaade *v.* be caught.

jinde [jin^nde] *(nde)* area where garbage is piled.

jindude *v.* be busy; need help.

jindere *(nde)* busy state.

jiŋde *v.* hang over.

jinditde [jin^ndidde] *v.* sell out.

jingande [jiŋ^ngande] *v.* favor; side with; give judgement to. *A jinganii mo* You sided with him.

jingoowo [jiŋ^ngoowo] *adj.* partial.

jingude [jiŋ^ngude] *v.* side with. *Ngon daa ko e jingude* You are being partial.

jinnaado *(o)* parent. ~ *debbo* a female parent. ~ *gorko* a male parent. *Ko o jinnaado maa* S/he is your parent.

jinne *(o)* spirit.

jinnéyél *(ngél)* imp.

jippaade *v.* 1) dismount; come down; 2) finish work; 3) be hosted. *Mi jippiima* I am off.

jippinde *v.* set down.

jipporde *(nde)* camp; temporary stop; rest area.

jippunde [jippu^nde] *(nde)* camp; temporary residence.

jirwude *v.* be pleasant; be happy.

jiwde *v.* be adolescent.

jiwo *(o)* girl.

jiyaado *(o)* captive; slave; servant. *Ko o jiyaado* He is a slave.

jo e jo frequently; often.

jobnotoodo *(o)* cashier.

jofe *(de)* liver; lungs.

jofnde [jof^nde] *(nde)* enclosure for animals.

joftagól *(ngól)* vengeance.

jogaade *v.* have; possess; own. ~ *hakkille* be thoughful.

jogagól *(ngól)* possession; ownership.

joganaade v. 1) hold for someone 2) hold a grudge.

joganiiɗo adj. rancorous.

jogiiɗo adj. wealthy; holder of.

joggaango [joggaaⁿgo] *(ngo)* morning crow of the cock.

jóggude v. crow.

jokkande v. sew for; put together for.

jokkande [jokkanⁿde] *(nde)* knot.

jokkere (nde) sequel; knot.

jókkitde [jókkidde] v. 1) finish up 2) break.

jókkóndiral [jokkóⁿdiral] *(ngal)* liaison; sequence.

jókkóndirde [jókkóⁿdirde] v. splice; connect.

jokkoowo (o) tailor.

jokkorde (nde) node.

jókkude v. continue; sew together; fasten; append.

jolde v. 1) get into; descend into a well; board 2) be fashionable. *Ko ɗum jóli* It is the new fashion.

jólirde (nde) boarding place. *Ko ɗoo woni jolirde nde* This is the area for boarding.

jolngo (ngo) boarding.

jólnude v. place in. ~ *leeteer* mail a letter.

jolɗo adj. fashionable.

jolfe (ɗe) Wolof language. *O mo nana jolfe* He speaks Wolof.

jolfo (o) Wolof person.

jom owner; self respect ~ *galle* husband. ~ *suudu* wife.

jóómiraaɗo (o) God.

jombaajo (o) a newly wed person.

jombo [jomᵐbo] *(ko)* tassel.

jómbinde [jómᵐbinde] v. flourish; come out.

jómbude [jómᵐbude] v. 1) flourish; come out 2) be happy.

jómmude v. point to.

jonde (nde) gathering.

joñde [joñje] v. discard; set aside.

joñgol (ngol) the setting aside of an object or a person.

joñoowo (o) person who sets something aside.

jonɗo adj. complete; reliable. *Ko o neɗɗo jon ɗo* He is a reliable person.

jóɗɗinde v. make sit; put on the floor.

jooɗaade v. sit down. *Jooɗo* Sit down.

jooɗorde (nde) seat; chair; bench. *Addan mo jooɗorde* Bring him a seat.

jooɗorgal (ngal) chair; place for sitting.

jooɗaade [joottaade] v. sit down again; sit tightly.

joodde v. salivate; slobber.

jóóɗól (ngól) saliva.

jooɗɗo [jooɗɗo] adj. cute; gorgeous; handsome; nice. *debbo* ~ a pretty woman.

joofaade v. point to.

jóófórdu (ndu) forefinger.

joofande [joofanⁿde] *(nde)* stop.

joofde v. stop; end; anchor; accost. *Ko ɗoo tindol ngol joofi* The tale ends here.

jóófirde (nde) berth; end.

jóófnirde (nde) end.

jóófnude v. achieve; accomplish; finish.

jookaaɗo (o) cornered person.

jookde v. corner; hedge. *Ko o jookaaɗo* He is cornered.

jóókdu (ndu) corner.

jookeede v. be cornered.

jóókirde (nde) place for cornering.

jooko (ngo) cornering.

Joolaa (o) Joolaa person.

joolaade v. betray.

joolo (ngo) betrayal.

jóóliiɗo (o) person who drowned. *yoolde* v.

jooloowo (o) person who drowns someone or something.

joom chief's title.

joomaade v. choke.

jóóni now; soon. ~ *jooni* right now; immediately. ~ *faade yeeso* henceforth.

jooraade v. be poured; come down.

joorde v. pour.

joortaade v. 1) be poured again; fall again 2) anticipate; expect. *Mbeɗe*

jóórtiiɗo (o) person who expects something.

joortinoo ɗum I expected it.

jootaaɗo adj. unfortunate.

joote (ɗe) misfortune; hardship.

jooteede v. undergo hardship; be unfortunate.

joowde v. pile.

óówóndirde [jóówó^{n}dirde] v. accumulate; pile up.

oowre (nde) pile; heap.

oowtude v. remove a pile.

oownde [joow^{n}de] (nde) heap.

ottaade v. miss.

óy num. five. **laabi** ~ five times.

oyaɓal (ngal) the fifth (part/share).

oyaɓo (o) the fifth in rank.

óyɓitde [jóyɓidde] v. be fifth.

óŶŶinde v. deposit.

óŶŶinoowo (o) person who places something somewhere.

ubaade v. extract butter from milk.

ubarde (nde) island. **jubare** (ɗe) pl.

ubbande v. set aside for.

ubbande [jubban^{n}de] (nde) a pinch; food set aside.

ubbude v. pinch.

ubból (ngól) braid.

uɓɓugól (ngól) cohesion.

ubde v. be deprived of sexual intercourse.

uɗande v. roast for someone; barbecue for.

juɗande [juɗan^{n}de] (nde) roast; barbecue.

juɗde [judde] v. roast; barbecue.

juɗoowo (o) cook; person who barbecues.

juggal (ngal) fold; enclosure **jugge** (ɗe).

juknude v. pawn.

juko (ngo) long rain. **jukóóji** (ɗi) pl.

jula (o) merchant; tradesman; monger. **julaaɓe** (ɓe) pl.

julaade v. buy with the intent of selling back at a later stage; trade.

julankaagal [julaŋkaagal] (ngal) trading; commerce.

julanke [julaŋke] (o) merchant; trader/tradesman; monger.

julotooɗo (o) merchant; tradesperson.

jullaare (nde) tree stump.

jullude v. eat watery substance with the hand.

jumaa (o) {ar.} mosque. **O yahii jumaa** He went to the mosque.

jumde v. 1) request; file a claim/suit 2) get honey from a hive.

jumpude v. jiggle a bucket in a well.

junaade v. stoop down with legs apart; bend.

jungo (ngo) [juŋ^{n}go] arm; hand; forearm. ~ **cómól** sleeve. **peewɗo** ~ marksman.

junnitbasel (ngél) acrobatics.

junnitde [junnidde] v. hold upside down.

jurminiiɗo adj. piteous; melancholic; sad.

jurmotooɗo adj. merciful.

jusaade v. kneel down.

jusande [jusan^{n}de] (nde) kneeling of an animal.

juulde v. pray; say one's prayers.

juulde (nde) prayer; major religious holiday. ~ **koorka** religious holiday commemorating the end of fasting.

juulɗo (o) Moslem; Muslim.

juulɗo adj. pious. **O wonaa juulɗo** He is not a Moslem.

juulirde (nde) place or rag used for praying.

juulirde v. pray with.

juulkinaade v. pretend to say one's prayers.

juulnude v. lead a prayer.

juumde v. make a mistake; be mistaken. **Ko mi juumɗo** I am mistaken.

juumnude v. mislead.

juuraade v. 1) pour water over oneself 2) land 3) pay a visit.

juurde v. 1) pour out 2) give money to an artist.

juurgal (ngal) money given to an artist.

juurtude v. 1) pour 2) lengthen sounds.

juurngól [juur^{n}gól] (ngól) dam; dike pl. juurli (ɗi).

juutde [juudde] v. be long; be tall.

juutgól (ngól) length. **laawol** ~ a long way.

juutnude [juunnude] v. elongate; lenthen; prolong.

juuti (o) tax collector. **yoɓde** ~ pay a tax to the tax collector.

juuwde v. ford/cross a stream.

juuwde (nde) ford.

K

ka *det.* the. *taasa* ~ the bowl.

Kaaba *(o)* *{ar.}* Kaaba.

kaadééki *(ki)* bitterness.

kaadi *(di)* folly; insanity; mania. *dum ko kaadi* That is insane.

kaangaado [kaaⁿgaado] *adj.* mad; fool; insane. *Ko o kaangaado* He is insane.

kaadtinoowo [kaattinoowo]*(o)* person who sets limits.

kaadtudi [kaattudi] *(ndi)* limit; boundary.

kaakaale *(de)* leaves.

kaake *(de)* 1) baggage; luggage; equipment 2) testicles. ~ *janane* someone else's belongings.

kaakte *(de)* spits.

kaala *(ka)* scarf. *fiilaade* ~ tie one's headscarf.

kaaldigal *(ngal)* dialogue. *Ko kaaldigal addi paamondiral* Through dialogue we come to a mutual understanding.

kaale *(o)* white horse.

kaalis *(o)* 1) money; cash; currency 2) silver.

kaamiilu *(o)* the Koran.

kaandi [kaaⁿdi] *(ndi)* lion.

kaani *(o)* red pepper. *O mo suusi kaani* He likes red pepper.

kaañééri *(ndi)* candleberry; wax.

kaari *(o)* someone.

kaata *(o)* ashes.

kaaw *(o)* uncle (mother's brother).

kaawaado *adj.* stunned; astonished; amazed.

kaawis *(o)* wonder; miracle *kaawisaaji (di)* pl.

kaaye *(de)* urine.

kaaᵞél *(ngél)* little stone. ~ *manaango* thunderbolt.

kaayit *(o)* *{wol.}* paper hello ~ page.

kaba *(ka)* bottle.

kabaaru *(o)* *{ar.}* piece of news; information. ~ *jam* good news. ~ *bone* bad news.

kabroowo *(o)* informant; an individual who informs.

kabayél *(ngél)* little bottle.

kabbannoodo *(o)* person who used to tie something.

kabboowo *(o)* person who ties.

kabbugol *(ngol)* fastening.

kabbale *(o)* corpse.

kabdigal *(ngal)* adversity.

kabdiido *(o)* opponent; adversary ~ *am* my adversary.

kabeteedo *(o)* fighter; militant; quarreller; warrior.

kabirde *(de)* armament.

kacitaagol *(ngol)* the act of eating breakfast.

kacitaari *(ndi)* breakfast. *Kacitaari maa buubii* Your breakfast is cold.

Kacitiido *(o)* person who ate breakfast.

kaddagól *(ngól)* 1) the tying of a skirt/sarong 2) circumcision.

kadi *foc.* also; yet; in addition.

kadu *(o)* nape of the neck.

kafe *(de)* coffee. *yarde* ~ drink coffee. *duudeede* ~ be addicted to coffee.

kafo *(o)* dye.

kafu (ngu) age set.

kaggu *(o)* shelf; platform for keeping milk. *kagguuji (di)* pl.

kahi *(ki)* tree.

kal *det.* the. *dihal* ~ the water.

kala *adv.* every; each; whatever; per. *neddo* ~ every person.

kalaas *(o)* *{fr.}* class.

kalabante *(o)* rascal.

kalandiriye [kalanⁿdiriye] *(o)* *{fr.}* calendar.

kalasal *(ngal)* hedge; stick; façade; fence.

kalbe *(de)* wallet; purse. ~ *keewde kaalis* a wallet full of money.

kalfaado *(o)* slave.

kalfinaado *(o)* guardian; warden.

kalfoowo *(o)* ruler; owner.

kalfudo *(o)* slave owner; owner.

kalhaldi *(ndi)* bull.

kaliifa *(o)* owner; master.

kallemme *(o)* small horse.

kallu *(o)* main road *pl. kalluuji (di)*.

kalmaade *v.* complain; report a complaint.

kalmagol *(ngol)* complaint.

lmotoodo *(o)* person who complains.

lumbam [kalu^mbam] *(dam)* water already used to wash rice or millet.

lwude *v.* pray.

lwugol *(ngol)* prayer.

am *pers. pron.* he; him. **Kam ari** S/he came.

ama *(o)* latrine.

amañaɳ *(o)* rice farm.

ambaane [kam^mbaane] *(o)* youth.

ambe *pers. pron.* them. ~ **koye mabbe** themselves.

amen *pers. pron.* they.

amiyoɳ *(o)* {fr.} truck; lorry.

ammonjawo [kammoⁿjawo] *(ngo)/(o)* millet ear that is not completely ripe.

ammu *(o)* sky. **asamaan** *alt.*

añ *pers. pron.* he; she.

aña *(o)* {wol.} big rat.

anappe *(o)* canopy.

andal [kanⁿdal] *(ngal)* fruit.

ande *(o)* basket.

ani *(o)* locust.

anje *(de)* okra.

ankaleewal [kaɳkaleewal] *(ngal)* duck; goose.

anko [kaɳko] *pron.* he; she.

aɳɳe *(o)* gold. **jawo** ~ a gold bracelet.

añtudi [kañcudi] *(ndi)* semen; sperm.

appe *(de)* yams.

araaje *(de)* empty area.

araas *(o)* dandruff. **O mo wondi e karaas** He has dandruff.

arafe *(o)* horse.

aral *(ngal)* half.

arallaagal *(ngal)* technique; intelligence; machinery.

arallo *(o)* expert; technician.

araw *(o)* porridge.

arawal *(ngal)* bald area.

ardumbal [kardu^mbal] *(ngal)* spindle.

are *(o)* {fr.} chalk. **windirde** ~ write with chalk.

armingol *(ngol)* the act of giving up something forever. **harminde** *v.*

armindo *adj.* person who gave up something forever.

armudum *adj.* forbidden; taboo.

karot *(o)* {fr.} carrot.

karsin *(o)* {fr.} kerosene.

karsirgal *(ngal)* rope tied around a neck.

kartal *(ngal)* {fr.} card **fettude karte** play cards.

kartuus *(o)* {fr.} bullet.

karwaas *(o)* {fr.} whip; lash. **fiirude** ~ whip.

kasanke [kasaɳke] *(o)* shroud.

kasikoño *(o)* cloth.

kaske *(o)* {fr.} helmet.

kasó *(o)* {fr.} cage; jail; prison. **O mon e kaso** He is in prison.

kastiloor *(o)* {fr.} pan.

katamaawu *(ngu)* tiger.

kaw *(o)* group of farmers.

kawasal *(ngal)* sock. **boornaade** ~ wear a sock. **kawase** *(de) pl.*

kawgel *(ngel)* game.

kawle *(de)* autumn.

kawral *(ngal)* truce; consensus; concord; agreement.

kawrugól *(ngól)* meeting. ~ **heen** chance.

kay *foc. part.* indeed. **Ko kanko kay** It is him indeed.

kayfal *(ngal)* upland tsetse fly.

kayre *pron.* it.

kebbe *(de)* burrs; thorns.

kebdo *(o)* recipient.

kébtingól *(ngól)* recognition.

kebtindo *(o)* person who recognized another person.

kecco *(o)* raw; fresh; wet.

kéccudo *(o)* elder.

keddam *(dam)* fresh milk.

kedde *(de)* remnants; rest; remains; residue; residual ~ **makko** his leftovers.

kééci *(ki)* back. ~ **muusóówi** backache.

keefeero *(o)* non Muslim.

keeferaagal *(ngal)* sin.

kééfgól *(ngol)* scraping.

kééfól *(ngól)* track left by scraping; trace.

keefoowo *(o)* person who scrapes.

kéélééli *(ki)* shrub growing at the bank of a river.

kééról *(ngól)* limit; scope; frontier; boundary; border **keeri** *(di) pl.*

kééróndiral *(ngal)* limit; bordering.

Keerotooɗo *(o)* person who sets limits.

kees *(o) {fr.}* box. ~ *tamaate* a box of tomatoes.

keewal *(ngal)* fullness; multitude; plethora; opulence. *Ngaree e keewal* Come in large numbers.

kééwɗi *adj.* numerous; many; several; various.

keewɗo *adj.* full.

kelal *(ngal)* fracture. ~ *koyngal* a broken leg. ~ *jungo* a broken arm.

kelgol *(ngol)* breaking.

keltagol *(ngol)* the breaking of items into smaller parts.

keloowo *(o)* person who breaks things.

kelle *(ɗe)* clappings; slappings. *Yo kelle ngar* Let us hear a round of applause.

kélli *(ki)* tree.

kéllifaaɗo *adj.* adolescent. *mawɗo* ~ a mature individual.

kéllifuya *(o)* adolescence. *maale* ~ signs of puberty.

kéllóóri *(ndi)* red dye.

kelme *(ɗe)* vocabulary; lexicon *helmere (nde) sing.*

kenal (kal) breeze; air; light wind. *kénééli (ɗi) pl.*

kéñiiɗo *(o)* a person who is in a hurry.

kerem *(o) {fr.}* cream.

keri (o) hoe; type of wood.

kersa *(o)* disgrace; scandal.

kersuɗo *adj.* ashamed. *Ko o kersuɗo* He is ashamed.

késniiɗo *(o)* widow.

keso *adj.* new. *galle* ~ a new house.

kétungól [kétuⁿgól] *(ngól)* cream**kéw** *(o)* party.

kewal *(ngal)* bamboo.

kewe *(ɗe) pl.*

kéwi *(ki)* bamboo plant.

kéyniraaɗo *(o)* wife's brother/sister to husband.

ki *det.* the. *lekki* ~ the tree.

kii *det.* this.

kiinnitiiɗo *(o)* selfish.

kiirimeewal *(ngal)* board placed on top of the dead.

kiitaaɗo *(o)* cursed person; unlucky individual. *Ko o kiitaaɗo* He is unlucky.

kiitangél [kiitaⁿgél] *(ngél)* little cursed person.

kiite *(ɗe)* curse; misfortune

kijgol *(ngol)* roar. *hijde v.*

kijoori *(ndi)* lion.

kijoowo *(o)* person who roars.

kikiiɗe *(o)* afternoon. *hande* ~ this afternoon.

kiliyaan *(o) {fr.}* customer; client.

kippu *(o)* trap.

kiram *(ɗam)* jealousy.

kiriŋtiŋ *(o)* bed.

kiriyoŋ *(o) {fr.}* pencil.

kirannooɗo *(o)* person who used to be jealous.

kirondiral *(ngal)* mutual jealousy/envy.

kiroowo *(o)* jealous person.

kirtiiɗo *(o)* person who ate supper.

kirtotooɗo *(o)* person who is eating or who eats supper.

kisal *(ngal)* safety.

kisiŋ *(o)* basket of palm fronds.

ko *foc.* focus particle. *Ko kanko ari* He is the one who came.

ko *det.* the. *haako* ~ the leaf/leaves.

kobjal *(ngal)* a strip; a rind; a tree shell/skin.

kodda *(o)* last born child.

kóɗdigal [kóddigal] *(ngal)* neighborhood.

kóɗdiiɗo [kóddiiɗo] *(o)* neighbor. *Ko min hoɗdiibe* He is my neighbor.

koɗɗo *(o)* inhabitant.

koɗo *(o)* guest; stranger. *Koɗo teddinte* guest should be treated well.

kodiije *(ɗe)* silver coins.

kojomból [kójóᵐból]*(ngól)* esophagus.

kokko *(o)* cocoa.

kolangal [kolaⁿgal] *(ngal)* farmland.

kolñet *interj.* sound of something that is broken.

kolloowo *(o)* person who shows.

komaak *(o)* rust.

koñ *det.* the; these.

kóndóróból [kónⁿdóróból] *(ngol)* throat.

kóngól [kóŋgól] *(ngól)* speech; speech act; talk; statement. ~ *nanondiraango* password. *Kongol ko ndiyam so rufi ɓoftotaako* What comes out of the mouth cannot be drawn back in.

koñjam [koñⁿjam] *(ɗam)* alcohol.

kóndirde [kónⁿdirde] *v. {fr.}* steer. *O kondirta ko oto makko* She drives her car.

kono *conj.* however; but ~ *noon* however.

konomo *(o)* greedy person.

kontoor *(o) {fr.}* against. *Ko mi kontoor maa* I am against you.

kóntuwaar *(o) {fr.}* counter.

kónu *(ngu)* 1) war; battle 2) booty. *honde v.*

kooba *(ba)* large antelope.

koolaaɗo *(o)* trustworthy; reliable. *Ko o koolaaɗo* She is trustworthy.

kooñoor *(o)* skinny and weak person.

koora musical instrument; game played with sticks and a ball.

koorka *(ka)* fasting.

kóótu *(ngu)* type of insect *kooti (ɗi) pl.*

koppoor *(o)* penny. *O alaa hay koppoor* He is penniless.

kóppu *(o)* {eng} cup.

kor *(o)* sound made to stop a donkey.

koraaɗo *adj.* worn out; poor.

koral *(ngal)* wild duck; big calabash.

kórél *(ngél)* little calabash.

korɗo *(o)* female slave.

kórééji *(ɗi)* kinsfolk. *Kó min kóreeji* We are related hóreeru *(ndu) sing.*

kóri *foc.* I hope. *Kóri oɗon njiindira* I hope you see each other.

kóriiɗo *adj.* pregnant.

korlal *(ngal)* lower leg; shank; shin. *korle (ɗe) pl.*

kornaal *(o)* horn.

koroy *(o)* sound made to show appreciation of a dish.

korsa *(ka)* love.

korsinaaɗo *adj.* beloved; cherished.

korsinɗo *(o)* person who loves or cherishes.

korsuɗo *adj.* beloved; cherished.

kosam *(ɗam)* milk. ~ *lammuɗam* curd; sour milk. ~ *biraɗam* fresh milk.

koso *(o)* fish.

koto *(o)* older brother.

kottal *(ngal)* big vigina.

kottu *(ngu)* vigina. *kaake debbo alt.*

kottude *v.* lie.

kottoowo *(o)* liar.

kottuɗo *(o)* liar.

kóy *foc.* emphatic particle.

koyɗe *(ɗe)* feet; legs. **koyngal** *(ngal) sing.*

koyɗo *adj.* 1) light. 2) ashamed. ~ *e léydi* agile.

koyeera *(o)* shame.

Koynoowo *(o)* person whose behavior makes others ashamed.

kóynuɗo *(o)* person who caused someone to be ashamed.

kóyli *(ki)* tree.

koyngal [koyⁿgal] *(ngal)* leg; foot.

kubbal *(ngal)* tax.

kuddu *(o)* spoon. ~ *luus* ladle *kudduuji (ɗi) pl.*

kuɗaaɗo *adj.* cursed.

kuɗɗi [kuddi] *(ndi)* curse.

kuɗoowo *(o)* person who lays a curse.

kuɗél *(ngél)* little straw.

kuɗól *(ngól)* straw; stalk; pen. ~ *almet* match.

kufne *(o)* hat. *boornaade* ~ wear a hat.

kulbinaaɗo *adj.* scared.

kulɗo *adj.* scared. ~ *réédu* a coward.

kulól *(ngól)* fear; fright; terror; dread. *Kulól nangi mi* I was caught by fear/I was afraid.

kulle *(ɗe)* things.

kumaandaɳ [kumaaⁿdaɳ]*(o)* *{fr.}* commissioner; major.

kume *(o)* gun.

kupe *(ɗe)* ball.

kurjuru *(o)* garbage; litter; trash. *rufde* ~ throw garbage away.

kurka *(o)* child; snipe; boy; tot.

kurkól *(ngól)* mortar.

kurkur *(o)* type of teapot **kurtungu** [kurtuⁿgu] *(ngu)* the moving of the bride to the groom's house.

kurum foc. part. very black. *Ina bawli kurum* It is really black.

kurus *(o)* prayer beads.

kus *(o)* sound used to chase hens; cocks.

kutal *(ngal)* bullet; ammunition. *Kutal ngal woorataa teɗɗinde becce mum buri* One must face what one cannot avoid *kute (ɗe) pl.*

kutindiɳ *(o)* steel trap.

kuudi *(ndi)* stools; feces.

kuugal *(ngal)* sanction. *fawde* ~ impose a sanction.

kuukuyi *(ki)* tree.

kuundal [kuuⁿdal] *(ngal)* scoop.

kuungi [kuuⁿgi] *(o)* bullroarer.

kuuraa *(o)* *{fr.}* electricity.

kuurde *v.* separate.

kuurgal *(ngal)* enclosed place.

kuutól [kuuroól] *(ngól)* bottom.

kuy *(o)* sound used to attract hens; cocks.

L

abal *(ngal)* hygiene; purification; cleanliness.

aɓde *v.* be clean. *O mo laaɓi* He is clean.

aɓɗo *adj.* clean. *neɗɗo ~* a clean person.

aɓtinde *v* clarify. *Ina foti laaɓtineede* It needs to be clarified.

ɓɓinde *v.* cleanse; to elucidate; deplete; make clean. *~ yeeso* put on a clear face.

abi *(ɗi)* 1) roads; ways 2) times. *~ ɗiɗi* twice.

aci *(ki)* tail. *laaceeje (ɗe) pl.*

adi *(ɗi)* grave.

adól *(ngól)* trace left by a snake. *laadol (ngól) sing.*

adóóri *(ndi)* snake; reptile.

dde *v.* creep; crawl. *O mo waawi laadde jooni* He can creep now.

afa *(ka)* cap. *ɓoornaade ~* wear a hat.

akira *(o) {ar.}* hereafter (hell). *faade ~* go to hell. *Faa laakira* Go to hell. *laakara alt.*

alaade *v.* rest.

alagal*(ngal)* broken calabash/watermelon. *laalakoñ; laalaaɗe (ɗe) pl.*

ale *(ɗe)* baobab trees.

ali *(ki)* baobab tree.

alndaade [laalⁿdaade] *v.* add laalo to steamed couscous.

alo *(ko)* powdered baobab leaf.

altaade *v.* lay mud on the wall. *O woni ko e laaltaade* He is laying mud on the wall.

amaade *v.* rule. *Ko kanko laamii* He is the president.

amɗo *(o)* king; ruler. *laamɓe (ɓe) pl.*

amiiɗo *(o)* king; ruler *laamiiɓe (ɓe) pl.*

amorde *(nde)* capital city. *Nuwaasoor woni laamorde.*

Muritani Nouakchott is the capital city of Mauritania.

amu *(ngu)* kingdom; reign; rule. *~ neɗɗo gooto* despotism.

amminde *v.* appoint a chief; elect a ruler.

amlaame *(ɗe)* skin fungus.

ana *(ka)* ship; boat; vessel. *~ cuurki* steamboat. *~ ndiwoowa* plane. *jom ~* sailor. *~ mawka* liner.

añal *(ngal)* arrow; arc.

laañoowo *(o)* 1) person who aims with arrows 2) person who hunts with arrows.

laañde *v.* aim with an arrow.

laaral *(ngal)* type of bird.

laarde *v.* observe; peer; gaze; stare; look at; look for. *Hol ko laarata* What are you looking for?

laaroowo *(o)* seeker; person who looks for.

laataade *v.* be; occur; happen.

laatagol *(ngol)* being.

laawaade *v.* be upset; be angry; hurt. *Gite ɗe ko laawiiɗe* His eyes are hurting.

laawde *v.* 1) upset 2) pour into boiling sauce.

laawól *(ngól)* alley; pathway; route; track. *ko rewaani ~* illicit. *dewɗo ~* law-abiding. *yahde ~ mum* take care of one's own business. *laabi (ɗi) pl.*

laaϒaade *v.* lick.

laayde *v.* be apart.

labaade *v.* choose. *Hol mo labi ɗaa* Which one did you choose?

labal *(ngal)* wooden bowl.

labbo *(o)* caste that specializes in woodwork. *Ko o labbo* He belongs to the wood worker caste.

labbu *(o)* a rice dish.

laɓande [laɓanⁿde] *(nde)* shave.

laɓde *v.* shave. *laɓaade alt.*

laɓi *(ki)* knife. *~ njuulaawi* dagger. *taϒirde ~* cut with a knife.

laɓɓinoowo *(o)* person who cleans.

laɓoowo *(o)* barber.

laɓorke *(ki)* razor.

lacciri *(ndi)* couscous. *~ e kosam* couscous and milk dish. *~ e haako* dinner spinach sauce and couscous dish.

ladde *(nde)* bush; wilderness. *faade ~* go to the bush; go away.

laddanke *(o)* person from the bush or rural area.

laggaade *v.* sharpen a knife.

lahal *(ngal)* vase; calabash; wooden bowl; wooden calabash.

lahdi *(ndi)* grave.

lahe *(nge)* brownish black cow.

lajal *(ngal)* 1) deadline 2) long wood closing a gate. *Lajal maa yonti* Your deadline is up.

lallitam *(ɗam)* water used to rinse/cleanse.

lallitde [lallidde] *v.* rinse; cleanse. ~ *kaake* rinse dishes.

lamburere [lam^mbureere] *(nde)* amber.

lambere [lam^mbere] *(nde)* bead.

lamɗam *(ɗam)* salt. *safde* ~ be pretty; have enough salt/to be salty enough.

lamkal (kal) a little salt.

lammeeki (ki) acidity.

lammeere (nde) bitterness *lamminde v.* 1) make sour 2) joke around 3) apppoint a chief. *Min ngoni ko e lamminde* We are just having fun.

lammude v. be sour; be bitter. *Ina lammi* It is sour.

lambude [lam^mbude] *v.* 1) be unsold 2) be unwed.

lammuki *(ki)* tree.

lamndaade [lam^ndaade] *v.* inquire; question; ask. *So a andaa lamndo* If you do not know ask.

lamndal [lam^ndal] *(ngal)* query; question; inquiry. *werlaade* ~ throw a question.

lamól *(ngól)* trailing stem (of calabash etc.).

lamolamongal [lamolamo^ngal] *(ngal)* salted ground.

lampa *(o) {fr.}* lamp. *huɓɓude* ~ switch the light on. *ñifde* ~ switch the light off. *lampaaji (ɗi) pl.*

lamƳindaade [lamƳi^ndaade] *v.* lick.

laƞde *v.* be stranded in a foreign country.

lañde [lañje] *v.* spread.

lañtude [lañcude] *v.* spread food in a bowl to cool off.

lankata [laƞkata] *(o)* type of braid.

lappaci *(ki)* a long line/trail.

lappól (ngól) track/trail; column. *lappi (ɗi) pl.*

lappirde *v.* strike with. ~ *loocol* hit with the whip.

lappude v. 1) hit; strike 2) thrash; remove grains from stalks.

laral *(ngal)* animal skin.

laru *(o)* dish.

lasal *(ngal)* circle.

lasde v. make a circle.

lasli *(o)* origin. *Hol ko woni lasli mum* Where does it originate?

laso *(o) {fr.}* whitewash; white lime.

latde *v.* kick.

lati *(o)* perfume. *waɗɗe* ~ wear perfume.

latikoloñ *(o)* perfume.

lattinaade *v.* lay down.

lattitaade *v.* change into.

law *adv* early. *dawde* ~ go early. *finde* ~ wake up early.

lawaade *v.* be aside.

lawake *(o)* noble.

lawde *v.* carve.

lawñandi [lawña^ndi] *(ki)* shrub.

lawo *(o)* tattooer.

lawtól *(ngól)* open space.

lawƳirgal *(ngal)* tool instrument for cleaning.

lawƳude v. clean; wash. ~ *haa laaɓa* wash clean. *O woni ko e lawƳude kaake* He is washing the dishes.

layde *v.* 1) be spread 2) speak. *Hol ko layataa* What did you say?

layo *(ngo)* spreading of plants such as bean plants.

laƳde [lajje] *v.* limp; hobble.

la Yoowo *adj.* cripple; lame; person who limps. *Ko o la Yoowo* He limps.

layru *(ndu)* a bow; dike.

layset *(o)* blade; a razor blade. *laysetaaji (ɗi) pl.*

layya *(o)* animal for holiday sacrifice. *Mi sóódii layya* I bought the sacrifice for the holiday.

layyaade v. sacrifice. *Mi layyiima ngaari* I sacrificed an ox.

lébbi *(ɗi)* moons; months. *lewru (ndu) sing.*

leɓde v. chat; prattle; prate; talk too much.

léɓdude v. talk with.

leɓo (ngo) incessant talk.

leɓoowo (o) chatterbox.

lebte *(ɗe)* torture.

léɓtude v. torture.

leebeede *v.* Be unfortunate. *Ko o leeɓaaɗo* He is unfortunate.

lééɓól *(ngól)* 1) hair 2) piece of music.

leefde *v.* be nonchalant; be weak. *O mo leefi* He is nonchalant.

gal *(ngal)* quarter; district. ~ *Baabaaɓe*
ɲe Ba extended family quarter.

ke *(ɗe)* swollen glands below
heekbones.

lde *v.* be late/slow ~ *jippaade* get off
ate. *O leelii* He is late.

lltinde *v.* delay; make late; procrastinate.
ɓo kanko leeltini min* He delayed us.

mde *v.* 1) beat 2) lay on one another.

muna *(o)* lime fruit. ~ *kaci* bitter
ranges.

n *(o)* *{fr.}* wool.

so *(ngo)* matt. *wertude* ~ spread a mat.
aggude ~ fold or roll up a mat.

wtaade *v.* slip away.

ol *(ngól)* strip of cloth; band; bandage.

pi *(ɗi)* pieces of clothing *sing lefól
ngól).*

gal *(ngal)* timber; wood.

gere *(nde)* solid wood; big stick.

de [leede] *v.* breathe lightly while
atching one's breath; gasp; pant. *O mon
eha* he is catching his breath.

ɲe *(ɗe)* wooden calabashes *sing lahal
ngal).*

ki *(ki)* 1) tree 2) medicine. *yarde ~ mum*
ake one's medicine. *Ɣettude ~ mum* take
ne's medicine. *A yarii lekki maa* Have
ou taken your medicine?

kol *(o)* *{fr.}* school. *yaltude* ~ quit
chool. *naatde* ~ start going to school. *O
aatii lekkol* He has started going to
chool.

kkoñ (koñ) little sticks.

laade *v.* lie down. *Hol to leloto ɗaa*
Where will you sleep?

lnde [lelⁿde] *(nde)* bed.

lnude *v.* lay.

lorde *(nde)* area for sleeping; bed.

ltaade *v.* go back to bed.

lla *(ba)* antelope; gazelle.

mbél [lémᵐbél] *(o)* second wife.

mbéɣél [léᵐbéɣél] *(ngél)* third wife.

mlémól *(ngól)* edge.

mpeteere *(nde)* strip of cloth worn by a
girl.

mso *(ngo)* incessant talk.

msude *v.* be talkative. *A ɗa lemsi* You talk
too much.

ñamleñaagu *(ngu)* racism.

léñól *(ngól)* descent; family tree; genealogy;
ethnicity. *yaltude* ~ be an outcast.

lenge [leŋⁿge] *(o)* derrick.

léngi [léŋⁿgi] *(ɗi)* celebration; celebration
songs.

lénguru *(ndu)* [léŋⁿguru] little bell.

léppinde *v.* soak; drench; wet. *A leppinii
mo* You got him wet.

léppude *v.* be wet; be soaked. *Ina leppi* It is
wet.

lériinde [lériiⁿde] *(nde)* between.

lértinde *v.* flatten.

lértude *v.* be flat.

les *prep.* beneath; under; underneath; below.
sakkude ~ place under.

lésɗinde *v.* lower; down; debase.

lésɗude *v.* be low. *Ina lesɗi* it is low.

lésɗugol *(ngol)* inferiority.

letaade *v.* glance over.

léttiɗɗe [léttidde] *v.* be squint-eyed.

letto *adj.* squint-eyed.

lewde *v.* clear bush for farming.

lewre *(nde)* cleared land; open space;
harpoon.

lewlewal *(ngal)* moonlight.

léwléwél *(ngél)* little flame.

léwléwndu [léwléwⁿdu] *(ndu)* flame.

léwñude *v.* twinkle.

léwru *(ndu)* month; moon. ~ *koorka*
Ramadan. ~ *dariindu* crescent. ~
maayndu ndu last month.

léydi *(ndi)* earth; country; land; ground;
floor; sand; state. ~ *ndemoteendi* arable
land. ~ *njiimaandi* colony.

léytude *v.* feel like; want.

leɣɣaade *v.* glance over.

liɓde *v.* throw on the floor. *O liɓii mo* He
threw him on the floor.

liɓiliɓtoo *v.* wrestle each other down in
turn.

liɓtaade *v.* wrestle someone down.

liddi *(ɗi)* several fish. *liingu (ngu) sing.*

liingu [liiⁿgu] *(ngu)* fish.

liirde *v.* spread out to dry.

liirtude *v.* remove what was spread out to
dry.

liirtaade *v.* become dilated.

liirtagol *(ngol)* dilation.

liggaade *v.* labor; fag; toil; work.

liggééy *(o)* profession; labor; career; vocation; function. ~ *galle* housework. ~ *juŋngo* handicraft.

ligginde *v.* employ.

ligginoowo (o) employer.

ligginteeɗo (o) employee.

liggitaade *v.* lose hold of.

liggódiiɗo (o) colleague; partner.

liggorde (nde) workplace; workshop.

liggorgal (ngal) tool.

liggotooɗo (o) clerk; laborer; employee; worker; agent.

liggude *v.* hang up; hang. *Liggu wutte maa* Hang your gown.

ligi (o) scolopendra.

liibaar (o) {fr.} half a kilogram; pound.

liide *v.* rest.

liigal (ngal) big cotton plant/field.

liige (nge) cotton field.

liirde *v.* spread out to dry. ~ *lacciri* spread out couscous to dry.

liirtude *v.* remove what was spread out to dry. ~ *cómci* remove clothing from the line.

liital (ngal) flute; trumpet. *wuttude* ~ play the flute.

liitde [liidde] *v.* play the flute.

liiteer (o) {fr.} liter *liiteruuji (ɗi) pl.*

liiʄaade *v.* waddle.

likʄere (nde) hiccup. *wondude e* ~ have a hiccup.

likʄude *v.* hiccup; have a hiccup.

limce (ɗe) pieces of rags; used clothing. *limsere (nde) sing.*

limcél (ngél) little rag.

limsere (nde) piece of rag; used clothing.

limde *v.* count.

limgol (ngol) the act of counting.

limoore (nde) 1) count; calculus 2) number. ~ *yimɓe* census. ~ *teelnde* an odd number.

limre (nde) number. ~ *teelnde* an odd number.

limtaade *v.* recount; count again. *Limto* Count again.

limtagol (ngól) recounting.

limto (ngo) alphabet; learning of the alphabet. *jangude* ~ learn the alphabet.

limtude *v.* 1) enumerate; list; count again 2) decipher. *O woni ko e limtude* He is learning the alphabet.

liminaat (o) {fr.} lemonade drink.

limoŋ (o) {fr.} lemon.

limpó (o) due; tax. *yoɓde* ~ pay taxes.

liñtitde [liñcidde] *v.* examine.

liwal (ngal) bait.

liweede *v.* take the bait.

liwóógu (ngu) namatee; seacow.

liyaade *v.* pour milk on the food; add sauce. *Liyo* Pour the milk.

liyam (ɗam) sauce.

liyorgal (ngal) calabash for pouring water.

loɓɓaade *v.* taste sauce by dipping a finger into it.

loɓɓagól (ngól) tasting of sauce by dipping a finger into it.

lobbere (nde) beauty.

lóbbiɗde [lóbbidde] *v.* be beautiful/good. *Ndaw ko lobbiɗi* She is so beautiful!

lobbo (o) beautiful; kind.

lóbbudu (ndu) corner; angle.

lócital (ngal) bathing a child before the naming ceremony.

lofaade *v.* be stuck in the mud. *Oto makko ko ko lofii* His car is stuck in the mud.

lofde *v.* be muddy. *Ina lofi* It is muddy.

lófól (ngól) muddy way.

lófu (ngu) muddy area.

loggaade *v.* be hooked; be stuck.

loggande [loggan"de] *(nde)* hook.

loggeede *v.* be hooked.

lóggirde (nde) hook.

lóggirgal (ngal) hook.

lóggitde *v.* unhook.

lóggude *v.* hook.

lohaade *v.* cut weeds.

lohde [loode] *v.* be tired; be useless; be nonchalant.

lohɗo [looɗo] *adj.* weak; feeble; nonchalant. *O mo lohi* He is weak.

lóhnude [lóónude] *v.* weaken.

lóhól (ngól) charm worn around the arm or the waist. *ɓoorno lohol maa* Put your charm on.

lojaade *v.* have debris in the eye.

lójól (ngól) debris in the eye.

lokaade v. stir; upset.

lókkitde [lókkidde] v. take out; remove.

lookde v. place in.

lolloŊeere (nde) a heavy lock.

lollinde v. make famous.

lóllude v. be famous. *O mo lolli* He is famous.

lómból [lóm^m ból] (ngól) strips of cloth with different colors.

lómbude [lóm^m bude] v. put inside; place in between.

lombaade [lom^m baade] v. be placed in. ~ *hakkunde yimɓe* squeeze oneself in.

lomtaade v. replace; supersede; supplant; succeed.

lomtiido (o) replacement.

lomtinde v. replace.

lomto (o) interim; substitute; replacement.

longaade [loŊ^n gaade] v. look with binoculars.

longorde (de) binoculars.

longere [loŊ^n gere] (nde) mouthful; handful. ~ *maaro* handful of rice.

lóŊdu (ndu) hook; long stick with hook on end used for picking.

looɓde v. be easily vexed. *O mo looɓi* He gets angry easily.

looɓdo adj. acerb.

looɓre (nde) anger.

lóócól (ngól) rod; stick for hitting. *looci* (di) pl.

loode (de) water holders.

loonde [loo^n de] (nde) water holder; (nde) vase for holding water.

loopal (ngal) muddy area; mud.

loorde v. 1) plant 2) lose one's voice; be hoarse.

lootaade v. wash oneself. *O woni ko e lootaade* He is taking a shower.

lootde [loodde] v. wash.

lóótirde (nde) place for cleansing the dead.

lootorde (nde) washing place; shower room.

lootorgal (ngal) bathing instrument.

lóótóyde v. to go and wash.

loowande v. fill for.

loowande [loowan^n de] (nde) load.

loowde v. pour out to fill; fill up.

loowdi (ndi) contents.

lópitaan (o) {fr.} hospital *lópitaanuuji* (di) pl.

loppaade v. 1) remain in a place 2) be crushed.

loppande [loppan^n de] (nde) crushed load in a mortar.

loppere (nde) crushed load in a mortar.

lóppude v. crush; pound into a paste. ~ *bunaa* pound dried fish into paste.

lóppitaade v. move.

loraade v. depend upon. *Ko e maa lórii mi* I depend on you.

loragól (ngól) dependence.

lorla (o) harm. *dum alaa lorla* There is no harm.

lórlude v. harm.

lorso (ngo) wheat.

lóskude v. inquire; ask; pry; minimize.

lóttundu [lóttu^n du] (ndu) sling.

lowre (nde) 1) duty; share 2) lot.

lówtude v. add fiber strings.

loɤde [lojje] v. drown.

luɓaade v. borrow; quote.

luɓal (ngal) borrowing; lending.

luɓde v. lend. *Neddo yo luɓ ko jeyi* One should not lend other people's belongings.

lubbude v. look under.

luggééndi [luggéé^n di] (ndi) depth. *Hol do luggeendi mum tólnii* How deep is it?

luggere (nde) deep area.

luggidde [luggidde] v. be deep. *Ina luggidi* It is deep.

luggiddum adj. profound; deep.

luggidinde v. deepen.

lugu (o) salamander.

lujum (o) vegetable.

lulaade v. spend days in the farm. *Ko ɓe luliiɓe* They live at the farm now.

lulnde [lul^n de] (nde) days spent in the farm.

lumbaade [lum^m baade] v. swim. *Mi waawaa lumbaade* I do not know how to swim.

lumbagól [lum^m bagól] (ngól) natation; swimming. *lumbaali* (di) pl.

lumbal [lum^m bal] (ngal) crossing.

lumbayru [lu^m bayru] (ndu) way of swimming.

lumbinde [lum^mbinde] *v.* take across water. *O woni ko e lumbinde nay* He is making the cows cross the river.

lumbirde [lum^mbirde] *(nde)* area for crossing the river.

lumbirgal [lum^mbirgal] *(ngal)* oar; a boat.

lumbude [lum^mbude] *v.* cross a river.

lumminde *v.* bend/shake one's bottom.

lumminaade *v.* bend over.

lundugal [lun^ndugal] *(ngal)* log tied to the neck of a cow.

lupuut foc. part. very.

lurde *v.* roar.

luttal *(ngal)* settling in a foreign country.

luttude *v.* miss; settle/remain in a foreign country.

luuɓde *v.* stink; smell bad. ~ *hunuko* have a bad smell.

luuɓnude *v.* make stink.

luuɓól *(ngól)* stinking smell.

luudde [luudde] *v.* cry.

luugal *(ngal)* pestle used for making holes for sowing.

luukaango [luukaa^ngo] *(ngo)* loud cry. *luukaali (ɗi) pl.*

luukde *v.* cry loudly; vociferate.

luumo *(ngo)* fair.

luural *(ngal)* disagreement; dissension; discrepancy; discord; conflict.

luurde *v.* be in disagreement; lack synchronization.

luurdeede *v.* have a disagreement; lack synchronization.

luurdude *v.* disagree with each other.

luutaade *v.* be in the rear-guard; be last.

luutde [luudde] *v.* be posthumous.

luuteede *v.* miss.

luuti *(o)* posthumous child. *Ko o luuti* He is a posthumous child.

luutndaade [luut^ndaade] *v.* disagree; go against the code.

luutndaare [luut^ndaare] *(nde)* disagreement.

luutndiɗum [luut^ndiɗum] *adj.* adverse; contrary.

luutndiiɗo [luut^ndiiɗo] *(o)* contra; con; adverse.

luutondiral [luuto^ndiral] *(ngal)* the act of missing one another.

luutondirde [luuto^ndirde] *v.* miss one another.

luwa *(o)* {fr.} law. *luwaaji (ɗi) pl.*

luwaas *(o)* {fr.} rent. *yoɓde* ~ pay rent.

luwde *v.* make holes for sowing seeds.

luwre *(nde)* holes for sowing seeds.

M

aa *poss.* 1) or 2) if 3) you; your. *hoore* ~ your head.

aada *poss.* your *(sing.). maa alt.*

abbe *poss.* their; theirs. *kaake* ~ their belongings.

aabde *v.* cover; put arms around.

aabo *(o)* potter; weaver. *Ko o maabo he* belongs to the weaver caste. *maabube (be) pl.*

aadde *v.* take a large handful of.

aafaade *v.* be tasty.

aafe *(de)* peanut butter sauce. *Maafe maa maafiima* Your peanut butter sauce dish is tasty.

aage *(o)* type of hat.

aaja *(o)* millet.

aajde [majje] *v.* salute; march; parade. *Omon maaja* He is marching.

aajgol *(ngol)* parading.

aajoowo *(o)* a person who is parading.

aaje *(de)* rivers.

aayo *(ngo)* river. ~ *Senegaal* Senegal river.

aale *(de)* signs. ~ *gabbe* granular. ~ *kellifuya* signs of puberty.

aama *(o)* grandparent.

aamaare *(nde)* ancestor; grandparent.

aamayél *(ngél)* granny.

aamiraado *(o)* grandmother.

aanaa *(o) {ar.}* meaning; explanation. *dum alaa maanaa* It is meaningless.

aande [maande] *(nde)* sign.

aandinde *v.* sign.

aani *(o)* someone. *kaari (o) alt.*

aarimilla *(o)* welcome.

aaro *(ko)* rice. ~ *e teew* rice and meat dish. ~ *e liddi* rice and fish dish.

aawaade *v.* cover.

aayde *(nde)* death. *Mo suwaa*

aayde tagdaaka Anything can happen to a live being.

aayde *v.* die. *O maayii* He is dead.

aaydo *adj.* dead person; defunct. ~ *pak* really dead. *Ko o maaydo* He is dead.

aayka *(ka)* nonsense. *haala* ~ nonsense. *dum ko maayka* That is nonsense.

maayo *(ngo)* river. *taccude* ~ cross the river.

ma?aade *v.* make a person intervene.

ma?ande *v.* intervene.

mabbaado *(o)* person suffering from a cold. *Ko mi mabbaado* I have a cold.

mabbeede *v.* have a cold. *Ngonmi ko e mabbeede* I am getting a cold.

mabbo *(ngo)* cold. ~ *muusngo* a bad cold.

mabbande [mabban^nde] *(nde)* seizing by closing on.

mabbude *v.* catch/seize by closing.

mabde *v.* circle; surround.

macaacaa *(o)* real slave.

macungaagu *(ngu)* slavery.

maccinaade *v.* be an obedient slave.

maccudo *(o)* slave; captive. *rimdinde* ~ free a slave. *maccube (be) pl.*

macculinde *v.* behave like a slave.

maccungal [maccu^ngal] *(ngal)* big slave.

mafñaade *v.* walk carelessly. *daccu mafñaade* Stop walking carelessly.

mafñeede *v.* have rash on one's bottom.

mahande *v.* build for someone. *O mahanii mo suudu* He built a room for him.

mahde [maadi] *v.* build; construct; edit; mold.

mahdi [maadi] *(ndi)* construction. ~ *tóówndi* a high- rise building.

mahdo [maado] *(o)* author; builder. *Hol mahdo nde deftere* Who is the author of this book?

mahgól [maagól] *(ngól)* construction.

mahngo [maa^ngo] *(ngo)* construction.

mahól *(ngól)* fake story.

mahoowo *(o)* mason. *Ko o mahoowo* He builds houses.

majaango [majaa^ngo] *(ngo)* lightning. ~ *yitere* a blink of the eye. *majaali (di) pl.*

majande [majan^nde] *(nde)* lightning.

majde [majje] *v.* wink; blink; flash. *Hol to maj* Do not blink.

majjere *(nde)* 1) loss 2) misconception. *dum ko majjere* That is a misconception.

majjinde *v.* bewilder; loose.

majjude *v.* stray; be lost. *Ko mi majjudo* I am lost.

makka *(o)* 1) corn 2) Mecca.

Makka *(ngo)* Mecca. *O artii Makka* S/he returned from her pilgrimage to Mecca.

makko *poss.* his; hers. *kaake* ~ his belongings.

malaaɗo *adj.* blessed; fortunate. *Ko a malaaɗo* You are blessed.

maleede *v.* be blessed; be fortunate.

malkisaaɗo *adj.* unlucky; unfortunate. *Ko o malkisaaɗo* He is unlucky.

malkiseede *v.* be unfortunate.

malu *(ngu)* blessing. *ɗum ko malu* It is a blessing.

malamlaaji *(ɗi)* butterflies.

malayka *(o)* *{ar.}* angel *malaykaaji (ɗi) pl.*

malde *v.* make an agreement.

mallól *(ngól)* indirect talk about someone; accusation. *Mallol so firtii jubbol so joomum hulaani yo o jaabo* One should respond to accusations about oneself. *malli (ɗi) pl.*

mallude *v.* talk indirectly about someone. *Ko aan o mallata* He is talking indirectly about you.

manaango [manaaⁿgo] *(ngo)* thunder. *kaaⱧel* ~ thunderbolt *manaali (ɗi) pl.*

mande *v.* praise. *O mo man maa no feewi* He praises you a lot.

manoore *(nde)* praise. *ɗum ko manoore mawnde* It is a major praise.

mantude *v.* exalt; thank; commend; eulogize; praise. ~ praise someone. *O mo mantu maa* He praises you.

mande [maⁿde] *inter.* when. *Mande njahataa* When are you leaving?

manganace [maⁿganace] shrub.

mankude [maⱧkude] *v.* *{fr.}* lack *Ⱨakkude* alt.

manna *(o)* 1) male first name 2) hat.

mandilde [manⁿdilde] *v.* be drunk. *Ko o mandilɗo* He is drunk.

mango [maⱧ]ⁿgo] (ko) mango fruit.

mangu [maⱧ]ⁿgu] *(ngu)* seniority.

manto *(o)* *{fr.}* mint.

marde *v.* 1) breed; raise 2) marry.

markere *(nde)* ball of mud *pl. marke (ɗe)*.

marmalle *(ɗe)* snow.

marsandiis *(o)* *{fr.}* merchandise; commodity.

marse *(o)* *{fr.}* market *pl. marsééji (ɗi)*. *O yahii marse* He went to the market.

martu *(o)* *{fr.}* hammer fiirude ~ hammer. *martuuji (ɗi) pl.*

Maruk *(o)* Morocco.

masde *v.* place diachritics. *Mas ɗum* Place the diachritics where they belong.

masgal *(ngal)* diacritic; accent *masɗe (ɗe)*.

masoowo *(o)* person who places diacritics.

masiⱧ] *(o)* *{fr.}* machine; sewing machine. *masiⱧaaji (ɗi) pl.*

maslaha *(o)* *{ar.}* reconciliation. *Mbaɗdee maslahaa* Try and settle the matter amicably.

masloowo *(o)* reconciler.

maslude *v.* reconcile.

masoⱧ] *(o)* *{fr.}* mason.

mata *(o)* weight measure. *mataaji (ɗi) pl.*

mawɗo *adj.* adult; gigantic; patriarch; senior. ~ *gadii ɗo* ancestor; forefather.

mawnikinaade *v.* put on airs; act important. *O mo mawnikinii* He acts important.

mawninde *v.* enlarge; celebrate; glorify.

mawniraaɗo *(o)* older sibling. ~ *gorko* older brother. ~ *debbo* older sister.

mawniraagal *(ngal)* act of being old.

mawnude *v.* be big; become adult. *O mawnii* He has become big/old.

mawnu ɗo *adj.* big; huge; large; immense.

mawnugól *(ngól)* growth; maturation.

mayonees *(o)* *{fr.}* mayonnaise.

Mayram female first name. *Mbiyetee mi ko Mayram* My name is Mayram.

méccude *v.* trim with scissors.

mecekke *(ɗe)* chisel; scissors.

meeɗde [meedde] *v.* taste. *So a meeɗii a jombat* If you taste it you would want more.

meeɗgól *(ngól)* taste.

meeɗnude [meennude] *v.* make someone taste something.

meeɗen *poss.* our. *comci* ~ our clothing. *men* alt.

men our; ours.

meenaango [meenaaⁿgo] *(ngo)* bleat. *meenaali (ɗi) pl.*

meende *v.* bleat.

méénélli *(ki)* tree.

meere *adj.* futile; nothing. *cfum ko meere* It is futile.

meernaade *v.* look away; put on airs.

mees *(o) {fr.}* wick.

meeteer *(o) {fr.}* meter. *meeteruuji (cfi) pl.*

méételól *(ngól)* turban.

mééwtude *v.* skim a liquid off.

mehde [meede] *v.* stutter; stammer.

mehgól [meegol] *(ngól)* stutter.

mehoowo *(o)* stutterer; stammerer. *Ko o mehoowo* He stutters.

meho *adj.* blank; hollow; vacant; naked; empty.

méhru *(ndu)* an empty room.

melde *(nde)* vagina.

melde *(nde)* flat floor.

melde *v.* flatten; make smooth; level off.

méldugal *(ngal)* tool for leveling floors.

melo *(ngo)* flattened area.

melléwól *(ngól)* flame.

méltirde *(nde)* steaming pot.

membaade [mem^mbaade] *v.* grope; feel for.

memde *v.* touch; feel. *Mem njiyaa* Touch and see.

mémirde *v.* touch with.

mémóndiral [memo^ndiral] *(ngal)* contact.

mémótóócfum *adj.* tangible; touchable.

memtaade *v.* masturbate.

mémtude *v.* touch again.

menkelde [meŋkelde] *(nde)* weight measure. *menkelle (cfe) pl.*

mentuŋeere *(nde)* tomato. *mentuŋeeje (cfe) pl.*

méppicfde [méppidde] *v.* have a small lower lip.

meppo *(o)* person with a lower lip smaller than the upper lip. *Ko o meppo* His lower lip is shorter than his upper lip.

merere *(nde)* mirage.

mértude *v.* have a clean cut.

mesde *v.* pour.

meselal *(ngal)* needle. *wuurtude* ~ thread a needle. *meselle (cfe) pl.*

mettaade *v.* lap; lick. *Metto juŋngo maa* Lick your hand.

metteede *v.* be licked.

metteede *v.* suffer.

metteende [mettee^nde] *(nde)* sadness; sorrow; suffering.

mettere *(nde)* suffering; sadness. *mette (cfe) pl.*

méttinde *v.* be displeased; be angry. *Ko o mettincfo* He is angry.

méttude *v.* be unpleasant.

mettucfo *adj.* unpleasant. *Ko o mettucfo* He is unpleasant.

méttéllu *(ngu)* red ant.

méytude *v.* be satiated.

méΥΥude *v.* close tightly; close. ~ *e nder suudu* lock someone in a room.

mi *pers. pron.* I. *Mi arii* I am here. ~*cfen* we are. ~*cfo* I am. *Mi cfo yiya* I can see.

miin *pron.* I; me; myself.

min *pron.* we. *Min ngarii* We arrived.

minen *pron.* we.

miijaade *v.* ponder; think; cogitate; conceive. *Hol ko miijoto cfaa* a penny for your thoughts.

miijo *(ngo)* thought; doctrine; position. ~ *wocfngo* alternative. *Hol ko woni miijo maa* What is your opinion?

miijotoocfo *adj.* pensive.

miijtagól *(ngól)* afterthought.

miirde *v.* itch.

miiro *(ngo)* itch.

mikró *(o) {fr.}* microphone.

miñiraacfo *(o)* younger sibling. ~ *gorko* younger brother. ~ *debbo* younger sister.

miñiraagal *(ngal)* sisterhood; brotherhood.

minise *(o) {fr.}* carpenter.

misiide *(nde) {ar.}* mosque.

miskiino *(o) {ar.}* person with modest means. *Ko o miskiino* He is not wealthy.

misooro *(o)* head scarf.

móbél *(ngél) {fr.}* automobile; car. *dognoowo* ~ a driver.

móccude *v.* make a cord; tend; heal.

móddinde *v.* stain; smudge; tarnish; dirty. *A moddinii comcolam* You stained my clothing.

móddinoowo *(o)* person who stains.

móddude *v.* 1) be thick 2) be unclear 3) be stained. ~ *haala* speak unclearly.

móddugól *(ngól)* thickness; stain.

mocfde [modde] *v.* swallow; absorb; gobble; gulp. *Mocf cfum* Swallow it.

modgól (ngól) swallowing.

módnude [mónnude] *v.* make someone swallow.

mofde *v.* hide; hold under the armpit. *O mof dum* He hid it under the arm.

mofoowo (o) person who hides things.

moggere *(nde)* hidden thing.

mógginaade v. hide oneself. *Hol to o mogginii* Where is he hiding?

mógginoowo (o) person who hides.

móggitaade v. come out of hiding.

móggitiido (o) person who came out of hiding.

móggude v. hide; protect.

mojde *v.* cover with a cloth, a sheet or a blanket.

mojaade v. cover oneself.

mola *(ba)* young animal. *moli (di) pl.*

mólfidde *v.* be bandy legged.

molfo (o) knock-kneed person. *Ko o molfo* He is knock-kneed.

momlaade *v.* rub something on oneself.

mómlude v. rub something on. *Momlu dum e yeeso maa* Rub it on your face.

momloowo (o) a person who rubs.

momtaade *v.* wipe oneself off. *Momto so a haljitii* Wipe your bottom when you finish defecating.

mómtude v. wipe off; erase; elide.

mómtugól (ngól) deletion.

mon *poss.* your (plural referent). *galle ~* your house.

moodon poss. your (plural). *kaake ~* your belongings.

monaade *v.* make the best of a deal.

moññaade *v.* be crushed; crumble away.

móññude v. crush; squeeze; to mash; smash; squash.

móngude [móꞇ]ⁿgude] *v.* be almost ripe.

mónginde [móꞇ]ⁿginde] *v.* be almost right; come out.

montoor *(o) {fr.}* watch; clock *montoraaji (di) pl.*

moobaare *(nde)* sinister.

moobde *v.* gather up.

moobre (nde) gathering.

moodde [moodde] *v.* gather.

móódibo *(o)* scholar; learned person.

móóftirde *(nde)* pouch; account. *~ kaake* depot. *~ kabirde, jaande walla hudo* barn. *~ kosam e nebam keccam* dairy.

mooftoowo (o) keeper.

móóftude v. keep; protect; conserve. *Móóftu dum haa ngarten* Keep it until we return.

mookaade *v.* swallow without chewing.

mool *(o)* one stringed guitar. *waawde ~* be a skilled one- stringed-guitar player.

moolaade *v.* seek protection.

moolagól (ngól) asylum; refuge.

moolde v. protect.

móóliido (o) person who sought asylum. *Ko o mooliido* He has thought asylum.

móólirde (nde) sanctuary.

moolotoodo (o) person seeking protection.

mooltaade *v.* come out of hiding; give up a shelter.

mooltoowo (o) person who takes something or someone from a hiding state.

moolanaande [moolanaaⁿde] *adj.* wonderful.

moomaade *v.* rub on oneself.

moomde v. caress; pamper; rub; fondle.

mooraade *v.* have one's hair braided.

moorde v. plait; braid.

mooreede v. be braided.

móórgól (ngól) braiding.

mooriido (o) a person with braided hair.

móóról (ngól) braid; plait *moori (di) pl.*

mooroowo (o) person who braids.

moosde *v.* smile. *Ndaw ko yaawi moosde* He smiles easily.

móósól (ngól) a smile. *móósóóji/móósóóooli (di) pl.*

móósturu *(ndu)* braid ornament.

mooyde *v.* be lazy.

mooYde [moojje] *v.* gnaw.

móó Yi (di) white ants; termites.

moo Yu (ngu) white ant; termite.

mooytaade *v.* approach slowly *mooyto* walk slowly.

mooytagól (ngól) slow and quiet walk.

morde *v.* breed; eat grass.

morle *(de)* balls of.

morlere (nde) ball of.

mórlude v. roll up.

morndolde [morndolde] *(nde)* ball of.

mórñitde [mórñidde] *v.* crush again into pieces.

morñitere *(nde)* piece.

mórñitte *(ɗe)* pieces.

mórñude *v.* crush.

mósól *(ngól)* path.

moto *(o) {fr.}* motorcycle. **mótóóji** *(ɗi) pl.* **waɗɗaade** ~ ride a motorcycle.

motoor *(o) {fr.}* engine **motoraaji** *(ɗi) pl.*

motto *(ngo)* thread.

mottoowo *(o)* spinner.

móttude *v.* 1) forget 2) spin.

moylaade *v.* twist; shuffle.

móylude *v.* hurry; walk faster **moylu** hurry up.

moylugol *(ngól)* speed walk.

moytaango *(ngo)* stroke; caress.

móytude *v.* stroke; caress; rub gently.

moYYere *(nde)* bounty; generosity; quality; kindness.

móYYinde *v.* make good; do well.

móYYinoowo *(o)* benefactor.

moYYo *(o)* good; reputable. **neɗɗo** ~ a kind person.

móYYude *v.* be good; be kind.

mubbitde *v.* open. ~ *gite* open one's eyes.

mubboowo *(o)* a person who closes.

mubbude *v.* seal; close; zip. **Mubbu hunuko maa** Close your mouth.

muccude *v.* suck.

muccoowo *(o)* sucker.

mudda *(o)* span; period; time; while. **oon** ~ at that time. **Wónii mudda** It has been a while.

muddere *(nde)* dummy state.

muddiɗde [muddidde] *v.* be dumb.

muddo *(o)* dummy. **Ko o muddo** He is a dummy.

muddaade *v.* pay/give a tithe.

muddu *(o)* weight measurement. ~ *hoore* tithe.

muk *foc.* never; not at all.

mum *poss.* his; her. **hoore** ~ himself; herself.

mumen *poss.* their.

muuɗum *poss.* his; hers; its.

mumaade *v.* remove grains from the ear.

mumi *(ɗi)* millet ears.

mumnude *v.* come out.

muumru *(ndu)* millet stalk. **muumi** *(ɗi) pl.*

muñal *(ngal)* patience. **famɗude** ~ lack patience. **heewde** ~ be very patient. **O alaa muñal** He is impatient. **ɓaawo muñal ko alhamdulillahi** Patience is always rewarded.

muñande *v.* have patience for.

muñde [muñje] *v.* bear; forbear; be patient.

muñɗo [muñYo] *adj.* patient.

muñótóóɗum *adj.* bearable.

muñtóriɗde [muñcóridde] *v.* lose patience.

mungaas [muɭŋgaas] *(o)* file.

muraade *v.* play deaf.

muraadu *(ndu)* work.

murde *v.* suck.

murliɗde [murlidde] *v.* be round. **Ina murliɗi** It is round.

murlo *adj.* round.

murtere *(nde)* revolt. **murte** *(ɗe) pl.*

murtude *v.* revolt; rebel; be defiant.

murtugól *(ngól)* revolt; insurrection.

murtóóki *(ki)* tree.

murtoonde *(nde)* fruit. **murtooɗe** *(ɗe) pl.*

muruk *interj.* sound of something that enters.

musidaagal *(ngal)* friendship.

musiɗɗo *(o)* dear; relative; friend. **musibɓe** *(ɓe) pl.*

musóndirde [musóⁿdirde] *v.* be a close friend of.

mutal *(ngal)* sinking of; disappearance. ~ *naange* sundown; sunset.

mutde [mudde] *v.* go under water; set; sink; disappear.

mutnude [munnude] *v.* sink; make go under the water; make disappear.

mutum *(o)* bird.

muuɗde [muudde] *v.* eat a floury substance.

muuɗgol *(ngól)* eating of floury substance.

muuɗoowo *(o)* a person who eats a floury substance.

muudo *(ngo)* measurement which equals four kilograms.

muufól *(ngól)* braid.

muukaade *v.* exceed the expected limits.

muukiiɗo *(o)* excessive person.

muumantél Alla *(ngel)* an animal.

muumdinde *v.* make someone dumb.

muumdude *v.* be dumb.

muumdudo *adj.* mute.

muumdugól (ngól) dumbness.

muumo (o) dumb person; mute. **Ko o** *muumo* He is dumb.

muumre (nde) dumbness.

muumnaade *v.* doze; nap; snooze. *O woni ko e muumnaade* He is taking a nap.

muurde *v.* cover; veil; hide.

muurnaade *v.* cover one's head. **Ko o** *muurniido* Her face is covered with a veil.

muurorde (nde) veil.

muus *(o)* sound made to attract a cat.

Muusaa *(o)* male first name.

muusaado *adj.* ailing; hurting. **Ko o** *muusaado* He is hurting.

muusde *v.* be painful. *Ina muusi* It is painful.

muuseede *v.* ail.

muusééki (ki) pain; suffering.

muusdum *adj.* sore; painful.

muusu (ngu) pain; ache. ~ *hoore* headache; migraine. ~ *góddól* / *dakañe* angina.

muuya *(o)* objective; purpose. *Hol ko woni muuyaa maa* What do you want?

muuyde *v.* desire; want.

muuyeede *v.* want; desire.

muuybude *v.* be sprained.

muyninde *v.* breastfeed; suckle.

muynude *v.* suck; breastfeed. *O mo muyna haa jooni* He is still breastfeeding.

muyningól (ngól) breastfeeding.

muynugól (ngól) breastfeeding.

MB [ᵐb]

baaɓattu [ᵐbaaɓattu](*ngu*) locust. *baaɓatti* *(ɗi) pl.*

baaddaagu [ᵐbaaddaagu] *(ngu)* lack of energy.

baaddi [ᵐbaaddi] *(ndi)* a nonchalant individual. *Ko a mbaaddi* You are weak.

baadi [ᵐbaadi] *(ndi)* feature; pattern; plight; type. *mo Ƴƴo* ~ a pretty lady; a handsome man. *mo Ƴƴude* ~ be pretty/handsome. *bonde* ~ be ugly.

baagaan [ᵐbaagaan] *(o)* bird. *mbaaganééji (ɗi) pl.*

baala [ᵐbaala] *(o)* fishing net. *mbaalaaji (ɗi) pl.*

baalu [ᵐbaalu] *(ngu)* sheep. *baali (ɗi) pl.*

baangu [ᵐbaaⁿgu] *(ngu)* spear.

baawka [ᵐbaawka] *(ka)* ability; means; skill; aptitude; proficiency. *Hollu am ɗo mbaawka maa tólnii* Show me what you can do.

baayan [ᵐbaayan] *(o)* calabash. *mbaayanééji (ɗi) pl.*

babba [ᵐbabba] *(ba)* donkey. ~ *hoore* louse. ~ *tugal* hog; pig. *waɗɗaade* ~ ride a donkey. *bamɗi (ɗi) pl.*

bajju [ᵐbajju] *(o)* blanket. *suddaade* ~ cover oneself with a blanket.

bake [ᵐbake] *(o)* horse.

bakku [ᵐbakku] *(o)* catapult; slingshot.

balka [ᵐbalka] *(ka)* water storage place.

balla [ᵐballa] *(o)* farm.

balndi [ᵐbalⁿdi] *(ndi)* bed. *feewnude* ~ make a bed.

bandu [ᵐbaⁿdu] *(o)* water holder. *mbanduuji (ɗi) pl.*

bar [ᵐbar] I hope. *Mbar aɗa selli* I hope you are well.

baraangu [ᵐbaraaⁿgu] *(ngu)* 1) horse 2) tithe.

barngu [ᵐbarⁿgu] *(ngu)* dam.

baróódi [ᵐbaróódi] *(ndi)* animal. *barooɗe (ɗe) pl.* ~ *leydi* a snake.

basu [ᵐbasu] *(ngu)* bag. ~ *coofe* bladder. *basi (ɗi) pl.*

bato [ᵐbato] *(o)* lizard.

bawgu [ᵐbaggu] *(ngu)* drum. *fiide* ~ play a drum. *bawɗi (ɗi) pl.*

mbayla [ᵐbayla] *(ka)* forge.

mbaylaandi [ᵐbaylaaⁿdi] *(ndi)* industry.

mbedda [ᵐbedda] *(o)* street. *ferde* ~ open a road. *uddude* ~ close a road. *mbeddaaji (ɗi) pl.*

mbéɗu [ᵐbéɗu] *(ngu)* cover.

mbéélu [ᵐbéélu] *(ngu)* silhouette; shadow. *Ko o mbeelu makko tan* He follows him like a shadow.

mbeewa [ᵐbeewa] *(ba)* goat. *bey (ɗi) pl.*

mbege [ᵐbege] *(o)* bicycle rim.

mbele [ᵐbele] *conj.* so that.

mbildi [ᵐbildi] *(ndi)* ceiling; mansard.

mbimƳa [ᵐbimƳa] *(ba)* egg lice.

mbiñcaan [ᵐbiñcaan] *(o)* millet.

mbindaan [ᵐbinⁿdaan](*o)* maid. *Ko o mbindaan* She is a maid.

mbir [ᵐbir] *(o)* wrestler. *mbiruuji (ɗi).*

mbiru [ᵐbiru] *(ngu)* woven reeds. *biri (ɗi) pl.*

mbóddi [ᵐbóddi] *(ndi)* poisonous snake.

mbolo [ᵐbolo] *(ngo)* forest. *mbólóóji (ɗi) pl.*

mbóódude [ᵐbóódude] *v.* denounce.

mbóólu [ᵐbóólu] *(ngu)* horse.

mboombaagu [ᵐbooᵐbaagu] *(ngu)* virginity. *mbóómri* [ᵐbóómri] *(ndi)* girl; virgin. *Ko o mbóómri* She is a virgin. *O wonaa mboomri* She is not a virgin.

mbóóngu [ᵐbóóⁿgu] *(ngu)* horse.

mbóótu [ᵐbóótu] *(ngu)* strip of fabric for carrying a baby.

mbórtu [ᵐbórtu] *(ngu)* baby goat.

mbulayse [ᵐbulayse] *(o) {fr.}* bakery.

mburɓuttu [ᵐburɓuttu] *(ngu)* baby toad.

mburu [ᵐburu] *(o)* bread. *lóócól* ~ a loaf of bread.

mburuutu [ᵐburuutu] *(ngu)* worm.

mbuubu [ᵐbuubu] *(ngu)* fly. ~ *ñaaku* a bee. *buubi (ɗi) pl.*

mbuuɗu [ᵐbuuɗu] *(ngu)* monetary unit. *ɗum jarata ko mbuuɗu* It costs a monetary unit.

mbuuwwa [ᵐbuuwwa] *(o)* bone marrow. *ɓuucaade* ~ eat bone marrow.

N

na *part.* process.

naaɗaade *v.* stretch oneself.

naaɗagól (ngól) stretching of oneself.

naafige *(o)* hypocrite. *Ko o naafige* He is a hypocrite. *naafigeeɓe (ɓe) pl.*

naafki *(ki)* armpit. *Naafki ma ina sicci* Your underarm smells badly. *naafɗe (ɗe) pl.*

naakaade *(nde)* wooden board for tanning.

naale *(ɗe)* dance.

naam *part.* yes (reply when called upon).

naamndaade [naamⁿdaade] *v.* question; inquire. *So a andaa aɗa foti naamndaade* If you do not know you should inquire.

naanaa *(o)* mint.

naane *(o)* a period ago. *Mi yii mo naane* I saw him earlier.

naangde *v.* be sunny; be hot.

naange [naaⁿge] (nge) sun; nadir. *puɗal ~* sunrise. *mutal ~* sunset.

naaraade *v.* be lazy.

naasaade *v.* be blocked.

naasde v. block.

naatɗam [naaɗɗam] *(ɗam)* flood water.

naatde [naadde] *v.* enter; infiltrate; meddle; penetrate; adhere. *~ e nder suudu* enter a room. *~ e fedde* enter an age group; belong to an age group.

naatgól (ngól) admission

naatirde (nde) entrance; inlet; access; entry; door. *Toon wonaa naatirde* That is not the entrance.

naatirde v. enter with/by. *Naatir damal fuɗnaange* Use the east entrance.

naatngo [naatⁿgo] *(ngo)* entering.

naatnude [naannude] *v.* put in; make enter; introduce; penetrate; admit. *~ ndiyam* irrigate.

naatóndiral [naatóⁿdiral]*(ngal)* caption.

naatóndirde [naatóⁿdirde] *v.* intermingle; grab other while wrestling.

naattinde v. make enter.

naattude v. be circumcised. *O naattii hande* He was circumcised today.

naawde v. grill; place on top of fire to burn hair.

naawɗude v. be light-skinned.

naawo(o) light-skinned person. *Ko o naawo* He is light-skinned.

naayaade *v.* bend onself.

naayde *v.* bend.

naɓde *v.* take.

naddere (nde) alt.

nadorde *(nde)* waist. *nadorɗe (ɗe) pl.*

naɗdal [naddal] *(ngal)* ravine.

naɗde [nadde] *(nde)* ravine. **nafde** *v.* benefit; be useful; serve. *ɗum nafataa* It is useless.

nafójum adj. useful; valuable.

nafoore (nde) importance; value; use; worth. *Ko/mo alaa ~* worthless. *nafooje (ɗe) pl.*

nafoowo (o) useful person.

nafqoowo (o) person who gives charity.

nafqude v. give charity.

naftoraade v. use something. *Yettu naftoro ɗaa* Take it and make a good use of it.

naftortooɗo (o) person who makes use of something.

nagge (nge) cow; zebu. *nay (ɗi) pl.*

nahre [naare] *(nde)* grass.

najde [najje] *v.* be astonished. *Kó mi najɗo* I am astonished.

najnajilo (o) astonishingly smart person.

najnude [naññude] *v.* petrify; astound; astonish.

najoore (nde) astonishment; consternation; mystery. *najooje (ɗe) pl.*

nammaadi *(ki)* tree.

nammanduru   [nammaⁿduru]   *(ndu)* abundance; plentiness.

nammude v. be abundant.

nambu [namᵐbu] *(o)* garden. *~ ñebbe* a bean garden.

nanal *(ngal)* left; left hand. *paɗal ~* left hand show.

nano (ngo) left; left hand. *jungo ~* left hand. *bange ~* left side.

nanalla *(o)* hearsay; piece of news. *ɗum ko nanalla* That is hearsay. *nanallaaji (ɗi) pl.*

nande v. hear; understand. *A nanii* Do you understand?

nanɗe (ɗe) hearing. *ko faati e ~* acoustic; aural.

nanirde v. listen with; hear with.

nadirde (nde) hearing device/part.

ióndiral [nanóⁿdiral] *(ngal)* accord; ɲreement.

ıóndirde [nanóⁿdirde] *v.* agree. *E ɓe anóndiri* They relate to each other very ɲell.

ıoowo *(o)* hearer. *O wonaa nanoowo* He ɔes not listen.

ıótóóɗum *adj.* audible; acceptable.

ɑtinde *v.* interpret; translate; repeat louder.

ɑtinoowo *(o)* translator. *Ko o nantinoowo* ɩe is a translator.

ɑtiiɗo *adj.* rich person.

ɑde [nañje] *v.* oppose.

ɑdal [nanⁿdal] *(ngal)* purge.

ɑdo [nanⁿdo] *(o)* person who is similar; ıalogous.

ıduɓe [nanⁿduɓe] *adj.* identical; similar.

ɑdude [nanⁿdude] *v.* resemble. *E ɓe ɑnndi* They look alike.

ɑdugól [nanⁿdugól]*(ngól)* similitude.

ıgal [naɿ]ⁿgal] *(ngal)* 1) tax; 2) eclipse. *~ ɑange* a solar eclipse.

ıgande [naɿ]ⁿgande] *v.* hold for. *~jungo* ɛlp; give a hand.

ɑgirde [naɿ]ⁿgirde] *v.* hold with.

ɑgóndiral [naɿ]ⁿgóⁿdiral] *(ngal)* solidarity.

ɑgude [naɿ]ⁿgude] *v.* 1) arrest; apprehend; ɑtch; hold. 2) repossess. *O nangaama* He ɩs been arrested.

ngugól [naɿ]ⁿgugól] *(ngól)* hold.

ɩkaaɗo *adj.* cad.

ɩól *(ngól)* anus.

ɑtal *(ngal)* picture; photograph. *~ makko* ɩs picture. *nate (ɗe) pl.*

ttinde *v.* stop.

ttude *v.* cease; die. *ɗum nattii* It has ɛased.

ɯande *v.* carry for. *Nawan mo* Take it for ɩm.

ɯde *v.* take; take along; transport. *~ ɩriyeer* impound.

ɯdude *v.* 1) liken 2) take along.

ɯliigu *(ngu)* polygamy. *Mi yiɗaa nawliigu* do not like polygamy.

ɯliraaɗo *(o)* cowife. *nawliraaɓe (ɓe) pl.*

ɯlirde *v.* be polygamous. *O nawlirii* He is ɔlygamous.

ɯorde *v.* carry with.

nawtude *v.* carry back; return. *Nawtu ɗum* Take it back.

nawdi *(ki)* tree.

nay *num.* four. *laabi ~* four times.

nayaɓal *(ngal)* quarter; fourth.

nayaɓo *(o)* the fourth (in rank).

nayeejo *(o)* old person; veteran. *Ko o nayeejo* He is old. *nayeeɓe (ɓe) pl.*

nayééwu *(ngu)* old age.

nayewaagu *(ngu)* old age.

naywinde *v.* make old.

naywude *v.* be old; act old. *O naywii* He is old.

naywuɗo *(o)* old person.

ne *part.* what about.

nebam *(ɗam)* oil. *~ keccam* butter. *~ defirteeɗam* cooking oil. *nebameeje (ɗe) pl.*

neɗɗo *(o)* person; someone; everyone; somebody. *~ kala* anybody; everyone. *ko faati e ~* human.

neeɓde *v.* be slow; be long.

neegde *v.* have no pity; be merciless. *O mo neegi* He is merciless.

neene *(o)* mother.

nééniraaɗo *(o)* mother.

néénó *(o)* mommy.

néésu *(ngu)* 1) culture 2) upbringing; education.

néétóriɗde [néétóridde] *v.* to be impolite. *O mo neetoriɗi* He is impolite.

neetaro *adj.* impolite; disrespectful; rude.

nefde *v.* resent; dislike; repulse. *Ina nefnii* It makes me want to throw up.

nefnaade *v.* be disgusting.

nefre *(nde)* dislike; resentment.

nehaade *v.* be well brought up; behave. *O mo nehii* He is polite.

nehde [neede] *v.* foster; upbring; train. *Ko kanko nehi mi* He is my foster parent.

néhdi [néédi] *(ndi)* behavior; character; upbringing. *mo ɯude nehdi* have good upringing. *bonde ~* be rude; be ill-bred.

néhiiɗo *adj.* polite.

nehoowo *(o)* person who provides upbringing.

nelaaɗo *(o)* messenger; emissary; envoy; Messiah. *~ Alla* Prophet Muhammad. *nelaaɓe (ɓe) pl.*

nelal (ngal) message; errand. *yettinde ~* deliver a message. *Nelal ko bakkaat* A message is a sin (One must deliver someone's message).

neldal (ngal) parcel. *Neldal maa yettiima* Your parcel has been delivered.

nelde v. send a person.

neldoowo (o) sender.

néldude v. send; wire. *~ kaalis* wire money.

néludo (o) sender.

newaade *v.* be easygoing. *O mo newii* He is flexible.

newaare (nde) kindness.

néwiido adj. flexible; easygoing.

néwidum *adj.* easy.

néwninde v. facilitate; make easy.

newnoowo (o) easygoing person.

néwnude v. ease; make easy. *Alla néwnii* It went well.

newde *v.* grease; oil.

newre *(nde)* palm (hand).

ni *part.* thus; negative particle.

niɓɓere *(nde)* gloom; darkness. *suusde ~* like darkness. *~ kurum* complete darkness.

niɓɓidde [niɓɓidde] *v.* be dark. *Ina niɓɓidi* It is dark.

niɓɓiddo adj. grim. *niɓɓo alt.*

niɓɓiddum adj. obscure; dim.

niɓɓidinde v. obscure; obfuscate.

niɓɓo (o) an obscure person.

niilnude *v.* negate.

niiwdude *v.* be cloudy.

niiwre (nde) cloudy weather.

niloɲ *(o) {fr.}* nylon.

nimsa *(o)* remorse; regret. *O alaa nimsa* He has no regret.

nimsitde [nimsidde] really regret.

nimsude v. regret. *Mi nimsii* I regret I did it.

nirkude *v.* grind.

no *part.* how. *No mbaddaa* How are you?

noddaango [noddaaⁿgo] *(ngo)* call. *noddaali (di) pl.*

nóddinde v. call to prayer.

nóddingól (ngól) a call for prayer.

nóddinoowo (o) muezzin.

nódditaade v. sniff in; draw snot back.

nódditde [nóddidde] *v.* recall.

nóddóndirde [nóddóⁿdirde] *v.* call on another.

noddoowo (o) caller.

nóddude v. call; convoke; denominate.

nóddu do (o) caller.

nóddugol (ngol) calling.

nófru (ndu) ear. *welde ~* have a good ea. hear easily.

nókitaade *v.* remove couscous from steamin utensil.

nokkande [nokkanⁿde] *(nde)* handful; shar*

nokkere (nde) handful.

nókkude v. take a handful of.

nókku *(o)* place; fief; lieu; region; secto area. *~ safaara* clinic; hospital. *~ godo* elsewhere. *~ deental* venue. *~ kal* everywhere. *nokkuuji (di) pl.*

nóllidde [nollidde] *v.* be beardless.

nollo *adj.* beardless. *Ko o nollo* He beardless.

nómból [nómᵐból] *(ngól)* charm.

noogaas *(o)* twenty. *~ e góó* twenty and on*

noon *adv.* thus. *dum ~* therefore; so.

noorde *v.* color.

nóórdi (ndi) color.

nóórdude v. change color.

nóóról (ngól) backbone; foundation. *~ kéé* spine.

nóóróó (o) alligator; crocodile. *nóódi (di) p*

noos *(o) {fr.}* celebration.

noosde *v. {fr.}* celebrate.

nootaade *v.* answer. *~ telefoɲ* answer th telephone.

nootaango [nootaaⁿgo] *(ngo)* answer.

nooyde *v.* be soft.

nuddinaade *v.* hide; squat.

nufaade *v.* go deep into mud.

nufde *v.* sink.

nuflude *v.* become unimportant. *O mo nuf* He is useless.

nuggaro *adj.* shy; timid.

nuundal *(ngal)* honesty; trust; integrit* probity. *Nuundal ina móɣɣi* Honesty good.

nuundude v. be truthful; be honest.

nuundudo adj. honest; trustworthy.

nuunde *v.* caponize.

ND [^{n}d]

aarde [^{n}daarde] *v.* look; seek. *Hol ko daarataa* What are you looking for? *'gonmi ko e ndaarde liggeey* I am looking for a job.

aaroowo [^{n}daaroowo] *(o)* 1) person who looks 2) seeker. ~ *liggééy* applicant.

aaroyde [^{n}daaroyde] *v.* seek; go and seek.

aartoowo *(o)* seeker.

aw [^{n}daw] *(o)* ostrich.

aw [^{n}daw] *interj.* interjection signaling exaggeration or admiration. *Ndaw ko eewi haala* He talks too much.

e [^{n}de] *part.* 1) when; upon 2) *det. Nde jiiɗaa mo nde o sellaano* When you saw im he was sick.

een [^{n}deen] *adv.* at that time. *Ndeen o laano toon* At that time he was not there.

een [^{n}deen] *det.* that. ~ *hoore* that head.

ema [^{n}dema] *(ka)* agronomy. *ko faati e ~ ngaynaaka* agricultural. ~ *e ngaynaaka.* gronomy. *So ndiyam alaa ndema oodataa* One cannot farm when there is o water.

nder [^{n}der] *adv.* in; among; inside. ~ *suudu* in the room.

ndi [^{n}di] *det.* the. *ngaari* ~ the ox.

ndiga *(o)* nothing.

ndimaagu [^{n}dimaagu] *(ngu)* honor; freedom. ~ *hooremum* independence. *heɓde* ~ *hooremum* be free from slavery or occupation. *O heɓii ndimaagu hoore makko* He is free.

ndiwri [^{n}diwri] *(ndi)* birds.

ndiwoowa [^{n}diwoowa] *(ka)* plane; airplane. *laana* ~ an airplane. *jolde e* ~ take a plane; fly.

ndiyam [^{n}diyam] *(ɗam)* water. ~ *gawYal* sap. ~ *njareteeɗam* drinking water. ~ *ngulɗam* hot water. ~ *buubɗam* cold water.

ndónu [^{n}dónu] *(ngu)* inheritance; patrimony

ndungu [^{n}dun^{n}gu] *(o)* rainy season. *Ndungu ngu moYYii* We had a good rainy season.

nduulaldi [^{n}duulaldi]*(ndi)* male lizard.

NG [^{n}g]

ngaameela [^{n}gaameela] *(ka)* laziness. *wondude e* ~ be lazy.

ngaandi [^{n}gaan^{n}di] *(ndi)* brain. **ngaari** *(ndi)* bull.

ngabu *(ngu)* hippopotamus. *gabi (ɗi).*

ngal *(det.)* the. *leggal* ~ the wood.

ngalu [^{n}galu] *(ngu)* fortune.

ngam *conj.* so that.

ngañaari [^{n}gañaari] *(ndi)* benefice; thrift. *ɗum alaa ngañaari* You cannot make a profit from that investment.

ngañgu [^{n}gañgu] *(ngu)* antipathy; hatred; loathing. *ɗum jibinta ko ngañgu* It breeds hatred.

ngaska [^{n}gaska] *(ka)* hole. *asde* ~ make a hole. *gasɗe (ɗe) pl.*

ngasu [^{n}gasu] *(ngu)* trench. *ngasuuji (ɗi) pl.*

ngaynaaka [^{n}gaynaaka] *(ka)* herding.

nge [^{n}ge] *det.* the. *nagge* ~ the cow.

ngel [^{n}gel] the (diminutive). *naggel* ~ the little cow.

ngeya *det.* that. *nagge* ~that cow over there.

ngeera [^{n}geera] *(o)* trap *ngeeraaji (ɗi) pl.*

ngelooba [^{n}gelooba] *(ba)* camel. *waɗɗaade* ~ ride a camel.

ngembe [^{n}gem^{m}be] *(o){wol.}* diaper.

ngéndi [^{n}gén^{n}di] *(ndi)* nation; motherland. *ko faati e* ~ national. *ɗemɗe* ~ national languages.

ngesa *(ba)* farm.

ngilngu [^{n}gil^{n}gu] *(ngu)* worm.

ngo [^{n}go] *det.* the.

ngol [^{n}gol] *det.* the. *laawol* ~ the path.

ngolwa [^{n}golwa]*(ba)* dragon.

ngóóróóndi [^{n}góóróó^{n}di] *(ndi)* 1) snake 2) foundation; basis. ~ *huɓeere* the foundatio of a building. *goorooɗe (ɗe) pl.*

ngoraagu [^{n}goraagu] *(ngu)* manhood; virility *waasde* ~ *mum* lose one's manhood.

ngóri [^{n}góri] *(o)* cock. *ngóriiji (ɗi) pl.*

ngu [^{n}gu]

ngulééki [^{n}gulééki] *(ki)* heat. *heewde* ~ ac important; put on airs.

nguli *(ki)* heat.

nguru [^{n}guru] *(ngu)* skin. ~ *hoore* scalp.

nguttu *(ngu)* pride.

nguufa [^{n}guufa] *(ka)* lather; foam.

nguunu [^{n}guunu] *(ngu)* chicken cage.

nguura [^{n}guura] *(ka)* victuals; food; foo supplies.

nguurndam [^{n}guur^{n}dam] *(ɗam)* life. *e* makko in his lifetime. ~ *njuutɗam* a lon life.

nguyka [^{n}guyka] *(ka)* fraud; larceny; razzi theft. *ɗum ko nguyka mawka* It is a majc fraud.

NJ [ⁿj]

ajééndi ["jaajééndi] *(ndi)* width.
uuteendi e ~ the size of. *Hol no
uuteendi e njaajeendi galle o póti* How
ʒ is the lot?

arééndi ["jaarééndi] *(ndi)* sand. ~
laneeri white sand.

atige ["jaatige] *(o)* host; sponsor. *Hol
ⁿdo njaatige maa* Who is your host?

utiraado ["jaatiraado] *(o)* 1) host 2) great
andchild; great grandparent.

mala ["jamala] *(ba)* 1) spider 2) giraffe.
ese ~ a cobweb.

mndi ["jamⁿdi] *(ndi)* metal; steel. ~ *pono
heel.* ~ *baleeri* iron.

ram ["jaram] *(dam)* beverage. *sarwude ~
rve drinks.

wdi ["jawdi] *(ndi)* ram. ~ *kalhaldi* ram.
yyaade ~ slaughter a ram for sacrifice.

ytam ["jaytam] *(dam)* water added to
ok a meal.

njeenaari["jeenaari] *(ndi)* bribery; reward. *O
mo suusi
njeenaari* He likes bribery.

njééygu ["jééygu] *(ngu)* sale; trade.

njiilaw ["jiilaw] *(o)* search; quest. *O woni ko
e njiilaw* He is searching.

njimri ["jimri] *(ndi)* song; carol. ~ *mbelndi* a
beautiful song. ~ *mettundi* a bad song.

njóbdi ["jóbdi] *(ndi)* salary; stipend; wages.
beydude ~ increase the salary. *ustude* ~
reduce the salary. *hebde* ~ be paid; get
one's salary.

njogoram ["jogoram] *(dam)* genitals. *Ko
faati e* ~ genital.

njoobaari ["joorta] *(ndi)* food set aside for a
trip.

njoorta ["joorta] *(o)* hope anticipation;
expectation. ~ *moYYa* expected good news.

njurum *(o)* ["jurum] *(o)* pity.

njuulaawi ["juulaawi] *(ki)* dagger.

njuumri ["juumri] *(ndi)* honey.

njuutééndi ["juutééⁿdi] *(ndi)* length. ~ *e
njaajeendi* the size of.

Ñ

ñaadde [ñaadde] v. be ill-tempered; be fierce.

ñaadahoore (o) unlucky individual; old person.

ñaafaade v. roll one's clothes up. O woni ko e ñaafaade He is rolling his clothing up.

ñaagaade v. request; beseech; appeal; implore; solicit; crave; pray for.

ñaagaro (o) person with endless needs.

ñaagotoodo (o) person who tries.

ñaagunde [ñaagunde] (nde) petition; plea; proposal; request.

ñaaki (di) bees.

ñaaku (ngu) bee. mbuubu ~ a bee.

ñaalal (ngal) white bird.

ñaaltaade v. trim; cut the upper part of the grass.

ñaamanduru [ñaamanduru] (ndu) abundance of food.

ñaamatééri (ndi) food supplies.

ñaamatinde [ñaamatinde] (nde) leftovers.

ñaamdaro (o) person who eats incessantly. ~ ñaamgawiijo voracious; greedy.

ñaamde v. eat. O woni ko e ñaamde He is eating.

ñaamdu (ndu) food; nutrition; way of eating. ñaamde (de) pl.

ñaamgawiijo adj. voracious; greedy. ñaamdaro ~ voracious; greedy.

ñaamirde v. eat with. ñaamrude alt.

ñaamoowo (o) person who eats. ~ yimbe cannibal. Ko o ñaamoowo He is eating.

ñaamówél (ngél) depredator.

ñaamre (nde) fine.

ñaamroowo (o) person who eats with.

ñaamrude v. eat with. ~ jungo eat with a hand. ~ kuddu eat with a spoon.

ñaamtaade v. rust.

ñaamo (ngo) right hand. bange ~ dexter. jungo ~ right hand.

ñaande [ñaande] (nde) pericarp; grain shells.

ñaantaade v. dress up.

ñaantagól (ngól) elegance.

ñaantude v. dress someone up.

ñaantungal [ñaantungal] (ngal) elegance; the act of dressing up.

ñaañde [ñaañje] v. play the fiddle.

ñaañóóru (ndu) fiddle; violin. O mo waaw ñaañóóru He is a skilled violin player.

ñaañoowo (o) fiddler.

ñaañte [ñaance] (de) carded cotton.

ñaañtude [ñaañcude] v. card cotton.

ñaarde v. shine.

ñaasal (ngal) scar.

ñaawde v. judge; adjudicate; adjudge doom. ~ goonga render a goo judgment/verdict. ~ fenaande render wrong judgment/verdict.

ñaaweede v. be judged.

ñaawoore (nde) trial; adjudication judgment. ñaawooje (de) pl.

ñaawoowo (o) judge. ~ goonga a goo judge.

ñaawoyde v. go and judge.

ñaayde v. eat crops. Nay di ñaayii nges ba The cows ate the crops.

ñaaygol (ngol) the eating of crops.

ñaayko (ko) stalks.

ñaakon (kon) small beads; small pearls.

ñaayre (nde) bead; pearl. ñaaYe (de) pl.

ñaaYal (ngal) slow pacing.

ñaaYde [ñaajje] v. flaunt; parade; wal slowly.

ñabbude v. pile/gather disorderly.

ñakkaade v. jump on; fall on. Mbaróó ndi ñakkii e makko The lion jumped o him.

ñakkeere (nde) pile of dead shrubs.

ñakkitaade v. redo a fence of shrubs.

ñakkude v. pile dead shrubs; fence wit shrubs.

ñakkudi (ndi) ornament pieces. ñakku (de) pl.

ñalaande [ñalaande] (nde) day; particula day.

ñalawma (o) day. ~ hande o today; th very day. ñaldi (di) pl.

ñallande [ñallande] (nde) day; the spendin of a day.

llande v. spend the day for. *Ko mi gardo* **ñawdo** *adj.* ill; sick.
tallande ma I came to spend the day at
our house.

llinde v. spend a day. *ñallinen doo* Let
s spend the day here.

llirde (nde) gathering place during the
lay; a place where people spend the day.

llude v. spend the day.

lnde [ñalⁿde] *(nde)* daily stay.

lngu [ñalⁿgu] *(ngu)* day.

nde [ñaⁿde] *(nde)* day; the day. ~ *kala*
lways; daily. ~ *ndeen* a particular time
go.

le (nge) heifer. *ñalbi (di) pl.*

lél (ngél) calf.

tllambero [ñallamᵐbero] *(o)* dear friend.

tmaande [ñamaaⁿde] *(nde)* debt; loan.
uusde ~ be eager to take loans. *hulde* ~
e reluctant to take loans.

tmlaade v. borrow. ~ *kaalis* borrow
money.

tmliido (o) indebted person; borrower.

tmlude v. loan; give on credit; lend.
tamlu mo ujundere dolaar Lend him one
thousand dollars.

tmakala *(o)* dependents; dependent
artists.

tmako *(ko)* pimento; red pepper.

tmambo [ñamamᵐbo] *(ko)* eyebrow
tiemambo (ko) alt.

tmminde v. feed; nourish ~ *sukaaɓe* feed
the children.

tmminoowo (o) person who feeds.

tmneejo (o) witch.

tmri (ndi) dish; meal; stodge; food. ~
ngulndi hot food. ~ *buuɓndi* cold food.

tmtude v. eat what is forbidden.

angere [ñaɗ]ⁿgere] *(nde)* rage; wickedness;
unkindness.

tngude [ñaɗ]ⁿgude] v. be fierce.

tngudo [ñaɗ]ⁿgudo] *adj.* naughty;
ferocious; fierce. *suka* ~ a fierce child.

appude v. 1) rain heavily; pour 2) lay on;
cover.

arde v. dress up.

atti *(o)* fish.

aw *(o)* disease; illness; sickness. ~ *gite*
conjunctivitis *ñabbuuli (di) pl.*

twande [ñawanⁿde] *(nde)* wound; abscess.

awde v. be sick.

ñawdo *adj.* ill; sick.

ñawndaade [ñawⁿdaade] v. have charms.

ñawndogal [ñawⁿdogal] *(ngal)* talisman;
charm.

ñawndude [ñawⁿdude] v. make a charm for
someone.

ñawnude v. sicken.

ñawlude v. be high. *Naange ñawlii* The sun
is high.

ñebbe(de) beans. *ñewre (nde)* sing.

ñéwñéwól (ngól) bean plant.

ñewre *(nde)* bean; fruit stone; pea. *ñebbe
(de) pl.*

ñedande [ñedanⁿde] *(nde)* a potful of (e.g.
water).

ñedde [ñedde] v. take a potful of.

ñédugal *(ngal)* small pot *ñédude (de) pl.*

ñeeɓaade v. shrug one's shoulders.

ñeeɓaango [ñeeɓaanⁿgo] *(ngo)* shrugging
of shoulders.

ñeekam *(dam)* sauce.

ñeeŋtaade v. creep.

ñeeñal *(ngal)* skill; experience.

ñeeñde [ñeeñje] v. 1) flatter 2) be skilled.

ñeeño *(o)* type of caste; artist caste; artisan.
Ko o ñeeño He belongs to the artisan
caste.

ñeeñre *(nde)* flattery.

ñéésól *(ngól)* cut on the face.

ñékkude v. trip along; canter; gallop; trot.

ñemambo [ñemamᵐbo] *(ko)* eyelash.

ñemboowo [ñemᵐboowo] *(o)* person who
mimics.

ñémbude [ñemᵐbude] v. emulate; imitate;
mime; simulate.

ñémtinde v. mimic; imitate; simulate. *Ó
wóni ko e ñemtinde ma* He is imitating
you.

ñengaade [ñeɗ]ⁿgaade] v. perform magic.

ñengi [ñeɗ]ⁿgi] *(di)* magic.

ñengotoodo [ñeɗ]ⁿgotoodo] *(o)* a magician.
Ko o ñengotoodo He is a magician.

ñenkilaade [ñeɗ]kilaade] v. lie sideways.

ñiɓaade v. be planted.

ñiɓande [ñiɓanⁿde] *(nde)* hole.

ñiɓde v. stab; plant.

ñiɓirde v. plant with.

ñiɓtaade v. transplant;.

ñifde v. turn off; put off; extinguish.

ñifdo adj. dummy. *Ko o ñifdo* He is stupid.

ñifdum adj. extinct.

ñihri [ñiiri] *(ndi)* dish made of millet grains and meat.

ñiibde *v.* stay long; last. *Aduna ñibaaki ko baarii* The world is not static/Things change.

niibdum *adj.* lasting.

ñiire *(nde)* tooth. *ñiiYe (de) pl.*

ñiiwa *(ba)* elephant. *ñiibi (di) pl.*

ñikle *(de)* tickles. *hulde* ~ be sensitive to tickles. *suusde* ~ be insensitive to tickles.

ñikleede v. be tickled.

ñiklude v. tickle.

ñimbude [ñimᵐbude] *v.* be grouped.

ñiŋde *v.* blame; reproach.

ñippude *v.* plant.

ñirbinaade *v.* show an angry face.

ñirtotal *(ngal)* worm.

ñittaade *v.* blow one's nose. *ñitto* blow your nose.

ñittere (nde) mucus.

ñittude v. blow someone's nose.

ñóbbude *v.* tan; beat; do leather.

ñóftude *v.* unfold.

ñohde [ñoode] *v.* gossip about someone; traduce.

ñohoowo (o) person who gossips.

ñohre (nde) gossip. ~ *mo YYaani* gossip is despised.

ñolde *v.* rot; putrefy; be rotten. *dum ñolii* It is rotten.

ñóldum adj. rotten.

ñólnude v. make rotten.

ñomaade *v.* hurry.

ñóndidde [ñónⁿdidde] *v.* nasalize one's speech.

ñóndo v. person whose speech is affected by nasalization.

ñóngude [ñoŋⁿgude] *v.* roll up.

ñongaade [ñoŋⁿgaade] *v.* wriggle; gather oneself up before leaping.

ñóngól [ñóŋⁿgól] *(ngól)* pleat.

ñoofaade *v.* curl up.

ñoofande [ñoofanⁿde] *(nde)* disorderly piled/packed items.

ñoofde v. pile in a bag disorderly.

ñóófól (ngol) fold.

ñóóju *(o)* hypocrite.

ñookaade *v.* squeeze oneself in.

nookde *v.* squeese in.

ñooleede *v.* have no means; be poor.

ñóólu (ngu) poverty.

ñoomre *(nde)* hay; dry grass for animal consumption.

ñootde [ñoodde] *v.* sew; stitch.

ñóótgól (ngól) the act of sewing.

ñóótirde v. sew with.

ñóótól (ngól) sewing; seam; sewing style.

ñootoowo (o) tailor; seamstress.

ñoraade *v.* raise one's clothes up.

norde v. roll/raise someone's clothes.

ñórbólól (ngól) wrinkle; plica. *ñórbolli (di) pl.*

ñórbude v. be wrinkled.

ñórngilaade [ñórⁿgilaade] *v.* show an angry/sad facial expression.

ñorgo *(ngo)* winnow.

ñosde *v.* be cheap. *Omo ñosi* He is cheap.

ñówtude *v.* dress up.

ñoynaade *v.* kneel.

ñoYYere (nde) pressure.

ñóYYitde [ñoYYidde] *v.* release from pressure.

ñóYYude v. apply pressure; compress; press on.

ñuggaade *v.* have one's hair braided temporarily.

ñuggoowo (o) person who provides temporary braiding of hair.

ñuggude v. braid temporarily.

ñukaade *v.* pick up dry wood.

ñukindaade [ñukiⁿdaade] *v.* pick up small dry wood.

ñukkindaade [ñukkiⁿdaade] *v.* spy. *daccu ñukkindaade* Stop spying.

ñukkóndirde [ñukkóⁿdirde] *v.* agglomerate, pile shrubs up.

ñumptaade *v.* whisper.

ñuumbaade [ñuumᵐbaade] *v.* to murmur whisper; sough.

ñuuñde [ñuuñje] *v.* lament.

ñuuñu *(ngu)* ant; pismire; black ant). *warde* ~ stay after eating. *ñuuYi (di) pl.*

ŋ

ablude *v.* yawn.

ablugól *(ngól)* yawn. **ŋaablaali** *(ɗi) pl.*

aaɓaade *v.* 1) be wide open 2) be spoilt.

aaɓal *(ngal)* opening.

aɓde *v.* open wide. **ŋaaɓ hunuko maa Ɔpen** your mouth.

ɓɓitaade *v.* be open wide apart.

ɓɓitde [ŋaɓɓidde] *v.* open wide apart. ~ **ŋunuko** open the mouth wide apart.

aacal *(ngal)* scratch. ~ **battingal** cicatrix.

acde *v.* scratch. *O ŋaaci mo e tiinde* She scratched his face.

acere *(nde)* scratch.

aafde *v.* claw.

aalde *(nde)* piece of watermelon.

aalde *v.* eat water melon.

aañaade *v.* scratch oneself. *Hol ko ŋaañotoɗa* Why are you scratching yourself?

aañande [ŋaañanⁿde] *(nde)* scratch.

aañde [ŋaañje] *v.* scratch.

aasde *v.* scratch.

abbirde *(nde)* ramp; ladder.

abbirde *v.* climb with. ~ *seel* climb with a ladder.

abbude *v.* ascend; climb. ~ *dow haayre* climb a mountain.

abbugól *(ngól)* climbing.

aɗaali *(ɗi)* sounds of the camel.

aɗde [ŋadde] *v.* make the sound of a camel.

addere *(nde)* crack.

addo *(ngo)* half of a cola nut. **ŋaddo ngo ŋónii** One half of the cola nut will suffice.

addude *v.* crack open.

akkere *(nde)* handicap; insufficiency; deficit; shortage. *E ɗen ngóndi e ŋakkere mawnde* We have a major deficit. **ŋakke** *(ɗe). pl.*

akkude *v.* lack; be short of. *Ina ŋakki* It is rare.

akkudi *(ndi)* shortage. **ŋakkule** *(ɗe) pl.*

akkuɗum *adj.* incomplete.

akkugól *(ngól)* deficit; deficiency.

alde *(nde)* space. ~ *mawnde* a bid space.

añňaade *v.* lower one's performance.

ŋappere *(nde)* bite.

ŋappo *adj.* insufficient; short.

ŋappude *v.* bite; have a bite.

ŋappudi *(ndi)* bite. **ŋappule** *(ɗe) pl.*

ŋarɗude *v.* be pretty.

ŋari *(ndi)* appearance. *móƳƳude* ~ be pretty. *bonde* ~ be ugly.

ŋatiwere *(nde)* pain prior to delivery.

ŋarwude *v.* be about to deliver.

ŋarwuɗo *(o)* parturient; person about to deliver. *Ko o ŋarwuɗo* She is about to deliver. **ŋarɗuɓe** *(ɓe) pl.*

ŋatande [ŋatanⁿde] *(nde)* bite.

ŋatde [ŋadde] *v.* 1) bite; tingle 2) be stubborn. *Ndaw ko ŋati* He is so stubborn.

ŋatere *(nde)* bite.

ŋati *(ɗi)* bugs; lice.

ŋatoŋato *(ngo)* insect(s); itching. **ŋatiŋati** *(ɗi) pl.*

ŋayloowo *(o)* climber.

ŋaylude *v.* climb. *O mon ŋayla e lekki* He is climbing up the tree.

ŋeerde *v.* be tight. *Ina ŋeeri* It is tight.

ŋéérnude *v.* tighten.

ŋeewaali *(ɗi)* purrs; baby cries.

ŋeewde *v.* purr; miaow.

ŋefde *v.* gnaw; nibble.

ŋeñde [ŋeñje] *v.* gild; adorn; embellish; decorate.

ŋeñema *(o)* earring. *boornaade* ~ *mum* wear one's earring. **ŋeñemaaji** *(ɗi) pl.*

ŋoɓande [ŋoɓanⁿde] *(nde)* fish bite; bite.

ŋoɓde *v.* bite.

ŋóɓdi *(ndi)* fish bite. **ŋóɓli** *(ɗi) pl.*

ŋómindaade [ŋoɓinⁿdaade] *v.* gnaw; chew at.

ŋolde *v.* nibble; chew at. *E ndun ŋola Ƴiyal ngal* The dog is chewing at the bone.

ŋómsinde *v.* squat.

ŋómsude *v.* flick a finger.

ŋoŋde *v.* be sleepy. *Mbeɗe ŋóŋi* I am sleepy.

ŋóŋgól *(ngól)* sleepiness; somnolence. **ŋóŋɗi** *(ɗi) pl.*

Ŋ̃ooɓde v. 1) make a face 2) be short. wudere ~ a short sarong.

Ŋ̃ooɗde [ŋoodde] v. be tired.

Ŋ̃óótóótu (ngu) bug. Ŋ̃óótóóti (ɗi) pl.

ŋooyre (nde) penis. diidol ~ truth.

Ŋ̃oral (ngal) lower bank of a river. ~ maayo lower bank of the river.

Ŋ̃uccere (nde) pinch. Ŋ̃ucce (ɗe) pl.

Ŋ̃uccude v. pinch. O Ŋ̃ucci mo e jungo She pinched his arm.

Ŋ̃uccugól (ngól) pinching. Ŋ̃uccule (ɗe) pl.

Ŋ̃uceede v. be pinched.

Ŋ̃urtuŋurtu (o) continuous small fights. ɗaccee Ŋ̃urtuŊ̃urtu Stop fighting.

Ŋ̃uslaango (ngo) lament; sigh. Ŋ̃uslaali (ɗi) pl.

Ŋ̃uslere (nde) sigh; lament.

Ŋ̃uslude v. sigh; lament.

Ŋ̃uuñde [ŋuuñje] v. make the cry of the hyena.

Ŋ̃uurde v. growl.

Ŋ̃uylude v. whine.

O

ɔ *det.* the; he; she. *neɗɗo* ~ the person. *O yahii* He left.

ɔɔ *det.* this. ~ *gorko* this man.

ɔɔn *det.* the; that. ~ *neɗɗo* that person. ~ *tuma* at that time.

ɔɗon *pers. pron.* you (plural). *O ɗon njiya* Can you see?

ɔn *pers. pron.* you (pural). *On njettii ma* You have arrived.

ɔnon you (plural).

ókkude *v.* hand over.

ɔlde *v.* loose leaves.

ɔlnde [ol^{n}de] *(nde)* cry.

ɔlowere *(nde)* sweat.

ɔmbaade [óm^{m}baade] *v.* be closed.

ómbirgal [óm^{m}birgal] *(ngal)* cover; lid.

ómbitde [óm^{m}bidde] *v.* open.

ɔmboode [om^{m}boode] *(nde)* lid; cover. *Yitere waɗanaaka omboode* Eyes do not have lids (Nothing is hidden to the eye).

ómbude [óm^{m}bude] *v.* close; cover.

ɔmo *part.*   he/she is. *O mo toon* S/he is there.

ómtude *v.* open.

ɔñde [oñje] *v.* remove grain shells.

ɔoɗaa *det.* that one. ~ *neɗɗo* that person.

ɔoɗoo *det.* this one. ~ *neɗɗo* this person.

ɔogde *v.* extract; rub.

óógirgal *(ngal)* extraction instrument.

ɔogo *(ngo)* extraction.

ɔogore *(nde)* rubbing stone.

ɔolaade *v.* cry.

óólél *(ngél)* echo.

óólɗude *v.* be yellow. *Ina oolɗi* It is yellow.

óólɗuɗum *adj.* yellow.

ɔolo *adj.* yellow.

Óólél *(o)* female first name.

óólél *(ngél)* echo.

ɔoñaade *v.* deviate; be bent; be unjust; be crooked. *O mo ooñii* He is unjust.

ɔoñaare *(nde)* aberrance; injustice.

oɔñde [ooñje] *v.* bend.

óóñiɗum *adj.* crooked; tortuous.

óóñiiɗo *(o)* crook.

óóñtude [óóñcude] *v.* straighten.

óóndu [óó^{n}du] *(ndu)* fish. *O jaggii oondu* He caught the fish called oondu.

oorde *v.* 1) go to pasture; go to graze 2) wander. *O oorii* He is wandering.

oornde [oor^{n}de] *(nde)* herd.

óórnude *v.* drive sheep to pasture. *O oornii nay* He drove the cattle to pasture.

óórtude *v.* return from pasture.

ooTaade *v.* fall.

ooyde *v.* be unwilling to share food.

ooyoowo *(o)* person unwilling to share food. *Ko o ooyoowo* He is unwilling to share his food.

ooyre *(nde)* unwillingness to share food.

oppaaɗo *adj.* feverish. *Kó mi oppaaɗo* I am feverish.

oppere *(nde)* fever. *O mo wondi e oppere* He is feverish.

óppude *v.* be feverish.

ormaade *v.* crush tobacco in one's palm.

ormanke [ormaŋke] *(o)* name used to designate a Haratine individual.

oto *(o)* {fr.} vehicle; car. *dognude* ~ drive a car.

otoraay *(o)* {fr.} train. *ɗannoraade* ~ travel by train.

ottaango [ottaa^{n}go] *(ngo)* groan.

óttude *v.* {fr.} groan.

owde *v.* be troubled.

ówlude *v.* sweat.

ównude *v.* trouble. ~ *hakkille* trouble someone.

oya *det.* that; that one. *neɗɗo* ~ that person.

óynude *v.* hold over fire.

oTTaade *v.* fall.

óTTude *v.* knock down.

P

paabi *(ɗi)* frogs. *faaburu (ndu) sing.*

paaɗɗo *adj.* 1) narrow 2) easily vexed. *Ko o paaɗɗo* He gets angry easily.

paafal *(ngal)* trace left after hoeing.

paalél *(ngél)* small gourd ~ *manna* an individual who gets upset easily. *Ko o paalel manna* He gets upset very easily.

paas *(o)* fare. *yoɓde* ~ *mum* pay one's fare. *Hol no paas o foti* What is the fare? *paasuuji (ɗi) pl.*

paasaase *(o) {fr.}* passenger.

paasde *v. {fr.}* iron. *O woni ko e paasde comci jom suudu makko* He is ironing his wife's clothes.

paasde *v.* {fr.} pass an exam. *O paasii* he passed his examination.

pasioꞁ *(o)* restaurant.

paaspoor *(o) {fr.}* passport.

Paate *(o)* male first name.

paayɗo *adj.* worried. *Aɗa nandi e paayɗo* You look worried.

paaygól (ngól) worry.

paɓɓingól *(ngól)* deferment; postponement; adjournment.

paccirgól *(ngól)* commentary.

paɗal *(ngal)* big shoe.

paɗe (de) shoes. *ɓoortude* ~ take off shoes. *ɓoornaade* ~ wear shoes. *ɓoortu paɗe maa* Take your shoes off. *faɗo (ngo) sing.*

padara *(o)* roll of cloth.

paddagól *(ngól)* ambush; ambuscade.

paggiri *(ndi)* wild millet.

paho *(o)* deaf person. *Ko o paho* He is deaf.

pajaas *(o)* mattress. *pajasuuji (ɗi) pl.*

pak *foc.* used for emphasis; really; completely. *maayde* ~ be really dead.

pakke *(o) {fr.}* liner.

pakket *(o) {fr.}* packet; box. ~ *suukara* a box of sugar.

pakketaaji (ɗi) pl.

palaat *(o) {fr.}* plate.

palal *(ngal)* a long piece of wood used to close a gate.

palanteeje *(ɗe)* windows. *udditde* ~ open the windows. *uddude* ~ close the windows. *falanteere (nde) sing.*

paltu *(o) {wol.}* uniform. *O ɓoorniima paltu makko* He is wearing his uniform.

pamarél *adj.* tiny.

pamaro adj. small; minute. *famɗude v.*

pañe *(o)* basket.

pante *(ɗe)* stripes. *fantere (nde) sing.*

pappaaya *(o)* pawpaw tree.

pappaaye *(o)* pawpaw fruit.

parasseewal *(ngal) {fr.}* umbrella.

parde *v.* {fr.} be ready. *Mi parii* I am ready. *Mi paraani tawo* I am not ready yet.

parti *(o) {fr.}* party. *Kamɓe ngondi e parti gooto* They are members of the same party.

pattuki *(ki)* tree. *pattuɗe (ɗe) pl.*

pawagol *(ngól)* dependence.

peccoowo *(o)* divider.

péccugól (ngól) partition.

péécól (ngól) partition; opening.

peel *(o) {fr.}* shovel. *asirde* ~ dig with a shovel.

peerɗo *adj.* lucid; intelligent. *neɗɗo* ~ a lucid person. *Ko o neɗɗo peerɗo* She is a very intelligent person.

péértuɗo adj. lucid; intelligent.

peesde *v.* {fr.} weigh. *O mon peesa maaro ko* He is weighing the rice.

péésirde v. weigh with.

péésirgal (ngal) scales *peesirɗe* (ɗe) *pl.*

peewal *(ngal)* decency; adequacy.

peewɗo adj. righteous; just; appropriate.

pééwnitaagól (ngól) the act of getting ready; preparation.

pééwnitoowo (o) repair person. ~ *otooji* a mechanic.

peewnoowo (o) maker. ~ *otooji* a car maker.

péllital *(ngal)* decision.

pelloowo *(o)* gunman.

pemboowo [pem^mboowo] *(o)* barber.

peꞁgal *(ngal)* stake; a planted stick; pillar; post. *peꞁɗe (ɗe) pl.*

Penda [pen^nda] *(o)* female first name.

péndél [pé^ndél] *(ngél)* undersarong. *péndélaaji (ɗi) pl.*

pendagól [pen^ndagól] *(ngól)* frost.

pendoowo [pen^ndoowo] *(o)* person who freezes.

penoowo *(o)* liar. *Aan ko a penoowo* You are a liar.

péntiir *(o)* *{fr.}* paint.

péntirde *v.* paint.

péntirgol *(ngól)* painting.

peragol *(ngól)* 1) expense 2) accident. *O mo suusi pere* He spends a lot of money.

perɗo *(o)* immigrant. *Ko o perɗo* He migrated.

pérlél *(ngél)* little hill.

péru *(ngu)* nail.

petto *adj.* single; alone; sole *gooto* ~ one and only.

pewjanoowo *(o)* plotter.

piɓól *(ngól)* knot.

piindi [pii^ndi] *(ndi)* bloom.

pijirgél *(ngél)* toy.

pijoowo *(o)* 1) actor; player 2) prostitute.

piliweer *(o)* *{fr.}* pullover; sweater. *ɓoorno piliweer maa ina jaangi* Wear your sweater because it is cold.

piliyaan *(o)* *{fr.}* deckchair.

pilñitiiɗo *adj.* furious; irate.

pingaade *v.* take a shot; be vaccinated.

pingu [piŋ^ngu] *(o)* 1) safety pin 2) shot. *pinguuji (ɗi) pl.*

pingude [piŋ^ngude] *v.* inject; give a shot. *O pingii mo* He gave him a shot.

pinal *(ngal)* vigilance; awareness; intelligence.

pinɗo *adj.* vigilant; intelligent; awake. *finde v.*

pinnuɗo *adj.* irate.

pinnugól *(ngól)* anger; passion.

pirlu *(ngu)* enclosure.

pittirgal *(ngal)* broom. *pittirɗi (ɗi) pl.*

pittugól *(ngól)* sweeping.

piye *(ɗe)* contributions. *fiyde v.*

poɗɗe *(ɗe)* seeds; pills. *yarde ~ mum* take one's pills. *foɗɗere (nde) sing.*

pógu *(ngu)* shelter. *póguuji (ɗi) pl.*

pokpokolam *(ɗam)* shallow area nearest to the bank. *Haaɗ e pokpokolam ɗam* Stay in the shallow area.

pólis *(o)* *{fr.}* police.

polise *(o)* *{fr.}* a police officer. *Ko o polise* He is a police officer.

pólótigi *(o)* *{fr.}* politics.

pom *(o)* *{fr.}* apple; deck. *Yakkude* ~ eat an apple.

pompe *(ɗe)* *{fr.}* pumps.

pómpude *v.* {fr.} spray.

pómpiteer *(o)* *{fr.}* potato.

póndugól [pón^ndugól] *(ngól)* comparison.

poobaar *(o)* *{fr.}* pepper. *Ina manki poobaar* I need to add more pepper.

póóɗgól *(ngól)* pulling *pooɗoowo (o)* drawer; person who pulls.

póófirgél *(ngél)* comma.

poofoowo *(o)* person who breathes.

poolaaɗo *(o)* defeated person.

pooldo *(o)* winner.

póólgól *(ngól)* victory.

poos *(o)* *{fr.}* pouch; pocket. ~ *julɗo* an empty pocket; a pocket with no money in it. *nder* ~ in the pocket.

pooYɗo *adj.* gaunt; lank; meager; skinny.

póóYtiiɗo *adj.* strict; straight; lawabiding; upright.

porogaraam *(o)* *{fr.}* program. *Hol ko woni porogaraam maa hande* What are you doing today?

portal *(ngal)* straight line / direction.

posone *(o)* *{fr.}* poison. *Ina waɗi posone* It is poisonous.

pot *(o)* *{fr.}* can. ~ *tamaate* a can of tomatoes.

potal *(ngal)* equality accuracy; parity.

pottal *(ngal)* meeting.

puccu *(ngu)* horse. *dognude* ~ ride a horse. *pucci (ɗi) pl.*

pucél *(ngél)* little horse.

pulaagu *(ngu)* Fulani pride.

Pullo *(o)* Fullani; Fula person. *Ko o Pullo* He is Fullani.

pulóók *(o)* cassava; yam.

pundi [pun^ndi] *(ndi)* dust. *Ina heewi pundi* It is dusty.

punaaɗo *(o)* twin.

puniiɗo *(o)* a person who gave birth to twins.

punotooɗo *(o)* person who gives birth to twins.

puñtinaade [puñcinaade] *v.* plunge into deep water.

pur *{fr.}* for.

purayél *(ngél)* little pigeon.

purto *(o)* type of bird **purtóóji** *(ɗi) pl.*

puttere *(nde)* **1)** fart; lie. **2)** nothing. *O andaa puttere* He knows nothing. *putte (ɗe) pl.*

puttoowo (o) liar.

puttude v. fart; lie. *A puttii* you lied.

puuɗdi [puuddi] *(ndi)* henna.

puuntaaɗo *(o)* a deceived individual.

puuntugól (ngól) deceit. *fuunti (o) alt.*

puuyɗo *(o)* stupid person.

puuyndam [puuyⁿdam] *(ɗam)* stupidity.

puƴe *(ɗe)* pimples. *fuƴere (nde) sing.*

puƴel (ngel) small pimple.

puƴoowo *(o)* person who kills lice.

R

raaɓde *v.* contaminate; transmit. *Ko aan raaɓi mi* You are the one who contaminated me.

raaɓeede *v.* be contaminated.

raaɓo *(ngo)* contamination.

raamde *v.* circle; caracole.

raamraamtude *v.* circle; caracole.

raayre *(nde)* nenuphar. *daaye (ɗe) pl.*

rabbere *(nde)* short size.

rabɓiɗde [raɓɓidde] *v.* be short. *Ina rabɓiɗi* It is short.

rabɓiɗinaade *v.* make short; shorten. *Rabɓiɗino* Make your intervention short.

rabɓiɗinde *v.* abbreviate; shorten; condense. ~ *haala* cut (speech) short.

raddo *(ngo)* hunt; hunting *yahde* ~ go hunting. *ɓe njahii raddo* They went hunting.

raddóyde *v.* go hunting. *O raddoyii* He went hunting.

raddude *v.* hunt.

raɗo *(ngo)* tendon; cartilage.

raɗtaade [rattaade] *v.* remove a pot from the stove.

rafde *v.* lack.

rafeede *v.* be sick. ~ *cellal* be sick. *Ko o dafaaɗo* He is sick.

rafi *(o)* illness; sickness. *O mo wondi e rafi* He is sick.

rajo *(ngo) {fr.}* radio. ~ *kankan* hearsay. *udditde* ~ switch the radio on. *ñifde* ~ switch the radio on. *rajóóji (ɗi) pl.*

rakkoor *(o) {fr.}* hose. *roosrude* ~ water with a hose.

ramde *v.* squat.

raŋalde *(nde)* backside. *O fii mo e raŋalde* He hit him on his backside.

raneere *adj.* white. *wudere* ~ white sarong.

ranwinde *v.* bleach; whiten.

ranwude *v.* be white. *Ina ranwi* It is white.

rañ ñeere *(nde)* tuft of grass.

rato *(o) {fr.}* rake. *ratooji (ɗi) pl.*

rawaandu [rawaa^{n}du] *(ndu)* dog; hound. ~ *fétél* trigger.

rawane *(o)* last year. ~ *ndeya* two years ago.

rawtane *(o)* three years ago.

rawtitaane *(o)* four years ago.

rawde *v.* pass.

rayteede *v.* be bewildered.

raytude *v.* bewilder.

raϒϒere *(nde)* tuft of grass.

reɓde *v.* spread. *Ko ko reɓata* It spreads around.

reedeede *v.* be born out of wedlock.

reedde *v.* be pregnant outside of marriage; bear out of wedlock.

réédu *(ndu)* stomach; belly; abdomen. ~ *muusooru* a stomach ache. ~ *mehru* an empty stomach.

réédunte *(o)* woman with pregnancies before marriage.

reenaade *v.* guard against; be careful.

reenande *v.* guard for.

reende *v.* supervise; watch over. ~ *waktu* be punctual. ~ *no feewi* control tightly.

reeneede *v.* be guarded against.

réénnude *v.* allocate; guard against.

réénoyde *v.* go and guard.

reentaade *v.* beware; guard oneself against; be careful. *Reento* Be careful.

rééntinde *v.* 1) warn; caution; forewarn; forestall; alert 2) gather again. *Mi reentinii mo* I warned him.

rééntondirde *v.* avoid one another.

réétude *v.* be skinny.

réftude *v.* follow again; repeat. *Reftu ɗo ndewno ɗaa* Go back the way you came/Repeat what you said.

regaade *v.* be smooth.

regde *v.* move slowly.

régginde *v.* lead; guide.

réggóndirde [réggóndirde] *v.* be aligned; follow one another.

remde *v.* plough; fallow; farm. ~ *ngesa mum* cultivate one's farm; take care of one's own business.

remnaade *v.* be employed as a farmer.

remmeraaɗo *(o)* mother's sister's child.

réndinde [rén^{n}dinde] *v.* 1) unite; blend; collect; compile 2) cause people to quarrel.

réndude [rén^{n}dude] *v.* gather; share.

rééntude *v.* meet; rally; merge; congregate.

reppeende [reppee^{n}de] *(nde)* deliberate offense.

réppude *v.* provoke deliberately.

resde *v.* 1) put aside 2) wed. *O resii* He got married.

resande *v.* marry for. *Mi resanii mo* I married his daughter.

résndude [rés^{n}dude] *v.* 1) to empower; entrust 2) keep.

rewanke [rewaᶅke] *(o)* northerner.

rewo *(ngo)* North. *huccude* ~ go north. *huccitde* ~ face north.

rewɓe *(ɓe)* women. ~ *mawɓe* old women. *debbo (o)* sing.

réwru *(ndu)* female. *rawaandu* ~ a female dog.

rewde *v.* 1) follow; persist; conform; pursue; revere; venerate 2) owe. ~ *laawol* be straight; be law-abiding.

reweede *v.* owe.

réwnude *v.* make something pass through and opening.

rewtaade *v.* follow one's footsteps again. *reftaade alt.*

ribaa *(o)* illicit profit(s)

riddo *(ngo)* chase.

riddude *v.* chase.

rido *(o) {fr.}* curtain. *tellinde* ~ lower the curtain. *ridooji (ɗi) pl.*

riiɗde [riidde] *(nde)* fart.

riiɗde [riidde] *v.* fart.

riimde *v.* tell lies.

riis *(o)* saw.

riiwde *v.* banish; dispel; expel; revoke; evict; drive off.

riiweede *v.* be revoked; be expelled. *O riiwaama ekkol* He was banned from school.

riiwoyde *v.* go and ban someone.

rimare *adj.* barren (use restricted to animals, cows specially).

rimde *v.* give birth (use restricted to animals).

rimɗinde *v.* free a slave; emancipate; abolish slavery; decolonize. ~ *jiyaaɗo* free a slave.

rimɗineede *v.* be freed.

rimɗude *v.* be noble.

rimndude [rim^{n}dude] *v.* load an animal. *dimngal (ngal) n.*

rimtude *v.* unload. ~ *dimngal* unload/to remove from the back of an animal. *dimtugol (ngól) n.*

rippó *(ngo)* dance.

rippude *v.* strike one's foot/feet on the ground.

roɓaande [roɓaa^{n}de] *(nde)* ears of millet gathered on the ground.

róɓtude *v.* pick millet ears gathered on the ground.

róbiné *(o) {fr.}* faucet; tap.

róggude *v.* strike on the head with the fist.

rojde [rojje] *v.* go early in the morning.

rókkude *v.* donate; provide; give.

rókkitde [rókkidde] *v.* give again.

ronde *v.* bequeath; inherit.

rónnude *v.* make someone inherit one's property.

ronkere [roᶅkere] *(nde)* poverty; inaptitude. *Sinno wonaano roᶅkere mami arane* If I had the means I would come for you.

rónkitde [róᶅkidde] *v.* be completely unable to perform.

rónkude [róᶅkude] *v.* be incapable of.

roondaade [roo^{n}daade] *v.* carry on the head. ~ *ko teddi* carry a heavy load.

roontaade *v.* 1) go the opposite direction of the current 2) take a load off; unload.

roosde *v. {fr.}* sprinkle; water. *O mon roosa huɗo ko* He is watering the grass.

rosaade *v.* lose one's hair. *Hoore makko rosiima* He is bald.

roso *(ngo)* disease that makes hair fall off.

rotere *(nde)* backside; buttock.

rottande *v.* serve food for someone.

róttude *v.* serve food. *Rottu min keyɗii* Serve the food, we are hungry.

róytude *v.* be burned out.

rubbere *(nde)* fruit.

ruɓde *v.* advance slowly.

rubundere [rubu^{n}dere] *(nde)* animal waste. *dubuuje (ɗe) pl.*

rufde *v.* 1) spill 2) throw away; dump. ~ *Ɲii Ɲam* bleed; cause someone to bleed.

rufo *(ngo)* overflow.

ruggude *v.* grind.

rujjaade *v.* strike with the head.

rullinde *v.* catch with a trap; entrap. *O rullinii sondu* He caught a bird with a trap.

rumtaade *v.* turn one's back.

ruŋaade *v.* leave a habit.

rungaade [ruŋⁿgaade] *v.* carry on the head without a head pad.

rungere [ruŋⁿgere] *(nde)* beehive.

ruttaade *v.* recede; retreat; return to a place. *Rutto toon* Go back there.

ruttitaade v. go back again.

ruttude v. 1) vomit 2) reimburse; refund; give change 3) repel. ~ *kaalis* give change back.

ruuɓde *v.* frighten.

ruuɗaade *v.* parry; duck down.

ruudde *v.* lag behind; linger; waddle; toddle; go slowly. *O mo ruudi* He is so slow.

ruufde *v.* do final pounding of (millet).

ruukde *v.* be noisy.

ruulde *(nde)* cloud. *duule (ɗe) pl.*

ruumde *v.* spend the rains; spend a long time.

ruy *(o)* thin and light porridge.

ruyde *v.* start going; move off.

S

saakaade *v.* be scattered; pervade; be destroyed.

saakde *v.* spread.

saaktaade *v.* be revealed. *Sirru o saaktiima* The secret has been revealed.

saaktude *v.* reveal. ~ *sirru* reveal a secret.

saakit *(o)* net.

saak *(o) {fr.}* bag; sack. ~ *maaro* a bag of rice. *saakuuji (ɗi) pl.*

saalde *v.* be unable to make a sound.

saalitde [saalidde] *v.* forget.

saamde *v.* fall. *ɗum saamii* It fell off.

saan *(o)* taenia; worm.

saañde [saañje] *v.* to be voracious; have a huge appetite.

saanga [saaⁿga] *(o)* period; moment; date; advent. *oon* ~ at that particular moment. ~ *e saangaaji* the old good days. *saangaaji (ɗi) pl.*

saaño *(ko)* husks; bran; husk; hull; pericarp.

saanóyde *v.* go to tether out.

saare *(nde)* town; village.

saasde *v.* have energy. *O mo saasi no feewi* He is full of energy.

saawandere [saawaⁿdere] *(nde)* dew.

saawde *v.* tie in a bundle.

saawdu (ndu) bundle.

saayaande [saayaaⁿde] *(nde)* bundle of hair. *ustude* ~ *mun* get a haircut.

saayde *v.* melt away; pass without breaking (storm). *Yiiwoonde nde saayii* The clouds gathered but it did not rain.

saayngo [saayⁿgo] *(ngo).* melting.

saaynude *v.* melt; dissolve.

saaynaade *v.* pick one's fiancee.

saaytinde *v.* make disappear.

saaysaaye *(o)* thug. *Ko o saaysaaye* He is a thug.

sabaabu *(o) {ar.}* cause. ~ *nde maa* thanks to you.

sabu (o) cause; sake.

sabba (o) about; skirt. ~ *waktuuji ɗiɗi* about two hours.

sabbinde *v.* nestle.

sabbbitde [sabbidde] *v.* remove from a nest.

sabbundu [sabbuⁿdu] *(ndu)* nest.

sabbitaade *v.* make an unhappy sound with the tongue; refuse.

sabbitde *v.* rinse; wash millet.

sabburlere (nde) fruit.

sadak *(o) {ar.}* alms; charity; sacrifice. *rokkude* ~ give charity. *sadakeeji (ɗi) pl.*

sadde [sadde] *v.* be difficult. *ina saɗi* it is difficult.

saɗnude [saannude] *v.* complicate.

saɗre (nde) difficulty; rarity.

saɗtinde [sattinde] *v.* 1) rarify 2) complicate.

saɗtude [sattude] *v.* be difficult; be rare. *Ina saɗti* It is hard to find.

saɗiwere (nde) ringworm.

safaara *(o)* medicine; remedy; cure. *ɗum alaa safaara* There is no cure for it.

safrorde (nde) hospital.

safrotooɓe (ɓe) patients. *cafrotooɗo (o) sing.*

safrude *v.* nurse; treat; cure. ~ *mo sellaani* treat a patient. ~ *kaaɗi* treat mental illness.

safde *v.* be tasty. ~ *lamɗam* have enough salt. *Ina safi* It is tasty.

safnude *v.* make tasty; sweeten.

saftude *v.* be too spicy; be tasteless. *ɗum saftii* It is too spicy.

saftaade *v.* fish. *wandaade alt.*

sagata *(o)* young man; adolescent. *sagataaɓe (ɓe) pl.*

sagginde *v.* start cooking. *Saggin ko mbaawɗaa ɓendinde* Start what you can finish.

saggitde *v.* 1) unhook 2) remind.

saggitorde (nde) dictionary. ~ *Pulaar* a Pulaar dictionary. *Yeew ɗum e nder saggitorde nde* Look it up in the dictionary.

saggude *v.* 1) be hanging 2) forget.

sago *(o)* desire. *sinno ko* ~ I wish I.

sahaa *(o)* period; moment; date; instant. ~ *sahaa* frequently; every now and then. ~ *kala* every time. *oon* ~ at that time. *sahaaji (ɗi) pl.*

sahde [saade] *v.* roast; fry. ~ *liɗɗi* fry fish.

saka *conj.* so that.

sake *(o)* warehouse. *sakééji (ɗi) pl.*

kkaade v. 1) give charity 2) be underneath. *Sakko jelotooɗo o* Give charity to the beggar.

kkóyaade v. go and give charity.

kke *(o)* leather worker; shoemaker. *Ko o akke* She belongs to the leather worker caste. *sakkeeɓe (ɓe) pl.*

kkitaade v. be last.

kkitóyaade v. go to meet someone again.

kkude v. 1) place below 2) wear under.

kkoos *(o) {fr.}* handbag. *weelnaade ~* old a bag.

la *(ka)* bridge. *salaaji (ɗi) pl.*

laade v. object; refute; abstain. *Salaade o waawaa jeyaaka e mbaaɗdaagu* Limiting oneself to what one can do is not a sign of weakness.

laare *(nde)* refusal; objection.

ltintinaade v. pretend to refuse.

laatu *(o)* prayer.

lɓaade v. lap.

lde *(nde)* junction.

llifana *(o)* two o'clock prayer time.

lligaade v. do one's ablution. *Salligo hadee maa juulde* Do your ablution before you say your prayers.

llige *(o)* ablution.

lminaango [salminaa^{n}go] *(ngo)* greeting.

lminde v. greet; salute. *Neɗɗo salminirta ko jungo ñaamo* You greet with the right hand.

lmitaade v. return greetings *Salmito mo* Return his greetings.

lnde [sal^{n}de] *(nde)* junction; confluent.

lndu [sal^{n}du] *(ndu)* branch; fork; a pillar. *calɗi (ɗi) pl.*

ltude v. branch off.

amba [sam^{m}ba] male first name.

amba tali [sam^{m}batali] *(o)* caterpillar; tractor.

amme *(o)* millet. *aawde ~* sow millet.

ammeere *(nde)* ear (of millet stalk). *~ jungo* wrist.

amminde v. drop; knock off.

ammitde v. remove poison.

ammitooɓe *(ɓe)* people who remove poison. *cammitoowo (o) sing.*

ammude v. knock fruit off trees. *Sammu ko njey ɗaa* take what belongs to you.

sammunde [sammun^{n}de] *(nde)* hedgehog.

samorde v. feel better; be better. *Mi samorii* I feel better.

sampaade v. thresh; separate.

samre *(nde)* chicken pox pimple.

sanajida *(o)* idolater.

sanam *(o)* idol; totem; fetish.

sandólicɗde [san^{n}dólidde] v. be stubborn; be rude. *A ɗa sandoliɗi* You are impolite.

sangalde [saŋ^{n}galde] *(nde)* porcupine.

sangara [saŋ^{n}gara] *(o)* beer; liquor; wine. *jaroowo ~* a drunkard.

sañde [sañje] v. weave; knit.

sañtaade [sañcaade] v. to undo one's hair.

sañtude [sañcude] v. to undo someone's hair.

saŋo *(o)* thorn fence.

saŋre *(nde)* hunchback.

sapato *(ko)* plant.

sappaade v. ready oneself for a battle.

sappaare *(nde)* brushwood.

sappoɓo *(o)* the tenth in rank.

sappo *num.* ten. *~ e jóy* fifteen. *~ e jééɗiɗi* seventeen. *~ e ɗiɗi* dozen.

sappóɓinde v. multiply tenfold; be ten years old.

sappinaade v. point.

sappórdu *(ndu)* forefinger.

sappitaade v. lay mud balls on a wall. *O woni ko e sappitaade* He is laying mud on the wall.

saqqa *(o) {ar.}* problem; need. *Holi saqqa maa* What do you need?.

sara *(o)* side; near; brink; vicinity; aside; nearby; edge. *~ makko* next to him. *saraaji (ɗi) pl.*

saraade v. be dispersed; be scattered.

sarde v. scatter. *~ yimɓe* create confusion/animosity amongst individuals.

sarbet *(o) {fr.}* towel.

sardiŋe *(o) {fr.}* garden. *roosde ~* water a garden.

saret *(o) {fr.}* cart.

sarfaade v. have a splinter.

sarfude v. cut a splinter.

sariya *(o)* islamic law.

sarwiis *(o) {fr.}* service.

sarwude v. *{fr.}* to serve.

sasa *(o)* leather bag. *sasaaji (ɗi) pl.*

sataade *v.* set a child across legs to urinate or defecate.

satalla *(ka)* kettle. *satallaaji (ɗi) pl.*

satde *v.* court.

satigi *(o)* king's title.

sawndaade [sawⁿdaade] *v.* be adjacent to.

sawndo [sawⁿdo] *(ngo)* side; nearby.

sawndóndirde [sawⁿdóⁿdirde] *v.* be next to each other.

sawru *(ndu)* stick. ~ *tuggortééndu* cane. *cabbi (ɗi) pl.*

sayeede *v.* be rabid. *rawaandu sayaandu* a rabid dog.

sayo *(ngo)* rabies.

saygalaare *(nde)* music.

sayyaade *v.* swing. *O woni ko e sayyaade* He is swinging.

sebbe *(ɓe)* warrior caste. *Ko ɓe sebbe* They belong to the warrior caste. *ceɗɗo (o) sing.*

sebde *v.* be slightly more than. *Ko kanko seb maa* He is a little bit taller than you.

seɗɗaade *v.* be strong.

seɗde [sedde] *v.* separate (bran & flour); sift.

seebde *v.* 1) be sharp 2) be intelligent; be perceptive. *Ndaw ko seeɓi* He is very perceptive.

séébnude *v.* sharpen.

seeɓre *(nde)* intelligence; sharpness.

seedaade *v.* witness; certify; attest; testify.

seede *(o)* witness. *Ko kanko woni seede am* He is my witness.

seedere *(nde)* cowrie shell.

seeɗa *(o)* few; scant; slight; bit; little. *seeɗa seeɗa* little by little.

seeɗde [seedde] *v.* spend the dry season.

sééɗirde *(nde)* camp for dry season.

seekande *v.* buy new clothing for. *Seekan mo wutte* Buy him a new gown.

seekande [seekaⁿde] *(nde)* tear.

seekde *v.* tear; mangle; rip.

seekoode *(nde)* notch.

seelde *v.* cut into strips.

sééltude *v.* Subdivide into smaller parts.

seeno *(ngo)* sandy area.

seerde *v.* separate; divorce; dissociate.

seereede *v.* 1) be divorced 2) be constipated.

séérndude [séérⁿdude] *v.* distinguish; separate; discriminate; sort. ~ *goonga e fenaande* tell right from wrong.

séértude *v.* be separated again; diverge; differ; part.

sééréér *(o)* individual from the Serer ethnic group.

seernaade *v.* be religious.

seese *adv.* slowly; softly; carefully *waarude.* ~ do gently.

sefaade *v.* loose fiber.

sefde *v.* draw up; lift up.

seggude *v.* filter.

sehde [seede] *v.* carve.

séhil *(o)* friend; ally; pal.

séhilaaɓe *(ɓe)* friends.

sekde *v.* be angry; be upset. *Ko o cekɗo* He is angry.

seknoraade *v.* scoff; deride; make fun of.

séknude *v.* upset; vex. *Ko kanko sekni mi* He got me upset.

sekre *(nde)* anger.

sekkaade *v.* carry on the side; hide.

sekkere *(nde)* cheek.

sekko *(ngo)* fence of woven reed; woven reed.

sélbude *v.* be thin/light (liquid).

selde *v.* 1) branch 2) be abnormal; get out of the way; go aside.

sélnude *v.* divert.

séllinde *v.* heal.

séllitde [séllidde] *v.* be well again.

séllude *v.* be well; be healed; recover. *O sellii* He has recovered from his illness.

sembaade [semᵐbaade] *v.* wash one's feet.

sembaan [semᵐbaan] *(o)* tall grass that grows on lower grounds.

sembe [semᵐbe] *(o)* force; vigor; strength. *jogaade* ~ be strong.

sémbinde [sémᵐbinde] *v.* fortify.

semteende *(nde)* lie.

sémtinde *v.* shame someone.

sémtude *v.* lie.

sende *v.* castrate.

sengo [seŋgo] *(ngo)* side; part.

seŋaade *v.* be hooked.

eŊde v. 1) join 2) put bait on the hook; affix.

éŊóndirde [séŊóⁿdirde] v. adjoin; connect.

éŊóndireede [séŊóⁿdireede] v. be joined.

éŊtude v. disjoin; disconnect.

éŊlude v. ring; toll.

éngu [seŊⁿgu] (o) {fr.} zinc leaf.

erde v. join; nibble.

érééndu [sérééⁿdu] (ndu) sunbeam; gleam; ray.

érkitde [sérkidde] v. laugh loudly.

érndu [sérⁿdu] (ndu) flute.

ertaade v. stretch.

ete (o) caravan. **sétééji** (ɗi) pl.

etéwól (ngól) a long caravan.

etto (ngo) sharpening.

éttude v. peel; pare.

ewde v. be thin. *O mo sewi* He is thin.

ewnde [sewⁿde] (nde) spring of water; water source.

éybude v. be pretty.

eytaane (o) {ar.} demon; devil.

i if.

iɓaade v. measure by spans.

iɓatinde [siɓatinⁿde] (nde) span.

iɓatindu [siɓatinⁿdu] (ndu) pinky.

iɓre (nde) span.

iɓɓere (nde) leftover.

iɓɓitde [siɓɓidde] v. pour.

iɓɓude v. pour.

iccere (nde) odd smell.

iccude v. smell odd. *Ina sicci* It smells odd.

idere (nde) carp.

ifaa (o) {ar.} description; type; kind; sort. *sifaaji* (ɗi) pl.

ifaade v. describe; depict. *A ɗa waawi sifaade mo* Can you describe him?.

iftinde v. remind. *Siftin am* Remind me.

iftorde v. remember; recollect; recall. *A siftorii* Do you remember?

iftoreede v. be remembered.

igaret (o) {fr.} cigarette.

ige (o) feather.

iiɓaade v. suck.

iidaade v. joke with.

iido (ngo) joke.

iifde v. ratify.

siikaango [siikaaⁿgo] (ngo) squeak.

siikde v. scream; squeak.

siiltude v. cease to rain. *Toɓo ngo siiltii* The rain has stopped.

siimtinde v. strain; drain away; drip.

siimtude v. drop; strain; trickle; drip.

siiñde [siiñje] v. bare teeth. ~ *ñii Ye mum* show one's teeth.

siiraŊ (o) seat.

siirde v. {fr.} be sure; be true.

siirtaade v. flee; swim fast.

siirtude v. cut meat by strips.

siiwde v. strain; pour; pour out.

siiweede v. be strained; be poured; be poured out.

siiwtude v. drain; decant; filter.

siiwre (nde) grass.

sikaade v. peck.

sikke (o) thought; opinion. *alaa* ~ no doubt.

sikkeede v. be a suspect.

sikkitaade v. suspect; doubt; have a hunch.

sikkude v. believe; think; presume; guess; suppose.

siko conj. but.

silaama (ka) sword.

silkitde [silkidde] v. cut into pieces.

simaa (o) {fr.} cement. *simoŊ* (o) alt.

simbude [simᵐbude] v. play the fiddle.

simis (o) {fr.} shirt. *simisaaji* (ɗi) pl.

simmaade v. smoke. *O mo simmoo* He smokes.

simme (o) tobacco. *ɗaccude* ~ quit smoking.

sinamaa (o) {fr.} movie. *yahde* ~ go to the movies.

siñtaan [siñcaan] (o) newly built village.

siñtude [siñcude] v. build a new village/compound.

sinde v. fix.

sindere [sinⁿdere] (nde) 1) tree fruit 2) extra organ.

sindude [sinⁿdude] v. fix to; tie to; follow; tow.

sinkaade [siŋkaade] v. adorn oneself.

sinkude [siŋkude] v. decorate; embellish; gild; adorn.

singóndirde [siŊⁿgóⁿdirde] v. to place each other's arms on shoulders.

singoore [siŋŋoore] *(nde)* cluster of (e.g. fruit).

sinno if only.

sippirde v. wrestle.

sippiro (ngo) wrestling.

sippirooɓe *(ɓe)* wrestlers.

sippooɓe *(ɓe)* people who buy or sell milk.

sippoyde v. go and buy or sell milk.

sippude v. buy or sell milk.

siññere *(nde)* shaking.

siññude v. shake; tremble; quake; flicker; quiver; shiver; thrill.

siññinde v. shake.

sippude v. buy milk.

Sira *(o)* female first name.

sirande [sirandе] *(nde)* bark removal.

sirde v. tear strips.

sirme *(o)* oil.

sirŋinaade v. be upset; be defiant.

siro *(ko)* strip.

siro   (o) *{fr.}* syrup.

sirpaade v. jump down.

sirƴude v. spit through the teeth.

sisó *(o) {fr.}* scissors. *ta ƴirde* ~ cut with scissors.

sitde [sidde] v. protect.

siwil *(o) {fr.}* civilian.

siwó   (o) *{fr.}* bucket; pail.

siwrude v. be drunk.

siyde v. leak. *Inan siya* It is leaking. *ciyam (ɗam)*.

so *conj.* if.

sóɓɓundu [sóɓɓundu] *(ndu)* clitoris.

soɓde v. be a nuisance; be useless.

soɓe (o) soil.

soble *(ɗe)* onions.

soblere *(nde)* onion.

soccaade v. brush clean.

sóccudde v. rub; scratch clean. ~ *ñii ƴe* brush teeth.

sodo *(ko)* plant.

sófru *(ndu)* chick.

sóftikinaade v. exercise.

sóftude v. be willing to exercise.

sóftinde v. exercise.

sóggude v. drive cattle.

sogone *(o)* length of arm from the elbow to the tip of the middle finger.

sohre [soore] *(nde)* viper.

sójjude v. be dry. *Mi sojjii* I am dry.

sokde v. lock; latch.

sokeede v. be locked. *Ko o cokaaɗo* He is in prison.

sóktude v. unlock.

sokkaade v. be crushed.

sókkude v. pound millet/corn stalks.

sokkola *(o) {fr.}* chocolate.

sokla *(o)* need; necessity. *Hol ko woni sokla maa* What do you need?

sóklude v. need; necessitate. *Mbeɗe soklu maa* I need you.

sokna *(o)* address for a woman.

soko *conj.* if.

solaade *(nde)* funnel.

soldaat *(o) {fr.}* serviceman; soldier.

solande v. remove a tooth for someone.

solde v. come out of; take out; remove. ~ *ñiire mum* have one's tooth out.

sólima *(o)* uncircumcised person.

sollaaru *(ndu)* dust.

solléwól *(ngól)* rolled fabric. *solleeji (ɗi) pl.*

solom *(o)* pipe; hose. *solomaaji (ɗi) pl.*

sombe [somᵐbe] *(o)* tool for digging.

sómpude v. establish.

somre *(nde)* roach.

sónkude [sóŋkude] v. quarrel.

sondaade [sondaade] v. choke.

sóndude [sondude] v. choke someone.

sondeel [sondeel] *(o) {fr.}* candle. *huɓɓude* ~ light a candle.

sondu [sóndu] *(ndu)* bird.

songo [soŋŋgo] *(ngo)* hunting; seizing; seizure.

sóngude [sóŋŋgude] v. seize a prey.

sontaade v. talk back; respond with no respect.

sontiŋ *(o)* type of bird.

soñde [soñje] to harvest; reap.

soñe *(nge)* cow.

sóññude v. make a light noise.

soodde v. purchase; buy.

soódnude v. make someone purchase something.

sóódtude [sóóttude] *v.* to redeem; buy back; buy from.

soodaade *v.* wash one's hands.

soofde *v.* be tasteless; urinate.

sóófnude *v.* 1) moisten; soak; wet 2) trivialize.

soolde *(nde)* penis.

soomaade *v.* wrap oneself up.

soomde v. wrap up; pack; envelop.

sooñde [sooñje] *v.* lack water.

sooño (ngo) dearth; hardship; water shortage; drought.

sooraade *v.* walk everywhere. ~ *wuru* walk all around the town.

soorde *v.* pour in a cooking pot.

sóórtude *v.* take out.

sóóró *(o)* minaret.

soos *(o)* *{fr.}* ragout; sauce.

sootaade *v.* weed.

sooye *(o)* silk.

sóóydude v. be fawn-colored.

sooyde *v.* be unwed for a long time.

sooynaade *v.* sight; catch sight of from far away.

sooynde [sooynde] *(nde)* open land.

sóóyru *(ndu)* parrot.

sópónduru [sóppónduru] *(ndu)* tree.

soppande [soppande] *(nde)* cut; slash.

sóppude v. 1) hack; cut; chop 2) bite.

sóppinaade *v.* squat.

sóppunde [sóppunde] *(nde)*   squat.

sorbo *(ngo)* courtship.

sórbude v. court.

sorbinaade *v.* put water in one's nostrils.

sórbóndirde [sórbóndirde] *v.* follow one another.

sórbude *v.* smell bad.

sorde *v.* creep under.

sorkaade v. enter; be inserted.

sorkeede v. be inserted.

sorkude v. make enter; insert.

sórnude v. place under/in.

sórsórtude v. go in and out repeatedly.

sortaade v. escape; slip away; withdraw; sneak out.

sórtude v. extract.

sóriwal *(ngal)* fish spear.

sórmitaade v. dress up; be elegant.

sórmitde [sórmidde] *v.* dress a person up.

sosaade *v.* be agitated.

sosde v. agitate; innovate; found; originate; begin.

sóttinde *v.* complete the shelling of grains.

sóttude v. pound grain (to remove the cover); shell grains by pounding.

sowaade *v.* be folded.

sowande [sowande] *(nde)* fold. *sowde v.* 1) fold; sag 2) multiply.

sowoore (nde) agnomen; euphemism; nickname.

sówti *(o)* insect. *sówtiiji (di) pl.*

soYYaade *v.* be broken.

soYYude v. break.

subaka *(o)* *{fr.}* forenoon; morning. *hande* ~ this morning. *subakaaji (di) pl.*

subalbe *(be)* fishermen *cubballo (o) sing.*

subaade *v.* choose; pick out; select; elect.

subde v. choose; pick up.

subngo (ngo) selection; choice.

suddaade *v.* cover oneself.

suddaare (nde) cover.

sudditde [suddidde] *v.* Uncover; expose.

suddude v. marry; cover someone. *O suddii* He has gotten married.

sudaade *v.* wear jewelery; adorn oneself.

sufde *v.* pick.

suftude v. extract.

suka *(o)* 1) child; kid 2) lover; mistress. ~ *debbo* girl. ~ *gorko* boy. *sukaabe (be) pl.*

sukkitaade *v.* be open.

sukkitde [sukkidde] *v.* open; uncork; clean holes out.

sukkoode (nde) cork.

sukkude v. 1) plug; cork; block up; cover 2) be next 3) be thick.

suknaade *v.* have a mistress.

sukñude *v.* be greedy.

sukuña (o) witch.

sukundu [sukundu] *(ndu)* hair.

sulle *(o)* loser. *sulleebe (be) pl.*

sulmaade *v.* wash one's face.

sulmude v. wash someone's face.

sumalle *(o)* gourd made of goat, sheep or lamb skin. *sumalléeji (di) pl.*

sumande [sumande] *(nde)* burn.

sumde v. burn.

sumeede v. be burnt.

sumbaade [sum^mbaade] v. take snuff.

sumbude [sum^mbude] v. dance.

suna *(o)* millet.

sunaade v. mourn; grieve; be sad.

sunaare v. chagrin; distress; mourning; sorrow.

suñtude [suñcude] v. to stack.

sunka [suŋka] *(o)* animal.

sunnaade v. spy.

sunnude v. taste good.

suntude v. slap.

suppitaade v. come up to surface; emerge; resurface.

suppome *(o)* cabbage.

suraade v. be protected.

surde v. hedge; prevent; stop.

surɓaade v. sip.

surga *(o)* young male; lad; chap; teenager.

suro *(ngo)* retaining of a person.

suruundu [suruu^ndu] *(ndu)* bag.

susde v. sniff.

susnaade v. sniff.

sutde [sudde] v. add.

sutu *(o)* group of shrubs. *sutuuji (ɗi) pl.*

suuɗaade v. hide oneself.

suuɗde [suudde] v. hide; veil; conceal; dissimulate.

suuɗeede v. be protected.

suuɗorde (nde) hideout; shelter; hiding place; chache.

suudu cabin; bedroom. *jom* ~ wife.

suufa *(o)* servant.

suukara *(o) {fr.}* sugar. ~ *wonni* vanilla sugar.

suulde v. defecate.

suumde v. cover the mouth.

suuméé *(o)* tattoo.

suumko *(ngo)* whiskers.

suumtaade v. suffer from overwork.

suumtude v. cause someone to suffer due to overwork.

suunde [suun^de] *(nde)* secret.

suuraade v. be protected; be statisfied.

suuraare (nde) protection; satisfaction.

suurde v. protect.

suurndu [suur^ndu] *(ndu)* cloud.

suuróndirde [suuró^ndirde] v. protect each other.

suurtaade v. be uncovered; be unprotected.

suurtude v. 1) reveal 2) be steam cooked.

suurkude v. smoke; fume.

suurtinde v. steam.

suurtinirde (nde) utensil for steaming food.

suurtude v. be rightly cooked; be steamed.

suusde v. dare; be brave.

suutaade v. leave one's husband's compound after a dispute.

suutde [suudde] v. raise; uplift; lift.

suuteede v. be lifted.

suuwde v. dip.

suwaa *imperf.* not yet; time is not up yet. ~ *tawo* not yet.

suwde v. dip.

suyde v. vaporize; evaporate.

T

abal *(ngal) {fr.}*.

abbaaje *(ki)* tree.

aɓaade *v.* step over something.

aɓande [taaɓanⁿde] *(nde)* stride. ~ *mawnde* a long stride.

adere *(nde)* grass used for animal consumption. *taade (ɗe) pl.*

akinaade *v.* pace slowly.

alde *v.* put oil in a pan.

alnande [taalnanⁿde] *(nde)* wound.

alnande *v.* inflict a wound on behalf of someone.

alnude *v.* wound.

alól *(ngól)* tale.

amaade *v. [ar.}* do ablutions with sand or a stone.

amaamuya *(o) {ar.}* ablutions performed with a stone or sand.

amorde *(nde)* stone used for ablution.

amotooɗo *(o)* person who performs ablutions with a stone or sand.

aniraaɗo *(o)* 1) grandchild 2) grandparent. ~ *gorko* grandfather. ~ *debbo* female grandmother.

ara *(o)* concubine. *taaraaɓe (ɓe) pl.*

araade *v.* 1) besiege; surround; circumvent 2) urinate. *ɗoo taaretaake* It is forbidden to urinate here.

arol *(ngol)* scenic route.

arorde *(nde)* restroom.

areede *v.* be surrounded.

arnude *v.* surround.

artaaról *(ngól)* scenic route.

artóyaade *v.* take a scenic route.

artude *v.* remove a fence.

asa *(ka)* bowl. *taasaaji (ɗi) pl.*

asande [taasanⁿde] *(nde)* lighter.

aske *(o)* religious holiday.

asnude *v.* polish.

astaade *v.* lay mud.

asto *(ngo)* laying of mud/cement on a wall/roof.

ataade *v.* trip; slide; slip. *O taati* He slipped.

atde [taadde] *v.* be slippery. *Ina taati* It is slippery.

taaynude *v.* cause to melt. ~ *nebam* melt butter.

taayre *(nde)* melting.

tabalde *(nde)* big bass drum. *fiide* ~ hit/play a big bass drum.

tabitde *v.* happen; be true.

taɓɓere *(nde)* waterlily.

taɓɓital *(ngal)* the third.

taɓɓitde [taɓɓidde] *v.* triple.

taɓɓitgal *(ngal)* the third.

taccude *v.* cross a river. *O taccii maayo ngo* He crossed the river.

taɗɗude *v.* jump over.

tafde *v.* forge. ~ *jawo* make a bracelet.

tafngo [tafⁿgo] *(ngo)* manner of forging; the making of metal products.

tafsiiru *(o)* commentary; translation.

tagaaɗo *(o)* human being.

tagande [taganⁿde] *(nde)* volume of a book.

tagde *v.* create. *Ko Alla tag maa* Allah created you.

tagdeede *v.* be fully created.

tagdude *v.* create simultaneously.

tagóódi *(ndi)* state; shape.

tagoore *(nde)* creation.

tagoowo *(o)* creator.

taggéé *(o)* death message broadcast on radio.

taggere *(nde)* something that is rolled.

taggude *v.* 1) roll up 2) close up.

takkaade *v.* stick to; stick oneself to.

takkél *(ngél)* little paw.

takkere *(nde)* claw; paw.

takkitde [takkidde] *v.* remove stick; unstick.

takko fringe; near; beside. ~ *maayo* near the river.

takkóndirde [takkóⁿdirde] *v.* agglutinate; get close.

takkórdi *(ndi)* stick.

takkude *v.* 1) stick 2) accuse. ~ *fenaande* make a false accusation.

Takko *(o)* female first name.

taksi *(o) {fr.}* taxi. *jolde e* ~ take a taxi.

taktako *(o)* person with leprosy.

taktakri *(ndi)* lion. *mbaroodi* ~ a lion.

tal *adv.* very white. *ranwude* ~ be very white.

talaata *(o)* Tuesday. *Hande ko talaata* Today is Tuesday.

talde *v.* cut a big piece of raw meat.

talde (nde) big piece of raw meat.

talkuru *(ndu)* charm.

talla *(o)* pillow.

tallaade *v.* roll.

tallande [tallanⁿde] *(nde)* roll.

tallinde *v.* cause to roll.

talloowo *(o)* person who rolls something.

tallorde *(nde)* place for rolling.

tallude *v.* roll.

tamande [tamanⁿde] *(nde)* handful; grip.

tamaroore *(nde)* date.

tamaróówi *(ki)* date tree.

tamatere *(nde)* *{fr.}* tomato. *tamate (ɗe) pl.*

tambaade [tamᵐbaade] *v.* carry in one's palm.

tambaɠ [tamᵐbaɠ] fish.

tamde *v.* hold with closed fingers; have a grip.

tamgól (ngól) grip.

tame *(o)* sieve. *tamééji (ɗi) pl.*

tampande *v.* work hard for. ~ *hoore mum* work for oneself.

tampere (nde) fatigue; tiredness. *wondude e* ~ be tired.

tampinde *v.* make someone tired; wear someone out. *A tampinii mo* You got him tired.

tampinoowo (o) a difficult individual.

tampude *v.* be tired. *Mi tampii* I am tired.

tampuɗo adj. weary; tired. *Ko mi tampuɗo* I am tired.

tamsindaade [tamsinⁿdaade] *v.* squeeze.

tamulde *(nde)* chiefs drum.

tan *foc.* only; alone. *aan* ~ you only.

tana *(o)* trouble. *ɗum alaa tanaa* It is no trouble. *tanaaji (ɗi) pl.*

tanka [taɠka] *(o)* smallest money unit. *tankaaji (ɗi) pl.*

tankere [taɠkere] *(nde)* load.

tangal [taɠ)ⁿgal] *(o)* candy.

tappale *(o)* rogue; rowdy.

tappi *(o)* *{fr.}* rug; carpet.

tappirgal *(ngal)* instrument used for ironing.

tappude *v.* *{fr.}* 1) type; strike; beat 2) castrate.

tappisaade *v.* bother someone; joke around. *Ngonmi ko e tappisaade mo* I am just joking with her.

taransu *(ngu)* shilling.

tarde *v.* graduate; complete one's education or training.

taro (ngo) learning.

tartude *v.* remove a person's sarong. ~ *wudere* untie the sarong.

tasa *(ka)* brass.

tasde *v.* finish; be finished. *Batu ngu tasii* the meeting is over. *fusde alt.*

tasngo [tasngo] *(ngo)* end.

tata *(ka)* wall; fort. *tataaji (ɗi) pl.*

tataɓal *ord.* the third.

tataɓo ord. third in rank.

tati *num.* three; trey.

tato num. three. *yimɓe* ~ three people.

tawaaɗo *adj.* present; found.

tawde v. find.

tawdeede v. be found with.

taweede v. be found; be present. *Mbeɗe tawanoo* I was present.

tawngo [tawⁿgo] *(ngo)* finding.

tawtoraaɗo (o) participant.

tawtude v. find again.

tawre *(nde)* block of butter; animal foot track.

tayde *v.* happen.

taƴaade *v.* secede.

taƴande [taƴanⁿde] *(nde)* piece of.

taƴande v. allocate; cut for.

taƴatinél (ngél) bit; piece.

taƴatinde [taƴatinⁿde] *(nde)* scrap; sop; piece.

taƴde [tajje] *v.* cut; amputate; dissect; clip; mutilate. ~ *daande* decapitate.

taƴgól (ngól) cut.

taƴkinaade v. pretend to cut.

taƴóndiral [taƴóⁿdiral] *(ngal)* scission; separation.

taƴoowo (o) person who cut.

taƴre (nde) piece; share; cut.

taylude *v.* pledge; pond.

tébbuuli *(ɗi)* meats.

tééw *(ngu)* meat; flesh. ~ *kolce* beef. ~ *mbabba tugal* bacon; ham.

tebɓaade *v.* toss and catch with the hand.

tebɓagol *(ngól)* tossing.

tébɓitaade *v.* be falling from a hook to fall from a hanging position. **téddééndi** [téddéé^{n}di] *(ndi)* weight.

tebɓotooɗo *(o)* juggler.

téddinde *v.* honor; treat with respect. ~ *koɗo* treat a guest well.

téddineede *v.* be treated with respect.

téddude *v.* 1) be heavy; be difficult 2) be pregnant. *Ko o teddu ɗo* She is pregnant.

téddungal (ngal)[téddu^{n}gal] respect.

teeɗde [teedde] *v.* bleat.

teelde *v.* be odd; be uneven; be alone. *limoore teelnde* an odd number.

téélnude *v.* make an odd number.

teelre *(nde)* solitude; oneness.

teeleende [teelee^{n}de] *(nde)* baldness. *teeleeɗe (ɗe) pl.*

teeltelal *(ngal)* file.

teemedere *(nde)* one hundred. ~ *neɗɗo* one hundred people.

téémódinde *v.* centuple. *O teemodinii* He is one hundred years old.

téémódinɗo *adj.* centennial. *neɗɗo* ~ a hundred year old person. *Ko o teemodinɗo* He is one hundred years old.

teende *v.* collect fire wood.

téénól *(ngól)* the collecting of firewood.

téénóyde *v.* go and collect firewood. *O teenoyii* He went to collect firewood.

teeŊde *v.* be tight. *Ina teeɲi* It is tight.

tééŊtinde *v.* insist; affirm; confirm.

teerde *v.* cast anchor; accost. *Ka teeri* The boat just stopped.

tééri *(o)* 1) port of call; temporary stop; friend 2) friend. *téériiji (ɗi) pl.*

teere *(nde)* current.

teetatééri *(ndi)* booty; plunder.

teetde [teedde] *v.* take by force; usurp. *rokka teeta* a person who gives and takes back what was given.

teetere *(nde)* looting; pillage.

teetgól *(ngól)* taking by force.

teeyde *v.* be calm. *O mo teeyi* He is calm.

teeyɗo *adj.* tactful; calm.

teeyteeyngal [teeyteey^{n}gal] *(ngal)* lake. *teeyteeyle (ɗe) pl.*

tefde *v.* calm; pacify; pursue; beg.

tefoowo *(o)* mediator.

teftaade *v.* revenge; hold a grudge.

teftagól *(ngól)* revenge; grudge.

téftóndiral [téftó^{n}diral] *(ngal)* bitterness.

téftóndirde [téftó^{n}dirde] *v.* bear a grudge for one another.

teheende [tehee^{n}de] *(nde)* camp.

tékkééndi [tékkéé^{n}di] *(ndi)* width; strength; thickness.

tékkinde *v.* stress; strengthen ~ *alkulal* stress a sound.

tékkude *v.* 1) be hard 2) roll up/use a head pad 3) be thick. *Tekku ɗum* Use it as a head pad.

tékkuɗo *adj.* vigorous; strong. *neɗɗo* ~ a strong person.

tekkere *(nde)* pad; rag. *tekke (ɗe) pl.*

téktékól *(ngól)* bowel; intestine; gut. *tekteki (ɗi) pl.*

teko *(ngo)* whooping cough.

tékum *adj.* tasteless; uninteresting; tedious. *ɗum ko tekum* It is tasteless.

telefoŊ *(o) {fr.}* telephone.

tellaade *v.* retrograde; to alight; dismount.

tellagól *(ngól)* dismount.

tellorde *(nde)* getting off place.

tembere [tem^{m}bere] *(nde) {fr.}* stamp.

témbinde [tém^{m}binde] *v.* level; line up.

témbude [tém^{m}bude] *v.* be leveled; be in line.

ténkude [téŊkude] *v.* wait for food without being invited.

ténkugól [téŊkugól] *(ngól)* the waiting for food without being invited.

tengaade [teŊ^{n}gaade] *(nde)* large cone shaped hat.

ténnude *v.* remove lice.

teŋde *v.* give dowry. *Mi teŊii ma gay sappo* I gave you ten oxen for your dowry.

teŋe *(ɗe)* dowry.

teŋkere *(nde)* locust.

teppaade *v.* be fixed.

teppere *(nde)* foot; step. *yabɓude e* ~ follow a person's footstep. *teppe (ɗe) pl.*

téppirgal *(ngal)* instrument for sowing.

téppitde [téppidde] *v.* remove what was fixed.

téppude v. sow; fix.

téppól *(ngól)* bridle.

teptere *(nde)* something that is picked.

teptude *v.* pick.

téptungo [téptuⁿgo] *(ngo)* picking.

terde *v.* chase. *Ɓe teri mo* They chased him away.

teret *(o)* trade season.

tergal *(ngal)* limb. *terɗe (ɗe) pl.*

termude *v.* use language skillfully.

termoowo (o) person who uses language skillfully.

teskaade *v.* remember; recall. *Mbeɗe teeski maa* I remember you.

téskuya *(o)* memory; remembrance; souvenir. *heewde* ~ have a good memory.

tetaanoos *(o) {fr.}* tetanus.

tete *(o)* toddler.

tewngo [tewⁿgo] *(ngo)* ambush.

teyde *v.* do deliberately. *Ko miin teyi* I did it on purpose.

tiba *(o)* 1) roof 2) one-room house. *tibaaji (ɗi) pl.*

tidɗude *v.* save space while storing.

tibde v. thatch.

tiggaade *v.* roll oneself up.

tiggere (nde) disorderly fold.

tiggitaade v. stretch.

tiggude v. fold disorderly.

tiggal *(ngal)* park for animals.

tiggu *(o)* newborn; baby.

tigi *foc.* very; himself; herself (used for emphasis). *Ko aan tigi* It is you.

tigirigi foc. very much. *tigitigi alt.*

tiiɗaaɗo *adj.* proud; concerned. *Mbeɗe tiiɗaa ɗum* It is important for me.

tiiɗde v. 1) be hard; be strong 2) be expensive 3) be important. *Ina tiiɗi* It is expensive.

tiiɗɗo adj. 1) robust; hale; tough 2) dear. ~ *jungo* miser; penurious.

tiiɗgól (ngól) strength.

tiiɗnaade [tiinnaade] *v.* strive; persist; be serious minded. *O mo tiiɗnii* He is a very conscientious individual.

tiiɗniiɗo [tiinniiɗo] *adj.* serious; valiant.

tiiɗnude [tiinnude] *v.* strengthen; assert; to harden; toughen; increase the price.

tiiɗtinde [tiittinde] *v.* 1) make difficult 2) affirm; emphasize; reinforce.

tiiɗtingól [tiittingól] *(ngól)* emphasis.

tiille *(ɗe)* rights.

tiindi [tiinⁿdi] *(ndi)* right.

tiimde *v.* 1) predict 2) stand over; overlook.

tiimgal (ngal) prediction.

tiimo (ngo) prediction; astrology.

tiimoowo (o) astrologer. *Ko o tiimoowo* He is an astrologer.

tiimorgal (ngal) mirror.

tiimtaade v. look in the mirror. *O woni ko e tiimtaade* He is looking at himself in the mirror.

tiinde *(nde)* forehead.

tiitoonde [tiitooⁿde] *(nde)* address. *Hol ko woni tiitoonde maa* What is your address?

tiirde *v.* be swollen.

tijjaade *v.* expect; hope. *Mbeɗe tijjii mo hande* I expect to see her today.

tijjinde v. inform/warn in advance.

tikka *(ka)* head tie.

tikkande v. be angry at someone. *Ko o tikkanɗo ma* He is angry at you.

tikkere (nde) anger. *tikke (ɗe) pl.*

tikkuɓe (ɓe) angry persons.

tikkude v. withdraw because of anger; be angry; sulk.

tikkuɗo (o) an angry person. *Ko o tikkuɗo* He is angry.

tilfaade *v.* be lost.

tilfere (nde) loss.

tilfude v. waste.

tilliisa *(o)* tent.

timde *v.* have nausea.

timmal *(ngal)* completeness.

timminde v. finish; complete; achieve.

timmingól (ngól) addendum.

timminoore (nde) adjective; adjunct; adverb.

timmude v. 1) be finished; be complete 2) die. *O timmii* He is dead.

timmuɗo adj. 1) complete 2) serious minded; trustworthy.

timpaade *v.* urinate while standing.

timpude *v.* draw the bow.

timtimól *(ngól)* rainbow. *timtimi (ɗi) pl.*

tiŋ *(o)* pain.

tinde *v.* be aware of; know; be informed. *Mi tinii ɗum* I am aware of it.

tini *(ɗi)* awareness.

tindinde [tinⁿdinde] *v.* explain; teach. *Tindin mo* Teach him.

tindingol [tinⁿdingól]*(ngol)* teaching.

tindól [tinⁿdól]*(ngól)* tale; riddle; adage; proverb; yarn. **tindude** ~ tell a tale.

tindude [tinⁿdude] *v.* tell a story; narrate.

tinól *(ngól)* awareness.

tintinde *v.* advertise; inform; alert. *Tintinee mo* Keep him informed.

tintine *(ɗe)* warnings.

tintingól *(ngól)* warning; advertisement.

tintinoowo *(o)* advertiser; announcer.

tintude *v.* notice; be aware of. *Mi tintii ɗum* I am aware of it.

tirde *v.* fasten; tie an animal load.

tiro *(ngo)* animal disease.

tisubaar *(o)* second daily prayer; second daily prayer time. *Tisubaar yoni* It is time for the second daily prayer.

titi *foc.* again.

to *inter.* to; there; away; where. *hol* ~ where. *Hol to paaɗaa* Where are you going?

tóbbude *v.* hobble; limp. *O mo tobba* He limps.

tobbaade *v.* stain; dirty.

tobbere *(nde)* drop; speck; spot; dot; stain. ~ *kosam* a drop of milk. ~ *ndiyam* a drop of water.

tóbbinde *v.* pour by drops.

tóbbude *v.* 1) aim 2) add water 3) make a dot with ink.

tobde *v.* rain; sprinkle. *Inan toba* It is raining.

tobeede *v.* be rained upon.

tobndoogam [tobⁿdoogam] *(ɗam)* rainwater.

tobo *(ngo)* rain. *tóbóóji (ɗi) pl.*

toboyal *(kal)* drizzle.

tóccinde *v.* hatch.

tóccingól *(ngól)* hatch; hatching.

tóccude *v.* be hatched.

tóccungo [toccuⁿgo] *(ngo)* emergence from an egg; hatching.

toccoonde *(nde)* little hill.

toɗɗaade *v.* 1) swallow 2) designate; concern. *ɗum toɗɗaaki ma* It is not your concern.

toggere *(nde)* tuft. *togge (ɗe) pl.*

tójjude *v.* be small.

tokara *(o)* namesake. *Tokara maa arii* Your namesake has arrived. *tokaraabe (be) pl.*

tokkande [tokkanⁿde] *(nde)* knot.

tókkude *v.* tie a knot.

tokñaade *v.* rub one's eyes.

tokooso *adj.* small; scrimp.

tókósél *adj.* small; tiny; wee.

tolde *v.* break.

tóllitaade *v.* complete.

tóllitde [tóllidde] *v.* complete.

tólluru *(ndu)* crest; hair left after shaving; tuft of hair.

tolnaade *v.* reach the same height or location; be located at. *Hol ɗo tolni ɗaa* At what stage are you?

tombaade [tomᵐbaade] *v.* wait for. *Ko kanko tombii mi* I am waiting for him.

tongaade [toŋⁿgaade] *v.* be hampered; be busy.

tóngirde [tóŋⁿgirde] *(nde)* place where animals are tied up.

tóngól [tóŋⁿgól] *(ngól)* rope for tying legs.

tóngude [tóŋⁿgude] *v.* tie up legs. ~ *neɗɗo* tie a person's legs.

tonkoŋ *(o)* corner.

tóndu [tónⁿdu] *(ndu)* lip. ~ *dow* the upper lip. ~ *les* the lower lip.

toŋde *v.* be short (clothing); shrink. *wudere toŋnde* a short sarong.

tóŋirde *(nde)* 1) slaughter house; butchery 2) rope 3) number.

toŋo *(ngo)* sale by retail; retail.

toŋoowo *(o)* butcher.

toŋƴaade *v.* hop.

toobal *(ngal)* fish.

toobde *v.* be unable to cross a river or a lake; be unable to make one's way. *Ko mi toobɗo* I am stuck here.

toobre *(nde)* forced interruption of a journey.

tooke *(ɗe)* venom; poison. *heewde* ~ be poisonous.

tookaaɗo *adj.* poisonous. *Ko ndi tookaandi* It is a poisonous snake.

tookeede v. rankle; be poisonous.

toole *(o)* fool.

toon *adv.* there. *Yah toon* Go there.

tooñaaɗo *(o)* victim.

tooñange [tooñaɭ]ⁿge] *(nge)* affront; abuse; aggression; foul; offense. *tooñangééji (ɗi) pl.*

tooñde v. [tooñje] to offend; abuse; provoke; spite; violate.

tooñɗo [tooñɭo] *adj.* culprit; felon.

tooraade v. seek charity.

toorde v. thicken sauce by adding flour.

Tooro *(ngo)* region in Futa.

toorodaagal *(ngal)* Tooroodo pride. *hollude* ~ show the Tooroodo pride.

Tooroodo *(o)* individual of the Toroodo caste. *Ko o Tooroodo* He belongs to the Toorodɓe caste.

toowde v. be high. *Ina toowi* It is high.

tóówééndi [tóówééⁿdi] *(ndi)* height; altitude; elevation. *Hol no tooweendi huɓeere nde foti* How tall is the building.

tóównude v. make high; elevate.

tóppitaade v. attend to; care for; maintain. *Toppito jom suudu maa* Take care of your wife.

tóppitaagól *(ngól)* care; maintenance.

toraade v. beg. *ɗaccu toraade* Stop begging.

tórkude v. be dirty.

tóskude v. lose its value.

tóttitde [tóttidde] v. give or hand again; give back.

tóttude v. give; hand. *Tottu mo kaake makko* Give him his belongings.

towde v. carry on one's shoulders.

tówdi *(ndi)* shoulder load.

tóɼɼude v. break.

tuɗande [tuɗanⁿde] v. pond.

tuɗde [tudde] v. be waterproof; collect water.

tuɗɗaade v. cover oneself.

tuɗɗaari *(ndi)* cover.

tuɗɗude v. 1) cover 2) be waterproof.

tufam *(ɗam)* mixture of milk, sugar and water.

tufande [tufanⁿde] *(nde)* hole.

tufande v. make a drink for someone which consists of a mixture of water, milk and sugar.

tufde v. 1) pierce 2) mix water and milk. ~ *noppi* pierce the ear.

tufirde *(nde)* tool for piercing.

tufnde [tufⁿde] *(nde)* wharf.

tuggaade v. lean against; rely on.

tuggorde *(nde)* support; beginning; origin.

tuggude v. 1) start 2) pole. ~ *laana* push a boat by means of a pole.

tugunde [tugunⁿde] *(nde)* place for pounding.

tukkaade v. bend forward; kneel down.

tukkude v. aim.

tulde *(nde)* hill. *dow* ~ uphill.

tulde v. be steel or iron proof.

tuleŋ *adv.* completely.

tullinaade v. be inflated.

tuma *(o)* time; period. *oon* ~ at that period.

tumarankaagal [tumaraŋkaagal] *(ngal)* foreignness.

tumaranke [tumaraɭ]ke] *(o)* foreigner. *Ko o tumaranke* He is a foreigner.

tumbude [tuᵐbude] *(nde)* calabash.

tumbuŋ [tumᵐbuɭ]] *(o)* deserted village.

tumbere [tumᵐbere] *(nde)* pregnancy.

tumbude [tumᵐbude] v. be pregnant. *Ko o tumbuɗo* She is pregnant.

tumpilaade v. fold oneself while lying down.

tundaram [tunⁿdaram] *(ɗam)* steel or iron-proof charm.

tundeede [tunⁿdeede] v. be made of steel or iron-proof.

tundude [tunⁿdude] v. be steel or iron proof.

tunde [tunⁿde] *(nde)* block of wood; log; chump; stump.

tunwinde v. dirty.

tunwude v. be dirty. *Ina tunwi* It is dirty.

tunwuɗo *adj.* messy; dirty; squalid.

tuundi [tuuⁿdi] *(ndi)* dirt; filth.

tuppaade v. have one's lips tattooed.

tuppude v. tattoo someone's lips.

tuppere *(nde)* thorn plant.

turaade v. bow; bend down. *Turo* Bend down.

turngo [turⁿgo] *(ngo)* bending.

rtaade v. 1) sit or stand erect again 2) plant again.

rki (o) shirt with a V-shaped neck.

rulde (nde) pile of egg watermelon.

uba (ba) pants; trousers. **cakkiiba** underpants. **tuubaaji** (ɗi) pl.

uubaako (o) white person.

uubakiri (o) white peoples' countries.

uubankoore (nde) white people's language(s).

ubande v. ask for forgiveness. **Mi tuubanii ma** Please forgive me.

ubde v. 1) repent 2) convert. **O tuubii** He has converted.

uɓde v. dip one's lips into a liquid.

uɗde [tuudde] v. throw off.

ufaade v. trap; decoy.

ufeere (nde) brick. fiide **tuufeeje** make bricks. **tuufeeje** (ɗe) pl.

ugorde (nde) reference.

tuugorgal (ngal) reference.

tuumaaɗo (o) suspect.

tuumal (ngal) allegation.

tuumde v. allege. **Ko kanko tuumaa** He is the alleged killer.

tuumo (ngo) suspicion; doubt.

tuure (nde) vomit. **tuute** (ɗe) pl.

tuutaaɗe (ɗe) spits.

tuutde [tuudde] v. throw up; vomit; spit.

tuutnude [tuunnude] v. make someone vomit.

tuuya (o) strong.

tuuyeede v. desire; long for; have a craving for. **Mbeɗe tuuyaa maaro e liɗɗi** I have a craving for the rice and fish dish.

tuwaabir (o) lamb.

tuⲄⲄam (ɗam) nose bleeding.

tuⲄⲄude v. bleeding from the nose. **Ko o tuⲄⲄuɗo** His nose is bleeding.

U

ubbaaɗo *adj.* buried.

ubbirgal *(ngal)* burial instrument.

ubbitaade *v.* be dug up. *ɗum ubbitiima* It has come out.

ubbitde [ubbidde] *v.* dig up.

ubbude *v.* bury. ~ *ngaska* fill a hole up.

ubbugól (ngól) burial.

uccitaade *v.* flow heavily.

uddaade *v.* be closed. *Ko ko uddii* It is closed.

uddirgal (ngal) gate; door.

uddital (ngal) the opening of a new mosque.

udditaare (nde) openess; fortune *udditde* [uddidde] *v.* open. ~ *hakkille mum* open one's mind; be open-minded.

uddoode (nde) gate. ~ *galle* a gate.

uddude *v.* shut; close. ~ *galle* close the gate/entrance.

uddugól (ngól) closure.

udumere (nde) door; gate.

ufaade *v.* stay home a lot.

ufde *v.* decompose; rot; taint. *ɗum ufii* It is rotten.

ufnaade *v.* disdain; be disgusted.

ujunere *(nde)* one thousand. *ujunnaaji (ɗe) pl.*

ukkude *v.* be too much.

ullude *v.* cover with dust; throw sand to.

ullundu [ulluⁿdu] *(ndu)* cat.

ullungal [ulluⁿgal] *(ngal)* big cat.

ullungél [ulluⁿgél]*(ngél)* kitten.

Umma *(o)* female first name.

ummaade *v.* uprise; arise; depart. *Ummo dow* Stand up.

umminde *v.* rouse.

ummital (ngal) resurrection.

ummoraade *v.* come by way of. *O ummorii ko hirnaange* He came from the West.

ummorde (nde) origin; base.

umsinaade *v.* clear one's throat.

unde *v.* pound. ~ *gawri* pound millet.

unirde *v.* pound with.

unoowo (o) pounder.

untaade *v.* pound again.

unu (ngu) pounding.

unugal (ngal) pestle; stamper.

urɓa *(o)* lottery.

urɓitde [urɓidde] *v.* annoy.

urɓude *v.* annoy.

urde *v.* spread perfume or incense.

urkinaade *v.* smoke.

urlude *v.* hem; dry. *Urlu tuuba makko bɑ* Hem his pants.

urmbitaare [urᵐbitaare](nde) reopening.

urmbitaade [urᵐbitaade] *v.* be reopened.

urñaade *v.* force one's way through obstacles.

urtulde *(nde)* piece of salt.

usrude *v.* keep a secret.

ustaade *v.* depreciate.

ustaare (nde) reduction; lowering of. *ɗum ko ustaare mawnde* It is a major loss.

ustagól (ngól) reduction; depreciation; devaluation.

usteede *v.* be diminshed.

ustiiɗo (o) crazy person.

ustude *v.* reduce; abate; subtract; decrease; discount.

ustugól (ngól) reduction; rebate.

usuru *(ndu)* tithe.

uttaade *v.* thump.

uubre *(nde)* furuncle; swelling. *uube (ɗe) pl.*

uulde *v.* sow before the rain.

uumaango [uumaaⁿgo] *(ngo)* groan *uumaali (ɗi) pl.*

uumde *v.* groan.

uurde *v.* smell good. *Ina uuri* It smells good.

uurdi (ndi) perfume.

uurnaade *v.* smell something.

W

aaɓde v. carry on one's back.

aade v. be like. *wayde alt.*

aadere *(nde)* drop. ~ *to ɓo* raindrop.

aado *(ngo)* umbrella.

aafaade v. be pulled.

aafde v. pull.

aaftude v. cut open.

aajaade v. preach; advise. *A ɗa waawi waajaade mo* You can advise him.

aajoore *(nde)* advice.

aaju *(o)* advice.

aakde v. cut.

aaktaade v. laugh.

aaktaango [waaktaaⁿgo] *(ngo)* laugh.

aalande [waalanⁿde] *(nde)* night spent.

aalde v. spend the night. ~ *ɗaanaade* sleep the night away.

aaldude v. spend the night with.

aalnde [waalⁿde] *(nde)* night spent somewhere.

allinde v. make spend the night; spend the night. *Mballinen ɗoo* Let us spend the night here.

aalo *(ngo)* lower ground close to the river. *jolde* ~ farm the lower grounds.

aamde v. flow; flood.

aame *(o)* deluge; flood; waterfall.

aamulde *(nde)* grave. *baamuule (ɗe) pl.*

aañ *(o)* kitchen.

aande [waaⁿde] *(nde)* ant hill.

aañde [waañje] v. hunt.

aaño *(ngo)* hunt.

aañditaade [waañⁿjitaade] v. duplicate; copy; dub.

aañdude [waañⁿjude] v. to pour.

aandu [waaⁿdu] *(ndu)* baboon; monkey.

aaraade v. bring to oneself.

aasde v. lack; be poor; lose. *Mi waasii gi ɗo* I lost a friend.

aasóóru *(ndu)* hyena.

aatde [waadde] v. swear; vow.

aatoore *(nde)* oath.

aawande v. be able to. *Mi waawanaa ɗum* I cannot do it.

waawde v. can; be able to. *O mo waawi windude* He can write.

waawnude v. compel; force; oblige; persuade; cajole.

waawtaade v. be stronger than a previously stronger opponent.

waay *foc.* emphatic word.

waaɼde [waajje] v. transpire; sweat.

waaɼo *(ngo)* sweat.

wabbunde [wabbuⁿde] *(nde)* torrent.

waccere *(nde)* fish scale.

waccoore *(nde)* nickname.

wacude v. praise.

wadere *(nde)* small pox pimple.

waɗande v. provide; perform for.

waɗɗe [wadde] v. do; commit; indulge in; perpetrate; practise.

waɗɗude [waddude] v. 1) put with 2) quarrel with. *Ko ɓe waɗɗuɓe* They quarrelled.

waɗtere [wattere] *(nde)* something that is redone.

waɗtude [wattude] v. redo; remake. ~ *hakkille* concentrate.

waɗɗaade v. straddle; ride; mount. ~ *mbabba* ride a donkey.

waɗɗinde v. help someone mount on something.

waɗɗorde *(nde)* saddle.

wafde v. cut with a sickle.

wafdu *(ndu)* scythe; sickle.

waggiɗde [waggidde] v. be unripe. *Ɲiye ɗe ko bagge* His bones are young.

wagginde v. recommend.

waho *(ngo)* slope.

wahre [waare] *(nde)* 1) beard 2) bundle of wood. ~ *leɗɗe* faggot; stack. ~ *huɗo* truss. ~ *raneere* a white beard. ~ *juutnde* a long beard.

wajjiɗde [wajjidde] v. be the only one.

wakkaade v. place on one's shoulder.

wakkinde v. 1) place on someone's shoulder 2) sew.

wakkilaade v. decide.

waklaade v. change oneself into; turn into.

waklude v. change.

waktu *(o)* *{ar.}* hour; time. *Waktu o yoniii* The time is up.

walabo *(ngo)* shoulder.

walde *v.* spread.

walɗude *v.* like meat and vegetables.

walla *conj.* or.

wallere *(nde)* humid and fertile soil.

wallifaade *v.* compose.

wallitde [wallidde] *v.* help; assist.

wallóndirde [wallón dirde] *v.* help one another.

wallude *v.* aid; upbear; help; assist.

waltunde [waltun de] *(nde)* water stream.

wambude *v.* carry a child on one's back. *Mi tampii wambude mo* I am tired of carrying him on my back.

wamde *v.* weave.

wana *(ka)* holster; sheath *wanaaji (ɗi) pl.*

wandaade [wan ndaade] *v.* fish. *O woni ko e wandaade* He is fishing.

wande [wan de] *(nde)* hook. *seŊde* ~ bait.

wangaade [waŊ ngaade] *v.* turn around a place; go around.

wano *(ngo)* leave.

wantirde *v.* undersell; sell at a giveaway price.

wantireede *v.* be sold a a giveaway price.

wañjalde [wañ jalde] *(nde)* pimple.

wañtinde [wañcinaade] *v.* to tip out.

wappaade *v.* feint; shirk; parry; leave unnoticed.

waraango [waraan go] *(ngo)* torrent; current.

warde *v.* eliminate; slay; execute; kill; decapitate. ~ *hoore* kill a human being.

wardude *v.* kill with.

warngo [war go] *(ngo)* killing.

wartaade *v.* commit suicide.

warñeende *(nde)* sweat.

warñude *v.* sweat. *A warñii* You are sweating.

warsude *v.* remove fish scales.

wasaade *v.* brag; vaunt; boast. *O mo waawi wasaade* He brags continuously.

wasaango [wasaan go] *(ngo)* small millet stalk.

wasalde *(nde)* onion.

wasiyaade *v.* *{ar.}* advise; recommend; give one's last wish.

wasorde *(nde)* gathering place for animals.

wattindaade [watti ndaade] *v.* be last; com last.

wattinde *v.* last; remain.

wawlere *(nde)* blister.

wayde *v.* resemble; seem.

waykala *(o)* small field; garden.

waylaade *v.* change; change oneself. *(wayliima* He has changed.

waylinaade *v.* work as a blacksmith.

waylitde [waylidde] *v.* change back.

wayliteede *v.* be changed back.

waylude *v.* change; process; forge; modify vary; transform; distort. ~ *tagoodi* deform.

waynaade *v.* say goodbye. *Waynaade in muusi* It is sad to say goodbye.

wayrondirde *v.* remain a long perio without seeing one another.

wayrude *v.* be a long time away. *Mi wayr yiide mo* I have not seen him for a lon time.

waywayko *(ko)* eyelashes.

waʕʕinde *v.* cook slightly.

waʕʕude *v.* be cooked slightly.

weccande *v.* 1) give change 2) buy new clothing for.

wéccit *(o)* change.

wéccude *v.* 1) change money 2) buy new clothing.

wecco *(ngo)* side; rib.

weddaade *v.* throw away.

wéduru *(ndu)* stick.

weɗaade *v.* be carried away by wind *ɗerewol ngol weɗiima* The sheet wa carried away by the wind.

weɗɗaade *v.* winnow.

wéɗɗitde [wéɗɗidde] *v.* Disclose; uncover

weebde *v.* be easy. *O mo weeɓi* He is easy.

wééɓnude *v.* facilitate; ease; simplify. *K kanko weeɓni ɗum* He made it easy fo me.

weejde *v.* [weejje] to be indiscrete.

wééjnude [wééññude] *v.* reveal in public.

weejre *(nde)* indiscreteness.

weelde *v.* dangle; be hanging.

wééltude *v.* hang down; hang around.

weemde *v.* be stupid. *A ɗa weemi* You ar stupid.

éémtude v. be sharp; be intelligent. *O mo weemti* She is sharp.

eeñde v. open apart.

ééndu [wééⁿdu] *(ndu)* lake; pond.

eerde v. spread out.

eetde [weedde] v. be morning. *Jamma o weetii* The night is over.

eetndoogo [weenⁿdoogo] *(ngo)* twilight; dawn.

eetndorde [weenⁿdorde] v. oversleep; wake up late.

eeyde v. fly.

eeyo *(ngo)* atmosphere; climate; space.

éftilde v. frighten. *Ko mi beftilaado* I am frightened.

ékkude v. cover seeds with sand.

elamma *(o)* pleasure; happiness; delight. *Mbede wondi e welamma* I am having fun.

elde v. be sweet; be sharp; be tasty. *~ Ÿii Ÿam* be friendly; be easy going. *~ hakkille* be intelligent. *Ina weli* It is tasty.

élnude v. 1) sweeten; animate 2) sharpen.

eltaade v. be happy; rejoice. *Mbede weltii no feewi* I am very happy.

eltaare *(nde)* enthusiasm; happiness; gratification; mirth.

éltinde v. satisfy; gratify; please someone.

velo *(o)* {fr.} bicycle.

vélsindaade [welsiⁿdaade] v. neglect; be careless. *A da welsindii* You are careless.

vélsindaare [wélsiⁿdaare] *(nde)* carelessness; negligence.

vempeŸere *(nde)* wave.

veñere *(nde)* fritter.

veñje [weñje] v. wear clothing improperly.

veñtude [weñcude] v.

verde v. clear space.

vero *(ngo)* cavity; hollow.

vergaade v. roll.

verlaade v. throw; cast; hurl; fling; to pitch; project.

vérlude v. spin round.

vértude v. spread out. *~ leeso* spread a mat.

vesde v. winnow.

véydude v. be beautiful.

véyginaade v. lay on one's back.

weytaade v. relax. *O mo weytii* He is relaxed.

weytaare *(nde)* fun; relaxation.

wibjo *(ngo)* wing.

wiccude v. splash; sprinkle water. *~ ndiyam* sprinkle.

widaade v. scratch the. ground.

widtude [wittude] v. analyze; research; investigate; inquire.

widto [witto] *(ngo)* analysis; research; investigation; inquisition.

wifaade v. fan oneself.

wifde v. fan; blow; ventilate.

wifngo [wifⁿgo] *(ngo)* fanning.

wiide v. say; express; mention; tell. *~ eey* say yes. *~ alaa* say no. *Hol ko mbiidaa* what did you say?.

wiiduru *(ndu)* large excavation.

wiige *(nge)* heifer.

wiinde [wiinⁿde] *(nde)* abandoned house/village.

wiinnude v. abandon a house or a village.

wiir *(o)* sail.

wiis *(o)* {fr.} screw.

wilde *(nde)* gin; trap. *tuufaade ~* lay a trap.

wilde v. 1) disorder 2) perform sorcery.

wiltude v. 1) arrange in the right order 2) put forth leaves. *Mi wiltii deftere nde* The pages of the book are in the right order.

willere *(nde)* type of antelope.

willude v. set aside.

wilwilnde [wilwilⁿde] *(nde)* bat.

winnaade v. manure fields; fertilize.

windande [winⁿdanⁿde] *(nde)* paragraph; lesson.

windande [winⁿdande] v. write for. *Windanam leeteer* Write a letter for me.

windere [winⁿdere] *(nde)* world; creation; nature.

windondirde [winⁿdonⁿdirde] v. write to one another.

windude [winⁿdude] v. write; record; transcribe; recruit. *~ bataake* write a letter.

wirdude v. do beads. *O woni ko wirdude* He is doing the beads.

wirnaade v. vanish; be out of vision; die. *O wirniima* He died.

wirnitaade v. come to vision.

wirtaade v. pass close to. *O wirti maa mami* He passed by me.

wiro *(ko)* cotton; wool.

wisde v. 1) water 2) cleanse. *Wis cukalel ngel* Cleanse the child.

wiŕŕere *(nde)* cotton seed.

woccaade v. eat grass.

woccoonde [woccooⁿde] *(nde)* egg.

woɗa *(o)* taboo. *ɗum ko woɗa* It is taboo.

woɗaade v. taboo. *Mbeɗe woɗii ɗum* It is forbidden for me.

woɗɗaade v. go far; be far.

wóɗɗinde v. move something away.

wóɗɗitaade v. move away; be away from.

wóɗɗóndirde [wóɗɗóⁿdirde] v. be far away from each other. *A min ngoɗɗondiri* We are far apart.

wóɗɗude v. be far. *ina woɗɗi no feewi* It is far away.

woɗeere adj. red.

wójjinde v. redden; blush. ~ *gite* be mad.

wójjude v. be red; blush.

wofde v. bark.

wojere *(nde)* rabbit; hare.

wokde v. spill over while boiling.

wolde *(nde)* army; war.

wólis *(o) {fr.}* valise.

wolsude v. vomit milk.

wolweere *(nde) {fr.}* pistol.

wómbilaade [wóᵐbilaade] v. rid of unwanted grains.

wómbude [wómᵐbude] v. buzz; supervise.

womnde [womⁿde] *(nde)* grave. *faade* ~ go to hell.

womre *(nde)* blow; fist.

wonande v. favor; side with.

wonde v. be; occur. *Ina wona wonata* There is a story that.

wóndude v. be with; associate; suffer from. ~ *e hoore muusoore* have a headache.

wóntude v. become; turn into.

wónki [wóᵭki] *(ki)* heart. *wónkiiji (ɗi)* pl.

woobde v. take a draught.

wooɓre *(nde)* draught.

woodde v. be; exist. *Ina woodi* It is true.

woofaade v. sit on eggs.

woofoonde [woofooⁿde] *(nde)* egg.

woofde v. 1) miss 2) sin. *O woofii Alla* H⟨e⟩ sinned.

wóófɗude v. be paralyzed; be paralytic.

woogde v. fill; sharpen.

wookoŕere *(nde)* little child.

woonde v. swear; make an oath.

woondoore [wooⁿdoore] *(nde)* oath.

wóóndu [wóóⁿdu] *(ndu)* hip.

woorde v. 1) avoid 2) be abnormal. *ɗun⟨?⟩ woorii mo* He escaped it.

woosde v. be crippled.

wootande v. *{fr.}* elect. *Ko aan ngootanm⟨i⟩* I voted for you.

wootde [woodde] v. vote.

woote (o) {fr.} vote.

wootere adj. unique; sole.

woowde v. be accustomed to; be used t⟨o⟩ *Mbeɗe woowi ɗum* I am used to it.

wóównude v. accustom; familiarize.

wóówtude v. adapt; acclimate; get used t⟨o⟩ *Mi woowtii mo* I am used to her.

woppere *(nde)* animal waste.

wóppude v. let go; leave alone. ~ *simm⟨e⟩* quit smoking. *ɗaccude alt.*

wóptude v. make a mistake.

woraade v. go around an obstacle.

worɓe *(ɓe)* men. *gorko (o) sing.*

worde (nde) male; masculine.

wórɗude v. 1) be infected 2) be selfish; b⟨e⟩ stingy. *O mo worɗi* He is stingy.

worganke [worgaᵭke] *(o)* Southerner.

worgo (ngo) South.

wormbolde [worᵐbolde] *(nde)* couscous grain.

woroɗde [worodde] *(nde)* misfortune.

woroore *(nde)* cola nut.

wórsude v. make/tie a slipknot.

wórsundu [wórsuⁿdu] *(ndu)* slipkno⟨t⟩ noose.

wosaade v. be thin. *Ina wosii* The sauce is thin.

wostaade v. exchange; swap.

wóstóndirde [wóstóⁿdirde] v. exchang⟨e⟩ swap. ~ *hakkillaaji* discuss.

wottaade v. eat lunch. *O woni ko wottaade* He is eating lunch.

wowlaango [wowlaaⁿgo] *(ngo)* utterance.

wówlude v. 1) be happy 2) pronounc⟨e⟩ utter.

wówru *(ndu)* mortar.

oyde v. cry; weep; mourn.

oykinaade v. pretend to cry.

oynude v. make someone cry.

oytaade v. lament; prosecute; complain.

oȲde [wojje] v. be interested; be concerned; be worried. *O mo woȠi mi* I am worried about her.

oȲeede v. be concerned.

oyndu [wóy^{n}du] *(ndu)* well; pit.

ubbude v. 1) cut grass 2) fish.

uccundu [wuccu^{n}du] *(ndu)* anus.

uddere *(nde)* hole. ~ *hinere* nostril.

uddinde v. make unclear.

uddude v. be unclear.

uddu *(ndu)* navel.

udere *(nde)* sarong. ~ *toȠnde* a short sarong.

uduru *(ndu)* watermelon.

udɗaade v. have insect holes; be pierced.

udɗe [wudde] v. make a hole; be rotten.

udɗinde v. make appear.

udɗude v. come out; appear.

ufnude v. bear a fruit.

uftude v. come out of the stalk.

ufȲaade v. rinse/clean one's mouth.

ufȲude v. rinse someone's mouth.

uga *(o)* male pigeon.

uggude v. repair; fix.

ujaade v. rub oil on oneself or on one's hair.

ujde [wujje] v. oil.

ujjude v. steal; abduct; cheat; embezzle; rob; defraud.

ujo *(ngo)* shell.

ukkitde [wukkidde] v. spit. *Wukkit ɗum* Spit it out.

ukkude v. come out; spit.

ulaango [wulaa^{n}go] *(ngo)* loud cry; howl.

ulde v. be hot.

uleede v. be hot. *Mbeɗe wulaa* I am hot.

ulnude v. heat.

ullinde v. make someone scream.

ullitaade v. complain; prosecute.

ullude v. scream; shout; sound the horn.

ulnude v. heat.

ultaade v. withdraw one's previous statement. *O wultiima* He changed his mind.

ultinde v. 1) heat 2) confront.

wulnde [wul^{n}de] *(nde)* knot; node.

wuluure *(nde)* thousand.

wumbilaade [wu^{m}bilaade] v. grope.

wumde v. be blind. *O wumii* He has become blind.

wumtude v. recover one's eyesight. *So gumɗo wumii wumtii andii ko gite nafata* One should learn from one's mistakes.

wumpude v. make butter.

wumsundere [wumsu^{n}dere] *(nde)* lung.

wunay *(nge)* dirty cattle.

wune *(o)* consideration; gratefulness; gratitude. *O alaa wune* He is ungrateful.

wuppude v. wash; launder.

wurbude v. scorch.

wure *(o)* gamble; lottery.

wuro *(ngo)* town; village; city.

wurwude v. whisk; batter.

wusuŋ *(o)* basket used to catch fish.

wutaandu [wutaa^{n}du] *(ndu)* millet or corn ear.

wutte *(o)* gown.

wuttude v. blow; puff.

wuttuldu *(ndu)* area below ribs.

wuttulo *(ngo)* side.

wuuɗaango [wuuɗaa^{n}go] *(ngo)* whistle.

wuuɗe [wuudde] v. whistle.

wuuduru *(ndu)* pumpkin.

wuufde v. be pregnant; hold in the mouth.

wuufdu *(ndu)* growing ear.

wuukeede v. have swollen genitals.

wuuko *(ngo)* disease which causes the swelling of the genitals.

wuulaade v. swim.

wuundaade [wuu^{n}daade] v. carry on one's shoulders.

wuuraade v. bend.

wuuranaade v. side with.

wuurde v. 1) live; be alive; subsist; survive 2) bend.

wuurnude v. sustain; activate; animate; actuate.

wuurtinde v. resurrect; resuscitate.

wuurtude v. 1) revive; come to life again 2) thread.

wuutufere *(nde)* forest.

wuyde v. be hairy; grow hair.

wuyeede v. be shaggy.

Y

yaaɓre *(nde)* jujube (fruit).

yaactaade [yaaccaade] *v.* speed up; hurry up; accelerate. *Yaacto* Hurry up.

yaafaade *v.* spare; pardon; forgive; divorce. *Yaafaade wonaa waaweede* Forgiveness does not imply weakness.

yaafnaade *v.* to apologize.

yaafuya (o) amnesty; apology; mercy; clemency; grace; pardon *ñaagaade* ~ ask for forgiveness.

yaafde *v.* be soft. *Ina yaafi* It is soft.

yaafngo [yaafⁿgo] *(ngo)* softness.

yaajde [yaajje] *v.* 1) be wide 2) be patient. *Ndaw ko yaaji* He is so patient.

yaajnude [yaaññude] *v.* widen; diffuse; expand; propagate; proliferate.

yaakaare *(nde)* hope. *fawde* ~ *e neddo* place one's hopes on someone.

yaalaade *v.* yawn.

yaalde *v.* begin.

yaalnude *v.* set to work.

yaali *(o)* dish; porridge. *gosi* ~ porridge.

yaama *adv.* maybe.

yaas *adv.* outside.

yaawde *v.* be quick/fast. ~ *jungo* have the propensity to hit. *O mo yaawi* He is fast.

yaawnaade v to speed up; hurry up; hie; accelerate. *Yaawno* Hurry up.

yaawnude *v.* hasten; quicken; precipitate; hurry.

yaay *(o)* mother.

yabere *(nde)* bead. *tellinde jabe* do the beads.

yaɓɓande [yaɓɓanⁿde] *(nde)* footstep. ~ *maa* your footstep.

yaɓɓirde (nde) foot; sole.

yaɓɓitde [yaɓɓidde] *v.* take off/remove one's foot.

yaɓɓude v. tread; walk. ~ *e demngal* take the words out of someone's mouth.

yahande *v.* go for. *ɓe njahanii mo* They went to get him.

yahde v. depart; proceed; go; walk. *O woni ko ekkaade yahde* He is making his first steps.

yahdu [yaadu] *(ndu)* walk; gait. ~ *juutndi* a long journey.

yahdude [yaadude] *v.* go with; accompany ~ *e jamaanu* go with the tide/flow.

yahnaade [yaanaade] *v.* stroll; ramble promenade. *O woni ko yahnaade* He is strolling.

yahrude [yaarude] *v.* go with. ~ *koydi* tramp; walk. ~ *yeeso* proceed; go forward.

yahre [yaare] *(nde)* scorpion.

yakkude *v.* spoil.

yalmitde [yalmidde] *v.* light.

yaltinde *v.* exclude; bring out; dislocate preclude; eject. ~ *leydi* expel.

yaltirde (nde) outlet; exit. *dum wonaa yaltirde* It is not an exit.

yaltoyde v. go and relieve oneself.

yaltude v. 1) go out 2) complete the widowhood reclusion period. *O yaltii He* went out.

yamdinde *v.* be flexible.

yamdude v. be easy going; be flexible. *C mo yamdi* He is easy going.

yamirde *v.* authorize; assent; order; ordain may; permit. *Mi yamirii ma* You have my permission.

yamiroore (nde) permission; warrant; order *Min padi ko yamiroore maa* We are waiting for your order.

yammere *(nde)* fruit.

yanaade *v.* joke with someone; joke about someone.

yanondirde v. joke with one another.

yanaande [yanaaⁿde] *(nde)* tomb; grave *genaale (de) pl.*

yananeede *v.* ascertain; be certain. *A di yananaa* Are you certain?

yande *v.* raid; tumble; fall. *Ko o jando He* fell.

yandinde v. make fall; demolish; topple tackle; down. *O yandinii lekki ki He* downed the tree.

yanirde *v.* fall on a particular side.

yardude *v.* drink with.

yantinde *v.* 1) include 2) calm. *Mbar c yantinii* Has he calmed down?

yantóndirde [yantóⁿdirde] *v.* join amalgamate; gather.

ntude v. participate; mingle; relapse; coalesce. *yanti heen* in addition. *Yantu e aaɓɓe* Go and join them.

nkinaare *(nde)* modesty.

rde v. drink.

rdude v. drink with.

rnude v. give to drink; make a person or an animal drink. *Yarnu ba* Give water to ne donkey.

rlaade v. forgive. *Yarlo mi* Forgive me.

waade v. resent; belittle; disdain.

waare *(nde)* disdain; resentment.

wde v. disdain; be dissatisfied. *Mbeɗe awi ɗum* I am dissatisfied with it.

wtude v. go past; pass.

wuur *(o)* yogurt.

ynaade v. light. ~ *lampa* switch the light n.

ynude v. light.

ccitaade v. look back. *dogde in yeccitoo* ɔok back while running.

ddondirde v. disagree; contradict one nother.

ddude v. contradict; deny; disagree.

ɗde [yedde] v. give.

ebaade v. be careless. *O mo yeebii* He is areless.

ebaare *(nde)* carelessness.

eɓde v. admire; contemplate. ~ *sinamaa* watch a movie.

edde v. be calm. *O yeedii* He has calmed lown.

ednude [yéénnude] v. calm; immobilize.

ego *(nge)* young ox.

elaa *(o)* griot dance/song.

ende v. 1) bribe; corrupt 2) reward. *Mi eenii ma gay sappo* I give you ten oxen 'or a reward.

endu [yééndu] *(ndu)* animal.

erde v. last.

esaade v. comb one's hair. *O woni ko e eesaade* He is combing his hair.

esde v. comb hair.

esoode *(nde)* comb.

eso *(ngo)* 1) beyond 2) front; face. *wonde* ~ be ahead. *ɗum woni ko yeeso* It is head.

eweede v. be lonely. *Mbeɗe yeewaa* I am onely.

yeeweende [yeeweende]*(nde)* solitude; loneliness.

yééwnitde [yééwnidde] v. desire to see again.

yééwnude v. long; be nostalgic. *Mi yeewnii ma* I miss you.

yeewtere *(nde)* interaction; chat; conversation.

yééwtude v. commune; chat; converse; argue; interact; be lively. *Ina yeewti* It is lively.

yeeYaade v. look back.

yeeyde v. sell; commercialize; peddle.

yeeytaade v. bargain; ask for the price of goods.

yééytóndirde [yééytóndirde] v. bargain; negotiate; transact.

yééytóndireede v. bargain; transact.

yééytude v. resell.

yééynude v. publicize. *O woni ko e yeeynude* He is making an announcement.

yéjjitde [yéjjidde] v. forget; omit. *Hol to yejjit* Please do not forget.

yelaade v. beg; ask charity.

yelde *(nde)* space between teeth; cavity.

yelloore *(nde)* fruit.

yelooko *(ko)* plant.

yenge *(nge)* wedding celebration.

yénnude v. decry; belittle; degrade; disparage; minimize.

yenoore *(nde)* disparage; degrading remark. *njennoor alt.*

yérɓude v. shake; quake. *Leydi ndi yerɓii* An earthquake has occurred.

yéru *(o)* example; instance. *hokkude* ~ give an example. *Hokkam yeru* Give me an example.

yerwaade v. make flour grains.

yettaade v. attain; arrive. ~ *e jam* arrive safely.

yéttinde v. forward. ~ *nelal* deliver a message.

yettoode *(nde)* last name. *Hol no njettete ɗaa* What is your last name?

yéttude v. praise; thank. ~ *Alla* praise Allah.

yeYde [yejje] v. shake; rock; lull.

yidde [yidde] v. love; yearn; wish; desire; want. *Yiɗde haɗii yiide* She is blinded by love.

yiɗóndirde [yiɗóⁿdirde] *v.* love each other. *E ɓe njiɗondiri no feewi* They love each other very much.

yiggaade *v.* rub oneself.

yiggude v. rub. ~ *e ɓandu* rub on the body.

yiigde *v.* scratch.

yiigirde (nde) instrument for scratching.

yiilaade *v.* 1) seek; prospect 2) gyrate; gravitate; rotate. *Ngonmi ko yiilaade mo* I am looking for him.

yiilde v. twirl; wind; turn. ~ *hoore* shake the head; say no.

yiilnude v. make turn.

yiiloraade v. search with; seek with. ~ *juuɗe* grabble.

yiiltude v. change direction.

yiiñde [yiiñje] *v.* qualm.

yijilere *(nde)* fruit. *gijile (ɗe) pl.*

yillaade *v.* sojourn; visit.

yimɓe *(ɓe)* folk; people *sing.* **neɗɗo** (o).

yimde *v. sing. O woni ko e yimde* He is singing.

yimre (nde) song.

yinaade *v.* swim.

yiraade *v.* swim.

yirgude *v.* rub.

yiriinde [yiriiⁿde] *(nde)* swirl.

yisɓude *v.* ponder; weigh.

yitere (nde) eye. *gite (ɗe) pl.*

yiyde [yiide] *v.* see; sight.

yiydude v. see one another.

yiytondirde v. find each other.

yiytude v. 1) discover; locate 2) trace; locate. *Mi yiytii ɗum* I found it.

yiwande [yiwanⁿde] *(nde)* wound.

yiwde v. 1) capsize; shipwreck; wreck 2) pierce; stab.

yiⲅⲅude *v.* be of the same age. *Kamɓe njiⲅⲅi* They were born the same year.

yoɓde *v.* 1) pay 2) pay back; reimburse. ~ *ñamaande* pay a debt.

yoɓeede v. be paid; earn.

yoɓnaade v. request payment.

yoftaade *v.* revenge; penalize; retaliate.

yoftanaade v. avenge.

yólbinde *v.* loosen.

yólbude v. be loose. *E ba yolbi* It is loose.

yólbitaade *v.* slip into a hole.

yolnde [yolⁿde] *(nde)* space; interval distance.

yomde *v.* womanize.

yómbinaade [yomᵐbinaade] *v.* wear a vei during wedding days.

yonde *v.* be sufficient. *ɗum yonii* It is sufficient.

yoneede v. be satisfied. *Mi yonaama* I am satisfied.

yongaade [yoɲ]ⁿgaade] *v.* look over.

yónkude [yóɲ]kude] *v.* shake milk.

yonta *(o)* nowadays; nowaday's youth, today's youth.

yontere *(nde)* week. ~ *ɓennunde nde* last week.

yóntinde v. complete a week; be a week old.

yóntude *v.* 1) turn mature 2) be up. *Waktu o yontii* It is time for the prayer.

yooɓaade *v.* take food supplies for a journey.

yooɗde [yoodde] *v.* be good-looking/pretty

yooɗnaade [yoonnaade] *v.* tog; dress up.

yóóɗnude [yóónnude] *v.* embellish.

yookeede *v.* have goiter.

yookoode (nde) goiter.

yoolaade *v.* be drowned.

yoolde v. drown. ~ *hujja mum* lose one's rights.

yoomde *v.* be pale.

yoorde *v.* be dry.

yoornude v. dry.

yooro (ngo) drought.

yorde *v.* be loose. *Tuuba maa yorii* Your pants are loose.

yornude v. loosen.

yórtude v. go down the slope.

yortinde v. Insert; swallow.

yowde *v.* place in a higher position; shelve.

yoweede v. be shelved.

yówirde (nde) shelf.

yowtude v. remove from a shelf.

yubɓinde *v.* adjust; accommodate; correct.

yubɓude v. agree; be correct.

yulde *v.* pierce; perforate.

yulnde [yulⁿde] *v.* strainer.

yumma *(o)* mother. *yummen Hawaa* Eve.

yummiraaɗo (o) mother; mom.

umtude *v.* be successful.

unginaade [yuɲⁿginaade] *v.* lower the head because of sadness.

uppude *v.* pour; transfer.

urmaade *v.* have pity. *Yurmo mo* Have pity on him.

urmeende [yurmeeⁿde] *(nde)* mercy; pity. *~ Alla* Allah's mercy.

yurmikinaade *v.* show pity.

yurminaade *v.* be sad; look sad.

yuude *v.* cry.

yuumɗude *v.* be bright; be shiny.

yuurnaade *v.* peep; look into.

yuurnitaade *v.* look into.

Ɣ

Ɣaaŋde *v.* stop by; transit. *Mi Ɣaaɲii mo* I stopped by his house.

Ɣaaraade *v.* winnow. *O woni ko e Ɣaaraade* He is winnowing.

Ɣaarngo [Ɣaarⁿgo] *(ngo)* winnow.

Ɣaaragól *(ngól)* winnow.

Ɣaartaade *v.* winnow again.

Ɣaggude *v.* be hard.

Ɣakkirde *v.* chew with.

Ɣakkude *v.* chew; masticate. *Ɣakku hadee maa moɗɗe* Chew before you eat.

Ɣakkuru *(ndu)* chew; chewing.

Ɣamaaɗo *(o)* fiancée.

Ɣamal *(ngal)* the act of asking someone's hand for marriage.

Ɣamde *v.* ask someone's hand for marriage. *O Ɣamii* He has tied the knot.

Ɣamɗo *(o)* fiancée.

Ɣamoowo *(o)* person asking someone's hand.

Ɣamrudi *(ndi)* gift to in-laws.

Ɣam Ɣamo *(o)* fiancé; fiancée. ~ *gorko* fiancé. ~ *debbo* fiancée.

Ɣaŋaade *v.* swim cross a river.

Ɣéékiraaɗo *(o)* one's husband's sister.

Ɣeeŋde *v.* 1) climb 2) get off 3) be outdated. *O Ɣeeɲii* He got off work. *ɗum Ɣeeɲii* It is out-of-date.

Ɣééɲɗum *adj.* outdated; out-of-date.

Ɣééɲirde *v.* climb with.

Ɣééɲirde *(nde)* ladder; stairs.

Ɣééɲirgal *(ngal)* ladder; stairs.

Ɣééɲoyde *v.* go and climb.

Ɣééɲtude *v.* 1) be old-fashioned 2) climb down 3) complete one's turn.

Ɣeewde *v.* stare; look at. *Hol ko Ɣeewataa* What are you looking at?

Ɣééwki *(ki)* stare.

Ɣeewtaade *v.* watch over; check; review. *O woni ko e Ɣeewtaade ɓiyii ko* He is checking his baby.

Ɣeewtagól *(ngól)* retrospect.

Ɣééwtindaade [Ɣééwtiⁿdaade] *v.* verify; check. *Ɣeewtindo ko kaala taa ko* Be careful about what you say.

Ɣéftude *v.* pick up; lift. *Ɣeftu ko njeyɗaa* Take what belongs to you.

Ɣéllitaade *v.* prosper. *O mo Ɣellitii* He is prosperous.

Ɣéllitaagól *(ngól)* growth; prosperity.

Ɣéllitaare *(nde)* growth; prosperity.

Ɣéllitde [Ɣéllidde] *v.* promote; emancipate. *ꞵamtude alt.*

Ɣéllitiiɗo *adj.* prosperous.

Ɣerde *v.* 1) lament; cry 2) be larger than; be higher than. *ɗaccu ko Ɣerataa ko* Stop crying.

Ɣettaade *v.* insult; curse; abuse. *O Ɣettii mo* He cursed him out.

Ɣetteede *v.* 1) be lifted up; be recruited 2) be insulted.

Ɣettoore *(nde)* insult; curse; abuse; affront; slur. *ɗum ko Ɣettore* It is an insult.

Ɣettude *v.* pick up.

Ɣiinaade *v.* be powerful or influential.

Ɣiinude *v.* be powerful or influential.

Ɣiiwde *v.* be cloudy. *Asamaan o ko Ɣiiwɗo* It is cloudy.

Ɣiiwoonde [Ɣiiwooⁿde] *(nde)* clouds forming prior to rain.

ƔiiƔam *(ɗam)* blood.

Ɣiyal *(ngal)* bone. ~ *koyngal* tibia. ~ *juꞵngo* radius. *Ɣiye (ɗe) pl.*

Ɣóꞵꞵude *v.* prod; tickle.

Ɣóꞵꞵugól *(ngól)* tickling.

Ɣongo [Ɣoɲ ⁿgo] *(ngo)* ford.

Ɣoogande *v.* draw or fetch water for. *Ɣooganam mi yoꞵ maa* Fetch water for me and I will pay you.

Ɣoogde *v.* draw water.

Ɣóógirde *v.* draw water with.

Ɣóógirgal *(ngal)* bucket for drawing water.

Ɣóógól *(ngól)* act of fetching water.

Ɣóógóyde *v.* go and fetch water. *O Ɣoogoyii* He went to fetch water.

Ɣoolde *(nde)* breast. *Ɣoole (ɗe) pl.*

ƔoꞮde [Ɣojje] *v.* be clever. *O mo ƔoꞮi* S/he is clever.

Ɣo Ɣɗo [Ɣo Ɣɗo] *adj.* astute; clever; genius; shrewd; sly. *neɗɗo* ~ an intelligent person.

Ɣo Ɣre *(nde)* intelligence.

ƔóꞮnude [Ɣóññude] *v.* 1) make someone intelligent 2) be feverish. *Ko o Ɣo Ɣnuɗo* He is feverish.

ɗ**lmere** *(nde)* coal. ~ *jayngol* a burning
ꞁiece of coal.

ꞁ**sde** *v.* sob.

ꞁ**ufde** *v.* be swollen.

ꞁ**ufnude** *v.* swell; cause to swell.

Ƴ**uugeede** *v.* be hunchbacked.

Ƴ**uugere** *(nde)* hunchback.

Ƴ**uulde** *(nde)* hump.

HIPPOCRENE STANDARD DICTIONARY

ENGLISH-PULAAR

A

a [a] *det.* gooto; petto ~ *book* deftere wootere.

aback [əbak] *adv.* surprise. *be taken* ~ najde; najneede.

abandon [əbandən] *v.* ɗaccude; accitde. ~ *a house/village* wiinnude.

abandoned [əbandənd] *adj.* ɗaccaɗum. ~ *house/village* wiinde *(nde)*

abandonment [əbandənmənt] *n.* ɗaccugol *(ngol)*.

abase [əbeyz] *v.* nuskude; téllinde.

abate [əbeyt] *v.* ustude.

abatement [əbeytmənt] *n.* ustugol *(ngól)*.

abattage [əbəta3] *n.* kirsugol jawdi.

abattoir [abətwar] *n.* hirsirde *(nde)*.

abbreviate [əbriyviyeyt] *v.* raɓɓiɗinde.

abbreviation [əbriyviyeyšən] *n.* daɓɓiɗingol *(ngól)*.

abdicate [abdəkeyt] *v.* jébbilaade; ɗaccude; yaafaade. ~ *the throne* ɗaccude laamu mum/fiiltude laamu mum. *He abdicated* O jebbiliima.

abdication [abdəkeyšən] *n.* jébbilaare *(nde)*. *This is an abdication* ɗum ko jebbilaare.

abdomen [abdəmin] *n.* réédu *(ndu)*.

abdominal [abdowminəl] *adj.* ko faati e réédu ~ *pain* reedu muusooru.

abduct [abdʌkt] *v.* wujjude; teetde. *He was abducted* O wujja.

abduction [abdʌkšən] *n.* nguyka *(ka)*; teetere *(nde)*.

abecedary [əbesədəri] *adj.* ko faati e limto.

abecederian [əbesəderiən] *n.* limtoowo *(o)* . *He is an abecederian* Ko o limtoowo.

aberrance [əberəns] *n.* ooñaare *(nde)*.

aberrant [abərənt] *adj.* ooñiɗum; kó óóñii; ko fooˠtaaki.

aberration [abəreyšən] *n.* ooñaare *(nde)*. *It is a major aberration* ɗum ko ooñaare mawnde.

abeyance [əbeyəns] *n.* leefgol *(ngol)*.

abhor [abhor] *v.* añde.

abhorrence [abhorəns] *n.* ngañgu *(ngu)*; elko *(ko)*.

abidance [əbaydəns] *n.* ɗowtaare *(nde)*.

abide [əbayd] *v.* ɗowtaade; rewde. ~ *by* heddade e; rewde e. *You must abide by the rules* Aɗa foti rewde sarɗiyeeji ɗi.

ability [əbiləti] *n.* mbaawka *(ka)*; gandal. *to the best of my* ~ mbaawka am fof. *Show your ability* hollu mbaawka ma.

abject [abjekt] *adj.* ko yurminii; kérsiniiɗum.

abjure [abjuwr] *v.* ɗaccitde. ~ *one's religion* yaltude e diine mum.

ablate [əbleyt] *v.* taˠde; ittude.

ablation [əbleyšən] *n.* ittugol *(ngól)*; taˠgol *(ngól)*.

ablaze [əbleyz] *v.* huɓɓude; jawwude.

able [eybəl] *adj.* baawɗo; kattanɗo. *He is able to do it* Omo waawi waɗde ɗum.

ablution [əbluwšən] *n.* sallige.

abnegate [abnegeyt] *v.* ɗaccude; haaytude.

abnormal [əbnɔrməl] *adj.* ko wóóri; celɗum; ko rewaani laawol. *It is abnormal* ɗum rewaani laawol.

abnormality [əbnəmaləti] *n.* huunde woornde.

aboard [əbɔrd] *v.* jolde. *to go* ~ jolde e laana.

abode [əbowd] *n.* jippunde *(nde)*; hoɗorde *(nde)*. *place of* ~ hoɗorde *(nde)*; galle *(o)*.

abolish [əboliš] *v.* ittude; rimɗinde; abolish. ~ *slavery* tellinde kalifaandi; rimɗinde jiyaaɓe.

abolition [əbəliyšən] *n.* ittugól *(ngól)*.

abomasum [əbowmasum] *n.* fulkuru *(ndu)*.

abominable [əbomənəbəl] *adj.* bóómójum; bónɗum.

abomination [əboməneyšən] *n.* moobaare *(nde)*; bonande *(nde)*. *a major* ~ moobaare mawnde.

abordage [əborda3] *n.* naatóndiral laaɗe.

abort [abɔrt] *v.* rufde réédu; boosde. *She aborted* O rufii reedu/O boosii.

abortion [abɔršən] *n.* boosgól *(ngól)*; dufgol reedu. *have an* ~ rufde reedu.

abound [əbawnd] *v.* ittude; nammude; ɗuuɗde.

about [əbawt] *prep.* sabba. ~ *three kilograms* sabba cilooji tati.

above [əbowv] *prep.* dow ~ *your head* dow hoore maa.

abrade [əbreyd] v. heefde.

abrasion [əbreyʒən] n. gaañande *(nde)*.

abreast [əbrest] adv. sawndo *(ngo)*; takko *(ngo)*. *keep ~ of the times* yahdude e aduna.

abri [abri] n. ɗuhorde *(nde)*.

abridge [eybrij] v. raɓɓiɗinde.

abridgement [eybrijmənt] n. daɓɓiɗingól *(ngól)*.

abroad [əbrɔd] adj. caggal léydi. *He is abroad* O woni ko caggal leydi.

abrogate [abrowgeyt] v. firtude.

abrupt [əbrʌpt] adj. ko tijjaaka.

abscess [abses] n. ñawande worɗinde.

abscind [absind] v. taɼde.

abscond [abskond] v. dogde ñaawoore.

absence [absəns] n. birnagól *(ngól)*. *in the ~ of* so ɗum alaa. *It happened during your absence* It happened during your absence.

absent [absənt] adj. birniɗum; mo tawaaka. *He was absent* O tawanooka.

absentee [absəntiy] n. mo tawaaka; mo tawtoraaka.

absolute [absoluwt] adj. timmuɗum; ko timmi.

absolve [absolv] v. yaafaade.

absorb [abzɔb] v. moɗɗe. *The child absorbed it* Suka o moɗii ɗum.

absorbent [abzɔbənt] adj. ko moɗata.

absorber [abzɔbə] n. moɗoowo *(o)*.

abstain [absteyn] v. haɗaade; salaade. *You should abstain* Aɗa foti salaade.

abstemious [abstemyəs] adj. naɼtiiɗo; caasɗo.

absterge [abstərʒ] v. fiifaade; ñittaade; momtude.

abstersion [abstərʒən] n. taamaamuya *(o)*.

abstract [abstrakt] adj. niɓɓiɗɗum.

abstruse [abstruwz] adj. niɓɓiɗɗum.

absurd [absərd] adj. ko yuɓɓaani; ko nannaaki. *It is absurd* ɗum nannaaki.

abundance [abʌndəns] n. ñaamanduru *(ndu)*; ɗuuɗal *(ngal)*.

abundant [abʌndənt] adj. keewɗum.

abundantly [abʌndəntli] adv. kó hééwi.

abuse [əbyuwz] n. tooñange *(nge)*.

abuse [əbyuwz] v. tooñde; ɓurtinde. *He is abusing his power* Omon ɓurtina.

abusive [əbyuwziv] adj. tooñoowo.

acacia [əkasya] n. caski (ki); ɓulki (ki); ciluki (ki).

academic [akədemik] adj. ko faati e jaɼde ~ *work* liggeey jaɼde.

acatelectic [əkatəlektik] adj. ko timmi; timmuɗum.

accede [aksiyd] v. laamaade; fiileede; jaɓde. ~ *to the throne* laamaade; fiileede. *He acceded to the throne* O fiilaama.

accelerate [aksələreyt] v. yaawnaade; yaactaade. *You need to accelerate* Aɗa foti yaawnaade.

acceleration [aksələreyšən] n. jaactagól *(ngól)*.

accent [aksənt] n. masgal *(ngal)*; masgal dow. *place the accent on* masde; tekkinde.

accent [aksənt] v. tékkinde; masde.

accentual [aksənčuwəl] adj. ko faati e masgal/masɗe.

accentuate [aksənčuweyt] v. tékkinde; tééɼtinde.

accept [aksept] v. jeɓbilaade; jaɓde. *I accept your proposal* Mi jaɓii miijo maa.

acceptable [akseptəbəl] adj. ko jaɓetee. *This behavior is not acceptable* ɗee golle njamiraaka.

access [akses] n. naatirde *(nde)*; damal *(ngal)*. *the ~ to the house* natirde galle

accessible [aksəsibəl] adj. ko heɓotoo; keɓotooɗum. *It is not accessible* ɗum heɓotaako.

accident [ɑksidənt] n. aksida *(o)*. *He was involved in a car accident this morning* Ko o baɗɗo aksida subaka hande o.

accidental [aksidentəl] adj. ko faati e aksidaa.

acclaim [əkleym] v. foɓɓande; hellande. *They acclaimed the president* ɓe poɓɓanii laamɗo *(o)*.

acclamation [akləmeyšən] n. kelle.

acclimate [akləmeyt] v. wóówtude nókku. *He has gotten acclimated* O woowtii.

acclimatize [akləmətayz] v. wóówtude. *become ~ʐed* woowtude.

accommodate [akəmədeyt] v. yuɓɓinde; hoɗnude. *I accommodated him* Mi hoɗniimo.

accommodation [akəmədeyšən] n. hoɗorde *(nde)*.

accompaniment [əkompənimənt] *n.* ɗóftugól *(ngól).*

accompany [akəmpəni] *v.* yahdude; ɗóftude. *You should accompany him* Aɗa foti yahdude e makko.

accomplice [akəmplis] *n.* dénduɗo maakaa/feere. *He is an accomplice* Kamɓe ndendi maakaa.

accomplish [akəmpliš] *v.* jóófnude; fééwnude; waɗde.

accord [akɔd] *n.* nanóndiral *(ngal);* kawral *(ngal). We have reached an accord* Min nanondirii.

accord [akɔd] *v.* nanóndirde; aadóndirde; hawrude.

accordance [əkɔdəns] *n.* juɓɓugól *(ngól). be in ~ with* tuugnaade e.

according to [əkɔdiŋtə] e wiide. *~ you* e wiide maa. *act ~ to the law* rewde laawol.

accost [akost] *v.* teerde; joofde.

account [əkawnt] *n.* móóftirde kaalis. *I have an account in your bank* Mbeɗe jogii mooftirde kaalis e nder banke ma.

accountant [əkawntənt] *n.* joɓoowo *(o);* Ƴeewtotooɗo ko faati e kaalis. *He is an accountant* Ko o joɓoowo.

accouterment [akuwtermənt] *n.* cómci *(ɗi);* cómcól *(ngól).*

accrete [akriyt] *v.* mawninde.

accretion [akriyšən] *n.* mawnugól *(ngól).*

acculturate [akʌlčəreyt] *v.* neesaade néésu ngóngu; naatnude e neesu mum.

accumulate [akyuwmələyt] *v.* jóówóndirde; fawóndirde.

accumulation [akyuwmələyšən] *n.* jóówóndiral *(ngal).*

accumulator [akyuwmələytə] *n.* jóówóndiroowo *(o).*

accuracy [akurəsi] *n.* potal *(ngal);* juɓɓugól *(ngól).*

accurate [akurət] *adj.* potɗum; juɓɓuɗum; gooddum. *take ~ aim* feewnude toɓɓugol mum. *It is accurate* Ina woodi.

accusation [əkyuwzeyšən] *n.* tuumal *(ngal). a serious ~* tuumal tiiɗngal.

accuse [əkyuwz] *v.* tuumde; jumde. *He is accused of robbery* O tuumaama nguyka.

accustom [akʌstəm] *v.* wóównude. *I am accustomed to this heat* Mi woowtii kii nguleeki.

ace [eys] *n.* aas *(o).*

acerb [asərb] *adj.* lammuɗum.

ache [eyk] *n.* muusu *(ngu);* ñaw *(ngu). stomach ~* reedu muusooru. *~s and pains* muusu *(ngu). I have a headache* Hooram ina muusa.

ache [eyk] *v.* muusde.

achieve [əčiyv] *v.* jóófnude; timminde; heɓde. *I achieved what I wanted* Mi heɓii ko njiɗnoomi.

acid [asid] *adj.* lammuɗum; kaadɗum.

acidify [asədəfay] *v.* lamminde; hetde.

acidity [asəditi] *n.* lammugól *(ngól).*

acidulate [asidyuwleyt] *v.* lamminde; hetde.

acknowledge [aknəwlej] *v.* jaɓde.

acme [akme] *n.* ceɓtam *(ɗam).*

acne [akne] *n.* puƳe *(ɗe).*

acoustic [akustik] *adj.* maale nanɗe; ko faati e nanɗe.

acquaint [akwent] *v.* hóllóndirde; andondirde. *be ~ed with* andude.

acquaintance [akwentəns] *n.* kollóndiral *(ngal).*

acquest [akwest] *n.* jawdi *(ndi);* jéy *(o).*

acquiesce [akyes] *v.* heɓde; dañde; jaɓde.

acquire [akwayə] *v.* heɓde; dañde. *I acquired it yesterday* Keɓmi ɗum ko hanki.

acquirement [akwayəmənt] *n.* kéɓgól *(ngól).*

acquisition [akwiziyšən] *n.* kéɓgól *(ngól);* dañal *(ngal).*

acquit [akwit] *v.* ɗaccude jagganooɗo; ɗaccitde. *He was acquitted* O ɗaccitaama.

acquittal [akwital] *n.* ɗaccitgól *(ngól).*

acre [eykə] *n.* ngesa *(ba).*

acrimonious [akrimonyəs] *adj.* ñanguɗum.

acrobat [akrobat] *n.* geewotooɗo. *He is a skilled acrobat* Ko o baawɗo geewaade.

acrobatic [akrəbatik] *adj.* ko faati e geewagól walla junnitbasél.

acrobatics [akrəbatiks] *n.* junnitbasél.

across [əkrɔs] taccugol *(ngol). walk ~ the road* taccude kallu. *get something ~* famminde.

act [akt] *v.* waɗde; amdaade; gollaade.

act [akt] *n.* gollal *(ngal). be caught in the ~ of doing something* jaggeede jungo e faandu. *Get one's ~ together* heytaade.

action [akšən] *n.* gollal *(ngal). take ~* gollaade.

activate [aktəveyt] v. wuurnude.
active [aktiv] adj. cóftuɗo. *She is very active* Omo softi.
activity [aktivəti] n. gollal *(ngal)*; liggééy; gollal.
actor [aktə] n. pijoowo *(o)*.
actual [akčwəl] adj. gooɗɗum; kó wóódi.
actuality [əkčwaləti] n. huunde woodnde.
actually [akcwəli] adv. woni goonga; e goonga.
actuate [əkčweyt] v. wuurnude; wélnude; sóftinde.
acuity [akwiti] n. ceeɓdi *(ndi)*.
acute [akyuwt] adj. ceeɓɗo; kó sééɓi. *It is acute* Ina seeɓi.
ad [ad] n. jeeyngal *(ngal)*.
adage [adaჳ] n. tindól *(ngól)*.
Adam [ɑdəm] n. Aadama *(o)*; baammen Aadama.
adamant [adəmənt] adj. jattiniiɗo.
adapt [ədapt] v. wóówtude. *I am adapting to his wishes* Mbeɗen woowta yiɗde makko.
add [ad] v. ɓeydude. ~ *insult to injury* ɓurtinde. *Add water to the milk* ɓeydu ndiyam e kosam ɗam.
addendum [adendəm] n. timmingól *(ngól)*; timmitingól.
adder [adə] n. ɓeydoowo *(o)*.
addict [adikt] n. duudeteeɗo *(o)*. *He is an addict* Ko o duudeteeɗo.
addiction [adikšən] n. duudo *(ngo)*.
addition [adiyšən] n. ɓeydaari *(ndi)*; ɓeydugol *(ngol)*. *in* ~ yanti heen.
additional [adiyšənəl] adj. ɓeydiɗum.
addle [adəl] v. jilɓinde.
addle [adəl] adj. ñólɗum.
address [adres] n. tiitoonde *(nde)*. *What is your address* Hol ko woni tiitoonde ma?
addressee [adresiy] n. bindaaɗo; mo ɓataake huccinaa e mum. *He is the addressee* Ko kanko windaa.
adduce [adyus] n. addude; hóllirde.
adept [adept] n. almuudo *(o)*; dewɗo *(o)*. *He is an adept of Ahmadu Bamba* Ko o almuudo Ahmadu Bamba.
adequacy [adekwəsi] n. peewal *(ngal)*; timmal *(ngal)*.
adequate [adekwət] adj. pééwɗum; móƔƔuɗum. *It is adequate* Ina feewi.

adhere [adhiyr] v. jaɓde; naatde. *I adhere to that suggestion* Mi jaɓii ɗum.
adherence [adhiyrəns] n. naatgól *(ngól)*.
adherent [adhiyrənt] adj. naatɗo e; jeyaaɗo e.
adhesion [adhiyჳən] n. naatgól *(ngól)*; jaɓgól *(ngól)*.
adiaphorous [adyafərəs] adj. hakkundeejo.
adieu [adyə] n. baynóndiral *(ngal)*.
adipose [adipowz] adj. payɗum; ɓuttiɗɗum.
adit [adit] n. naatirde *(nde)*; laawól *(ngól)*. *Here is the adit* Ko ɗoo woni naatirde nde.
adjacency [ajeysənsi] n. ɓadtóndiral *(ngal)*.
adjacent [ajeysənt] adj. ko ɓadtondiri; ɓadtóndirɗum; takkondirɗum. *They are are adjacent* Eɗi takkondiri.
adjectival [ajektayvəl] adj. ko faati e timminoore; timminoojum.
adjective [ajektiv] n. timminoore *(nde)*. *It is an adjective* ɗum ko timminoore.
adjoin [ajoyn] v. séƖ)ondirde.
adjourn [ajərn] v. faɓɓinde. *The meeting is adjourned* Deental ngal faɓɓinaama.
adjournment [ajərnmənt] n. paɓɓingól *(ngól)*.
adjudge [ajʌj] v. ñaawde; yamirde.
adjudicate [ajudəkeyt] v. ñaawde; yamirde.
adjudication [ajudəkeyšən] n. ñaawoore *(nde)*; yamiroore *(nde)*.
adjunct [ajʌŋkt] n. timminoore *(nde)*.
adjust [ajʌst] v. fééwnitde; yuɓɓinde.
adjustment [ajʌstmənt] n. pééwnitgól *(ngól)*; juɓɓingól *(ngól)*.
adjuvant [ajuwvənt] adj. balloowo; ko wallata.
administer [administer] v. laamaade; jiimde; ardaade. *He is administering this locality* Ko kanko jiimi oo nokku.
administration [administreyšən] laamorde nókku.
admirable [admayrəbəl] adj. jeeɓeteeɗo; jeeɓeteeɗum.
admire [admayə] v. yeeɓde. *I admire you* Mbeɗe yeeɓ maa.
admissible [admisəbəl] adj. jaɓaɗum; jamiraaɗum; naatnaɗum.
admission [admiyšən] n. naatnugól *(ngól)*; naatgól *(ngól)*; yamiroore *(nde)*. *Your*

admission was rejected Naatgol maa yamiraa ka.

admit [admit] *v.* naatnude; jaɓde. *He has been admitted* O naatii.

admix [admiks] *v.* rendinde.

admonish [admoniš] *v.* waajaade; rééntinde.

admonition [admoniyšən] *n.* waajuya *(o)*.

adolescence [adolesəns] *n.* kéllifuya *(o)*; kellifaagal *(ngal)*; cagataagal *(ngal)*.

adolescent [adolesənt] *n.* kéllifaaɗo *(o)*; sagata *(o)*;

adopt [adopt] *v.* jaɓde; nehde.

adoptive [adəptiv] *adj.* nehɗo; nehɓe; nehaaɗo; nehaaɓe. *He is my adoptive parent* Ko kanko nehi mi.

adoration [adəreyšən] *n.* déwgól *(ngól)*; jééɓgól *(ngól)*.

adore [adowr] *v.* rewde; yeeɓde. *I adore you* Mi rewii ma.

adorn [adɔn] *v.* siŋkude. *~ oneself* suɗaade; ɓoornaade cuɗaari.

adornment [adɔnmənt] *n.* ñéŋkudi *(ndi)*.

adroit [adroyt] *adj.* peewɗo; peewɗo jungo.

adulate [adyuleyt] *v.* ɗowtaade.

adult [adʌlt] *adj.* mawɗo; mawnuɗo; kellifaaɗo. *He is an adult* Ko o kellifaaɗo.

adulterer [adʌltərə] *n.* jinoowo *(o)*. *He is an adulterer* Ko o jinoowo.

adulteress [adʌltərəs] *n.* debbo jinoowo; debbo pijoowo; garbotooɗo *(o)*.

adultery [adʌltri] *n.* jinaa *(o)*. *Adultery is forbidden* Jinaa ina harmi.

advance [advɑns] *v.* yahrude yeeso; Ɣéllitaade. *You need to advance* Aɗa foti yahrude yeeso.

advancement [advɑnsmənt] *n.* jahrugól yeeso.

advancer [advɑnsə] *n.* jahroowo yeeso.

advantage [advɑntij] *n.* ɓural *(ngal)*. *What is the advantage of this procedure* Hol ko woni ɓural ndee feere?

advantageous [advɑnteyjəs] *adj.* ɓurɗum.

advent [advent] *n.* saanga *(o)*; waɗnde *(nde)*.

adventure [advenčə] *n.* jiilagól *(ngól)*; njiilaw *(o)*.

adverb [advərb] *n.* timminoore *(nde)*.

adversary [advərsəri] *adj.* kaɓdiiɗo *(o)*. *He is my adversary* Ko min haɓdiiɓe.

adverse [advərs] *adj.* luutndiiɗo; luutndiɗum.

adversity [advərsiti] *n.* kaɓdigal *(ngal)*.

advertisement [advətayzmənt] *n.* tintingól *(ngól)*; jeeyngal *(ngal)*. *The advertisement was very useful* Jeeyngal ngal nafii no feewi.

advertiser [advətayzə] *n.* jeeynoowo *(o)*; tintinoowo *(o)*. *The advertiser has not arrived yet* Jeeynoowo o araani tawo.

advertise [advətayzə] *v.* tintinde; yééynude. *It has been advertised* ɗum yeeynaama.

advice [advays] *n.* waajuya *(o)*.

advise [advayz] *v.* waajaade. *He is advising you* O woni ko e waajaade ma.

advisee [advayzi] *n.* bajeteeɗo *(o)*.

adviser [advayzə] *n.* baajotooɗo *(o)*. *He is my adviser* Ko kanko woni baajotooɗo mi.

advocate [advəkeyt] *v.* heedande.

aerate [ereyt] *v.* naatnude héndu.

aerial [eriyəl] *adj.* ko faati e weeyo.

aeroplane [eyrpleyn] *n.* abiyoŋ.

aesthetic [esθetik] *adj.* jóóɗɗum.

aestival [estivəl] *adj.* ko faati e cééɗu.

afar [afar] *adv.* góɗɗuɗum.

affability [afəbiləti] *n.* belgól ƳiiƳam.

affable [afabəl] *adj.* belɗo ƳiiƳam.

affair [afer] *n.* haaju *(o)*; hafeere *(nde)*.

affect [afekt] *v.* heɓde.

affection [afekšən] *n.* jiɗgól *(ngól)*; gilli *(ɗi)*.

affiance [afiyəns] *n.* fodande *(nde)*; hoolaare *(nde)*.

affiliate [afilyet] *v.* jókkóndirde.

affirm [afərm] *v.* tééɫtinde; tiiɗtinde.

affirmation [afərmeyšən] *n.* tééɫtingól *(ngól)*.

affirmative [afərmeyšən] *adj.* ko teeɫtinaa; tééɫtinaaɗum.

affix [afiks] *v.* jókkude; seŋde.

affixation [afikseyšən] *n.* jokkere *(nde)*.

afflict [aflikt] *v.* sunnude. *He is afflicted* Ko o cuniiɗo.

affliction [aflikšən] *n.* sunaare *(nde)*; metteende *(nde)*.

affluence [afluwəns] *n.* garaangal e keewal; ɗuuɗal. *Their affluence was noted* Keewal maɓɓe tinaa ma.

affluent [afluwənt] *adj.* galo; alɗuɓe. *He is affluent* Ko o galo.

afford [afɔrd] *v.* jogaade; waawande. *I cannot afford it* Mi ala naa ɗum doole / Mi jogaaki.

affranchize [əfrənčayz] *v.* rimɗinde.

affray [əfrey] *n.* hare *(nde)*.

affrayer [əfreyə] *n.* kaɓeteeɗo *(o)*.

affright [əfrayt] *v.* hulɓinde.

affront [afront] *n.* tooñange *(nge);* Yettoore *(nde)*. *It is an affront* ɗum ko Yettoore.

afloat [əflowt] *adj.* kayojum; kumbojum.

afoot [afuwt] *adj.* jahroowo koyngal.

afore [afowr] *adj.* ko adii

afraid [əfreyd] *adj.* kulɗo; kulɓinaado. *He is afraid of him* Ko o kulɗo mo.

Africa [afrikə] *n.* Afirik.

African [afrikən] *adj.* afiriknaajo.

after [aftə] *conj.* ɓaawo; caggal ~ *you* ardo. *What are you after* hol ko cokluɗaa / Hol ko ɗekkataa.

aftermath [aftəmɑθ] *n.* caggal.

afternoon [aftərnuwn] *n.* kikiiɗe *(o)*. *I will see you in the afternoon* Ma mi yiye hande kikiiɗe.

afterthought [aftəθɔt] *n.* Yeewtagól *(ngól)*; miijtagól *(ngól)*.

afterward [aftəwɔd] *caggal* ɗum.

again [əgeyn] *adv.* titi; kadi ~ *and* ~ laabi keewɗi.

against [əgeynst] kontoor.

agape [əgeyp] *adj.* ŋaabiɗum (hunuko).

age [eyj] *n.* duuɓi. ~ *set* kafu. *old* ~ nayééwu *(ngu)*; nayewaagu *(ngu)*. *How old are you* No duuɓi maa poti?

aged [eyjd] *adj.* nayeejo; naywuɗo; naywuɗum; nayeeɓe; naywuɓe.

agent [eyjənt] *n.* baɗoowo *(o);* liggotooɗo *(o);*.

agential [eyjənšəl] *adj.* ko faati e liggotooɗo.

agglomerate [agloməreyt] *v.* ñukkóndirde.

agglomeration [agloməreyšən] *n.* ñukkóndiral *(ngal)*.

agglutinate [aglyuwtneyt] *v.* ɗakkondirde; takkóndirde; jókkóndirde.

aggrandize [əgrəndayz] *v.* mawninde.

aggravate [əgrəveyt] *v.* urɓitde.

aggravation [əgrəveyšən] *n.* urɓitgól *(ngól)*.

aggregate [agrəgeyt] *v.* réndinde.

aggress [agres] *v.* tooñde; yande e; fiide.

aggression [agrešən] *n.* tooñange *(nge)*.

aggressor [agresə] *n.* tooñoowo *(o)*. *He is the aggressor* Ko kanko tooñi; ko kanko yani e makko.

agile [əjayl] *adj.* koyɗo; koyɗo e leydi. *He is agile* Omo hoyi e leydi.

agility [əjiləti] *n.* kóygól é léydi.

agitate [ajəteyt] *v.* sosde; awYitde; dillinde.

agitation [ajəteyšən] *n.* dillere *(nde)*; dillingól *(ngól)*.

agitator [ajəteytə] *n.* urɓoowo *(o)*. *He is an agitator* Ko o urɓoowo.

agnomen [agnowmen] *n.* sowoore *(nde)*.

ago [əgow] *adv.* ko ɓenni; ɓennuɗum. *two days* ~ hecci haŊki. *three days* ~ heccitaawel hecci hanki. *four days* ~ waɗii balɗe nay.

agonize [agənayz] *v.* fitaade. *He is agonizing* Omon fitoo.

agrarian [agreriyən] *adj.* ko faati e léydi walla e ndema.

agree [agriy] *v.* hawrude; jaɓde; aadóndirde. *I agree* Mi jaɓii.

agreeable [agriyəbəl] *adj.* ɓelɗum.

agreement [agriymənt] *n.* ahdi *(ndi)*. *Our agreement holds* Ahdi men ina heddii.

agricultural [agrikʌlčərəl] *adj.* ko faati e ndema e ngaynaaka.

agriculture [agrikʌlčə] *n.* ndema e ngaynaaka.

agronomy [agrownəmi] *n.* jangde léydi e ndema. *He is studying agronomy* O jangata ko jangde leydi e ndema e ngaynaaka.

ahead [əhed] *adv.* ko wóni yeeso. *It is ahead of you* ɗum woni ko yeeso.

ahem [ahem] *n.* dirmaango (ngo); dirmaali *(ɗi)*.

aid [eyd] *v.* wallude.

aid [eyd] *n.* ballal *(ngal)*. *Your aid was valuable to us* Ballal maa nafii min.

ail [eyl] *v.* muuseede.

ailing [eyliŋ] *adj.* muusaaɗo.

ailment [eylmənt] *n.* ñaw *(ngu)*.

aim [eym] *v.* toɓɓude; tukkude. *He is aiming at the bird* Omon toɓɓa.

aimless [eymles] *adj.* mo alaa haaju.

ir [eyr] *n.* kenal *(kal)*; hendu *(ndu)*.

irplane [eyrpleyn] *n.* ndiwoowa *(ka)*.

irport [eyrpɔt] *n.* kandaa abiyoŋ. *They went to the airport* ɓe njahii kanda abiyoŋ.

jar [ajɑr] *adj.* ko uddaaki; ko hiɓɓaaki; gudditiiɗum.

kin [eykin] ko faati e. ~ *to* ko faati e.

lar [alɑr] *adj.* ko faati e wibjo/bibje.

larm [alɑm] *n.* kulól *(ngól)*; jeerto (ngo).

larmed [alɑm] *adj.* kulɗo; jeertiiɗo. *Tell him not to be alarmed* Hol to soklu.

lbino [albayno] *n.* fuuñéé *(o)*.

lbumen [albyumən] *n.* ndanééri ɓoccoonde.

lcohol [alkohowl] *n.* alkol *(o);* konjam *(ɗam)*. *He drinks alcohol* Omo yara konjam.

lcoholic [alkəhowlik] *adj.* ko faati e koñjam.

leph [alef] *n.* alkulal *(ngal)*; alliif *(o)*.

lert [alərt] *v.* tintinde; rééntinde *The army is under alert* Soldateeɓe ɓe ko reentinaaɓe.

lexia [aleksyə] *n.* ñaw ngaandi.

lgebra [aljəbra] *n.* kiisagól *(ngól)*.

lgebraic [aljəbrayik] *adj.* ko faati e kiisagól.

lgorithm [algoriðəm] *n.* feere *(nde)*. *What is your algorithm* Hol ko woni feere maa?

lien [eyliyən] *n.* arani *(o);* tumaranke *(o)*.

lienist [eyliyenist] *n.* cafroowo kaaɗi.

light [əlayt] *v.* tellaade.

light [əlayt] *adj.* kuɓɓaɗum; kuɓɓojum; kuɓɓaaɗi.

lign [əlayn] *v.* réggóndirde.

lignment [əlaynmənt] *n.* déggóndiral *(ngal)*.

like [əlayk] *adj.* nanduɗi; nanduɓe. *They are alike* Kamɓe nandi.

liment [aləmənt] *n.* ñamri *(ndi)*.

limentary [aləməntəri] *adj.* ko faati e ñamri.

limentation [alimənteyšən] *n.* ñamri *(ndi)*.

limony [aləmoni] *n.* nguura ceeraaɗo.

live [əlayv] *adj.* guurɗo; wuurɓe; ko wuuri. *They are alive* Eɓe nguuri.

all [ɔl] *adv.* dendaagal; fóf. *you* ~ onon kala.

Allah [alah] *n.* Alla.

allay [əley] *v.* dééɣnude; ɓuuɓnude.

allegation [aləgeyšən] *n.* tuumal *(ngal)*. *This is a serious allegation* Ngal tuumal ko tiiɗngal.

allege [alej] *v.* tuumde.

allegiance [aliyjəns] *n.* ɗowtagól *(ngól)*; ɗowtaare *(nde)*.

allegiant [aliyjənt] *adj.* ɗówtiiɗo.

alleviate [əliyvyeyt] *v.* hóybinde.

alleviation [əliyvyešən] *n.* kóybingól.

alley [ɑliy] *n.* laawól *(ngól)*. *Use this alley* Rew ngol laawol.

alliance [alayəns] *n.* jantóndiral *(ngal)*. *They formed an alliance* ɓe njantondirii.

alligator [aligeytə] *n.* nóóróó *(o)*.

allocate [aləkeyt] *v.* taɣande; réénnude; joñde.

allot [alot] *v.* taɣande; réénnude.

allow [əlaw] *v.* yamirde; jaɓande. *You are allowed to come in* a yamiraama yo a naat.

alloy [əloy] *adj.* jilluɗum.

ally [alay] *n.* séhil; gonanɗo.

almighty [almayti] *adj.* Allah.

almost [ɔlmowst] *v.* ɗesde.

alms [ɔlmz] *n.* sadakééji *(ɗi)*; sadak. *He gives alms every day* Omon sakkoo.

alone [əlown] *adj.* gooto; petto.

along [əloŋ] *prep.* njuutééndi *(ndi)*.

alongside [əloŋsayd] *n.* sara *(o);* takko *(o)*.

aloof [əluwf] *adj.* góɗɗuɗum.

aloud [əlawd] *adj.* mawnuɗum; mawnunde; mawnde.

alpha [alfə] *n.* alkulal *(ngal)*.

alphabet [alfəbet] *n.* alkule; limto (ngo).

already [ɔlredi] *adj.* ko ɓénni; ɓennuɗum.

also [ɔlso] *adj.* kadi; yanti heen.

alter [ɔltə] *v.* waylude. *The plan has been altered* Feere nde waylaama.

alteration [ɔltəreyšən] *n.* baylugol *(ngól)*; baylagol *(ngól)*; ñoottagól *(ngól)*.

altercate [ɔltərkeyt] *v.* dukde.

altercation [ɔltərkeyšən] *n.* duko (ngo).

alternative [ɔltərnətiv] *n.* feere wonde; miijo wongo; cuɓagól *(ngól)*. *What alternative solution are you suggesting* Hol miijo wongo njogiɗaa?

although [ɔlðow] *conj.* hay so.

altitude [altəčuwd] *n.* tóówééndi *(ndi)*.

altitudinal [altəčuwdinəl] *adj.* ko faati e tóówééndi.

altogether [ɔltəgeðə] *adv.* fóf; kañum fóf.

always [ɔlweyz] *adv.* ñande kala. *He is always there* Omo toon sahaa kala.

amalgamate [amalgəmeyt] *v.* yantóndirde; réndinde.

amass [əmɑs] *v.* réndinde.

amateur [amatər] *n.* jeeɓoowo; jiɗɗo.

amaze [ameyz] *v.* haawnude It is amazing Ina haawnii.

amazement [ameyzmənt] *n.* haawniinde *(nde).*

ambassador [ambasadə] *n.* ambaasadeer *(o);* gonanɗo léydi mum caggal léydi.

amber [ambə] *n.* lambureere *(nde).*

ambiguous [ambigyus] *adj.* ko yuɓɓaani; ko leeraani. *This speech act is ambiguous* kongol ngol leeraani.

ambitious [ambišəs] *adj.* jiɗɗo Ɣéllitaade.

amble [ambəl] *v.* yahnaade; daagaade.

ambulance [ambiləns] *n.* ambilaas *(o).*

ambulate [ambyuleyt] *v.* yahde.

ambuscade [ambyuskeyd] *v.* paddagól *(ngól).*

ambush [ambuš] *v.* faddaade; taɣde. *He was ambushed* ɓe paddi mo.

ameliorate [amelyoreyt] *v.* samorde; fééwnitde.

amen [amen] *interj.* aamiin.

amend [amend] *v.* fééwnitde; waylude This decree needs to be amended Sarɗi o ina foti feewniteede.

amendment [amendmənt] *n.* baylugól *(ngól);* peewnitgol *(ngól).*

amends [amendz] *n.* njóɓdi *(ndi).*

American [əmerikən] *adj.* amerike; ameriknaajo.

amiable [amyəbəl] *adj.* belɗo; neɗɗo belɗo Ɣiiɣam.

amicable [amikəbəl] *adj.* belɗo Ɣiiɣam.

amid [amid] *prep.* hakkunde; nder.

amigo [amiygo] *n.* séhil *(o).*

amity [amiti] *n.* céhilaagal *(ngal).*

ammunition [amoniyšən] *n.* kute *(ɗe)* ; cóndi kute.

amnesty [amnesti] *n.* yaafuya *(o).*

among [əmoŋ] *prep.* hakkunde; nder.

amongst [əmoŋst] *prep.* nder.

amorous [əmowrəs] *adj.* ko faati e gilli.

amorphous [əmowrfəs] *adj.* ko alaa tagóódi.

amount [əmawnt] *v.* fotde; jarde.

amount [əmawnt] *n.* cóggu *(ngu);* keewal *(ngal).*

amphibious [amfibyəs] *adj.* ko wuurata e léydi e ndiyam.

ample [ampəl] *adj.* jaajɗum; jónɗum.

amplify [ampləfay] *v.* yaajnude; mawninde. *It needs to be amplified* Ina foti mawnineede.

amputate [ampyuwteyt] *v.* taɣde The doctor amputated his leg Ko cafroowo o taɣi koyngal makko.

amputee [ampyuwti] *n.* neɗɗo mo tergal mum taɣaa.

amulet [amyuwlet] *n.* talkuru *(ndu).*

amuse [amyuwz] *v.* jalnude.

amusing [amyuwziŋ] *adj.* ko jalnii; jalniiɗo; jalniɗum. *Your grandfather is amusing* Taane ina jalnii.

anaconda [anəkonda] *n.* ngaadaada.

analeptic [analeptik] *n.* kó sémbinta.

analogous [analəgəs] *adj.* nando; nanduɗi; ko nandi. *They are analogous* Kanji nandi.

analphabet [analfəbet] *n.* humam binne.

analphabetic [analfəbetik] *adj.* mo jaɲngaani taraani.

analysis [analəsis] *n.* widto (ngo).

analyze [anəlayz] *v.* widtude; séérndude.

anatomical [anətomikəl] *adj.* ko faati e jaɲde terɗe.

anatomy [ənɑtəmi] *n.* jaɲde terɗe *the ~ of the human body* jaɲde terɗe ɓalli.

ancestor [ansestə] *n.* mawɗo gadiiɗo; maamaare *(nde).*

ancestral [ancestrəl] *adj.* ko faati e mawɗo gadiiɗo.

anchor [aŋkə] *v.* joofde; teerde.

ancient [anšənt] *adj.* ɓooyɗo; ɓooɣɗum; ɓooynde; ɓooɣɓe; ko ɓóóyi. *an ~ custom* aada ɓooyɗo *and* [ɑnd] *conj.* e. *you ~ him* aan e makko.

anemia [əniymiya] *n.* ñaw *(o).*

anew [anyew] *adv.* ko hésɗi.

angel [anjəl] *n.* malayka *(o).*

angelic [anjelik] *adj.* ko nandi e malayka.

anger [aŋgə] *n.* looɓre *(nde);* tikkere *(nde);* sekre *(nde).*

ᴀgina [anjiynə] *n.* muusu góddól; naw ɗakañe.

ᴀgle [ɑŋgəl] *n.* lóbbudu *(ndu).*

ᴀgry [ɑŋgri] *adj.* cekɗo; pilnitiiɗo; ɓernuɗo; mettinɗo. *He is angry* ko o cekɗo.

ᴀguish [ɑŋgwiš] *n.* sunaare *(nde).*

ᴀima [animə] *n.* fittaandu *(ndu).*

ᴀimal [animəl] *n.* jawdi *(ndi)*; mbaroodi *(ndi).*

ᴀimate [anəmeyt] *v.* wuurnude; wélnude.

ᴀimator [anəmeytə] *n.* belnoowo *(o).*

ᴀimosity [anəmowzəti] *n.* ngañgu *(ngu).*

ᴀkle [ɑŋkəl] *n.* hólɓundu *(ndu). sprain one's* ~ forñude. *He sprained his ankle* Ko o porñuɗo.

ᴀnex [aneks] *v.* jókkude; ɓéydude.

ᴀnihilate [aniyhəleyt] *v.* boomde.

ᴀnounce [ənawns] *v.* jaaynude.

announcement [ənawnsmənt] *n.* jaaynde *(nde). He is making an announcement* O woni ko e jaaynude.

ᴀnoy [ənoy] *v.* urɓude; urɓitde; haaɓnude; seknude. *She annoyed him* O sekni mo.

ᴀnoyance [ənoyəns] *n.* mettere *(nde)*; mettingol *(ngól).*

ᴀnual [anyəwəl] *adj.* hitaande kala.

ᴀnulation [anyəleyšən] *n.* pirtugól *(ngól).*

ᴀnunciate [anʌnšyeyt] *v.* habrude.

ᴀnunciation [anʌnšyeyšən] *n.* kabaaru *(o).*

ᴀnonymous [anəniməs] *adj.* mo innde mum andaaka. *an* ~ *person* neɗɗo mo inde mum andaaka.

ᴀnopheles [ənofəliyz] *n.* ɓówngu *(ngu).*

ᴀnother [ənowðə] *adj.* goɗɗo; góɗɗum. *help one* ~ wallondirde.

ᴀnswer [ansə] *v.* jaabaade; nootaade. ~ *back* sontaade. *He is answering your question* Omon jaaboo lamndal maa.

ᴀnswer [ansə] *n.* nootaango *(ngo)*; jaabawol *(ngól).*

ᴀnt [ɑnt] *n.* ñuuñu *(ngu)*; goololo *(ngól).*

ᴀntagonism [antagənizm] *n.* luural *(ngal)*; luutndagól *(ngól).*

ntagonize [antagənayz] *v.* luutndaade; añde.

ᴀntecede [antəsiyd] *v.* adaade.

ᴀntecedent [antəsiydənt] *adj.* gadiiɗo; adiiɓe.

ᴀntedate [antədeyt] *v.* héccude.

antelope [antəlopi] *n.* lella *(ba)*; willere *(nde)*; jaawre *(nde).*

antenna [antena] *n.* anteen.

anterior [antiyryə] *adj.* gadiiɗo; gadiɗum; ko adii. *His request was anterior to yours* lamndal makko adii lamndal maa.

anthropophagy [anθrəpowfəji] *n.* cukñaagu *(ngu).*

anti [anti] luutndiiɗo.

anticarious [antikeyrəs] *n.* ko haɗata ñihre yulde.

anticipant [antisəpənt] *adj.* jóórtiiɗo.

anticipate [antisəpeyt] *v.* joortaade; ɗaminaade. *I anticipate that things will work out* Mbeɗe joortii moYYere.

anticipation [antisəpeyšən] *n.* njoorta *(o).*

anticipatory [antəsipətəri] *adj.* ko faati e njoorta.

antidote [antidowt] *n.* lékki posone.

antipathy [antipəθi] *n.* ngañgu *(ngu).*

antique [antiyk] *adj.* ɓóóyɗum; ɓooyɗi.

antiquity [antikwiti] *n.* jamaanu ɓooyɗo ɓénnuɗo.

anurous [anyuwrəs] *adj.* ko alaa laaci.

anus [eynəs] *n.* nasól *(ngól)*; bunna *(o); gaɗa (o).*

anxiety [aŋzayti] *n.* sokla *(o).*

any [eni] *adj.* kala.

anybody [enibodi] *pron.* neɗɗo kala. *Anybody can do it* Neɗɗo kala ina waawi waɗde ɗum.

anyone [eniwan] *pron.* neɗɗo kala.

anyplace [enipleys] *adv.* nókku kala.

anything [eniθiŋ] *pron.* huunde kala.

anytime [enitaym] *adv.* sahaa kala.

anywhere [eniwer] *adv.* nókku kala.

apart [əpɑrt] *adj.* ceerɗi; ceertuɗi; ko séérti; ko joñaa.

apartment [əpɑrtmənt] *n.* hoɗorde *(nde).*

ape [eyp] *n.* déémóóru *(ndu).*

apex [eypeks] *n.* ceɓtam (dam).

aphrodisiac [afrowdiyziyak] *adj.* ko finninta.

apiece [apiys] *adv.* hoore kala; geɗal kala.

apish [eypiš] *n.* ko nandi walla ko faati e déémóóru.

aplenty [aplenti] *adj.* kééwɗum; ko heewi.

apologize [apowləjayz] *v.* yaafnaade. *I apologize for the mistake* Tiinno yaafo juumre nde.

apology [apowləji] *n.* yaafuya *(o)*. *Please accept my apology* Tiinno yaafo mi.

apostasy [apostəzi] *n.* daccugól diine.

apostle [aposəl] *n.* nelaado *(o)*; nulaado *(o)*.

appall [apɔl] *v.* hulɓinde.

apparent [apiyrənt] *adj.* ko yiyotoo.

apparition [apəriyšən] *n.* peeñal *(ngal)*.

appeal [apiyl] *n.* ñaagunde *(nde)*.

appeal [apiyl] *v.* ñaagaade. *I appeal to you* Mbede ñaago maa.

appear [apiyr] *v.* feeñde; feerde. *He appeared yesterday* Ko hanki o feeñi.

appearance [apiyrəns] *n.* 1) ŋari *(o)* 2) peeñal *(ngal)*.

appease [apiyz] *v.* dééɤnude.

appelation [apəleyšən] *n.* inde *(nde)*; noddaango (ngo).

append [apend] *v.* jókkude; ɓéydude.

applaud [aplɔd] *v.* hellude; fóɓɓude. *They applauded the chief* ɓe poɓɓanii laamdo.

applause [aplɔz] *n.* kelle *(de)*.

apple [ɑpəl] *n.* pom *(o)*. *He ate an apple* O ñaamii pom o.

applicant *n.* [aplikənt] ndaaroowo (liggééy) *The applicant is here* Ndaaroowo liggeey o arii.

apply [əplay] *v.* moomde;. ñóɤɤude.

appoint [apwent] *v.* fiilde; lamminde. *They appointed the chief* ɓe piilii laamdo o.

apportion [aporšən] *v.* féccude.

appose [apɔz] *v.* sawndondirde.

appraise [apreyz] *v.* yisɓude.

appreciate [apriyšeyt] *v.* usde.

apprehend [aprehənd] *v.* 1) naŋngude; jaggude 2) faamde.

apprehension [aprəhenšən] *n.* kulól *(ngól)*.

apprehensive [aprehensiv] *adj.* kuldo.

apprentice [aprentəs] *n.* ekkotoodo.

apprenticeship [aprentəšip] *n.* ekko (ngo).

approach [aprɔč] *v.* ɓattaade. *He is approaching the building* Omon ɓattoo huɓeere nde.

appropriate [əpropret] *v.* héɓtude.

appropriate [əpropret] *adj.* peewdo; ko fééwi.

approve [əpruwv] *v.* jaɓde *The decree has been approved* Sardi o jaɓaama.

apron [eyprən] *n.* haddaare *(nde)*.

apt [apt] *adj.* baawdo.

aptitude [aptətyuwd] *n.* mbaawka *(ka)*.

aquatic [akwatik] *adj.* ko faati e ndiyam.

Arab [eyrəb] *n.* aarabe *(o)*.

Arabic [arəbik] *n.* aarabeere *(nde)*.

arable [arabəl] *adj.* léydi ndémétééndi.

arbitrate [ɑrbətreyt] *v.* ñaawde.

arbitration [ɑrbiteyšən] *n.* ñaawoore *(nde)*.

arc [ɑrk] *n.* laañal *(ngal)*.

arcade [arkeyd] *n.* laawól *(ngól)*.

arcane [arkeyn] *adj.* ko niɓɓidi; sirru.

archaic [arkayik] *adj.* kó ɓóóyi; ko ɓénni It is archaic dum ɓooyii.

archer [ɑrčə] *n.* laañoowo *(o)*.

archery [ɑrčəri] *n.* laañgol *(ngól)*.

arduous [ɑrjewəs] *adj.* ko tiidi; tiiddum.

area [erya] *n.* nókku *(o)*.

arena [əriynə] *n.* dingiral *(ngal)*. *They entered the arena* ɓe naati e dingiral ngal.

argent [arjənt] *n.* kaalis.

argental [arjəntəl] *adj.* ko faati walla ko nandi e kaalis.

argue [ɑrgyuw] *v.* yéddóndirde; fóódóndirde. *I do not want to argue* Mi yidaa foodondireede.

argument [ɑrgyəmənt] *n.* póódóndiral *(ngal)*.

argumentation *n.* póódóndiral *(ngal)*.

arid [arid] *adj.* kó yóóri.

arise [arayz] *v.* fudde; ummaade.

arithmetics [ariθmetiks] *n.* kiisagól *(ngól)*; hiisa *(o)*.

arm [ɑm] *n.* jungo (ngo). *your* ~ jungo maa.

armament [ɑməment] *n.* kaɓirde *(de)* ; kaɓirgal *(ngal)*; njógitaari *(ndi)*.

armed [ɑmd] *adj.* jógitiido. *He is armed* Omo jogiti.

armistice [ɑmistis] *n.* dartingól hare.

armless [ɑmless] *adj.* guddo.

armlet [ɑmlet] *n.* cééltól *(ngól)*.

armoire [ɑrmwar] *n.* armoor *(o)*.

armory [ɑmori] *n.* móóftirde kaɓirde.

armpit [ɑmpit] *n.* naafki (ki).

army [ɑmi] *n.* wolde *(nde)*; soldateeɓe *(ɓe)*.

around [ərawnd] *prep.* hedde

arouse [ərawz] *v.* findinde.

arrange [əreynj] *v.* fééwnude.

arrest [ərest] *v.* jaggude; nangude.

arrival [ərayvəl] *n.* jettagól *(ngól)*.

arrive [ərayv] *v.* yettaade. *He arrived yesterday* O yettii ko hanki.

arrogance [arogəns] *n.* neetaraagal *(ngal)*; bon nehdaagal.

arrogant [arogənt] *adj.* ñaadɗo; neetaro.

arrow [arow] *n.* bamforo

arrowhead [arowhed] *n.* cééɓééndi bamfaro.

arsenal [ɑsənəl] *n.* móóftirde kaɓirɗe.

art [ɑt] *n.* fannu *(o)*.

artery [ɑtəri] *n.* ɗaɗól *(ngól)*.

article [ɑtikəl] *n.* windande *(nde)*.

artisan [ɑtizən] *n.* ñeeño *(o)*.

artistic [ɑtistik] *adj.* ko faati e fannu.

as if [asif] *adv.* éllééy; ɓayri.

ascend [asend] *v.* ŋabbude; ŋaylude.

ascension [asenšən] *n.* ŋabbugól *(ngól)*; ŋaylugól *(ngól)*.

ascertain [asərtən] *v.* yananeede.

ascribe [askrayb] *v.* takkude.

ascription [askripšən] *n.* iwdi *(ndi)*.

ashamed [ašeymd] *adj.* kérsuɗo.

ash [ɑš] *n.* ndoondi *(ndi)*; kaata. ~ *used for making soap* cekkiri *(ndi)*.

aside [asayd] *adv.* sara.

ask [ɑsk] *v.* lamndaade. ~ *for forgiveness* yaafnaade; tuubande.

asleep [asliyp] *adj.* ɗaaniiɗo *He is asleep* Ko o ɗaaniiɗo.

aspirant [aspərənt] *n.* ɗabɓoowo *(o)*. *He who aspires must be patient* ɗabɓoowo muñat.

aspiration [aspəreyšən] *n.* ɗamaawu *(o)*; naatnugol foofaango.

aspirin [aspərən] *n.* aspirin *(o)*.

ass [ɑs] *n.* kuutól *(ngól)*.

assail [aseyl] *v.* ñakkaade e.

assailant [aseylənt] *n.* ñakkiiɗo e.

assassin [asəsin] *n.* barɗo hoore. *He is the assassin* Ko kanko wari hoore.

assassinate [asasəneyt] *n.* warde hoore. *He was assassinated last year* O waraa ko rawane.

assassination [asasəneyšən] *n.* war hoore.

assault [asɔlt] *v.* yande; ñakkaade.

assay [asey] *v.* etaade; éndude.

assemble [asembəl] *v.* réndinde; mooɓde.

assembled [asembəld] *adj.* daakaade.

assembly [asembli] *n.* deental *(ngal)*.

assent [asent] *v.* yamirde; jaɓde.

assert [asərt] *v.* tiidɗnude; tééŋtinde.

assess [ases] *v.* hiisaade.

assessor [asesə] *n.* kiisotooɗo *(o)*.

asset [aset] *n.* dañal *(ngal)*.

assign [asayn] *v.* tóttude; heednude.

assignment [asaynmənt] *n.* liggééy *(o)*.

assimilate [asiməleyt] *v.* waade; naattinde; waawde.

assist [asist] *v.* wallude. *You should assist your teacher* Aɗa foti wallude ceerno maa.

assistance [asistəns] *n.* ballal *(ngal)*; doftal *(ngal)*.

assistant [asistənt] *n.* balloowo *(o)*.

associate [asowšeyt] *v.* wóndude.

association [asowšeyšən] *n.* deental *(ngal)*.

assoil [asoyl] *v.* yaafaade.

assort [asɔt] *v.* séérndude.

assortment [asɔtmənt] *n.* cééndugól *(ngól)*.

assume [asyuwm] *v.* sikkude; jikkude; miijaade. *I assume he is here* Mbeɗe jikki omon ɗoo.

assumption [asʌmpšən] *n.* sikke *(o)*; miijo (ngo).

asthma [ɑsma] *n.* aasmo.

astonish [astəniš] *v.* najnude. *I was astonished* Mi naj.

astonished [astəništ] *adj.* najɗo; kaawaaɗo.

astonishment [astənišmənt] *v.* najoore *(nde)*.

astound [astawnd] *v.* najnude.

astral [astrəl] *adj.* ko faati e.

astray [astrey] *adj.* ko majji; majjuɗum. *The letter went astray* ɓataake o majjii.

astrologer [astrowlojə] *n.* tiimoowo *(o)*. *He is an astrologer* Ko o tiimoowo.

astrology [astrowləji] *n.* tiimgal *(ngal)*; tiimgol *(ngól)*.

astronomy [astrownəmi] *n.* jangde windere.

astute [astyuwt] *adj.* YoYɗo. *He is really astute* Omo YoYi no feewi.

asylum [əsayləm] *n.* moolagól *(ngól).*

at [at] *prep.* nder; dow; to. ~ *his request* e wiide makko; e yamiroore makko.

atelier [atəlye] *n.* nókku liggorde.

athletic [aɵletik] *adj.* dóólnuɗo; cembinɗo.

atmosphere [atmosfiyr] *n.* weeyo (ngo).

atmospheric [atmosfiyrik] *adj.* ko faati e weeyo.

atonement [atownment] *n.* tuubgól *(ngól);* njóɓdi *(ndi).*

atop [atop] *prep.* ceptam *(ɗam).*

atrocious [atrowšəs] *adj.* bonɗo.

atrocity [atrowsəti] *n.* bonande *(nde).*

attach [atɑč] *v.* haɓɓude.

attachment [atɑčment] *n.* kaɓɓugól *(ngól);* takkagól e neɗɗo.

attack [atak] *v.* yande e; ñakkaade e. *They attacked him* ɓe njani e makko.

attain [ateyn] *v.* heɓde; yettaade.

attainable [ateynəbəl] *adj.* ko heɓotoo; keɓotooɗum.

attempt [atempt] *n.* ekko (ngo); ekkagól *(ngól);* etagol *(ngól).*

attempt [atempt] *v.* endude; etaade.

attend [atend] *v.* toppitaade. ~ *school* jangude lekkon.

attention [atenšən] *n.* battugól hakkille.

attentive [atentiv] *adj.* battuɗo hakkille.

attenuate [atenyuweyt] *v.* ustude.

attest [atest] *v.* seedaade. *Can you attest to that* Aɗa waawi seedaade ɗum?

attire [atayə] *n.* cómci *(ɗi);* cómcól *(ngól).*

attract [atrakt] *v.* fooɗde.

attractive [atraktiv] *adj.* jooɗɗo. *You are very attractive* Aɗa yooɗi no feewi.

attribute [atribyuwt] *v.* andinde iwdi.

auction [ɔkšən] *v.* yeeyde; wantirde.

auctioneer [ɔkšəniyə] *n.* jeeyoowo *(o).*

audacious [ɔdeyšəs] *adj.* cuusɗo.

audacity [ɔdasəti] *n.* cuusal *(ngal).*

audible [ɔdibəl] *adj.* ko nanotoo; ko nanetee.

audience [ɔdyəns] *n.* yimɓe tawtoraaɓe.

audition [ɔdiyšən] *n.* keɗtagól *(ngól).*

auditor [ɔdito] *n.* kéɗiiɗo *(o);* keɗotooɗo *(o).*

auditory [ɔdətowri] *adj.* ko faati e nanɗe.

augment [ɔgment] *v.* ɓeydude.

augmentation [ogmənteyšən] *n.* ɓéydugól *(ngól);* ɓeydaari *(ndi).*

augmenter [ɔgmentə] *n.* ɓeydoowo *(o).*

aunt [ɔnt] *n.* górgilaaɗo *(o).*

aura [ɔra] *n.* fooyre *(nde).*

aural [ɔrəl] *adj.* ko faati e nanɗe.

auricular [ɔrikyuwlə] *adj.* ko faati e nanɗe.

auspice [ospis] *n.* jiimgol *(ngól);* njiimaandi *(ndi)*

austerity [ɔsterəti] *n.* sooño (ngo); baasal *(ngal).*

author [ɔɵə] *n.* binduɗo; mahɗo.

authority [əɵorəti] *n.* baawal *(ngal);* yamiroore *(nde).*

authorize [əɵorayz] *v.* yamirde. *You are authorized to remain in the country* A yamiraama yo a heddo e leydi ndi.

automobile [ɔtəmowbiyl] *n.* móbél *(o).*

autonomous [ɔtownəməs] *adj.* ko jiimaaka *an autonomous region* nokku mo jiimaaka.

autonomy [ɔtownəmi] *n.* ndimaagu hooremum.

autumn [ɔtəm] *n.* kawle *(ɗe).*

avail [aveyl] *v.* nafde.

available [aveyləbəl] *adj.* kéɓiiɗo.

avarice [avəris] *n.* tiiɗgól jungo.

avenge [avenj] *v.* yoftanaade.

avenue [avenyu] *n.* laawól jaajngól.

average [avrij] *n.* hakkunde.

aversion [avərʒən] *n.* ngañgu *(ngu);* elko *(ko).*

avid [avid] *adj.* kuuñɗuɗo; jiɗɗo.

avidity [avidəti] *n.* kuuñɗugól *(ngól)*

avoid [avoyd] *v.* woorde.

await [aweyt] *v.* fadde.

awake [aweyk] *v.* findinde.

awaken [aweykən] *v.* findinde.

aware [aweyr] *adj.* tinɗo. *I am aware of it* Mbeɗe tini ɗum.

awareness [aweyrnes] *n.* tingól *(ngól).*

away [awey] *adv.* goɗɗuɗum right away jooni jooni.

awe [ɔ] *n.* kulól *(ngól).*

awful [ɔful] *adj.* bónɗum; kó bóni.

awl [ɔl] *n.* tufirde *(nde).*

ax [aks] *n.* jambere *(nde).*

azan [azan] *n.* nóddingól *(ngól).*

Azrael [azrel] *n.* jaraaʔiilu.

B

aa [bɑ] *n.* meengol *(ngól)*; meenaali *(ɗi)*.

abble [babəl] *n.* haala ka laaɓaani.

abbling [babliŋ] *n.* haala ka laaɓaani.

aboon [babuwn] *n.* waandu *(ndu)*.

aby [beybi] *n.* biɗɗo *(o)*; tiggu *(o)*.

achelor [bačələ] *n.* surga; mo resaani *He is a bachelor* Ko o surga.

ack [bak] *n.* keeci *(ki)*; ɓaawo *(ngo)*; caggal *(ngal)*. ~ *up* wallude; heedande. *I will back him up* Ma mi wallu mo. *talk behind someone's* ~ ñohde. *come* ~ artude.

ackache [bakeyk] *n.* kééci muusóówi *I have a backache* Mbeɗe wondi e keeci muusoowi.

ackbone [bakbown] *n.* noorol *(ngól)*.

ackground [bakgrawund] *n.* néésu *(ngu)*.

ackside [baksayde] *n.* raŋalde *(nde)*; rotere *(nde)*.

ackward [bakwɔrd] *adj.* ko yahri caggal.

acon *n.* [beykən] tééw mbabba tugal *I do not eat bacon* Mi ñaamataa teew mbabba tugal.

ad [bad] *adj.* bonɗo; bonɗum. *go* ~ bonde.

adly [badli] *adv.* kó bóni; ko feewani; bónɗum.

affle [bafəl] *v.* jiiɓde.

ag [bag] *n.* boot *(o)*; saak *(o)*; mbasu *(ngu)*; bata *(o)*; suruundu *(ndu)*. *be in the* ~ fandineede; nder poos.

aggage [bagij] *n.* kaake *(ɗe)*

ail [beyl] *n.* njoɓdi *(ndi)*.

ail [beyl] *v.* yaltinde cokaaɗo. *I bailed him out* Mi yoɓanii mo ko o rewetenoo.

ait [beyt] *n.* céŋdi *(ndi)*.

ake [beyk] *v.* defde e nder fuur.

aker [beykə] *v.* bulanse *(o)*; piyoowo mburu.

akery [beykəri] *n.* mbulayse *(o)*.

alance [balans] *v.* fóndude. *They are not balanced* ɗi potaani.

ald [bɔld] *adj.* jom teeleende.

aldness [bɔldnes] *n.* teeleende *(nde)*.

alk [bɔlk] *v.* daraade.

all [bɔl] *n.* kupe; bal *(o)*.

allet [bale] *n.* ngamri *(ndi)*.

alloon [baluwn] *n.* bal *(o)*.

bambara [bambara] *n.* bambaranke *(o)*.

bamboo [bambuw] *n.* kewal *(ngal)*.

ban [ban] *v.* haɗde. *He is banned from the group* O yaltinaama fedde.

banana [banana] *n.* banaana *(o)*.

band [bɑnd] *n.* léfól *(ngól)*; turup *(o)*.

bandage [bandij] *n.* bandaas *(o)*; léfól *(ngól)*.

bandit [bandit] *n.* bonɗo *(o)*.

bandy [bandi] *v.* wérlóndirde.

bandy-legged [bandileged] *adj.* molfo; molfiɗɗo. *He is bandy-legged* Ko o molfo.

bang [baŋ] *v.* buɓɓude. *Please do not bang the door* Holto buɓɓu baafal ngal.

bangle [baŋgəl] *n.* jawo *(ngo)*.

banish [banish] *v.* riiwde.

banishment [banišment] *n.* diiwgól *(ngól)*.

bank [baŋk] *n.* banke.

banker [baŋkə] *n.* liggotooɗo e baŋke.

bankrupt [baŋkrʌpt] *adj.* baasɗo; piɗɗuɗo. *I am bankrupt* Ko mi piɗɗuɗo.

banquet [baŋkwet] *n.* kew *(o)*.

banter [bantə] *v.* gaajóndirde; yanóndirde.

baobab fruit *n.* [bawbab fruwt] ɓohre *(nde)*; ɓohe *(ɗe)*.

baobab tree [bawbab triy] *n.* laali *(ki)*; ɓokki *(ki)*; ɓówdi *(ki)*.

baptize [baptayz] *v.* innude. *He was baptized yesterday* Ko hanki o innaa.

bar [bɑr] *n.* leggal *(ngal)*; palal *(ngal)*.

barb [bɑrb] *n.* lóŋdu *(ndu)*.

barbecue [bɑrbəkyuw] *v.* juɗde.

barbecued meat [barbəkyuwd miyt] *n.* afara *(o)* *You really like barbecued meat* Kooli ko aan yiɗi afara.

barber [bɑrbə] *n.* pemboowo *(o)*.

barbet [bɑrbet] *n.* sóndu *(ndu)*.

bare [beyr] *adj.* meho; ɓolo.

bargain [bɑrgen] *v.* haaldeede; yeeytóndireede; waɗɗeede ustu ɓeydu. *I am tired of bargaining* Mi tampii yeeytaade.

bargaining [bɑrgeniŋ] *n.* jeeytagól *(ngól)*; ustu ɓeydu.

bark [bɑrk] *n.* ɓokko *(ko)*.

bark [bɑrk] *v.* wofde.

barn [bɑrn] *n.* móóftirde kaɓirɗe/jaande/huɗo.

barrack [barak] *n.* suudu soldateeɓe.

barrage [baraj] *n.* haɗiinde *(nde).*

barren [baren] *adj.* dimaro; rimare (used for animals).

barricade [barikeyd] *n.* heɗɗaawo *(ngo).*

barricade [barikeyd] *v.* howde.

barrier [bariyǝ] *n.* heɗɗaawo *(ngo)*; galle *(o).*

barrow [barow] *n.* burwet *(o).*

bartender [bɑrtendǝ] *n.* jeeyoowo sangara/njaram.

barter [bɑrtǝ] *n.* barja *(o);* haaɗi haaɗa *(o).*

basal [beysǝl] *adj.* ko faati e ngóóróóndi léydi.

base [beyz] *n.* ummorde *(nde)*; ngóóróóndi *(ndi).*

bashful [bɑšful] *adj.* nuggaro *He is bashful* Ko o nuggaro.

basic [beysik] *n.* fuɗɗorde *(nde).*

basis [beysis] *n.* ngóóróóndi *(ndi).*

bask [bask] *v.* wulnaade e les naange; saaɗnaade.

basket [basket] *n.* sufirdu; *(ndu)* pañe *(o);* wusuŋ *(o).*

bastard [bastǝd] *adj.* deedaaɗo; mo alaa baaba mum You are a bastard Aan ko a deedaaɗo.

bat [bat] *v.* fiide. ~ *an eyelid* majde.

bat [bat] *n.* wilwilnde *(nde)*; bilbilel.

bate [beyt] *v.* ustude.

bathe [beyð] *v.* ɓuftaade. *He is bathing* Omon ɓuftoo.

bathing [beyðiŋ] *n.* ɓuftagol *(ngól).* ~ *instrument* lootorgal *(ngal)*/lootirgal *(ngal).* ~ *area* = lootorde *(nde).*

bathos [beyθos] *n.* ɓuutdi *(ndi).*

batten [batǝn] *v.* wuurnude.

batter [batǝ] *v.* wurwude; fiide.

battery [batǝri] *n.* batiri *(o).*

battle [bɑtǝl] *n.* hare *(nde).* *a major* ~ hare mawnde.

bawd [bɔd] *n.* garbotooɗo.

bazaar [bazar] *n.* jeere *(nde).*

be [biy] *v.* wonde. ~ *wrong* fende; tooñde.

beach [biyč] *n.* fongo gééc.

bead [biyd] *n.* ñaayre *(nde).* *do one's* ~*s* wirdude; tellinde jabe.

beak [biyk] *n.* hoggo *(ngo).*

beam [biym] *n.* leggal *(ngal).*

bean [biyn] *n.* ñewre *(nde).* *He loves beans* Ndaw ko yiɗi ñebbe.

bear [ber] *v.* 1) wufnude 2) muñde.

beard [biyrd] *n.* wahre *(nde)*

beardless [birdles] *adj.* nollo.

beast [bist] *n.* mbaróódi *(ndi).*

beat[biyt] *v.* leemde; fiide; tappude; lappude. ~ *the rice* lappee maaro (ko).

beater [biytǝ] *n.* piyoowo *(o).*

beautiful [biyuwtiful] *adj.* jooɗɗo; lobbo. *She is very beautiful* Ndaw ko yooɗi.

beauty [biyuwti] *n.* njooɗndam *(ɗam).*

because [bikɔz] *conj.* sabu.

beck [bek] *n.* hoggo *(ngo).*

beckon [bekon] *v.* dillinde hoore; jaɓde; jamminde.

become [bekʌm] *v.* wonde; wontude. *He has become greedy* Omo aybi.

bed [bed] *n.* mbaldi *(ndi)*; *(ndi)*; kiriŋtiŋ *(o);* lelorde *(nde).* *He went to bed early* O yaawii lelaade.

bedding [bediŋ] n. darabuuji e mbajjuuji.

bedroom [bedrum] n. suudu *(ndu).* *Where is your bedroom* Hol to suudu maa woni?

bee [biy] *n.* ñaaku *(ngu)*

beef [biyf] *n.* tééw kolce.

beefy [biyfi] *adj.* ɓéllinɗo.

beer [biyǝ] *n.* sangara *(o);* koñjam *(ɗam).*

beetle [biytǝl] *n.* somre *(nde).*

before [bifowr] *adv.* hadee; ko adii. *Wash your hands before you eat* Sooɗo hadee maa ñaamde.

beg [beg] *v.* toraade; yelaade; ñaagaade. *I am begging your forgiveness* Mbeɗe ñaagi maa yaafuya.

beget [biget] *v.* jibinde.

beggar [bega] *n.* jelotooɗo *(o).* *Beggars can't be choosers* Ñaadottoɗo suɓotaako. *Give charity to the beggar* Sakko jelotooɗo o.

begin [bigin] *v.* yaalde; tuggude; fuɗɗaade. ~ *afresh* fuɗɗitaade.

beginning [biginiŋ] *n.* fuɗɗoode *(nde)*; arwan *(o);* adan.

beguile [bigayl] *v.* fuuntude.

behave [biheyv] *v.* feewde; nehaade.

behavior [biheyviyǝ] *n.* néhdi *(ndi).* *good* ~ nehdi moƳƳiri.

behead [bihed] *v.* taƳde daande.

ehind [bihaynd] *n.* ɓaawo *(ngo)*; caggal *(o)*; gaɗa *(o)*. *He is behind you* Omon caggal maa.

ehold [bihold] *v.* Yeewde.

eing [beiŋ] *n.* aadéé. *a human* ~ innama aadee. *for the time* ~ jooni; hadee ndeen.

elay [biley] *v.* fiilde; taarnude.

elch [belč] *n.* ahre *(nde)*.

elch [belč] *v.* ahde.

elief [beliyf] *n.* déwgol *(ngól)*; dewal *(ngal)*; sikke *(o)*; góóŋɗingól *(ngól)*.

elieve [biliyv] *v.* gooŋɗinde; jaɓde; sikkude. *I believe in Allah* Mbeɗe gooŋɗini Alla.

eliever [biliyvə] *v.* jaɓɗo Alla.

elittle [bilitəl] *v.* yénnude; biskitde.

ell [bel] *n.* hulnde *(nde)*. *little* ~ leŋnguru *(ndu)*.

elligerence [belijerəns] *n.* hare *(nde)*.

ellow [below] *v.* huunde.

ellow [below] *n.* huunaango *(ngo)*.

elly [beli] *n.* réédu *(ndu)*. *big* ~ déériŋgi; deeral *(ngal)*.

elong [biloŋ] *v.* jeyeede. *The book belongs to me* Ko miin jey deftere nde.

elonging [biloŋiŋ] *n.* halal *(ngal)*; jey *(o)*.

elow [bilow] *prep.* les.

elt [belt] *n.* dadorgal *(ngal)*; duhól *(ngól)*; dadól *(ngól)*.

ench [benč] *n.* jooɗorde *(nde)*.

end [bend] *v.* wuuraade; ooñde; junaade; hofde. ~ *down* turaade; Yukkaade ~ *over* wuññinaade. ~ *oneself* naayaade ~ *forward* tukkaade.

ender [bendə] *n.* kofoowo *(o)*.

eneath [biniyθ] *prep.* les.

enediction [benedikšən] *n.* baraaji; duwaawu.

enefaction [benefakšən] *v.* nafoore *(nde)*.

enefactor [benefaktə] *n.* móYYinoowo; balloowo *(o)*.

enefic [benefik] *adj.* nafojum; ko nafata.

enefice [benefəs] *n.* ngañaari *(ndi)*.

eneficient [benefišənt] *adj.* nafojum; ko nafata.

enefit [benefit] *v.* nafde. *He did not benefit from it* ɗum nafaani mo.

enevolent [benevələnt] *adj.* ko wóni Allah meho; Alla meho.

equeath [bikwiθ] *v.* rónnude.

bequest [bikwest] *n.* ndónu *(ngu)*.

bereave [biriyv] *v.* héɓtude; haɗde.

beret [bəret] *n.* beere *(o)*.

berry [beri] *n.* ɓingél leɗɗe.

berth [bərθ] *n.* jóófirde *(nde)*; tufnde *(nde)*.

beseech [bisiyč] *v.* ñaagaade.

beset [biset] *v.* yande e; ñakkaade e.

beside [bisayd] *prep.* takko; sara.

besiege [bisiyj] *v.* taaraade.

best [best] *adj.* ɓurɗo fof; ɓurɗo fof móYYude.

bestial [besčəl] *adj.* ko faati e jawdi.

bestow [bistow] *v.* yeɗde; rókkude.

bet [bet] *v.* fawde; tegde. *How much did you bet* No foti tegɗaa?

betray [bitrey] *v.* janfaade; joolaade. *They betrayed him* ɓe njanfii mo.

betrayal [bitreyəl] *n.* joolo *(ngo)*; janfa *(o)*.

betroth [bitrowθ] *v.* Yamde; humande.

better [betə] *adj.* ɓurɗo móYYude.

better [betə] *v.* moYYinde.

betterment [betəment] *n.* ɓural *(ngal)*.

between [bitwiyn] *n.* leriinde; hakkunde.

beverage [bevrij] *n.* njaram *(ɗam)*.

bewail [beweyl] *v.* sunaade.

beware [beweyr] *v.* reentaade. ~ *of the dog* reento rawaandu *(ndu)*.

bewilder [biwildə] *v.* raytude; majjinde; jiiɓde.

beyond [biyond] *prep.* dow; yeeseo.

bi [bay] *pref.* ɗiɗi.

bicycle [baysikəl] *n.* biskalet *(o)*.

bid [bid] *v.* yamirde.

biennial [bayeniyəl] *adj.* ko kewata duuɓi ɗiɗi kala.

biff [bif] *n.* womre *(nde)*.

bifurcate [bifirkeyt] *v.* selde.

big [big] *adj.* mawɗo; ko mawni.

bigwig [bigwig] *n.* koohoowo *(o)*.

bijou [biju] *n.* cuɗaari *(ndi)*.

bilingual [bayliŋwəl] *n.* kaaloowo ɗemɗe ɗiɗi. *He is bilingual* Omo haala ɗemɗe ɗiɗi.

bilk [bilk] *v.* salaade yoɓde ñamaande.

bill [bil] *n.* ɗéréwól *(ngól)*.

billow [bilow] *n.* wempeYere *(nde)*.

billy [bili] *n.* sawru *(ndu)*.

bind [baynd] *v.* jókkondirde; haɓɓude.

binder [baynda] *n.* kaɓɓoowo *(o)*.

binoculars [binowkalaz] *n.* loŋŋorɗe *(ɗe)*.

birch [bərč] *n.* lékki *(ki)*.

bird [bərd] *n.* sondu *(ndu)*. *A bird in the hand is worth two in the bush* ɓamde ko rokkaa ɓuri sooynaade ko heɓataa.

birdcatcher [bərdkača] *n.* tuufotooɗo cólli.

birdie [bərdi] *n.* cólél tókósél.

birdlime [bərdlaym] *n.* wilde *(nde)*.

birl [bərl] *v.* yiilde; yuppude; yuppande.

birth [bərθ] *n.* jibingól *(ngól)*; jibinande *(nde) to give* ~ jibinde.

birthmark [bərθmɑk] *n.* toɓɓere nde neɗɗo jibidinaa e mum.

birthright [bərθrayt] *n.* tiinde *(nde)*.

bis [bis] *adv.* laabi ɗiɗi.

bisect [baysekt] *v.* féccude; eeɓde.

bit [bit] *n.* seeɗa *(o); ta*Ɣatinel (ngel).

bitch [bitč] *n.* joorɗo gite; caga.

bite [bayt] *n.* soppande *(nde)*; fiɗande *(nde)*; ŋatande; ŋoɓande.

bite [bayt] *v.* ŋatde; ŋoɓde; ŋappude *(ndi)*.

biter [bayta] *n.* ŋatoowo.

bitter [bita] *adj.* lammuɗum; kaaɗɗum.

bitter end [bitarend] *n.* gasirde *(nde)*; wattan *(o)*.

bitterness [bitarnes] *v.* mettere *(nde)*; mettingol *(ngól)*.

bizarre [bizɑr] *adj.* kaawniɗum; kaawniiɗo. *He is very bizarre* Omo haawnii no feewi.

blab [blab] *v.* tindude; saaktude sirru.

black [blak] *adj.* ɓaleejo; ɓalejum. ~ *person* ɓaleejo *(o)*. ~ *ant* ñuuñu *(ngu)*. ~ *color* ɓaléwól *(ngól)*; ɓalééri *(ndi)*; ɓawlugól. *very* ~ kurum.

blacken *v.* [blakən] ɓawlinde ~ *oneself* ɓawlinaade.

blackmail [blakmeyl] *v.* waawnude.

blackness [blaknes] *n.* ɓalewol *(ngól)*.

blacksmith [blaksmiθ] *n.* baylo *(o)*. ~ *shop* mbayla *(ka)*.

bladder [bladə] *n.* mbasu coofe.

blade [bleyd] *n.* layset *(o); jalo (ngo)*.

blame [bleym] *n.* ñiŋoore *(nde)*.

blame [bleym] *v.* ñiŋde.

blameless [bleymles] *adj.* laaɓɗo; mo alaa ñiŋoore.

blanch [blanč] *v.* ranwinde.

blank [blaŋk] *adj.* meho.

blanket [blaŋket] *n.* mbajju *(o)*.

blaspheme [blasfiym] *v.* hééfóriɗde.

blasphemy [blasfəmi] *n.* fanoore *(nde)*; keeferaagal *(ngal)*.

blaze [bleyz] *v.* jawwude.

bleach [bliyč] *v.* ranwinde.

bleat [bliyt] *n.* meenaango *(ngo)*.

bleat [bliyt] *v.* meende.

bleed [bliyd] *v.* tuƔƔde; rufde ƔiiƔam. *He is bleeding* ko a tuƔƔuɗo.

bleeder [bliydə] *n.* tuƔƔuɗo *(o)*.

bleeding [bliydiŋ] *n.* tuƔƔam (ɗam).

blemish [blemiš] *v.* bónnude.

blend [blend] *v.* réndinde.

blender [blendə] *n.* déndinoowo *(o)*.

bless [bles] *v.* duwanaade. *I bless you* Mi duwani maama.

blessed [blesd] *adj.* duwanaaɗo; malaaɗo; barkinɗo.

blessing [blesiŋ] *n.* malu *(ngu)*; barke *(ɗe)*; baraaji *(ɗi)*.

blight [blayt] *n.* ñaw leɗɗe.

blind [blaynd] *adj.* gumɗo *(o)*. *turn a ~ eye to* faalkisaade.

blindness [blayndnes] *n.* ngumndam *(ɗam)*.

blink [bliŋk] *v.* léwñude; majde.

bliss [blis] *n.* weltaare *(nde)*.

blister [blistə] *n.* wawlere *(nde)*; faandu *(ndu)*.

blister [blistə] *v.* fuɗtude.

bloat [blowt] *v.* ɓuutde.

block up [blokʌp] *v.* sukkude.

blood [blʌd] *n.* ƔiiƔam; ƔiiƔe *(ɗe)*.

bloom [bluwm] *n.* piindi *(ndi)*.

blossom [blosəm] *n.* piindi *(ndi)*.

blot [blot] *n.* toɓɓere *(nde)*.

blotch [bloč] *n.* toɓɓere.

blow [blow] *v.* wuttude; fuufde; wifde. ~ *one's nose* fiifaade; ñittaade. ~ *someone's nose* ñittude.

blubber [blʌbə] *v.* woyde.

blue [bluw] *adj.* bulo. ~ *cloth* baka.

blunder [blʌndə] *n.* juumre *(nde)*.

blunt [blʌnt] *adj.* muddiɗɗum; ko muddiɗi.

blush [blʌš] *n.* kersa *(o)*; gacce *(ɗe)*.

bluster [blʌstə] *v.* baabaade.

board [bord] *n.* dukuduku. ~ *for tanning leather* ɗatirde *(nde)*; kiirimmeewal *(ngal)*.

boast [bowst] *v.* wasaade; huunaade.

boaster [bowstə] *n.* basotoodo (o).

boat [bowt] *n.* laana (ka); lumbirgal (ngal).

bob [bopʌp] *v.* suppitaade; fiide.

bodily [bodili] *adv.* ko faati e banndu.

body [bodi] *n.* bandu (ndu).

bodyguard [bodigard] *n.* deenoowo neddo.

boggy [bogi] *adj.* lofdum; ko lófi.

boil [boyl] *v.* dalde; fasde; fasnude. *The water is boiled* Ndiyam dam fasii.

boisterous [boystərəs] *adj.* keewdo/keewdum dille.

bold [bowld] *adj.* tekkinaadum; kó tékkinaa.

bolero [bolero] *n.* ngamri (ndi).

bolster [bolstə] *n.* talla (ka); njegenaawe(o).

bond [bond] *n.* jiyaado (o); maccudo (o); kalfaado (o).

bondage [bondij] *n.* kalifaandi (ndi).

bone [bown] *n.* Yiyal (ngal). *feel something in ones's* ~ ejde.

bonfire [bonfayə] *n.* dudal (ngal).

bonny [boniy] *adj.* kó yóódi; jóóddum.

boo [buw] *v.* wullude; wullude neddo.

book [buk] *n.* deftere (nde).

booklet [buklet] *n.* déftél (ngel).

boost [buwst] *v.* béydude.

booster [buwstə] *n.* beydoowo (o).

boot [buwt] *v.* boornaade pade.

booty [buwtiy] *n.* jawdi teetaandi.

booze [buwz] *n.* koñjam (dam); saŋngara (o).

border [bordə] *n.* kééról léydi.

bore [bowr] *v.* yulde.

born [born] *adj.* jibinaado. *be* ~ *with* jibidineede e. *first* ~ afo (o). ~ *out of wedlock* deedaado (o).

borrow [borow] *v.* ñamlaade; lubaade

borrowing [borowiŋ] *n.* lubal (ngal); ñamaande (nde).

bosom [buzum] *n.* éndu (ndu).

boss [bos] *n.* gardiido (o).

botanical [bowtanikəl] *adj.* ko faati e ledde.

both [bowθ] *adj.* didi/dido kala.

bother [boðə] *v.* tappisaade; haljinde.

bottle [botəl] *n.* butel (o); kaba. *little* ~ kabayel.

bottom [botəm] *n.* gada (o); les.

bough [bow] *n.* catal lékki.

bounce [bowns] *v.* diwde ina doYYoo.

bound [bownd] *v.* kabbaado; keeraado.

boundary [bowndri] *n.* kééról (ngól).

boundless [bowndles] *adj.* ko alaa happu.

bounteous [bownteyəs] adj. kaaraysire; moYYo.

bountiful [bowntiful] *adj.* moYYo (o).

bounty [bownti] *n.* moYYere (nde).

bow [bow] *v.* turaade.

bow [bow] *n.* baylol (ngól); layru (ndu).

bowel [bowəl] *n.* téktékól (ngól).

bowl [bowl] *n.* labal (ngal); lahal (ngal); tumbude (nde); taasa (ka); bool (o).

bowman [bowmən] *n.* laañoowo (o).

box [boks] *n.* boyet; pakket (o); kees (o).

box [boks] *v.* lukkude; gobbaade.

boy [boy] *n.* suka (o); cukalél (ngel).

boyish [boyiš] *adj.* ko faati e cukaagu.

bracelet [breyslet] *n.* jawo (ngo); jawél (ngél).

brag [brag] *v.* wasaade.

bragger [bragə] *n.* basotoodo (o).

braid [breyd] *v.* moorde; sañde. ~ *temporarily* ñuggude.

braid [breyd] n.; móóról (ngól); jubból (ngól). ~ *ornament* móósturu (ndu).

braided [breydid] *adj.* mooraado; mooradum.

braider [breydə] *n.* mooroowo (o).

braiding [breydiŋ] *n.* móórgól (ngól).

brain [breyn] *n.* hakkille (o).

brake [breyk] *n.* fereŋ (o)

bran [bran] *n.* saaño (ko); ñaande (nde).

branch [branč] *v.* saltude; selde.

branch [branč] *n.* catal (ngal). *tree ~es* cate (de).

brandish [brandiš] *v.* hóllirde.

brangle [braŋgəl] *v.* dukde.

brass [bras] *n.* njamndi jillundi.

brat [brat] *n.* cukalél (ngel).

brave [breyv] *adj.* cuusdo. *He is a brave man* Omo suusi reedu.

bravery [breyvri] *n.* cuusal (ngal).

brawl [browl] *n.* hare (nde).

bray [brey] *v.* hande.

bread [bred] *n.* mburu (o).

breadth [bredθ] *n.* njaajééndi.

break [breyk] *v.* helde; fusde; tolde. ~ *off* héltude. ~ *by pounding* aYYude. ~ *a* *fasting ritual* taˈɗe koorka; hoortude. ~ *into pieces* morñitde. ~ *a promise* firtude ahdi.

break [breyk] *n.* helande *(nde)*; aˈˈere *(nde)* **breaker** [breykə] *n.* keloowo *(o)*.

breakfast [brekfast] *n.* kacitaari *(ndi)*.

breast [brest] *n.* endu *(ndu)*; ˈoolde *(nde)*.

breastfeed [brestfiyd] *v.* muyninde.

breath [breϴ] *n.* foofaango *(ngo)*. *You are wasting your breath* Holto tampin hoore ma.

breathe [briyð] *v.* foofde. ~ *one's belly in* ɗehaade. ~ *lightly while catching one's breath* lehde.

breathing [briyðing] *n.* foofaango *(ngo)*.

breech [briyč] les.

breed [briyd] *v.* jibinde; diwnude. *ill-bred* neetaro. *well-bred* nehiiɗo.

breeze [briyz] *n.* kenal subaka.

brevity [breviti] *n.* huunde rabbiɗnde.

bribe [brayb] *v.* yeende.

bribe [brayb] *n.* njeenaari *(ndi)*. *He takes bribes* Omo jaɓa yeeneede.

briber [braybə] *n.* jeenoowo *(o)*.

bribery [braybəri] *n.* njeenaari *(ndi)*.

brick [brik] *n.* tuufeere *(nde)*.

bride [brayd] *n.* debbo dambiiɗo. ~ *room* dambórdu *(ndu)*. ~ *groom* gorko dambiiɗo (jombaajo gorko).

bridge [brij] *n.* sala *(o)*

bridle [braydəl] *n.* faram *(o)*.

brief [briyf] *adj.* ɗaɓɓiɗɗum; ko rabbiɗi. *Be brief* Raɓɓiɗino.

brigand [brigənd] *n.* taˈoowo *(o)*.

bright [brayt] *adj.* jalbuɗum; ko jalbi; juumɗuɗum; ko yuumɗi.

brighten [braytən] *v.* yuumɗinde; fóóynude.

brightness [braytnes] *n.* annoore *(nde)*; jalbugól *(ngól)*.

brilliant [brilyənt] *adj.* jalbuɗum; ko jalbi.

bring [briŋ] *v.* addude. ~ *near* ɓattinde. ~ *up* nehde. ~ *with* addorde. ~ *for someone* addande. ~ *the wife to one's compound* hurtinde. ~ *to oneself* waaraade.

brink [briŋk] *n.* sara *(o)*.

brisket [brisket] *n.* becce jawdi.

bristle [brisəl] *n.* lééɓól *(ngól)*; lééɓi *(ɗi)*.

brittle [britəl] *v.* bonde.

broad [browd] *adj.* jaajɗum; ko yaaji.

broadcast [browdcast] *v.* habrude.

broadcaster [browdcastə] *n.* kabroowo *(o)*.

broaden [browdən] *v.* yaajnude.

brocade [browkeyd] *n.* bagi *(o)*.

broil [broyl] *v.* juɗde.

broke [browk] *adj.* baasɗo; mo alaa kaalis.

bronchitis [broŋkaytəs] *n.* ñaw jofe.

broody [bruwdi] *adj.* dikkale.

broom [bruwm] *n.* pittirgal *(ngal)*.

broth [broϴ] *n.* ñeekam *(ɗam)*.

brother [brɑϴə] *n.* miñiraaɗo gorko; mawniraaɗo gorko.

brother-in-law [brɑϴəinlɔ] *n.* keyniraaɗo *(o)*.

brotherhood [brɑðərhud] *n.* jiidigal *(ngal)*.

brow [braw] *n.* ñemembo (ko).

browse [brawz] *v.* ˈeewndaade; ˈeewde.

bruise [bruwz] *n.* gaañande *(nde)*; ŋaacal *(ngal)*.

brumal [bruwməl] *adj.* ko faati e dabbunde.

brush [brʌš] *v.* fiɗɗuude; soccude.

brushwood [brʌšwud] *n.* sappaare *(nde)*.

brutal [bruwtəl] *adj.* ñaŋŋguɗo; bonɗo; mo teeyaani.

bubble [bʌbəl] *v.* fattude; fasde.

buck [bʌk] *v.* tuuɗde; jattinaade.

bucker [bʌkə] *n.* tuuɗoowa *(ba)*.

bucket [bʌket] *n.* siwó. ~ *for drawing water* ˈoogirgal *(ngal)*.

bucolic [byuwkowlik] *adj.* ko faati e ngaynaaka.

bud [bʌd] *n.* wuufre *(nde)*.

buddy [bʌdi] *n.* séhil *(o)*; jahdiiɗo *(o)*.

buffalo [bʌfəlow] *n.* eda *(ba)*

bug [bʌg] *n.* ŋóótóótu *(ngu)*.

build [bild] *v.* mahde; feˈde. ~ *a shelter* fogde. ~ *a dike* ambude. ~ *a new village or compound* siiñtude. ~ *for someone* mahande.

builder [bildə] *n.* mahoowo *(o)*.

building [bildiŋ] *n.* huɓeere *(nde)*; mahdi *(ndi)*.

bulge [bʌlj] *n.* ˈuulde *(nde)*.

bull [bul] *n.* ngaari *(ndi)*; kalhaldi *(ndi)*.

bullet [bulet] *n.* kartuus *(o)*; kutal *(ngal)*.

bullion [bulyən] *n.* kaŋŋe(o).

bullock [bulok] *n.* gayél (ngel).

bully [buli] *adj.* kaɓeteeɗo; ñaŋŋguɗo.

nch [bʌnč] *n.* éndu *(ndu).*

ndle [bʌndəl] *n.* saawdu *(ndu).* ~ ***of hair*** aayaande *(nde).*

r [bər] *n.* nguru *(ngu).*

r [bər] *v.* sókkude.

rden [bərdən] *n.* fawaare *(nde)*; doŋngal *gal).*

rglar [bərglə] *n.* gujjo *(o).*

rglarize [bərglərayz] *v.* wujjude.

rglary [bərgləri] *n.* nguyka *(ka).*

rial [bəriyəl] *n.* ubbugol *(ngól).* ~ ***nstrument*** ubbirgal *(ngal).*

rke [bərk] *v.* warde.

rly [bərli] *adj.* ɓutto.

rn [bərn] *n.* sumande *(nde).*

rn [bərn] *v.* duppude; nuccude; naawde. ~ ***o ashes*** roytinde.

rned [bərnd] *adj.* kuɓɓuɗum; doytuɗum.

rner [bərnə] *n.* fehre *(nde).*

rning [bərniŋ] *n.* kuɓɓugol *(ngól)*; cumu *ngu).* ~ ***piece of wood*** docotal *(ngal).*

rr [bər] *n.* hebbere *(nde).*

rrow [bʌrow] *v.* asde.

rst [bərst] *v.* fuccitde; fuccitaade; féttude; usde; feɗɗitaade. ~ ***into tears*** woyde.

rst [bərst] *n.* fusande *(nde).*

ry [bəri] *v.* ubbude; irde.

bush [buš] *n.* ladde *(nde).* ***~fowl*** gerlal *(ngal).* ~ ***dog*** saafaandu. ~ ***fire*** cumu ladde.

business [biznes] *n.* fii(o); haaju *(o).*

bust [bʌst] *v.* fusde; féɗɗitaade.

bustard [bʌstəd] *n.* doobal *(ngal)*; caygal *(ngal).*

busy [bizi] *adj.* kaljuɗo. ***I am busy*** Mbeɗe halji.

but [bʌt] *conj.* kono.

butcher [butčə] *n.* toŋoowo *(o);* buuse *(o).*

butler [bʌtlə] *n.* carwoowo *(o);* deenoowo *(o).*

butt [bʌt] *v.* hawde.

butter [bʌtə] *v.* wumpude.

butter [bʌtə] *n.* nebam keccam; malamlaaji.

buttock [bʌtok] *n.* rotere *(nde).*

button [bʌtən] *n.* butoŋ *(o)*

buy [bɑy] *v.* soodde. ~ ***milk*** sippude. ~ ***new clothing for*** hettande. ~ ***clothing for someone*** hóltinde. ~ ***new clothing*** héttude. ~ ***back*** sóódtude.

buyer [bɑyə] *n.* coodoowo *(o).*

buying [bɑyiŋ] *n.* cóggu *(ngu)*

buzz [bʌz] *v.* wombude.

by [bɑy] *adv.* sara; takko dów. ~ ***train*** yahrude laana njoorndi.

bygone [bɑygon] *adv.* hanki men.

bypass [bɑypas] *n.* sodorde *(nde).*

bypass [baypass] *v. sodaade.*

C

cab [kab] *n.* taksi *(o)*.

cabaret [kabare] *n.* pasioŋ *(o)*.

cabbage [kabij] *n.* suppome *(o)*.

cabin [kabin] *n.* suudu *(ndu)*; jééwru *(ndu)*.

cable [keybəl] *n.* ɓóggól *(ngól)*.

cache [kaš] *n.* suudorde *(nde)*; faawru *(ndu)*.

cachet [kaše] *n.* tampoŋ *(o)*.

cackle [kakəl] *v.* herde (gertogal).

cacophonous [kakəfownəs] *adj.* luurducfum; ko yahdaani.

cad [kad] *n.* naskaado *(o)*.

cadaver [kadavə] *n.* neddo maaydo; jiiba.

cadaverous [kadavrəs] *adj.* ko faati e jiiba.

caddy [kadi] *n.* boyet *(o)*.

cadet [kadet] *n.* ɓidoo battindiido jibineede.

cadge [kaj] *v.* ñaagaade.

cadger [kajə] *n.* ñaagotoodo *(o)*.

cafe [kafe] *n.* pasioŋ tokooso.

caftan [kaftən] *n.* kaftaan *(o)*.

cage [keyj] *n.* kasó *(o)*.

cagey [keyji] *adj.* dééntiido.

cajole [kajowl] *v.* waawnude; fuuntude.

cajolery [kajowlri] *n.* fuunti *(o)*.

cake [keyk] *n.* ñamri *(ndi)*.

calabash [kalabaš] *n.* lahal *(ngal)*; ceŋalal *(ngal)*; tumbude *(nde)*; ewre *(nde)*; mbaayan *(o)*. **broken** ~ laalagal. ~ *for milking* ɓirdugal *(ngal)*. **big** ~ geworgal *(ngal)*; koral *(ngal)*. ~ *for pouring sauce or milk* liyorgal *(ngal)*.

calamitous [kəlamətəs] *adj.* boomojum; ko faati e boomaare.

calamity [kəlamiti] *n.* boomaare *(nde)*.

calculate [kalkyuleyt] *v.* hiisaade.

calculus [kalkiləs] *n.* limoore *(nde)*; hiisa *(o)*.

calendar [kalendə] *n.* kalandiriye.

calf [kɑf] *n.* gool *(o)*; ñale *(nge)*.

caliph [kalif] *n.* kiliifa *(o)*.

call [kɔl] *v.* noddude; eeraade. ~ *for prayer* eewnaade; nóddinde. ~ *one another* noddondirde. *He called him a name O* tooñii mo.

call [kɔl] *n.* noddaango *(ngo)*; eewnaango *(ngo)*.

caller [kɔlə] *n.* noddoowo *(o)*.

calling [kɔliŋ] *n.* eewnaango; noddaango.

calligraphy [kaligrəfi] *n.* bindól jódngc bindi jóóddi.

callous [kaləs] *adj.* mo wondaaka.

calm [kɑm] *v.* deΥΥinde; daayd deeΥnude; tefde; yeedde; teeyde. ~ *dow* deeΥ.

calm [kɑm] *n.* deeyre *(nde)*

caltrop [kaltrop] *n.* tuppere *(nde)*.

calumet [kalumet] *n.* jardugal *(ngal)*.

calumniate [kaləmneyt] *v.* ñohde.

calumniation [kaləmneyšən] *n.* ñoh *(nde)*.

calumniator [kaləmneytə] *n.* ñohoowo *(o,*

calumny [kaləmni] *n.* ñohre *(nde)*.

calve [kɑv] *v.* jibinde ñale.

calyx [kaliks] *n.* morlere *(nde)*.

camaraderie [kamradəri] *n.* céhilaag *(ngal)*; musidaagal *(ngal)*.

camel [kaməl] *n.* ngelooba *(ba)*.

camera [kamərə] *n.* foto.

cameraman [kamərəmən] *n.* potoowo *(o)*

camion [kamiyon] *n.* kamiyoŋ *(o)*.

camp [kamp] *n.* jippunde *(nde)*. ~ *for dr season* séédirde *(nde)*.

camper [kampə] *n.* jippiido *(o)*.

can [kan] *v.* waawde that cannot be du waawaa wonde.

can [kan] *n.* pot *(o)*.

canal [kənal] *n.* gaawol *(ngól)*.

canalize [kanəlayz] *v.* asde gaawól.

canard [kənard] *n.* kankaleewal *(ngal)*.

cancel [kansəl] *v.* firtude; haaytude.

cancellation *n.* [kansəleyšən] kaaytugc *(ngól)*; pirtugól *(ngól)*.

cancer [kansə] *n.* ñaw.

candid [kandid] *adj.* nuundudc goongante.

candidate [kandideyt] *n.* dabɓoowo *(o* ndaaroowo *(o)*.

candle [kandəl] *n.* sondeel *(o)*.

candleberry [kandəlberi] *n.* kaañééri *(ndi)*

candlelight [kandəlayt] *n.* léwléwnd sondeel.

candor [kandə] *n.* nuundal *(ngal)*.

dy [kandi] *n.* tangal *(o)*.

e [keyn] *n.* sawru tuggortééndu.

ister [kanistə] *n.* boyet *(o)*.

nibal [kanibəl] *adj.* ñaamoowo yimɓe.

ny [kani] *adj.* dééntiiɗo.

oe [kanow] *n.* laana kahi.

opy [kanəpi] *n.* kanappe *(ɗe)*.

taloupe [kantəluwp] *n.* dende *(nde)*.

teen [kantiyn] *n.* bitik soldateeɓe.

ter [kantə] *v.* ñékkude.

ter [kantə] *n.* jelotooɗo *(o)*.

tle [kantəl] *n.* taƴande *(nde)*.

vas [kanvəs] *n.* bagi *(o)*.

vass [kanvəs] *v.* ndaarde wootooɓe.

[kap] *n.* laafa *(ka)*.

ability [keypəbiliti] *n.* mbaawka *(ka)*.

able [keypəbəl] *adj.* baawɗo.

ital city [kapitəlsiti] *n.* laamorde *(nde)*.

itulate [kapyuwtileyt] *v.* jébbilaade.

itulation [kapyuwtileyšən] *n.* jébbilaare *de)*.

on [keypon] *n.* ngóri *(o)*.

onize [keypowniz] *v.* sende.

ricious [kapriyšəs] *adj.* jaawɗo waylude iijo mum.

ricorn [kaprəkorn] *n.* ɓota *(ba)*.

riole [kapriyol] *v.* ƴeeraade (puccu).

size [kapsayz] *v.* yiwde (laana yiwde); ppaade.

tion [kapšən] *n.* naatóndiral *(ngal)*; ppiro *(ngo)*.

tivate [kaptəveyt] *v.* nangude hakkille.

tive [kaptiv] *adj.* jiyaado; maccuɗo; ggaaɗo.

ture [kapčə] *v.* jaggude; dahde.

[kɑ] *n.* oto *(o)*; móbél *(o)*.

acole [karəkowl] *v.* raamraamtude.

amel [kaməl] *n.* karaameel *(o)*; tangal).

avan [karəvan] *n.* setéwol *(ngól)*; sete); jiggoore *(nde)*.

avel [karəvel] *n.* laana *(ka)*.

bine [karbayn] *n.* fetel *(o)*.

cass [karkəs] *n.* jiiba *(o)*.

rd [kɑd] *n.* kartal *(ngal)*. *He threw up is own cards* O ɗamtindiima.

diac [kardyak] *adj.* ko faati e ɓernde.

diology [kardyoləji] *n.* jangde ɓernde.

care [keyr] *n.* toppitaagol *(ngól)* take care of him toppito mo.

care [keyr] *v.* tóppitaade; hinnaade. *I don't care* Mi wondaaka.

career [keriyə] *n.* liggééy *(o)*.

careful [keyrful] *adj.* dééntiiɗo. *be ~* reento.

carefully [keyrfuli] *adv.* seese.

careless [keyrles] *adj.* jeebiiɗo; yeebiiɓe.

carelessness [keyrlesnes] *n.* yeebaare *(nde)*.

caress [kares] *v.* moytude; moomde.

caress [kares] *n.* moytaango *(ngo)*.

carious [karyəs] *adj.* julɗum; yulnde; ko yuli (ñiire).

carnage [kɑrnij] *n.* warngo yimɓe heewɓe.

carnal [kɑnəl] *adj.* ko faati e yimɓe/aduna.

carnivorous [karnəvorəs] *adj.* ko ñaamata tééw.

carol [kerol] *n.* njimri *(ndi)*; jimól *(ngól)*.

carp [karp] *n.* sidere *(nde)*.

carpenter [karpentə] *n.* minise *(o)*; labbo.

carpet [kɑrpet] *n.* tapis *(o)*.

carrier [keriyə] *n.* bilanka *(o)*; doondotooɗo.

carrion [karyon] *n.* jiiba *(o)*.

carrot [kerot] *n.* karot *(o)*.

carry [keri] *v.* roondaade. *~ in one's palm* tambaade. *~ with* naworde. *~ on one's back* waaɓde. *~ on the head* roondaade. *~ back* nawtude. *~ for* nawande. *~ a load on the head without a head pad* rungaade. *~ on one's shoulders* towde. *~ a child on one's back* wambude.

cart [kɑt] *n.* saret *(o)*. *They put the cart before the horse* Nay njardii laaceeje.

carton [katən] *n.* boyet *(o)*.

cartouche [kartuwš] *n.* kutal *(ngal)*.

cartridge [kɑtrij] *n.* kutal *(ngal)*.

carve [kɑv] *v.* sehde.

carving [kɑviŋ] *n.* sehngo *(ngo)*.

case [keys] *n.* suudu *(ndu)*. *in any ~* ko waawi wonde kala.

casern [kəzərn] *n.* hoɗorde *(nde)* soldateeɓe.

cash [kɑš] *n.* kaalis. *pay ~* yoɓde jungo e jungo.

cashier [kašyə] *n.* joɓnotooɗo.

casque [kask] *n.* kaske *(o)*.

cassava [kasava] *n.* pulóók *(o).*
casserole [kasərol] *n.* kastiloor *(o).*
cassette [kaset] *n.* banda *(o).*
cast [kast] *v.* werlaade.
caste [kɑst] *n.* hinde *(nde).*
castle [kɑsəl] *n.* hoɗorde laamɗo.
castrate [kastreyt] *v.* sende; tappude. *~ed bullock* ngaari ɓujiri *(ndi).*
casual [kazəl] *adj.* ko tiiɗaani.
casualty [kazəlti] *n.* maayɓe e wolde/hare.
cat [kat] *n.* ullundu *(ndu)*
cataclysm [cataklizm] *n.* jérɓugól léydi.
catalog [katəlog] *n.* defte limtaaɗe.
catapult [katəpʌlt] *n.* mbakku *(o).*
cataract [katərakt] *n.* ndanééri yitere.
catastrophe [katəstrowfi] *n.* boomaare *(nde);* bonande mawnde.
catch [kač] *v.* heɓɓaade; hirɓaade. *~ up with* heɓtaade. *~ with a trap* rullinde. *~ fire* boyde. *~ by closing in on* maɓɓude.
catcher [kačə] *n.* keɓɓootooɗo.
categorize [katəgowrayz] *v.* sifaade fannuuji.
category [katəgowri] *n.* fannu *(o).*
cater [keytə] *v.* defande; sarwude yimɓe kéw.
caterer [keytərə] *n.* carwoowo yimɓe kéw.
caterpillar [katerpilə] *n.* samba tali.
cattle [katəl] *n.* jawdi *(ndi). ~ food* jaandere *(nde). ~ market* daral *(ngal).*
caught [kɔt] *adj.* jaggaaɗo
causal [kɔzəl] *adj.* cabobinɗum; ko faati e sabaabu.
cause [kɔz] *n.* sabaabu *(o).*
cause [kɔz] *v.* sabobinde. *~ people to quarrel* réndinde. *~ to melt* taaynude.
caution [kɔšən] *v.* rééntinde.
cautious [kɔšəs] *adj.* dééntiiɗo.
cave [keyv] *n.* ngaska *(ka).*
cavern [kavən] *n.* ngaska mawka *(ka).*
cavity [kavəti] *n.* yelde *(nde);* ngaska *(ka).*
cavort [kavɔt] *v.* birgude.
cease [siyz] *v.* nattude; daraade. *~ to rain* siiltude. *~ fire n.* dartingól hare/jéyli.
ceaseless [siyzles] *adj.* ɗuumiɗum; ko nattataa.
cecum [siykəm] *n.* jokkorde téktéki.
ceil [siyl] *v.* bilde (huɓeere).

ceiler [siylə] *n.* biloowo *(o).*
ceiling [siyliŋ] *n.* mbildi *(ndi).*
celebrate [seləbreyt] *v.* mawninde; noosd wuurtinde.
celebration [seləbreyšən] *n.* noos *(o* mawningol *(ngól)* **celebrity** [seləbri *n.* lóllugól *(ngól).*
celerity [seləri] *n.* yaawre *(nde).*
celestial [seləsčəl] *adj.* ko faati e weeyo.
celibate [seləbət] *n.* neɗɗo n resaani/resaaka.
cellar [selə] *n.* faawru *(ndu).*
cement [səment] *n.* simaa *(o);* simoŋ *(o).*
cemetery [semetri] *n.* baamuule *(ɗe)* ; cel *(ɗe).*
cense [sens] *v.* urde.
censer [sensə] *n.* feere cuuraay.
censor [sensə] *n.* koɗoowo *(o).*
censorship [sensəšip] *n.* kuugal *(ngal).*
censure [sensə] *v.* haɗde.
census [sensəs] *n.* limoore yimɓe.
cent [sent] *n.* taka *(o).*
centenarian [sentəneyryən] *adj.* jom duul teemedere; téémódinɗo.
centennial [sentəniyəl] *adj.* teemodinɗ teemodinɓe; ko téémódini.
center [sentə] *n.* hakkunde.
central [sentrəl] *adj.* ko faati e hakkunde.
centuple [sentyuwpəl] *v.* fiyde laa teemedere; téémódinde.
century [sentri] *n.* duuɓi teemedere.
cereal [siryəl] *n.* gawri *(ndi).*
cerebral [serəbrəl] *adj.* ko faati e ngaandi.
ceremony [serəmoni] *n.* dillere *(nde).*
certain [sərtən] *adj.* jananaaɗo.
certes [sert] *n.* ko goonga.
certificate [sərtifikeyt] *n.* sertifika *(o).*
certification [sərtifikeyšən] *n.* ceedagól.
certify [sərtifay] *v.* seedaade.
certitude [sərtityuwd] *n.* huunde n neɗɗo yananaa.
cessation [seseyšən] *n.* dartingól *(ngól).*
chagrin [šəgrin] *n.* sunaare *(nde).*
chain [čeyn] *n.* tóngude.
chain [čeyn] *n.* ceen *(o);* callal *(ngal).*
chair [čeyr] *n.* jooɗorde *(nde).*
chairman [čeyrmən] *n.* gardiiɗo *(o).*
chalk [čɔk] *n.* kare *(o).*

hallenge [čalənj] v. salaade.

hallenger [čalənjə] n. caliiɗo (o); cippirteeɗo (o).

hamber [čeymbə] n. suudu (ndu).

hameleon [kamelyən] n. dooñoo (o).

hampion [čampyən] n. pooldo (o).

hance [čans] n. kawrugól heen.

hange [čeynj] v. waylude; firtude. ~ back waylitde. ~ oneself waylaade. ~ color noordude. ~ into lattitaade. ~ shape ɓoome. ~ places heedtude. ~ direction aaltaade. ~ money weccude.

hange [čeynj] n. weccit (o). I have no change Mi alaa weccit.

hangeable [čeynjəbəl] adj. ɓaylottoɗum; ko waylotoo.

hannel [čanəl] n. céékól (ngól).

hanson [šanson] n. jimól (ngól).

hant [čant] v. yimde. ~ the praises of awlude.

hanter [čantə] n. jimoowo (o).

haos [kewos] n. jilɓere (nde).

haotic [kewotik] adj. jilɓuɗum; ko faati e jilɓere.

hap [čap] n. surga (o); sehil (o).

hapeau [šapɔ] n. laafa (ka).

haracter [karaktə] n. jikku (o); néhdi (ndi).

haracterization n. sifaa (o).

haracterize [karaktərayz] v. sifaade.

harade [šərad] n. ciftól (ngól).

harcoal [čarkol] n. Yulɓe (ɗe); Yulmere (nde).

harge [čarj] v. rimndude. ~ with the head (used mainly for animals) hawde. be in ~ of defaade; ardaade. free of ~ Alla meho.

haritable [čaritəbəl] adj. karambure; kaaraysire.

harity [čarəti] n. sadak (o). njelaari (ndi). give ~ sakkaade.

harlatan [šarlətan] n. bileejo (o); biloowo (o).

harlatanism [šarlətanizm] n. mbileew (ngu).

harm [čɑm] n. ñawndogal (ngal); nombol (ngól); talkuru (ndu); lohol (ngól) ~ for attraction ɓayre (nde).

harming [čɑmiŋ] adj. belɗo.

hary [čari] adj. dééntiiɗo.

hase [čeys] n. riddo (ngo).

chase [čeys] v. terde; riddude; huɓde v.; rewde ~. birds off fields hiwde. ~ birds away hartude.

chaser [čeysə] n. diddoowo (o).

chasseur [šasər] n. baañoowo (o).

chaste [čeyst] adj. laaɓɗo.

chastise [čəstayz] v. léɓtude; waɗɗe kuugal.

chastity [častəti] n. laaɓal (ngal).

chat [čat] n. yeewtere (nde). They are having a chat ɓe ngoni ko e yeewtude.

chat [čat] v. yeewtude.

chatter [čatə] v. leɓde.

chatterbox [čatəbɑks] n. leɓoowo (o).

chatterer n. [čatərə] leɓoowo (o).

chauffeur [šɔfər] n. dognoowo oto.

chaw [čaw] v. Yakkude.

cheap [čiyp] adj. ɓeeɓɗum; ko wééɓi.

cheapen [čiypən] v. wééɓnude.

cheat [čiyt] v. wujjude.

cheater [čiytə] n. gujjo (o).

check [ček] v. Yeewtaade.

checkers [čekəz] n. cokki (ɗi); wóli (o).

cheek [čiyk] n. aɓugo (ngo); gabgal (ngal); sekkere (nde).

cheer [čiyr] v. wéltinde; hóybinde sunaare.

cheerful [čiyrful] adj. béltiiɗo.

cheery [čiyri] adj. béltinoowo.

cheetah [čiytəh] n. céwngu (ngu).

chef [šef] n. defoowo (o).

cherish [čeriš] v. horsinde.

cherished [čerišd] adj. korsuɗo; kórsinaaɗo. be ~ hórsineede.

chess [čes] n. cókki (ɗi).

chest [čest] n. becce (ɗe). get something off of one's ~ yaltinde ko woni e ɓernde mum.

chesty [česti] adj. jom becce mawɗe.

chevy [ševi] adj. riddude.

chew [čuw] v. Yakkude. ~ the cud aactaade. ~ at ŋolde.

chew [čuw] n. Yakkuru (ndu).

chic [šik] adj. jooɗɗo; kó yóóɗi.

chicane [šəkeyn] v. fuuntude.

chick [čik] n. sófru (ndu).

chicken [čikən] n. gertogal (ngal). ~ pox pimple samre (nde). ~ pox amumal (ngal).

chide [čayd] v. furaade; hartaade.

chief [čiyf] n. gardiiɗo (o); jaarga (o); amiiru (o); arɗo (o); jamiroowo (o); almaami (o).

child [čayld] n. kurka (o); suka (o); boobo (o); biɗɗo (o); cukalel (ngél). ~ gum disease addo (ngo). little ~ wookoƴere (nde); bingél; cukayél (ngél). ~hood cukaagu (ngu).

childish [čayldiš] adj. ko faati e golle suka/sukaaɓe.

children [čildrən] n. sukaaɓe (ɓe); biɓbe (ɓe).

chill [čil] n. buuɓól (ngól).

chilly [čili] adj. buuɓɗum; ko buuɓi.

chimney [čimni] n. yaltirde cuurki.

chimpanzee [čimpənzi] n. deemooru (ndu); waandu (ndu).

chip [čip] n. elal (ngal).

chippy [čipi] n. debbo pijoowo.

chirk [čərk] v. wéltinde.

chirp [čərp] v. siikde.

chirping [čərpiŋ] n. siikaango (ngo).

chisel [čizəl] v. taƴde; méccude.

chisel [čizəl] n. mecekke (ɗe).

chitchat [čitčat] n. yeewtere (nde).

chitter [čitə] v. siññude.

chocolate [čowklet] n. sokkola (o).

choice [čoys] n. suɓngo (ngo); cuɓagól (ngól).

choke [čowk] v. ɗeɗɗaade; joomaade; sondaade. ~ someone sóndude; ɗéɗɗude; feɲde.

choker [čokə] n. ɗeɗɗoowo.

choose [čuwz] v. suɓaade; suɓde; labaade; faltaade.

chop [čop] v. sóppude; dóttude; féƴƴude.

chopper [čopə] n. peƴƴoowo (o); coppoowo (o).

chopping [čopiŋ] n. feƴƴere (nde).

chore [čowr] n. liggééy nder galle.

chosen [čowzən] adj. cuɓaaɗo.

chow [čaw] n. ñamri (ndi).

Christ [krayst] n. Annabi Iisaa.

Christian [krisčən] adj. mo wonaa juulɗo.

chronic [kronik] adj. duumiɗum; jokkiɗum; ko jokkii; ko duumii.

chronology [krənowləji] n. kiisagól sahaa.

chum [čʌm] n. góndiiɗo e suudu; séhil.

chump [čʌmp] n. tunde (nde).

churn [čərn] n. sumalle (o).

churn [čərn] v. yónkude.

chute [šut] v. yande.

cicatrix [sikətriks] n. ŋaacal battingal; fesoode (nde).

cichlid [sikləd] n. liingu (ngu).

cigar [sigɑ] n. simme (o).

cigarette [sigəret] n. sigaret (o); simme (o).

circle [sərkəl] n. lasal (ngal).

circle [sərkəl] v. taaraade; lasde.

circumcise [sərkəmsayz] v. haddinde; ɓóórninde; duhde.

circumcised [sərkəmsayz] adj. boorniiɗo; duhiiɗo.

circumcision [sərkəmciyzən] n. kaddingól (ngól); kaddinaagól; duhagol (ngól). person who performs ~ boornoowo; kaddinoowo.

undergo ~ boornaade.

circumspect [sərkumspekt] adj. dééntiiɗo.

circumvent [sərkəmvent] v. taaraade; réwrude.

cite [sayt] v. luɓaade kóngól jananól; limtude.

citizen [sitəzən] n. biɗɗo léydi.

city [siti] n. wuro (ngo)

civet [sivet] n. ullundu ladde.

civic [sivik] n. ko faati e wuro.

civilian [sivilyən] n. siwil (o).

civilization [siviləzeyšən] n. neɗɗaagu (ngu); néésu (ngu).

clad [klad] adj. ɓóórniiɗo cómci/cómcól.

claim [kleym] v. lamndaade. ~ someone's belongings happaade.

claimer [kleymə] n. lamndiiɗo.

clairvoyance [klervoyəns] n. péérgól (ngól).

clairvoyant [klervoyənt] adj. peerɗo.

clam [klam] v. rendinde.

clamber [klamə] v. ŋaylude; ƴeeŋde.

clamor [klamə] n. dillere mawnde.

clan [klan] n. fedde (nde); hinde (nde).

clandestine [klandestən] adj. cuuɗiiɗo; ko suuɗii/suuɗaa.

clannish [klaniš] adj. ko faati e hinde.

clap [klap] v. hellude; fóɓɓude.

clap [klap] n. hello (ngo).

pper [klapə] *n.* poɓɓoowo *(o)*.

pping [klapiŋ] *n.* kelle *(ɗe)*.

rify [klarəfay] *v.* laaɓtinde.

rity [klarəti] *n.* laaɓal *(ngal)*.

sh [klaš] *v.* fiindirde; fuɓɓóndirde.

ss [klas] *n.* kalaas *(o)*.

ssification [klasfikeyšən] *n.* céérndugól *ŋgól)*.

ssify [klasəfay] *v.* séérndude.

vicle [klavəkyuwl] *n.* Ƴiyal walabo.

w [klɔ] *n.* takkere *(nde)*.

w [klɔ] *v.* ŋaafde; ŋaacde

y [kley] *n.* ɓakkere *(nde)*.

an [kliyn] *v.* lawƳude; laɓɓinde. ***be ~* ɩaɓde. *make ~*** laɓɓinde. ***~ holes out*** ɩkkitde. ***~ one's mouth*** wufƳaade.

aner [kliynə] *n.* lawƳoowo *(o)*.

anliness [klenlines] *n.* laaɓal *(ngal)*.

anse [klens] *v.* laɓɓinde.

anser [klenzə] *n.* laɓɓinoowo *(o)*.

ar [cliyr] *v.* laɓɓinde. ***~ weeds*** duggude. ***weeds a second time*** beytaade. ***~ bush r farming*** lewde. ***~ one's throat*** ɩmsinaade; haaktaade.

arance [cliyrəns] *n.* laɓɓingol *(ngól)*.

econd ~ of weeds beyaat *(o)*.

ared [kliyrd] *adj.* laaɓɗum; ɩɓɓinaaɗum. ***~ land*** lewre *(nde)*.

avage [kliyvij] *n.* seekoode *(nde)*; péról ɩgól)*; céérndugól *(ngól)*.

ave [kliyv] *v.* seekde; feecde; ferde aawól); sóppude; eeɓde.

mency [clemənsi] *n.* yaafuya *(o)*.

ment [klemənt] *adj.* jaafotooɗo.

nch [klenč] *v.* muɓɓude; hamƳude.

rk [klərk] *n.* liggotooɗo *(o)*.

ver [klevə] *adj.* Ƴoƴɗo.

ck [klik] *n.* saɓɓitaango *(ngo)*; aɓɓitaagól *(ngól)*; wowlaango *(ngo)*.

ck [klik] *v.* saɓɓitaade; wowlude.

ent [klayənt] *n.* kiliyan *(o)*.

mate [klaymit] *n.* weeyo *(ngo)*.

matology [klaymətoləji] *n.* jangde ɩeeyo.

mb [klaym] *v.* ŋabbude; Ƴeeŋde; ɩaylude. ***~ with*** Ƴééŋirde.

mber [klaymə] *n.* ŋayloowo *(o)*; ɩabboowo; Ƴeeŋoowo *(o)*.

mbing [klaymiŋ] *n.* ŋabbugól *(ngól)*.

cling [kliŋ] *v.* takkaade e; heddaade e.

clingy [klinji] *adj.* takkiɗum; takkiiɗo; ko takkii.

clinic [klinik] *n.* nókku safaara.

clinical [klinikəl] *adj.* ko faati e nókku safaara.

clink [kliŋk] *v.* séŋlude; siŋlinde.

clinker [kliŋkə] *n.* ciŋlinoowo *(o)*.

clip [klip] *v.* taƳde.

clipper [klipə] *n.* taƳoowo *(o)*.

clique [kliyk] *n.* fedde *(nde)*.

clitoris [klitowrəs] *n.* sóɓɓundu *(ndu)*.

cloak [klowk] *n.* cómcól *(ngól)*.

clobber [klobə] *v.* fiide.

clock [klok] *n.* montoor *(o)*.

clocker [klokə] *n.* deenoowo waktu.

clod [klɑd] *n.* ɓoodde léydi.

clog [klɑg] *v.* sukkude.

close [klowz] *v.* uddude. ombude; sukkude; hiɓɓude. ***~ tightly*** hokde; hiɓɓude. ***~ the way to*** faddaade. ***~ one's eyes*** gumbinaade/wumbinaade.

close [klowz] *adj.* ɓattiɗum. ***be ~ to one another*** ɓadóndirde. ***be ~*** uddaade. ***make ~ ɓadinde. *be ~ to*** ɓadaade; ɓallaade; ɓattaade; faandaade.

closer [klowzer] *n.* guddoowo *(o)*.

closure [klowzə] *n.* uddugól *(ngól)*.

clot [klot] *v.* hetde.

clot [klot] *n.* heɗɗere *(nde)*.

cloth [kloθ] *n.* comcol *(ngól)*; bagi *(o)*; tekkere *(nde)*. ***~ for tying a child on one's back*** bambu *(ngu)*.

clothe [klowð] *v.* hóltinde.

clothing [klowðiŋ] *n.* cómci *(ɗi)*; comcol *(ngól)*. ***strip of ~*** léfól *(ngól)*; tekkere *(nde)*. ***remove someone's ~*** ɓoorde. ***remove one's ~*** ɓoortaade. ***own many pieces of ~*** holtude.

cloud [klawd] *n.* ruulde *(nde)*; suurndu *(ndu)*; guttere *(nde)*. ***~s forming prior to rain*** Ƴiiwoonde *(nde)*.

cloudy [klawdi] *adj.* Ƴiiwɗum; ko Ƴiiwi. ***~ weather*** niiwre *(nde)*; Ƴiiwoonde *(nde)*.

clove [klowv] *n.* kobjal *(ngal)*; nguru *(ngu)*.

club [klʌb] *n.* **1)** sawru *(ndu)*; ɓóóldu *(ndu)* **2)** fedde *(nde)*.

clubber [klʌbə] *n.* piyoowo *(o)*.

cluck [klʌk] *v.* saɓɓitaade; herde.

cluster   combinatior

cluster [klʌstə] *n.* endu *(ndu).* ~ *of fruit* singoore *(nde);* éndu *(ndu).*

clutter [klʌtə] *v.* sarde.

co-wife [kowayf] *n.* nawliraaɗo *(o).* pl. nawliraaɓe *(ɓe).*

coach [kowč] *v.* janginde; ékkinde.

coach [kowčə] *n.* janginoowo *(o);* ékkinoowo *(o).*

coagulate [kowagyəleyt] *v.* fendaade.

coal [kowl] *n.* Yulɓe *(ɗe);* Yulmere *(nde).*

coalesce [kowales] *v.* yantude; rééntude; yantóndirde; naatóndirde.

coalition [kowəliyšən] *n.* jantondiral *(ngal).*

coarse [kɔrs] *adj.* neetaro.

coast [kowst] *n.* fongo *(ngo).*

coax [kowks] *v.* ééltude.

cob [kob] *n.* Yuulde *(nde).*

cobble [kobəl] *v.* ɗakkude (e.g paɗe).

cobbler [koblə] *n.* ɗakkoowo *(o).*

cobweb [kobweb] *n.* geesa njamala.

cock [kok] *n.* ngóri *(o).*

cockle [kɔkəl] *n.* honoldu *(ndu).*

cockroach [kɔkrɔč] *n.* somre *(nde);* mbóótu *(ngu).*

cocky [kɔki] *adj.* YoYɗo; peerɗo.

coddle [kɔdəl] *v.* béwnude; fasnude.

code [kowd] *n.* laawól *(ngól).* *go against the* ~ luutndaade

coerce [kowers] *v.* waawnude.

coercion [kowəršən] *n.* baawnugól *(ngól).*

coff [kɔf] *v.* soodde; dañde.

coffee [kowfi] *n.* kafe *(ɗe).*

coffer [kowfə] *n.* wakande *(nde);* móftirde *(nde).*

coffin [kofin] *n.* balankaar *(o).*

cogitate [kowjəteyt] *v.* miijaade.

cogitation [kowjəteyšən] *n.* miijagól *(ngól).*

cognition [cogniyšən] *n.* gandal *(ngal).*

cognizance [kognəzəns] *n.* gandal (ngal).

cohabit [kowhabit] *v.* hóɗdude.

cohere [kowhiyr] *v.* yuɓɓude; réndude.

coherent [kowhiyrənt] *adj.* juɓɓuɗum; ko yuɓɓi; kó réndi.

cohesion [cowhiyʒən] *n.* juɓɓugól *(ngól).*

coincidence [koynsədens] *n.* kawrital *(ngal).*

cola nut [kowlənʌt] *n.* woroore *(nde).* *halɟ of a* ~ ŋaddo *(ngo);* felso *(ngo);* félsitere *(nde).*

cold [kowld] *n.* 1) jaangol *(ngól);* ɓuuɓó *(ngól).* 2) maɓɓo *(ngo).* *be ~ agaiɲ* ɓuuɓtude. *be ~* jaangde; ɓuuɓde. *have ɑ* ~ maɓɓeede; haakeede. *~ weatheɲ* jaangól *(ngól). feel ~* jaangeede.

colic [kɔlik] *n.* réédu muusóóru; reedu dógóóru.

collaborate [kolabəreyt] *v.* wallóndirde.

collaboration [kolabəreyšən] *n.* ballóndira *(ngal).*

collapse [kolaps] *v.* fukkaade.

collar [kola] *n.* cakka *(ka)*

collateral [kəlatərəl] *adj.* ko héédi sara.

colleague [koliyg] *n.* liggóddiiɗo.

collect [kolekt] *v.* réndinde. *~ firewooc* teende.

collection [kolekšən] *n.* déndigól. *~ oɟ firewood* téénól *(ngól);* teengol *(ngól)* collector [kolektə] *n.* déndinoowo *(o).*

college [kɑlij] *n.* jangirde *(nde);* duɗa *(ngal).*

collide [kolayd] *v.* fuɓɓóndirde.

collision [kəliyʒən] *n.* aksida *(o).* puɓɓóndiral *(ngal).*

collocate [koləkeyt] *v.* yahdude.

collude [kolyuwd] *v.* réndude maakaa waɗdude jungo e faandu.

colon [kowlən] *n.* toɓɓe ɗiɗi (:).

colonial [kolownyəl] *adj.* ko faati e jiimde.

colonize [kolənayz] *v.* jiimde.

colony [koləni] *n.* léydi njiimaandi.

color [kolə] *v.* noorde. *~ blue* bulde.

color [kolə] *n.* noordi *(ndi).*

colorful [kolərfəl] *adj.* kó yóóɗi; jóóɗɗum

colossal [kələsəl] *adj.* mawɗo mawnuɗum; ko mawni.

colt [kowlt] *n.* mola *(ba).*

column [kowlum] *n.* lappól *(ngól).*

comb [kom] *n.* yeesoode *(nde).*

comb [kom] *v.* yeesde. *~ one's haiɲ* yeesaade.

combat [kombət] *v.* haɓde; haɓeede.

combat [kombət] *n.* hare *(nde).* kareeli *(ɗi,* pl.

combination [kombəneyšən] *n.* déndingó *(gol).*

142

nbine [kombayn] v. réndinde.

mbustible [kombəstəbəl] adj. ko ubbata; kubbojum.

mbustion [kombʌsčən] n. kubbugól.

me [kɑm] v. arde; yettaade. ~ down ɔoraade; jippaade ~ down heavily oɣɣaade. ~ out of a hiding place ɩóggitaade. ~ for arande. ~ out of solde. ~ out wuddude. ~ from iwde. ~ by way 'f iwrude. ~ with ardude. ~ out (color) vukkude. ~ from iwde. ~ up to surface uppitaade. ~ up fudde. ~ up again udtude. ~ out wuftude; fulfitde.

median [komiyjən] n. jalnoowo (o).

mer [komə] n. garoowo (o).

mestible [kəmestəbəl] adj. ko ñaametee.

mfortable [komfətəbəl] adj. kó ééwnitii; pééwnitiido.

mic [komik] adj. jalniido; jalnidum; ko alnii.

mma [kowmə] n. póófirgél (ngél).

mmand [komand] v. hoonaade; ardaade.

mmemorate [koməmə reyt] v. mawninde.

mmence [komens] v. fuddaade.

mmend [komend] v. jaarde.

mment [koment] n. haala (ka).

mmentary [komentri] n. paccirgól ngól).

mmerce [komərs] n. julankaagal (ngal).

mmercial [koməršəl] adj. ko faati e ulankaagal.

mmercialize [koməršəlayz] v. yeeyde.

mmiserate [komisəreyt] v. réndude e eddo sunaare.

mmission [komiyšən] n. yamiroore (nde).

mmisioner [komiyšənə] n. kumaandaɲ 'o).

mmit [komit] v. wadde.

mmittee [komitiy] n. deental oodotoongal; deental cubangal.

mmix [komiks] v. réndinde.

mmodity [kəmowditi] n. marsandiis.

mmon [kamən] adj. dendadum; ko rendaa.

mmune [komyuwn] v. haalde; yééwtude.

mmunicate [komyuwnəkeyt] v. haaldude; jókkóndirde.

mmunication [komyunəkeyšən] n. kaaldigal (ngal); jókkóndiral (ngal).

community [komyuwnəti] n. yimbe wuurdube.

commutation [kəmyuwteyšən] n. gostagól (ngól).

commute [kəmyuwt] v. waylude.

compact [kəmpakt] adj. kó réndi.

companion [kəmpanyən] n. góndiido; jahdiido.

company [kəmpəni] n. gondiido (o). part ~ seertude.

compare [kəmpeyr] v. fóndude; nawdude.

comparison [kəmparəsən] n. póndugól.

compassion [kəmpašən] n. yurmeende.

compatible [kəmpatəbəl] adj. ko yahdi; ko yahdata.

compel [kəmpel] v. waawnude.

compensate [kəmpənseyt] v. yobde.

compensation [kəmpənseyšən] n. njóbdi.

compete [kəmpiyt] v. fóólóndirde; fóódóndirde.

competence [kompətəns] n. gandal (ngal); mbaawka (ka).

competition [kəmpətiyšən] n. póódóndiral.

compile [kəmpayl] v. réndinde.

complain [kəmpleyn] v. wullitaade.

complaint [kəmpleynt] n. gullitaagól (ngól); goytagól (ngól).

complete [kəmpliyt] v. gasnude; timminde; tóllitde; tóllitaade.

completely [kəmpliytli] adv. tuleɲ.

completeness [kəmpliytnes] n. timmal (ngal).

complex [kəmpleks] adj. caddum; ko sadi.

complexion [kəmplekšən] n. nóórdi neddo.

compliance [kəmplayəns] n. dowtagól.

complicate [kəmpləkeyt] v. sadnude.

compliment [kəmplimənt] v. njettoor (o).

comply [kəmplay] v. dowtaade; rewde.

component [kəmpownənt] n. gedal jeyangal e.

compose [kəmpowz] v. wallifaade.

composition [kəmpəzišən] n. ballifaagól; mahgól (ngól).

composure [kəmpowзə] n. deeɣre (nde).

compound [kəmpawnd] n. hodorde (nde); galle (o).

comprehend [kəmprəhend] v. faamde.

comprehension [kəmprəhenšən] *n.* faamaamuya.

comprehensive [kəmprəhensiv] *adj.* kó réndini kó hééwi.

compress [kəmpres] *v.* ñóꞮꞮude.

comprise [kəmprayz] *v.* rééntude.

compromise [kəmprəmayz] *v.* accóndirde.

comrade [komrad] *n.* séhil *(o)*

con [kɔn] *v.* jangude.

con [kɔn] *n.* luutndiiɗo.

concatenate [kənkatəneyt] *v.* séꞱóndirde.

concatenation [kənkatəneyšən] *n.* céꞱóndiral *(ngal)*.

concave [kənkeyv] *adj.* naɗɗiɗɗum; ko naɗɗiɗi.

conceal [kənsiyl] *v.* suuɗde.

concede [kənsiyd] *v.* jaɓde.

conceit [kənsiyt] *v.* miijaade.

conceit [kənsiyt] *n.* miijo *(ngo)*.

conceive [kənsiyv] *v.* miijaade.

concentrate [konsəntreyt] *v.* waɗtude hakkille; féndude.

concentration [konsəntreyšən] *n.* battugól hakkille e.

concept [kənsept] *n.* annama *(o)*; miijo *(ngo)*.

concern [kənsərn] *n.* hammu *(o)*; haaju *(o)*; woꞮa *(o)*. *That should not be your concern* ɗum wonaa haaju maa.

concerned [kənsərnd] *adj.* goꞮaaɗo.

concert [kənsərt] *v.* diisnóndirde; féwjude.

conciliate [kənsəlyeyt] *v.* wélditinde.

conciliator [kənsəlyeytə] *n.* bélditinoowo.

concise [kənsayz] *adj.* juɓɓuɗum; ko yuɓɓi.

conclude [kənkluwd] *v.* jóófnude; gasnude.

conclusive [kəkluwziv] *adj.* jóófɗum; ko joofi.

concoct [kənkɑt] *v.* féwjude.

concord [kənkord] *n.* kawral *(ngal)*; juɓɓugol *(ngól)*.

concordance [kənkordəns] *n.* kawral *(ngal)*; juɓɓugol *(ngól)*.

concordant [kənkərdənt] *adj.* kawruɗum; juɓɓuɗum; ko hawri.

concourse [kənkɔs] *n.* deental *(ngal)*.

concrete [kənkriyt] *adj.* gooɗɗum; kó wóódi.

concubine [kənkəayn] *n.* taara *(o)*.

concur [konkər] *v.* hawrude; yuɓɓude.

concurrence [kənkərəns] *n.* nanodiraꞱ *(ngal)*.

condemn [kəndem] *v.* felde.

condensate [kəndenseyt] *v.* féndude.

condense [kəndens] *v.* rabɓiɗinde.

condisciple [kəndəsaypəl] *n.* jangidiiɗo.

condition [kəndiyšən] *n.* sarɗi *(o)*.

conditional [kəndiyšənəl] *adj.* ko faati e sarɗi.

condole [kəndowl] *v.* duwanaade; réndude e neɗɗo sunaare.

condolence [kəndələns] *n.* duwaawu *(o)*.

condone [kəndown] *v.* wonande; jingande; yaafaade.

conduce [kəndyuws] *v.* jibinde; addude.

conduct [kəndʌkt] *n.* néhdi *(ndi)*.

conductor [kəndʌktə] *n.* gardiiɗo *(o)*.

confabulate [kənfəbyuwleyt] *v.* yééwtude.

confect [kənfekt] *v.* fééwnude.

confederate [kənfədəreyt] *v.* rééntude.

confederation [kənfədəreyšən] *n.* deental *(ngal)*.

conference [kənfərəns] *n.* deental *(ngal)*; góstóndiral hakkillaaji.

confess [kənfes] *v.* haaltude.

confide [kənfayd] *v.* hoolaade; haalande neɗɗo sirru mum.

confidence [kənfidəns] *n.* hoolaare *(nde)*.

confident [kənfidənt] *adj.* kooliiɗo.

confidential [kənfidənšəl] *adj.* ko faati e sirru.

confine [kənfayn] *v.* haaɗnude.

confirm [kənfərm] *v.* tééꞱtinde.

confirmation [kənfəmeyšən] *n.* tééꞱtingól *(ngól)*.

confiscate [kənfiskeyt] *v.* héɓtude.

conflict [kənflikt] *n.* luural *(ngal)*; hare *(nde)*.

conflicting [kənfliktiŋ] *adj.* luutondirɗum; kó luutóóndiri.

confluence [kənfluwəns] *n.* kawrital *(ngal)*.

conform [kənform] *v.* rewde.

confound [kənfawnd] *v.* jiiɓde.

confrere [kənfrer] *n.* liggodiiɗo *(o)*.

confront [konfrənt] *v.* wultinde.

confuse [kənfyuwz] *v.* jiiɓde.

confused [kənfyuwzd] *adj.* kawjuɗo.

nfusion [kənfyuwzən] *n.* jiiɓru *(ndu)*.

nfute [kənfyuwt] *v.* fénnude.

ngeal [kənjiyl] *v.* fendaade; féndude.

ngelation [kənjəleyšən] *n.* pendagól *ngól)*.

ngest [kənjest] *v.* ɓurtinde; ñukkóndirde.

nglomerate [kəŋgloməreyt] *v.* réndinde.

nglutinate [kəŋglutəneyt] *v.* ɗakkóndirde.

ngratulate [kəŋgrəčəleyt] *v.* yéttude.

ngratulation *n.* njettoor *(o)*.

ngregate [kəŋgrəgeyt] *v.* rééntude.

ngregation [kəŋgrəgeyšən] *n.* deental *(ngal)*.

ngruity [kəŋgruwəti] *n.* kawral *(ngal)*.

njoin [kənjoyn] *v.* réndinde.

njugal [kənjuwgəl] *adj.* ko faati e dewgal.

njunctivitis *n.* ñaw gite.

njuration [kənjəreyšən] *n.* duwaawu *(o)*; cappagól *(ngól)*.

njure [kənjuwr] *v.* dabaade; liggaade.

nnect [kənekt] *v.* jókkóndirde; séɠóndirde.

nnection [kənekšən] *n.* jókkóndiral *(ngal)*.

nnective [kənektiv] *adj.* jokkojum; ko jokkata.

nnector [kənektə] *n.* jokkoowo *(o)*.

nnivance [kənivəns] *n.* maakaa.

nquer [koŋkə] *v.* foolde; honde.

nqueror [koŋkərə] *n.* poolɗo *(o)*.

nquest [konkwest] *n.* póólgól *(ngól)*.

nsanguinity [konsaŋgwinəti] *n.* jiidigal *(ngal)*; bandiraagal *(ngal)*.

nscience [konšəns] *n.* pinal *(ngal)*; gandal *(ngal)*.

nsciousness [konšəsnəs] *n.* gandal *(ngal)*.

nsecutive [konsekyətiv] *adj.* ɗewondirɗum; kó réwóndiri.

nsensus [kənsensəs] *n.* pottal *(ngal)*; kawral *(ngal)*; ahdi *(o)*.

nsent [kənsent] *v.* jaɓde.

nsequence [konsəkwens] *n.* wattan.

nservation [kənzərveyzən] *n.* móóftugól.

nserve [konsərv] *v.* móóftude.

nsider [kənsidə] *v.* miijaade.

considerable [kənsidəbəl] *adj.* mawnuɗum; jaajɗum; ko mawni.

consideration [kənsidəreyšən] *n.* miijo *(ngo)*; wune *(o)*.

console [kənsowl] *v.* déɍɍinde; yeɍde.

consolidate [kənsalədeyt] *v.* tiiɗnude.

consolidation [kənsalədeyšən] *n.* tiiɗtingól *(ngól)*.

consonance [kansənəns] *n.* kawral *(ngal)*.

consonant [kansənənt] *n.* alkulal *(ngal)*.

consort [kənsərt] *n.* jom galle/suudu.

conspiracy [kənspirəsi] *n.* maakaa *(o)*.

conspire [kənspayə] *v.* fewjande.

constant [kanstənt] *adj.* ko waylaaki.

constellate [kanstəleyt] *v.* ñukkóndirde.

constellation [kanstəleyšən] *n.* koode ñukondirɗe.

consternate [konstərneyt] *v.* najnude.

consternation [konstəneyšən] *n.* najoore *(nde)*.

constipated [konstəpeytid] *adj.* ceeraaɗo; gonduɗo e seero.

constipation [konstəpeyšən] *n.* seero *(ngo)*.

constituency [konstəčəwənsi] *n.* yimɓe nókku; nókku.

constitution [konstətyuwšən] *n.* laabi léydi.

constrain [kənstreyn] *v.* waawnude; haɗde.

constrict [kənstrikt] *v.* tóɠnude; lééltinde.

construct [kənstrʌkt] *v.* mahde.

construction [kənstrʌkšən] *n.* mahdi *(ndi)*; mahngo *(ngo)*.

construe [kənstruw] *v.* firde; faamde.

consult [kənsʌlt] *v.* diisnaade.

consultant [kənsʌltənt] *n.* diisniiɗo *(o)*.

consumable [kənsyuwməbəl] *adj.* ko ñaametee.

consume [kənsyuwm] *v.* ñaamde.

consummate [kənsyuwmeyt] *v.* gasnude; fééwnude.

contact [kəntakt] *n.* mémóndiral *(ngal)*.

contagion [kənteyʒən] *n.* daaɓgól; raaɓo.

contagious [kənteyjəs] *n.* daaɓojum; ko raaɓata.

contain [kənteyn] *v.* wonde e nder.

contemplate [kontəmpleyt] *v.* yeeɓde.

contemporary [kəntempəreri] *adj.* ko faati é jóóni.

contempt [kəntempt] *n.* ɗuurtagól *(ngól)*; ufnagol *(ngól)*.

contemptuous [kəntempčəs] *adj.* gañɗo.

contend [kəntend] *v.* fóóɗóndirde.

content [kəntent] *n.* weltaare *(nde)*.

contentious [kəntenšəs] *adj.* póóɗóndirteeɗo.

contentment [kəntentmənt] *n.* weltaare *(nde)*.

contest [kəntest] *v.* hakde; salaade.

contestation [kəntəsteyšən] *n.* salaare *(nde)*.

contested [kəntestəd] *adj.* calaaɗo; ko salaa.

contiguity [kəntəgwiti] *n.* jókkóndiral *(ngal)*.

contiguous [kəntiygiwəs] *adj.* jokkondirɗum; kó jókkóndiri.

continence [kontənəns] *n.* heytaare *(nde)*.

contingency [kontənjənsi] *n.* fawaare *(nde)*.

contingent [kəntenjənt] *adj.* pawiɗum e; ko fawii e.

continual [kəntinyəl] *adj.* jokkiɗum; kó jókkii.

continually [kəntinyəli] *adv.* jokkiɗum; kó jókkii; ko duumii.

continue [kontinyuw] *v.* jókkude.

continuity [kantənwiti] *n.* jókkóndiral *(ngal)*.

continuous [kantənyus] *adj.* jokkiɗum; kó jókkii.

contort [kəntɔt] *v.* haaⵏde.

contra [kəntrə] *n.* luutndiɗo *(o)*.

contraceptive [kəntrəseptiv] *adj.* ko haɗata réédu.

contract [kəntrakt] *n.* ahdi *(o)*.

contradict [kontrədikt] *v.* yéddude.

contradiction [kontrədikšən] *n.* géddi *(ɗi)*.

contrary [kontrəri] *adj.* luutndiɗum; ko luutndii.

contrast [kəntrast] *v.* luutndaade.

contrastive [kəntrastiv] *adj.* ko luutndii.

contravene [kontrəviyn] *v.* luutndaade.

contravention [kontrəvenšən] *n.* luutndagól *(ngól)*.

contribute [kontrəbyuwt] *v.* fiide.

contrive [kəntrayv] *v.* féwjude.

control [kəntrowl] *v.* reende; heytaade.

controller [kəntrowlə] *n.* ⵏeewtotooɗo.

controversy [kontrəvərsi] *n.* luural *(ngal)*.

contumacy [kəntyuwməsi] *n.* murtugól.

contusion [kəntyuwzən] *n.* ɓuutdi *(ndi)*.

conundrum [kənəndrʌm] *n.* ciftól *(ngól)*.

convalescent [kənvələsənt] *adj.* camorɗo; camoranaaɗo.

convalesce [kənvales] *v.* samorde; samoraneede.

convene [kənviyn] *v.* reentude.

convenient [kənviynyənt] *adj.* jubɓuɗum; peewɗum; ko yuɓɓi; ko fééwi; kó fééwnitii.

convention [kənvenšən] *n.* deental; nanóndiral.

converge [kənvərj] *v.* hawrude.

convergence [kənvərjəns] *n.* kawral *(ngal)*.

conversation [konvərseyšən] *n.* yeewtere *(nde)*.

conversational [konvəseyšən] *adj.* ko faati e yeewtere.

converse [kənvərs] *v.* yééwtude.

conversion [konvərʒən] *n.* baylagól *(ngól)*; gostagól *(ngól)*.

convert [kənvərt] *v.* tuubde; waylaade; wostaade.

convey [kənvey] *v.* yettinde; nawde.

conveyor [kənveyə] *n.* nawoowo; ko nawata.

convict [kənvikt] *adj.* tooñɗo.

convince [kənvins] *v.* ɗahde.

convive [kənviyv] *n.* ñaamdiiɗo.

convoke [kənvowk] *v.* nóddude.

convoy [kənvoy] *v.* reende.

convulsion [kənvʌlšən] *n.* karlagól *(ngól)*; muusu *(o)*.

cook [kuk] *n.* defoowo *(o)*.

cook [kuk] *v.* defde. ~ *slightly* waⵏⵏinde. ~ *with* défrude; defirde. ~ *for* defande.

cooked [kukt] *adj.* ɗefaɗum; ɓenduɗum. *be ~ improperly* hirde (used for fish).

cooker [kukə] *n.* masiꞑ defoowo.

cooking [kukiŋ] *n.* ndefu *(ngu)*. ~ *oil* diwlin *(o)*. ~ *pot* barme *(o)*; fayande *(nde)*.

cool [kuwl] *v.* ɓuuɓnude; dééⵏnude.

cooler [kuwlə] *n.* nokku ɓuuɓnoowo.

cooperate [kowpəreyt] *v.* walloóndirde.

cooperation [kowpəreyšən] *n.* ballóndiral *(ngal)*.

coordinate [kowrdəneyt] v. réndinde.

cope [kowp] v. wadɗude heen; tiiɗnaade.

copier [kowpiyə] n. baañjittooɗo (o).

copious [kowpyəs] adj. kó hééwi; kééwɗum.

copula [kowpyuwlə] n. kó réndinta.

copulate [kowpyuwleyt] v. hoowde; yiindirde.

copy [kɑpi] v. waañjitaade.

cord [kɔd] n. ɓóggól (ngól); dóggól (ngól). ~ for guiding an animal ginól (ngól).

cordial [kɔjəl] adj. belɗo YiiYam.

cordon [kordən] n. ɓógól (ngól).

cork [kɔk] n. sukkoode (nde).

cork [kɔk] v. sukkude.

corn [kɔn] n. makka (o)

corner [kɔnə] v. jookde.

corner [kɔnə] n. lobbudu (ndu); jóókdu (ndu); tonkoŋ (o).

cornered [kɔnəd] adj. jookaaɗo.

cornering [kɔnəriŋ] adj. jooko (ngo).

cornet [kornet] n. liital (ngal).

cornstalk [kɔnstɔk] n. gawYal (ngal); gombal (ngal).

corporal [kɔpərəl] adj. ko faati e ɓandu.

corpse [kɔrps] n. kabbale; maayɗo (o).

corpulence [kɔrpyuwləns] n. doole (ɗe) ; sembe (o).

corpulent [kɔrpyuwlənt] adj. dóólnuɗo; cémbinɗo.

corrade [koreyd] v. rosaade; ŋeemtaade.

correct [korekt] v. fééwnitde.

correction [korekšən] n. pééwnitgól (gol).

corrector [korektə] n. pééwnitoowo (o).

correlate [kowrileyt] v. naatnaattondirde.

correlation [kowrəleyšən] n. naatnaattóndiral (ngal).

correspond [korespɑnd] v. jókkóndirde; windóndirde

correspondence [kərespəndəns] n. bindóndiral (ngal).

corroborate [kərowbəreyt] v. sémbinde; tééŋtinde.

corroboration [kərowbəreyšən] n. tééŋtingól; cémbingól (ngól).

corrode [kərowd] v. ŋeemtaade.

corrosion [kərowʒən] n. ŋeemtagól (ngól).

corrugate [kərəgeyt] v. ñórɓólinde.

corrupt [kərʌpt] v. yeende.

corrupt [kərʌpt] adj. jeeneteeɗo; mo feewaani.

corvée [korve] n. gollal ngal Alla meho.

cosmic [kozmik] adj. ko faati e weeyo.

cosmology [kozmowloji] n. jangde weeyo.

cosmopolitan [kozmowpəlitən] adj. kuɓtódinɗum.

cosset [kɔset] v. béwnude.

cost [kost] n. cóggu (ngu).

costly [kostli] adj. caɗɗum; kó tiiɗi.

cottage [kɑtij] n. huɓeere tokosere.

cotton [kɑtən] n. wiro (ko) ~ thread geese (ɗe). ~ field liige (nge). ~ seed wiYYere (nde).

couch [kawč] n. leeso (ngo).

cough [kɔf] v. ɗojjude.

cough [kɔf] n. ɗojjere (nde)

council [kawnsəl] n. deental (ngal).

counsel [kawnsəl] v. tóppitaade; waajaade.

counselor [kawnsələ] n. tóppitiiɗo (o); baajotooɗo (o).

count [kawnt] n. limoore (nde).

count [kawnt] v. limde ~ again limtaade.

countable [kawntəbəl] adj. limotooɗum; ko limotoo.

countenance [kawntənəns] n. mbaadi; yeeso.

countenance [kawntənəns] n. deeYre (nde).

counter [kawntə] n. kontuwaar.

country [kʌntri] n. léydi (ndi).

county [kawnti] n. nókku (o); yimɓe nókku.

couple [kʌpəl] v. réndinde.

couple [kʌpəl] n. ɗiɗi.

coupler [kəplə] n. déndinoowo.

coupon [kyuwpon] n. taYatinde.

courage [kərij] n. tiiɗnaare (nde); cuusal (ngal).

courageous [kəreyjəs] adj. cuusɗo.

courier [kuriye] n. nelaaɗo; nulaaɗo.

course [kɔs] v. tiindaade; huccude.

court [kɔt] v. satde; gerde

court [kɔt] n. ñaaworde (nde)

courtesy [kərtəsi] n. néhdi móYYiri.

courtier [kurče] n. batilo (o).

courtly [kɔtli] adj. néhiiɗo.

courtship [kɔtšip] *n.* sorbo *(ngo).*

courtyard [kɔtyɑd] *n.* boowal galle.

couscous [kuskus] *n.* lacciri *(ndi).* ~ **grain** wormbolde *(nde).*

cousin [kazin] *n.* déndiraado *(o);* baabiraado *(o).* **first** ~ ɓii miñum/mawnum yumma.

couteau [kutɔ] *n.* laɓi *(ki).*

covenant [kɔvnənt] *n.* ahdi *(o).*

cover [kɑvə] *n.* hippoode *(nde);* omboode *(nde);* suddaare *(nde);* mbedu *(ngu).* **take** ~ sudaade.

cover [kɑvə] *v.* hippude; suddude; muurde; buumde. ~ **seeds with sand** wékkude. ~ **with dust** ullude. ~ **with leather** aalde. ~ **one's head** muurnaade. ~ **the mouth** muɓɓude; suumde. ~ **oneself** tuddaade. ~ **oneself** suddaade. ~ **with cloth** mojde. ~ **with sand** irde.

covert [kowvərt] *adj.* cuudidum; ko suudii; ko suudaa.

covet [kovət] *v.* hirde; yidde kaake janane.

coveter [kovətə] *n.* kiroowo *(o);* kirdo *(o).*

cow [kaw] *n.* nagge *(nge);* haange *(nge);* jebe *(nge);* soñe *(nge).* ~ **dung** jaañe *(de)*

coward [kawəd] *adj.* kuldo réédu.

cowardice [kawədis] *n.* kulól réédu.

co-wife [kowayf] *n.* nawliraado.

cowlick [kawlik] *n.* atturu.

cowrie [kawri] *n.* wujo *(ngo).* ~shell seedere *(nde).*

coy [koy] *adj.* nuggaro.

crack [krak] *n.* gewol *(ngól);* ŋaddere *(nde).*

crack [krak] *v.* feecde; feecaade; ŋaddude.

craft [kraft] *n.* mbaawka *(ka);* gandal *(ngal);* ñeeñal *(ngal).*

craftsman [kraftsmən] *n.* liggortoodo juude mum; ñeeño *(o).*

cram [kram] *v.* hébbinde; ñoofde; ñookde; ɓittondirde.

cramp [kramp] *n.* jaadre *(nde)*

crap [krap] *n.* jaañe *(de)* ; kuudi *(ndi).*

crash [kraš] *v.* móññude.

crate [kreyt] *n.* wakande *(nde).*

crave [kreyv] *v.* ñaagaage. ~ **for** tuuyeede; yidde.

crawl [krɔwl] *v.* ladde.

crawler [krɔwlə] *n.* ladoowo *(o).*

crawling [krawliŋ] *n.* ladól *(ngól).*

crayon [kreyon] *n.* kiriyoŋ *(o).*

craze [kreyz] *v.* feecde.

crazy [kreyzi] *adj.* kaangaado; ustiido.

creak [kriyk] *v.* ɓiicde.

creak [kriyk] *n.* 1) ɓiicaango *(ngo);* ɓiicgol *(ngól)* 2) caadngol *(ngól).*

cream [kriym] *n.* ketungol *(ngól);* kerem *(o).*

crease [kriys] *v.* ñórɓólinde.

create [kryeyt] *n.* tagde. ~ **simultaneously** tagdude.

creation [kryeyšən] *n.* windere *(nde);* tagoore *(nde).*

creator [kryeyrə] *n.* tagoowo *(o).*

creature [kriyčə] *n.* innama aadéé *(o);* muumantél *(ngél);* aadee.

credible [kredibəl] *adj.* koolaado.

credit [kredit] *n.* hoolaare *(nde);* ñamaande *(nde).*

creditor [kreditə] *n.* ñamloowo *(o).*

creed [kriyd] *n.* cappagól *(ngól);* duwaawu *(o).*

creek [kriyk] *n.* caadngól *(ngól).*

creep [kriyp] *v.* sorde; ladde. ~ **along** ɓodde.

creeper [kriypə] *n.* ladoori *(ndi).*

cremate [krimeyt] *v.* sumde; duppude.

crepitate [krepiteyt] *v.* féttude.

crescent [kresənt] *n.* léwru dariindu.

crest [krest] *n.* jubudu *(ndu);* tólluru *(ndu);* gééjól *(ngól).*

cretin [krətin] *n.* puuydo *(o).*

crew [kruw] *n.* yimɓe liggotooɓe.

crib [krib] *n.* ndaddudi cukalél.

cricket [kriket] *n.* tenkere *(nde).*

crier [krayə] *n.* goyoowo *(o);* jeeynoowo *(o).* ~ **cry** luukgol *(ngól);* eewnagol *(ngól);* wulaango *(ngo).*

crime [kraym] *n.* tooñange *(nge);* aŕŕiiba *(o);* bonande *(nde).*

criminal [kriminəl] *adj.* ko faati e bonande.

crimp [krimp] *v.* sowde; ñóngude.

cripple [kripəl] *adj.* laŕoowo; boofo.

crippled [kripəld] *adj.* boofo

critic [kritik] *adj.* loskoowo; ŕeewtotoodo.

criticize [kritəsayz] *v.* lóskude.

crochet [krowše] *n.* lóŋdu *(ndu).*

crocodile [krowkədayl] *n.* nooroo *(o).*

croft [krɑft] *n.* sardiɲɲe *(o);* gesel *(ngél).*

crook [kruwk] *n.* óóñiiɗo *(o).*

crooked [kruked] *adj.* óóñiiɗo; ooñiɗum.

croon [kruwn] yimde; ŋuuñde.

crop [krop] *n.* coñaandi *(ndi).*

cropper [kropə] *n.* demoowo *(o).*

cross [kros] *v.* taccude; lumbude; Yaɲaade. ~ *one's legs while sitting* ferlaade. ~ *off* momtude.

cross [kros] *n.* céli.

crossbow [krosbaw] *n.* laañal *(ngal).*

crossing [krosiŋ] *n.* lumbal *(ngal).*

crouch [krawč] *v.* hofaade.

crow [kraw] *v.* jóggude.

crow [kraw] *n.* joggaango *(ngo).*

crowd [krawd] *n.* yimɓe heewɓe.

crucify [kruwsəfay] *v.* warde hono warngo Annabi Iisaa.

crude [kruwd] *adj.* keccidɗum; ko ɓendaani; ko waylaaka.

crudity [kruwdəti] *n.* huunde héccidnde.

cruel [kruwl] *adj.* bonɗo; ñanguɗo.

crumble [krʌmbəl] *v.* moññaade.

crumb [krʌm] *n.* taYatinde.

crumple [krʌmpəl] *v.* hamYude.

crunch [krʌnč] *v.* Yakkude.

crusade [kruwseyd] *n.* péllugól diine.

crusade [kruwseyd] *v.* féllude diine.

crush [krʌš] *v.* moññude; bojjude. ~ *up* lóppude. ~ *tobacco in one's palm* ormaade. ~ *into pieces again* mórñitde.

crushed [krʌšt] *adj.* ko loppaa; loppaaɗo; loppaɗum; moññaaɗo; moññaɗum; cokkaaɗo; cokkaɗum.

cry [kray] *v.* woyde; Yerde; Yekkitde; luuɗde (dog); ŋuuñde (hyena).

cub [kʌb] *n.* bingel *(ngél).*

cud [kʌd] *n.* aaYtere *(nde).*

cuddle [kʌdəl] *v.* hibɓóndirde.

cuddy [kʌdi] *n.* cuurél nder laana.

cuff [kʌf] *v.* fiide hello.

cuisine [kwiysiyn] *n.* ndéfu *(ngu);* waañ *(o);* défirde *(nde).*

cul-de-sac [kʌldəsak] *n.* laawól ngól yulaani.

cull [kʌl] *v.* suɓaade.

culminate [kʌlməneyt] *v.* heɓde ceɓtam.

culpable [kʌlpəbəl] *adj.* tooñɗo.

culprit [kʌlprit] *adj.* tooñɗo.

cult [kʌlt] *n.* bóri *(o).*

cultivate [kʌltəveyt] *v.* remde.

cultivation [kʌltiveyšən] *n.* ndémri *(ndi).*

cultivator [kʌltiveytə] *n.* demoowo *(o).*

cultural [kʌlčərəl] *adj.* ko faati é néésu.

culture [kʌlčə] *n.* néésu *(ngu).*

cumber [kʌmbə] *v.* haljinde.

cumbersome [kʌmbəsəm] *adj.* ko haljinta.

cumulate kyuwmyəleyt] *v.* fawóndirde; joowondirde.

cumulus [kyuwmyələs] *n.* ruulde *(nde).*

cunning [kʌniŋ] *n.* YoYre *(nde);* gandal *(ngal).*

cup [kʌp] *n.* kóppu *(o).* *It is not my cup of tea* ɗum wona ko am.

cupidity [kyuwpidəti] *n.* tiiɗgól jungo.

curable [kyuwrəbəl] *adj.* ko safrotoo.

curative [kyuwrətiv] *adj.* cafrojum; ko safrata.

curd [kərd] *n.* kosam lammuɗam; kosam pendaɗam.

cure [kyuwr] *v.* safrude; sellinde. ~ *by body contact* hokondirde.

curious [kyuryəs] *adj.* jiɗɗo andude.

curl [kərl] *v.* hofde. ~ *up* ñoofaade.

currency [kərənsi] *n.* kaalis *(o).*

current [kərənt] *n.* teere *(nde);* waraango *(ngo).*

currently [kərəntli] *adv.* jóóni.

currish [kəriš] *adj.* ñanguɗo.

curse [kərs] *v.* Yettaade; huɗde.

curse [kərs] *n.* Yettore *(nde);* kuɗdi *(ndi).*

cursed [kərst] *adj.* kiitaaɗo; kuɗaaɗo.

curt [kərt] *adj.* daɓɓo; ko raɓɓiɗi.

curtail [kərteyl] *v.* raɓɓidinde.

curtain [kərtən] *n.* rido *(o).*

curtsy [kərtsi] *n.* diccagól *(ngól).*

curve [kərv] *v.* ooñde.

curved [kərvd] *adj.* kogiɗum; ooñiɗum.

cushion [kʌšən] *n.* talla *(o);* ngaflaari *(ndi).*

cushy [kuši] *adj.* beeɓɗum; kó wééɓi; kó wéli.

custodian [kʌstowjən] *n.* deenoowo *(o).*

custody [kʌstədi] *n.* dééngól *(ngól);* ndeenka *(ka).* *He is in custody* Ko o jaggaaɗo.

custom [kʌstəm] *n.* nèésu *(ngu)*; jikku *(o);* aada *(o).*

customary [kʌstəməri] *adj.* ko faati e nèésu.

customer [kʌstəmə] *n.* kiliyaan *(o);* coodoowo *(o).*

customs [kʌstəmz] *n.* duwaañ.

cut [kʌt] *v.* taɼde; soppude. ~ *oneself accidentally* ɗeeɗaade. ~ *with a sickle* wafde. ~ *up* seelde. ~ *meat into strips.* siirtude ~ *fish into parts.* ande ~ *someone's ear* fañaade. ~ *open* waaftude. ~ *a splinter* sarfude. ~ *into strips* seelde ~ *grass* wubbude; hesde.

cut [kʌt] *n.* taɼande *(nde);* taɼre *(nde);* soppande *(nde);* ɗeeɗol *(ngól);* ééból *(ngól).*

cute [kyuwt] *adj.* jooɗdo.

cutler [kʌtlə] *n.* peewnoowo paakaaji; jeeyoowo paakaaji.

cutlet [kʌtlet] *n.* taɼande *(nde).*

cutoff [kʌtəf] *n.* taɼande *(nde).*

cutter [kʌtə] *n.* taɼoowo *(o).*

cycle [saykəl] *v.* dógnude. welo.

cyst [sist] *n.* basél *(ngél).*

D

dabble [dabəl] v. léppinde; wiccude.
dacker [dakə] v. daaldaalnude.
dad [dad] n. baabiraaɗo (o).
daffing [dafiŋ] n. kaaɗi (ɗi); ɗaayre (nde).
daft [daft] adj. ɗaaydo.
dagger [dagə] n. laɓi (ki).
daggle [dagəl] v. daasde.
daily [deyli] adj. ñalawma kala; ñande kala.
dainty [deynti] adj. kó yóóɗi; kó wéli.
dairy [deyri] n. móóftirde kosam e nebam keccam.
daleth [daleƟ] n. alkulal (ngal); alkulal deel.
dam [dam] n. mbarngu (ngu).
damage [damij] v. bónnude.
damage [damij] n. bonande (nde).
dame [deym] n. debbo (o).
damnable [damnəbəl] adj. ko añaa; kó félnii.
damp [damp] adj. ɓaytuɗum; ɓayɗum [dampən] v. ɓaytinde.
dampness [dampnes] n. ɓayto (ngo).
dance [dans] n. ngamri (ndi).
dance [dans] v. amde. make someone ~ amnude.
dancer [dansə] n. gamoowo (o)
dander [dandə] n. sekre (nde).
dandle [dandəl] v. yeɣde cukalel.
dandruff [dandrʌf] n. karaas (o).
danger [deynjə] n. bone (ɗe); ko gaañata.
dangerous [deynjərəs] adj. bonnojum; lorlojum; ko bonnata; ko lorlata.
dangle [daŋgəl] v. weelde.
dap [dap] v. saftaade.
dare [der] v. suusde.
daring [deriŋ] n. cuusal (ngal).
dark [dɔrk] adj. niɓɓidɗum; iirɗuɗum. after ~ so hiirii.
darken [darkən] v. ɓawlinde.
darkle [darkəl] v. niɓɓidinde.
darkness [darknes] n. niɓɓere (nde).
darling [darliŋ] n. giɗo (o); giɗél (ngél).
darn [darn] v. ñootde.
dash [daš] v. fiide; furtaade.
dasher [dašə] n. piyoowo (o).
data [deytə] n. kabaaru (o).

date [deyt] n. 1) saanga; sahaa. out of ~ ko ɓenni; ko jolti 2) tamaroore (nde).
daughter [dɔtə] n. biɗɗo debbo.
daunt [dɔnt] v. hulɓinde.
dauntless [dɔntles] adj. cuusɗó reedu.
dawn [dɔn] n. weetndoogo.
day [dey] n. ñalnde (nde); nalawma (o); nalngu (ngu); ñallande (nde); nalaande (nde). ~ off ñalawma fooftere.
day-to-day [deytədey] adj. ñalawma kala.
daze [deyz] v. hawjinde.
dead [ded] n. maayɗo (o); birniiɗo (o). ~ as mutton maayɗo pak.
deadline [dedlayn] n. lajal (ngal); ahdi (o).
deadly [dedli] adj. ko warata.
deaf [def] adj. paho. ~ person paho (o).
deafen [defən] v. faaɗnude.
deafness [defnes] n. paaɗgól (ngól).
deal [diyl] v. yeeyde; feccude.
dealer [diylə] n. jeeyoowo (o).
dealership [diyləšip] n. njééygu (ngu).
dear [diyə] adj. tiiɗɗo; misiɗɗo. ~ friend ñallambero (o); musiɗɗo (o).
dearth [derƟ] n. sooño (ngo); heege (nge).
deary [deri] n. giɗo.
death [deƟ] n. maayde (nde). ~ message broadcast on the radio taggéé (o).
deathly [deƟli] adj. barojum; ko warata.
deave [diyv] v. faaɗnude.
debase [dibeyz] v. lésɗinde; bónnitde.
debatable [dibeytəbəl] adj. ko hoolnaaki.
debate [dibeyt] v. wóstóndirde hakkillaaji.
debonair [deboner] adj. belɗo hakkille.
debt [det] n. ñamaande (nde). He is discharging a debt omon yoɓa ñamaande nde.
debtor [detə] n. ñamliiɗo (o).
debutant [debyuwtənt] n. puɗɗiiɗo golle.
decade [dekeyd] n. duuɓi sappo.
decadence [dekədəns] n. nuflugól (ngól).
decadent [dekədənt] adj. nufluɗo.
decaliter [dekalitə] n. liitéruuji sappo.
decameter [dekamitə] n. meeteruuji sappo.
decant [dekənt] v. siiwtude.
decapitate [dekəpiteyt] v. warde; taɣde daande.

decay [dikey] *n.* ŋeemtaade; ñolde.

decease [disiyz] *v.* maayde.

deceased [disiyzd] *adj.* maayɗo.

deceit [disiyt] *n.* fuunti *(o).*

deceitful [disiytfəf] *adj.* puuntoowo; ko fuuntata.

deceive [disiyv] *v.* fuuntude.

decelerate [dicələreyt] *v.* ustude yaawre.

decenary [desənəri] *adj.* ko faati e duuɓi sappo.

decency [diysənsi] *n.* peewal *(ngal).*

decennial [desiynyəl] *adj.* ko faati e duuɓi sappo.

decent [disent] *adj.* ko fééwi.

deception [disepšən] *n.* fuunti *(o).*

deceptive [disəptiv] *adj.* ko fuuntata; puuntojum.

decide [disayd] *v.* wakkilaade; haajde; féllitde.

decimate [desəmeyt] *v.* boomde.

decipher [disayfə] *v.* hijjude; limtude; jangude.

decision [disiyʒən] *n.* péllital *(ngal).*

deck [dek] *n.* pom *(o).*

deckchair *n.* [dekčer] piliyaan *(o).*

declare [dikleyr] *v.* hóllirde; habrude.

declinate [dikləneyt] *v.* tellaade.

declination [dikləneyšən] *n.* tellagól *(ngól).*

decline [diklayn] *v.* tellaade; ustaade.

decode [dikowd] *v.* firde; faccirde.

decoder [dicowdə] *n.* piroowo *(o).*

decollate [dikəleyt] *v.* taɼde daande.

decolonize [diykələnayz] *v.* rimɗinde leydi; jiimtude léydi.

decompose [diykəmpowz] *v.* ufde; jiiɓde; séérndude; ñolde.

decorate [dekəreyt] *v.* ŋeñde; sinkude.

decorticate [dikərtikeyt] *v.* feɼde.

decortication [dikərtikeyšən] *n.* péɼgól *(ngól).*

decoy [dikoy] *v.* fuuntude; tuufaade.

decrease [dikriys] *v.* ustude.

decrease [dikriys] *n.* ustaare *(nde);* ustugól *(ngól).*

decree [dikriy] *n.* yamiroore *(nde).*

decrement [dikrəmənt] *n.* ustaare *(nde);* ustugól *(ngól).*

decrial [dikrayəl] *n.* njennoor *(o).*

decry [dikray] *v.* bónnitde; yénnude.

decuple [dekyuwpəl] *v.* fiide laabi sappo.

dedicate [dedikeyt] *v.* ɗowtaade.

dedication [dedikeyšən] *n.* ɗowtaare *(nde).*

deduct [didʌkt] *v.* ustude; ittude.

deduction [didʌkšən] *n.* ustaare *(nde).*

deed [diyd] *n.* gollal *(ngal).*

deem [diym] *v.* miijaade.

deep [diyp] *adj.* luggiɗɗum; ko luggiɗi. ~ *area* luggere *(nde).* ~ *mourning* sunaare mawnde.

deepen [diypən] *v.* luggiɗinde.

deeply [diypli] *adv.* ko luggiɗi; luggiɗɗum.

defalcate [dəfalkeyt] *v.* wujjude.

defalcation [dəfəlkeyšən] *n.* nguyka *(ka).*

default [diyfɔlt] *n.* ella *(o).*

defaulter [diyfɔltə] *n.* jom ella.

defeat [difiyt] *v.* foolde

defeated [difiytəd] *adj.* poolaaɗo.

defecate [dəfəkeyt] *v.* suulde; huwde; aɗɗitde. ~ *in one's clothing* bonnitaade.

defect [difekt] *n.* ella *(o)*

defend [difend] *v.* dartaade.

defendant [difendənt] *n.* tuumaaɗo.

defense [difens] *n.* hare *(nde);* dartagól *(ngól).*

defer [difər] *v.* faɓɓinde.

deferment [difərmənt] *n.* paɓɓingól.

deferring [difəriŋ] *n.* paɓɓingól.

defiance [difayəns] *n.* salaare *(nde).*

defiant [difayənt] *adj.* caliiɗo; cirŋiniiɗo.

deficiency [defiyšənsi] *n.* ŋakkere *(nde).*

deficient [defiyšənt] *adj.* ŋakkuɗum; ustiɗum.

deficit [defisit] *n.* ŋakkere *(nde).*

defile [dəfayl] *v.* tunwinde.

define [difayn] *v.* hókkude maanaa.

definite [defnət] *adj.* laaɓɗum; ko laaɓi; ko lééri.

definition [defniyšən] *n.* maanaa *(o).*

deflagrate [dəfləgreyt] *v.* huɓɓude.

deflate [difleyt] *v.* péérnude; yaltinde héndu pono.

deflect [diflekt] *v.* filtinde.

defloration [dəfləreyšən] *n.* jiidgól *(ngól).*

deform [difɔm] *v.* waylude tagóódi.

defraud [dəfrowd] *v.* wujjude; tooñde.

defray [dəfrey] *v.* yoɓde.

defunct [difʌŋkt] *adj.* maayɗo.

defy [difay] *v.* jattinaade.

degrade [diygreyd] *v.* bónnitde; hérsinde.

degrading [digreydiŋ] *adj.* kersiniiɗum; kó hérsinii.

degree [digriy] *n.* degere *(o).*

degression [digreyšǝn] *n.* ustaare *(nde);* ustagól *(ngól).*

déjà vu [deʒavu] *n.* ko yiyaa haa bénni; ko hesɗaani.

delay [diley] *v.* lééltinde. *without* ~ ɗoon e ɗoon.

delectable [dilektǝbǝl] *adj.* belɗum; kó wéli; dakmuɗum.

delegate [delǝgeyt] *v.* nelde; halfinde.

delegate [dǝlǝgeyt] *n.* nulaaɗo *(o);* nelaaɗo *(o).*

delegation [dǝlǝgeyšǝn] *n.* nelaabe *(be);* halfinaabe *(be).*

delete [dǝliyt] *v.* mómtude.

deleterious [dǝlǝtǝryǝs] *adj.* ko ñawnata.

deletion [dǝliyšǝn] *n.* mómtugól.

deliberate [dǝlibrǝt] *adj.* ko amdaa; ko naatni amdaare.

delicious [dǝliyšǝs] *adj.* dakmuɗum; belɗum; ko dakmi; ko wéli.

delight [dǝlayt] *n.* welamma *(o).*

delighted [dǝlaytǝd] *adj.* béltiiɗo.

delightful [dǝlaytfǝl] *adj.* kó wéltinta; béltinoowo; beltinoojum.

delimit [dilimit] *v.* heertaade.

delineate [dǝlinyeyt] *v.* amminde; sifaade.

deliquesce [dǝlǝkwes] *v.* saayde.

deliration [dǝlǝreyšǝn] *n.* duuytugól.

delirious [dǝlǝryǝs] *adj.* duuytoowo.

deliver [dǝlivǝ] *v.* yéttinde; tottude; jibinde.

delude [dǝlyuwd] *v.* fuuntude.

deluge [dǝluwʒ] *n.* amo *(ngo).*

delve [delv] *v.* asde; luggiɗinaade; wittude.

demagogue [dǝmǝgog] *n.* puuntoowo *(o).*

demagogy [dǝmǝgoji] *n.* fuunti *(o).*

demand [dǝmand] *v.* lamndaade hakke mum. *This merchandise is in great demand* Marsandiis o ina soklaa no feewi.

demarcate [dǝmǝrkeyt] *v.* heertaade.

demarcation [dǝmǝrkeyšǝn] *n.* keertagól *(ngól).*

dement [dǝment] *v.* haaɭɗinde.

dementia [dǝmenčǝ] *n.* kaaɗi *(ɗi).*

demi [dǝmi] *pref.* feccere *(nde);* hakkunde.

demise [dǝmayz] *v.* nattude.

demission [dǝmišǝn] *n.* ɗaccingól hoore mum golle.

demit [dǝmit] *v.* ɗaccinde hoore mum golle.

demolish [demǝliš] *v.* yandinde.

demon [diymǝn] *n.* seytaane *(o).*

demoniac [dǝmonyak] *adj.* ko faati e seytaane.

demonstrate [dǝmǝnstreyt] *v.* hóllude; tééɭtinde.

demonstrator [dǝmǝnstreytǝ] *n.* kolloowo *(o).*

demount [dǝmawnt] *v.* téllinde.

demure [demyuwr] *n.* nuggaro *(o).*

denial [dǝnayǝl] *n.* géddi *(ɗi).*

denier [dǝnayǝ] *n.* jéddudo *(o).*

denigrate [dǝnigreyt] *v.* bónnitde.

denominate [dǝnǝmineyt] *v.* innude; nóddude.

denomination [dǝnǝmineyšǝn] *n.* inde.

denounce [dǝnawns] *v.;* féññinde.

dense [dens] *adj.* cukkuɗum; ko sukki.

dent [dent] *v.* bobbude.

dental [dentǝl] *n.* ko faati e ñiiⱤe/ñiire.

dentist [dentist] *n.* doktoor ñiiⱤe.

denude [dǝnyuwd] *v.* waɗde meho; labbinde; lewde.

deny [dinay] *v.* yeddude.

depart [dipɑt] *v.* yahde; ummaade.

departure [dipɑčǝ] *n.* ummagól *(ngól).*

depend [dipend] *v.* fawaade e; loraade e.

dependable [dǝpendǝbǝl] *adj.* koolaaɗo.

dependence [dǝpǝndǝns] *n.* pawagol *(ngól);* loragól(ngol); fawaare *(nde).*

dependency [dǝpǝndǝnsi] *n.* fawaare *(nde).*

depict [dǝpikt] *v.* sifaade.

depilate [dǝpileyt] *v.* borde léébi.

deplete [dipliyt] *v.* gasnude; labbinde.

deplore [diplowr] *v.* woytaade.

deploy [dǝploy] *v.* sarde.

deplume [dǝplyuwm] *v.* borde.

deport [dǝpɔrt] *v.* yaltinde léydi.

deportee [dǝpɔrti] *n.* jaltinaaɗo léydi.

depose [dǝpowz] *v.* fiiltude.

deposit [dǝpowzǝt] *v.* jóⱤⱤinde.

depot [dəpɔ] *n.* móóftirde kaake.

deprave [dəpreyv] *v.* bónnude.

depreciate [dəpriyšeyt] *v.* ustaade; ustude.

depreciation n.[dəprəšyeyšən] ustaare *(nde)*.

depredate [dəprədeyt] *v.* honde; wujjude.

depredator [dəprədeytə] *n.* ñaamówél *(ngél)*; bónnówél *(ngél)*.

depress [dəpres] *v.* sunaade.

deprive [dəprayv] *v.* haɗde.

depth [depθ] *n.* luggééndi *(ndi)*.

depurate [dəpyuwreyt] *v.* laɓɓinde.

deputy [dəpyəti] *n.* dipite *(o)*; lomto *(o)*.

deracinate [diyrasəneyt] *v.* ɗoofde; ɗuggitde.

derange [dəreynj] *v.* sarde. *He is deranged* Hoore makko dillii.

deride [dərayd] *v.* jalkitde; seknoraade.

derision [dəriyʒən] *n.* jalkitgól *(ngól)*; ceknoraagól *(ngól)*.

derive [dərayv] *v.* ummaade e.

dermatology [dərmətoləji] *n.* jangde nguru.

derogatory [dirogətəri] *adj.* kó téllinta; ko lésɗinta.

derrick [derik] *n.* lenge *(o)*.

descend [disend] *v.* tellaade; jippaade. ~ *into a well* jolde e ɓundu.

descent [dəsent] *n.* léñól *(ngól)*.

describe [diskrayb] *v.* sifaade

description [dəskrəpšən] *n.* sifaa *(o)*.

descriptive [dəskrəptiv] *adj.* ko faati e sifaa.

desegregate [disəgrəgeyt] *v.* haɗde leñamleñaagu.

desert [dizərt] *n.* ladde yoornde.

deserted [dizərtid] (adj) biinnuɗum; nokku biiɗɗuɗo.

desertion [dizəršən] *n.* dógdu *(ndu)*.

deserve [dəzərv] *v.* haandude.

desiccate [dəsəkeyt] *v.* yóórnude.

desiccator [dəsəkeytə] *n.* joornoowo *(o)*.

desiderate [dəsidəreyt] *v.* yiɗde; yééwnude.

design [dizayn] *v.* amminde.

designate [dəsigneyt] *v.* toɗɗaade; suɓaade.

desirable [dəzayrəbəl] *adj.* jiɗaɗum; ko yiɗaa.

desire [dəzayə] *v.* yiɗde; faaleede; muuyde; góddude; fiimlude; duudeede; tuuyeede.

desire [dəzayə] *n.* sago; tuuya *(o)*; muuya *(o)*.

desist [dəzist] *v.* daraade; ɗaccude.

desolate [dəsəlet] *v.* wiinnude.

despair [disper] *v.* ɗamtindaade.

despise [dispayz] *v.* yawaade; hutaade.

despite [dispayt] *n.* hutaare *(nde)*.

despoil [dispoyl] *v.* teetde; wujjude.

despot [despot] *n.* laamɗo mo laamu mum rendaaka.

dessert [dəzərt] *n.* ñamri *(ndi)*.

destiny [destəni] *n.* hóddiro *(ngo)*.

destitute [dəstətuwt] *adj.* baasɗo.

destitution [dəstətuwšən] *n.* baasal *(ngal)*.

destool [dəstuwl] *v.* fiiltude laamɗo.

destroy [distroy] *n.* halkude; bónnude; boomde.

destroyed [distroyd] *adj.* boomaaɗo; boomaɗum.

destroyer [distroyə] *n.* bonnoowo *(o)*.

destructible [distrʌktəbəl] *adj.* bonnojum; ko bonata.

destruction [distrʌkšən] *n.* halkaare *(nde)*; bonande *(nde)*.

destructive [distrʌktəv] *adj.* ko bonnata; ko halkata.

detach [ditač] *v.* ɓabbitde; séérndude.

detached [ditačt] *adj.* ceerɗum; ko seerti.

detail [diteyl] *n.* geɗal *(ngal)*; huunde *(nde)*; feccere *(nde)*.

detain [diteyn] *v.* sokde; jaggude.

detainer [diteynə] *n.* jaggoowo *(o)*; cokoowo *(o)*.

detect [ditekt] *v.* yiide.

detention [ditənšən] *n.* jaggugól *(ngól)*; cókgól *(ngól)*.

deter [ditər] *v.* haɗde.

deterge [ditərj] *v.* lawⱤude.

deteriorate [dətəryowreyt] *v.* bónnude.

determinate [dətərmənət] *v.* heertaade; firde; faccirde.

determination [dətərməneyšən] *n.* anniya *(o)*; wakkilaare *(nde)*.

deterrent [ditərənt] *n.* huunde haɗoore; ko haɗata.

detest [ditest] *v.* añde.

detestation [ditəsteyšən] *n.* ngañgu *(ngu)*.

ethrone [diΘrown] v. fiiltude laamɗo.

etour [dətuwr] n. taartaaról (ngól).

etractor [dətraktə] n. gaño (o).

etriment [dətrimənt] n. bonande (nde).

etrimental [dətrəmentəl] adj. bonnojum; ko bonnata.

euterogamy [dyuwtərəgəmi] n. dewgal diɗaɓal.

evaluate [divalweyt] v. ustude; ustude nafoore.

evaluation [divalweyšən] n. ustagól (ngól).

evastate [dəvəsteyt] v. bónnude.

evastation [dəvəsteyšən] n. bonande (nde).

develop [dəvəlop] v. Ɏéllitde; mawninde.

development [dəvəlopmənt] n. Ɏéllitaare (nde); Ɏéllitaagól (ngól).

deviate [divyeyt] v. ooñaade; selde.

deviation [dəvyeyšən] n. célgól (ngól); célól (ngól).

devil [devəl] n. seytaane.

devious [diyvyəs] adj. ko liilti; laawól liiltungól.

devise [dəvayz] v. mahde; fééwnude; sosde.

devoid [dəvoyd] adj. ko alaa.

devoir [dəvwar] n. fotde (nde).

devote [dəvowt] v. tóppitaade.

devoted [dəvowtəd] adj. ɗowtiiɗo.

devotion [dəvowšən] n. ɗowtaare (nde).

devour [dəvawə] v. moɗde; ñaamde.

devout [dəvawt] adj. góóɈɗinɗo; dewɗo; ɗówtiiɗo.

dew [dəw] n. saawandere (nde)

dexter [dekstə] adj. ñaamo; baɈɈe ñaamo; peewɗo; ñeeñɗo.

dexterous [dekstrəs] adj. peewɗo jungo.

diabetes [daybiytiz] n. ñaw.

diabolic [daybowlik] adj. ko faati e golle seytaane.

diacritic [daykrətik] n. masgal (ngal).

diagnose [daygnowz] v. Ɏeewde maale.

dialect [daylekt] n. haala nókku.

dialectal [daylektəl] adj. ko faati e haala nókku.

dialectology [daylektowləji] n. jangde haala nókku.

dialogic [daylowjik] n. ko faati e kaaldigal.

dialogue [daylog] n. kaaldigal (ngal).

diametre [dayamitə] n. diidól hakkunde.

diamond [daymənd] n. haayre jamaa.

diaper [daypə] n. ngembe cukalél.

diaphragm [dayəfram] n. biiwól (ngól).

diarrhea [dayryə] n. ɓoccitel (ngél) ɓóccitél (ngél); réédu dógóóru.

dichotomize [daykətəmayz] v. féccude pecce ɗiɗi.

dichotomy [daykətəmi] n. péccugól pecce ɗiɗi.

diction [dikšən] n. tinndól.

dictionary [dikšənəri] n. saggitorde (nde).

didactic [daydəktik] adj. ko faati e jangde.

diddle [didəl] v. wujjude; bonnude.

die [day] v. maayde; jiibde.

diet [dayet] n. ñamri (ndi).

dietary [dayətəri] adj. ko faati e ñamri.

dietetic [dyetətik] adj. ko faati e ñamri.

differ [difər] v. séértude.

difference [difrəns] n. ceerndugol (ngól); huunde séérndunde.

different [difrənt] adj. ceerɗum; ko séérti.

differentiate [difrənšeyt] v. séérndude.

differentiator [difrənšeytər] n. ceerndoowo.

difficult [difkʌlt] adj. caɗɗum; ko saɗi.

difficulty [difkʌlti] n. saɗre (nde).

diffident [difʌdənt] adj. nuggaro (o).

diffuse [difyuwz] v. yaajnude; saaktude.

diffusion [difyuwʒən] n. caaktugól (ngól).

dig [dig] v. asde. ~ itself asaade. ~ out aawtaade; aastaade; iirtude. make someone ~ asnude. ~ for asande. ~ up ubbitde; aaftaade; duggude.

digamy [digəmi] n. dewgal diɗaɓal.

digest [dayjest] v. dolde

digger [digə] n. gasoowo (o).

digging [digiŋ] n. gasgol (ngól) (ɗe).

digit [dijit] n. fédééndu (ndu).

dignified [dignəfayd] adj. ɗimɗuɗo; dimo.

dignitary [dignətəri] n. koohoowo (o).

dignity [dignəti] n. ndimaagu (ngu).

digress [daygres] v. selde.

dike [dayk] n. haɗiinde (nde).

dilacerate [dələsəreyt] v. taƳde; seekde.

dilapidate [dələpədeyt] v. bónnude.

dilate [dayleyt] v. Ɏuufde; yaajde.

dilemma [dilemə] *n.* jaakre *(nde)*; ngaanumma *(o)*. *be in a* ~ aande; jaakde.

diligence [dilijəns] *n.* tiicnaare *(nde)*.

diligent [dilijənt] *adj.* tiicniico.

dilute [dayluwt] *v.* sélbinde.

dilution [dayluwšən] *n.* célbingól.

dim [dim] *adj.* nibbiccum; ko nibbici.

dimension [dəmensən] *n.* njuutééndi; njaajééndi.

diminish [diminiš] *v.* ustude.

diminished [diminišd] *adj.* ustiico; ko ustii

diminution [diminušən] *n.* ustaare *(nde)*; aayaare *(nde)*.

dindle [dindəl] *v.* siññude.

dine [dayn] *v.* hirtaade.

diner [daynə] *n.* kirtotoodo *(o)*.

dinghy [diŋgi] *n.* laanél *(ngél)*.

dinky [diŋki] *adj.* pamaro.

dinner [dinə] *n.* hiraande *(nde)*.

dint [dint] *n.* sembe *(o)*.

diotic [dayotik] *adj.* ko faati e nóppi.

dip [dip] *v.* suuwde. ~ *one's lips into a liquid* tuubde.

diphtheria [difƟeryə] *n.* ñaw.

dire [dayə] *n.* cactucum; ko sacti.

direct [dərekt] *v.* hóllude; amminde; huccinde.

direction [dərekšən] *n.* huccaango *(ngo)*.

director [dərektə] *n.* gardinaado *(o)*; gardiico *(o)*.

directory [dərektəri] *n.* deftere incfe e tiitoode.

dirk [dərk] *n.* njuulaawi *(ki)*.

dirt [dərt] *n.* tuundi *(ndi)*. *eat* ~ hoyde; hoyneede.

dirty [dərti] *v.* tunwinde.

disability [disəbələti] *n.* ronkere *(nde)*.

disable [diseybəl] *v.* rónkinde.

disabled [diseybəld] *adj.* dónkucdo; boofo; gumcdo; taktako.

disaccord [disəkɔd] *n.* luural *(ngal)*.

disadvantage [disədvəntij] *n.* huunde nde alaa nafoore.

disagree [disəgriy] *v.* luurdude.

disagreement [disəgriymənt] *n.* luural *(ngal)*.

disallow [disəlaw] *v.* hacde.

disappear [disəpiyr] *v.* majjude; wirnaade.

disapproval [disəpruwvəl] *n.* salaare *(nde)*.

disapprove [disəpruwv] *v.* salaade.

disarm [disarm] *v.* hébtude kabircfe.

disarrange [disəreynj] *v.* firtude.

disassemble [disəsəmbəl] *v.* firtude.

disaster [dizastə] *n.* bonande *(nde)*.

disavow [disəvow] *v.* wultaade.

disbelieve [disbəliyv] *v.* waasde góóŋcinde.

disburse [disbərs] *v.* yobde.

discard [discɑd] *v.* joñde.

discern [disərn] *v.* seerndude, yiide.

discharge [disčɑj] *n.* rimtude.

disciple [dəsaypəl] *n.* almuudo *(o)*.

discipline [dəsəplin] *n.* néhdi *(ndi)*.

disclaim [diskleym] *v.* wultaade; yaafaade.

disclose [disklowz] *v.* haaltude; féññinde.

disclosure [disklow3ə] *n.* péññingól *(ngól)*.

discolor [diskələ] *v.* waylude nóórdi.

disconnect [diskənekt] *v.* séŋtude; séérndude.

discontent [diskəntent] *adj.* mo weltaaki; mettinco.

discontinue [diskəntənyu] *v.* haacnude; dartinde.

discord [diskɔd] *n.* luural *(ngal)*.

discordance [diskɔdəns] *n.* luural *(ngal)*.

discount [diskawnt] *v.* ustude.

discourse [diskɔs] *n.* haala; haala mbinndaaka.

discover [diskɑvə] *v.* yiitude.

discovery [diskɑvri] *n.* jiitugól *(ngól)*.

discredit [diskrədit] *v.* fénnude.

discreet [diskriyt] *n.* mooftoowo sirru; dééntiico; nibbo.

discrepancy [diskrepənsi] *n.* luural *(ngal)*.

discretion [diskrešən] *n.* yamiroore hooremum.

discriminate [diskrəməneyt] *v.* séérndude.

discrimination *n.* céérndugól.

discuss [diskʌs] *v.* yééwtude; wóstóndirde hakkillaaji.

discussion [diskʌšən] *n.* yeewtere *(nde)*; haala *(ka)*.

disdain [disdeyn] *n.* elko; elgól; yawaare *(nde)*.

disdain [disdeyn] *v.* añde; elde.

disdainer [disdeynə] *n.* eloowo *(o)*.

disdainful [disdeynfəl] adj. elɗo; eloowo.

disease [diziyz] n. ñaw (ngu).

disembark [disembɑrk] v. tellaade.

disengage [disiŋgeyj] v. yaltinde.

disentangle [disenteŋgəl] v. séérndude.

disgrace [disgreys] n. gacce (ɗe) ; kersa (o).

disgust [disgʌst] v. nefnaade.

disgusting [disgʌstiŋ] adj. nefniɗum; ko nefnii.

dish [diš] n. ñamri (ndi).

dishonest [disonest] adj. mo nuunɗaani.

disintegrate [disintəgreyt] v. seerde; moññaade.

disjoin [dijoyn] v. seɳtude; séérndude.

disjunct [disjʌŋkt] adj. ko séérti.

dislike [dislayk] n. nefre (nde); ngañgu (ngu).

dislike [dislayk] v. añde; nefde.

dislocate [disləkeyt] n. ittude é nókku; yaltinde.

dismantle [dismantəl] v. firtude.

dismay [dismey] n. kulól (ngól).

dismiss [dismis] v. riiwde.

dismount [dismawnt] v. tellaade; jippaade; jippinde; tellinde.

disobedient [disobiyjənt] adj. mo ɗowtaaki; caliiɗo.

disobey [disobey] v. salaade.

disorder [disordə] v. wilde; sarde.

disparage [dispərij] v. yénnude; felde.

disparagement [dispərijmənt] n. yennoore (nde); feloore (nde).

disparate [dispareət] adj. ceerɗi; kó sééri.

dispart [dispɑt] v. séérndude.

dispatch [dispɑč] v. néldude.

dispel [dispel] v. riiwde; sarde.

disperse [dispərs] v. sarde.

dispersed [dispərst] adj. cariɗum; ko sarii.

displace [displeys] v. ittude e nokku; ittude; dirnude.

display [displey] v. hóllirde.

displease [displiyz] v. séknude.

displeased [displiyzd] adj. mettinɗo; mo weltaaki.

displeasure [displeʒə] n. metteende (nde).

dispute [dispyuwt] n. duko (ngo). beyond ~ ko alaa geddi.

disrepute [disrəpyuwt] adj. télliiɗo; koyɗo.

disrespect [disrispekt] n. yawaare (nde).

disrespect [disrispekt] v. aybinde; bonde nehdi.

disrespectful [disrispektfəl] adj. neetaro.

disrupt [disrʌpt] v. bonnude; haljinde.

dissect [disekt] v. taϒde.

disseminate [disəmineyt] v. yaajnude; habrude.

dissension [disənšən] n. luural (ngal).

dissidence [disədəns] n. luural (ngal).

dissident [disədənt] adj. luutndiiɗo.

dissimulate [disəmyuwleyt] v. suuɗde.

dissipate [disəpeyt] v. suyde; saraade.

dissociate [disowšeyt] v. séérndude; seerde.

dissolve [disolv] v. saaynude.

distance [distəns] n. góɗɗóndiral (ngal); ɓadóndiral (ngal).

distant [distənt] adj. goɗɗuɗum; kó wóɗɗi; góɗɗuɗo.

distasteful [disteystfəl] adj. tékum; kó métti.

distinct [distiŋkt] adj. ko séérti; ko laaɓi.

distinction [distiŋkšən] n. céérndugól (ngól).

distinguish [distiŋgwiš] v. séérndude.

distort [distɔt] v. waylude; fende.

distress [distres] n. sunaare (nde).

distressful [distresfəl] adj. ko addata sunaare.

distribute [distrəbyuwt] v. yeɗde; tóttude; feccude.

distributor [distrəbyuwtə] n. jeɗoowo (o).

distrust [distrʌst] v. hóólkisaade.

disturb [distərb] v. haljinde.

disturbance [distərbəns] n. kaljingól.

ditch [dič] n. gaawól (ngól).

ditcher [dičə] n. gasoowo gaawi.

diurnal [dyurnəl] adj. ko faati e ñalawma; ñande kala.

divagate [divəgeyt] v. selde.

dive [dayv] v. fiyaade e ndiyam; puñtinaade.

diver [dayver] n. piyotooɗo e ndiyam.

diverge [dəvərj] v. séértude.

divergent [dəvərjənt] adj. kó séérti.

diverse [dayvərs] adj. ko séérti.

divert [divərt] v. sélnude.

divest [dayvest] v. ɓoorde; ittude.

divide [dəvayd] v. feccude. ~ *for* feccande.

divider [dəvaydə] n. peccoowo (o).

divine [dəvayn] adj. ko faati e joomiraaɗo.

divisible [dəvizəbəl] adj. ko feccotoo.

division [dəviyʒən] n. péccugól (ngól).

divisor [dəvayzə] n. ko feccata; peccoowo.

divorce [dəvors] n. ceergal (ngal).

divorce [dəvors] v. seerde

divorcee [dəvorsi] n. deboo ceerɗo/ceeraaɗo; diwo (o).

divulge [dəvʌlj] v. féññinde; saaktude sirru.

dizzy [dizi] adj. hakkille miirɗo; miirɗo.

djin [jin] n. jinne (o).

do [du] v. waɗde. ~ *again* waɗtude. ~ *ablutions with sand or a stone* taamaade. ~ *deliberately* amdaade; teyde. ~ *with haste* heñaade; fulsinde. ~ *one's ablutions* salligaade. ~ *twice* ɗimmitde.

docile [dowsayl] adj. deeŕɗo; eeltaaɗo; mo ñaaɗaani.

doctor [doktə] n. doktoor (o); cafroowo (o).

doctrine [doktrən] n. miijo (ngo).

document [dokyuwmənt] n. kayit (annama kayit juddu).

dodder [dodə] v. siññude.

dodge [doj] v. ruuɗaade; wappaade.

doer [duwə] n. baɗoowo (o).

dog [dog] n. rawaandu (ndu). *wild* ~ safaandu (ndu).

doll [dol] n. ɓiɗɗo tekke.

dolt [dolt] adj. beemɗo.

domestic [dəmestik] adj. ko faati e galle.

domesticate [dəmestəkeyt] v. eeltude.

domicile [doməsil] n. hoɗorde (nde).

dominant [domənənt] adj. poolɗo; ɓurɗo.

dominate [dəməneyt] v. foolde; ɓurde.

donate [doneyt] v. rókkude.

donation [doneyšən] n. dokkal (ngal).

donkey [doŋki] n. mbabba (ba)

donor [dono] n. dókkuɗo (o); dokkoowo (o).

doom [dum] n. hóddiro.

doom [dum] v. hóddirde.

doomsday [dumsdey] n. buutufal (ngal).

door [dor] n. damal (ngal); baafal (ngal); udumere (nde); naatirde (nde). indoors nder galle.

dormant [dormənt] adj. ɗaaniiɗo; ɗaankiniiɗo.

dorsal [dorsəl] adj. ko faati é kééci.

dot [dot] n. toɓɓere (nde); póófirgél (ngél).

dote [dowt] v. yiɗde; horsinde.

double [dʌbəl] n. ɗiɗi.

double [dʌbəl] v. ɗimmitde.

doubt [dawt] n. sikkitaare (nde); hoolkisaare (nde). *I have my doubts* Mbeɗe hoolkisii ɗum.

doubt [dawt] v. sikkitaade.

doubtful [dawtfəl] adj. cikkitiiɗo.

doubtless [dawtles] adj. ko alaa sikkitaare.

dough [dow] n. cóndi njiiɓaandi.

douse [dowze] v. wisde; léppinde.

douser [dowzə] n. biccoowo (o); léppinoowo (o).

dove [dowv] n. fóóndu (ndu).

down [dawn] prep. les.

down [dawn] v. lésɗinde; yandinde.

dowry [dawri] n. teŋe (ɗe).

doze [dowz] v. muumnaade.

dozen [dozən] n. sappo e ɗiɗi.

drabble [drabəl] v. léppinde.

draft [draft] n. bindól gadanól; héndu (ndu).

drag [drag] v. daasde. ~ *oneself* daasaade.

drain [dreyn] v. siiwtude.

drainage [dreynij] n. ciiwtugól.

drained [dreynd] adj. ko siiwtaa; ciiwtaɗum.

draining [dreyniŋ] n. ciiwtugol (ngól).

drape [dreyp] v. soomde.

draper [dreypə] n. jeeyoowo bagi.

draught [draft] n. wooɓre (nde). *take a* ~ wooɓde.

draw [drɔ] v. 1) diidde 2) fooɗde; sefde; daasde. ~ *water* Ŕoogde. ~ *water with* Ŕóógirde. ~ *a plan* éɓɓude. ~ *up* sefde. ~ *the bow* timpude. ~ *back* naattinde.

drawer [drɔwə] n. pooɗoowo (o).

drawing [drɔwiŋ] n. urɓa; natal (ngal); annama (o).

drawl [drɔwl] v. juurtude (alkule).

dread [dred] v. hulde.

dread [dred] n. kulól (ngól); atturu (ndu).

dreadful [dredfəl] adj. ko hulɓinii; kulɓiniiɗum.

dreadlock [dredlok] n. atturu (ndu).

ːream [driym] *v.* hoyɗude.

ːream [driym] *n.* koyɗol *(ngól)*.

ːreary [dreri] *adj.* ko addata sunaare.

ːredge [drej] *v.* fullude.

ːrench [drenč] *v.* léppinde.

ːress [dres] *v.* ɓoornaade. ~ *up* ñaantaade; ñarde; ñówtude; sórmitde. ~ *someone up* ñaantude; sórmitde.

ːressed [drest] *adj.* ɓoorniiɗo comci.

ːresser [dresə] *n.* boornoowo *(o)*.

ːried [drayd] *adj.* joorɗo; ~ *fish* bunaa *(o)*.

ːrier [drayə] *n.* joornoowo *(o)*; ko yoornata.

drill [dril] *v.* asde; yulde.

drink [driŋk] *v.* yarde

drinker [driŋkə] *n.* jaroowo *(o)*.

drip [drip] *v.* siimtude; siimtinde.

drive [drayv] *v.* dognude. ~ *cattle* sóggude. ~ *off* riiwde *They drove him mad* ɓe kaaɳɗin mo.

driver [drayvə] *n.* dognoowo *(o)* ; gardiiɗo *(o)*.

driving [drayviŋ] *n.* dógnugól *(ngól)*.

drizzle [drizəl] *n.* toɓoyal *(ngal)*.

droll [drol] *v.* gaajaade.

droop [drup] *v.* mutde.

drop [drop] *n.* waadere *(nde)*; toɓɓere *(nde)*.

drop [drop] *v.* yandinde; siimtinde. ~ *waste* fóccude.

dropout [dropawt] *n.* jaltuɗo jangde; ɗaccuɗo jangde; mo ɓaaraani.

droppings [dropiŋz] *n.* focco *(ngo)*.

drought [drawt] *n.* yooro *(ngo)*; sooño *(ngo)*.

drown [drawn] *v.* yoolaade; yoolde.

drowse [drawz] *v.* ŋoɳde.

drowsy [drawzi] *adj.* ŋoɳɗo.

drug [drʌg] *n.* foɗɗere safaara.

drum [drʌm] *n.* mbaggu *(ngu)*. *little* ~ baggel *(ngél)*. *bass* ~ tabalde *(nde)*. *talking* ~ buubaa *(o)*.

drummer [drʌmə] *n.* piyoowo mbaggu; piyoowo buubaa.

drumstick [drʌmstik] *n.* sawru buubaa.

drunk [drʌŋk] *adj.* jarɗo; cirwuɗo; mandilɗo.

drunkard [drʌŋkəd] *n.* mandiloowo *(o)*.

dry [dray] *v.* yoornude; aɗde. *be* ~ yoorde; sójjude. ~ *stream bed* gulumból *(ngól)*.

dual [duwəl] *adj.* ko faati e ɗiɗi.

dub [dʌb] *v.* innude; waañjitaade.

dubiety [dyuwbidi] *n.* sikkitaare *(nde)*.

dubious [dyuwbyəs] *adj.* ko laaɓaani.

dubitative [dyuwbitətiv] *adj.* ko faati e sikkitaare.

duck [dʌk] *n.* kankaleewal *(ngal)*. *wild* ~ koral *(ngal)* *due* [du] *n.* kó yónti yoɓeede; limpó *(o)*. *in* ~ *time* so ndeen yontii; ndee sahaa o yonti.

dug [dʌg] *adj.* gubbitaaɗum; ko ubbitaa.

dulcet [dʌlset] *n.* kó wéli heɗaade.

dull [dʌl] *adj.* beemɗo; mo feeraani; muddo. *He is dull of hearing* O welaani nanɗe.

dullness [dʌlnes] *n.* weemre *(nde)*.

dumb [dʌm] *n.* muumo *(o)*.

dumbness [dʌmnes] *n.* muumɗugól *(ngól)*; muumre *(nde)*.

dumminess [dʌmines] *n.* muddere *(nde)*.

dummy [dʌmi] *n.* muddo *(o)*; ñifɗo *(o)*.

dump [dʌmp] *v.* rufde; samminde.

dung [dʌŋg] *n.* rubundere *(nde)*.

dunk [dʌŋk] *v.* suuwde.

duo [dwo] *n.* yimɓe ɗiɗo.

dup [dʌp] *v.* fuuntude.

duplicate [dyuwpləkeyt] *v.* waañjitaade.

durable [dyuwrəbəl] *adj.* ko ɓooyata.

duration [dyuwreyšən] *n.* ɓooygol *(ngól)*.

dusk [dʌsk] *n.* futuro *(o)*; mutal *(ngal)*.

dust [dʌst] *n.* pundi *(ndi)*; sollaaru *(ndu)*; collaay *(o)*. *throw* ~ *in someone's eyes* ullude leydi e gite neɗɗo.

duster [dʌstə] *n.* piɗɗoowo pundi.

dustpan [dʌstpan] *n.* ɓóftirgél *(ngél)*.

duty [dyuwti] *n.* lowre *(nde)*; fotde *(nde)*.

dwell [dwel] *v.* juutnaade e.

dwindle [dwindəl] *v.* ustaade.

dye [dɑy] *n.* goobu *(ngu)*; bóru *(ngu)*; kafo *(o)*. *red* ~ kelloori *(ndi)*.

dye [dɑy] *v.* goobde; borde; noorde. ~ *blue* bakde.

dyer [dɑyə] *n.* gooboowo *(o)*.

dynasty [daynəsti] *n.* laamu *(ngu)*.

dysentery [dizənteri] *n.* réédu dógóóru.

E

e [iy] *n.* alkulal *(ngal)*.

each [iyč] *adj.* kala; nedɗo kala. ~ *one* gooto kala.

eagerness [iygənes] *n.* heñaare *(nde)*.

ear [iyə] *n.* nofru *(ndu)*. *I am all ears* Mbeɗe heɗi maa.

earthquake [ərθkweyk] *n.* jérɓugól léydi.

earthy [ərθi] *adj.* ko faati e léydi; ko faati e aduna.

easily [iyzəli] *adv.* beeɓɗum; newiɗum; ko wééɓi; kó néwii.

easy [iyzi] *adj.* ko weeɓi. beeɓɗum. *It is easy* Ina weeɓi.

easterner [iystənə] *n.* Fuɗnanke *(o)*.

eatable [iytəbəl] *adj.* ñaameteeɗum; ko ñaametee.

eatery [iytəri] *n.* ñaamirde *(nde)*; paasioŋ.

eating [iytiŋ] *n.* ñaamdu *(ndu)*.

eavesdrop [iyvzdrop] *v.* ñukkindaade.

eccentric [eksəntrik] *adj.* celɗum; kó séli.

echoic [ekowik] *adj.* ko faati e óólél.

eclectic [eklektik] *adj.* cuɓaɗum; ko suɓaa.

eclosion [eklowzən] *n.* tóccingól *(ngól)*.

economic [ekənəmik] *adj.* ittuɗum; ko itti. *It is not economical* ɗum fuɗɗiima hande.

economize [ekənəmik] *v.* ittinde; resde; mooftude.

ecstasy [ekstəzi] *n.* welaare *(nde)*.

ecstatic [ekstətik] *adj.* béltiiɗo.

ecumenical [ekyəmenikəl] *adj.* ko huɓtódini; kuɓtódinɗum.

edify [edəfay] *v.* nehde; janginde.

educator [edəkeytə] *n.* janginoowo *(o)*. *He is an educator* Ko o jaŋnginoowo.

efface [ifeys] *v.* mómtude.

effective [ifektiv] *adj.* ko hawri. *It is effective today* ɗum fuɗɗiima hande.

effervesce [efərvəs] *v.* fuɗtude; fasde; addude paali.

effervescent [efərvəsənt] *adj.* ko addata paali.

efficient [efiyšənt] *adj.* ko hawri.

effloresce [eflores] *v.* fiindude.

effractor [efraktə] *n.* gujjo *(o)*.

effuse [efyuwz] *v.* yaajnude; rufde.

effusion [efyuwʒən] *n.* dufgól *(ngól)*.

egest [ijest] *v.* yaltinde.

egestion [ijesčən] *n.* jaltingól *(ngól)*.

eggression [igrəšən] *n.* jaltugól *(ngól)*.

ego [iygow] *n.* hooram; ko faati e nedɗo.

egoism [igowizm] *n.* hooram hooram.

egoist [igowist] *adj.* hooram hooreejo.

egress [igres] *v.* yaltude.

eighty [eyti] *num.* capanɗe jeetati.

eighteen [eytiyn] *num.* sappo e jéétati.

either [iyðə] *pron.* gooto; kala. ~ *side* bangeeji kala.

ejaculator [ejəkyuwleytə] *n.* kañoowo *(o)*.

ejection [ejekšən] *n.* jaltingól.

eke [iyk] *v.* yaajnude;   mawninde.

elapse [ilaps] *v.* ɓénnude. *Two hours have already elapsed* Waktuuji ɗiɗi ɓennii.

elate [ileyt] *v.* wéltinde.

elated [ileytəd] *adj.* béltiiɗo. *I am elated* Mbeɗe weltii.

elation [ileyšən] *n.* weltaare *(nde)*.

elect [ilekt] *v.* suɓaade. *Who did you elect* Hol mo cuɓiɗon?

election [ilekšən] *n.* cuɓagól *(ngól)*; woote *(o)*.

elector [ilektə] *n.* cuɓotooɗo; gootoowo *(o)*.

electorate [ilektrət] *n.* suɓotooɓe *(ɓe)*; wootooɓe *(ɓe)*.

electrocute [ilektrəkyuwt] *v.* wardude jéyngól kuuraa.

elegant [eləgənt] *adj.* jooɗɗo; jooɗɗum; kó yóóɗi; ko hawri.

elegize [eləjayz] *v.* woytaade.

elegy [eləji] *n.* yimre *(nde)*.

elicit [eləsit] *v.* yaltinde.

eliminator [eləmineytə] *n.* jaltinoowo *(o)*; baroowo *(o)*.

elision [elyzən] *n.* mómtugól *(ngól)*.

elk [elk] *n.* kooba *(ba)*.

ellipsis [elipsəs] *n.* mómtugól *(ngól)*.

eloign [eloyn] *v.* wóɗɗitaade.

elongation [eləngeyšən] *n.* juutnugól *(ngól)*; juurtugól *(ngól)*.

else [els] *adv.* goɗɗo. *something ~* huunde wonde.

elucidate [elyuwsədeyt] *v.* laɓɓinde.

de [elyuwd] v. wappaade; majjinde.

anate [eməneyt] v. ummaade e; iwde e.

ancipation [emənsəpeyšən] n. dimaagu *(ngu)*; Yéllitaare *(nde)*. ~ *from* avery keɓgol ndimaagu yimɓe. *women's* Yellitaare rewɓe.

bargo [embagow] v. haɗde.

bark [embak] v. jolde e laana.

barrass [embarəs] v. jiiɓde; hérsinde. *I m really embarrassed* Mi hersii no ɛewi.

bitter [əmbitə] v. lamminde; hartude.

blaze [əmbleyz] v. huɓɓude; jawwude.

boss [əmbos] v. Yuulnude.

end [əmend] v. saatde; fééwnitde.

igrate [eməgreyt] v. ferde; hoɗde e léydi janandi.

igration [eməgreyšən] n. fergo *(ngo)*.

inence [eminəns] n. lolla *(o)*; lóllugól *igól)*.

inent [eminənt] adj. lólluɗo.

it [emit] v. yaltinde.

iperor [emprə] n. laamɗo *(o)*.

iplace [empleys] v. waɗde é nókku.

iployment [imploymənt] n. liggééy *(o)*; ollal *(ngal)*. *He is unemployed* O ggaaki.

able [ineybəl] v. wallude. *This rocedure will enable you to see better* Aa ɗum ɓeydu giile maa.

cephalon [insefəlon] n. ngaandi *(ndi)*.

chant [inčənt] v. dabaade.

chanter [inčəntə] n. dabotooɗo *(o)*.

compass [iŋkompəs] v. réndinde; aatnude.

core [aŋkor] n. kadi.

courage [iŋkərij] v. wallude. *He needs to e encouraged* Omo foti walleede.

couragement [iŋkəŋrij] n. ballital *(ngal)*.

cumber [iŋkəmbə] v. haɗde; lééltinde.

demic [endəmik] adj. ko faati e nókku valla e yimɓe.

dless [endles] adj. duumiɗum; ko ɣasataa; ko duumii. *His talk is endless* aala makko gasataa.

dorse [əndors] v. jaɓde; sémmbinde; vonande. *We endorse your bid* Ko aan nin ngonani.

dow [indaw] v. rókkude.

energetic [enərjətik] adj. caasɗo; dóólnuɗo.

enervate [enərveyt] n. lóhnude; tampinde.

enfeeble [enfiybəl] v. lóhnude; tampinde.

enfold [enfowld] v. soomde.

engage [iŋgeyj] v. waɗde; wonde e ; haljude.

engaged [iŋgeyjd] adj. 1) kaljuɗo 2) kumanaaɗo. *He is engaged* O humanii; Omo halji.

engrave [ingreyv] v. windude.

enhance [inhens] v. tééɭtinde.

enigma [ənigmə] n. huunde nde laaɓaani.

enjoin [injoyn] v. weltaade.

enlighten [inlaytən] v. janginde.

enlistee [enlistiy] n. bindaaɗo; bindiiɗo.

ennui [anwi] n. haaɓre *(nde)*.

enough [inʌf] adv. jonɗum; ko yoni. *It is enough* ɗum yonii.

enormous [inərməs] adj. mawnuɗum; ko mawni.

enrage [inreyj] v. séknude.

enrich [ənrič] v. alɗinde. *They enriched the country* ɓe ngalɗinii leydi ndi.

enroll [inrowl] v. windude neɗɗo.

enrollment [inrowlmənt] n. bindagól *(ngól)*.

ensconce [inskans] v. suuɗaade; suuɗde.

entail [inteyl] v. jibinde.

entente [əntant] n. nanóndiral *(ngal)*.

entertain [əntərteyn] v. wéltinde.

enthuse [ənθyuwz] v. weltaade.

enthusiastic [ənθyuzyəstək] adj. béltiiɗo.

entire [intayə] adj. fóf. *the ~ population* Yimɓe leydi fof.

entity [entəti] n. huunde woodnde.

entourage [antəraj] n. 1) wóndiiɓe *(ɓe)* 2) saraaji *(ɗi)*.

entrain [əntreyn] v. jolde e laana njóórndi.

entrant [əntrənt] n. naatoowo *(o)*.

entreat [əntriyt] v. ñaagaade.

entrepôt [əntrəpɔ] n. móóftirde kaake.

enumeration [ənyuwməreyšən] n. limtugól *(ngól)*.

enunciate [enənšeyt] v. wówlude.

enunciation [enʌnšeyšən] n. wowlaango *(ngo)*.

environment [invayrənmənt] n. sara *(o)*; saraaji *(ɗi)*.

envisage [envəzeyj] v. miijaade.

envy [envi] n. kiram (ɗam). He is watching you with envy Omo waɗti e maa yiitere.

envy v. waɗtude yiitere.

epenthesis [epenƟəsis] n. naatnugól wowlaango.

epicene [epəcen] adj. ko faati e debbo e gorko.

epidemiology [epidəmyələji] n. jangde ñabbuuli. He studies epidemiology O jangata ko jangde ñabbuuli.

epidermis [epədərməs] n. nguru (ngu).

epiglottis [epəglowtəs] n. ɗakañe (o).

epilate [epəleyt] v. borde lééɓi.

epilepsy [epəlepsi] n. ciññel gujjo.

epileptic [epəlektik] adj. ko faati e ciññél gujjo.

epilogue [epəlowg] n. haala (ka).

epistle [episəl] n. bataake (o).

epitaph [epətaf] n. binndi e yanaande.

epoch [epək] n. sahaa (o); saanga (o); mudda (o).

equality [ikwaləti] n. potal (ngal).

equalize [ikwəlayz] v. fóndude.

equilibrate [ekwələbreyt] v. fóndude.

equitation [əkwəteyšən] n. dógnugól puccu.

equity [ekwəti] n. potal (ngal).

equivocal [ekwivowkəl] adj. ko laaɓaani; niɓɓiɗɗum.

eradicate [eradəkeyt] v. mómtude; ittude.

erasure [irey3ə] n. mómtugól (ngól).

ergot [ergət] n. ñaw leɗɗe.

err [er] v. selde; lówwirde.

error [erə] n. juumre (nde). He made an error O juum.

eruct [erʌkt] v. ahde.

eructate [erʌkteyt] v. ahde.

erupt [erʌpt] v. fuccitaade.

eruption [erʌpšən] n. puccitaagól (ngól).

escalade [eskəleyd] n. ŋabbirgól seel.

escalate [eskəleyt] v. ɓeydude.

eschew [esčuw] v. woɗaade.

escort [eskɔt] v. yahdude e; ɗóftude.

esophagus [əzowfəgəs] n. kójómból (ngól).

esperance [espərens] n. ɗamaawu (o).

espionage [əspyownaj] n. ñukindaare (nde).

espouse [espawz] v. Ýéttude; naatde e. I do not espouse that point of view Mi alaa e ngoon miijo.

essence [esəns] n. ngóóróóndi (ndi); qiimaa (o).

estate [esteyt] n. léydi (ndi).

estimation [estəmeyšən] n. hiisa (o).

estivate [estəveyt] v. seeɗde.

estrange [estreynj] v. séérndude; seerde.

estreat [estriyt] n. bindi gadani; ko waañjaaka; ko waañjitaaka.

étape [etap] n. jippunde (nde); yahdu ñalawma kuurɗo.

eternity [itərnəti] n. huunde nde alaa happu; abada.

ethnic [eƟnik] adj. ko faati e léñól/ngendi. the Fulani ~ group ngendi Fulɓe.

ethnology [eƟnowləji] n. jangde léÝÝi.

etiolate [ətiyəleyt] v. ranwinde.

etude [etud] n. jangde (nde).

eudemonia [yuwdəmownyə] n. weltaare (nde).

eulogize [yuwləjayz] v. mande; mantude.

euphonious [yuwfownyəs] adj. bélɗum; kó wéli.

euthermic [yuwƟermik] adj. gulnojum; ko wulnata.

evacuate [ivakyəweyt] v. yaltinde. Evacuate the building Njaltee e huɓeere nde.

evactuation [evəkyuweyt] n. jaltingól (ngól).

evanesce [evənes] v. majjude; wirnaade.

evasion [ivey3ən] n. ɓóccitaagól (ngól).

evening [iyvniŋ] n. jamma (o).

ever [evə] adv. gila. ~ and anon sahaa sahaa. ~ since gila. ~ more haa abada.

every [evri] adj. kala. ~body neɗɗo kala; móni kala. ~ day ñande kala.

evict [evikt] v. yaltinde. He was evicted from his house O yaltina e galled makko.

evidence [evidəns] n. huunde tééɌtinoore; sabaabu (o). You have no evidence A alaa sabaabu.

evident [evidənt] adj. laaɓɗum; paamniɗum; ko yalti; ko laaɓi; ko faamnii.

evil [iyvəl] n. bone (ɗe); bonande (nde). the ~ eye yiitere bonde.

evince [əvins] v. hóllirde.

evocation [evowkeyšən] n. ciftingól.

evoke [evowk] v. siftinde.

exaggeration [egzəjəreyšən] n. pantingól (ngól); ɓurtingol (ngól).

exalt [egzalt] v. mande; mantude.

exaltation [egzəlteyšən] n. manoore (nde).

exasperate [egzəspəreyt] v. séknude; haaɓnude.

excavator [ekskəveytə] n. gasoowo (o).

excerpt [eksərpt] n. windande ittaande e deftere.

excise [eksayz] n. lémpóó (o); duwaañ (o).

exclusion [ekskluwzən] n. jaltingól (ngól).

excrete [ekscriyt] v. séérndude; yaltinde.

excursion [ekskərjən] n. ɗangal daɓɓal.

excuss [ikskəs] v. teetde; héɓtude.

execrate [ekskreyt] v. añde.

executor [egzəkitə] n. baɗoowo (o); baroowo (o).

exemplary [egzəmpləri] adj. kó fóti ñémtineede; ñemtinteeɗum.

exhale [eksheyl] v. yaltinde foofaango.

exhaust [egzɔst] v. 1) gasnude 2) tampude. I am exausted Mbeɗe tampi.

exhaustion [egzɔsčən] n. tampere (nde).

exhort [egzɔt] v. waajaade.

exhume [egzuwm] v. ubbitde.

existent [egzəstənt] adj. gooɗɗum; kó wóódi.

exogamy [egzowgəmi] n. dewgal ngal wonaa hakkunde fasiraaɓe.

exorbitant [egzɔbətənt] adj. ɓurtuɗum; kó ɓurti.

exorcise [egzɔsayz] v. wilde; riiwde sukuña walla jinne.

exorcist [egzɔsəst] n. bileejo (o).

exotic [egzowtik] adj. ko jeyaaka é léydi.

expatriate [ekspətreyt] v. yaltinde léydi.

expectorate [ekspektowreyt] v. haaktaade.

expedite [expədayt] v. yaawnude.

expeller [expelə] n. diiwoowo (o); jaltinoowo (o).

expend [ekspend] v. feraade.

expire [ekspayə] v. gasde; joofde. The delay expires today Lajal ngal gasata ko hande.

explicit [eksplɘsit] adj. ko laaɓi; ko faamnii.

explosion [eksplow3ən] n. puccitaagól (ngól)

expound [ekspawnd] v. faccirde.

express [ekspres] v. haalde; wiide. You need to express your opinion Aɗa foti hollirde miijo maa.

expression [eksprəšən] n. haala (ka); kóngól (ngól).

expulsion [ekspəlšən] n. jaltingól (ngól); diiwgól (ngól).

expunge [ekspʌnj] v. mómtude.

exquisite [ekskwəzət] adj. kó yóóɗi; jóóɗɗum.

exscind [eksind] v. taɽde.

extant [ekstənt] adj. goɗɗuɗum; kó wóódi.

extemporize [ekstəmpərayz] v. haalde.

extend [ekstend] v. juutnude. ~ a welcome jaɓɓaade.

extensible [ekstensəbəl] adj. portotooɗum; ko ina fortoo; ko ina fortee.

extension [ekstenšən] v. portagól (ngól); pooɽtagol (ngól).

extent [ekstənt] n. njuutééndi (ndi); njaajééndi (ndi).

extol [ekstowl] v. mande; mantude.

extractor [ekstraktə] n. oogoowo (o).

extradition [ekstrədiyšən] n. nawtugól móóliiɗo.

extrajudicial adj. caggal ñaawoore; ko yalti ñaawoore.

extrapolate [ekstrəpəleyt] v. hiisaade; miijaade.

extravagance [ekstrəvəgəns] n. ɓurtugol (ngól).

extreme [ekstriym] adj. ɓurtuɗum; ko ɓurti. carry to ~s ɓurtinde.

extremist [ekstriyməst] n. ɓurtuɗo (o).

extricate [ekstrəkeyt] v. jiktude.

exult [egzʌlt] v. weltaade.

F

fable [feybəl] *n.* tindól *(ngól).*

fabric [fabrik] *n.* bagi *(o).* **strips of** ~ léppi *(ɗi).* **rolled** ~ sollewól *(ngól).* **strip of** ~ *for carring a baby* mbóótu *(ngu).*

fabricate [fabrəkeyt] *v.* fééwnude.

fabrics [fabrəks] *n.* bagiiji *(ɗi).*

façade [fasad] *n.* galle *(o);* gaalɗi *(ɗi);* kalasal *(ngal).*

face [feys] *n.* yeeso *(ngo).* **side of the** ~ hanawere. *make a* ~ ŋoobde. *face to face* kuccondiral *(ngal).*

face [feys] *v.* huccitde. *You face the east when you say your prayers* So aɗa juula kuccittaa ko Fuɗnaange.

facial [feyšəl] *adj.* ko faati e yeeso.

facilitate [fəsələteyt] *v.* wéébnude.

fact [fakt] *n.* huunde woodnde. *It is a fact that cannot be denied* Eɗum woodi tigi.

factor [faktə] *n.* sabaabu *(o).* *One must take this factor into consideration* Aɗa foti Yeewde o sabaabu.

factual [fakčəl] *adj.* gooddum; ko wóódi.

fade [feyd] *v.* furde; iwde. *The color has faded away* ɗum furii.

faeces [fiysiz] *n.* jaañe *(ɗe);* kuudi *(ndi).*

fag [fag] *v.* liggaade; tampinde.

fagot [fagət] *n.* wahre leɗɗe.

fail [feyl] *v.* ronkude; horaade. ~ *to recognize* faaytude. *My sight is failing* Giilaam inan ngustoo.

failure [feylə] *n.* ronkere *(nde).*

fain [feyn] *adj.* béltiiɗo.

faint [feynt] *v.* faɗɗaade he fainted ko o paɗɗiiɗo. **fainting** [feyntiŋ] *n.* paɗɗagól *(ngól).* *recover from* ~ ɗiftude. *He has recovered from fainting* O faɗɗinooma kono o ɗiftii.

fair [fer] *adj.* hakkundeejo; laabɗo.

faith [feyθ] *n.* diiné *(o).* *put* ~ *in* hoolaade.

faithful [feyθfəl] *adj.* ɗowtiiɗo.

fake [feyk] *v.* wontinaade. *He faked his death* O maaykini.

falcon [falkən] *n.* ciilal *(ngal).*

fall [fɔl] *n.* libre *(nde).*

fall [fɔl] *v.* yande; fukkaade; saamde; bobbaade; bappaade. ~ *on* ñakkaade. ~ *on one's bottom* deppaade. ~ *from*

aggitaade. ~ *from a hook* tébbitaade. *to* ~ *out with* luurdude.

fallacious [faləšəs] *adj.* puuntoowo; puuntojum; ko fuuntata.

fallow [falow] *v.* remde; ɗoofde.

false [fɔls] *adj.* ko yubbaani; ko faati e fenaande; ko wonaa goonga. *He made a false accusation* A haalaani goonga.

falsify [fɔlsəfay] *v.* waylude.

falter [fɔltə] *v.* juumde.

fame [feym] *n.* daraja *(o);* lóllugól *(ngól).*

familiar [femiylyə] *adj.* goowɗo. *I am not familiar with this area* Mi woowaani nokku o.

familiarize [fəmiylyərayz] *v.* wóównude; anndinde.

family [faməli] *n.* besngu *(ngu).* ~ *tree* léñól *(ngól).* **Where is your family** Hol to galle maa woni?

famine [famən] *n.* heege *(nge).*

famous [feyməs] *adj.* darjuɗo he is really famous Omo darji.

fan [fan] *n.* bokkirgal *(ngal);* bokkirde *(nde);* taafiya *(o).*

fan [fan] *v.* wifde; bokkude. ~ *flies away* bokkude. ~ *insects away from oneself* bokkaade.

fancy [fansi] *n.* miijo.

fancy [fansi] *v.* miijaade; yiɗde. *Fancy meeting you here* Mi miijanooki yiide ma ɗoo. *I fancy you* Aɗa weli mi.

fanning [faniŋ] *n.* wifngo *(ngo);* bifgol *(ngól).*

far [fɑ] *adv.* goɗɗuɗum; pooɗtiɗum. ~ *side* baŋŋe ñaamo. *It is far* Ina woɗɗi.

farce [fars] *n.* gaajaare *(nde).*

fare [fer] *n.* paas *(o).* *How much is the fare* No paas o foti.

farewell [ferwel] *n.* baynóndiral *(ngal);* baynagól *(ngól).*

farm [fɑm] *n.* ngesa *(ba).* ~ *at the bank of a river* falo *(ngo).*

farm [fɑm] *v.* remde.

farmer [fɑmə] *n.* demoowo *(o).* *group of* ~ *s* kaw *(o).*

fart [fart] *n.* riiɗde *(nde);* puttere *(nde).*

fart [fart] *v.* puttude; riiɗde.

arther [faröə] adj. ko ɓuri woɗɗude. ~
end joofnirde (nde).

ascinate [fasəneyt] v. haawde.

ashion [fašən] n. huunde jolnde; ko jóli; ko
kewi.

ashionable [fašənəbəl] adj. jolɗo; kewɗo;
ko joli.

ast [fast] v. hoorde. I am fasting Ko mi
koorɗo.

asting [fastiŋ] n. koorka (ka); hoorngo
(ngo).

asten [fasən] v. 1) jókkude; haɓɓude 2)
tirde. Fasten your belt Haɓɓu dadorde
maa.

astigious [fətiyjəs] adj. tiiɗɗum; ko tiiɗi.

at [fat] n. ɓellere (nde).

at [fat] adj. payɗo; ɓutto ɓellinɗo.

atal [feytəl] adj. barojum; ko warata.

ather [faðə] n. baaba (o); baabiraaɗo (o);
puɗɗuɗo (o). ~ in-law esiraaɗo gorko.
like ~ like son O artii baaba makko.

athom [faθəm] n. kiisorgal luggééndi.

atigue [fətiyg] n. tampere (nde).

atness [fatnes] n. fayfayru (ndu).

atten [fatən] v. faynude; ɓuttiɗinde.

aucet [fawset] n. róbiné (o).

auna [fownə] n. barooɗe (ɗe)

avor [feyvə] v. jingande; wonande.

avorite [feyvrit] adj. cuɓaaaɗo; ɓurɗo.

awn-colored [fɔnkaləd] adj. cóóyɗuɗo.

ear [fiyə] n. kulól (ngól). He has no fear
Alaa ko o huli.

earless [fiyəles] adj. cuusɗo réédu. He is
fearless Alaa ko o huli.

easible [fiyzəbəl] adj. ko wonata.

east [fiyst] n. botoboto (o); kew.

eather [feðə] n. sige (o); ɓoro (ngo).

eature [fiyčə] n. mbaadi (ndi).

eck [fek] n. doole (ɗe)

ecund [fekʌnd] adj. jibinoowo; ko jibinta.

ed [fed] adj. ñamminaaɗo. ~ up kaaɓɗo.

ee [fiy] n. njóɓdi (ndi); alamaan (o). You
should pay the fee Aɗa foti yoɓde
alamaan.

eeble [fiyɓəl] adj. lohɗo; mo doolnaani.

eed [fiyd] v. ñamminde. He is feeding the
child Omon ñammina cukalel ngel.

eeder [fiydə] n. ñamminoowo (o).

feeding [fiydiŋ] n. ñammingól (ngól);
durnugól (ngól).

feel [fiyl] v. ɓoɗɗude; memde. ~ better
ɗiftude. ~ for membaade. to ~ one's way
membaade.

feet [fiyt] n. teppe (ɗe) ; koyɗe (ɗe). Lower
your feet Tellin koyɗe maa.

feint [feynt] v. wappaade.

felicitate [fələsəteyt] v. yéttude.

felicity [fələsiti] n. welamma (o).

fellow [feləw] n. jahdiiɗo (o); góndiiɗo (o).
He is my fellow countryman Minen
njeydaa e nokku gooto.

felon [felən] n. tooñɗo (o).

female [fiymeyl] adj. réwru; jarlal; njarlu.

feminine [fəmənin] adj. réwru; ko faati e
debbo.

fence [fens] n. kalasal (ngal); galle. woven
reed ~ hurgo (ngo).

fend [fend] v. tiiɗnaade.

ferocious [fərowšəs] adj. ñangudo.

ferry [feri] n. baag (o).

ferryboat [feribowt] n. baag (o).

fertile [fərtayl] adj. ko jibinta; jibinoowo. ~
soil wallere (nde).

fertilizer [fərtəlayzə] n. angare (o).

fetch [feč] v. addoyde. ~ water for
Yoogande.

fetish [fetiš] n. sanama (o).

fetter [fetə] n. tóngól (ngól).

feud [fyuwd] n. hare (nde); luural (ngal).

fever [fiyvə] n. ayto (ngo); oppere (nde);
paawngal (ngal).

feverish [fivriš] adj. oppaaɗo; paawnudo.
He is feverish Ko mi paawngudo.

few [fyuw] pron. seeɗa; ko heewaani.

fiancé [fyanse] n. Yamᴧamo gorko;
kumanɗo; kumanaaɗo.

fiancée [fyanse] n. Yamᴧamo debbo;
kumanaaɗo.

fib [fib] n. fenaande (nde).

fiber [faybə] n. baami

fiddle [fidəl] n. ñaañóóru (ndu).

fiddler [fidlə] n. ñaañoowo (o).

fidelity [fidələti] n. ɗowtaare (nde);
ɗowtagól (ngól).

fief [fyef] n. nókku (o).

field [fiyld] n. waykala (o); ngesa (ba).

fierce [fiyrs] adj. ñangudo.

fifteen [fiftiyn] *num.* sappo e jóy.

fifth [fifθ] *ord.* joyabo(o); joyabal *(ngal)*.

fiftieth [fifčeθ] *ord.* capanɗe joyabo.

fight [fayt] *n.* hare *(nde)* **small** ~ ŋurtuŋurtu *(o)*

fight [fayt] *v.* habde; habeede. ~ **back** habtaade. *They are fighting* Eben kaba.

figure [figə] *n.* tagóódi *(ndi)*.

file [fayl] *v.* mooftude.

fill [fil] *v.* hébbinde. ~ *for* loowande. ~ **up** hebbinde.

filly [fili] *n.* mbóómri *(ndi)*.

film [filəm] *n.* sinamaa *(o)*.

filter [filtə] *v.* siiwtude.

filth [filθ] *n.* tuundi *(ndi)*.

filthy [filθi] *adj.* ko tunwi; tunwuɗum. *The place is filthy* Nokku o ina tunwi.

filtrate [filtreyt] *v.* siiwtude.

final [faynə] *adj.* battano.

finalist [faynəlist] *n.* battindiiɗo *(o)*.

find [faynd] *v.* yiitude; tawde. ~ **again** tawtude. *I will find you there* Ma mi tawe toon.

finding [fayindiŋ] *n.* tawngo *(ngo)*; jiitugol *(ngól)*.

fine [fayn] *n.* alamaan *(o)*; ñaamre *(nde)*. *How much is the fine* no alamaan o foti?

finger [fiŋə] *n.* feɗeendu *(ndu)*. **point with** *one's* ~ yobnaade.

finish [finiš] *v.* gasnude; joofnude; timminde. ~ **work** jippaade. ~ **wedding** *days* dambitaade.

finished [finišt] *adj.* gasɗum; ko gasi. **be** ~ bantude; gasde; fusde; timmude; tasde The food is finished ñamri ndi gasii.

finite [faynayt] *adj.* ko jogii happu.

fire [fayə] *n.* jayngol *(ngól)*. *Put out the fire* Nif jayngol ngol.

fire [fayə] *v.* 1) riiwde 2) féllude. *He was fired yesterday* O riiwaama hanki.

firefly [fayəflay] *n.* sówti *(o)*.

fireplace [fayəpleys] *n.* haatande *(nde)*.

firm [fərm] *adj.* kó tiiɗi; kó tékki.

firmament [fərməmənt] *n.* kammu *(o)*.

first [fərst] *ord.* gadano. **be** ~ idaade. ~ *of all* ko adii kala.

firstborn [fəstborn] *n.* afo *(o)*. *He is my first born* kanko woni afo am.

fish [fiš] *n.* liingu *(ngu)*. ~ *bite* ŋobdi *(ndi)*.

fish [fiš] *v.* awde; saftaade; wanⁿdaade; bisaade; wubbude.

fisherman [fišəmən] *n.* 1) gawoowo *(o)*; bandotooɗo *(o)* 2) cubballo *(o)*.

fishing [fišiŋ] *n.* awo *(ngo)*. ~ *net* mbaala *(ka)*; jalla. ~ *net with hooks* dóóliŋŋe *(o)* **fissure** [fišə] *n.* ééból *(ngól)*.

fist [fist] *n.* womre *(nde)*. ~ *fight* gobbondiral *(ngal)*.

fit [fit] *v.* heïde; fotde. *The pants do not fit* Tuuba ba fotaani.

fitting [fitiŋ] *n.* póndugól *(ngól)*.

five [fayv] *num.* joy.

fix [fiks] *v.* feewnude; feewnitde; teppude; sinde; wuggude. *He is fixing the car* O woni ko e feewnude oto o.

fixed [fikst] *adj.* deeïɗum; peewnitaaɗum; ko feewnitaa.

fizgig [fizgig] *n.* debbo pidduɗo.

flaccid [flasəd] *adj.* lééfɗum; leefɗo.

flag [flag] *n.* araaraay *(o)*.

flake [fleyk] *n.* hóbbitande *(nde)*.

flame [fleym] *n.* lewlewndu *(ndu)*; mélléwól *(ngól)*. *burst into -s* jawwude; jappude.

flank [flaŋk] *n.* wuttuldu *(ndu)*.

flap [flap] *v.* fiide.

flash [flaš] *n.* majaango *(ngo)*.

flash [flaš] *v.* majde; ilbude; hubbude.

flat [flat] *adj.* berkaɗum; lértuɗum. **lay** ~ hippaade

flatten [flatən] *v.* bérkude; melde; lértinde.

flatter [flatə] *v.* awlude; ñeeñde; fuuntude.

flatterer [flatərə] *n.* batilo *(o)*.

flattery [flatəri] *n.* ñeeñre *(nde)*; fuunti *(o)*.

flaunt [flɔnt] *v.* ñaaïde; hóllirde.

flavor [fleyvə] *n.* dakam *(ɗam)*; dakame *(ɗe)*.

flay [fley] *v.* huttude.

flea [fliy] *n.* hoowoyre *(nde)*.

flee [fliy] *v.* dogde. ~ *fast* siirtaade.

fleer [fliyə] *v.* jalkitde; seknoraade.

flesh [flesh] *n.* tééw *(ngu)*.

flick [flik] *v.* ŋómsude; fiɗɗude; siññude.

flight [flayt] *n.* diwgól *(ngól)*; diwal *(ngal)*.

flinch [flinč] *v.* ruuɗaade; wappaade.

fling [fliŋ] *v.* werlaade.

flint [flint] *n.* haayre *(nde)*.

flirt [flərt] *v.* gerde; tappisaade.

oat [flowt] *v.* humbude; hayde. *The boat is still floating* Ekan haya haa jooni.

ɔating [flowtiŋ] *n.* hayngo *(ngo)*; kummbugol *(ngól)*.

ood [flʌd] *n.* ilam *(ɗam)*; waame *(o)*; amo *(ngo)*; feeteeto *(ngo)*.

ood [flʌd] *v.* waamde; ilde.

oor [flɔr] *n.* léydi *(ndi)*. *take the* ~ ʔettude kongol.

ora [flowrə] *n.* leɗɗe *(ɗe)*.

our [flawə] *n.* cónndi *(ndi)*. *steamed* ~ ḷacciri *(ndi)*.

ourish [fləriš] *v.* fiindude; ʔéllitaade.

out [flawt] *v.* jalkitde; añde.

ow [flow] *v.* waamde; bulde; faccude. ~ *heavily* uccitaade.

ower [flawə] *n.* piindi *(ndi)*.

u [flu] *n.* ayto *(ngo)*.

uff [flʌf] *v.* juumde.

ute [fluwt] *n.* liital *(ngal)*; sérndu *(ndu)*; cóórumbal *(ngal)*.

utter [flʌtə] *n.* dillere *(nde)*.

y [flay] *n.* mbuubu *(ngu)*.

y [flay] *v.* diwde; weeyde. *make* ~ diwnude.

●al [fowl] *n.* pucél.

●am [fowm] *n.* nguufa *(ka)*.

●cus [fowkəs] *v.* teeʔtinde; waɗtude hakkille.

●ld [fold] *n.* cowol *(ngól)*.

●ld [fold] *v.* sowde. ~ *oneself while lying down* tumpilaade. ~ *disorderly* tiggude.

●liage [folyəj] *n.* baramléfi *(ɗi)*.

●lk [fɔk] *n.* yimbe *(be)*. *my* ~*s* koreeji am.

●llow [fɑlow] *v.* rewde; abbaade; siindaade. ~ *one's footsteps again* rewtaade ~ *again* abbitaade; réwtude. ~ *one another* abbondirde; réggóndirde; sórbóndirde.

●lly [fɑli] *n.* kaaɗi *(ɗi)*.

●ment [foment] *v.* ʔéllitde.

●nd [fɑnd] *adj.* jiɗɗo. *I am fond of her* Mbeɗe yiɗi mo.

●ndle [fɑndəl] *v.* moomde.

●od [fuwd] *n.* ñamri *(ndi)*. ~ *supplies* ñaamatééri *(ndi)*.

●ol [fuwl] *n.* kaangaaɗo *(o)*; ɗaayɗo *(o)*. *You are a fool* ko a kaangaaɗo.

foolish [fuwliš] *adj.* puuyɗo; puuyɗum; kaangaaɗo; kaangaɗum; ɗaayɗum.

foolishness [fuwləšnes] *n.* ɗaayre *(nde)*.

foot [fuwt] *n.* teppere *(nde)*; yabbirde *(nde)*. ~ *of an animal* holsere *(nde)*. ~ *track* felo *(ngo)*.

football [fuwtbɔl] *n.* fuku *(o)*.

footprint [fuwtprint] *n.* felo *(ngo)*; yabbande *(nde)*.

footstep [fuwtstep] *n.* felo *(ngo)*; yabbande *(nde)*.

for [fər] *conj.* pur; sabi. *I did it for you* Ko aan tagi mi waɗde ɗum.

foray [fərey] *v.* honde.

forbear [forber] *v.* muñde.

forbid [fəbid] *v.* hajaade; haɗde; harminde.

forbidden [fərbidən] *adj.* karmuɗum; ko harmi; ko haɗaa. *It is forbidden* Ko ko haɗaa.

force [fɔs] *n.* sembe *(o)*; forso *(o)*; doole *(ɗe)*.

force [fɔs] *v.* waawnude; forsude. *take by* ~ teetde. ~ *one's way through obstacles* urñaade.

ford [fɔd] *n.* juuwde *(nde)*.

ford [fɔd] *v.* juuwde.

fore [fowr] gadiiɗo.

forearm [forɑm] *n.* jungo *(ngo)*.

forefather [forfɑðə] *n.* mawɗo gadiiɗo.

forefinger [forfiŋə] *n.* sappordu *(ndu)*.

forefront [forfrənt] *n.* yeeso *(ngo)*.

forego [forgow] *v.* aditaade.

forehead [forhed] *n.* tiinde *(nde)*.

foreign [foren] *adj.* tumaranke; caggal léydi.

foreigner [forenə] *n.* tumarake *(o)*; arani *(o)*. *He is a foreigner* Ko o tumaranke.

foreignhood [forenhud] *n.* tumarakaagal *(ngal)*.

forenoon [fornuwn] *n.* subaka.

foresight [forsayt] *n.* tijjagól *(ngól)*.

forest [fowrest] *n.* wuutufere *(nde)*; mbolo *(ngo)*; ladde leɗɗe.

forestall [forstɔl] *v.* rééntinde.

forewarn [forwɔrn] *v.* rééntinde.

forfeit [forfət] *v.* hebteede; haɗeede ~ *one's word* luutndaade kongol mum.

forge [fɔj] *n.* mbayla *(ka)*.

forge [fɔj] *v.* tafde; waylude.

forging [fɔjiŋ] *n.* tafŋgo *(ngo).*

forget [fɔrget] *v.* yéjjitde; diwde hakkille; saalitde. *I forgot to tell you* Mi yejjit haalande ma.

forgetful [forgetfəl] *adj.* jéjjitoowo; keewɗo jejji.

forgetfulness [forgetfəlnes] *n.* jéjji *(ɗi).*

forgive [forgiv] *v.* yaafaade; yarlaade; accande. *Please forgive me* Tiinno yaafo mi.

forgiveness [forgivnes] *n.* yaafuya *(o).*

fork [fɔk] *n.* furset *(o);* salndu *(ndu).*

former [fɔmə] *adj.* gadiiɗo.

fornicate [fɔrnəkeyt] *v.* jinde.

forsake [fərseyk] *v.* harminde; ɗaccude.

fortieth [forčef] *ord.* capanɗe nayaɓo.

fortify [fortəfay] *v.* sémbinde.

fortnight [fortnayt] *n.* jonte ɗiɗi.

fortunate [forčnət] *adj.* malaaɗo; gaabɗo. *He is very fortunate* Omo malaa no feewi.

fortune [forčən] *n.* ngalu *(ngu);* dañal *(ngal). ~ teller* tiimoowo *(o).*

forty [fɔti] *num.* capanɗe nay.

forward [fɔwəd] *v.* yéttinde.

forward [fɔwəd] *adv.* ko faati e yeeso; ko fayi arde.

foster [fostə] *v.* nehde; diwnude.

foul [fawl] *n.* tooñange *(nge).*

found [fawnd] *v.* sosde.

found [fawnd] *adj.* tawaaɗo.

foundation [fawndeyšən] *n.* nóóról *(ngól).*

founder [fawndə] *n.* cosɗo *(o);* puɗɗuɗo *(o). He is the founder of this town* Ko kanko sosi ngo wuro.

fourteen [fɔtiyn] *num.* sappo e nay.

fourth [fɔθ] *ord.* nayaɓo; nayaɓal.

fowl [fawl] *n.* gerlal *(ngal).*

fox [fɔks] *n.* bóy *(o).*

fracture [frakčə] *v.* helde; tokkitde.

fracture [frakčə] *n.* helande *(nde);* kelal *(ngal).*

fragment [fragmənt] *n.* helande *(nde);* ta ʄande *(nde).*

frankly [fraŋkli] *adj.* e nuunɗal.

fraud [frɔd] *n.* nguyka *(ka);* fuunti *(o).*

fraudulent [frɔdyuwlənt] *adj.* ko faati e nguyka walla fuunti.

free [friy] *v.* ɗaccude; jooktude; ɓiltude; ɗaccitde. *~ one's arm suddenly* bikkitaade. *~ something suddenly* bikkitde. *~ a slave* rimɗinde.

freeborn [friyborn] *n.* dimo *(o).*

freedom [friydəm] *n.* jey hooremum; ndimaagu hooremum.

freeman [friymən] *n.* dimo *(o).*

French [frenš] *n.* farayse *(o);* faranse *(o).*

frequency [friykwənsi] *n.* jó é jó.

frequent [friykwənt] *adj.* ko wóni sahaa sahaa kala.

fresh [freš] *adj.* ɓuubɗum; kecco; kecciɗɗum. *~ milk* biraɗam *(ɗam);* keɗɗam *(ɗam).*

freshness [frešnes] *n.* kéccól *(ngól);* ɓuuɓol *(ngól).*

Friday [fraydi] *n.* aljumaa *(o).*

friend [frend] *n.* sehil *(o);* giɗo *(o);* tééri *(o);* musiɗɗo.

friendly [frendli] *adj.* cakalo.

friendship [frendšəp] *n.* cehilaagal *(ngal);* musidaagal *(ngal).*

fright [frayt] *n.* kulól *(ngól).*

frighten [fraytən] *v.* hulɓinde; wéftilde; ruuɓde; gidde. *It is frightening* Ina hulɓinii.

frightened [fraytənd] *adj.* gidaaɗo; kulɗo; beftilaaɗo.

fringe [frinj] *n.* sara *(o);* takko *(o);* cilɓi *(ɗi).*

frisk [frisk] *v.* birgude.

fritter [fritə] *n.* weñere *(nde).*

frog [frog] *n.* faaburu *(ndu).*

frolic [frɔlik] *v.* birgude.

from [frəm] *prep.* iwdi. *Where are you from* Hol to njeyaɗaa? *I am from ɓoghe* Njeyaami ko ɓoghe.

frond [frond] *n.* léfól *(ngól);* baramlefol *(ngól).*

front [front] *n.* tiinde *(nde);* yeeso ngo.

frontier [frəntiyə] *n.* kééról *(ngól). The Senegal river is the frontier between Senegal and Mauritania* Ko maayo Senegal woni keerol hakkunde Muritani e Senegaal.

frost [frost] *n.* penndagol *(ngól).*

froth [froθ] *n.* nguufa *(ka).*

frown [frawn] *v.* ñirɓinaade.

frozen [frowzən] *adj.* ko fenndii. *It is frozen* Ko ko fendii.

fruit [fruwt] *n.* ɓingel leɗɗe.

fruitful [fruwtfəl] *adj.* ko nafata. *It was not a fruitful meeting* Deental ngal nafaani.

frustrate [frʌstreyt] *v.* haaɓnude; haljinde. *I am frustrated* Mi haaɓi.

fry [fray] *v.* sahde. *Are you going to fry that meat* Ko a cahoowo teew ngu?

fry [fray] *n.* andoonde *(nde)*; bujubuju *(o)*.

fuck [fʌk] *v.* ɓolkude; hoowde.

fugitive [fyuwjətiv] *n.* dogɗo *(o)*. *He is a fugitive* Ko o dogɗo.

Fula [fulə] *n.* ɗemngal Fulɓe.

Fulani [fulani] *n.* Fulɓe *(ɓe)*; Pullo *(o)*.

fulfill [fulfil] *v.* timminde; waɗde. *Destiny has been fulfilled* Fodoore ñaawaama.

full [ful] *adj.* keewɗo; ko hééwi; kaarɗo. ~ *moon* baata. *I am full* Mi haarii.

fullness [fulnes] *n.* keewal *(ngal)*.

fumble [fʌmbəl] *v.* ɓóccitoreede.

fume [fyuwm] *v.* suurkude; dumaade.

fun [fʌn] *n.* weytaare *(nde)*.

function [fʌŋkšən] *n.* liggééy *(o)*; nafoore *(nde)*.

funeral [fyuwnərəl] *n.* janayse *(o)*.

funny [fʌni] *adj.* jalniiɗo; ko jalnii. *He is funny* Omo jalnii.

furious [fyuwryəs] *adj.* pilñitiiɗo.

furtive [fərtiv] *adj.* gujjittooɗo.

furuncle [fyuwrəŋkəl] *n.* uure *(nde)*.

fuse [fyuwz] *v.* saayde.

fusion [fyuwzən] *n.* caaygól *(ngól)*; deental *(ngal)*.

fussiness [fʌsənes] *n.* looɓre *(nde)*.

fussy [fʌsi] *adj.* looɓɗo.

futile [fyuwtayl] *adj.* ko nafataa.

future [fyuwčə] *n.* ko fayi arde *in the* ~ ko fayi arde.

Fuuta [fuwtə] *n.* Fuuta. *person from* ~ fuutanke *(o)*.

G

gabble [gabəl] v. leɓde.

gabby [gabi] adj. lemsucɗo; keewcɗo haala.

gaffe [gaf] n. juumre (nde).

gag [gag] v. sukkude hunuko necɗɗo.

gage [geyj] v. juknude.

gaiety [geyti] n. weltaare (nde).

gain [geyn] n. dañal (ngal)

gain [geyn] v. dañde; yoɓeede. ~ strength niggude. He gained strength O dañii doole.

gainless [geynles] adj. ko alaa ngañaari.

gait [geyt] n. yahdu (ndu).

gala [gala] n. kéw (o).

gale [geyl] n. héndu mawndu.

gall [gal] n. taɤre (nde); ɗeecɗagól (ngól).

gallantry [galəntri] n. cuusal (ngal).

galley [galiy] n. laana (ka).

gallop [galəp] v. ñékkude; dogde.

galore [gəlor] n. keewal (ngal).

gamble [gambəl] n. wure (o).

gamble [gambəl] v. wuraade. He gambles every day Omo wuroo ñalawma kala mo Alla addi.

gambol [gambəl] v. birgude.

game [geym] n. fijirde (nde). play a ~ fijde. He is playing a game with his children O woni ko e fijjude e sukaaɓe makko.

gamma [gamə] n. alkulal (ngal).

gang [gaŋ] n. fedde (nde).

gang [gaŋ] v. yantondirde. They ganged up against his leadership ɓe calii gardagol makko.

gangster [gaŋstə] n. bandi (o).

gantlet [gantlət] n. laabi laana njóórndi.

gap [gap] n. yelde (nde); yolnde (nde). generation ~ yolnde hakkunde sukaaɓe e mawɓe.

gar [gar] v. waawnude.

garage [gəraʒ] n. móóftirde oto.

garbage [gabij] n. kurjuru (o). Throw the garbage away Rufoy kurjuru (o).

garble [gabəl] v. jiiɓde.

garden [gadən] n. nambu (o); sardiŋe (o). He is watering his gardern Omon roosa sardiŋŊe makko.

gargle [gagəl] v. wufɤaade.

garment [garmənt] n. cómcól (ngól).

garner [gɑnə] n. faawru (ndu)

garnish [gɑniš] v. ñénkude.

garniture [gɑničə] n. ñénkudi (ndi).

garrulous [garələs] adj. leɓoowo.

gas [gɑs] n. esaas (o). Put some gas in your car loow esaas e oto maa.

gasconade [gaskəneyd] v. wasaade.

gash [gaš] n. ñiɓande (nde); yiwande (nde).

gasp [gasp] v. lehde.

gastric [gastrik] adj. ko faati é réédu.

gastrology [gastrowləji] n. jangde mbaadi e ñabbuuli réédu.

gate [geyt] n. damal (ngal); uddoode (nde). Open the gate Uddit damal ngal.

gather [gaðə] v. rendude; rendinde; mooɓde. ~ oneself up ñongaade. ~ crops in a crop gathering area gérnude. ~ up mooɓde; ɓóftude.

gathering [gaðəriŋ] n. déndingól (ngól); daakande (nde).

gauge [geyj] v. hiisaade.

gauger [geyjə] n. kiisotoocɗo (o).

gaunt [gɔnt] adj. pooɤcɗo.

gavial [gavyəl] adj. piyóóri.

gawk [gɔk] v. laarde; fulñitde gite.

gay [gey] adj. 1) béltiicɗo 2) debati gorkati. He is gay Omo weltii.

gaze [geyz] v. laarde; fulñitde gite.

gazelle [gəzel] n. lella (ba).

geld [geld] v. sende puccu.

geminate [jəminet] v. tékkinde.

geminate [jəminet] n. alkulal tékkinaangal.

gemination [gəmineyšən] n. tékkingól (ngól).

gender [jendə] n. réwru walla wórdu. male ~ wordu; gorko; ngoraagu. female ~ rewru; debbo.

genealogy [jenyaləji] n. asko (ngo); innitoore (nde). Please tell me my genealogy Tiinno askinam.

general [genərəl] adj. kuɓtódindɗum.

generate [genəreyt] v. wóódnude; jibinde.

generator [genəreytə] n. 1) ko woodnata; goodnoowo (o). 2) masiŋ (o).

generosity [genərowsəti] n. moɤɤere (nde); yaajre (nde).

generous [genərəs] *adj.* moƳƳo; jaajɗo. *She is very generous* Omo weeɓi jungo.

genesis [jiynəsis] *n.* iwdi *(ndi).*

genetics [jənetiks] *n.* jangde ndónu.

genial [jiynyəl] *adj.* ƳoƳɗo.

genie [jeni] *n.* jinne *(o).*

genital [jənitəl] *adj.* ko faati e njogoram.

genius [jiynyəs] *n.* ƳoƳɗo *(o)*; peerɗo *(o)*; péértuɗo *(o). He is a genious* Ndaw ko ƳoƳi.

genocide [jənəsayd] *n.* moobaare *(nde)*; warngo yimɓe léñól.

genre [janr] *n.* sifaa *(o).*

gentle [jentəl] *adj.* baɗiroowo seese; belɗo ƳiiƳam; teeyɗo.

gently [jentli] *adv.* seese; jamjam. *Do it gently* waaru seese.

genuine [jenwin] *adj.* kó fééwi; kó hóólnii; ko ñembaaka.

geology [jeloji] *n.* jangde léydi.

geomancy [jewomənsi] *n.* tiimgól *(ngól)*; dabare *(ɗe).*

georgic [jorjik] *adj.* ko faati e ndema.

geriatrics [jeryatriks] *n.* safaara e tóppitaagól nayeeɓe.

germ [jərm] *n.* puɗdi *(ndi)*; iwdi *(ndi).*

germane [jermeyn] *adj.* ko faati e.

germinate [jermineyt] *v.* fuɗde.

germinative [jermənətiv] *adj.* ko fuɗata.

gestate [jəsteyt] *v.* wonde réédu; teddude.

gestation [jəsteyšən] *n.* réédu *(ndu).*

gesticulate [jəstəkyuleyt] *v.* amminirde jungo.

gesture [jesče] *v.* amminde.

get [get] *v.* heɓde; wonde. ~ *into* jolde. ~ *with* heɓirde. ~ *one's first bath* fukeede. ~ *ready* hebaade. ~ *ready for a prayer* heblaade. ~ *away* daɗde. ~ *off* tellaade; jippaade. ~ *closer slowly and quietly* mooytaade. ~ *closer* ɓallade; ɓallitaade.

getable [getəbəl] *adj.* ko heɓotoo.

ghetto [getow] *n.* leegal *(ngal).*

ghost [gowst] *n.* fittaandu *(ndu).*

giant [jayənt] *adj.* mawɗo; ko mawni; mawnuɗum. *He is a giant* Ndaw ko mawni.

gibberish [gibəriš] *n.* haala ka faamnaaki.

gibbon [gibən] *n.* waandu *(ndu).*

gibe [jayb] *v.* 1) gaajaade   2) jalkitde; seknoraade.

gift [gift] *n.* silafanda *(o)*; dokkal *(ngal).* ~ *to inlaws* Ƴamrudi *(ndi).*

gifted [giftəd] *adj.* ñeeñuɗo; jom ñeeñal.

gig [gig] *n.* laana *(ka).*

gigantesque [jaygəntesk] *adj.* ko mawni.

gigantic [jaygəntik] *adj.* mawɗo; ko mawni.

giggle [gigəl] *v.* jalde; ŋooɓde.

gild [gild] *v.* sinkude; ŋeñde.

gill [gill] *n.* suka debbo.

gimel [giməl] *n.* alkulal *(ngal).*

gimlet [gimlet] *v.* yiwde; yulde.

gin [jin] *n.* wilde *(nde).*

gingival [jinjayvəl] *adj.* ko faati e ɗakkudi.

gingivitus [jinjəvaytəs] *n.* ñaw ɗakkudi.

giraffe [jərɑf] *n.* njamala *(ba).*

gird [gərd] *v.* taarnude; howde.

girdle [gərdəl] *n.* wudere *(nde).*

girl [gərl] *n.* suka debbo; mbóómri *(ndi)*; jiwo *(o).* ~*friend* suka/sehilaaɗo debbo.

girlish [gərliš] *adj.* ko faati e suka debbo.

girth [gərθ] *v.* taarnude.

gist [jist] *n.* qiimaa *(o).*

give [giv] *v.* rokkude; hokkude; yeɗde. ~ *each other* hókkóndirde. ~ *birth for the first time* dikkaade. ~ *thanks* jaarde. ~ *up* haaytude. ~ *money to an artist* juurde. ~ *birth* jibinde. ~ *birth to twins* funaade. ~ *charity* sakkaade; nafqude. ~ *a reward* yeende. ~ *away used items* ɓiirtinde. ~ *a child his first bath* fukaade. ~ *on credit* ñamlude. ~ *change* weccude; weccande. ~ *dowry* teŊde *He gave in* O ɗaccii.

give-and-take [givənteyk] *adj.* maslahaa *(o).*

glacé [glase] *adj.* ɓuuɓɗum.

glad [glad] *adj.* béltiiɗo. *He is glad that you arrived safely* Omo weltii e jettagol maa e dow jam e cellal.

gladden [gladən] *v.* wéltinde.

glair [gler] *n.* ndanééri ɓoccoonde.

glaive [glev] *n.* jaasi *(ki)*; silaama *(ka).*

glamorous [glamərəs] *adj.* jooɗɗum; kó yóóɗi.

glance [glans] *v.* leƳƳaade; letaade; sunnaade.

glare [gleyr] *v.* futtinde gite; fulñitde gite.

glary [gleri] *adj.* jalbuɗum; ko jalbi.

glass [glas] *n.* daarorgal *(ngal)*; weer *(o). a looking* ~ daarorgal *(ngal)*.

glaucoma [glowkəmə] *n.* ñaw gite.

glaze [gleyz] *v.* Ɣeewde; laarde.

gleam [gliym] *n.* sérééndu *(ndu)*.

glean [gliyn] *v.* réndinde.

gleaning [gliyniŋ] *v.* déndigól *(ngól)*.

glebe [gleb] *n.* léydi *(ndi)*.

glee [gliy] *n.* weltaare *(nde)*.

gleet [gliyt] *n.* mbórdi *(ndi)*.

glib [gləb] *adj.* kébiiɗo; borwuɗum.

glide [glayd] *v.* weeyde.

gilde [glayd] *n.* alkulal *(ngal)*.

glider [glaydə] *n.* beeyoowo *(o)*.

glimmer [glimə] *v.* léwñude.

glimpse [glimps] *v.* leɣɣaade.

glint [glint] *v.* jalbude.

glitter [glitə] *v.* jalbude *~ing eyes* gite jalbuɗe.

gloaming [glowmiŋ] *n.* futuro.

gloat [glowt] *v.* weltaade.

global [glowbəl] *adj.* ko hubtódini; kubtódinɗum.

gloom [gluwm] *n.* nibbere *(nde)*.

gloomy [gluwmi] *adj.* nibbidɗum; ko nibbidi.

glorify [glowrəfay] *v.* mawninde; mantude.

glory [glowri] *n.* dówlugól *(ngól)*; manoore *(nde)*.

glossary [glosəri] *n.* limto kónguɗi.

glow [glow] *v.* hubbude; jawwude.

gloze [glowz] *v.* faccirde.

glue [gluw] *v.* ɗakkude.

glue [gluw] *n.* ɗaccere *(nde)*.

glunch [glʌnč] *v.* ñirbinaade.

glut [glʌt] *v.* hébbinde.

gluteal [gluwtiyl] *adj.* ko faati e dote.

glutton [gletən] *n.* gaybuɗo *(o)*.

glycerin [glisərin] *n.* nebam poppeteeɗam; gilcérin.

gnash [naš] *v.* Ɣakkude; hérɣóndirde ñiiɣe.

gnaw [now] *v.* ŋefde.

gnostic [nostik] *adj.* ko faati e gandal.

go *v.* yahde. *~ far* wóɗɗóyde. *~ and meet* hawróyde. *~ under water* mutde. *~ back again* ruttitaade. *~ to help* faabóyaade. *~ with* yahdude. *~ around an obstacle*

woraade. *~ down the slope* yórtaade. *~ with* yahdude. *~ in and out repeatedly* sórsórtude. *~ and collect firewood* teende; teenoyde. *~ and bring* addoyde. *~ herding* aynoyde. *~ and play* fijóyde. *~ to work in the morning* dawde. *~ and watch over* dóókóyde. *~ for* yahande. *~ early in the morning* rojde. *~ and shop groceries* duggóóyde. *~ and get* hébóyde. *~ and wash* lóótóyde. *~ out* yaltude. *~ earlier than usual* héjjude. *~ slowly* ruudde. *~ aside* selde; ikkaade. *~ the opposite direction* roontaade. *~ and fetch water* Ɣóógóyde. *~ and sleep again* ɗaantóyaade. *~ and look for* ɗabbóyde. *have a ~* etaade.

go-ahead [gowəhed] *n.* yamiroore *(nde)*.

go-between [gowbitwiyn] *adj.* neɗɗo hakkundeejo.

goal [gowl] *n.* muuya *(o)*; yiɗde *(nde). My goal is to finish first* Njiɗmi ko adaade gasnude.

goat [gowt] *n.* ndamndi *(ndi). female ~* mbeewa *(ba)*.

gob [gob] *v.* hébbinde.

gobble [gobəl] *v.* albaade; moɗde.

God [god] *n.* joomiraaɗo(o); alla *(o)*; jabbaaru *(o). in the name of ~* bismillaay

godless [godles] *adj.* mo jabaani jóómiraaɗo.

godly [godli] *adj.* kó réwi diine.

goer [gowə] *n.* jahoowo *(o)*.

goggles [gowgəlz] *n.* lone mawɗe.

going [gowiŋ] *n.* yahdu *(ndu)*.

goiter [gwatə] *n.* yookoode *(nde). have a ~* yookeede.

gold [gold] *n.* kaŋŋe *(o)*

golden [goldən] *adj.* ko faati e kaŋŋe. *a ~ watch* montoor kaŋŋe.

gondola [gondəla] *n.* laana *(ka)*.

gonorrhea [gonəriyə] *n.* fiɗo *(ngo)*.

good [gud] *adj.* moɣɣuɗum; ko moɣɣi. *make ~* móɣɣinde. *be ~* móɣɣude; feewde.

good-for-nothing [gudfənəθiŋ] *adj.* mo alaa nafoore.

good-humored [gudhyuwməd] *adj.* belɗo Ɣiiɣam.

good-tempered [gudtempəd] *adj.* muñɗo; belɗo Ɣiiɣam.

od-bye [gudbay] *n.* baynondiral *(ngal)*.
Ie said good-bye to you O wayni maama.
od-looking [gudlukiŋ] *adj.* jooɗɗo. *He*
s good-looking omo yooɗi/Omo moƳƳi
nbaadi.
odness [gudnes] *n.* moƳƳere *(nde)*.
ods [duwdz] *n.* kaake *(ɗe)*; marsandiis
:o).
of [guwf] *v.* fogoreede.
ose [guwz] *n.* kankaleewal *(ngal)*; caygal.
osy [guwzi] *adj.* ko nandi e kankaleewal.
rge [gorj] *n.* goddol *(ngól).* *What you*
re doing makes my gorge rise Ko mbaɗa
aa ko ina nefñii.
rgeous [gorjəs] *adj.* jooɗɗo. *She is*
gorgeous Ko o debbo jooɗɗo.
rilla [gorələ] *n.* déémóóru *(ndu)*.
rmandize [gormandayz] *v.* aybude.
ssip [gɑsip] *n.* ñohre *(nde)*.
ssip [gɑsip] *v.* ñohde. *She likes to gossip*
Ɔmo waawi ñohde.
urd [gɔd] *n.* faandu *(ndu)*; horde *(nde)*;
šumalle *(o)*; boliiru *(ndu)*; hudusuru *(ndu)*.
small ~ paalél (ngél).
urde [gurd] *n.* kaalis *(o)*.
urmand [gərmənd] *adj.* gaybuɗo; jiɗɗo
ĩaamde.
vern [gɑvən] *v.* ardaade; laamaade.
vernment [gɑvənmənt] *n.* laamu *(ngu)*.
vernmental [gɑvənməntəl] *adj.* ko faati
e laamu.
wn [gawn] *v.* wutte *(o)*. *I like your gown*
Wutte maa ina yooɗi.
rab [grab] *v.* jaggude; nangude. *~ a*
handful of jikkude. *~ each other while*
wrestling naatondirde. *I grabbed his hand*
Njaggu mi jungo makko.
rabble [grabəl] *v.* membaade; yiiloraade
juuɗe.
race [greys] *n.* yaafuya *(o)*.
racious [greyšəs] *adj.* moƳƳo.
radation [grədeyšən] *n.* huunde yahroore
taƳre.
radual [grajwəl] *adj.* ko yahrata
taƳre/taƳe.
radually [grajwəli] adv. taƳre taƳre.
rain [greyn] *n.* abbere *(nde)*.
rainy [greyni] *adj.* ko nandi e abbere;
maale abbere.
ram [gram] *n.* garaam *(o)*.

grammar [gramə] *n.* celluka *(ka)*. *His*
grammar is not sound Haala makko ka
sellaani.
grammarian [grameryən] *n.* gando célluka.
grammatical *adj.* [grəmətikəl] ko faati e
celluka; ko selli; haala celluka.
granary [granəri] *n.* faawru *(ndu)*.
grand [grand] *adj.* ko mawni.
grandchild [grančayld] *n.* taaniraaɗo *(o)*.
grandeur [grandər] *n.* mangu *(ngu)*;
Ƴéllitaagól *(ngól)*.
grandfather [grandfɑðə] *n.* taaniraaɗo
gorko.
grandmother [granmɔðə] *n.* taaniraaɗo
debbo.
grandiose [grandyowz] *adj.* mawɗo; ko
mawni.
grandparent [grandperənt] *n.* taaniraaɗo
(o); maama *(o)*.
grandson [grandsʌn] *n.* taaniraaɗo gorko.
granny [grani] *n.* maamayel (ngél).
grant [grant] *v.* jaɓande. *to ~ a pardon*
yaafaade. *He was granted permission to*
leave Jahgol makko yamiranooma.
granular [granyulə] *n.* maale abbere.
granulate [granyuleyt] *v.* mónginde.
granule [granyuwl] *n.* gabbél *(ngél)*.
grasp [grasp] *v.* jaggude; faamde.
grass [gras] *n.* huɗo *(ko)*. *He is mowing*
the grass Omon taƳa/hesa huɗo.
grassless [grasles] *adj.* nalduɗo.
grate [greyt] *v.* séknude; haljinde.
grateful [greytfəl] *adj.* jettuɗo. *I am*
grateful to you Mbeɗe yettu maa.
gratification [gratifəkeyšən] *n.* weltaare
(nde).
gratify [gratəfay] *v.* wéltinde.
gratis [gratis] adv. Allah meho.
gratitude [gratətyud] *n.* njettoor *(o)*. *I wish*
to express my most sincere gratitude to
you Mbeɗe yettu maa kaaɗi njettoor.
gratulate [gračəleyt] *v.* yéttude.
grave [greyv] *n.* añ̃ñeere *(nde)*; lahdi *(ɗi)*;
yanaande *(nde)*; womnde *(nde)*; góóski
(ki).
graveyard [greyvyɑd] *n.* baamuule *(ɗe)*.
gravitate [grəvəteyt] *v.* yiilaade.
gravitation [grəvəteyšən] *n.* jiilagól *(ngól)*.
gravure [gravur] *n.* natal *(ngal)*.

gravy [greyvi] *n.* ñeekam *(ɗam)*.

grayish [greyiš] *adj.* purɗuɗum; ko furɗi

graze [greyz] *v.* durde.

grease [griyz] *v.* newde.

great [greyt] *adj.* mawnuɗum; ko mawni.

greater [greytə] *adj.* ɓurɗo mawnude.

greatest [greytəst] *adj.* ɓurɗo fóf mawnude.

greatness [greytnes] *n.* mangu *(ngu)*.

greed [griyd] *n.* aybeende *(nde)*; reedunteya. *accuse someone of* ~ aybinde.

greediness [griydənes] *n.* aybeende *(nde)*; aybanduru *(ndu)*.

greedy [griydi] *adj.* gaybuɗo; cukñuɗo; kuuñɗuɗo. ~ *person* konomo. *He is a greedy individual* Ndaw ko aybi.

green [griyn] *adj.* ko wayi no noordi haako ñebbe.

greet [griyt] *v.* salminde; hinnude. *I greet you all* Mi salminii on.

greeting [griytiŋ] *n.* salminaango *(ngo)*. *my ~s to your folks* Mi salminii ko reeji maa.

grenade [grəneyd] *n.* garnaad *(o)*.

grey [grey] *adj.* purɗuɗu; ko furɗi. *His color is grey* Omo furɗi.

griddle [gridəl] *n.* pool *(o)*.

grief [grief] *n.* sunaare *(nde).* *with* ~ wondude e sunaare.

grievance [grievəns] *n.* tooñange *(nge)*; gullitaagól *(ngól)*.

grieve [griyv] *v.* sunaade.

grievous [griyvəs] *adj.* cuniiɗo.

grill [gril] *v.* naawde; juɗde.

grillade [grilad] *n.* juɗgól tééw.

grim [grim] *adj.* niɓɓiɗɗo; ñaaɗɗo; niɓɓo. *The future looks grim* Alla andi ɗo paaɗen.

grimace [griməs] *v.* ɓiiñde

grime [graym] *v.* tunwinde.

grime [graym] *n.* tuundi *(ndi)*.

grin [grin] *v.* ɓiiñde.

grind [graynd] *v.* ruggude; nirkude. ~ *peanuts* dirde; ɓursude.

grinder [grayndə] *n.* nirkoowo *(o)*; duggoowo *(o)*.

griot [griyo] *n.* gawlo *(o)*; bambaaɗo *(o)*; jalli *(o)*; jaawando *(o)*; jaareejo *(o)*

grip [grip] *n.* jaggugol *(ngól)*; tamande *(nde).* *have a good* ~ naŋtaade no moƳƳi.

gripe [grayp] *v.* jaggude; hamƳude.

gripple [gripəl] *adj.* boroodo; tiiɗɗc jungo.

gris-gris [grigri] *n.* ñawndogal *(ngal)*.

grist [grist] *n.* rogere unu.

gritty [griti] *adj.* bakkiliiɗo.

grizzle [grizəl] *v.* furɗude.

groan [grown] *n.* ottaango *(ngo)* uumaango *(ngo)*.

groan [grown] *v.* uumde; óttude.

grocer [grosə] *n.* jeeyoowo ñamri.

groceries [grosəriz] *n.* nduggu *(ngu)*.

groom [gruwm] *n.* gorko dambiiɗo jombaajo gorko.

grope [growp] *v.* membaade; wumbilaade.

groping [growpiŋ] *n.* membagól *(ngól)*.

gross [grɔs] *adj.* mo wondaaka; nefniɗum.

grotto [groto] *n.* ngaska *(ka)*.

ground [grawnd] *n.* léydi *(ndi).* *Put the shoes on the ground* Faw paɗe ɗe e dow leydi ndi.

group [grup] *n.* fedde *(nde)*.

group [grup] *v.* réndinde. *Group them together* Rendin ɓe.

grouse [graws] *v.* dumaade; woytaade.

grouty [grawti] *adj.* ñanguɗo.

grove [growv] *n.* laadde *(nde)*.

grow [grow] *v.* 1) mawnude 2) remde. *He grows millet* Ko o demoowo gawri.

grower [growə] *n.* demoowo *(o)* gaawoowo *(o)*.

growl [growl] *v.* ŋuurde

growler [growlə] *n.* ŋuuroowo *(o)* ŋuurooru *(ndu)*.

grown-up [grownʌp] *n.* neɗɗo kéllifaaɗo kellifaaɗo.

growth [growθ] *n.* mawnugól *(ngól)* Ƴellitaare *(nde)*; mangu *(ngu)*.

grudge [grʌj] *n.* téftóndiral *(ngal)*; teftagó *(ngól).* *hold a* ~ teftaade; tikkande.

gruel [gruwəl] *n.* ruy *(o)*.

grumble [grʌmbəl] *v.* dumaade.

grunt [grʌnt] *v.* óttude.

guarantee [garəntiy] *v.* tééŋtinde; fodande *I guarantee you will win* Mbeɗe fodar maa hawde.

guard [gɑd] *n.* garde *(o)*.

guard [gɑd] *v.* reende. ~ *against* reentinde. ~ *for* reenande. ~ *oneself against* reenaade; reentaade.

guard [gɑd] *n.* garde *(o).*

guarded [gɑdəd] *adj.* deenaaɗo.

guardian [gɑdyən] *n.* kalfinaaɗo *(o);* deenoowo *(o). She is my guardian* Ko kanko kalfinaami.

guddle [gʌdəl] *v.* jaggude.

guerilla [gerəla] *n.* hare béttugól.

guess [ges] *n.* sikke *(o)* miijo *(ngo).*

guess [ges] *v.* sikkude; miijaade. *take a* ~ miijo. *What is your guess* Hol ko woni miijo maa?

guest [gest] *n.* koɗo *(o). I am treating my guest to dinner* Mbeɗen teddina koɗo am.

guffaw [gəfɔ] *v.* hékitde.

guidance [gaydəns] *n.* gardagól *(ngól).*

guide [gaydəns] *n.* ɗowoowo *(o);* dabi *(o);* gardiiɗo *(o).*

guild [gild] *n.* fedde *(nde).*

guile [gayl] *n.* feere *(nde);* fuunti *(o).*

guilt [gilt] *n.* nimsa *(o);* tooñange *(nge).*

guilty [gilti] *adj.* tooñɗo. *He is guilty* ko kanko tooni.

guinea fowl [ginifawl] *n.* jaawngal *(ngal).*

guise [gayz] *v.* ɓoornaade.

guitar [gitɑ] *n.* hoɗdu *(ndu). one stringed* ~ mool *(o).*

guitarist [gitɑrist] *n.* koɗoowo *(o).*

gull [gʌl] *v.* fuuntude.

gullet [gʌlət] *n.* góddól *(ngól).*

gullible [gʌləbəl] *adj.* beeɓɗo hoore; beeɓɗo fuuntude.

gulosity [gəlosəti] *n.* aybeende *(nde).*

gulp [gʌlp] *v.* moɗde; sondaade.

gum [gʌm] *n.* 1) ɗakkudi *(ndi)* 2) ɗaccere *(nde).*

gumbo [gʌmbo] *n.* kañnje *(ɗe).*

gun [gʌn] *n.* fetel *(o);* kume *(o).*

gun [gʌn] *v.* fellude. *He was gunned down* O wardaama fetel.

gunfight [gʌnfayt] *n.* péllóndiral *(ngal).*

gunfire [gʌnfayə] *n.* fiyande *(nde).*

gunnery [gʌnəri] *n.* pellugol *(ngól).*

gunpowder [gʌnpowdə] *n.* cóndi fétél.

gunshot [gʌnpowdə] *n.* fiyande *(nde). I heard a gunshot* Fiyande dillii.

guru *n.* janginoowo *(o);* ceerno *(o).*

gusset [gʌset] *n.* jawo jungo reentorteengo.

gust [gʌst] *n.* héndu mawndu.

gut [gʌt] *n.* téktékól *(ngól).*

gutter [gʌtə] *n.* baltirgal *(ngal).*

guzzle [gʌzəl] *v.* yarde; ɓurtinde njaram.

gymnasium [jimneyzyəm] *n.* nókku coftal balli.

gynarchy [jənɑrki] *n.* laamu debbo.

gynecology [gaynəkoloji] *n.* jangde terɗe e ñabbuuli rewɓe.

gyrate [jayreyt] *v.* yiilaade.

gyration [jayreyšən] *n.* jiilagól *(ngól).*

H

haberdasher [habədašə] n. jeeyoowo cómci worɓe.

habile [habəl] adj. baawɗo; ñeeñɗo.

habiliment [habələmənt] n. cómci (ɗi).

habit [habit] n. néésu (ngu); jikku (o).

habitable [habitəbəl] adj. nókku koɗeteeɗo.

habitant [habitənt] n. neɗɗo koɗɗo.

habitat [habətat] n. hoɗorde (nde).

habitation [habəteyšən] n. hoɗorde (nde).

habitual [habəčəl] adj. ko faati e jikku.

habituate [habəčweyt] v. wóównude.

habitude [habəčud] n. ngoowka (ka); jikku (o).

hacienda [hasyendə] n. hoɗorde (nde).

hack [hack] v. sóppude; féΥΥude.

hackney [hakni] n. puccu (ngu).

hadith [hadiyθ] n. hadiis (o).

hafiz [hafiz] n. dursuɗo (o); gando (o).

haft [haft] v. serde.

haft [haft] n. ɓande jambere.

hag [hag] n. debbo coofɗo; bonɗo.

haggard [hagəd] adj. béftilaaɗo.

hail [heyl] v. eeraade. I hail you Mi eeri maama.

hair [her] n. lééɓól (ngól); sukundu (ndu). She is washing her hair Omon lawΥaa sukundu makko.

hairy [heri] adj. guyɗo; ko wuyi.

hajj [haj] n. hajju (o).

hale [heyl] adj. célluɗo; tiiɗɗo.

hale [heyl] v. daasde; foodde; séllinde.

half [haf] n. feccere (nde); karal (ngal); gennewalla (o).~ an hour feccere waktu.

half [haf] v. feccude.

hallow [halow] v. rewde; téddinde.

hallucinate [halusəneyt] v. ruuytude.

hallucination [halusəneyšən] n. duuytugól (ngól).

hallway [hɔlwey] n. bólééru (ndu).

halo [heylo] n. sérééndu (ndu).

halt [hɔlt] v. daraade; dartinde.

halve [halv] v. féccude; felsude.

ham [ham] n. tééw mbabba tugal.

hammer [hamə] v. fiirude martu. prov. Strike the hammer while the iron is hot ɓakke mahetee gila ko ɗe kecce.

hammer [hamə] n. martu (o).

hamper [hampə] v. haɗde.

hamstring [hamstriŋ] n. códdungól (ngól).

hamza [hamza] n. alkulal (ngal).

hand [hand] n. jungo (ngo). from ~ to ~ jungo e jungo.

hand [hand] v. tottude; rókkude. Hand it over to me Heɓnam ɗum.

hand-feed [handfiyd] v. ñamminirde jungo.

handbag [handbag] n. sakkoos (o). Where is your handbag Hol to sakkoos maa woni?

handcraft [handkraft] v. fééwnirde jungo.

handcuff [handkʌf] v. sokde juuɗe; ceende. They handcuffed him ɓe ceenii juuɗe makko.

handful [handfəl] n. nokkande (nde); nokkere (nde); jikkande (nde); tamande (nde). He is a handful Omo fiddi.

handicap [handəkap] n. ŋakkere (nde); ronkere (nde).

handicraft [handəkraft] n. liggééy jungo.

handkerchief [hankəčiyf] n. tekkere ñittorteende.

handle [handəl] n. ɓande (nde); jungo (ngo).

handle [handəl] v. toppitaade.

handsome [handsəm] adj. jooɗɗo. He is handsome Ko o gorko jooɗɗo.

handwork [handwərk] n. liggééy jungo.

handwrite [handrayt] v. windirde jungo.

handwriting [handraytiŋ] n. bindol jungo. Your handwriting is difficult to read Bindi maa ina metti jangude.

hang [haŋ] v. liggude. ~ down wééltude. ~ around doomde.

hangar [haŋər] n. caali (ki).

hanger [haŋə] n. liggirgal (ngal). Where is the hanger Hol to liggirgal ngal woni?

hanging [haŋiŋ] n. beelgol (ngól); liggugol (ngól)

hanker [haŋkə] v. yiɗde.

haphazard [haphazəd] adj. ko tijjaaka; ko tijjanooka.

hapless [haples] n. malkisaaɗo (o).

pen [hapən] *v.* waɗde; wonde. *What* ***ppened to him** Hol ko heɓi mo?

piness [hapines] *n.* weltaare *(nde).*

py [hapi] *adj.* béltiiɗo. *He is happy to* *e you* Omo weltii e garaangal maa.

angue [həraŋ] *n.* haala.

ass [heras] *v.* haljinde.

bor [habə] *n.* tééri *(ɗi).*

bor [habə] *v.* moolde; ɗuhde; oolaade; ɗuhaade.

d [had] *adj.* tiiɗɗum; jaɗɗuɗum; ɗtuɗum; tékkuɗum. *He is trying very* *ard* Omo tiinnii no feewi.

den [hadən] *v.* tiiɗnude; saɗtinde; agginde.

dener [hadənə] *n.* Yagginoowo *(o).*

dihood [hadihud] *n.* sembe *(o);* ɗnaare *(nde).*

diness [hadines] *n.* tiiɗnaare *(nde).*

dship [hadšəp] *n.* joote (de); baasal *gal).*

dy [hadi] *adj.* caasɗo; mo hulaani mpere.

e [her] *n.* wojere *(nde).*

k [hak] *v.* heɗaade; heɗtaade.

l [hal] *v.* daasde; fooɗde.

lot [halət] *n.* debbo pijoowo; jinoowo *).*

m [ham] *n.* lorla *(o);* bone *(ɗe);* ɔnande *(nde). He caused no harm* O rlaani hay gooto.

m [ham] *v.* lorlude.

mattan [hamətan] *n.* héndu émminaare.

mful [hamfəl] *adj.* ko gaañata; ko rlata.

monic [hamownik] *adj.* ko yahdi.

monious [hamownyəs] *adj.* ko yahdi.

monize [hamənayz] *v.* yahdinde.

ness [hanes] *n.* habɓude; jókkóndirde.

poon [hapuwn] *n.* deŋŋere *(nde).*

ry [hari] *v.* haljinde; tooñde.

sh [haš] *adj.* ko muusi.

shen [hašən] *v.* muusnude.

vest [havest] *n.* coñal *(ngal);* ɓultagol ʒgól).*

vest [havest] *v.* ɓultaade; soñde.

vester [havestə] *n.* coñoowo *(o).*

haste [heyst] *n.* heñaare *(nde). Do not do it* *with haste* Hol to heño?.

hasten [heysən] *v.* yaawnude.

hastily [heystəli] *adv.* ko yaactii; ko heñoraa.

hasty [heysti] *adj.* kéñiiɗo.

hat [hat] *n.* tengaade *(nde);* laafa *(ka);* kufne *(o);* maage *(o);* manna. *Wear your* *hat because it is hot outside* ɓoorno laafa sabi naange nge ina wuli.

hatch [hač] *v.* tóccinde.

hatch [hač] *n.* tóccungo *(ngo);* toccingol *(ngól).*

hatchet [hačet] *n.* jambél *(ngél). bury the ~* welditde.

hate [heyt] *v.* añde. *~ one another* añondirde. *~ forever* añtude. *I hate it* Mbeɗe añi ɗum.

hated [heytəd] *adj.* gañaado *(o).*

hatred [heytrəd] *n.* ngañgu *(ngu).*

hatter [hatə] *n.* peewnoowo laafaaji.

haul [howl] *v.* fooɗde; daasde.

hauler [howlə] *n.* pooɗoowo *(o);* daasoowo *(o).*

haunted [hontid] *adj.* ko hoɗaa; ɗó jinnééji kóɗi. *a ~ house* galle koɗaaɗo.

have [hav] *v.* jogaade; dañde; jeyde. *I had* *rather stay home today* ɓurani mi ko heddaade galle hande.

haven [heyvən] *n.* tééru; duhorde *(nde).*

haversack [havəsak] *n.* mbasu *(ngu).*

havoc [havək] *n.* bonande *(nde).*

hawk [hɔk] *v.* yeeyde; waañde.

hay [hey] *n.* ñoomre *(nde). make ~ while* *the sun shines* mahde ɓakke gila koɗe kecce.

hazard [hazəd] *n.* huunde bonnoore.

hazy [heyzi] *adj.* ko laaɓaani.

he [hi] *pron.* o; omo; kam; kañ; kanko He is eating lunch O woni ko e wottaade.

head [hed] *n.* hoore *(nde). ~ tie* tikka. *~* *load* dongal *(ngal). Where is your head* Hol to hakkille maa woni? **head** [hed] *v.* ardaade. *~ toward* faade; tiindaade; huccude. *Where are you headed* Hol to paa ɗaa?

headache [hedeyk] *n.* muusu hoore; hoore muusoore. *I have a headache* Hooram ina muusa.

headless [hedles] *adj.* ko/mo alaa hoore.

headstall [hedstɔl] *n.* faram *(o).*

headstrong [hedstrɔŋ] *adj.* ŋatɗo.

heal [hiyl] *v.* séllinde; móccude.

healed [hiyld] *adj.* célluɗo; cellinaaɗo.

healer [hiylə] *n.* caroowo *(o);* cellinoowo *(o).*

health [helƟ] *n.* cellal *(ngal). He is in good health* Omo selli.

healthy [helƟi] *adj.* célluɗo.

heap [hiyp] *n.* joowre *(nde);* joowde *(ɗe).*

hear [hiyə] *v.* nande. *I have not heard from him ever since he left* Mi heɓaani kabaruuji makko gila o yahi.

hearer [hiyrə] *n.* nanoowo *(o).*

hearing [hiyriŋ] *n.* nanɗe *(ɗe).*

hearsay [hiyrsey] *n.* nanalla *(o).*

heart [hɑt] *n.* ɓernde *(nde);* wónki *(ki).* *~ache* ɓernde muusoore. *~burn* cum ɓerel

heart-to-heart [hɑtəhɑt] *adj.* nuunɗuɗo.

hearth [hɑrƟ] *n.* haatande *(nde).*

heartless [hɑtles] *adj.* ko/mo alaa ɓernde; joorɗo ɓernde.

heat [hiyt] *v.* wulnude; wultinde. *~ oneself* aɗɗaade; saaɗnaade.

heat [hiyt] *n.* ngulééki *(ki).*

heathen [heðən] *n.* neɗɗo mo rewaani jóómiraaɗo; keefeero *(o).*

heave [hiyv] *v.* Ƴéttude.

heaven [heven] *n.* aljanna *(o). He is in heaven* O naatii aljanna.

heavenly [hevenli] *adv.* ko faati e aljanna.

heavy [hevi] *adj.* tédduɗum; ko téddi. *This task is a heavy burden* ɗum ina teddi e am.

hebdomad [hebdəmad] *n.* balɗe jééɗiɗi.

hebetate [hebəteyt] *v.* muuddiɗde; muddiɗinde.

hebetude [hebətyuwd] *n.* muddiɗgól *(ngól).*

heckle [hekəl] *v.* haljinde.

hedge [hej] *n.* kalasal *(ngal)*

hedge [hej] *v.* jookde; howde; surde.

hedgehog [hejhog] *v.* sammunnde *(nde).*

hedonic [hiydownik] *adj.* ko faati e welamma/weltaare.

heed [hiyd] *n.* baɗtugol hakkille. *pay ~ to* waɗtude hakkille.

heed [hiyd] *v.* waɗtude hakkile.

heedless [hiydles] *adj.* mo waɗtaa hakkille e.

heel [hiyl] *n.* teeppere *(nde). show one's ~* dogde.

heft [heft] *n.* téddééndi *(ndi).*

hefty [hefti] *adj.* tekkuɗum; tedduɗum; k tékki; ko sélli; ko téddi.

hegemony [hejəmoni] *n.* gardagól *(ngói* jiimgól *(ngól);* njiimaandi *(ndi).*

heifer [hayfə] *n.* ñale *(nge);* wiige *(nge).*

height [hayt] *n.* tooweendi *(ndi);* darnɔ *(nde).*

heighten [haytən] *v.* tóównude; mawninde

heinous [henəs] *adj.* gañɗo.

heir [er] *n.* dono *(o);* donoowo *(o).*

heirdom [erdəm] *n.* ndónu *(ngu).*

heiress [erəs] *n.* debbo donɗo/donoow dono.

hell [hel] *n.* jéyngól jahannama. *raise* finnude; dukde. *He will go to hell* Ma naat e jayngol.

hello [helow] *n.* salminaango *(ngo).*

helmet [helmet] *n.* kaske *(o).*

help [help] *n.* ballal *(ngal).*

help [help] *v.* wallude; faabaade; hakkitd *~ one another* wallóndirde. *~ yourse* wallu hoore maa.

helper [helpə] *n.* balloowo *(o);* jagganoow jungo

helpful [helpfəl] *adj.* ko wallata; balloowo

helve [helv] *n.* ɓande *(nde).*

hem [hem] *v.* hombude.

hemal [hiyməl] *adj.* ko faati e ƳiiƳam.

hematic [hiymatik] *adj.* ko faati e ƳiiƳam.

hemi [hemi] *pref.* feccere.

hemisphere [hemisfiyə] *n.* fecce léydi/weeyo.

hemmer [hemə] *n.* komboowo *(o).*

hemophobia [hiyməfowbyə] *n.* kul ƳiiƳam.

hen [hen] *n.* gertogal *(ngal);* jarlal *(ngal).*

hence [hens] *adv.* ɗum waɗi/noon; gila.

henceforth [hensforƟ] *adv.* ko fayi arɗ jóóni faade yeeso.

henna [henə] *n.* puuɗdi *(ndi). lay ~ ɔ one's arms or feet* fuuɗaade.

hepatic [hepatik] *adj.* ko faati e jofe.

her [hər] *poss. pron.* mum; muuɗu makko. *~ shoes* paɗe makko.

ald [herəld] *v.* andinde; habrude; **tinde.**

b [hərb] *n.* huɗo *(ko).*

baceous [hərbeyšəs] *adj.* ko faati e **ɗo.**

bivorous [hərbivərəs] *adj.* ko ñaamata **ɗo/leɗɗe.**

d [hərd] *n.* oornde *(nde);* coggal *(ngal).*

d [hərd] *v.* aynude. *make someone ~* ninde. *~ for someone* fullinaade.

der [hərdə] *n.* gaynoowo *(o);* gaynaako **ɗ**; aga *(o).*

dsman [hərdsmən] *n.* gaynaako *(o);* aga *).*

e [hiyə] *adv.* ɗoo; gaa; gaay; gaayenne. *and there* ɗoo e ɗaa.

eafter [hiyraftə] *n.* laakara *(o).*

editary [herədətəri] *adj.* ko ronetee; ko naa.

edity [herədəti] *n.* ndónu *(ngu).*

esy [herəsi] *n.* luutndagól *(ngól).*

itable [heritəbəl] *adj.* ko ronetee.

itage [heritəj] *n.* ndónu *(ngu). It is **portant to know one's heritage* Neɗɗo a foti andude hoore mum.

itor [herətə] *n.* gorko donoowo.

itress [herətres] *n.* debbo donoowo.

metic [hərmetik] *n.* ko hiɓɓii.

mit [hərmit] *n.* guddiiɗo *(o);* jóñiiɗo *).*

mitage [hərmitej] *n.* joñorde *(nde).*

self [hərself] pron. kanko hoore makko ebbo).

itant [hezitənt] *adj.* mó féllitaani.

itate [hezəteyt] *v.* waasde féllitde.

eroclite [hətərəklayt] *adj.* neɗɗo celɗo.

erogenous [hətərowjənəs] *adj.* ko onaa góótum.

h [heð] *n.* alkulal *(ngal).*

w [hyuw] *v.* sóppude.

x [heks] *v.* liggaade (dabare).

day [heydey] *n.* naange huunde walla **eɗɗo.** *in his ~* e naange makko.

tus [hyatəs] *n.* ŋalde *(nde).*

iscus [həbiskəs] *n.* follere *(nde).*

cup [hikʌp] *n.* likʸere *(nde). He has a **ccup* O mo wondi e likʸere.

cup [hikʌp] *v.* likʸude

hidden [hidən] *adj.* kó suuɗii; cuuɗiɗum. *~ meaning* maanaa cuuɗiiɗo.

hide [hayd] *v.* sekkaade; mofde; suuɗde; nuɗɗinde; móggude. *~ oneself* suuɗaade; mógginaade.

hide-and-seek [haydənsiyk] *n.* suuɗó suuɗóóndu.

hideous [hidyəs] *adj.* bónɗum; kulɓiniiɗum.

hideout [haydawt *n.* suuɗorde *(nde).*

hider [haydə] *n.* mooftoowo *(o);* mofoowo *(o).*

hie [hay] *v.* yaawnude; yaawnaade.

hieroglyphics [hiyərəglifiks] *n.* alkule *(ɗi);* bindol *(ngól).*

higgle [higəl] *v.* haaldeede; yeeytaade.

high [hay] *adj.* ko tóówi; toowɗum. *The price is high* ina tiiɗi.

higher [hayə] *adj.* ɓurɗo toowde; ko ɓuri toowde.

highest [hayəst] *adj.* ko ɓuri fóf toowde.

highlight [haylayt] *n.* tééɭtinde.

highway [haywey] *n.* kallu *(o).*

hike [hayk] *v.* yahde yahdu wóɗɗundu.

hilarious [hələryəs] *adj.* béltiiɗo.

hill [hill] *n.* tulde *(nde);* ferlo *(ngo). ant~* waande *(nde).*

hilly [hili] *adj.* nókku keewɗo tule; tulnuɗo; ko tulni.

him [him] pron. kanko (gorko).

himself [himself] pron. kanko hooremakko (gorko).

hinder [hində] *v.* haɗde; lééltinde.

hindrance [hindrəns] *n.* kaɗgól *(ngól).*

hint [hint] *v.* jeertaade.

hint [hint] *n.* jeertagól *(ngól);* jeerto *(ngo).*

hip [hip] *n.* wóóndu *(ndu);* buhal.

hipjoint [hipjoynt] *n.* asangal *(ngal).*

hippophagist [hipəfajəst] *n.* ñaamoowo tééw puccu.

hippopotamus [hipəpətaməs] *n.* ngabu *(ngu).*

hire [hayə] *v.* ligginde; ʸettude. *They hired him yesterday* O ʸettaama hanki.

his [hiz] pron. muuɗum; makko; mum (gorko).

hiss [his] *v.* fuufde; sóññude; wuuɗde; siikde; salaade.

historian [histowryən] *n.* bittoowo hanki men.

179

historical [histərikəl] *adj.* ko faati e hanki men.

history [histri] *n.* hanki men; jangde hanki men.

hit [hit] *n.* fidde; fiide. bammude; lappude. ~ *a target* fidde. ~ *with a car* feraade. ~ *the nail on the head* fiide e hoore.

hitch [hič] *v.* habbude; jókkóndirde.

hither [hiðə] *adv.* sara; takko.

hitherto [hiθerto] *adv.* haa jóóni.

hoard [hɔd] *n.* ndesaari *(ndi)*.

hoarse [hɔs] *adj.* ko loori; daande loornde.

hoax [hɔks] *v.* fuuntude.

hoax [hɔks] *n.* fuunti *(o)*.

hobble [hɔbəl] *v.* tóbbude; laɼde.

hobbler [hɔblə] *n.* tobboowo *(o)*; laɼoowo *(o)*.

hoe [how] *n.* jalo *(ngo)*; kéri.

hoe [how] *v.* remde.

hog [hɑg] *n.* mbabba tugal.

hoist [hoyst] *v.* ŋabbinde.

hold [hold] *v.* jaggude; nangude; tamde. ~ *in the mouth* wuufde. ~ *in the hand* tamde. ~ *a child in the lap* lendaade. ~ *for* nangande. ~ *with* nangirde. ~ *in arms* huufde.

hold [hold] *n.* nangugol *(ngól)*.

holder [holdə] *n.* jógiido *(o)*; jaggudo *(o)*.

holdup [holdʌp] *n.* nguyka *(ka)*.

hole [howl] *n.* wuddere *(nde)* ngaska *(ka)*; tufannde *(nde)*. ~ *for sowing seeds* eño *(ngo)*. *ass~* wuddere gada.

holey [hɑli] *adj.* ko yuli; juldum.

holiday [hɑlədey] *n.* hurjo *(ngo)*; guurti *(di)*.

holler [hɑlə] *v.* siikde; wullude.

hollow [hɑlow] *adj.* meho; méhum.

hollow [hɑlow] *n.* ngaska *(ka)*; dóórumaaru *(ndu)*.

holster [holstə] *n.* wana *(ka)*.

home [howm] *n.* hodorde *(nde)*; galle *(o)*. *He went home yesterday* O hooti galle mabbe hanki. *There is no place like home* Neddo hadtetee ko do jeyaa.

homeland [howmlənd] *n.* ngéndi *(ndi)*.

homeless [howmles] *adj.* mo alaa hodorde. *He is homeless* O alaa do o woni.

homicide [homəsayd] *n.* war/warngo hoore.

homogeneity [homowjəneyti] *n.* nandug *(ngól)*.

homogeneous [homowjiynyəs] *adj.* nanndi.

homologate [hɑmələgeyt] *v.* jabde.

homonym [hɑmənim] *n.* tokara *(o)*.

homosexual [həmowsekšəl] *n.* deba gorkati.

hone [hown] *v.* wélnude; séébnude.

honest [honest] *adj.* nuundudo.

honesty [honesti] *n.* nuundal *(ngal)*.

honey [hɑni] *n.* njuumri *(ndi)*.

honor [onə] *n.* fulla *(o)*; faayiida *(c* neddaagal *(ngal)*. *man without* ~ nedc mo alaa fulla alaa faayiida.

honorarium [onəreryəm] *n.* njobdi *(ndi)*.

hood [hud] *n.* hippoode *(nde)*.

hoodoo [huwdu] *v.* malkiseede

hoodoo [huwdu] *n.* malkisaare *(nde)*.

hoof [huf] *n.* holsere *(nde)*.

hook [huk] *n.* wande *(nde)*; lóggirde *(nde* lóŋdu *(ndu)*; loggande *(nde)*; lóggirg *(ngal)*.

hook [huwk] *v.* hogde; loggude.

hooked [hukt] *adj.* loggiido; ko loggii.

hooker [hukə] *n.* garbotoodo *(o)*.

hookworm [hukwɔm] *n.* saan *(o)*

hooligan [huligən] *n.* aawaseejo *(c* aawase *(o)*.

hooliganism [huləgənizm] *n.* aasaag *(ngal)*.

hoot [huwt] *v.* wullude (neddo).

hop [hop] *v.* toŋɼaade. ~ *in* jolde.

hope [howp] *n.* damaawu *(o)*; yaakaa *(nde)*. *prov. While there is life, there hope* Guurdo fotaani damtindaade.

hope [howp] *v.* daminaade; yaakoraade. *hope to see him* Mbede yaakorii yiide m

hopeful [howpful] *adj.* daminiido.

hopeless [howples] *adj.*
1) damtindiido 2) mo alaa nafoore.

hopper [hopə] *n.* toŋɼotoodo *(c* toŋɼoowo *(o)*.

hopping [hɑpiŋ] *n.* toŋɼagól *(ngól)*.

hopple [hopəl] *v.* tongude.

hora [hora] *n.* ngamri *(ndi)*.

horal [horəl] *adj.* ko faati e waktu.

horde [hɔd] *n.* deental yimbe; deental.

horn [hɔn] *n.* allaadu *(ndu)*; kornaal *(o)*.

rologic [horowləjik] *adj.* ko faati e waktu.

rrible [horəbəl] *adj.* bóndʼum; kulɓiniidʼum.

rrid [horid] *adj.* bóndʼum; kulɓiniidʼum.

rrific [horəfik] *adj.* kulɓiniidʼum.

rrified [horəfayd] *adj.* kuldʼo; gijaadʼo.

rrify [horəfay] *v.* hulɓinde; gijde.

rror [horo] *n.* kulól *(ngól).*

rse [hɔs] *n.* puccu *(ngu).* **hold one's ~es** wadʼ seese.

rsy [hɔsi] *adj.* ko faati e puccu.

se [howz] *n.* rakkoor *(o).*

spice [hospis] *n.* jipporde *(nde);* dʼuhorde *(nde).*

spitable [hospitəbəl] *adj.* kottoowo; moƳƳo.

spital [hospitəl] *n.* safrorde *(nde);* lópitaan *(o).* **He works at the hospital** O liggotoo ko lopitaan.

spitality [hospətaləti] *n.* kóttugól.

st [howst] *n.* njaatige *(o).* **I am your host** Ko miin woni njaatige maa.

stage [howstij] *n.* jaggaadʼo *(o).*

stess [hostes] *n.* njaatige debbo.

stile [hostayl] *adj.* bondʼo; gaño; luutndiidʼo.

stility [hostəliti] *n.* ngañgu *(ngu);* luutndagól *(ngól).*

t [hɑt] *adj.* guldʼum; ko wuli; kaadʼdʼum. **This pepper is hot** O kaani ko kaadʼdʼo.

ound [hawnd] *n.* rawaandu *(ndu).*

our [awə] *n.* waktu *(o)*

ouri [huri] *n.* debbo aljanna.

ourly [awəli] *adv.* waktu kala.

ouse [haws] *n.* galle *(o);* suudu *(ndu);* hodʼorde *(nde).* **~ breaking** nguyka *(ka).*

ousehold [hawshowld] *n.* yimɓe galle.

ousekeeper [hawskiypə] *n.* deenoowo galle; mbindaan *(o).*

ousemaid [hawsmeyd] *n.* mbindaan *(o).*

ousewife [hawswayf] *n.* debbo galle.

ousework [hawswɔk] *n.* liggééy galle.

ow [haw](question word)no; hol no. **How are you** Hol no mbadʼdʼaa?

owever [hawevə] *adv.* kono; kono noon; dʼum fóf e waade noon.

owl [hawl] *v.* ŋuurde.

owler [hawlə] *n.* ŋuuróóru *(ndu).*

hubbub [hʌbʌb] *n.* gulaali *(dʼi).*

hubby [hʌbi] *n.* jom galle. **Where is my hubby** Hol to jom galle am woni?

huckster [hʌkstə] *n.* jeeyoowo *(o).*

huddle [hʌdəl] *v.* ñukkóndirde.

huff [hʌf] *n.* sekre *(nde);* mettere *(nde).*

huge [hyuwj] *adj.* mawdʼo; ko mawni.

hull [hʌl] *n.* saaño *(ko);* nguru *(ngu).*

hum [hʌm] *v.* uumde.

human [yuwmən] *adj.* ko faati e nedʼdʼo. **~ being** nedʼdʼo; innama aadee.

humanist [yuwmənist] *n.* jidʼdʼo yimɓe.

humanity [yuwmanəti] *n.* nedʼdʼaagu *(ngu);* nedʼdʼankaagal *(ngal).*

humble [hʌmbəl] *adj.* jankiniidʼo. **He is a humble man** Omo yankinii.

humbleness [hʌmbəl] *n.* yankinaare *(nde).*

humbug [hʌmbʌg] *n.* fuunti *(o).*

humectant [hyuwmektənt] *adj.* kó léppinta.

humerus [hyuwmərəs] *n.* Ƴiyal jungo.

humid [hyuwmid] *adj.* ko léppi; leppudʼum.

humidify [hyuwmidəfay] *v.* léppinde.

humidity [hyuwmidəti] *n.* ɓayto *(ngo);* léppugól *(ngól).*

humiliate [hyuwməlyeyt] *v.* hérsinde.

humiliation [hyuwməlyeyšən] *n.* koyeera *(ka);* gacce *(dʼe).*

humility [hyuwmələti] *n.* yankinaare *(nde).*

humming [hʌmiŋ] *n.* uumgól *(ngól).*

hummock [hʌmok] *n.* tulde *(nde).*

hummocky [hʌmoki] *adj.* kó hééwi tule.

humor [hywmə] *n.* gaajaare *(nde);* janondiral (ngal). **He has a good sense of humor** Omo weli yanondirde.

humorous [hyuwmərəs] *n.* ko jalnii; jalnidʼum.

hump [hʌmp] *n.* Ƴuulde *(nde).*

hunch [hʌnč] *v.* jeertaade.

hunch [hʌnč] *n.* jeerto *(ngo);* jéértungo *(ngo).* **I had a hunch** Mi jeerti.

hundred [hʌndred] *n.* teemedere *(nde).*

hunger [hʌŋgə] *n.* heege *(nge).*

hunger [hʌŋgə] *v.* hooƳeede; heegeede; héydʼude.

hungry [hʌŋgri] *adj.* keydʼudʼo; kooƳaadʼo. **I am hungry** mbedʼe heydʼi.

hunker [hʌŋkə] *v.* soppinaade.

hunt [hʌnt] *v.* waañde; raddude.

hunt [hʌnt] *n.* waaño *(ngo)*; raddo *(ngo)*.

hunter [hʌntə] *n.* daddoowo *(o)*; danna *(o)*; baañoowo *(o)*.

hunting [hʌntiŋ] *n.* raddo *(ngo)*; waaño; fiifiire *(nde)*; songo *(ngo)*.

hurdle [hərdəl] *v.* diwde.

hurl [hərl] *v.* werlaade.

hurling [hərliŋ] *n.* berlagól *(ngól)*.

hurricane [hʌrəkeyn] *n.* héndu mawndu.

hurry [hʌri] *v.* yaawnaade; heñaade; yaawnaade; ñomaade. ~ *up* yaawno.

hurry [hʌri] *n.* heñaare *(nde)*.

hurt [hʌrt] *adj.* gaañiiɗo; gaañaaɗo.

hurt [hʌrt] *v.* gaañde. *You hurt my feelings* A metti nii bernde am.

hurter [hərtə] *n.* gaañoowo *(o)*.

hurtful [hərtful] *adj.* ko gaañata. gaañojum; gaañoowo.

hurtle [hərtəl] *v.* yaawnaade; heñaade.

husband [hʌzbənd] *n.* jom galle. *one's ~ 's sibling* Ɣéékiraaɗo *(o)*.

hush [hʌš] *n.* deeɣre *(nde)*.

husk [hʌsk] *n.* saaño *(ko)*; nguru *(ngu)*.

hustle [hʌsəl] *v.* yaawnaade e golle.

hut [hʌt] *n.* suudu huɗo.

hutch [hʌč] *n.* cuurél wojere.

hybrid [haybrəd] *adj.* jilluɗo; ko jilli.

hybridize [haybrədayz] *v.* jillinde.

hydraulic [haydrɔlik] *adj.* ko faati e ndiyam ndogojam.

hydraulics [haydrɔliks] *n.* jangde ndiyam ndogojam.

hyena [hayiynə] *n.* waasooru *(ndu)*; fowru *(ndu)*; huttooru *(ndu)*.

hyetography [haytəgrafi] *n.* jangde toɓo e caragól mum.

hygiene [hayjiyn] *n.* laaɓal *(ngal)*.

hygienic [hayjiynik] *adj.* ko faati e laaɓal.

hymn [him] *n.* njimri *(ndi)*.

hyperdactylia [haypədaktəlya] *n.* péɗééli burtuɗi (annama peɗeeli jeegom).

hyphen [hayfən] *n.* jókkirde (-); diidél déndinóówél.

hyphenate [hayfəneyt] *v.* jókkude.

hypocrite [hipəkrit] *n.* ñóóju *(o)*; naafige *(o)*.

hypostasize [haypəstəsayz] *v.* sikkude.

hypothecate [haypowθəkeyt] *v.* juknude.

hypothesis [haypowθesis] *n.* miijo *(ngo)*.

hypothetical [haypowθetikəl] *adj.* ko faati e miijo; ko sikkini.

hysteria [histerya] *n.* filñitaare *(nde)*, pilñitaagól *(ngól)*.

hysterical [histerikəl] *adj.* pilñitiiɗo; ko faati e filñitaare. *He became hysterical* O filñitii.

I

ay] pron. mi; miin. *I saw this morning* Mi yii mo naane subaka.

nb [iyam] *n.* kijjaancfe cficfi.

ada [ibada] *n.* ngóóróóndi diine.

ex [aybeks] *n.* ndamndi *(ndi).*

n [ibn] *n.* bii.

[ays] *n.* galaas *(o).* ~ *cream* kerem alaas.

berg [aysbərg] *n.* tulde galaas.

man [aysmən] *n.* jeeyoowo galaas.

ea [aydiyə] *n.* miijo *(ngo). His idea works etter* Ko miijo makko buri moYYude.

eal [aydiyl] *n.* sago *(ngo). The ideal is to ave both of you here* Sinno ko sago, non cficfo kala on ngonanno cfoo.

eally [aydiyli] adv. sinno ko sago.

eate [aydiyeyt] *v.* miijaade.

eation [aydiyšən] *n.* miijagól *(ngól).*

eational [aydyšənəl] *adj.* ko faati e miijagól.

entic [aydentik] *adj.* nanducfi; ko nandi. *They are identic* kambe nandi.

entical [aydentikəl] *adj.* nanducfi; ko andi; nandube.

entification *n.* féññinoore.

entify [aydentətay] *v.* féññinde; hebtinde.

eology [aydiyəloji] *n.* miijo *(ngo).*

iocy [idyəsi] *n.* puuyndam *(cfam).*

iom [idyəm] *n.* haala *(ka);* kongol *(ngól).*

iosyncrasy [idyəsinkrəsi] *n.* maale uunde/neďdo.

iot [idyət] *adj.* mo YoYaani; puuycfo. *He 's an idiot* Ko o puuycfo.

iotic [idyowtik] *adj.* ko fuuyi; puuycfum.

le [aydəl] *adj.* mo liggaaki; mo haljaani. ~ *hands* juucfe cfe kaljaani.

ol [aydol] *n.* sanam *(o);* bóóri *(o).*

olater [aydəladə] *n.* sanajida *(o).*

olize [aydəlayz] *v.* sanójinde.

yll [aydəl] *n.* yimre *(nde).*

yllic [aydəlik] *adj.* ko faati e yimre.

[if] *conj.* si tay; sinno; soko; so; si. *even* ~ hay so.

loo [iglu] *n.* suudu *(ndu).*

ignite [ignayt] *v.* hubbude.

igniter [ignaytə] *n.* kubboowo *(o).*

ignition [igniyšən] *n.* kubbugól *(ngól).* ~ *key* coktirgal kubbowal oto.

ignoble [ignowbəl] *adj.* bondo; mo wonaa dimo.

ignominy [ignowmini] *n.* kersa *(o)/*(ka); gacce *(cfe).*

ignorance [ignərəns] *n.* majjere *(nde). It is a sign of ignorance* cfum ko maale majjere.

ignorant [ignərənt] *adj.* Majjucfo; humambinne *(o). He is so ignorant* Kooli ko aan majji.

ignore [ignowr] *v.* humpeede; waasde anndude; faalkisaade. *You should ignore him* Potcfaa ko faalkisaade mo.

iguana [igwana] *n.* huttooru *(ndu);* elo *(o).*

ill [il] *adj.* ñawcfo; dafaacfo. *I am ill* Mi sellaani.

ill-bred [ilbred] *adj.* neetaro.

ill-mannered [ilmanəd] *adj.* neetaro.

ill-tempered [iltempəd] *adj.* ñaacfcfo.

illegal [iliygəl] *adj.* ko rewaani laawól. *What you are suggesting is illegal* Miijo maa ngo rewaani laawol.

illegalize [ilygəlayz] *v.* luutndaade laawól.

illegible [ilejəbəl] *adj.* ko jangotaako. *Your handwriting is illegible* Bindi maa njangotaako.

illegitimate [iləjətəmet] *adj.* ko yamiraaka; ko rewaani laawól. *an* ~ *child* mo alaa baaba mum.

illicit [iləsit] *adj.* ko rewaani laawól.

illimitable [iləmitəbəl] *adj.* ko heeraaka/heertaaka.

illiteracy [ilətərəsi] *n.* majjere *(nde);* humambinnaagal *(ngal).*

illiterate [ilətret] *adj.* majjucfo; mo jangaani; humam binne.

illness [ilnes] *n.* ñaw *(o);* rafi *(o).*

illude [iluwd] *v.* fuuntude.

illuminate [iluwməneyt] *v.* jalbinde; fóóynude.

illumination [iluwməneyšən] *n.* póóynugól.

illusion [iluwʒən] *n.* sikke *(o)*; fuunti *(o)*.

illusionary [iluwʒənəri] *adj.* ko faati e sikke.

illusory [iluwsri] *adj.* ko faati e fuunti.

illustrate [ilʌstreyt] *v.* famminde; faccirde. *Let me illustrate this with an example* Mi famminir maa yeru.

illustration [ilʌstreyšən] *n.* yéru *(o)*.

illustrious [ilʌstryəs] *adj.* dówlud̃o.

image [imij] *n.* annama *(o)*; ayaawo *(ngo)*. *I saw his image* Ayaawo makko ari e am.

imagery [imijri] *n.* miijo *(ngo)*.

imaginable [iməjənəbəl] *adj.* ko ina miijee.

imagination [iməjəneyšən] *n.* miijo *(ngo)*. *throw one's* ~ werlaade miijo mum.

imagine [imajin] *v.* miijaade.

imam [imam] *n.* almaami *(o)*. *Who is the imam of the mosque* Hol gond̃o almaami jumaa?

imbalance [imbaləns] *n.* ko fotaani.

imberbe [imbərb] *adj.* nollo.

imbibe [imbayb] *v.* léppinde; mod̃de.

imbrue [imbru] *v.* móddinde.

imitable [imitəbəl] *n.* ñembeteed̃um; ñemtinteed̃um; ko ina ñemboo/ñémtinoo.

imitate [iməteyt] *v.* ñemtinde; ñémmbude.

imitation [iməteyšən] *n.* ñémtingól *(ngól)*.

imitative [imətətiv] *adj.* kó ñémtinta.

immaculate [imakələt] *adj.* laabd̃um; ko laaɓi; ko alaa toɓɓere.

immature [iməčuwr] *adj.* baggo; ko waggid̃i; ko ɓendaani; ko mawnaani.

immeasurable [imeʒrəbəl] *adj.* ko waawaaka hiiseede.

immediate [imiydyət] *adj.* jóóni jóóni; ko yaactii.

immediately [imiydyətli] adv. jooni jooni.

immemorial [iməmoryəl] *adj.* kó ɓénni walla ko yalti miijo; kó ɓóóyi.

immense [imens] *adj.* mawnud̃um; ko mawni.

immerge [imərj] *v.* mutde.

immerse [imərs] *v.* mutnude.

immigrant [imigrənt] *n.* perd̃o *(o)*; arani *(o)*.

immigrate [imigreyt] *v.* ferde.

immigration [imigreyšən] *n.* fergo *(ngo)*.

immobile [imobəl] *adj.* deeỸd̃o; ko dééỸi.

immobility [imobələti] *n.* deeỸre *(nde)*.

immobilize [imowbəlayz] *v.* dééỸnude(yéédnude. *The limb needs to b(immobilized* Ed̃en poti yeednude terga(ngal.

immodest [imodest] *adj.* mo yankinaaki.

immolate [imowleyt] *v.* warde; sakkaade.

immortal [imɔtəl] *adj.* mo maayataa.

immortality [imɔtaləti] *n.* nguurndam ha(abada.

immortalize [imɔtəlayz] *v.* wuurnude ha(abada.

immune [imyuwn] *adj.* tunndud̃o; tuld̃o *He is immune to insults* O wondaak(Ỹettoore.

immunity [imyuwnəti] *n.* tundaram *(d̃am)*.

immunize [imyuwnayz] *v.* tundude; fesde.

immure [imyuwr] *v.* howde; jóókrude ɓale.

imp [imp] *n.* jinnéyél *(ngél)*.

impair [imper] *v.* bónnude.

impalpable [impəlpəbəl] *adj.* m(muusetaake.

impart [impɑt] *v.* rókkude; anndinde(habrude; sarde; jaajnude; janginde.

impartial [impɑšəl] *adj.* peewd̃o; m(jingaani / wuuraaki. *He is impartial* Ko (peewd̃o.

impatient [impeyšənt] *adj.* képpud̃o(muñtorid̃d̃o.

impeach [impyč] *v.* tuumde; fiiltude.

impeccable [impekəbəl] *adj.* ko hawri.

impede [impiyd] *v.* had̃de; lééltinde.

impediment [impedəmənt] *n.* huund(haljinoore; ko haljinta, ko had̃ata.

impel [impel] *v.* nawrude yeeso.

imperceptible [impersəptəbəl] *adj.* k(nanotaako; ko yiyotaako.

imperfect [impərfekt] *adj.* ko wad̃i ella; k(jógii ella.

imperialism [imperyəlizm] *n.* jiimgó(nókkuuji janani; jiimgol leyd̃eele janane.

imperishable [imperišəbəl] *adj.* k(bonataa.

impermeable [impərmiyəbəl] *adj.* k(tud̃ata.

impermissible [impərməsəbəl] *adj.* k(yamiraaka.

impertinent [impərtənənt] *adj.* k(soklaaka.

imperturbable [impərtərbəbəl] *adj* deeỸd̃o.

etus [impətəs] *n.* Υéllitgól *(ngól)*; ɛ́llitaare *(nde)*.

ious [impyəs] *adj.* mo rewaani ómiraaɗo.

lant [implant] *v.* ñiɓde.

lement [impləment] *v.* waɗde; ɛnninde.

lore [implor] *v.* ñaagaade. *I implore u* Mbeɗe ñaagi maa.

olite [impəlayt] *adj.* neetaro; bonɗo hdi.

ort [impɔrt] *v.* naatnude e nder léydi.

ortance [impɔtəns] *n.* nafoore *(nde)*. *hat is the importance of this paper* Hol woni nafooree ngol ɗerewol?

ortant [impɔtənt] *adj.* nafojum; ko fata. *It is a very important factor* Eɗum ewi nafoore no feewi.

orts [imports] *n.* kaake gummiiɗe ggal léydi.

ose [impowz] *v.* waawnude; fawde ugal; yamirde.

osition [impəziyšən] *n.* baawnugól góĺ); lorla *(o)*.

ossible [impɑsəbəl] *adj.* ko wonataa.

ostor [impostə] *n.* gujjo *(o)*.

otent [impətənt] *adj.* maayraaɗo. *He is npotent* Ko o maayraaɗo.

ound [impawnd] *v.* nawde furiyeer.

overish [impavriš] *v.* ñóólnude.

precise [imprəsayz] *adj.* ko yuɓɓaani; ko taani.

pression [imprešən] *n.* ejo *(ngo)*; sikke).

prison [imprizən] *v.* sokde.

prisonment [imprizənmənt] *n.* cókgól góĺ).

probable [imprəbəbəl] *adj.* ko aminaaka; ɗamtindaaɗum.

proper [imprəpə] *adj.* ooñiɗum; ko ewaani; ko rewaani laawal.

propriety [imprəprayəti] *n.* ooñaare nde).

prove [impruv] *v.* móΥΥinde; fééwnitde.

provement [impruvmənt] *n.* móΥΥingól ngól). *It is a major improvement* ɗum uri feewde.

pudence [impyədəns] *n.* neetaraagal ngal).

pudent [impyədənt] *adj.* neetaro.

impure [impyur] *adj.* jilluɗum; ko jilli.

impurity [impyurəti] *n.* tuundi *(ndi)*; soɓe *(o)*.

imputation [impyuwteyšən] *n.* taΥgól *(ngól)*.

in [in] *prep.* heen; e; nder. **in-law** [inlɔ] *n.* esiraaɗo *(o)*. *an ~ relationship* esiraagal *(ngal)*.

inaccessible [inəksesəbəl] *adj.* ko heɓotaako.

inaccurate [inəkəret] *adj.* ko fotaani; ko woodaani. *This is an inaccurate statement* A haalaani goonga.

inadequate [inədəkwit] *adj.* ko feewaani.

inadvertant [inədvərtənt] *adj.* mo waɗtaani hakkille.

inanimate [inənanəmit] *adj.* maayɗum; ko wuuraani.

inapt [inapt] *adj.* lohɗo; mo waawaa; mo hattanaani.

inaptitude [inaptətyud] *n.* lohre *(nde)*; ronkere *(nde)*; donkal *(ngal)*.

inaugurate [inɔgəreyt] *v.* fuɗɗude.

incandesce [iŋkəndes] *v.* jawwude.

incandescence [iŋkəndəsəns] *n.* jawwugól *(ngól)*.

incant [inkənt] *v.* sappaade.

incantation [iŋkənteyšən] *n.* cappagól *(ngól)*; móccugól *(ngól)*.

incapable [iŋkeypəbəl] *adj.* donkuɗo; koriiɗo.

incarcerate [iŋkarsəreyt] *v.* sokde; uddude.

incendiary [insəndyəri] *adj.* ko sumata; cumojum.

incense [insens] *n.* cuuraay *(o)*.

inception [insepšən] *n.* fuɗɗorde *(nde)*.

incessant [insesənt] *adj.* jokkiɗum; duumiɗum; kó jókkii. *~ talk* leɓo *(ngo)*; lemso *(ngo)*.

incinerate [insinəreyt] *v.* huɓɓude.

incise [insayz] *v.* taΥde; jelde.

incision [insiyʒən] *n.* taΥgól *(ngól)*.

incline [iŋklayn] *v.* wuurde; wuuraade. *I am inclined to say no* Mbeɗe anniyii salaade.

include [iŋkluwd] *n.* naatnude; yantinde.

inclusion [iŋkluwʒən] *n.* naatnugól e.

incoherent [iŋkowhiyrənt] *adj.* ko yuɓɓaani. *His speech is incoherent* Haala makko ka yuɓɓaani.

income [iŋkəm] *n.* dañal *(ngal)*; njóɓdi *(ndi)*.

incomer [iŋkəmə] *n.* garoowo *(o)*; garɗo *(o)*.

incoming [iŋkəmiŋ] *adj.* ko fayi arde.

incomparable [iŋkəmperəbəl] *adj.* ko nawdetaake.

incompatible [iŋkəmpatəbəl] *adj.* ko yahdaani; ko yuɓɓaani.

incomplete [iŋkəmpliyt] *adj.* ko ŋakki; ko timmaani; ko joofaani. *This sentence is incomplete* Ngol kongol timmaani.

incompliant [iŋkəmplayənt] *adj.* mo ɗowtaaki.

incomprehensible *adj.* ko faamnaaki.

inconsiderate [iŋkənsədrət] *adj.* mo wondaaka. *He is a very inconsiderate individual* O wondaaka hay dara.

inconvenient [iŋkənviynyənt] *adj.* ko haljinta.

incorrect [iŋkərekt] *adj.* ko feewaani; kó wonaa goonga.

incorrupt [iŋkərʌpt] *adj.* nuunɗuɗo.

increase [iŋkriys] *v.* ɓéydude; ɓéydugól. *Can you please increase the volume* ɓeydu daande nde.

increment [iŋkrəmənt] *n.* ɓeydaari *(ndi)*; beydagól *(ngól)*.

incubate [iŋkyəbeyt] *v.* woofaade.

inculcate [iŋkʌlkeyt] *v.* janginde.

incult [iŋkʌlt] *adj.* mo jangaani; humambinne.

incur [iŋkər] *v.* defaade.

incurable [iŋkərəbəl] *adj.* ko safrotaako.

incursion [iŋkərʒən] *n.* naatgól e.

indebted [indəted] *adj.* ñamliiɗo; dewoowo kaalis.

indecent [indiysənt] *adj.* ko suuraaki.

indeed [indiyd] *adv.* kay; tigi.

indelible [indələbəl] *adj.* ko momtotaako.

indemnify [indəmnəfay] *v.* yoɓde.

indent [indent] *v.* ɓóɓɓude.

independence [indəpendəns] *n.* ndimaagu hooremum.

independent [indəpendənt] *adj.* dimo; mo fawaaki; mo jiimaaka. *Senegal is an independent country* Leydi Senegal jiimaaka.

indescribable *adj.* ko sifotaako; ko ammintaako.

index [indeks] *n.* sappórdu *(ndu)*; jóófórc *(ndu)*.

indicant [indəkənt] *n.* huunde holloore.

indicate [indəkeyt] *v.* aarnude; hóllud jamminde.

indicator [indəkeytər] *n.* kolloowo *(o* huunde holloore.

indict [indayt] *v.* felde; fawde kuugal. *I. was indicted today* Kuugal fawaama makko hannde.

indictment [indaytmənt] *n.* feloore *(nde* kuugal *(ngal)*.

indifferent [indifrənt] *adj.* mo wondaaka.

indigent [indəjənt] *adj.* ñoolaaɗo.

indigestible [indəjəst] *adj.* ko dolotaako.

indigo [indəgo] *n.* bóru *(ngu)*.

indiscipline [indəsəplin] *n.* neetaraag *(ngal)*.

indiscrete [indiskriyt] *adj.* beejɗo.

indispensable [indəspensəbəl] *adj.* k hatojinaa; ko soklaa.

indistinct [indistiŋkt] *adj.* ko laaɓaani.

individual [indəviyjəl] *n.* neɗɗo *(o)*.

individual [indəviyjəl] *adj.* ko faati neɗɗo.

individually [indəviyjəli] *n.* neɗɗo kala.

indivisible [indivizəbəl] *adj.* ko feccotaakc

indocile [indowsayl] *adj.* ko/mo/n eeltaaka.

indoor [indɔr] *adj.* nder.

indubitable [indyuwbətəbəl] *adj.* ko ala sikke.

induce [indyuws] *v.* waawnude; waɗnude.

indulge [indʌlj] *v.* waɗde.

indulgent [indʌljənt] *adj.* jaafotooɗo.

indurate [indyuwreyt] *v.* tékkinde.

industrial [indʌstriyəl] *adj.* ko faati mbaylaandi.

industrious [indʌstriyəs] *adj.* cuusd liggééy.

industry [indʌstri] *n.* mbaylaandi *(ndi)*.

inedible [inedəbəl] *adj.* ko ñaametaake.

ineffable [inefəbəl] *adj.* ko sifotaako; k haalotaako.

inept [inept] *adj.* dónkuɗo; leefɗo.

inequitable [inekwitəbəl] *adj.* ko fotaani.

inert [inərt] *adj.* ko maayi; ko dillataa.

inestimable [inestiməbəl] *adj.* k hiisetaake.

evitable [inevitəbəl] *adj.* ko woorataa.

exact [inegzakt] *adj.* ko hawraani/fotaani.

existent [inegziztənt] *adj.* ko woodaani.

expensive [inekspənsiv] *adj.* ko tiidaani.

explicit [inekspləsit] *adj.* ko leeraani.

famous [infəməs] *adj.* bondo.

fancy [infənsi] *n.* cukaagu *(ngu).*

fant [infənt] *n.* suka *(o);* kurka *(o).*

fanticide [infəntəsayd] *n.* warngo ʃuka/sukaaɓe.

fantile [infəntayl] *adj.* ko faati e cukaagu.

fect [infekt] *v.* ñawnude; raaɓde.

fected [infektəd] *adj.* ñawdum; ɟordudum.

fection [infekʃən] *n.* ñaw *(ngu).*

fecund [infekʌnd] *adj.* dimaro; rimare.

fer [infər] *v.* miijaade; sikkude; faamde. *I infer from that he is not feeling well* Paammi e majjum ko o wonaa celludo.

ference [infərəns] *n.* miijo *(ngo);* sikke *(o).*

ferior [infiyryə] *adj.* ko ɓuri lésdude.

fernal [infərnəl] *adj.* bondum; kó bóni; ko faati é jéyngól.

fertile [infərtəl] *adj.* dimaro.

fidel [infədəl] *n.* keefeero *(o);* neddo mo rewaani jóómiraado.

filtrate [infəltreyt] *v.* naatde.

finite [infənit] *adj.* ko alaa kééról walla happu.

firm [infərm] *adj.* ñosdo; mo doolnaani; leefdo; laYoowo.

flame [infleym] *v.* huɓɓude; jawwude.

flammable [inflaməbəl] *adj.* ko huɓɓata.

flammation [infləmeyʃən] *n.* ɓuutdi *(ndi).*

flate [infleyt] *v.* tullinde; wuttude.

flated [infleytəd] *adj.* guttadum; tullinaadum.

flexible [infləksibəl] *adj.* ko hofotaako; mo wuurotaako.

flict [inflikt] *v.* wadde.

fluence [influwəns] *v.* yiinude; wadnude. *He is under the influence of alcohol* Ko o jardo /Ko o cirwudo/Ko o mandildo.

form [infɔrm] *v.* tintinde; habrude; humpitde; daawnude; haalande. *I want to inform you that he arrived safely* Mbede yidi andinde ma wonde o yettii ma e dow jam e cellal.

informant [infɔmənt] *n.* kaaloowo *(o);* gandinoowo *(o);* kabroowo *(o).*

information [infɔmeyʃən] *n.* kabaaru *(o).*

informed [infɔmd] *adj.* kumpitiido.

informer [infɔmə] *n.* kabroowo *(o).*

infraction [infrəkʃən] *n.* tooñange *(nge).*

infringe [infrinj] *v.* tooñde.

infuriate [infyuwreyt] *v.* séknude.

infuse [infyuwz] *v.* naatnude; yuppude.

infusion [infyuwʒən] *n.* naatnugól *(ngól);* juppugól *(ngól).*

ingenious [injiynyəs] *adj.* YoYdo.

ingenuity [injənwiti] *n.* YoYre *(nde).*

ingest [injest] *v.* modde.

ingrate [iŋgreyt] *adj.* mo alaa wune.

ingress [iŋgres] *n.* naatnugól *(ngól).*

ingurgitate [iŋgərjəteyt] *v.* alɓaade; modde.

inhabit [inhabit] *v.* hodde.

inhabitant [inhabitənt] *adj.* koddo. *~s of ɓoghe* ɓoggeenaaɓe.

inhale [inheyl] *v.* naatnude foofaango; sórɓinaade.

inherent [inhiyrənt] *adj.* gooddum; ko wóódi e.

inherit [inherit] *v.* ronde. *I inherited my share* Mi ronii gedalaam.

inheritable [inheritəbəl] *adj.* doneteedum; ko ronetee.

inheritance [inheritəns] *n.* ndónu *(ngu).*

inheritor [inherətə] *n.* donoowo *(o);* donor *(o).*

inhibit [inhibit] *v.* hadde.

inhume [ihyuwm] *v.* ubbude.

iniquity [inəkwiti] *n.* tooñange *(nge).*

initial [iniyʃəl] *adj.* ko faati e fuddorde. *My initial reaction was not good* Miijo am adano ngo moYYaano.

initiate [iniyʃeyt] *v.* fuddude; hasde.

inject [injekt] *v.* pingude; naatnude.

injure [injə] *v.* gaañde. *He was injured in the accident* O gaañii ko e aksidaa o.

injurious [injəryəs] *adj.* gaañojum; ko gaañata.

injury [injəri] *n.* gaañande *(nde).*

injustice [injʌstəs] *n.* ooñaare *(nde).*

ink [iŋk] *n.* dahaa *(o).*

inky [iŋki] *adj.* ko ɓawli.

inlet [inlet] *n.* naatirde *(nde).*

inmate [inmeyt] *n.* góndiiɗo e suudu.

inn [in] *n.* jipporde *(nde).*

innate [ineyt] *adj.* ko neɗɗo jibidinaa e mum.

inner [inə] *adj.* nder.

innocent [inəsənt] *adj.* laabɗo; mo tooñaani.

innominate [inamənət] *adj.* ko/mo alaa innde.

innovate [inəveyt] *v.* waylude; fuɗɗude; sosde.

innovation [inəveyšən] *n.* cosgol *(ngól).*

innumerable [inʌmrəbəl] *adj.* kó hééwi; kééwɗum; ko limotaako.

inoculate [inowkyuwleyt] *v.* fesde; naatnude e.

input [imput] *v.* naatnude.

input [imput] *n.* miijo *(ngo).*

inquietude [inkyetud] *n.* sokla *(o).*

inquire [iŋkwayə] *v.* lamndaade; lóskude; wittude. *I am inquiring about your past* Ngon mi ko e wittude hanki ma.

inquiry [iŋkwəri] *n.* lamndal *(ngal);* witto *(ngo).*

inquisition [iŋkwəziyšən] *n.* lamndal *(ngal);* witto *(ngo).*

inquisitive [iŋkwəzətiv] *adj.* loskoowo *(o). You are very inquisitive* Aɗa waawi loskude.

insane [inseyn] *adj.* kaangaaɗo.

insanity [insanəti] *n.* kaaɗi *(ɗi).*

insatiable [inseyšəbəl] *adj.* mo/ko haarataa.

inscribe [inskrayb] *v.* windude.

inscription [inskrəpšən] *n.* bindól *(ngól).*

inseminate [insəmineyt] *v.* aawde.

insert [insərt] *v.* bilde e nder; naatnude e. *Insert it between the doors* bilɗum e hakkunde dame ɗe.

inside [insayd] nder.

insider [insaydə] *n.* neɗɗo gonɗo e nder.

insinuate [insənyweyt] *v.* baagaade.

insipid [insipəd] *adj.* tékum.

insist [insist] *v.* téélŋtinde.

insistence [insəstəns] *n.* téélŋtingól *(ngól).*

insolence [insələns] *n.* bonehdagaal *(ngal);* neetaraagal *(ngal).*

insolate [insəleyt] *v.* saaɗnude; saaɗnaade.

insoluble [insoləbəl] *adj.* ko saayataa.

insomniac [insəmnyak] *adj.* dónkuɗo ɗaanaade.

insouciant [insusyənt] *adj.* mo wondaaka.

inspect [inspekt] *v.* Ƴeewtaade; yuurnitaade.

inspection [inspekšən] *n.* juurnitaagol *(ngól). upon closer* ~ nde njuurnitii mi.

inspector [inspektə] *n.* juurnittooɗo *(o).*

inspire [inspayə] *v.* naatnude foofaango.

install [instɔl] *v.* fawde.

instance [instəns] *n.* yéru. *for* ~ yeru.

instant [instənt] *n.* sahaa *(o);* saanga *(o).*

instantly [instəntli] adv. ɗoon e ɗoon

instigate [instəgeyt] *v.* urbude.

instigator [instəgeytə] *n.* urboowo *(o);* puɗɗuɗo.

institute [instətyuwt] *v.* waɗde; mahde.

instruct [instrʌkt] *v.* janginde.

instruction [instrʌkšən] *n.* jangde *(nde).*

instructor [instrʌktə] *n.* janginoowo *(o);* ékkinoowo *(o)*

insufficiency [insəfiyšənsi] *n.* ŋakkere *(nde).*

insufficient [insəfiyšənt] *adj.* ŋakkuɗum; ko ŋakki.

insult [insʌlt] *n.* Ƴettoore *(nde).*

insult [insʌlt] *v.* Ƴettaade.

insupportable [insəpɔtəbəl] *adj.* ko muñotaako.

insurmountable *adj.* huunde nde bennotaako.

insurrection [insərekšən] *n.* murtugól *(ngól).*

intact [intakt] *adj.* ko waylaaki. *The building is intact* Hubeere nde waylaaki hay dara.

integer [intəjə] *n.* limoore *(nde).*

integrate [intəgreyt] *v.* réndinde; naatnude e.

integrity [intəgriti] *n.* nuunɗal *(ngal).*

integument [intəgyəmənt] *n.* nguru *(ngu).*

intelligence [intəlijəns] *n.* ƳoƳre *(nde)* karallaagal *(ngal);* seebre *(nde).*

intelligent [intəlijənt] *adj.* ƳoƳɗo; peerɗo pesiiɗo. *He is very intelligent* O mo feert no feewi.

intelligible [intəlijəbəl] *adj.* ko faamotoo ko faamnii.

intend [intend] *v.* fibde; anniyaade. *I intend to finish the work today* Mbeɗe anniyi gasnude golle ɗe hande.

intensify [intensəfay] *v.* téélŋtinde.

tent [intent] *n.* anniyya *(o)*; fiɓre *(nde)*.

tention [intenšən] *n.* anniyya *(o)*; fiɓre *nde)*.

tentional [intənšənəl] *adj.* ko anniyaa; ko aati e anniya.

teract [interakt] *v.* yeewnude.

tercalate [interkəleyt] *v.* ɓilde.

tercede [intersiyd] *v.* maslude; wéltinde.

tercept [intersept] *v.* heɓɓaade; faddaade.

terchange [interčeynj] *n.* góstóndiral *ngal)*.

terchange [interčeynj] *v.* wóstóndirde; ʋóstóndireede.

terconnect [intəkənekt] *v.* jókkóndirde; eŋondirde.

tercourse [intəkɔs] *n.* jiindiral *(ngal)*.

terdict [intədikt] *v.* haɗde.

terdiction [intədikšən] *n.* haɗnde *(nde)*; uunde haɗaande.

terfere [intərfiyə] *v.* naatde e ko wonaa aaju mum; haɗde.

terim [intərəm] *n.* lomto *(o)*; mudda *(o)*.

terior [intiyryə] *n.* nder.

terlocutor [intələkutə] *n.* kaaldiiɗo *(o)*; :aaldeteeɗo *(o)*.

termarriage [intəmarij] *n.* dewgal akkunde léƳƳi.

termediary [intəmiydyəri] *n.* akkundeejo *(o)*.

terminable [intərminəbəl] *adj.* ko ;asataa.

termingle [intəmiŋgəl] *v.* naatóndirde.

termit [intərmit] *v.* dartinde.

ternal [intərnəl] *adj.* kó wóni nder. ~ *ffairs* golle nder leydi.

ternational [intənašənəl] *adj.* hakkunde eyɗeele.

ternee [intərniy] *n.* jaggaaɗo *(o)*; :okaaɗo *(o)*.

terpersonal [intəpərsənəl] *adj.* hakkunde ʼimɓe.

terpose [intərpowz] *v.* ɓilde.

terpret [intərprit] *v.* firde; nantinde; accirde.

terpreter [intərpritə] *n.* piroowo *(o)*; antinoowo *(o)*.

terracial [intəreyšəl] *adj.* hakkunde éƳƳi.

terrelate [intəriyleyt] *v.* naatondirde; aatnaattóndirde.

interrelation [intərəleyšən] *n.* naatondiral *(ngal)*; naatnaattóndiral *(ngal)*.

interrogate [intərəgeyt] *v.* lamndaade.

interrogation [intərəgeyšən] *n.* lamndagól.

interrogator [intərəgeytə] *n.* lamndotooɗo.

interrupt [intərʌpt] *v.* héɓɓitaade; feraade haala. *I do not mean to interrupt you* Wonaa feraade haala maa.

interruption [intərʌpšən] *n.* peragol haala; kéɓɓitaagól *(ngól)*.

intersect [intəsekt] *v.* yantóndirde; hawrude.

interspace [intəspeys] *n.* yelde *(nde)*; ŋalde *(nde)*.

interval [intəvɔl] *n.* yolnde *(nde)*.

intervene [intəviyn] *v.* maʔaade; lombaade. *He intervened to stop the fight* O lombii hakkunde maɓɓe.

interview [intəvyuw] *n.* kaaldigal *(ngal)*.

interview [intəvyuw] *v.* haaldude e.

interviewee [intəvyuwiy] *n.* lamndeteeɗo *(o)*.

interviewer [intəvyuwə] *n.* lamndotooɗo *(o)*.

interweave [intəwiyv] *v.* sañóndirde.

intestinal [intəstinəl] *adj.* ko faati é téktékól.

intestine [intəstin] *n.* téktékól *(ngól)*.

intimidate [intimədeyt] *v.* hulɓinde.

into [intu] *prep.* nder.

intolerable [intələrəbəl] *adj.* ko muñotaako.

intolerant [intələrənt] *adj.* looɓɗo; mo muñataa.

intort [intɔt] *v.* haaƳde.

intractable [intraktəbəl] *adj.* ŋatɗo.

intransigent [intrənzijənt] *adj.* mo hofotaako.

intravenous [intrəviynəs] *adj.* nder ɗaɗól.

intricate [intrəkət] *adj.* kó jikkóndiri.

intrigue [intriyg] *n.* sirru *(o)*.

intrinsic [intrənsik] *adj.* ko jeyaa e huunde.

introduce [intrədyuws] *v.* naatnude; hóllondirde. ~ *oneself* innitaade.

introduction [intrədʌkšən] *n.* kóllóndiral *(ngal)*.

introductory [intrədʌktri] *adj.* ko faati e puɗɗagól.

introspect [intrəspekt] *v.* Ƴeewde e nder mum.

intrude [intruwd] *v.* naatde e ko wonaa ko mum. *You are intruding* Aɗan naata eko wonaa ko maa.

inundate [inʌndeyt] *v.* waamde.

inure [inyuwr] *v.* tékkinde.

invade [inveyd] *v.* naatde; hébtude nókku janano. *They invaded his house* be naati e galle makko.

invaginate [invəjəneyt] *v.* naatnude e nder wana.

invalid [invalid] *adj.* 1) laƳoowo; boofo 2) ko feewaani.

invaluable [invalyəbəl] *adj.* kó hééwi nafoore.

invariable [invəryəbəl] *adj.* ko waylotaako

invasion [inveyʒən] *n.* naatgól *(ngól)*.

invective [invektiv] *n.* Ƴettoore *(nde)*; tooñange *(nge)*.

invent [invent] *v.* fuɗɗude; sosde.

inventor [inventə] *n.* puɗɗuɗo *(o)*; cosɗo *(o)*.

inverse [invərs] *adj.* kó hippii.

invert [invərt] *v.* hippude.

investigate [invəstigeyt] *v.* wittude.

investigation[invəstigeyšən] *n.* witto *(ngo)*.

inveterate [invətərət] *v.* dóólnuɗo e huunde.

invigorate [invigəreyt] *v.* tékkinde; sémbinde.

invincible [invinsəbəl] *adj.* mo fooletaake.

invisible [invəzəbəl] *adj.* ko/mo yiyotaako.

invocate [invəkeyt] *v.* ñaagaade.

invocation [invəkeyšən] *n.* ñaagunde *(nde)*.

invoke [invowk] *v.* ñaagaade.

involve [involv] *v.* naatnude; réndinde. *I am not involved in that project* Mi alaa heen.

invulnerable [invəlnərəbəl] *adj.* ko tundi.

inward [inwəd] *adj.* nder.

inwardly [inɔdli] *adv.* ko faati e nder.

irascible [irasəbəl] *adj.* loobɗo.

irate [ayreyt] *adj.* pilñitiiɗo; pinnuɗo; cekɗo.

irenic [ayriynik] *adj.* ko faati e deeƳre.

iritis [ayraytəs] *n.* ñaw gite; gite gójjuɗe.

irk [ərk] *v.* séknude; haabnude.

irksome [ərksʌm] *adj.* kaabniɗum; kaabniiɗo.

iron [ayrən] *v.* paasde.

iron [ayrən] *n.* 1) feer *(o)*; tappirgal *(ngal* tappirde *(nde)* 2) njamndi *(ndi)*. *The iro is hot* Feer o wulii   **ironer** [ayrənə] ʋ paasoowo *(o)*.

irradiate [iradyeyt] *v.* jalbinde; fóóynude.

irrecoverable [irəkəvrəbəl] *adj.* k hebtotaako; ko yalti ñaamɗe.

irreducible [irədyuwsəbəl] *adj.* k ustotaako.

irregular [iregilə] *adj.* ko luutndii.

irreligious [irəliyjəs] *adj.* ko/mo rewaar diine.

irreparable [irepərəbəl] *adj.* k fééwnittaako.

irreplaceable [iriypleysəbəl] *adj.* k lomtetaake.

irresolute [irəzolyuwt] *adj.* mo wakkilaaki.

irreversible [irivərsibəl] *adj.* k waylotaako.

irrigate [irəgeyt] *v.* naatnude ndiyam.

irrigation [irəgeyšən] *n.* naatnugól ndiyam.

irritable [iritəbəl] *adj.* loobɗo.

irritate [irəteyt] *v.* séknude.

irruption [irʌpšən] *n.* puccitaagól *(ngól)* puɗgol *(ngól)*.

is [iz] *v.* wóni; wóódi.

Islam [izlam] *n.* lislaam *(o)*. *I believe i Islam* Mbeɗe goongɗini diine Islam.

island [aylənd] *n.* duunde *(nde)*; jubard *(nde)*; dujal *(ngal)*.

islander [ayləndə] *n.* koɗɗo e duunde.

islet [aylət] *n.* duunde tokosere.

isolate [aysəleyt] *v.* ambude; séérndude.

issue [išyuw] *v.* yaltinde.

it [it] *pron.* ɗum; huunde *(nde)*. *Give it t him* Rokku mo ɗum.

itch [ič] *n.* miiro *(ngo)*; feɗɗo *(ngo)*.

itch [ič] *v.* miirde; feɗɗude; feɗɗeede ŋatde. *My hand is itching* Jungam ng ina ŋata.

itchy [iči] *adj.* ko ŋati.

iterate [itəreyt] *v.* reftaade.

itinerary [aytinərəri] *n.* laawól *(ngól)*.

its [its] *det.* ko mum; ko muuɗum.

itself [itself] *pron.* hoore mayre.

J

b [jab] *v.* Yobbude; gobbude.

bber [jabə] *n.* haala njaawka.

ck [jak] *n.* suutirde *(nde)*.

ckal [jakəl] *n.* bóy *(o)*.

cket [jaket] *n.* cómcól *(ngól)*.

cob [jeykəb] *n.* yaaquub; annabi yaaquub.

cquerie [jakri] *n.* murtugól *(ngól)*.

dder [jadə] *n.* keloowo kaaYe.

g [jag] *v.* yiwde; taYde.

il [jeyl] *n.* kasó *(o)*. *He is in jail* ko o okaado.

iler [jeylə] *n.* deenoowo kasó.

ilhouse [jeylhaws] *n.* kasó *(o)*.

m [jam] *v.* duñde.

maica [jəmeykə] *n.* jamayik.

mboree [jambəriy] *n.* deental sukaab e.

mpack [jampak] *v.* hébbinde haa heewa.

ngle [jaŋgəl] *v.* siŊlude.

nitor [janətə] *n.* gorko deenoowo nókku. *Where is the janitor* Hol to deenoowo o woni?

nitress [janətres] *n.* debbo deenoowo nókku.

nuary [janəri] *n.* saawiye *(o)*.

pe [jeyp] *v.* gaajaade.

r [jar] *v.* dillude.

unt [jɔnt] *v.* dannaade dangal dabbal.

velin [javəlin] *n.* mbaangu *(ngu)*.

w [jɔ] *n.* golgolal *(ngal)*; gabgal *(ngal)*.

alous [jiyləs] *adj.* kirdo. *He is jealous* Ko o kirdo.

alousy [jiyləsi] *n.* kiram *(dam)*.

ep [jiyp] *n.* oto.

er [jiyə] *v.* seknoraade.

erer [jiyrə] *n.* ceknortoodo *(o)*.

l [jel] *v.* fendaade.

remiad [jerəmyad] *n.* gullitaagól *(ngól)*.

rk [jərk] *v.* rippude; diwde e doYYaade.

ss [jes] *v.* tóngude.

st [jest] *v.* gaajaade.

st [jest] *n.* gaajaare *(nde)*.

sus [jiyzəs] *n.* annabi Iisaa.

tliner [jetlaynə] *n.* ndiwoowa *(ka)*.

tport [jetport] *n.* kandaa abiyoŊ.

w [juw] *n.* yahuudiyanke.

jewel [juwəl] *n.* cudaari *(ndi)*.

jeweler [juwələ] *n.* baylo *(o)*.

jib [jib] *v.* turaade; lééltinde.

jibe [jayb] *v.* hawrude.

jigger [jigə] *n.* gamoowo *(o)*.

jiggle [jigəl] *v.* jumpude; diwde ina doYYoo.

jihad [jihad] *n.* péllugól diine.

jimp [jimp] *adj.* cewdum; kó séwi.

jingle [jiŋgəl] *v.* séŊlude; siŊlude. *~ bell* hulnde.

jinn [jin] *n.* jinné *(o)*.

jinx [jiŋks] *n.* kiitaado.

jitter [jitə] *n.* kulól *(ngól)*.

job [job] *n.* liggééy *(o)*; gollal *(ngal)*. *~ holder* jom liggééy. *I am looking for a job* Ko mi ndaaroowo liggeey.

jobless [jobles] *adj.* mo alaa liggééy.

jockey [jokiy] *n.* dognoowo puccu.

jocose [jowkowz] *adj.* jalnidum; ko jalnii.

jocund [jowkənd] *adj.* béltiido.

jocundity [jowkəndəti] *n.* weltaare *(nde)*.

jog [jog] *v.* dogde. *Jogging is good for you* Dogdu ina moYYi e maa.

joggle [jogəl] *v.* dillinde.

join [joyn] *v.* seŊondirde; seŊde; jókkóndirde. *Let us join forces* Njantondiren.

joinder [joyndə] *n.* céŊóndiral *(ngal)*.

joined [joynd] *adj.* ko seŊondiraa.

joiner [joynə] *n.* minisé *(o)*; labbo *(o)*.

joint [joynt] *n.* jokkere *(nde)*; jokkorde *(nde)*.

joke [jowk] *n.* gaajondiral *(ngal)*; gaajaare *(nde)*.

joke [jowk] *v.* gaajaade. *~ around* lamminde. *~ with* siidaade. *He is joking* O woni ko e gaajaade.

joker [jowkə] *n.* gaajotoodo *(o)*.

jolly [joli] *adj.* béltiido.

jolt [jolt] *v.* dillinde.

jostle [josəl] *v.* felmaade.

jot [jot] *v.* windude. *Jot the sentence down* Windu kongol ngol.

jotter [jotə] *n.* bindoowo *(o)*.

jounce [jowns] *v.* diwde ina doYYoo.

191

journey [jərni] *v.* ɗangal (ngal.) *Have a safe journey* yo Alla waɗ jaanje.

jovial [jowvyəl] *adj.* belɗo ƔiiƔam.

joviality [jowvyəlti] *n.* bélgól ƔiiƔam.

joy [joy] *n.* welamma *(o)*; weltaare *(nde)*.

joyful [joyfəl] *adj.* béltiiɗo.

joyless [joyles] *adj.* mo weltaaki.

joyous [joyəs] *adj.* béltiiɗo.

jubilant [juwbilənt] *adj.* béltiiɗo.

jubilate [juwbəleyt] *v.* weltaade.

jubilation [juwbəleyšən] *n.* weltaare *(nde)*.

judge [jʌj] *n.* ñaawoowo *(o)*.

judge [jʌj] *v.* ñaawde.

judgement [jʌjmənt] *n.* ñaawoore *(nde)*.

judicature [juwdikəčur] *n.* ñaawoore *(nde)*.

judicial [juwdiyšəl] *adj.* ko faati e ñaawoore.

judiciary [juwdiyšəri] *adj.* ko faati e ñaawoore.

judicious [juwdiyšəs] *adj.* peewɗo.

judo [juwdow] *n.* sippiro *(ngo)*.

juggle [jʌgəl] *v.* tebbaade.

juggler [jʌglə] *n.* tebbotooɗo.

jugglery [jʌgləri] *n.* tebbagól *(ngól)*.

jugulate [juwgyəleyt] *v.* warde.

juice [juws] *n.* ndiyam bingél leɗɗe.

jujube *n.* [juwjub] yaabre *(nde)*.

jumble [jʌmbəl] *v.* réndinde.

jump [jʌmp] *n.* diwal *(ngal)*; diwgól *(ngól)* *high* ~ diwal dow.

jump [jʌmp] *v.* diwde. ~ *in* bed dimbaade. ~ *over* taɗɗude. ~ *down* sirpaade. ~ *around* folde; diwde inɑ doƔƔoo.

jumper [jʌmpə] *n.* diwoowo *(o)*.

jumping [jʌmpiŋ] *n.* diwgol *(ngól)*; diwa *(ngal)*.

junction [jʌŋkšən] *n.* déndingól *(ngól)* salnde *(nde)*.

jungle [jʌŋgəl] *n.* ladde tuulaa heelaa.

junior [juwnyə] *n.* suka *(o)*.

junk [jʌŋk] *n.* kurjuru *(o)*.

jural [juwrəl] *adj.* ko faati ñaawoore/laawól.

jurisprudence [juwrisprudəns] *n* ñaawoore *(nde)*; laawól *(ngól)*; luwaa *(o)*.

jurist [juwrist] *n.* ñaawoowo *(o)*.

just [jʌst] *adj.* peewɗo.

justice [jʌstis] *n.* ñaawoore goonga.

justification [jʌstifəkeyšən] *n.* sabaabu *(o)*.

justify [jʌstəfay] *v.* sabóbinde.

juvenile [juwvənayl] *adj.* ko faati suka/sukaabe.

K

aba [kɑbə] *n.* kaaba *(ka)*.
bob [kabəb] *n.* taˠatine tééw.
f [kaf] *n.* alkulal Aarabeere.
aftan [kaftən] *n.* kaftaan.
akapo [kakəpo] *n.* sóndu.
olin [kalin] *n.* ɓakkere raneere.
arat [karət] *n.* ɓétirde kaŋŋe; ɓetirde amaa.
atamorphism [katəmorfizm] *n.* baylagól *(ngól)*.
eel [kiyl] *n.* ñaw kankaleewal.
een [kiyn] *adj.* kó wéli; belɗum.
eep [kiyp] *v.* mooftude. ~ *a secret* usrude; mooftude sirru. ~ *one's word* reende kongol mum; heddaade e kongol mum. *Keep the noise down* Ustee dille.
eeper [kiypə] *n.* mooftoowo *(o)*. *house* ~ deenoowo galle.
eg [keg] *n.* barigal tokasal.
elt [kelt] *n.* jiiba *(o)*.
epi [kepi] *n.* laafa *(ka)*.
ernel [kərnəl] *n.* aaludere *(nde)*.
erchief [kərčəf] *n.* misooro *(o)*.
erosene [kerowsin] *n.* karsin
etch-up [kečʌp] *n.* soos *(o)*.
ettledrum [ketəldrʌm] *n.* tabalde *(nde)*.
ettle [ketəl] *v.* satalla *(ka)*.
ey [kiy] *n.* coktirgal *(ngal)*. ~ *to success* maale ˠellitaagol.
eynote [kiynowt] *n.* qiimaa *(o)*.
ibble [kibəl] *v.* unde; lóññude; féccude.
ick [kik] *v.* dampude; féttude. ~ *accidentally* feraade. *Kick the ball* Fettu bal o.
icking [kikiŋ] *n.* dampugol *(ngól)*.
ickoff [kikəf] *n.* puɗɗagól *(ngól)*.
id [kid] *n.* boobo *(o)*; suka *(o)*.
id [kid] *v.* gaajaade. *I am just kidding* Ngonmi ko e gaajaade.
iddy [kidi] *n.* suka *(o)*.
idnap [kidnap] *v.* diftaade; saaynaade; suuɗde.
idney [kidniy] *n.* ɓooˠere *(nde)*.
ill [kil] *v.* warde. ~ *lice* fuˠde.
iller [kilə] *n.* baroowo *(o)*.

killing [kiliŋ] *n.* warngo *(ngo)*; war hoore.
kilogram [kiləgram] *n.* cilo *(o)*. *two ~s* cilooji ɗiɗi.
kilo [kilow] *n.* cilo *(o)*.
kilometer [kilowmitə] *n.* ujunere meeteer.
kin [kin] *n.* bandiraaɗo *(o)*.
kind kaynd] *adj.* lobbo; néwiiɗo. *He is very kind* ko o neɗɗo moˠˠo/newiiɗo.
kind [kaynd] *n.* sifaa *(o)*. *what* ~ hol sifaa.
kindly [kayndli] (adv) ko faati e moˠˠere.
kindness [kayndnes] *n.* newaare *(nde)*; moˠˠere *(nde)*.
kindle [kindəl] *v.* hubɓude.
kindling [kindliŋ] *adj.* ko yaawi hubɓude. ~ *wood* camalle.
kinfolk [kinfɔk] *n.* bandiraaɓe *(ɓe)*; koreeji *(ɗi)* **king** [kiŋ] *n.* laamɗo *(o)*; buur *(o)*; laamiiɗo *(o)*. *He is the king* ko kanko laamii; ko kanko woni laamɗo.
kingdom [kiŋdəm] *n.* laamu *(ngu)*.
kingfisher [kiŋfišə] *n.* hammayeroyél *(ngél)*.
kinsfolk [kinsfɔk] *n.* kórééji *(ɗi)*; banndiraaɓe (be).
kinship [kinšip] *n.* jiidigal *(ngal)*; bandiraagal *(ngal)*.
kiss [kis] *n.* ɓuucagol *(ngól)*
kiss [kis] *v.* ɓuucaade. ~ *each other* ɓuucondirde.
kitchen [kičən] *n.* waañ *(o)*. *in the* ~ nder waañ.
kite [kayt] *n.* ciilal *(ngal)*.
kitten [kitən] *n.* ullungél *(ngél)*.
kittle [kitəl] *v.* ˠóbɓude.
kleptomaniac [kleptowmenyək] *n.* gujél *(ngél)*; mo jeyaa jungo mum.
knave [neyv] *n.* neɗɗo mo nuunɗaani.
knead [niyd] *v.* jiiɓde.
knee [niy] *n.* hofru *(ndu)*. *Down on your knees* Dicco.
kneecap [niykap] *n.* tumude hófru.
kneel [niyl] *v.* diccaade; ñoynaade. ~ *down* tukkaade; ˠukkaade.
kneeling [niyliŋ] *n.* diccande *(nde)*.
knife [nayf] *n.* laɓi *(ki)*
knit [nit] *v.* sañde.
knitting [nitiŋ] *n.* cañu *(ngu)*.

knock [nok] *v.* hongude. ~ *fruit off trees* sammude. ~ *down* sammude; óⲅⲅude.
knock-kneed [nokniyd] *adj.* molfo.
knot [not] *n.* piɓol *(ngól)*; jokkere *(nde)*; jokkande *(nde)*; fiɓre *(nde)*; wulnde *(nde)*. *tie the* ~ haɓɓude; fiɓde; humande.
know [now] *v.* andude. ~ *about someone* andande. *I know him* Mbeɗe anndi mo.
knowable [nowəbəl] *adj.* ko andotoo.

knowledge [nowlej] *n.* gandal *(ngal)*. *to my* ~ e gandalam **knowledgeable** [nowlejəbəl] *adj.* gando.
known [nown] *adj.* dowluɗo; gandaaɗo. *well* ~ darjuɗo; lólluɗo.
knuckle [nʌkəl] *n.* jokkere *(nde)*.
kob [kɔb] *n.* lella (ba).
kola nut [kowlənʌt] *n.* goro *(ko)*.
Koran [kowran] *n.* quraan *(o)*.
kowtow [kowtow] *v.* fiide tiinde é léydi.

L

ager [lɑgə] n. jippunde (nde).

bor [leybə] v. liggaade; gollade.

bor [leybə] n. liggééy (o); gollal (ngal). manual ~ liggeey jungo.

borer [leybərə] n. liggotoodo (o); gollotoodo (o).

brum [leybrəm] n. tóndu (ndu).

ce [leys] n. bóggól pade.

cerate [lasəreyt] v. taⲅde.

ceration [lasəreyšən] n. taⲅgól (ngól).

ck [lak] n. hokkere (nde); donkal (ngal); baasal (ngal).

ck [lak] v. hókkude; waasde; mankude. ~ water soofñde; hókkude. ~ clothing holde.

conic [ləkonik] adj. dabbiddum; ko rabbidi.

cuna [ləkyuwnə] n. ŋakkugól (ngól).

d [lad] n. suka gorko; surga (o).

dder [ladə] n. ⲅééŋirde (nde); seel (o); ⲅeeŋirgal (ngal).

de [leyd] v. fawde; rimndude.

dle [ladəl] n. kuddu luus; kuundal (ngal).

dy [leydi] n. sokna (o); debbo (o). ladies and gentlemen rewbe e worbe.

g [lag] v. ruudde; bodde; leelde.

ggard [lagəd] adj. leeldo.

goon [laguwn] n. teeyteeyngal (ngal).

ir [leyə] n. lowol (ngól).

ke [leyk] n. teeyteeyngal (ngal); deedal (ngal).

m [lam] v. fiide.

mb [lam] n. 1) mbaalu (ngu); dammuhol (ngól) 2) teew dammuhol.

mbda [lamdə] n. alkulal (ngal).

me [leym] adj. laⲅoowo. walk ~ laⲅde.

ament [ləment] v. woytaade; ⲅerde; sunaade; woyde.

ament [ləment] n. uumaango (ngo); ŋuslere (nde); goytagol (ngol.

aminate [laməneyt] v. séérndude.

amp [lamp] n. lampa (ka).

ance [lans] n. deⲏⲏere (nde); baawal (ngal).

ance [lans] v. yiwde.

and [land] n. léydi (ndi). make ~ teerde; joofde.

andless [landles] adj. mo alaa léydi.

landmark [lanmɑk] n. kééról (ngól).

landslide[lanslayd] n. jooragól leydi; dirtugól léydi.

language [laŋgwij] n. demngal (ngal). Fula ~ s demngal Fulfulde; Fulfulde.

languid [laŋgwid] adj. lohdo; leefdo.

languish[laŋgwiš] v. lohde; leefde; lééfdude.

lank [laŋk] adj. pooⲅdo.

lantern [lantərn] n. lampa (ka).

lap [lap] v. mettaade.

lapidate [lapədeyt] n. wardude kaaⲅe.

lapse [laps] n. juumre (nde); fuujoore (nde).

larcener [larsənə] n. gujjo (o).

larceny [larsəni] n. nguyka (ka).

lard [lard] n. bellere mbabba tugal.

large [lɑj] adj. mawnudum; ko mawni; jaajdum.

largess [lɑjes] n. moⲅⲅere (nde).

lark [lɑk] v. gaajaade.

larva [larva] n. bingél (ngél).

lash [laš] n. karwaas (o).

lash [laš] v. fiide.

lassie [lasi] n. suka debbo; bóómbél (ngél).

lassitude [lasityuwd] n. tampere (nde).

last [last] v. wadtinde; booyde; yeerde; booyde. be ~ wadtindaade; sakkitaade; luutaade.

last [last] adj. battano. ~ born child kodda (o). ~ but one cukko battano. ~ night hanki jamma.

latch [lač] v. sokde.

latchet [lačit] n. bóggél pade.

late [leyt] adj. leeldo. be ~ leelde; jéngude. He is late O leelii arde/o tardii.

lately [leytli] adv. ko booyaani.

latent [laytənt] adj. ko suudii; cuudidum.

lateral [latərəl] adj. ko faati e baⲏⲏe.

laterite [latərit] n. léydi mbódééri.

latest [leytəst] adj. kó buri fóf hésdude.

lath [laθ] n. bokko (ko).

lather [laðə] n. nguufa (ka).

latrine [latrin] n. firlorde (nde).

latter [latə] adj. battindiido. the former and the ~ gadiido e battindiido.

laud [lɔd] v. mantude.

laudable [lɔdəbəl] adj. mantindo.

laugh [laf] *v.* jalde. *make someone* ~ jalnude.
~ *loudly* waaktaade; sérkitde. ~ *down*
jalkitde. *He is laughing at you* O woni ko e
jalde ma.
laughable [lafəbəl] *adj.* jalniɗum; ko jalnii.
laughter [laftə] *n.* jaleeɗe *(ɗe)*.
launch [lɔnč] *v.* werlaade; jólnude. ~ *an
attack* yande e.
launch [lɔnč] *n.* laana *(ka)*.
launder [lɔndə] *v.* wuppude.
launderette [lɔndəret] *n.* wuppirde *(nde)*.
laundromat [lɔndrəmat] *n.* wuppirde *(nde)*.
laundry [lɔndri] *n.* cómci guppétééɗi; guppól
(ngól). *I am doing my laundry* Mbeɗen
wuppa comci am.
lava [lava] *n.* léydi ngulndi ngummiindi nder
léydi.
lavalava [lavalava] *n.* wudere *(nde)*.
lavation [laveyšən] *n.* guppól *(ngól)*.
lave [leyv] *v.* lootde; ɓuftude.
lavish [laviš] *v.* ɗuuɗɗe; heewde.
law [lɔ] *n.* luwaa *(o)*; laawól *(ngól)*.
law-abiding [lɔwabaydiŋ] *adj.* dewɗo
laawól; póóɣtiiɗo.
lawful [lɔfə] *adj.* ko dagii; kó rewi laawól;
dagiɗum; pooctiɗum; jamiraaɗum.
lax [laks] *adj.* mo wondaaka.
laxative [laksətiv] *n.* lékki seero.
lay [ley] *v.* lelaade; lelnude. ~ *straight*
fortaade. ~ *an egg* ɓoccinde; furtude. ~
down lattinaade. ~ *mud on the wall*
sappitde. ~ *on* ñappude. ~ *off* riiwde. ~ *out*
wértude. ~ *on ones' back* ajjaade;
wéyginaade. ~ *something or someone on
the back* ajjinde. ~ *on ones' back* hippaade.
layette [ləyet] *n.* cómci e kaake cukalél.
layover [leyowvə] *n.* jippunde *(nde)*.
laziness [leyzines] *n.* aamre *(nde)*.
lazy [leyzi] *adj.* gaamɗo you are lazy aɗa
aami.
lead [liyd] *n.* 1) gardagol *(ngól)* 2) bedek *(o)*.
~*in* fuɗɗorde *(nde)*.
lead [liyd] *v.* ardaade; regginde. ~ *a holiday
prayer* fumminde. ~ *a prayer* juulnude. ~
the blind ɗowde. ~ *again* arditaade. *Lead
the prayer* Juulnu en.
leader [liydə] *n.* gardiiɗo *(o)*.
leadership [liydəšip] *n.* gardagól *(ngól)*.
leading [liydiŋ] *n.* gardagol *(ngól)*; ɗówgól
(ngól).

leaf [liyf] *n.* baramléfól *(ngól)*.
leaflet [liyflet] *n.* kayitél *(ngél)*; ɗéréwól
bindangól e dów mum.
leafy [liyfi] *adj.* ko sukki; cukkuɗum.
league [liyg] *n.* deental *(ngal)*; fedde *(nde)*.
He does not belong to that league O
jeyaaka e ndeen fedde.
leak [liyk] *n.* ciyam *(ɗam)*.
leak [liyk] *v.* siyde. *There was a leak
somewhere* Won kaaltuɗo.
lean [liyn] *adj.* cewɗo; ko fayaani.
lean [liyn] *v.* 1) ɓaarde; ɓaggude 2)
Ɣukkaade. ~ *against* tuggaade; ɓaaraade;
ɓaggaade. ~ *oneself on* ɓaaraade.
leaning [liyniŋ] *n.* Ɣukkagól *(ngól)*; turagól
(ngól).
leap [liyp] *v.* diwde.
learn [lərn] *v.* jangude; ekkaade. ~ *again*
ekkitaade. *Learn your lesson* Jangu
windande ma.
learned [lərnd] *adj.* janguɗo.
learner [lərnə] *n.* jangoowo *(o)*.
learning [lərniŋ] *n.* jangde *(nde)*.
lease [liys] *v.* luwde.
leash [liyš] *n.* ginól *(ngól)*.
least [liyst] *adj.* ɓurɗo fóf famɗude.
leather [leðə] *n.* nguru *(ngu)* -*bag* sasa *(ka)*.
~ *worker* garanke *(o)*; sakke *(o)*.
leave [liyv] *v.* 1) ɗaccude 2) yahde; fokkitde.
~ *for someone* accande. ~ *unnoticed*
wappaade. ~ *early morning* huudaade. ~ *in
the afternoon* hirndude. ~ *a trace* battinde.
~ *for someone* accirde; accande. ~ *a habit*
ruɳaade. ~ *over* héddude. ~ *one's
husband's compound after a dispute*
suutaade. ~ *alone* wóppude; ɗalde. *I am
leaving today* Ko hande njahatmi.
lector [lektə] *n.* janginoowo *(o)*; jangoowo
(o).
lecture [lekčə] *v.* janginde.
lecturer [lekčərə] *n.* janginoowo *(o)*.
ledge [lej] *n.* sara *(o)*; hawngo *(ngo)*.
leech [liyč] *n.* mbuutu *(ngu)*.
left [left] *adj.* baɳɳe nano; nano; jungo nano.
~ *hand* jungo nano; nanal *(ngal)*. ~ *handed*
nannano.
leftover [leftowvə] *n.* kedde (de); siɓɓere
(nde); ñaamatinde *(nde)*.

g [leg] *n.* koyngal *(ngal)*; cakutal *(ngal)*. *ower* ~ korlal *(ngal)*. *pull someone's* ~ ñuuntude; gaajaade.

gacy [legəsi] *n.* ndónu *(ngu)*.

gal [liygəl] *adj.* jamiraaɗum; ko réwi aawól; ko yamiraa.

galize [liygəlayz] *v.* yamirde. *It must be* ***egalized*** Ina foti yamireede.

gerity [lejərəti] *n.* yaawre *(nde)*.

gged [legəd] *adj.* ko jogii koyɗe.

gible [lejibəl] *adj.* jangotooɗum; ko angotoo.

gislation [lejəsleyšən] *n.* ñaawoore *(nde)*.

gislative [lejəslətiv] *adj.* ko ñaawata.

gitimate [ləjitmət] *adj.* kó réwi laawól; ko yamiraa; jamiraaɗum.

gless [legles] *adj.* guddo.

isure [liyzə] *n.* weytaare *(nde)*.

man [lemən] *n.* giɗo *(o)*; suka *(o)*.

mon [lemən] *n.* limoƴ *(o)*.

monade [leməneyd] *n.* njaram liminaat.

nd [lend] *v.* luɓde; aslude; ñamlude. *Lend* ***me a hand*** Rokkam jungo; wallam. *Lend* ***me some money*** Ñamlam kaalis.

ndable [lendəbəl] *adj.* luɓeteeɗum; ko luɓetee.

nding [lendiŋ] *n.* luɓal *(ngal)*.

ngth [leŋθ] *n.* njuuteendi *(ndi)*.

ngthen [leŋθən] *v.* juutnude. ~ *sounds* juurtude **lengthy** [leŋθi] *adj.* ko juuti; juutɗum.

niency [linyənsi] *n.* maslaha *(o)*; yaafuya *(o)*.

nient [liynyənt] *adj.* jaafotooɗo.

per [lepə] *n.* góndudo e baras.

prosy [leprəsi] *n.* baras *(o)*.

sion [liyჳən] *n.* gaañande *(nde)*.

ss [les] *adj.* ko jaasi.

ssen [lesən] *v.* dajde; ustude.

sson [lesən] *n.* windande *(nde)*. *He learned* ***a lesson*** So mawɗo wumii wumtii anndii ko gite nafata.

ssor [leso] *n.* luwoowo *(o)*.

st [lest] *adj.* koyɗo é léydi.

t [let] *v.* woppude; accude. *to let in* naatnude.

thargy [leθərji] *n.* ngaameela *(ka)*.

tter [letə] *n.* 1) alkulal *(ngal)* 2) ɓataake *(o)*. *I sent you a letter* Mi winndii ma ɓataake. *I am waiting for your reply* Mbeɗe fadi jaabtawol ma.

lettered [letəd] *adj.* gando; janguɗo.

levade [ləveyd] *v.* Ƴeeraade (puccu).

levant [ləvant] *n.* ummagol *(ngól)*.

level [levəl] *v.* fóndude. ~ *off* melde. ~ *out* fondude.

levelled [levəld] *adj.* pondaɗum; berkaɗum.

leveling [levəliŋ] *n.* berko *(ngo)*.

levigate [levəgeyt] *v.* ruggude; unde.

levitate [levəteyt] *v.* weeyde.

levy [levi] *v.* askude.

levy [levi] *n.* límpóó *(o)*.

lexical [leksikəl] *adj.* ko faati e kelme.

lexicography [leksikowgrəfi] *n.* bindól e jande caggitorɗe.

lexicon [leksəkon] *n.* kelme *(ɗe)*.

liability [layəbiləty] *n.* ñamaande *(nde)*.

liaison [liyezon] *n.* jókkóndiral *(ngal)*.

liar [layə] *n.* penoowo *(o)*. *He is a liar* Ko o penoowo.

libation [laybeyšən] *n.* cakkagól *(ngól)*.

libel [laybəl] *v.* takkude neɗɗo.

liberate [libəreyt] *v.* ɗaccitde; accitde; humtude. *He was liberated today* Ko hande o ɗaccitaa.

liberty [libəti] *n.* jéy hoore mum.

library [laybrəri] *n.* móoftirde defte.

lice [lays] *n.* bamɗi hoore; bamɗi comci. *egg* ~ mbimƴa *(ba)*.

licit [lisit] *adj.* jamiraaɗum; ko réwi laawól/ko yamiraa.

lick [lik] *v.* salɓaade; mettaade; laaƴaade; lamƴindaade.

licked [likt] *adj.* mettaɗum

lid [lid] *n.* hippoode *(nde)*; ombirgal *(ngal)*; omboode *(nde)*. *Put the lid on the pot* Hippu barme o.

lie [lay] *v.* 1) lelaade 2) fende; semtude. ~ *sideways* ñenkilaade.

lie [lay] *n.* puttere *(nde)*; fenaande *(nde)*. *He told a lie* ɗum ko fenaande.

lieu [luw] *n.* nókku *(o)*.

life [layf] *n.* nguurndam *(ɗam)*. ~*guard* deenoowo *(o)*.

lift [lift] *v.* ɓamtude; huñde; sefde; suutde. ~ *while wrestling* fooɓnaade.

lift-off [liftəv] *n.* diwgól *(ngól)*.

lifted [liftəd] *adj.* cuutaaɗo.

lifting [liftiŋ] *n.* cuutgol *(ngól)*; Γettugol *(ngal)*.

ligate [ligeyt] *v.* haɓɓude.

ligature [ligəčə] *n.* kaɓɓugól *(ngól)*.

light [layt] *adj.* koyɗo; koyɗum. *He is light-headed* Omo weeɓi hoore.

light [layt] *n.* fooyre *(nde)*. *Do you have a light* Aɗa jogii jayngol/Aɗa jogii kuɗol? almet.

light [layt] *v.* huɓɓude; yaynude; yalmitde; yaynaade.

light-skinned [laytskind] *adj.* naawo.

lightning [laytniŋ] *n.* majaango *(ngo)*; majande *(nde)*; manaango *(ngo)*.

like [layk] *conj.* elleey.

like [layk] *v.* waade; nandude e. *I like him* O mo weli mi.

likeable [laykəbəl] *adj.* belɗo Γiiam; belɗo.

liken [laykən] *v.* nawdude; nandinde.

likeness [layknes] *n.* nandugól *(ngól)*.

liking [laykiŋ] *n.* jiɗgól *(ngól)*.

limb [limb] *n.* tergal *(ngal)*.

limbo [limbow] *v.* amde.

lime [laym] *n.* leemuna *(o)*.

limit [limit] *v.* haaɗnude.

limit [limit] *n.* happu *(o)*; haaɗtirde *(nde)*; kééról *(ngól)*. *without* ~ ko alaa happu.

limitation [liməteyšən] *n.* kééról *(ngól)*; happu *(o)*.

limited [limətid] *adj.* keeraɗum.

limitless [limətles] *adj.* ko heeraaka.

limp [limp] *v.* laΓde

line [layn] *v.* reggondirde; rewondirde. ~ *up* témbinde. *be in* ~ témbude.

line [layn] *n.* diidol *(ngól)*; ciifól *(ngól)*; góról *(ngól)*.

lineage [liynij] *n.* asko *(ngo)*; léñól *(ngól)*.

linen [linen] *n.* cómci *(ɗi)*; darabuuji *(ɗi)*.

liner [laynə] *n.* pakke *(o)*; laana mawka; laana *(ka)*.

linger [liŋə] *v.* ruudde; heddaade e.

lingerie [lenʒəri] *n.* njodom; comci baalirteeɗi.

lingual [liŋwəl] *adj.* ko faati e ɗemngal.

linguistic [liŋgwistik] *adj.* ko faati e ɗemngal.

linguistics [liŋgwistik] *n.* jangde ɗemɗe.

lingworm [lingwɔm] *n.* saɗiwere *(nde)*.

link [liŋk] *n.* jókkóndiral *(ngal)*.

link [liŋk] *v.* jokkondirde.

lint [lint] *n.* gaaraaji *(ɗi)*; gaarawól *(ngól)*.

lion [layən] *n.* taktakri *(ndi)*; kaandi *(ndi)*. ~*'s share* geɗal laamɗo.

lip [lip] *n.* tondu *(ndu)*

lippen [lipən] *v.* hoolaade.

liquefaction [likwəfakšən] *n.* caaynugól *(ngól)*.

liquefy [likwəfay] *v.* saayde; saaynude.

liqueur [likər] *n.* koññjam *(ɗam)*; sangara *(o)*.

liquid [likwid] *n.* male ndiyam; ko faati e ndiyam.

liquidate [likwideyt] *v.* 1) yoɓde; yeeyde 2) warde.

liquidator [likwideytə] *n.* jeeyoowo *(o)*.

liquor [likə] *n.* sangara *(o)*.

Lisbon [lisbən] *n.* laamorde Portugal.

list [list] *v.* limtude; windude. *He is listing their names* O woni ko e windude inɗe maɓɓe.

listing [listiŋ] *n.* limtugól *(ngól)*.

listen [lisən] *v.* heɗaade. ~ *carefully* heɗtaade; héɗtindaade. *I am listening to you* Mbeɗe heɗi maa.

literacy [litrəsi] *n.* jangde *(nde)*; gandal *(ngal)*.

literate [litret] *adj.* janguɗo.

litter [litə] *n.* kurjuru *(o)*.

litter [litə] *v.* rufde walla werlaade kurjuru.

little [litəl] *adj.* tokooso; tokosel.

live [layv] *v.* wuurde; hoɗde. ~ *with* hóddude. *I live here* Ko ɗoo koɗmi.

livelihood [layvlihud] *n.* nguura *(ka)*.

lively [layvli] *adj.* guurɗum; ko wuuri.

liven [layvən] *v.* wuurnude; wélnude.

liver [livə] *n.* jofe *(ɗe)*.

liverish [livriš] *adj.* ko nandi e jofe.

livestock [layvstok] *n.* jawdi *(ndi)*.

living [liviŋ] *n.* nguurndam *(ɗam)*.

lizard [lizəd] *n.* mbato *(o)*; gundo; huttoóru *(ndu)*; basawal *(ngal)*; nduulaldi *(ndi)*.

load [lowd] *n.* loowande *(nde)*; dongal *(ngal)*; dimngal *(ngal)*. *a heavy* ~ dimngal teddungal.

load [lowd] *v.* loowde; rimndude. ~ *a gun* bannude.

loaded [lowdid] *adj.* dimndaaɗo; teddudʼo; loowaaɗo; ko loowaa. *The gun is loaded* Kute ina e nder fetel o.

loaf [lowf] *n.* lóócól mburu.

loafer [lowfə] *n.* nedʼdʼo gaamdʼo.

loan [lown] *v.* ñamlude; luɓde.

loan [lown] *n.* ñamaande *(nde)*; luɓal *(ngal)*. *a ~ word* kongol luɓangol.

loathe [lowθ] *v.* añde.

loathing [lowθiŋ] *n.* ngañgu *(ngu)*.

lobster [lobstə] *n.* sippak *(o)*.

locality [lokaləti] *n.* nókku *(o)*.

locate [lokeyt] *v.* fawde e nókku; yiitude; héédnude.

location [lokeyšən] *n.* nókku *(o)*.

locative [lokətiv] *n.* jamminoore *(nde)*; huunde jamminoore nókku.

lock [lok] *n.* beddal *(ngal)*; kannaat *(o)*; lolloƭjeere *(nde)*.

lock [lok] *v.* sokde; méƮƮude.

locomotive [lowkəmotiv] *n.* laana njóórndi.

locus [lokəs] *n.* nókku *(o)*.

locust [lokʌst] *n.* mbaaɓattu *(ngu)*; tenkere.

loft [loft] *n.* faawru *(ndu)*.

log [log] *n.* tunde *(nde)*. *I slept like a log* dʼaaniimi ko dʼoyngol belngol/juutngol.

loin [loyn] *n.* njogoram *(dʼam)*

lone [lown] *adj.* petto; gooto.

loneliness [lownlənes] *n.* yeeweende *(nde)*.

lonely [lownli] *adj.* jeewaadʼo. *I am lonely* Mbedʼe yeewaa.

long [loŋ] *adj.* juutdʼo; ɓooydʼo. *in the ~ run* ko ɓooyi juutde kala.

long [loŋ] *v.* yééwnude; tuuyeede.

longlife [loŋlayf] *n.* nguurndam *(dʼam)*; njuutdʼam *(dʼam)*; baldʼe juutdʼe.

look [luk] *v.* Ƴeewde; laarde. *~ in the mirror* tiimtaade. *~ over* yongaade. *~ back* yeeƳaade; yéccitaade. *~ under* lubbude. *~ into* yuurnaade. *~ up* hooynaade. *~ out* reentaade. *Look out* Reento.

loom [luwm] *n.* cañirgal *(ngal)*; kandal *(ngal)*.

loophole [luwphowl] *n.* ella *(o)*.

loose [luws] *adj.* jolɓudʼum; jordʼum; ko yoori. *get ~* ɓoccitaade.

loosen [luwsən] *v.* yólbinde; firtude.

loot [luwt] *n.* jawdi konaandi.

loot [luwt] *v.* honde; bónnude; wujjude.

lop [lop] *v.* férƳude; féƮƮude.

loquacious [lokweyšəs] *adj.* keewdʼo haala; beldʼo dʼemngal.

lord [lod] *n.* jóómiraadʼo *(o)*.

lorry [lori] *n.* kamiyoƭj *(o)*.

lose [luwz] *v.* majjude; majjinde. *~ consciousness* fadʼaade; fekkoreede. *~ leaves* olde. *~ hair/feathers* ɓoraade. *~ value* lóskude. *~ fiber* sefaade. *~ one's hair* rosaade. *~ one's mind* haangeede.

loser [luwzə] *n.* nedʼdʼo poolaadʼo; sulle *(o)*.

loss [los] *n.* majjere *(nde)*; tilfere *(nde)*. *Your loss is mine* Enen ndendi sunaare.

lost [lost] *adj.* majjudʼo. *I am lost* Ko mi majjudʼo.

lot [lot] *n.* lowre *(nde)*.

loud [lawd] *adj.* mawnudʼum; ko mawni; mawnde. *a ~ voice* daande mawnde.

lounge [lawnj] *v.* weytaade.

louse [laws] *n.* mbabba hoore/comci.

love [lʌv] *n.* gilli *(dʼi)*.

love [lʌv] *v.* yidʼde. faaleede; hoowde. *~ each other* yidʼóndirde. *I love you* Mbedʼe yidʼ maa.

lovely [lʌvli] *adj.* joodʼdʼo; kó yóódʼi.

lover [lʌvə] *n.* suka *(o)*; nedʼdʼo jidʼdʼo.

low [low] *adj.* ɓappidʼdʼum; lésdʼudʼum. *It is low* Ina lesdʼi.

lower [lowə] *v.* ustude; lésdʼinde.

lowering [lowəriŋ] *n.* ustaare *(nde)*; ustugól *(ngól)*.

lowing [lowiŋ] *n.* huunaango *(ngo)*.

loyal [loyə] *adj.* dʼówtiidʼo.

loyalty [loyəlti] *n.* dʼowtagol *(ngól)*.

lucent [luwsənt] *adj.* jalbudʼum; ko jalbi.

lucid [lusid] *adj.* peerdʼo; péértudʼo; paamnidʼum.

luck [lʌk] *n.* aaɓre *(nde)*.

luckless [lʌkles] *adj.* malkisaadʼo.

lucky [lʌki] *adj.* gaaɓdʼo He is lucky Omo aaɓi.

lucrative [luwkrətiv] *adj.* ko wadʼi ngañaari; gaaɓdʼum.

lug [lʌg] *v.* daasde; foodʼde.

luggage [lʌgij] *n.* kaake *(dʼe)*

lull [lʌl] *v.* yeƳde.

lump [lʌmp] *n.* ɓoodde *(nde)*.

lumpy [lʌmpi] *adj.* kó hééwi boodʼe.

lunacy [luwnəsi] *n.* kaadʼi *(dʼi)*.

lunch [lʌnč] *n.* bottaari *(ndi). Let's eat lunch* Ngotto ɗen.

lunch [lʌnč] *v.* wottaade.

luncheon [lʌčən] *n.* bottaari *(ndi).*

lune [luwn] *n.* léwru *(ndu).*

lung [lʌŋ] *n.* wumsundere *(nde).* ~s jofe *(ɗe).*

lunt [lʌnt] *n.* cuurki *(ki).*

lure [luwr] *n.* fuunti *(o).*

lure [luwr] *v.* fuuntude.

lurk [lərk] *v.* faddaade.

lute [luwt] *n.* hóɗdu *(ndu).*

luxuriant [lʌgȝuryənt] *adj.* keewɗum; kó hééwi.

lynch [linč] *v.* warde.

M

acadam [makədəm] n. laawól (ngól).
acaque [makak] n. waandu (ndu).
machete [mašəti] n. jaasi (ki).
machinate [mašəneyt] v. fééwnude.
machine [məšiyn] n. masiŋ (o). a sewing ~ masiŋ ñootoowo.
machinist [məšiynist] n. dognoowo masiŋ.
macro [makro] adj. mawɗo; ko mawni.
maculate [makyuwleyt] v. tunwinde.
mad [mad] adj. kaangaaɗo; cekɗo. be ~ haangeede. They drove him mad 6e kaangɗinii mo.
madam [madəm] n. debbo (o).
madden [madən] v. haangɗinde; séknude.
madman [madmən] n. kaangaaɗo (o).
madness [madnes] n. kaaɗi (ɗi).
magic [majik] n. dabare (ɗe); ñengi (ɗi). perform ~ ñengaade.
magic [majik] n. ko faati e dabare.
magical [mjikəl] adj. ko faati e dabare. ~ lotion aaye (o).
magician [məjiyšən] n. ñengotooɗo (o).
magnate [magneyt] adj. koohoowo; mawɗo.
magnet [magnet] n. huunde fooɗoore; njamndi póóɗóóri jamɗe.
magnified [magnəfayd] adj. mawninaaɗum; ko mawni naa.
magnify [magnəfay] v. mawninde.
Mahdi [mahdi] n. maadii (o).
Mahomet [mahəmet] n. annabi Muhammad; nelaaɗo Alla.
maid [meyd] n. mbindaan (o); mbóómri (ndi). I work as a maid Ko mi bindiiɗo.
maiden [meydən] n. mbóómri (ndi).
maigre [megr] adj. pooŸŸo; póóŸɗum; kó fóóŸi.
mail [meyl] v. jólnude 6ataake. I mailed your letter today Mi jolnii 6ataake maa hande.
maillot [mayo] n. cómcól (ngól).
main [meyn] adj. ko 6uri himmude; kimmuɗum; ngóóróóndi. ~ road kallu mawɗo.
maintain [menteyn] v. heddaade; tóppitaade; jókkude.

maintenance [mentənəns] n. tóppitaagól (ngól).
maize [meyz] n. makka (o).
major [meyjə] n. kumaandaŋ (o).
major [meyjə] adj. ko mawni; mawnuɗo.
majority [majowrəti] n. ko 6uri heewde.
make [make] v. wadde; feewnude. ~ love hoowde. ~ an appointment aadondirde sahaa.
maker [maykə] n. peewnoowo (o). bread ~ piyoowo mburu.
making [meykiŋ] n. pééwnugól (ngól).
maladroit [maladroyt] adj. mo feewaani jungo.
malady [malədi] n. ñaw (ngu); rafi (o).
malapropos [maləpropo] adv. ko feewaani; ko haanaani.
malcontent [malkəntent] adj. mó fééwnitaaki; mo weltaaki.
male [meyl] adj. worde; wordu; gorko.
malediction [malədikəšən] n. kuɗɗi (ndi).
malefactor [malefaktə] n. bonnoowo (o).
malefic [malefik] adj. bonnojum; ko bonnata.
malevolence [malevoləns] n. ngañgu (ngu).
malice [malis] n. ngañgu (ngu).
malign [məlayn] v. tooñde; fende.
malleable [məliyəbəl] adj. ko jii6otoo.
malodorous [malədrəs] adj. luu6ɗum; ko luu6i; ko sicci.
malt [mɔlt] n. gawri coofnaandi.
mamba [mambə] n. ngaadaada (ba).
mammock [mamɔk] v. helde.
man [man] n. gorko. little ~ górél (ngél). ~hood ngoraagu. head- gardiiɗo (o).
manacle [manəkəl] v. tóngude.
manage [manij] v. ardaade. I can manage Ma mi waɗɗu heen.
management [manajmənt] n. gardagól (ngól).
manager [manajə] n. gardiiɗo (o). Who is the manager Hol gardiiɗo?
manatee [manəti] n. liwóógu (ngu).
manche [manš] n. jungo cómcól (kaftaan/simis).
mandate [mandeyt] v. halfinde.
mandatory [mandətəri] adj. kó fóti wonde.

manege [manij] *n.* ekko *(ngo)*; ekkagol *(ngól)*.

maneuvre [manuwvə] *v.* dógnude.

mangle [mangəl] *v.* seekde.

mangle [mangəl] *n.* tappirde *(nde)*; tappirgal *(ngal)*.

mango [mangow] *n.* mango *(ko)*.

mania [manya] *n.* kaaɗi *(ɗi)*.

maniac [manyak] *n.* kaangaaɗo *(o)*.

manic [manik] *adj.* ko faati e kaaɗi.

manifest [manəfest] *adj.* ko laaɓi; ko yiyotoo.

manifold [mənifowld] *adj.* kó hééwi; keewɗum.

mankind [mankaynd] *n.* windere *(nde)*.

manlike [manlayk] *n.* ko wayi no neɗɗo. ~ *behavior* golle gorko.

manna [manə] *n.* ñamri *(ndi)*.

manner [manə] *n.* fasoɭ *(o)*; feere *(nde)*. *He has no manners* O nehaaki.

mansard [mansard] *n.* mbildi *(ndi)*.

mansion [manšən] *n.* huɓeere mawnde.

manslaughter [manslɔtə] *n.* war hoore.

manual [manyəl] *adj.* ko waɗirtee jungo; ko faati e jungo.

manufacture [manyuwfakčə] *v.* fééwnude.

manufacturer [manyuwfakčərə] *n.* peewnoowo *(o)*.

manure [manyuwr] *n.* dorde *(nde)*; dubuuje *(ɗe)*.

many [məni] *adv.* kééwɗi. ~ *a* laabi keewɗi. ~ *times* cile keewɗe; laabi keewɗi.

map [map] *v.* amminde.

mar [mar] *v.* bónnude.

marabou [marəbu] *n.* ginal *(ngal)*.

marabout [marəbut] *n.* ceerno *(o)*.

marathon [maraθon] *n.* dógdu *(ndu)*; daɗóndiral *(ngal)*.

maraud [mərɔd] *v.* wujjude.

march [mɑč] *v.* march; maajde; yahrude koyɗe. *the ~ing band* maajooɓe *(ɓe)*.

mare [mer] *adj.* njarlu.

margin [mɑjin] *n.* kééról *(ngól)*.

marginate [mɑjəneyt] *v.* heeraade.

marinade [marəneyd] *v.* marine.

marital [maritəl] *adj.* ko faati e dewal.

maritime [marətaym] *adj.* ko faati e gééc.

mark [mɑk] *n.* diidol *(ngól)*; jeloode *(nde)*. maantoore *(nde)*; maantorde *(nde)*; toɓɓe *(ɗe)*.

mark [mɑk] *v.* jelde. ~ *with a hoe* faafde.

marker [mɑkə] *n.* diidoowo *(o)*; jeloowo *(o)*.

market [mɑket] *n.* jeere *(nde)*; marse *(o)*. *She went to the market* O yahii jeere.

marketable [mɑketəbəl] *adj.* kó wééɓi yeeyde; kó njééygu mum wééɓi.

marksman [mɑksmən] *n.* peewɗo jungo; mo woofataa. *He is a marksman* Ndaw ko feewi jungo.

marriage [marij] *n.* dewgal *(ngal)*.

married [marid] *adj.* cudduɗo; cuddaaɗo. *He is married* Ko o desɗo.

marrow [marow] *n.* mbuuwwa *(ka)*.

marry [mari] *v.* resde; suddude; marde. *I married her* Mi resii mo.

marshy [mɑši] *adj.* ko faati e leydi.

mart [mɑt] *n.* jeere *(nde)*.

martial [mɑšəl] *adj.* jiɗɗo hare.

martingale [mɑtingeyl] *n.* faram *(o)*; ginól *(ngól)*.

martyr [mɑtə] *n.* cahódinɗo *(o)*.

martyrdom [mɑtərdəm] *n.* cahódingól *(ngól)*.

mascara [maskəra] *n.* fino *(ngo)*.

masculine [maskilin] *adj.* worde.

mash [maš] *v.* móññude; nirkude.

mason meysən] *n.* mahoowo *(o)*; masoɭ *(o)*.

mass [mas] *n.* deental keewngal.

massacre [masakə] *n.* war hoore.

massage [masaj] *v.* ɓoosde; ɓoosgol *(ngól)*. *Give him a massage* ɓoos mo.

masseur [masər] *n.* gorko ɓoosoowo.

masseuse [masuwz] *n.* debbo ɓoosoowo.

mast [mast] *n.* jaalal *(ngal)*; leggal wiir.

master [mastə] *n.* kaliifa *(o)*. *headmaster* gardiiɗo ekkol.

master [mastə] *v.* dursude; ɗigginde; waawde.

mastery [mastəri] *n.* gandal *(ngal)*.

masticate [mastəkeyt] *v.* ʼYakkude.

masturbate [mastərbeyt] *v.* memtaade.

masturbation [mastərbeyšən] *n.* memtagól *(ngól)*.

mat [mat] *n.* leeso *(ngo)*; daago *(ngo)*. *spread a* ~ wertude daago *(ngo)*.

match [matč] *n.* kuɗól almet. *I need a match* Mbeɗe sokli kuɗol almet.

match [matč] *v.* fotde; fóndude. *They do not match* ɗi potaani.

mate [meyt] *n.* jóm suudu; jom galle; góndiiɗo. *He is my roommate* Minen ndenndi suudu.

material [matiyryəl] *n.* abaari.

materialize [matiyryəl] *v.* wonde.

maternity [matərniti] *n.* ɓesngo *(ngo).*

mathematical [maθəmatikəl] *adj.* ko faati e hiisa walla kiisagól.

mathematics [maθəmatiks] *n.* kiisagól *(ngól).*

matriarchy [matreyarki] *n.* laamu rewɓe; gardagól rewɓe.

matrimonial [matremownyəl] *adj.* ko faati e dewgal.

matrimony [matreməni] *n.* cuddungu *(ngu)*; dewgal *(ngal).*

matron [meytrən] *n.* debbo deenoowo.

matter [matə] *v.* nafde. *It does not matter* ɗum bonnataa hay huunde.

matter [matə] *n.* alhaali *(o).*

mattress [matres] *n.* pajaas *(o).*

maturate [mačureyt] *v.* ɓénndude; héllifeede.

nature [mačur] *v.* hellifeede.

nature [mačur] *adj.* kéllifaaɗo. *He is mature* O hellifaama.

maturity [mačuwrəti] *n.* kéllifuya *(o).*

maul [mɔl] *v.* fiide.

mausoleum [mɔzɔleyəm] *n.* yanaande *(nde).*

maxim [maksim] *n.* tindól *(ngól).*

maximum [maksimʌm] *n.* huunde ɓurnde fóf.

may [mey] *v.* yamirde. *You may go* A yamiraama yo a yah.

mayonnaise [mayənez] *n.* mayonees *(o).*

mayor [meyə] *n.* meer *(o). He is the mayor of Toulde* Ko kanko woni meer Toulde.

me [miy] *pron.* miin; mi; kam. *He saw me* O yii kam.

meager [miygə] *adj.* pooYɗo; póóYɗum.

meal [miyl] *n.* ñamri *(ndi).*

mean [miyn] *n.* 1) hakkunde 2) muuya *(o).*

mean [miyn] *adj.* bonɗo.

mean [miyn] *v.* firtude. *Your support means a lot to me* Ballal maa ngal ina tiiɗi mi no feewi.

meaning [miyniŋ] *n.* maanaa *(o).*

meaningful [miyniŋ] *adj.* kó jógii maanaa. *That statement is not meaningful* Kaan haala alaa maanaa.

meaningless [miyniŋles] *adj.* ko alaa maanaa.

means [miynz] *n.* baawal *(ngal). by any ~* no ina wonira kala.

meantime [miyntaym] *adv.* hadee; ndeen; ɗo e ndeen. *in the ~* ɗoo e ndeen.

measles [miyzəlz] *n.* came *(ɗe).*

measurable [meʒrəbəl] *adj.* ko ɓetotoo.

measure [meʒrəbəl] *v.* ɓetde; hiisaade; fónndude. *~ with* ɓetirde. *~ by spans* siɓaade.

measure [meʒə] *n.* ɓetgol *(ngól).*

measurement [meʒərmənt] *n.* 1) ɓétgól *(ngól)*; póndugól *(ngól)* 2) ɓetirgal *(ngal)* 3) diraa *(o)* 4) hamdaat *(o).*

meat [miyt] *n.* teew *(ngu). piece of ~* hettere *(nde)*; husere *(nde). big piece of ~* talde *(nde). raw ~* teew keccu. *cooked ~* teew ɓendungu. *barbecued ~* teew juɗaaɗo; afara.

meaty [miyti] *adj.* tebbinɗum; kó hééwi tééw.

Mecca [mekə] *n.* Makka. *He went on a pilgrimage to Mecca* O hajjoyii.

mechanic [mekanik] *n.* peewnitoowo móbélaaji. *He is a mechanic* Ko o peewnitoowo otooji.

mechanical [mekanikəl] *adj.* ko faati e masiƲaaji.

meddle [medəl] *v.* naatde e ko wonaa haajumum; jiiɓde.

meddling [medliŋ] *n.* naatgól e ko wonaa haaju mum.

medial [miydyəl] *adj.* hakkundeejo.

mediate [miydyeyt] *v.* wélditinde.

mediator [miydyeytə] *n.* bélditinoowo *(o)*; nelaaɗo *(o).*

medicable [medikəbəl] *adj.* ko safrotoo; cafrotooɗum.

medical [medikəl] *adj.* ko faati e safaara.

medicament [medikəmənt] *n.* lékki *(ki).*

medicinal [mediysinəl] *adj.* ko faati é safaara.

medicine [medəsin] *n.* lékki *(ki)*; safaara *(o).* **take one's** ~ yarde lekki mum.

mediocre [miydyowkə] *adj.* hakkundeejo.

meditate [medəteyt] *v.* miijaade.

medium [miydyəm] *n.* hakkunde *(nde).*

meek [miyk] *adj.* muñɗo.

meet [miyt] *v.* fottude; hawrude. ~ **accidentally** feraade. ~ **again** hawritde. *I* **met him today** Mi hawrii e makko hande. **We have already met** A min ngandondiri.

meeting [miytiŋ] *n.* batu *(ngu)*; deental *(ngal).* *I* **attended the meeting** Mi tawtoraama batu ngu.

melancholic [meləŋkowlik] *adj.* jurminiiɗo.

melder [meldə] *n.* rogere *(nde).*

mell [mel] *v.* jiiɓde.

melodious [melowjəs] *adj.* kó wéli heɗaade.

melon [melən] *n.* dende *(nde).*

melt [melt] *v.* taayde; saayde; saaynude. ~ **into tears** woyde.

melting [meltiŋ] *n.* saayngo *(ngo)*; taayre *(nde).*

member [membə] *n.* jeyaaɗo e. *He is a* **member of the Fulani community** Ko o Pullo.

memento [məmentow] *n.* huunde siftinoore.

memoir [memwar] *n.* hakkille *(o).*

memorable [memrəbəl] *adj.* ko haani siftoreede.

memorize [memərayz] *v.* huñaade.

memory [memri] *n.* téskuya *(o).*

men [men] *n.* worɓe *(ɓe)*

menace [mənas] *v.* baabaade.

mend [mend] *v.* ɓasde; waɗde.

mendacity [məndəsiti] *n.* fenaande *(nde).*

mender [mendə] *n.* ɓasoowo *(o)*

mendicity [məndəsiti] *n.* jelagól *(ngól).*

menial [miynyəl] *adj.* kersiniiɗum; kó hérsinii.

menses [mensiz] *n.* ella.

menstruate [menstrəweyt] *v.* yiide ella.

mental [mentəl] *adj.* ko faati e hakkille.

mention [menšən] *v.* wiide; innude. *Do not* **forget to mention it to him** Hol to yejjit haalande mo.

meow [miyow] *v.* ŋeewde.

mercantile [mərkəntəl] *adj.* ko faati e julankaagal.

merchandise [mərčəndayz] *n.* marsandiis *(o).*

merchant [mərčənt] *n.* julanke *(o).*

merciful [mərsəful] *adj.* jaafotooɗo; jurmotooɗo.

merciless [mərsəles] *adj.* mo alaa njurum; mo yurmotaako; neegɗo.

mercy [mərsi] *n.* yurmeende *(nde)*; yaafuya *(o).*

merengue [mereŋg] *n.* ngamri.

merge [mərj] *v.* rééntude; yantóndirde.

merger [mərjə] *n.* jantóndiral *(ngal).*

merit [merit] *v.* haandude.

mermaid [mərmeyd] *n.* debbo jom maayo.

merry [meri] *adj.* béltiiɗo.

mess [mes] *n.* bonande *(nde)*; tuundi *(ndi).*

message [mesij] *n.* nelal *(ngal)*; nulal *(ngal).* **deliver a** ~ yettinde nulal.

messenger [mesenjə] *n.* nelaaɗo *(o);* nulaaɗo *(o)*

messiah [mesayəh] *n.* nelaaɗo *(o).*

messy [mesi] *adj.* tunwuɗo.

metal [metəl] *n.* njamndi *(ndi).*

metallic [metalik] *adj.* ko faati e njamndi.

metalproof [metəlpruf] *adj.* tunduɗo; tunduɗum; tulɗo; ko tuli. ~ **charm** tundaram *(ɗam).*

metamorphose [metəmorfowz] *v.* waylaade; waylude.

metamorphosis [metəmorfəsis] *n.* baylagól *(ngól).*

mete [miyt] *v.* ɓetde; yeɗde.

meteorology [miytyorləji] *n.* jaŋde weeyo.

method [meθod] *n.* feere *(nde).*

meticulous [metikiləs] *adj.* ɽeewtotooɗo; dééntiiɗo.

metier [meče] *n.* golle; liggeey.

metis [metis] *n.* jilluɗo.

metre [miytə] *n.* meeteer *(o).*

metropolis [metrowpəlis] *n.* wuro mawngo.

mettle [metəl] *n.* cuusal *(ngal).*

mew [myuw] *v.* uddude; ŋeewde.

miaow [myaw] *v.* ŋeewde.

micturate [mikčureyt] *v.* taaraade; soofde; ɓuuɽeede.

mice [mays] *n.* dóómbi *(ɗi).*

micro [maykro] *adj.* pamaro; pamarum.

microphone [maykrəfon] *n.* mikró *(o).*

mid [mid] *n.* hakkunde *(nde).* ~ *way* feccere laawol.

midday [midey] *n.* fanaa *(o)*

middle [midəl] *n.* hakkunde *(nde).*

midmorning [midmɔniŋ] *n.* beetawe *(o).*

midnight [midnayt] *n.* feccere jamma.

midst [midst] *n.* hakkunde *(o);* hakkundere *(nde).*

might [mayt] *n.* doole *(ɗe).*

mighty [mayti] *adj.* dóólnuɗo.

migraine [maygreyn] *n.* hoore muusoore; muusu hoore.

migrate [maygreyt] *v.* ferde; férlude; éggude.

migration [maygreyšən] *n.* fergo *(ngo).*

mild [mayld] *adj.* ko hakindii; ko ɓurtaani.

mildew [milduw] *n.* komaak *(o).*

militant [milətənt] *n.* daraniiɗo *(o);* kaɓeteeɗo *(o).*

milk [milk] *n.* kosam *(ɗam).* **sour** ~ kaaɗɗam; fedannde *(nde).* **fresh** ~ ɓiraɗam **milk** [milk] *v.* ɓirde; saafde. ~ *for someone* ɓirande. ~ *again* ɓirtaade.

milker [milkə] *n.* ɓiroowo *(o).*

milking [milkiŋ] *n.* ɓirgól *(ngól).*

milkman [milkmən] *n.* ɓiroowo *(o).*

milky [milki] *adj.* kó jógii mbaadi kosam.

mill [mil] *n.* masiŋ gunoowo.

millenary [miləneri] *adj.* ko faati e ujunere/ujunere hitaande.

millet [milet] *n.* gawri *(ndi).* **shelled** ~ cottaandi *(ndi).* ~ *stalk* g a w Ɣ a l *(ngal).*

millier [milye] *n.* ujunere *(nde).*

mime [maym] *v.* ñémbude; ñémtinde.

mimic [mimik] *v.* ñémbude, ñémtinde.

mimic [mimik] *n.* ñemmboowo *(o).*

mimicry [mimikri] *n.* ñémtingól *(ngól).*

minaret [minəre] *n.* sóóróó *(o).*

mince [mins] *v.* taɣde taɣatinon.

mind [maynd] *v.* wondeede. *I don't mind* ɗum bonnataa hay dara/ɗum haljintaa kam.

mind [maynd] *n.* hakkille *(o). It went out of my mind* ɗum yaltu hakkillam.

mindless [mayndles] *adj.* mo ɣoɣaani.

mine [mayn] *pron.* ko am; jey am. *The book is mine* Ko miin jey deftere nde.

mingle [miŋgəl] *v.* yantude; jillondirde.

minify [minəfay] *v.* famɗinde; ustude.

minimize [minəmayz] *v.* famɗinde; lóskude.

minimum [minəmʌm] *adj.* ko ɓuri fóf famɗude.

minor [maynə] *n.* sukaajo *(o);* pamaro *(o). He is a minor* Ko o suka.

mint [mint] *n.* manto *(o);* naanaa *(o). I like mint tea* Ataaye baɗɗo naanaa ina weli mi.

mint [mint] *v.* tafde.

minute [maynuwt] *n.* pamaro.

minute [minit] *n.* hojom *(o).*

miracle [mirəkəl] *n.* haawniinde *(nde).*

miraculous [mirakiləs] *adj.* ko haawnii.

mirage [miraj] *n.* merere *(nde)/(ɗe).*

mire [mayr] *n.* ɓakkere *(nde).*

mirror [mirə] *n.* tiimtorgal *(ngal);* daaroggal *(ngal). look in the* ~ tiimtaade.

mirth [mərθ] *n.* weltaare *(nde).*

misbehave [misbəheyv] *v.* bonde jikku.

miscarry [miskəri] *v.* boosde.

mischief [misčiyf] *n.* bonande *(nde).*

misconduct [mikəndʌkt] *n.* bon nehdaagal *(ngal);* nehtaraagal *(ngal).*

miscount [mikawnt] *v.* juumde limoore.

mise [miz] *n.* ahdi *(o).*

miser [mayzə] *n.* tiiɗɗo jungo.

misfit [misfit] *v.* waasde fotde.

misfortune [misfɔčən] *n.* woroɗde *(nde);* bone *(o);* joote *(o).*

mislead [misliyd] *v.* juumnude; fuuntude.

misogynistic [mizəjiynistik] *adj.* gañɗo rewɓe.

miss [mis] *v.* haɗtaade; woofde; jottaade. ~ *one's mark* woofde. *I miss him* Mbeɗe yeewni mo.

mission [mišən] *n.* nelaaɓe *(ɓe);* nelal *(ngal).*

missive [misiyv] *n.* ɓataake *(o).*

mistake [misteyk] *n.* fuujoore *(nde);* ɓóccitorel *(ngél);* fergitaare *(nde);* pergitaagol *(ngól). make a* ~ fogoreede.

mistress [mistres] *n.* suka *(o);* taara *(o).*

mistrust [mistrʌst] *v.* hóólkisaade.

misty [misti] *adj.* ko leeraani.

misunderstand [misʌndəstənd] v. waasde faamde. *I miunderstood what you said* Mi faamaano ko mbid̃aa ko.

mitigate [mitəgeyt] v. famdinde; ustude.

mix [miks] v. iirtondirde; jiiɓde; réndinde. ~ *water and milk* tufde. ~ *it* fiindirde.

mixed [mikst] adj. jillondird̃um; ko jillondiri.

mixture [miksčə] n. jiiɓre *(nde)*; jilɓere *(nde)*; jillande *(nde)*.

moan [mown] v. angude.

mob [mob] n. deental mawngal.

mobile [mowbayl] adj. ko dirata.

mobilize [mowbəlayz] v. réndinde.

mock [mok] v. seknoraade.

mockery [mokri] n. jalkitgól *(ngól)*.

mode [mowd] n. fasoŋ *(o)*.

model [mowdəl] n. fasoŋ *(o)*.

moderate [modret] adj. kakindiidum; ko hakindii.

moderation [modəreyšən] n. hakindaare *(nde)*.

modern [modən] adj. kó yónti; kó hésdi.

modernism [modənizm] n. yonta *(o)*.

modest [modest] adj. jankiniid̃o. *He is modest* O mo yankinii.

modesty [modesti] n. yankinaare *(nde)*.

modification [mowdəfikəyšən] n. baylugól *(ngól)*.

modify [mowdəfay] v. waylude.

moil [moyl] v. tampande.

moist [moyst] adj. leppudum; kó léppi.

moisten [moystən] v. soofnude; leppinde.

moisture [moyščə] n. ɓayo *(ngo)*; ɓayto *(ngo)*.

molar [molə] n. aggitere *(nde)*; aggutere *(nde)*.

mold [mowld] v. mahde.

molest [molest] v. haljinde; memde.

mollify [moləfay] v. dééʳnude.

molt [mowlt] v. hesde; ñóórtude nguru (ngóóróndi).

moment [mowmənt] n. saanga *(o)*; sahaa *(o)*; mudda *(o)*. *at that* ~ oon sahaa.

momentary [mowməntəri] adj. ko duumaaki; ko ɓooyataa.

momentum [mowməntəm] n. doole *(d̃e)*.

Monday [mʌndi] n. altine *(o)*.

monetary [monətri] adj. ko faati e kaalis. *smallest* ~ *unit* tanka *(o)*.

money [moni] n. kaalis *(o)*. ~ *given to an artist* juurgal *(ngal)*. ~ *unit* mbuudu *(ngu)*. *borrow* ~ ñamlaade kaalis.

monger [mɑŋgə] n. jula *(o)*; julanke *(o)*.

mongrel [moŋgrəl] n. jilludo *(o)*.

monkey [mʌŋki] n. waandu *(ndu)*; buŋjéé *(o)*.

mono [mownə] n. gooto; petto.

monster [mʌnstə] n. barogal mawngal.

month [mʌnθ] n. léwru *(ndu)*. *this month* lewru dariindu ndu. *last* ~ lewru maayndu ndu. *two* ~s *ago* lewru maayndu nudya.

monthly [mʌnθli] adj. ko faati é léwru; lewru dariindu kala.

monumental [monyuwməntəl] adj. ko mawni.

moo [muw] v. huunde.

moon [muwn] n. lewru *(ndu)*. *new* ~ lewru dariindu.

moonlight [muwnlayt] n. lewlewal *(ngal)*.

moony [muwni] adj. ko faati é léwru.

Moor [muwr] n. capaato *(o)*.

mop [mop] v. 1) fóppude 2) ñirɓinaade.

moppet [mopet] n. suka *(o)*; boobo *(o)*.

moral [mowrəl] n. tindól *(ngól)*.

more [mowr] adj. kó ɓuri. *Give him more food* ɓeydan mo ñaamri.

moreover [mowrəwvə] adv. yanti heen.

morgue [morg] n. nókku dو maayɓe njoñetee.

moribund [mowrəbʌnd] adj. mo wod̃d̃aani maayde.

morning [mɔniŋ] n. subaka *(o)*; bimmbi; beetawe *(o)*. *early* ~ fajiri *(o)*. *this* ~ hande subaka.

Morocco [moroko] n. maruk.

morphology [morfowloji] n. tafngo kelme.

mortal [mɔtəl] adj. ko maayata; maayoowo.

mortality [mɔtaləti] n. maayde *(nde)*.

mortar [morta] n. wowru *(ndu)*.

mortification [mortəfikeyšən] n. koyeera *(o)*.

mortify [mortəfay] v. hóynude.

Moslem [mozləm] n. juuldo *(o)*.

mosque [mosk] n. jumaa *(o)*; misiide *(nde)*. *He went to the mosque* O yahii jumaa

mosquito [muskiyto] n. ɓówngu *(ngu)*. *big* ~ bippameernoo *(o)*.

ost [mowst] *adj.* kó buri fóf.

otel [motey] *n.* jipporde *(nde)*.

other [mʌðə] *v.* nééniraado *(o);* inna *(o);* yummiraado *(o);* neene *(o);* yumma *(o).* ~ *land* ngenndi *(ndi).* **grand**~ taaniraado debbo.

otherhood [mʌðəhud] *n.* yummiraagal *(ngal).*

otif [mowtif] *n.* 1) miijo *(ngo)* 2) sabaabu *(o).*

otion [mowšən] *n.* dirtugól *(ngól).*

otionless [mowšənles] *adj.* ko darii.

otive [mowtiv] *n.* sabaabu *(o). What is the motive* Hol ko saabii dum?

otor [mowtə] *n.* masiɲ *(o).*

otorcycle [mowtəsaykəl] *n.* moto *(o).*

ound [mownd] *n.* galle *(o).*

ount [mawnt] *v.* ɲabbude. ~ *an animal* waddaade.

ourn [mɔn] *v.* woyde; sunaade.

ourner [mɔnə] *n.* cuniido *(o);* goyoowo *(o).*

ournful [mɔnfəl] *adj.* cuniido.

ourning [mɔniŋ] *n.* sunaare *(nde).*

ouse [maws] *n.* dóómburu *(ndu).*

outh [mawθ] *n.* hunuko *(ko). Open your mouth* Mubbit hunuko maa.

outhful [mawθfəl] *n.* woobre *(nde);* longere *(nde).*

ovable [muwvəbəl] *adj.* ko dirtintee.

ove [muwv] *v.* dillude; dirde; eggude. ~ *while agonizing* fafaade; fettaade. *make someone* ~ egginde. ~ *while sitting* bafde. ~ *a little* bosde. ~ *over* dirtude. ~ *something to another place* héédtinde. ~ *away* wódditaade. ~ *to the husband's compound* hurtaade **movement** [muwvmənt] *n.* dillugol *(ngól);* dillere *(nde).*

ovie [muwvi] *n.* sinamaa *(o).*

ow [mow] *v.* hesde. *He is mowing the grass* Omon hesa hudo ko.

uch [mʌč] *adv.* pakitdum; pantudum; burtudum. *be too* ~ burtude.

nud [mʌd] *n.* bakkere *(nde).* ~ *ball* markere *(nde).*

nuddle [mʌdəl] *v.* jiibde.

nuddy [mʌdi] *adj.* lofdum; jilbudum; bakolindum. ~ *area* loopal *(ngal);* lófu *(ngu)*

nuezzin [myezen] *n.* nóddinoowo *(o).*

muffle [mʌfəl] *v.* soomde.

mug [mʌg] *n.* kóppu *(o).*

mule [myuwl] *n.*bingél puccu e mbabba.

multilingual [mʌltiliŋgwəl] *adj.* gandudo ko buri demngal gootal.

multiply [mʌltəplay] *v.* fiyde laabi kééwdi. ~ *tenfold* fiide laabi sappo.

multitude [mʌltəčuwd] *n.* keewal *(ngal).*

mum [mʌm] *adj.* déɣudo.

mumble [mʌmbəl] *v.* dumaade; sontaade.

mundane [mʌndeyn] *adj.* ko faati e aduna.

mural [myuwrəl] *adj.* ko faati e balal.

murder [mərdə] *n.* war hoore.

murder [mərdə] *v.* warde hoore. *He was murdered today* Ko hande o waraa.

murk [mərk] *n.* nibbere *(nde).*

murmur [mərmə] *v.* ñuumbaade.

muse [myuwz] *v.* miijaade.

music [myuwzik] *n.* léébi e bawdi.

musket [muskət] *n.* fétél *(o).*

Muslim [mozləm] *n.* juuldo *(o). He is a Muslim* Ko o juuldo.

must [mʌst] *v.* fotde. *You must go* A da foti yahde.

mustache [mʌstaš] *n.* suumko *(ngo).*

mustang [mʌstaš] *n.* puccu *(ngu).*

muster [mustə] *v.* réndinde.

mutable [myuwtəbəl] *adj.* ko waylotoo.

mutation [myuwteyšən] *n.* baylagól *(ngól).*

mute [myuwt] *adj.* muumo; muumdudo; déɣudo.

mutilate [myuwčəleyt] *v.* taɣde; gaañde; taɣde tergal.

mutiny [myuwtəni] *n.* jattinaare *(nde);* murtugól *(ngól).*

mutism [myuwtizm] *n.* deɣɣere *(nde).*

mutton [mʌtən] *n.* tééw njawdi; tééw mbaalu; tééw mbeewa; tééw ndamndi).

muzzle [mʌzəl] *n.* hoggo *(ngo).*

my [may] -am; ko am. ~ *bag* sakkoosam.

myriad [miryəd] *n.* kééwééndi *(ndi).*

myself [mayself] *pron.* miin; miin hooram.

mysterious [mistiyryəs] *adj.* kaawnidum; ko haawnii.

mystery [mistri] *n.* haawniinde *(nde).*

mystify [mistəfay] *v.* fuuntude.

N

nabob [nabob] *n.* galo *(o).*

nadir [nadir] *n.* ceɓtam *(ɗam);* naange *(nge).*

nag [nag] *v.* tooñde.

nag [nag] *n.* pucél *(ngél).*

nail [neyl] *v.* feɳde. *hit on the* ~ fiide e hoore. *pay on the* ~ yoɓde jungo e jungo

naissance [nesans] *n.* jibinande *(nde).*

naive [neyv] *adj.* beeɓɗo fuuntude.

naked [neykəd] *adj.* ɓóórtiiɗo; meho. *He is naked* Ko o meho.

namable [neyməbəl] *adj.* ko innotoo.

name [neym] *v.* innude. ~ *after* innirde. *He was named after his father* O inniraa ko baaba makko.

name [neym] *n.* inde *(nde) last* ~ yettoode *(nde). What is your name* Hol no mbiyete ɗaa?

namesake [neymseyk] *n.* inniraaɗo *(o);* tokara *(o)*

naming [neymiŋ] *n.* inde *(nde);* innugol *(ngól).* ~ *ceremony* inde *(nde).*

nance [nans] *n.* debati gorkati.

nap [nap] *v.* muumnaade. *take a* ~ muumnaade. *He is napping* Ko o muumniiɗo.

nape [neyp] *n.* kaɗu; hóɣɣudu *(ndu);* géénól *(ngól).*

narcissism [narsəsizm] *n.* gilli hoore mum; hooram hooram.

narrate [nəreyt] *v.* tindude; jaɳtaade.

narration [nəreyšən] *n.* tindól *(ngól);* jaɳtagól *(ngól).*

narrative [narətiv] *n.* tindól *(ngól).*

narrow [narəw] *adj.* paaɗɗum; ko faaɗi. *be in* ~ *circumstances* faaɗeede.

nasal [neyzəl] *adj.* ko faati e hinere.

nascent [neysənt] *adj.* ko fuɗɗii.

nasty [nasti] *adj.* bonɗo; tunwuɗo.

natal [neytəl] *adj.* ko faati e jibinde/jibinande.

natant [neytənt] *adj.* ko lumbii; ko hayi.

natation [neyteyšən] *n.* lummbagól *(ngól).*

natator [neyteytə] *n.* lumbotooɗo *(o).*

nates [neyts] *n.* dote *(ɗe).*

nation [neyšən] *n.* ngéndi *(ndi).*

national [našənəl] *adj.* ko faati e ngéndi. ~ *languages* ɗemɗe ngendi.

nationalism [našənəlizm] *n.* ɗowtagól kisal ngéndi.

nationalist [našənəlist] *n.* ɗówtiiɗo kisal ngéndi.

nationalize [našənəlayz] *v.* jéynude ngéndi; heɓtande ngendi.

native [neytəv] *n.* jibinaaɗo e nókku. *He is a native of this town* O jibinaa ko e ngoo wuro.

nature [neyčə] *n.* ladde *(nde);* leydi *(ndi);* mbaadi *(ndi);* ɣiɣam *(ɗam)* good natured belɗo ɣiiɣam; nehiiɗo.

natter [natə] *v.* woytaade.

naught [nɔt] *n.* dara *(o);* hay huunde.

naughty [nɔti] *adj.* bonɗo; ñanguɗo.

nausea [nɔzeya] *n.* ɓernde yiiñnde; tim ɓérél.

nauseate [nɔzeyet] *v.* yiiñde.

naval [neyvəl] *adj.* ko faati e laana/laaɗe.

navel [neyvəl] *n.* wuddu *(ndu)*

navigable [nəvigəbəl] *adj.* ɗo laana waawi rewde.

nay [nay] *adv.* alaa.

near [niyə] *prep.* sara *(o);* takko *(o).* ~ *the river* takko maayo.

nearby [niyəbay] *adv.* sara.

neat [niyt] *adj.* laaɓɗo; peewɗo.

nebulize [nebyəlayz] *v.* niɓɓiɗde; niɓɓiɗinde.

necessary [nesəsəri] *adj.* ko soklaa. *It is necessary* Ina soklaa.

necessitate [nesəsəteyt] *v.* sóklude.

necessity [nesəsəti] *n.* sokla *(o).*

neck [nek] *n.* daande *(nde);* géénól *(ngól);* hóɣɣudu *(ndu). save one's* ~ dandude hoore mum.

necklace [nekləs] *n.* cakka *(ka).*

need [niyd] *v.* haajde; sóklude. *I need your help* Mbeɗe sokli ballal maa.

need [niyd] *n.* sokla *(o);* haaju *(o).*

needle [niydəl] *n.* meselal *(ngal).*

needless [niydles] *adj.* ko soklaaka.

needy [niydi] *adj.* cókluɗo; katojinɗo heen.

negate [nəgeyt] *v.* niilnude.

negation [nəgeyšən] *n.* niilnugól *(ngól).*

egative [negətiv] *adj.* ko niilnaa.

eglect [nəglekt] *v.* wélsindaade.

eglect [nəglekt] *n.* wélsindaare *(nde).*

eglectful [nəglektfəl] *adj.* bélsindiiɗo. *He is so neglectful* Ndaw ko welsindii.

egligence [neglejəns] *n.* wélsindaare *(nde).*

egligent [neglejənt] *adj.* bélsindiiɗo.

egociate [nəgowšeyt] *v.* haaldude; yééytóndirde; haaldeede.

egotiable [nəgowšəbəl] *adj.* ko ina haaldoo. *The price is negociable* Coggu ngu ina waɗdee ustu ɓeydu.

egotiation [nəgowšeyšən] *n.* kaaldigal *(ngal).*

egro [niygro] *n.* ɓaleejo *(o).*

eigh [neyh] *v.* hijde

eighborhood [neybəhud] *n.* sara *(o);* takko *(o).*

eighbor [neybə] *n.* kóɗdiiɗo *(o). He is my next door neighbor* Ko kanko woni koɗdiiɗo am takkiiɗo mi.

enuphar [nenuwfar] *n.* raayre *(nde).*

eoteric [newotərik] *adj.* keso; kesum.

ephew [nefyuw] *n.* baaɗiraaɗo *(o).*

epotism [nepətizm] *n.* leñamleñaagu *(ngu).*

erval [nərvəl] *adj.* ko faati e ɗaɗól.

erve [nərv] *n.* ɗaɗol *(ngól). lose one's ~* ɓernude; mettinde; sekde.

ervous [nərvəs] *adj.* mo hakkille mum deeɤaani; looɓɗo.

est [nest] *n.* sabbundu *(ndu)*

est [nest] *v.* sabbinde.

estle [nesəl] *v.* sabbinde.

estling [neslĩ] *n.* ɓingél sóndu.

et [net] *n.* saakiti *(o).*

eural [nyuwrəl] *adj.* ko faati e ɗaɗi.

eutral [nyuwtrəl] *adj.* hakkundeejo; mo wuuranaaki.

ever [nevə] *adv.* abada; muk. *Never give up on a good thing* Neɗɗo ina foti jaggude e ko moɤɤi.

evertheless [nevəðəles] *adv.* kono noon.

ew [nyuw] *adj.* keso; kesum. *the ~ moon* lewru dariindu *(ndu).*

ewborn [nyuwborn] *n.* tiggu *(o).*

news [nyuwz] *n.* kabaruuji *(ɗi);* nanallaaji *(ɗi). -man* kabroowo *(o). Have you heard the news* A nanii kabaaru o?

next [nekst] dewɗo heen; cukko; cukkuɗo.

nib [nib] *n.* cééɓééndi kuɗól; hoggo *(ngo).*

nibble [nibəl] *v.* ŋolde; mooɤde; serde; ŋefde.

nice [nays] *adj.* jooɗɗo; moɤɤo. *He is nice* Omo moɤɤi.

nickname [nikneym] *n.* waccoore *(nde);* sowoore *(nde)*

nictate [nikteyt] *v.* majde.

nidificate [nidəfikeyt] *v.* sabbinde.

nidify [nidəfay] *v.* sañde sabbundu; sabbinde.

niece [niys] *n.* baaɗiraaɗo debbo.

niggard [nigəd] *adj.* borooɗo.

nigh [nay] *v.* faandaade; ɓattaade.

night [nayt] *n.* jamma *(o). last ~* jamma hanki.

nihilism [nihilizm] *n.* luutndagól *(ngól).*

nimble [nimbəl] *v.* koyɗo e léydi.

nine [nayn] *num.* jeenay.

ninefold [naynfowld] *adj.* laabi jeenay.

nineth [naynθ] *ord.* jeenayo.

ninety [naynti] *num.* capanɗe jeenay.

nip [nip] *v.* taɤde; ŋuccude.

nit [nit] *n.* mbimɤa *(ba).*

nix [niks] *n.* dara *(o);* hay huunde

no [now] *adv.* alaa.

nobble [nowbəl] *v.* yeende; soodde.

nobility [nowbələti] *n.* ndimaagu *(ngu).*

noble [nowbəl] *n.* dimo *(o);* lawake *(o).*

nobleman [nowbəlmən] *n.* dimo *(o).*

nobody [nowbədi] pron. hay gooto.

nocent [nowsənt] *adj.* ko gaañata.

nocturnal [noktərnəl] *adj.* ko faati e jamma; ko diwata jamma.

nod [nod] *v.* dillinde hoore; jaɓde.

node [nowd] *n.* wulnde *(nde);* jokkorde *(nde).*

noggin [nogin] *n.* hoore neɗɗo; koppu *(o).*

noise [noiz] *n.* dille *(ɗe);* dillere *(nde);* gulaali *(ɗi).*

noisy [noyzi] *adj.* kó hééwi dille; keewɗo dille. *be ~* heewde dille.

nominal [nowmənəl] *adj.* ko faati e innde.

nonchalant [nənšələnt] *adj.* mo wondaaka.

none [nown] hay huunde; hay dara.

nonsense [nonsəns] n. maayka *(ka)*; ko alaa maanaa. *What you are saying is nonsense* Haala maa kaa daraa ki.

nook [nuwk] n. lóbbudu *(ndu)*.

noose [nuwz] n. wórsundu *(ndu)*.

norm [norm] n. huunde yamiraande; huunde rewnde laawól.

normal [nɔməl] *adj.* kó réwi laawól.

normalize [nɔmǝlayz] v. réwnude laawól.

north [norθ] n. rewo *(ngo)*.

northeast [norθiyst] n. fuɗnaange rewo.

northerner [norðənə] n. rewanke *(o)*.

northwest [norθwest] n. hirnaange rewo.

nose [nowz] n. hinere *(nde)*. ~ *bleeding* tuΥΥam *(ɗam)*. *blow one's* ~ fiifaade; ñittaade.

nostalgia [nostəljə] n. yeeweende *(nde)*.

nostalgic [nostəljik] *adj.* jééwnuɗo.

nostril [nostrəl] n. wuddere hinere.

not [not] *adv.* alaa. ~ *yet* suwaa; suwaa tawo. ~ *even* hay. ~ *at all* muk.

notable [nowtəbəl] n. koohoowo *(o)*.

notation [nowteyšən] n. bindól *(ngól)*.

notch [nɔtč] v. seekoode *(nde)*.

note [nowt] n. kóngól bindangól.

noteworthy [nowtwərði] *adj.* ko haandi e.

nothing [noθiŋ] n. meere *(nde)*; dara *(o)*; futtere *(nde)*.

notice [nowtis] v. tintude; yiide; teskaade. *I did not notice it* Mi teskaaki ɗum.

notice [nowtis] n. kabaaru *(o)*.

notification [nowtǝfikeyšǝn] n. kabaaru *(o)*; tintingól *(ngól)*.

notify [nowtǝfay] v. tintinde; andinde; habrude.

notion [nowšən] n. miijo *(ngo)*.

notorious [nowtǝryǝs] *adj.* dówluɗo.

nought [nɔt] n. hay huunde.

noun [nawn] n. inde *(nde)*.

nourish [nuriš] v. ñamminde.

nourishment [nurišmǝnt] n. nguura; ñamri *(ndi)*.

novel [nowvǝl] *adj.* kó hésɗi.

novelty [nowvǝlti] n. huunde hésɗunde.

novice [nowvis] n. ekkotooɗo *(o)*; keso.

now [naw] *adv.* jóóni. *every* ~ *and then* sahaa sahaa kala.

noxious [nokšǝs] *adj.* ko bonnata.

noyade [nuwayad] n. yoolaare *(nde)*.

nub [nʌb] n. ɓoodde *(nde)*.

nubile [nyuwbǝl] debbo jóntuɗo reseede.

nude [nyuwd] *adj.* meho; ɓóórtiiɗo.

nudge [nʌj] v. ɓaaΥde.

nuisance [nusǝns] n. huunde haaɓniinde. *He is a nuisance* Omo haaɓnii.

null [nʌl] n. hay huunde.

nullify [nʌlǝfay] v. niilnude.

numb [nʌm] *adj.* jaaɗɗum; ko jaaɗi.

number [nʌmbǝ] n. limoore *(nde)*; limre *(nde)*. ~ *one* limoore adiinde.

numerable [nuwmǝrǝbǝl] *adj.* ko limotoo.

numeral [muwmǝrǝl] *adj.* ko faati e limoore.

numerate [nuwmǝret] v. limde.

numeration [nuwmǝreyšǝn] n. limoore *(nde)*.

numerous [nuwmǝrǝs] *adj.* kééwɗi; keewɗum; kó hééwi.

nuptial [nupšǝl] *adj.* ko faati e dewgal.

nurse [nǝrs] v. safrude.

nurture [nǝrčǝ] v. diwnude; nehde.

nut [nʌt] n. woroore *(nde)*.

nutrition [nuwtriyšǝn] n. ñaamdu *(ndu)*.

nylon [naylǝn] n. niloɈ *(o)*.

O

oaf [owf] *n.* nedɗo muddo.

oar [owr] *v.* awˠude.

oar [owr] *n.* awˠal *(ngal)*; lummbirgal *(ngal)*.

oat [owt] *n.* naskaaɗo.

oath [owθ] *n.* waatoore *(nde)*; woondoore *(nde).* **make an** ~ woonde. *be under* ~ woonde.

obdurate [objuwrət] *adj.* jattiniiɗo.

obedience [obiyjəns] *n.* ɗowtaare *(nde).*

obedient [obiyjənt] *adj.* ɗówtiiɗo.

obese [owbiyz] *adj.* béllinɗo; butto; buttiɗɗo.

obey [owbey] *v.* ɗowtaade. *You must obey him* Aɗa foti ɗowtaade mo.

obfuscate [obfəskeyt] *v.* nibbiɗinde; hawjinde.

obituary [owbičəri] *n.* taggéé *(o).*

object [objekt] *v.* salaade. *I object to that proposal* Mi jaɓaani ngoon miijo.

object [objekt] *n.* huunde *(nde).*

objection [objekšən] *n.* salaare *(nde).*

objective [objektiv] *n.* muuya *(o). The objective is to finish early* Njiɗɗen ko haljitde law.

obligate [obləgeyt] *v.* waawnude.

obligation [obləgeyšən] *n.* fotde *(nde).*

oblige [oblayj] *v.* waawnude.

oblique [obliyk] *adj.* ko fortaaki.

obliterate [oblətəreyt] *v.* mómtude.

obliteration [oblətəreyšən] *n.* mómtugól *(ngol).*

oblivion [obləvyən] *n.* jéjji *(ɗi).*

oblivious [obliyvyəs] *adj.* jéjjitɗo; jéjjitoowo.

obnoxious [obnokšəs] *adj.* kaabniiɗo.

obscene [obsiyn] *adj.* kóngól bóngól.

obscurant [obskyuwrənt] *n.* nibbiɗinoowo *(o).*

obscure [obskyuwr] *adj.* nibbiɗɗum.

obscurity [obskyuwrəti] *n.* nibbere *(nde).*

observable [obzərvəbəl] *adj.* ko yiyotoo.

observation [obzəveyšən] *n.* laargól *(ngól)*; ˠééwki *(ki).*

observe [obzərv] *v.* laarde.

obsess [obses] *v.* woˠeede; woˠde.

obsession [obsešən] *n.* woˠa *(o)*; ngoˠa *(o).*

obsolescence [obsowləsəns] *n.* nayewaagu *(ngu).*

obsolete [obsəliyt] *adj.* kó ˠééɳi; ko natti huutoreede.

obstacle [obstəkəl] *n.* haɗiinde *(nde).*

obstinate [obstənət] *adj.* jattiniiɗo; ɳatɗo.

obstruct [obstrʌkt] *v.* haɗde.

obtain [obteyn] *v.* hebde.

obtainable [obteynəbəl] *adj.* ko hebotoo.

obturate [občəreyt] *v.* mubbude; sukkude.

obvious [əbvyəs] *adj.* ko fééñi; peeñɗum. *It is obvious* Eɗum laabi.

occasion [okeyʒən] *n.* sahaa *(o).*

occasional [okeyʒənl] *adj.* sahaa sahaa.

occasionally [okeyʒənəli] *adv.* sahaa sahaa; sahaa kala.

occidental [oksədəntəl] *adj.* ko faati e hirnaange.

occlude [okluwd] *v.* sukkude; mubbude.

occult [okʌlt] *adj.* ko faati e dabare.

occupant [okyuwpənt] *n.* koɗɗo *(o)*; gonɗo *(o).*

occupation [okyuwpeyšən] *n.* liggééy *(o).*

occupy [okuwpay] *v.* wonde e.

occur [okər] *v.* wonde; laataade; waɗde. *The accident occurred today* Ko hande aksida o waɗi.

ocean [oyšən] *n.* gééc *(o).*

oceanic [oyšəyanik] *adj.* ko faati e gééc.

octa [oktə] *pref.* jeetati.

octogenarian [oktəjəneyryən] *n.* jom duubi capanɗe jeetati fayi jeenay.

ocular [okyələ] *adj.* ko faati e yitere/gite/giile.

oculist [okyəwləst] *n.* cafroowo gite.

odd [od] *adj.* teelɗum; ko teeli. *an ~ number* limoore teelnde. *be ~* waasde yubbude.

odious [ojəs] *adj.* ko añaa.

odor [odə] *n.* uurééki *(ki)*; luubééki *(ki).*

off [əf] *prep.* kó wóɗɗi. *be* ~ tellaade; jippaade; juumde.

offal [ofəl] *n.* kurjuru *(o).*

offcast [əfkast] *adj.* ko joñaa.

offend [ofend] v. tooñde; alɓaade. *He was offended by your remarks* A sectnii mo.

offense [ofens] n. tooñange *(nge)*.

offer [ofə] v. hókkude. *Make me an offer* haalanam ko njogi ɗaa.

offering [ofriŋ] n. dokkal *(ngal)*.

office [ofis] n. biró *(o)*. *He went to the office* O yahii biro makko.

official [ofiyšəl] *adj.* ko yamiraa.

officiate [ofiyšeyt] v. gollaade gollal mum.

offspring [ofspriŋ] n. ɓésngu *(ngu)*.

often [oftən] *adv.* jó é jó; sahaa sahaa kala.

ogle [ogəl] v. laarde.

ogre [ogə] n. mbaróódi *(ndi)*.

oil [oyl] n. nebam *(ɗam)*; diwlin *(o)*.

oil [oyl] v. wujde; newde. *~ someone's hair* wujde.

ointment [oyntmənt] n. lékki póppétééki.

okra [owkrə] n. kanje *(ɗe)* old [owld] *adj.* ɓooyɗo; naywuɗo; kiiɗɗo. *~ fashioned* ko ƴeeɗi; ko jolti. *How old are you* No duuɓi maa poti. *I am three years old* Mi dañii duuɓi tati.

older [owldə] *adj.* kéccuɗo. *~ sibling* deede *(o)* ; mawniraaɗo *(o)*. *be ~ than* héccude. *He is older than you* Ko kanko heccu maa.

oldest [owldəst] *adj.* ɓurɗo fóf heewde duuɓi.

olympic [olimpik] *adj.* ko faati e pijirlóóji hakkunde leyɗeele.

omelet [omlet] n. omolet *(o)*.

omit [omit] v. yéjjitde; joñde.

omnipotent [omnəpowtənt] n. jóómiraaɗo *(o)*.

omniscient [omnəšənt] *adj.* gando.

on [on] *prep.* e; dów.

once [wans] *adv.* góótól.

oncoming [onkəmiŋ] n. ɓattagól *(ngól)*.

one [wan] *num.* góó ; gooto *(o)*. *~ person* neɗɗo gooto. *~ book* deftere wootere.

one-eyed [wanayd] *adj.* ɗokko.

oneiric [ownərik] *adj.* ko faati e kóyɗól/kóyɗi.

oneness [wanes] n. wootere *(nde)*.

onerous [onərəs] *adj.* ko tiiɗi; tiiɗɗum.

oneself [wanself] pr. hooremum.

onion [onyən] n. wasalde *(nde)*; soblere *(nde)*.

only [onli] *adj.* tan; gooto; petto; bajjo.

onset [onsət] n. fuɗɗorde *(nde)*.

onward [onwəd] *adv.* faade yeeso.

oology [owloji] n. jangde ɓoccooɗe cólli.

opaque [owpeyk] *adj.* ko tunndi lewlewal.

open [owpən] *adj.* ŋaabiɗum; gudditiiɗum. *~ space* dingiral *(ngal)*. *be wide ~* ŋaabaade; ŋabɓitaade. *~ land* sooynde *(nde)*. *The door is open* Damal ngal uddaaki.

open [owpən] v. sukkitde; udditde; mubɓitde; ombitde. *~ halfway* aarde. *~ half way* feerde. *~ apart* weeñde; ŋaabde. *~ eyes widely* fulñitde. *~ fire* fellude.

opener [owpnə] n. gudditoowo *(o)* ; huunde uddittoore.

opening [owpniŋ] n. udditgol *(ngól)*; uddital *(ngal)*.

operate [owpreyt] v. dógnude.

operation [owpreyšən] n. dógnugól *(ngól)*.

ophthalmic [oftəlmik] *adj.* ko faati e gite/yitere.

ophthalmologist n. cafroowo gite.

opine [owpayn] v. hóllude miijo.

opinion [owpiynyən] n. miijo *(ngo)* sikke *(o)*. *in my ~* e wiide am. *What is your opinion* Holko woni miijo maa.

opponent [opownənt] n. kaɓdiiɗo *(o)*.

opportune [opəčuwn] n. ko hawri.

opportunity [opəčuwnəti] n. dañal *(ngal)*; keɓagol *(ngól)*. *I have not had the opportunity to go there* Mi dañaani no njahrumi toon.

oppose [opowz] v. nañde; luutndaade.

opposite [opəzit] *adj.* kó luutóndiri; ko luutndii. *the ~ sex* gorko; debbo; wordu; rewru.

opposition [opəziyšən] n. luutndagól *(ngól)*.

oppress [opres] v. hiiɗaade; ɓittude. *They are oppressed* Ko ɓe ɓittaaɓe.

oppression [oprešən] n. kiiɗagól *(ngól)*; ɓittugól *(ngól)*.

opt [opt] v. suɓaade.

optical [optəkəl] *adj.* ko faati e gite.

optician [optiyšən] n. peewnoowo lone; jeeyoowo lone.

optimal [optiməl] *adj.* ɓurɗo fóf; kó ɓuri fóf.

optimism [optəmizm] n. ɗamaawu *(o)*.

ptimist [optəmist] *n.* necɗo ɗaminiiɗo.
ptimum [optəməm] *n.* huunde burnde fóf.
ption [opšən] *n.* cubagól *(ngól).* *What are my options* Hol ko mbaawmi wacɗe/Hol ko mbaawmi subaade?
ptional [opšənəl] *adj.* ko faati e cubagól.
pulence [opyuwləns] *n.* keewal *(ngal).*
pulent [opyuwlənt] *adj.* keewraaɗo; keewɗum; ko heewi.
r [or] *conj.* walla; maa.
racle [orəkəl] *n.* baajotooɗo *(o).*
ral [owrəl] *adj.* ko faati e hunuko.
range [orənj] *n.* soraas *(o).*
rator [owreytə] *n.* kaaloowo *(o).*
rchard [ɔčəd] *n.* ngesa bibbe leɗɗe.
rdain [ɔrdeyn] *v.* yamirde.
rder [ɔdə] *n.* 1) déwóndiral *(ngal)* 2) yamiroore *(nde).*
rder [ɔdə] *v.* yamirde.
rderly [ɔdəli] *adj.* kó réwóndiri; ko réggóndiri.
rdinance [ɔdəli] *n.* yamiroore *(nde).*
rdure [ordyuwr] *n.* kurjuru *(o);* dubuuje *(ɗe).*
rgan [orgən] *n.* tergal *(ngal).* *extra* ~ sindere *(nde).*
rganism [ɔgənizm] *n.* muumantél Alla.
rganization [ɔgənəzeyšən] *n.* fedde *(nde).* *What is the purpose of your organization* Hol ko woni muuyaa fedde mon?
rient [oryənt] *n.* fuɗnaange *(nge).*
rient [oryənt] *v.* huccinde.
riental [oryəntəl] *adj.* ko faati e fuɗnaange.
rientation [oryənteyšən] *n.* kuccingól *(ngól).*
rifice [ɔrəfays] *n.* wuddere *(nde).*
rigin [orəjin] *n.* iwdi *(ndi);* lasli *(o).* *What is the origin of the Fulani* Hol ko woni lasli Fulbe?
riginate [orəjəneytə] *v.* sosde; iwde.
riginator [orəjəneytə] *n.* cosɗo *(o)* ; puɗɗuɗo *(o).*
rnament [ornəmənt] *n.* ñakkuɗi *(ndi).*
rnamental [ornəməntəl] *adj.* ko faati e ñakkudi.
rnate [orneyt] *v.* sinkude.
rphan [ɔfən] *n.* alyatiimu *(o)* ; baayo *(o).*

orphanage [ɔfənij] *n.* alyatiimaagu *(ngu);* alyatimaagal *(ngal).*
orthographer [orθogrəfə] *n.* jom bindól.
orthography [orθogrəfi] *v.* bindol *(ngól).*
orthopedics [orθopediks] *n.* safaara koyɗe.
os [os] *n.* Yiyal *(ngal).*
oscillate [osəleyt] *v.* yiilaade; dillude.
oscillation [osəleyšən] *n.* jiilagól *(ngól).*
osculate [oskyuwleyt] *v.* buucaade.
osculation [oskyuwleyšən] *n.* buucagól *(ngól).*
ossify [osəfay] *v.* Yiynude.
ostrich [ostrič] *n.* ndaw *(o)*
other [oðə] *adj.* goɗɗo. ~ *ones* góɗɗi *(ɗi).* *the* ~ *book* deftere ndeya.
otherwise [oðərwayz] *adv.* so wonaa ɗum.
otology [otələji] *n.* jangde nófru.
otter [otə] *n.* muumantél Alla.
ought [owt] *v.* fotde.
our [awə] *det.* amen; meeɗen; ko men. ~ *baby* bingel amen.
ours [awəz] *pron.* ko men. *The book is ours* ɗum ko deftere men.
ourselves [awəselvz] *pr.* enen koyemen; minen.
oust [awst] *v.* yaltinde; riiwde.
ouster [awstə] *n.* jaltingól *(ngól).*
out [awt] *prep.* boowal *(ngal).*
out-of-date [awtəfdeyt] *adj.* kó Yééŋi; ko jolti. *be* ~ Yeeŋde; joltude.
outdated [awtdeytid] *adj.* kó Yééŋi.
outdoor [awtdɔ] *n.* boowal *(ngal).*
outfit [awtfit] *n.* cómcól *(ngól).*
outgoing [awtgowiŋ] *adj.* cakalo.
outgrow [awtgrəw] *v.* burtaade.
outlaw [awtlɔ] *n.* luutndiiɗo laawól.
outlet [awtlet] *n.* yaltirde *(nde).* *This is not an outlet* ɗum wonaa yaltirde.
outline [awtlayn] *n.* kééról *(ngól).*
outline [awtlayn] *v.* amminde.
outpace [awtpeys] *v.* daɗtaade.
output [awtput] *n.* coñaandi *(ndi).*
outrage [awtreyj] *n.* tooñange *(nge);* gaañande *(nde).*
outright [awtrayt] *adj.* ɗoon e ɗoon.
outrun [awtrʌn] *v.* daɗde.

outset [awtset] *n.* fuɗɗoode *(nde)*; fuɗɗorde *(nde). from the* ~ gila adan; gila fuɗɗii.

outside [awtsayd] *n.* boowal *(ngal).*

outsider [awtsaydə] *n.* mo jeyaaka e.

outskirts [awtskərt] *n.* saraaji *(ɗi).*

oval [owvəl] *adj.* kó jógii tagóódi 6occoonde.

ovate [owveyt] *adj.* ko jógii tagóódi 6occoonde.

oven [owvən] *n.* fuur *(o).*

over [owvə] *prep.* dów. *be* ~ gasde; fusde.

overdo [owvədu] *v.* 6urtinde.

overdue [owvəjuw] *adj.* kó 6énni.

overeat [owvəriyt] *v.* 6uuteede.

overflow [owvəfləw] *n.* rufo *(ngo).*

overlap [owvəlap] *v.* 6urtude; yantude; naatondirde.

overlook [owvəluk] *v.* tiimde.

overrule [owvəruwl] *v.* haɗde.

overseas [owvəsiyz] *n.* caggal gééc.

oversee [owvəsiy] *v.* reende; ardaade.

oversleep [owvəsliyp] *v.* weetndorde. *I overslept this morning* Ko m beetndorɗo.

overtake [owvəteyk] *v.* daɗtaade.

overtime [owvətaym] *n.* waktuuji 6urtuɗi.

overwhelm [owvəwelm] *v.* foolde.

ovine [owvayn] *adj.* ko faati e baali.

ovoid [ovoyd] *adj.* kó jógii tagóód 6occoonde.

owe [ow] *v.* rewde. *I owe you fifty francs* Mbeɗe rewmaa buuɗi sappo/Mbeɗe jogani maa duu6i sappo.

owl [awl] *n.* puppu6al *(ngal).*

own [own] *v.* jogaade; halfude; jeyde. *I own a car* Mbeɗe jogii oto.

owner [ownə] *n.* jeyɗo; jom; kaliifa *(o). He is the owner of the house* Ko kanko jey galle o.

ownership [ownəšip] *n.* jeyal *(ngal).*

ox [oks] *n.* ngaari *(ndi). young* ~ yeegc *(ngo)*; gayel *(ngél).*

oyster [oystə] *n.* wujo *(ngo).*

P

[pa] *n.* baabiraaɗo *(o)*.

e [peys] *v.* daasnaade; daagaade; hnaade. **go at a slow** ~ yahrude yeeso.

:er [peysə] *n.* daasnotooɗo *(o)*; **ʌ**agotooɗo *(o)*; jahnotooɗo *(o)*.

ific [pasəfik] *adj.* deeɣɗo; jiɗɗo :eɣal.

:ifier [pasəfayə] *n.* deeɣnoowo *(o)*.

:ifism [pasəfizm] *n.* deeɣre *(nde)*; jam **).**

:ify [pasəfay] *v.* dééɣnude.

:ing [peysiŋ] *n.* ñaaɣal *(ngal)*.

:k [pak] *v.* soomde; haɓɓude. ~ **one's** *othing* feewnude comci mum.

:ker [pakə] *n.* coomoowo *(o)*.

:ket [paket] *n.* pakket *(o)*.

:king [pakiŋ] *n.* cóómgól *(ngól)*; ʌɓɓugól *(ngól)*.

:t [pakt] *n.* aadóndiral *(ngal)*.

d [pad] *n.* tekkere *(nde)*; jappeere *(nde)*.

ddle [padəl] *n.* awɣal *(ngal)*; awɣirgal ʌgal).

ddle [padəl] *v.* awɣude.

ddler [padlə] *n.* awɣoowo *(o)*.

ddling [padliŋ] *n.* awɣugól *(ngól)*.

dishah [padəša] *n.* laamɗo.

dlock [padlok] *n.* udumere *(nde)*.

en [peyən] *n.* jimól *(ngól)*.

gan [peygən] *n.* mo wonaa juulɗo.

ge [peyj] *n.* hello kayit; baŋŋe kaayit. *ou can write on this page* Aɗa waawi ʌindude e ngo hello.

ginal [pajinəl] *adj.* ko faati e hello kaayit.

ginate [pajəneyt] *v.* limde kelle ʌaayitaaji.

il [peyl] *n.* siwóó *(o)*.

illasse [palyas] *n.* pajaas *(o)*.

in [peyn] *n.* **1)** muusu *(o)*; mettere *(nde)*; ʌɪ]; muusééki *(ki)* **2)** Ŋatiwere *(nde)*. *I eel your pain* Enen ndendi sunaare.

ined [peynd] *adj.* gaañiiɗo; cuniiɗo.

inful [peynfəl] *adj.* kó muusi; muusɗum. *t is painful* Ina muusi.

int [peynt] *n.* pentiir *(o)*

inted [peyntəd] *adj.* kó péntiraa.

inter [peyntə] *n.* péntiroowo *(o)*.

painting [peyntiŋ] *n.* natal *(ngal)* péntirgol *(ngól)*.

pair [per] *n.* ɗiɗi.

pajamas [pajaməz] *n.* cómci baaldirteeɗe.

pal [pal] *n.* séhil *(o)*.

palace [palis] *n.* hoɗorde laamɗo.

palatal [palətəl] *adj.* ko faati e ɗakañe.

palate [palət] *n.* ɗakaañe *(o)*.

palaver [paləvə] *n.* yeewtere *(nde)*.

pale [peyl] *adj.* joomɗo.

palfrey [palfrey] *n.* puccu *(ngu)*.

palisade [paləseyd] *n.* galle *(o)*.

pallbearer [polberə] *n.* jahoowo janayse; nawoowo maayɗo to qabri mum.

pallet [palet] *n.* daago *(ngo)*.

palliasse [palyas] *n.* pajaas *(o)*.

palliate [palyeyt] *v.* dééɣnude.

palm [pɑm] *n.* **1)** newre *(nde)* **2)** lekki *(ki)*. *grease someone's* ~ yeende.

palmar [pɑmə] *adj.* ko faati e newre jungo.

palmer [pɑmə] *n.* kajjuɗo.

palpable [palpəbəl] *adj.* ko yiyitoo; ko memotoo.

palpate [palpeyt] *v.* memde.

palpitate [palpəteyt] *v.* diwde.

palpitation [palpəteyšən] *n.* lukkere *(nde)*.

paltry [poltri] *adj.* nuskuɗum (seeɗa).

pamper [pampə] *v.* bónnude; hórsinde; béwnude; moomde.

pan [pan] *n.* kastiloor *(o)*.

panache [pənaš] *n.* jombo *(ko)*; ñakkudi *(ndi)*.

pancake [paŋkeyk] *n.* weñere *(nde)*.

pandemic [pandemik] *adj.* ko yaaji; ko huɓtódini.

pandit [pandit] *n.* gando *(o)*.

pandy [pandi] *v.* fiide e jungo.

pang [paŋ] *n.* sunaare *(nde)*.

panhandle [panhandəl] *n.* jungo kastiloor.

panhandle [panhandəl] *v.* ñaagaade; yelaade.

panic [panik] *n.* jeeɣere *(nde)*; kulól *(ngól)*.

panic [panik] *v.* jééɣude; hulde; weftileede.

pannier [panye] *n.* pañe *(o)*.

pant [pant] *v.* lehde; féttude.

panter [pantə] *n.* pettoowo *(o)*.
panther [panƟə] *n.* céwngu *(ngu)*.
pantry [pantri] *n.* faawru *(ndu)*.
pants [pants] *n.* tuuba *(ba)*. *wear one's* ~ ɓoornaade tuuba mum.
pap [pap] *n.* éndu *(ndu)*.
papaya [papayə] *n.* pappaaye *(o)*.
paper [peypə] *n.* kaayit *(o)*
par [par] *n.* kó fóti.
parachute [parəšuwt] *n.* téllinde; tellaade.
parade [pəreyd] *v.* ñaaⲅde; maajde.
parade [pəreyd] *n.* ñaaⲅal *(ngal)*.
paradigm [parədaym] *n.* yéru *(ngu)*.
paradise [parədayz] *n.* aljanna *(o)*. *go to* ~ naatde aljanna.
paragraph [parəgraf] *n.* windande *(nde)*.
parallel [parəlel] *adj.* laabi tiindiiɗi nókku gooto ɗi pottataa.
paralytic [parəlitik] *adj.* boofo; góófɗuɗo.
paralyzed [parəlayzd] *adj.* góófɗuɗo; boofo.
paraphrase [parəfreyz] *v.* sifaade; reftaade e.
parasite [parəsayt] *adj.* pawiiɗo.
parasol [parəsol] *n.* paraseewal *(ngal)*.
parcel [pasəl] *n.* neldal *(ngal)*.
parch [pač] *v.* yóórnude.
pardon [padən] *n.* yaafuya *(o)*. *I beg your pardon* Ko mbiiɗaa.
pardon [padən] *v.* yaafaade.
pardoner [padənə] *n.* jaafotooɗo *(o)*.
pare [par] *v.* séttude; taⲅde.
parent [perənt] *n.* jinnaaɗo *(o)*.
parental [perəntəl] *adj.* ko faati e jinnaaɗo.
parenthood [perənthud] *n.* enɗam *(ɗam)*.
parenticide [perəntəsayd] *n.* neɗɗo barɗo jinnaaɗo/jinnaaɓe mum.
parity [parəti] *n.* potal *(ngal)*.
park [pak] *n.* galle *(o)* jawdi/muumantééji Alla.
parlance [paləns] *n.* haala *(ka)*.
parlay [paley] *v.* fawde; tegde.
parley [paley] *n.* yeewtere *(nde)*.
parlous [paləs] *adj.* ⲅoⲅɗo.
parol [pərowl] *n.* nanalla *(o)*.
parole [pərowl] *v.* ɗaccitde cokanooɗo. *be on* ~ jaggeede e kongol.

parricide [parəsayd] *n.* barɗo jinnaaɗ mum.
parrot [parət] *n.* sóóyru *(ndu)*.
parry [pari] *v.* ruuɗaade; wappaade.
parse [pas] *v.* sifaade.
parsimony [pasəmowni] *n.* tiiɗɗo jungo.
part [pat] *n.* sengo *(ngo)*; feccere *(ndɛ* geɗal *(ngal)*. *be* ~ *of* jeyeede e.
part [pat] *v.* séértude.
partake [pateyk] *v.* féccude; taweede.
parted [patid] *adj.* ko feccaa.
partial [pašəl] *adj.* 1) ko faati e geɗal jingoowo; guuraniiɗo.
partiality [pašyələti] *n.* jingere *(nde)*.
partible [patəbəl] *adj.* ko ii seerndoo/feccoo.
participant [pərtisipənt] *n.* jantuɗo *(ɛ* tawtoraaɗo *(o)*.
participate [pərtəsəpeyt] *v.* yantud taweede; tawtoreede.
particle [patəkəl] *n.* géɗél *(ngél)*.
particular [patikilə] *adj.* ko faati e.
particularly [patikiləli] *adv.* tééⲅti noon ɛ
parting [patiŋ] *n.* ceergal *(nga* céérndugól.
partisan [patizən] *n.* gonanɗo *(ɛ* góndaɗo *(o)*.
partite [pertayt] *adj.* ko feccaa.
partition [pərtiyšən] *n.* péccugól *(ngól)*.
partitioning [pərtiyšəniŋ] *n.* séérndad féccude.
partner [patnə] *n.* liggódiiɗo *(o)*; góndiiɗ *(o)*.
partridge [patrij] *n.* gerlal *(ngal)*.
parturient [partyuwryənt] *adj.* ɳarwuɗo.
party [pati] *v.* kéwnude.
party [pati] *n.* parti *(o)*; kéw *(o)*.
parure [paruwr] *n.* cuɗaari *(ndi)*.
pass [pas] *v.* ɓennude; daɗde; daɗtaad yawtude; rewde. ~ *again* ɓénnitde. ~ *t* *normal limits* muukaade. ~ *close* wirtaade. ~ *without breaking* saayde.
passable [pasəbəl] *adj.* ko ɓennata; ɗo ii rewoo.
passage [pasij] *n.* laawól *(ngól)*; windan *(nde)*.
passenger [pasenjə] *n.* paasaase *(o)*.
passer [pasə] *n.* jahoowo *(o)*; ɓennoow *(o)*; berlotooɗo *(o)*. ~ *by* jahoowo *(o)*.

ssion [pašən] *n.* pinnugól *(ngól)*.

ssive [pasiv] *adj.* mo dillataa; nuggaro.

ssport [pasport] *n.* paaspoor *(o)*.

ssword [paswərd] *n.* kóngól nandiraagól.

st [past] *n.* hankimen. **go** ~ ɓénnude; awtude; faataade.

storal [pastowrəl] *adj.* ko faati e gaynaaka.

sture [pasčə] *v.* óórnude; durnude.

t [pat] *v.* bérkude.

tch [patč] *v.* ɗakkude.

tchy patči] *adj.* ɗakkaɗum.

tent [patənt] *adj.* ko laaɓi; ko fééñi.

ternal [patərnəl] *adj.* ko faati e baaba. ~ **unt** górgól *(o)*; górgilaaɗo *(o)*.

th [paθ] *n.* bólól *(ngól)*; laawól *(ngól)*.

thology [paθowloji] *n.* jangde ñabbuuli.

thway [paθwey] *n.* laawól *(ngól)*.

tience [peyšəns] *n.* muñal *(ngal)*.

tient [peyšənt] *adj.* muñɗo *(o)*.

tri [patri] *n.* baaba *(o)*.

triarch [patryərk] *n.* mawɗo gadiiɗo.

trimonial [patrəmownyəl] *adj.* ko faati e dónu.

trimony [patrəmowni] *n.* ndónu *(ngu)*.

triot [peytryot] *adj.* jiɗɗo ngéndi mum.

trol [pətrowl] *v.* jéértoyaade; reende.

tron [peytrən] *n.* balloowo *(o)*; gardiiɗo *(o)*; jiimɗo *(o)*.

tter [patə] *v.* saalaade.

ttern [patən] *n.* mbaadi *(ndi)*.

ucity [pɔsəti] *n.* ŋakkere *(nde)*.

unch [pɔnč] *n.* réédu mawndu.

uper [pɔpə] *n.* neɗɗo baasɗo.

uperism [pɔpərizm] *n.* baasal *(ngal)*.

use [powz] *n.* deeⱮre *(nde)*; dartagól *(ngól)*.

ve [peyv] *v.* ferde; fééwnude laawól. ~ **he way for** udditde/ferde laawol.

vilion [pəvilyən] *n.* tilliisa *(o)*.

w [pɔw] *n.* takkere *(nde)*. **little** ~ takkél *(ngél)*.

wn [pɔwn] *n.* juknude.

wnbroker [pɔwnbrowkə] *n.* juknoowo *(o)*.

wpaw [pawpaw] *n.* pappaaye *(o)*.

pay [pey] *v.* yoɓde. ~ **part of a debt** dawlude. ~ **back** yoɓde; ~ **attention** dankaade; waɗtude hakkille.

payable [peyəbəl] *adj.* kó fóti yoɓeede.

payee [peyi] *n.* joɓaaɗo *(o)*; joɓeteeɗo *(o)*.

payer [peyə] *n.* joɓoowo *(o)*.

payment [peymənt] *n.* njoɓdi *(ndi)*.

payoff [peyof] *n.* njóɓdi *(ndi)*.

payroll [peyrol] *n.* inɗe yimɓe yoɓeteeɓe.

pea [piy] *n.* ñewre *(nde)*.

peace [piys] *n.* jam *(o)*. ~ **of mind** deeⱮre hakkille.

peaceful [piysfəl] *adj.* deeⱮɗo.

peach [piyč] *n.* janfaade.

peak [piyk] *n.* ceɓtam *(ɗam)*.

peanut [piynʌt] *n.* yertere *(nde)*; gerte *(ɗe)*; dege *(ɗe)*. thick. ~ **butter sauce** maafe *(ɗe)*; **thin** ~ **butter sauce** domoda *(o)*; baase *(ɗe)*.

pear [per] *n.* ɓingél leɗɗe.

pearl [pərl] *n.* ñaayre *(nde)*.

peasant [pezənt] *n.* demoowo *(o)*.

pebble [pebəl] *n.* haayre *(nde)*.

peccant [pekənt] *adj.* tooñɗo; bakkodinɗo.

peck [pek] *v.* sikaade.

pectoral [pektowrəl] *adj.* ko faati e becce.

peculate [pekyuwleyt] *v.* wujjude.

pecuniary [pekyuwnəri] *adj.* ko faati e kaalis.

pedagogical [pedəgowjəkəl] *adj.* ko faati e jangde.

pedagogics [pedəgowjiks] *n.* jangde jangingól.

pedagogy [pedəgoji] *n.* jangingól *(ngól)*; ko faati e jangingól.

pedal [pedəl] *n.* alkabeere *(nde)*.

peddle [pedəl] *v.* yeeyde.

peddler [pedlə] *n.* baanabaana *(o)*.

pederast [pedərast] *n.* baanabaana *(o)*.

pedestal [pedəstəl] *n.* jaalal *(ngal)*.

pedestrian [pedəstryən] *n.* jahroowo koyɗe.

pediatrics [pedyatriks] *n.* jangde cellal e laaɓal sukaabe.

pedicure [pedəkyuwr] *n.* safaara koyɗe.

pediform [pedəform] *adj.* ko wayi no koyngal.

pedigree [pedəgriy] *n.* asko *(ngo)*.

pedlar [pedlə] *n.* jeeyoowo *(o)*; doondotooɗo ina yoɓee.

pedology [pedəloji] *n.* jangde léydi.

peduncule [pedəŋkyuwl] *n.* gawⲅal *(ngal).*

pee [piy] *v.* taaraade.

peek [piyk] *v.* yuurnaade.

peel [piyl] *v.* hooltaade; séttude; esde.

peel [piyl] *n.* cettol *(ngól);* gufi *(ɗi);* nguru *(ngu).*

peeler [piylə] *n.* cettoowo *(o).*

peeling [piyliŋ] *n.* céttugól *(ngól).*

peep [piyp] *v.* yuurnaade.

peer [piyr] *v.* laarde.

peerless [piyrles] *adj.* mo hono mum woodaani; mo alaa giⲅiraaɗo.

peeve [piyv] *v.* séknude.

peewee [piywiy] *adj.* pamaro.

peg [peg] *n.* sukkoode *(nde).*

pelage [pəlaʒ] *n.* lééɓi.

pelican [pəlikan] *n.* ginal *(ngal).*

pellicle [pelikəl] *n.* nguru.

pen [pen] *n.* kuɗól *(ngól).*

penal [piynəl] *adj.* ko faati e kuugal.

penalize [piynəlayz] *v.* yoɓnaade tooñange; yoftaade; fawde kuugal e.

penalty [penəlti] *n.* kuugal *(ngal).* *pay the* ~ tellinde kuugal.

pencil [pensəl] *n.* kiriyoⲅ *(o).*

pend [pend] *v.* liggude; yowde.

pending [pendiŋ] *adj.* haa. ~ *approval* so jaɓaama; haa jaɓee.

penetrate [penətreyt] *v.* naatde; naatnude.

penetration [penətreyšən] *n.* naatnugól *(ngól);* naatgol *(ngól).*

penis [piynəs] *n.* soolde *(nde);* kaake gorko.

penitent [pənitənt] *adj.* tuuɓɗo.

penitentiary [pənitənšəri] *n.* kasó.

penknife [penayf] *n.* laɓél *(ngél).*

penniless [penəles] *adj.* baasɗo.

penny [peni] *n.* koppoor *(o).*

pensile [pensəl] *adj.* ko weelata; ko liggaa.

pensive [pensiv] *adj.* miijotooɗo.

penta [pentə] *pref.* jóy.

penult [piynⲗlt] *n.* cukko battano.

penurious [penyuwryəs] *adj.* tiiɗɗo jungo; baasɗo.

penury [penyuwri] *n.* baasal *(ngal).*

people [piypəl] *n.* yimɓe *(ɓe)*

pepper [pepə] *n.* poobaar *(o).*

peppery [pepəri] *adj.* kó hééwi poobaar.

peptic [peptik] *adj.* ko dolnata.

per [pə] *adv.* kala.

percale [pərkeyl] *n.* percale.

perceive [pərsiyv] *v.* yiide.

perch [pərč] *n.* 1) fooftorde *(nde)* 2 coorgal *(ngal).*

percolate [pərkowleyt] *v.* siiwtude.

percolation [pərkowleyt] *n.* ciiwtugɗ *(ngól).*

percuss [pərkʌs] *v.* fiide.

perdu [pərdu] *adj.* ko suuɗii.

peregrinate [pərəgrineyt] *v.* ɗaanaade.

peregrination [pərəgrəneyšən] *n.* ɗangа *(ngal).*

perennial [pərənyəl] *adj.* ko duumii; ha abada.

perfect [pərfekt] *adj.* ko timmi; ko hawri.

perfection [pərfekšən] *n.* timmal *(ngal)* peewal *(ngal).*

perfidious [pərfiyjəs] *adj.* mo nuunɗaani.

perforate [pərforeyt] *v.* yulde.

perform [perform] *v.* waɗde; gollaade. *for* waɗande.

perfume [perfyuwm] *n.* latikoloñ *(o);* lat uuratééri.

perhaps [pərhaps] ina wona; ina waawi.

pericarp [perikarp] *n.* saaño *(ko);* ngur *(ngu).*

peril [perəl] *n.* halkaare *(nde);* bonand *(nde).*

perilous [perələs] *adj.* ko halkata.

period [piyryəd] *n.* 1) dumunna *(o);* mudd *(o);* sahaa *(o);* saanga *(o).* ~ *before daw* weetndoogo *(ngo)* 2) fiilayru *(ndu).*

periodic [piyryowdik] *adj.* ko kewata saha kala.

peripheric [pərifiyrik] *adj.* ko faati kééról.

periphery [pərifəri] *n.* kééról *(ngól).*

periplus [pəriplʌs] *n.* ɗangal *(ngal).*

perish [periš] *v.* halkaade.

perishable [perišəbəl] *adj.* ko bonata; k ñolata.

perjure [pərjə] *v.* jumde.

perjury [pərjri] *n.* jumre *(nde).*

permanent [pərmənənt] *adj.* ko duumii.

rmissible [pərmisəbəl] *adj.* ko yamiraa.

rmission [pərmiyšən] *n.* yamiroore ıde).

rmit [pərmit] *v.* yamirde.

rmute [pərmyuwt] *v.* waylude.

rorate [pərowreyt] *v.* leɓde.

rpend [pərpend] *v.* yisɓude.

rpetrate [pəpətreyt] *v.* waɗde.

rpetual [pərpəčuwəl] *adj.* ko duumii.

rpetuity [pərpəčwiti] *n.* haa abada.

rplex [pərpleks] *v.* wéémnude; jiiɓde.

rplexed [pərplekst] *adj.* beemɗo.

rplexity [pərpleksəti] *(nde)* weemre ıde); jiiɓru *(ndu)*.

rsecute [pərsekyuwt] *v.* tooñde; iiɗaade.

rsecution [pərsekyuwšən] *n.* tooñange ıge); kiiɗagól *(ngól)*.

rsevere pərsəviyr] *v.* tiiɗnaade; waasde ʾaacude; rewde heen.

rsist [pərsist] *v.* tiiɗnaade; rewde.

rson [pərsən] *n.* neɗɗo *(o)*. *old* ~ ayeejo *(o)*; naywuɗo *(o)*. *strong heavy* ~ ,orbal *(ngal)*. *chosen* ~ ɓurnaaɗo *(o)*; ʉɓaaɗo *(o)*. *useless* ~ ɓottere *(nde)*. *in* ~ anko hoore makko.

rsonable [pərsənabəl] *adj.* jooɗɗo.

rsonal [pərsənəl] *adj.* ko faati e neɗɗo.

rsonality [pərsənaləti] *n.* néésu *(ngu)*; ,éhdi *(ndi)*.

rsonnel [pərsənel] *n.* liggotooɓe.

rspective [pərspektiv] *n.* miijo *(ngo)*; ıigól *(ngól)*.

rspicacious [pərspəkeyšəs] *adj.* ceeɓɗo; :aqqilɗo.

rspicacity [pərspəkasəti] *n.* cééɓgól ıakkille; hakkilantaagal *(ngal)*.

rspire [pərspayə] *v.* warñude.

rsuade [pərsweyd] *v.* waawnude; heɓde ıakkille neɗɗo.

rtain [pərteyn] *v.* jeyeede; jeyde.

rtinent [pərtinənt] *adj.* ko faati e.

rturb [pətərb] *v.* haljinde.

ruse [pəruwz] *n.* jangude.

rvade [pərveyd] *v.* saraade; saakaade.

rverse [pərvərs] *adj.* luutndiiɗo.

rversion [pərvəršən] *n.* luutndagól ʾngól).

rvert [pərvərt] *v.* luutndaade.

pesky [peski] *adj.* ko haljinta.

pessimist [pesəmist] *n.* neɗɗo mo ɗaminaaki.

pester [pestə] *v.* haljinde.

pestilence [pestələns] *n.* ñaw ndaaɓóówu; ñaw *(ngu)*.

pestle [pesəl] *n.* unugal *(ngal)*.

petit [pəti] *adj.* pamaro.

petite [pətiyt] *adj.* pamaro.

petition [pətišən] *n.* ñaagunde.

petrify [pətrəfay] *v.* jiiɓde ɓakke; hulɓinde; najnude.

petrol [pətrowl] *n.* esaas *(o)*.

petrology [pətrowloji] *n.* jangde kaaⱱe.

petty [peti] *adj.* seeɗa; ko famɗi.

phagocytize [fagowsətayz] *v.* ñaamde.

phantasm [fantazm] *n.* peeñal *(ngal)*.

phantom [fantəm] *n.* peeñal *(ngal)*.

pharynx [fariŋks] *n.* góddól *(ngól)*; hulquum *(o)*.

pheno [feno] *pref.* ko jalbi; ko jalbata.

philander [filandə] *v.* fijde; gerde.

philanthropy [fəlanθrəpi] *n.* gilli aduna.

philately [filatəli] *n.* jangde tembe.

philology [filələji] *n.* jangde bindi.

philosopher [filosəfə] *n.* gando *(o)*; keewɗo miijo.

philosophy [filosəfi] *n.* miijo *(ngo)*.

philter [filtə] *n.* ɓayre *(nde)*.

phlegm [flem] *n.* ɗuurtagól *(ngól)*; paalkisaagól *(ngól)*.

phlegmatic [flemətik] *adj.* ko faati e ɗuurtagól/paalkissagól.

phobia [phowbyə] *n.* kulól *(ngól)*.

phonate [fowneyt] *v.* wówlude.

phonation [fowneyšən] *n.* wowlaango *(ngo)*.

phone [fown] *n.* wowlaango *(ngo)*.

phoneme [fowniym] *n.* wowlaango *(ngo)*; helmere *(nde)*.

phonemics [fowniymiks] *n.* jangde gowlaali.

phonetic [fownetik] *adj.* ko faati e gowlaali/woowlaango.

phonetics [fownetiks] *n.* jangde gowlaali.

phonic [fɔnik] *adj.* ko faati e gowlaali/wowlaango.

phonology [fənowləji] *n.* jangde gowlaali.

phosphorescent [fəsforesənt] adj. ko jalbi/jalbata.

photo [fowto] n. fooyre (nde); huunde hubboore.

photocopy [fowtəkɑpi] n. natal (ngal).

photogenic [fowtəjenik] adj. peewɗo e natal.

photograph [fowtəgraf] n. natal (ngal).

photographer [fowtəgrafə] n. potoowo (o).

photographic [fowtəgrafik] adj. ko faati e natal/nate.

photophobia [fowtəfobya] n. kulól fooyre.

phrase [freyz] n. kóngól timmungól.

phrasing [freyziŋ] n. lélnugól kóngól.

physic [fizik] n. lékki; safaara (o); cafrugol (ngól).

physical [fizikəl] adj. ko faati e tagóódi/bandu.

physicality [fizikəli] n. tagóódi (ndi).

physician [fiziyšən] n. cafroowo (o).

physiology [fizyowloji] n. jangde nafoore terɗe.

physiotherapy [fizyowθerəpi] n. safaara (o).

physique [fiziyk] n. tagóódi (ndi).

picaroon [pikəruwn] gujjo.

pick [pik] v. bóggude; pick; sufde; téptude. ~ up small pieces of wood ñukaade. ~ out subaade. ~ millet ears róbtude. ~ up subde; hóccude; Yéftude; Yeftude.

picking [pikiŋ] n. teptungo (ngo); cubgól (ngól).

picklock [piklok] n. gujjo (o).

pictorial [piktoryəl] adj. ko faati e natal.

picture [pikčə] n. natal (ngal); annama (o).

picturesque [pikčəresk] adj. kó yóóɗi.

pie [pay] n. ñamri (ndi). as easy as ~ newiiɗo.

piece [piys] n. heltinde (nde); taYitande (nde); taYande (nde).

piecemeal [piysmiyl] n. seeɗa seeɗa.

pierce [piyrs] v. yulde; tufde.

piety [payəti] n. dewal Allah.

piffle [pifəl] n. haala maayka.

pig [pig] n. mbabba tugal.

pigeon [pijən] n. foondu (ndu). little ~ purayél (ngél). male ~ uuga (o).

pigment [pigmənt] n. nóórdi (ndi).

pike [payk] n. laawól (ngól).

pilaf [piləf] n. ñamri (ndi).

pile [payl] n. joowre (nde).

pile [payl] v. joowde. ~ shrubs ñakkude ~ dirty clothes ñabbude. ~ disorderl ñoofde.

pilfer [pilfə] v. wujjude.

pilferage [pilfərij] n. nguyka (ka).

pilgrim [pilgrim] n. alhajji (o); kajjuɗo (o) kajjoowo (o).

pilgrimage [pilgrəmij] v. hajjóyde; hajjude.

pilgrimage [pilgrəmij] n. hajju (o).

pill [pil] n. foɗɗere (nde).

pillage [pilij] v. honde; teetde.

pillage [pilij] n. teetere (nde); teetgo (ngól).

pillar [pilə] n. jaalal (ngal).

pillion [pilyən] n. jappeere (nde).

pillow [pilow] n. talla (ka)/(o); ngaflaaɛ (ndi); njegenaawe (o).

pilot [paylət] n. donoowo laana ndiwoowa.

piloti [piləti] n. ngóóróóndi hubeere.

pilule [pilyuwl] n. foɗɗere (nde).

pimento [pəmento] n. ñamako (ko).

pimple [pimpəl] n. wadere (nde); puYéɛ fuYere (nde);wañnjalde.

pin [pin] n. pingu (o).

pin [pin] v. baasde.

pinch [pinč] n. bóttugól (ngól); Ŋuccerɛ (nde); jubbande (nde).

pinch [pinč] v. Ŋuccude; bóttude.

pinched [pinčt] adj. Ŋuccaaɗo; bottaaɗo.

pinching [pinčiŋ] n. Ŋuccugól (ngól).

pine [payn] v. yééwnude.

pinfold [pinfowld] n. galle jawdi.

pink [piŋk] v. yiwde; tufde.

pinky [piŋk] adj. sibatindu (ndu).

pinnace [pinis] n. laana (ka).

pinnacle [pinəkəl] n. cebtam.

pinpoint [pinpoynt] v. foofaade; sifaade.

pioneer [payəniyə] v. fuɗɗude; ardaade.

piosity [payəsiti] n. dewal Alla.

pious [payəs] adj. juulɗo; dewɗ. jóómiraaɗo; dewɗo Alla.

pip [pip] n. foɗɗere (nde).

pipage [paypij] n. gaawól (ngól).

pipe [payp] n. 1) solom (o) 2) jarduɢ (ngal).

uant [piykənt] *adj.* ko yiwata.

ue [piyk] *v.* tooñde.

acy [payrəsi] *n.* nguyka *(ka)*.

ate [payrət] *n.* gujjo *(o)*.

ogue [piyrowg] *n.* laana *(ka)*.

ouette [pirəwet] *n.* jiilagól *(ngól)*.

cator [piskato] *n.* gawoowo *(o)*.

ces [paysiyz] *n.* licɗi *(ɗi)*.

mire [pismayə] *n.* ñuuñu *(ngu)*.

s [pis] *v.* taaraade; soofde.

tol [pistəl] *n.* fétél *(o)*.

[pit] *v.* asde.

[pit] *n.* wóyndu *(ndu)*.

ch [pitč] *v.* 1) werlaade 2) feŋde; arnude caali.

cher [pitčə] *n.* berlotooɗo *(o)*; dufoowo *)*.

eous [piyteyəs] *adj.* jurminiiɗo.

h [piθ] *n.* mbuuwwa *(o)*.

iable [pityebəl] *adj.* jurminiiɗum; ko urminii.

iless [pitəles] *adj.* mo yurmotaako.

y [piti] *v.* yurmaade. *have ~ on* urmaade.

y [piti] *n.* yurmeende *(nde)*.

za [pidza] *n.* ñamri *(ndi)*.

cable [plakəbəl] *adj.* jaafotooɗo.

cate [plakeyt] *v.* dééɣnude.

ce [pleys] *v.* fawde; lombude. *~ in* ɔokde. *~ in front of someone* huufnude. *diacritics* masde. *~ across* falde. *~ under* ɔrnude; sakkude.

ce [pleys] *n.* nokku *(o)*.

cid [pləsid] *adj.* deeɣɗo; kó dééɣi.

fond [plafond] *n.* mbildi *(ndi)*.

giarism [pleyjərizm] *n.* nguyka *(ka)*.

ague [pleyg] *n.* bonande *(nde)*; ñaw *ngu)*.

ain [pleyn] *adj.* laabɗum. *~ truth* goonga aabɗo.

aint [pleynt] *n.* gullitaagól *(ngól)*.

aintiff [pleyntəf] *n.* gullitiiɗo *(o)*.

ait [pleyt] *v.* moorde.

ait [pleyt] *n.* móóról *(ngól)*.

an [plan] *n.* feere *(nde)*; eɓɓere *(nde)*.

an [plan] *v.* fewjude. *~ for someone* ewjande.

plane [pleyn] *n.* laana ndiwoowa. *The plane took off* Ndiwowa ka diwii.

planet [planet] *n.* jaayre *(nde)*.

planetary [planetəri] *adj.* ko faati e jaayre.

planish [planiš] *v.* méldude.

planner [planə] *n.* pewjoowo *(o)*.

plant [plant] *v.* aawde; feŋde; ñiɓde.

plantation [planteyšən] *n.* ngesa *(ba)*.

planted [plantid] *adj.* ñiɓaɗum; peŋaɗum.

planter [plantə] *n.* gaawoowo *(o)*.

plaque [plak] *n.* ñakkudi *(ndi)*.

plaster [plastə] *n.* ɓakkere *(nde)*.

plaster [plastə] *v.* ɓasde.

plate [pleyt] *n.* taasa *(ka)*; palaat *(o)*.

platter [platə] *n.* lahal *(ngal)*.

plausible [plɔzəbəl] *adj.* ko ina wona.

play [pley] *v.* fijde. *~ deaf* muraade; faaɗkinaade. *~ the fiddle* ñaañde; simbude. *~ the flute* liitde.

player [pleyə] *n.* pijoowo *(o)*.

playwright [playrayt] *n.* bindoowo *(o)*.

plea [pliy] *n.* ñaagunde *(nde)*.

plead [pliyd] *v.* ñaagaade.

pleasant [plezənt] *adj.* belɗo; jirwuɗo.

pleasantry [plezəntri] *n.* gaajaare *(nde)*.

please [pliyz] *v.* wéltinde. *I am pleased* Mi weltiima; mbeɗe welti.

pleasure [pleʒə] *n.* welamma *(o)*.

pleat [pliyt] *n.* ñóngól *(ngól)*.

pledge [plej] *v.* taylude.

plenary [plenəri] *adj.* kó timmi.

plenish [pleniš] *v.* hébbinde.

plenitude [plenətyuwd] *n.* keewal *(ngal)*.

plentiness [plentines] *n.* nammanduru *(ndu)*; haaranduru *(ndu)*.

plenty [plenti] *adj.* keewɗum; ko heewi. *live in ~* neemaade.

plethora [plətora] *n.* keewal *(ngal)*.

plethoric [pletorik] *adj.* kééwɗum; kó hééwi.

pliable [playəbəl] *adj.* ko hofotoo.

pliant [playənt] *adj.* jaawɗo wuuraade.

plica [plikə] *n.* ñórɓólól *(ngól)*.

plight [playt] *n.* mbaadi *(ndi)*.

plink [pliŋk] *v.* soññude.

plop [plop] *v.* deppaade.

plot [plot] *v.* fewjande.

plotter [plotə] *n.* pewjanoowo *(o)*.

plow [plaw] v. remde.

pluck [plʌk] v. borde; sufde.

plug [plʌg] v. sukkude.

plumage [plʌmij] n. sigééji (ɗi).

plume [pluwm] n. sige (o).

plump [plʌmp] adj. béllinɗo.

plunder [plʌndə] v. honde.

plunderage [plʌndəreyj] n. kónu (ngu); kongol (ngól).

plunge [plʌnj] v. puñtinaade.

plural [pluwrəl] n. keewal (ngal).

plus [plʌs] adv. beydaari (ndi).

plutocracy [pluwtowkrəsi] n. laamu ngalu/alɗube.

pluvial [pluwvyəl] adj. ko faati e tobo.

ply [play] v. liggaade; gollaade; golloraade.

pneumonia [nyuwmownya] n. tiggere (nde).

poach [powč] v. wujjude.

poacher [powčə] n. gujjo (o).

pocket [poket] n. jeyba (o); poos (o).

pods [podz] n. gufi (ɗi).

podsol [pɑdsol] n. léydi (ndi).

poem [pom] n. jimól (ngól).

pogrom [pogrəm] n. boomaare (nde).

poignant [poynyənt] adj. ko faati e sunaare.

point [poynt] v. sappinaade; joofaade; jómmude.

pointer [poyntə] n. joofotooɗo (o).

pointy [poynti] adj. kó séébi; ceebɗum.

poison [poyzən] n. posone (o); tooke (ɗe). ~ healer cammitoowo (o).

poisonous [poyzənəs] adj. tookaaɗo.

poke [powk] v. duñtude; hubbude; Yóbbude.

poker [powkə] n. duñtoowo (o).

pole [powl] n. coorgal (ngal). ~ star ɗaccuki (ki).

polemic [polemik] n. luutndagól (ngól).

poler [powlə] n. tuggude laana.

police [pəliys] n. poliis.

policy [pɑləsi] n. yamiroore laamu.

polish [pɑliš] v. taasnude; dirkude.

polite [polayt] adj. néhiiɗo.

politeness [polaytnes] n. néhdi móYYundi.

politic [pɑlitik] n. dééntiiɗo (o).

political [pɑlitikəl] adj. ko faati e polotigi.

politics [pɑlitiks] n. pólótigi (o).

pollen [polən] n. bumangal (ngal).

pollute [polyuwt] v. wuddinde wuddiɗinde.

poltroon [poltruwn] n. kulɗo réédu.

polygamous [poləgaməs] adj. nawlirɗo.

polygamy [poliygəmi] n. nawliigu (ngu).

polyglot [poliglot] n. gando ɗemɗe keewɗe; kaaloowo ɗemɗe keewɗe.

polysemy [polisemi] n. maanaaji kééwɗi.

pomade [pomeyd] n. pomaate.

pond [pɑnd] v. juknude; taylude.

pond [pɑnd] n. tuɗande (nde); wééndu (ndu).

ponder [pɑndə] v. yisbude; miijaade.

pony [poni] n. pucél tókósél.

pool [puwl] n. deental (ngal)

poop [puwp] v. tampinde; lóhnude.

poor [puwr] adj. miskiino; koraaɗo paaɗaaɗo. ~ person dooba.

pop [pop] v. naatde; YaaNde.

popgun [popgʌn] n. fétél cukalél.

poplin [poplin] n. bagi (o).

popple [popəl] v. fasde (ndiyam).

popular [popyuwlə] adj. ko darji; darjuɗo lolluɗo.

popularity [popələrəti] n. daraja (o) lollugol (ngól)

popularize [popələrayz] v. darjinde.

populate [popyuwleyt] v. hoɗde.

population [popyuwlešən] n. yimbe nókku

populous [popyuwləs] adj. nókku keewɗ(yimbe.

porcupine [porkyuwpayn] n. sangald((nde).

pore [powr] v. miijaade; laarde.

pork [pork] n. tééw mbabba tugal.

porous [powrəs] adj. kó hééwi gudde.

porridge [pərij] n. gósi (o)

port [port] n. tééri (o).

portable [portəbəl] adj. ko ina jogee.

portal [portəl] n. damal (ngal).

porter [pɔtə] n. doondotooɗo.

portion [pošən] n. geɗal (ngal); taYand((nde).

portrait [portreyt] n. natal (ngal); annam; (o).

osition [pəziyšən] *n.* 1) miijo *(ngo)* 2) nokku *(o)*.

ositive [pɑzitiv] *adj.* kó móƳƳi.

ossess [pozes] *v.* jogaade; jeyde.

ossession [pozešən] *n.* halal *(ngal)*; jogagól *(ngól)*; jawdi *(ndi)*.

ossessive [pozesiv] *adj.* ko faati e dañal/jeyal.

ossessor [pozesə] *n.* jeyɗo *(o)*.

ossibility [pɑsəbiləti] *n.* huunde wonoore; feere *(nde)* **possible** [pɑsəbəl] *adj.* ko wonata.

ost [powst] *v.* jólnude bataake. *I will keep you posted* Ma mi tintine.

ost [powst] *n.* doygal *(ngal)*.

ostal [powstəl] *adj.* ko faati e poosto.

ostbox [powstbɑks] *n.* wakande ɓataake.

osterior [postiyryə] *n.* caggal *(o)*; kó héédi caggal.

osterity [postəriti] *n.* ɓésngu *(ngu)*.

osthumus [postəməs] *n.* luuti *(o)*.

ostman [powstman] *n.* jéttinoowo ɓatakééji.

ostpone [powstpone] *v.* faɓɓinde. *Our meeting has been postponed* Deental men faɓɓinaama.

ostponement [powstpownmənt] *n.* paɓɓingól *(ngól)*.

ostscript [powstskript] *n.* ɓeydaari *(ndi)*.

ostulant [powsčuwlənt] *n.* ɗaɓɓoowo.

ostulate [powstyuwleyt] *v.* ɗaɓɓude.

ostulator [powstyuwleytə] *n.* ɗaɓɓoowo *(o)*.

ot [pɑt] *n.* barme *(o)*.

otable [powtəbəl] *n.* ndiyam laaɓɗam; ndiyam njareteeɗam.

otato [powteyto] *n.* pómpiteer *(o)*.

otent [powtənt] *adj.* dóólnuɗo.

otentiality [powtənšaləti] *n.* mbaawka *(ka)*.

otful [pɑtfəl] *n.* ñeɗande *(nde)*.

otion [powšən] *n.* lékki *(ki)*

otter [pɑtə] *n.* maabo *(o)*.

ottery [potəri] *n.* mahgól looɗe.

ouch [pawč] *n.* poos *(o)*; móóftirde *(nde)*; danga *(o)*; bata *(o)*.

ounce [pawns] *v.* 1) junnitde; junnitaade 2) ñakkaade e.

pound [pawnd] *v.* unde. ~ *again* untaade. ~ *grain stalks* sókkude. ~ *grains into flower* hórtinde. ~ *into paste* lóppude.

pound [pawnd] *n.* liibaar *(o)*.

pounded [pawndid] *adj.* unaɗum.

pounder [pawndə] *n.* unoowo *(o)*.

pounding [pawndiŋ] *n.* unu *(ngu)*. *place for* ~ tugunde *(nde)*.

pour [puwr] *v.* yuppude; joorde; juurde; ~ *water over oneself* juuraade. ~ *into boiling water* laawde. ~ *by drops* tóɓɓinde. ~ *out to fill* loowde.

pout [pawt] *v.* ɓiiñde.

poverty [pɑvəti] *n.* baasal *(ngal)*; ronkere *(nde)*; ñóólu *(ngu)*.

powder [pawdə] *v.* fullude.

powder [pawdə] *n.* cóndi *(ndi)*. *gun-* condi fetel.

powdered [pawdəd] *adj.* laalndaɗum.

power [pawə] *n.* sembe *(o)*; mbaawka *(ka)*; doole *(ɗe)*; baawal *(ngal)*.

powerful [pawəfəl] *adj.* cémbinɗo; dóólnuɗo.

practicable [praktikəbəl] *adj.* baɗotooɗum; ko ina waɗoo.

practise [praktis] *v.* waɗde.

practitioner [praktiyšənə] *n.* gollotooɗo.

praise [preyz] *v.* yéttude; mande. *Praise the lord* Yettu Alla.

praise [preyz] *n.* manoore *(nde)*.

prance [prans] *v.* birgude.

prang [praŋ] *v.* fuɓɓaade e.

prate [preyt] *v.* leɓde.

prattle [pratəl] *v.* leɓde.

pray [prey] *v.* 1) juulde; fummude 2) duwaade; bismaade. ~ *for* ñaagaade; duwanaade. ~ *in the name of* duworaade. ~ *with* juulirde.

prayer [preyə] *n.* 1) juulde *(nde)*; duwaawu *(o)*; faddungo *(ngo)* 2) juuloowo *(o)*. ~ *beads* kurus *(o)*. *two o'clock* ~ sallifanaa. *sunset* ~ futuro *(o)*.

pre [pri] *pre.* hadee; ko adii.

preach [priyč] *v.* waajaade

preacher [priyčə] *n.* baajotooɗo *(o)*.

preamble [priyəmbəl] *n.* fuɗɗorde *(nde)*.

precarious [priykeyryəs] *adj.* ko siiraani.

precaution [priykɔšən] *n.* deentagól *(ngól)*.

precede [prisiyd] *v.* adaade; aditaade; ardaade.

precedence [presədəns] *n.* gardagól *(ngól)*.
precedent [presədənt] *adj.* ko bénni; ko adii.
preceptor [preseptə] *n.* janginoowo *(o)*.
precinct [priysint] *n.* kééról *(ngól)*.
precious [prešəs] *adj.* kó hééwi nafoore.
precipitate [presəpiteyt] *v.* yaawnude.
precise [prəsayz] *adj.* kó fóti.
precision [prəsiyʒən] *n.* huunde fotnde.
preclude [prekluwd] *v.* hadde; yaltinde.
predecessor [pridesəso] *n.* gadiido *(o)*.
predicate [predəkət] *v.* wiide; tééɲtinde.
predict [predikt] *v.* tiimde; gisde; tombaade; tijjaade.
prediction [predikšən] *n.* tiimgal *(ngal)*; tiimgol *(ngól)*.
predominate [priydəminet] *v.* burde sémbinde; foolde; burde.
preexist [priyegzist] *v.* adaade woodde.
preface [prefis] *n.* fuddorde *(nde)*.
prefer [prifə] *v.* burande; burnude; labaade.
preference [prefrəns] *n.* bural *(ngal)*.
pregnancy [pregnənsi] *n.* reedu *(ndu)*; tumbere *(nde)*. *first* ~ dikkuru *(ndu)*.
pregnant [pregnənt] *adj.* reedu. *be* ~ *outside marriage* reedde. *be* ~ halde; tumbude; wuufde; duñde.
prejudice [prejədəs] *n.* miijo *(ngo)*.
prejudicial [prejədiyšəl] *adj.* ko bonnata.
preliminary [preləminəri] *adj.* ko adii.
prelude [preluwd] *n.* fuddoode.
premature [premačuwr] *adj.* ko timmaani.
premier [primir] *adj.* gardiido.
premises [premisiz] *n.* nókku *(o)*; hodorde *(nde)*.
preoccupied [priyokəpayd] *adj.* cókludo.
preparation [prepəreyšən] *n.* peewnugol *(ngól)*; pééwnitaagól *(ngól)*.
prepare [priper] *v.* fééwnude.
prepared [pripeyd] *adj.* peewnitiido.
preponderant [priypɑndərənt] *adj.* kó buri sémmbinde.
prerogative [prirogətiv] *n.* hakke *(o)*; durwaa *(o)*.
presage [prəzaʒ] *n.* maale.
prescind [presind] *n.* séérndude.
prescription [preskripšən] *n.* órdinaas *(o)*.

present [prezənt] *n.* dokkal *(ngal)*. *make a* ~ rokkude; yedde.
present [prezənt] *adj.* gooddo; tawaado; tawtoraado. *be* ~ taweede; tawtoreede.
present [prezənt] *v.* hóllude.
present-day [prezəntdey] *adj.* aduna jóóni o.
preserve [prizərv] *v.* móóftude; hisnude.
preside [prəzayd] *v.* ardaade.
president [prezidənt] *n.* gardiido *(o)*.
press [pres] *v.* ñóɣɣude.
presser [presə] *n.* ñoɣɣoowo *(o)*.
pressing [presiŋ] *adj.* ko heñoraa.
pressure [prešə] *n.* ñoɣɣere *(nde)*.
prest [prest] *adj.* kebiido; pardo.
prestige [prestiyʒ] *n.* lóllugól *(ngól)*.
prestigious [prestiyjəs] *adj.* lólludo; darjudo; kó lólli.
presume [prəzyuwm] *v.* miijaade; sikkude.
presumption [prezʌmpšən] *n.* sikke *(o)*.
pretend [pritend] *v.* wonkinaade. ~ *to be dead* maaykinaade.
pretty [priti] *adj.* jooddo; jooddum; ŋardudo.
prevail [priveyl] *v.* hawde; foolde.
prevalent [prevlənt] *adj.* ko saaktii.
prevent [priyvent] *v.* ambude; surde; falaade; hadde **preventer** [priyventə] *n.* kadoowo *(o)*; palotoodo *(o)*.
previous [priyvyəs] *adj.* bénnudo; ko adii.
price [prays] *n.* cóggu *(ngu)*
pricer [praysə] *n.* piyoowo cóggu.
prick [prik] *v.* yiwde. ~ *up the ears* darnude noppi.
pride [prayd] *n.* faaro *(ngo)*; fayfayru *(ndu)*. *take* ~ *in* faarnoraade.
primacy [prayməsi] *n.* gardagól *(ngól)*.
primary [prayməri] *adj.* burdo fóf.
prime [praym] *adj.* gardiido.
primitive [primətiv] *adj.* ko adii.
primordial [priymɔjəl] *adj.* gadiido; ko adii.
prince [prins] *n.* biddo laamdo gorko.
princess [prinses] *n.* biddo laamdo debbo.
principal [prinsəpəl] *adj.* gardiido *(o)*.
prior [prayə] *adj.* ko adii.
prison [prizən] *n.* kasó *(o)*. *break out of* ~ boccitaade kaso.

risoner [priznə] *n.* cokaacfo *(o)*.

rivate [prayvit] *adj.* keertacfum; jananum.

rize [prayz] *n.* njeenaari *(ndi)*.

ro [prow] *n.* gonancfo. ~s *and cons* wonanɓe e luutndiiɓe.

robable [prowbəbəl] *adj.* ko ina wona.

robe [prowb] *v.* wittude; lóskude.

robity [probiti] *n.* nuuncfal *(ngal)*.

roblem [probləm] *n.* saqqa *(o)*; haaju *(o)*.

rocedure [prəsiyjə] *n.* feere *(nde)*.

roceed [prowsiyd] *v.* yahde; yahrude yeeso.

rocess [proses] *v.* fééwnude; waylude.

rocession [prosešən] *n.* déggóndiral *(ngal)*.

roclaim [prokleym] *v.* wiyde; yaajnude.

rocrastinate [prokrastəneyt] *v.* faɓɓinde; saɓɓitaade.

rocrastination *n.* paɓɓingol *(ngól)*; caɓɓitaagól *(ngól)*; leeltingol *(ngól)*.

rocreate [prokryeyt] *v.* jibinde.

roctor [proktə] *n.* deenoowo *(o)*.

rocurable [prokyuwrəbəl] *adj.* ko heɓotoo; keɓotoocfum.

rocure [prokyuwr] *v.* heɓde.

rod [prod] *v.* Yóɓɓude.

rodigious [prodiyjəs] *adj.* mawnde.

roduce [prowjuws] *v.* coñaandi *(ndi)*.

roductive [prowdʌktiv] *adj.* ko jibinta.

rofane [profeyn] *adj.* kééfóricfo.

rofanity [profanəti] *n.* keeferaagal *(ngal)*; haala mbonka.

rofess [profes] *v.* jéértinde.

rofession [profešən] *n.* gollal *(ngal)*; ligééy *(o)*.

rofessor [profesə] *n.* janginoowo *(o)*.

roficiency [prowfiyšənsi] *n.* baawal *(ngal)*; mbaawka *(ka)*.

roficient [prowfiyšənt] *adj.* gando; keewcfo ñeeñal.

rofile [prowfayl] *n.* baɲɲe *(o)*.

rofit [prowfit] *n.* ɓurtaari *(ndi)* ; ngañaari *(ndi)*. *He made a profit* o dañii ngañaari.

rofitable [prowfitəbəl] *adj.* ko wacfi ngañaari.

rofound [profawnd] *adj.* ko luggicfi; luggicfcfum.

rofundity [profʌnditi] *n.* luggéendi *(ndi)*.

profuse [profyuwz] *adj.* keewcfum; kó hééwi.

profusion [profyuwzən] *n.* keewal *(ngal)*; cfuucfal *(ngal)*.

progenitor [prowjənitə] *n.* gardiicfo *(o)*; pucfcfucfo léñól.

progeny [projəni] *n.* ɓésngu *(ngu)*.

program [program] *n.* porogaraam *(o)*.

progress [progres] *n.* ɓamtaare *(nde)*; jahrugól yeeso.

progress [progres] *n.* yahrude yeeso; ɓamtaade.

progressive [progresiv] *adj.* ko faati e ko fayi yeeso.

prohibit [prohibit] *v.* hacfde.

project [projekt] *v.* werlaade; cfaminaade.

projectile [projektayl] *n.* huunde werlaande; huunde fettaande.

proletariat [proleterya] *n.* liggotooɓe.

proliferate [prolifəreyt] *v.* Yaajnude.

prolific [prolifik] *adj.* ko jibinta.

prolong [proloŋ] *v.* juutnude; faɓɓinde.

promenade [promənad] *v.* yahnaade.

prominence [promənəns] *n.* ɓamtagól *(ngól)*; mawnugól *(ngól)*.

promiscuous [prosmikyuwəs] *n.* pijoowo.

promise [promis] *v.* ahdande; aadde.

promise [promis] *n.* ahdi *(o)*. *break a ~* firtude ahdi.

promote [promowt] *v.* Yéllitde.

promoter [promowtə] *n.* Yélitoowo *(o)*.

promotion [promowšən] *n.* Yellitgól.

prompt [prompt] *adj.* jaawcfo.

promulgate [prowmulgeyt] *v.* andinde.

pronounce [pronawns] *v.* wówlude.

pronunciation [pronʌnseyšən] *n.* wowlaango *(ngo)*.

prop [prop] *v.* Yaañde.

prop [prop] *n.* jaalal *(ngal)*.

propaganda [propəgənda] *n.* parbagaan *(o)*.

propagate [propəgeyt] *v.* yaajnude.

propel [propel] *v.* yahrinde yeeso.

propeller [propelə] *n.* ko nawrata yeeso.

proper [propə] *adj.* kó fééwi; ko laaɓi; peewcfum; laaɓcfum.

property [propəti] *n.* halal *(ngal)*.

prophecy [profesi] *n.* jéértingól *(ngól)*.

prophesy [profəsay] *v.* jéértinde.

prophet [prowfət] *n.* annabi *(o)*; nulaaɗo; nelaaɗo; annabiijo *(o)*.

prophylactic [prowfəlaktik] *adj.* ko haɗata ñaw.

propine [prəpiyn] *v.* rókkude.

propitiate [propəšeyt] *v.* dééɣnude; wélditinde.

proposal [propowzəl] *n.* miijo *(ngo)*.

propose [propowz] *v.* hóllude miijo.

proprietor [propraytə] *n.* jom *(o)*; jeyɗo *(o)*.

prorate [proreyt] *v.* féccude.

proscribe [proskrayb] *v.* haɗde.

prosecute [prosekyuwt] *v.* wullitaade; woytaade.

proselyte [prozelayt] *n.* neɗɗo bayluɗo miijo/diine mum.

prospect [prospekt] *v.* yiilaade.

prosper [prospə] *v.* ɣéllitaade.

prosperity [prospəriti] *n.* ɣéllitaare *(nde)*.

prosperous [prospərəs] *adj.* ɣéllitiiɗo.

prostitute [prostəčuwt] *v.* garbaade.

prostitute [prostəčuwt] *n.* garbotooɗo *(o)*; garba *(o)*.

prostrate [prostreyt] *v.* turaade; juulde.

protect [protekt] *v.* reende; suurde; moolde; sitde; sitde; móóftude. ~ *one another* suurondirde. ~ *with a prayer* faddinde.

protected [protektid] *adj.* deenaaɗo; cuuraaɗo; moolaaɗo.

protection [protekšən] *n.* suuraare *(nde)*. *person seeking* ~ moolotooɗo. *person who sought* ~ móóliiɗo. *give due* ~ *to* teddinde koɗo.

protective [protektiv] *adj.* ko suurata; ko mooftata.

protector [protektə] *n.* deenoowo *(o)*.

protest [protest] *v.* salaade.

prototype [protətip] *n.* yéru *(ngu)*.

protract [protrakt] *v.* juutnude.

protrude [protruwd] *v.* fulñitde gite.

protuberance [prowčuwbərəns] *n.* ɣuulnugól *(ngól)*.

protuberant [prowčuwbərənt] *adj.* ko ɣuulni.

proud [prawd] *adj.* béltiiɗo; tiiɗaaɗo; paarniiɗo.

prove [pruwv] *v.* teeŋtinde; góóngɗinde; fénnude.

provenance [provənans] *n.* iwdi *(ndi)* ; lasli *(o)*.

proverb [provərb] *n.* tindól *(ngól)*.

provide [provayd] *v.* rókkude; waɗande.

provident [providənt] *adj.* dééntiiɗo; paggiiɗo.

province [provins] *v.* diiwaan *(o)*. *He comes from that province* O jeyaa ko oon diiwaan.

provisional [proviyʒənəl] *adj.* ko duumaaki.

provoke [provowk] *v.* tooñde. ~ *deliberately* réppude.

prowess [prowəs] *n.* jaambaraagal *(ngal)*; cuusal *(ngal)*.

proximate [proksəmet] *adj.* ɓadtiiɗo; ko ɓadtii; ko ɓadii; takko.

proximity [proksimiti] *n.* ɓadagól *(ngól)*.

prude [pruwd] *adj.* jamyamo; jankiniiɗo.

prudence [pruwdəns] *n.* deentagól *(ngól)*.

prudent [pruwdənt] *adj.* deentiiɗo.

prudish [pruwdiš] *adj.* ko faati e jankiniiɗo/yankinaare.

pry [pray] *v.* yuurnaade; lóskude.

psalm [sɔm] *n.* jimól *(ngól)*.

psellism [selizm] *n.* mehgól *(ngól)*.

psychiatrist [saykaytrist] *n.* cafroowo kaaɗi.

psychiatry [saykaytri] *n.* jangde e safaara kaaɗi.

psychology [saykowləji] *n.* jangde hakkille.

psychopath [saykowpaθ] *n.* kaangaaɗo *(o)*.

psychopathy [saykowpaθi] *n.* kaaɗi *(ɗi)*.

puberty [pyuwbərti] *n.* kéllifuya *(o)*.

pubes [pyuwbz] *n.* faasko *(ko)*.

pubic [pyuwbik] *adj.* ko faati e lééɓi faasko *(ngo)ó*.

public [pʌblik] *adj.* ko faati e yimɓe/laamu.

publicity [pʌbləsiti] *n.* jaaynde *(nde)*.

publicize [pʌbləsayz] *v.* jaaynude; andinde.

publish [pʌbliš] *v.* lóllinde; saaktude.

pucker [pʌkə] *n.* ñórɓólól *(ngól)*.

puddle [pʌdəl] *v.* irñitde.

puerile [pyuwrəl] *adj.* ko faati e cukaagu.

puff [pʌf] *v.* wuttude.

puffer [pʌfə] *n.* guttoowo *(o)*.

pugilism [pyuwjəlizm] *n.* góɓɓóndiral *(ngal)*; fijirde goɓɓe.

puke [pyuwk] *v.* tuutde; ruttude.

pule [pyuwl] *v.* Ƴusde.

pull [pul] *v.* fooɗde; aggitde. ~ *weeds out* ɗooftaade. ~ *on ends* fóóɗondirde. ~ *off* ɓoorde. ~ *out* ɗoofde. ~ *up feathers* ɓorde.

pullover [pulowvə] *n.* piliweer *(o).*

pulmonary [pʌlmonəri] *n.* ko faati e jofe.

pulpit [pʌlpit] *n.* jéértingól *(ngól).*

pulsate [pʌlseyt] *v.* diwde (ɓernde).

pulse [pʌls] *v.* diwde.

pulverize [pʌlvərayz] *v.* móññude; ruggude; fuufde.

pumpkin [pʌmpkin] *n.* wuuduru *(ndu).*

pump [pʌmp] *v.* pompe *(ɗe)*

pun [pʌn] *v.* fiide; tappude.

punch [pʌnč] *v.* góɓɓude; fiyde womre.

punctual [pʌŋkčwəl] *adj.* timmuɗo; garɗo e waktu; deenɗo waktu.

punctuate [pʌŋkčweyt] *v.* tóɓɓude.

puncture [pʌŋkčə] *v.* fusde.

punish [pʌniš] *v.* waɗde/fawde kuugal.

punishment [pʌnišmənt] *n.* kuugal *(ngal).*

punitive [pyuwnətiv] *adj.* ko faati e kuugal.

punter [pʌntə] *n.* pettoowo *(o).*

pup [pʌp] *n.* ɓoosaaru *(ndu).*

pupil [pyuwpəl] *n.* almuudo *(o);* fósin *(o).*

puppy [pʌpi] *n.* ɓoosaaru *(ndu).*

purchase [pərčis] *v.* soodde.

purchaser [pərčəsə] *n.* coodoowo *(o).*

pure [pyuwr] *adj.* laaɓɗum; ko laaɓi.

purge [pərj] *v.* laɓɓinde.

purge [pərj] *n.* nandal *(ngal)*

purification [pyuwrəfikeyšən] *n.* laaɓal *(ngal).*

purify [pyuwrəfay] *v.* laɓɓinde.

purity [pyuwrəti] *n.* laaɓal *(ngal).*

purl [pərl] *v.* ñuumbaade.

purpose [pərpəz] *n.* muuyaa *(o). on* ~ e belaaɗe; e teyaaɗe.

purr [pər] *n.* ŋeewde.

purse [pərs] *n.* kalbe debbo.

pursue [pərsyuw] *v.* rewde; tefde.

pursuivant [pərswiyvənt] *n.* dewɗo *(o);* dewoowo e.

pus [pʌs] *n.* mbórdi *(ndi).*

push [puš] *v.* duñde *v.* yérƳude. ~ *out* yaltinde. ~ *in* naatnude.

push [puš] *n.* duñannde *(nde).*

pusher [pušə] *n.* duñoowo *(o).*

puss [pʌs] *n.* ullundu *(ndu).*

put [put] *v.* fawde. ~ *together* fedde. ~ *aside* faltaade. ~ *out* ñifde. ~ *forth* wiltude. ~ *perfume or incense* urde. ~ *upside down* junnitde. ~ *on below* sakkude. *aside* resde. ~ *on airs* mawnikinaade. ~ *inside* lómbude. ~ *with* waɗdude. ~ *down* diiñde. ~ *with* muñde. ~ *someone in a dilemma* aannude.

putrefy [pyuwtrəfay] *v.* ñólnude; ñolde.

puzzle [pʌzəl] *n.* ciftól *(ngól);* haawniinde *(nde).*

puzzled [pʌzəld] *adj.* kaawaaɗo; jaakɗo.

puzzling [pʌzliŋ] *adj.* kaawniɗum;.

python [payθən] *n.* sohre *(nde).*

Q

Qadiriya [kadiriyya] *n.* laawól Qaadiriyya.

quadregenarian *n.* jom duuɓi capanɗe nay.

quadrilingual [kwadrəliŋgwəl] *adj.* ko faati e ɗemɗe nay.

quadrisect [kwadrəsekt] *v.* féccude pecce nay.

quadruped [kwadruwpet] *n.* muumantél jahrowél koyɗe nay.

quadruple [kwadrupəl] *v.* fiyde laabi nay.

quaff [kwaf] *v.* yarde.

quail [kweyl] *v.* jébbilaade.

quake [kweyk] *v.* yérɓude; siññude; dillude.

qualification [kwaləfikeyšən] *n.* sifaa *(o)*; gandal *(ngal)*.

qualifier [kwaləfayə] *n.* cifotooɗo *(o)*.

qualify [kwaləfay] *v.* sifaade.

quality [kwaləti] *n.* moȲȲere *(nde)*.

qualm [kwam] *n.* nimsa *(o)*; ɓernde yiiñde.

quandary [kwandri] *n.* jaakre *(nde)*.

quantity [kwantəti] *n.* potal *(ngal)*.

quarrelsome [kwarəlsʌm] *adj.* kaɓeteeɗo.

quarrel [kwarəl] *n.* hare *(nde)*. ~ *with* waɗdude.

quarreller [kwarələ] *n.* kaɓeteeɗo *(o)*.

quarter [kɔtə] *n.* nayaɓal *(ngal)*; leegal *(ngal)*. *from all* ~*s* bangeeji kala.

quarterly [kɔtəli] *adj.* lébbi nay kala.

quartet [kwartət] *n.* deental nayo.

quash [kwaš] *v.* móññude.

quasi [kwayzay] *adj.* annama; ko wayi no.

quay [key] *n.* tééri.

quean [kwiyn] *n.* garbotooɗo *(o)*.

queasy [kwiyzi] *adj.* ko timnata ɓernde.

queen [kwiyn] *n.* laamɗo debbo.

queer [kwiyr] *adj.* ko hoolnaaki; ko luutndii.

quench [kwenč] *v.* ɗómɗitde

querulous [kwerələs] *adj.* keewɗo gullitaali.

query [kwiyri] *n.* lamndal *(ngal)*.

query [kwiyri] *v.* lamndaade.

quest [kwest] *n.* njiilaw *(o)*.

question [kwasčən] *n.* lamdal *(ngal)*. *ask a* ~ lamndaade.

question [kwasčən] *v.* lamndaade; naamndaade.

queue [kyuw] *v.* réggóndirde.

quick [kwik] *adj.* jaawɗo; jaawɗum. *be* ~ yaawnaade.

quicken [kwikən] *v.* yaawnude.

quickly [kwikli] *adv.* ko yaawi; jaawɗum; ko yaawi.

quiescence [kwiysəns] *n.* deeȲre *(nde)*.

quiescent [kwiysənt] *adj.* deeȲɗo.

quiet [kwayt] *adj.* deeȲɗo. *He is a quiet person* O heewaani haala..

quietude [kyetuwd] *n.* deeȲre *(nde)*.

quill [kwil] *v.* sige.

quinquagenarian *n.* jom duuɓi capanɗe jóy.

quinsy [kwinsi] *n.* sefo *(ngo)*.

quintal [kwintəl] *n.* teemedere cilo.

quintet [kwintət] *n.* deental ngal jóy.

quintuple [kwintyuwpəl] *v.* fiide laabi jóy.

quit [kwit] *v.* ɗaccude; accude.

quite [kwayt] *adv.* ko timmi; fóf.

quits [kwits] *adj.* fotɓe.

quiver [kwivə] *v.* siññude.

quorum [kowrʌm] *n.* deental jongal.

quota [kowtə] *n.* geɗal *(ngal)*.

quotation [kowteyšən] *n.* luɓal *(ngal)*.

quote [kowt] *v.* luɓaade.

quotidian [kowtiyjən] *adj.* ñande kala; ñalawma kala.

Quran [kuran] *n.* Quraana *(o)*.

R

Rabat [rabat] *n.* laamorde Maruk.
rabbit [rabit] *n.* wojere *(nde). little ~* bojel *(ngél). big ~* bojal *(ngal).*
rabble [rabǝl] *n.* deental yimɓe.
rabid [rabid] *adj.* cayaaɗo.
rabies [rabiz] *n.* sayo *(ngo).*
race [reys] *n.* dógdu *(ndu);* dandu *(ndu);* léñól *(ngól).*
race [reys] *v.* dogde.
racer [reysǝ] *n.* dognoowo *(o);* dogoowo *(o).*
racial [reyšǝl] *adj.* ko faati e léñól; leñamlñaagu *(ngu).*
racing [reysiŋ] *n.* dogdu *(ndu). ~ instrument* dógnirgal *(ngal).*
racism [reysizm] *n.* leñamleñaagu *(ngu).*
rack [rak] *v.* firtude; bónnude.
racket [raket] *n.* gulaali *(ɗi).*
radiant [reydyǝnt] *adj.* ko jalbi.
radiate [radyeyt] *v.* jalbude.
radical [radikǝl] *adj.* ko faati e iwdi.
radio [radyow] *n. {fr.}* rajo *(ngo).*
radius [radyǝs] *n.* Ƴiyal jungo.
radix [reydiks] *n.* ɗaɗól *(ngól).*
raffle [rafǝl] *n.* lótóri *(o).*
rafter [raftǝ] *n.* salndu mbildi; jaalal *(ngal).*
rag [rag] *n.* limsere *(nde);* tekkere *(nde). little ~* limcél *(ngél). piece of ~* limsere *(nde).*
rage [reyj] *n.* ñangere *(nde).*
ragged [raged] *adj.* kó wónti limce/limsere.
ragout [ragu] *n.* soos *(o);* suppu *(o).*
raid [reyd] *v.* yande; honde.
raillery [ralǝri] *n.* gaajaare *(nde).*
railroad [reylrowd] *n.* laawól laana njóórndi.
railway [relwey] *n.* laawól laana njóórndi.
raiment [reymǝnt] *n.* cómcól *(ngól);* comci *(ɗi).*
rain [reyn] *n.* toɓo *(ngo). light ~* fajjo *(ngo). ~ outside rainy season* bowte *(ɗe).*
rain [reyn] *v.* toɓde. *~ heavily* ñappude.
rainbow [reynbaw] *n.* timtimol *(ngól).*
raindrop [reyndrop] *n.* waadere *(nde).*
rainfall [reynfɔl] *n.* toɓo *(ngo).*

rainout [reynawt] *n.* huunde nde toɓo haaytini.
rainy [reyni] *adj.* ko toɓata. *~ season* ndungu *(ngu).*
raise [reyz] *v.* suutde. *~ a person's clothes* ñorde. *~ one's clothes up* ñoraade. *~ one's head* turtaade.
raised [reyzd] *adj.* cuutaɗum; ko suutaa. *~ platform* danki *(ki).*
rake [reyk] *n.* rato *(ngo)*
rally [rali] *n.* deental *(ngal).*
rally [rali] *v.* rééntude.
ram [ram] *n.* njawdi *(ndi).*
Ramadan [ramǝdan] *n.* léwru koorka; koorka.
ramble [rambǝl] *v.* yahnaade.
rambler [ramblǝ] *n.* jahnotooɗo *(o).*
ramification [ramǝfikeyšǝn] *n.* caltugól *(ngól);* jibingól *(ngól).*
ramify [ramǝfay] *v.* saltude; reɓde.
ramp [ramp] *n.* ŋabbirde *(nde);* célól *(ngól).*
rampaging [rǝmpeyjiŋ] *n.* ñangere *(nde).*
rampant [rempǝnt] *adj.* ñanguɗo.
rancid [ransid] *adj.* ko aamti; ko luuɓi; ko ufi.
rancorous [rankǝrǝs] *adj.* joganiiɗo.
randy [randi] *adj.* neetaro.
ranger [reynjǝ] *n.* deenoowo *(o).*
rankle [raŋkǝl] *v.* haaɓnude; seknude.
ransack [ransak] *v.* honde; wujjude.
ransom [ransʌm] *n.* cooɗtaari *(ndi).*
rant [rant] *v.* haalde.
rap [rap] *v.* fiide.
rape [reyp] *v.* wujjude; waawnude.
rapid [rapid] *adj.* jaawɗo; ko yaawi.
rapidity [rapǝditi] *n.* yaawre *(nde).*
rapprochement [raprošmǝnt] *n.* ɓattóndiral *(ngal).*
rare [reyr] *adj.* caɗɗum; caɗtuɗum; ko saɗti.
rarefy [rarefay] *v.* saɗtinde.
rarity [rarǝti] *n.* saɗre *(nde).*
rascal [raskǝl] *n.* kalabante *(o).*
rash [raš] *n.* amumal *(ngal).*
rasp [rasp] *v.* heefde.
rat [rat] *n.* doomburu *(ndu). big ~* kaña *(o).*

rate [reyt] *n.* coggu *(ngu).* **at any ~ ko** waawi wonde kal.

rathole [rathowl] *n.* ngaska dóómburu.

ratification [ratǝfikeyšǝn] *n.* ciifgól *(ngól).*

ratify [ratǝfay] *v.* siifde.

ration [reyšǝn] *n.* nguura *(ka).*

rattle [ratǝl] *v.* dillinde; sóññude.

ravage [ravij] *v.* bónnude.

rave [reyv] *v.* ruuytude.

ravel [ravǝl] *v.* jiktude.

ravine [raviyn] *n.* naddere *(nde)*; naddal *(ngal)*; gargulal *(ngal).*

raw [rɔw] *adj.* kecco; kó héccicɗi.

rax [raks] *v.* fortaade.

ray [rey] *n.* sérééndu *(ndu).*

rayon [reyon] *n.* gaarowól *(ngól).*

raze [reyz] *v.* mómtude; ittude; helde; yandinde.

razor [reyzǝ] *n.* laɓorke *(ki)*; layset *(o).*

razzia [razya] *n.* nguyka *(ka).*

re [ri] *prep.* ko faati e...

re [ri] *pref.* ɗimmitde; wacɗtude

reach [riyč] *v.* heɓde; tolnaade. **~ with the arm** ballaade. **~ the same height or location** tolnaade..

reachable [riyčǝbǝl] *adj.* ko heɓotoo.

reactivate [riyaktǝveyt] *v.* wuurtinde.

read [riyd] *v.* jangude.

readable [riydǝbǝl] *adj.* ko jangotoo.

reader [riydǝ] *n.* jangoowo *(o).*

reading [riydiŋ] *n.* jangde *(nde).*

ready [redi] *adj.* parcɗo; kebiicɗo. **~ oneself** hebaade. **~ ready oneself for prayer** heblaade.

real [riyl] *adj.* kó wóódi; gooddɗum.

realia [riylya] *n.* huundééji.

reality [riyalǝti] *n.* huunde woodnde.

realize [riylayz] *v.* faamde; anndude.

ream [riym] *v.* yaajnude.

reanimate [riyanǝmeyt] *n.* wuurtinde.

reap [riyp] *v.* soñde.

reaper [riypǝ] *n.* coñoowo *(o).*

rear [riyr] *v.* nehde.

rear [riyr] *n.* caggal *(ngal).*

reason [riyzǝn] *n.* sabaabu *(o).*

reason [riyzǝn] *v.* miijaade.

reasonable [riyznǝbǝl] *adj.* ko aamnii; ko wonata.

reave [riyv] *v.* teetde.

rebate [riybeyt] *n.* ustugól *(ngól).*

rebate [riybeyt] *v.* ustde.

rebel [riybel] *v.* murtude

rebellion [riybelyǝn] *n.* murtugól *(ngól).*

rebellious [riybelyǝs] *adj.* murtucɗo.

rebuild [riybild] *v.* mahtaade.

rebuke [riybyuwk] *v.* felde.

rebut [riybʌt] *v.* salaade.

rebuttal [riybʌtǝl] *n.* salaare *(nde).*

rebutter [riybʌtǝ] *n.* calotoocɗo.

recalcitrant [riykǝlsitrǝnt] *adj.* caliicɗo.

recalcitrate [riykǝlsǝtret] *v.* salaade.

recall [riykɔl] *v.* siftorde; nódditde.

recall [riykɔl] *n.* ciftorgol *(ngól).*

recant [riykǝnt] *v.* wultaade.

recapture [riykapčǝ] *v.* heɓtude.

recede [riysiyd] *v.* ruttaade.

receive [risiyv] *v.* heɓde.

receiver [risiyvǝ] *n.* keɓoowo *(o).*

recent [riysǝnt] *adj.* ko ɓooyaani.

receptacle [riyseptǝkǝl] *n.* nókku *(o).*

recess [riyses] *v.* yahrude caggal; duttagol *(ngól).*

recess [riyses] *n.* guurti *(cɗi).*

recipient [resǝpyǝnt] *n.* keɓcɗo.

recision [resiyzǝn] *n.* kaaytugól *(ngól).*

recitation [rǝsiyteyšǝn] *n.* kuñagól *(ngól).*

recite [riysayt] *v.* huñaade.

reck [rek] *v.* woƴeede; wondeede.

reckless [rekles] *adj.* mo woƴaaka; wondaaka.

reckon [rekǝn] *v.* limde; miijaade.

recline [riyklayn] *v.* téllinde; léscɗinde.

recognition [rikǝgniyšǝn] *n.* kéɓtingól *(ngól).*

recognize [riykǝgnayz] *v.* annditde; héɓtinde.

recollect [riykǝlekt] *v.* siftorde.

recommence [riykǝmens] *v.* fucɗcɗitaade.

recommend [riykǝmend] *v.* wagginde; wasiyaade.

recommendation *n.* wasiya *(o).*

recompense [riykǝmpens] *v.* yeende.

reconcile [riykǝnsayl] *v.* maslude.

reconciler [riykǝnsaylǝ] *n.* masloowo *(o).*

reconciliation *n.* maslahaa *(o).*

reconsider [riykənsidə] *v.* miijtaade.

reconstruct [riykənstrʌkt] *v.* fééwnitde.

record [rikɔd] *v.* windude; jaggude.

recorder [rikɔdə] *n.* bindoowo *(o)*.

recount [rikawnt] *v.* limtaade.

recounting [rikawntiŋ] *n.* limtagól *(ngól)*.

recover [rikovə] *v.* ɗiftude; séllude; yiitude.

recovery [rikovri] *n.* ɗiftere *(nde)*; ɗiftugól *(ngól)*.

recreant [rikreyənt] *n.* kulɗo reedu.

recrudescence [rəcruwdəsəns] *n.* bamtagól *(ngól)*; bamtugol *(ngól)*.

recruit [rikruwt] *n.* bindaaɗo *(o)*; Yettaaɗo *(o)*.

recruit [rikruwt] *v.* windude; yettude.

recta [rekta] *n.* baawooji *(ɗi)*.

rectifiable [rektəfayəbəl] *adj.* kó fééwnittoo.

rectify [rektəfay] *v.* fééwnitde.

rectitude [rektičuwd] *n.* peewal *(ngal)*.

rectum [rektəm] *n.* baawo *(ngo)*.

recuperate [rekyuwpəreyt] *v.* hébtude.

recusant [rekyuwzənt] *adj.* caliiɗo.

recuse [rekyuwz] *v.* salaade.

red [red] *adj.* boɗeejo; bóɗéjum. *very ~* coy. *~ pepper* ñamako *(ko)*; kaani *(o)*. *~ ants* góólóóli *(ɗi)*. *be ~* wójjude. *~ ant* méttéllu *(ngu)*; góólólól *(ngól)*.

redact [ridakt] *v.* winditaade; wiindude.

redden [redən] *v.* wójjinde.

rede [riyd] *v.* waajaade.

redeem [ridiym] *v.* soodde; wostaade; soodtude. *~ oneself* soodtaade.

redemption [ridempšən] *n.* cooɗtagól *(ngól)*.

redness [rednes] *n.* bóɗéwól *(ngól)*; mbóɗééri *(ndi)*

redo [riydu] *v.* waɗtude; ɗimmitinde. *~ a fence of shrubs* ñakkitaade.

redoubtable [riydawtəbəl] *adj.* ko hulbinii; kulbiniiɗum.

redress [riydres] *v.* wuurtude.

reduce [ridyuws] *v.* ustude; dajde. *~ to silence* deYYinde.

reduced [ridyuwsd] *adj.* gustiɗum; gustaɗum; gaayiɗum. *be ~* aayaade.

reducer [ridyuwsə] *n.* gustoowo *(o)*.

reduction [ridʌkšən] *n.* aayaare *(nde)*; aayandere *(nde)*; ustaare *(nde)*.

redundancy [rədəndənsi] *n.* deftagól *(ngól)*.

reed [riyd] *n.* celal *(ngal)* celi *(ɗi)*. *woven ~* mbiru *(ngu)*; sekko *(ngo)*.

reeducate [riyedəkeyt] *v.* ééltude.

reek [riyk] *n.* luubééki *(ki)*; cuurki.

referee [refəri] *n.* ñaawoowo *(o)*.

reference [refrəns] *n.* ruttorde *(nde)*.

refine [riyfayn] *v.* móYYinde.

reflect [riflekt] *v.* miijaade.

reflection [riflekšən] *n.* miijo *(ngo)*.

reflective [riyflektiv] *adj.* ko faati e miijo; miijotooɗo.

reform [riyform] *v.* fééwnitde.

reformer [riyformə] *n.* pééwnitoowo *(o)*.

refrain [riyfreyn] *v.* woɗaade.

refrigerate [refrəjəreyt] *v.* buubnude.

refrigerator [refrəjəreytə] *n.* filsideer *(o)*.

refuge [refyuwj] *n.* moolagól *(ngól)*. *take ~* moolaade; suuɗaade.

refugee [refyuwji] *n.* móóliiɗo *(o)*.

refund [riyfʌnd] *v.* ruttude.

refusal [rəfyuwzəl] *n.* salaare *(nde)*. *~ to give food* ɗawre *(nde)*.

refuse [rəfyuwz] *v.* salaade. *pretend to ~* saltintinaade. *~ food* géddude. *~ food to someone* ɗawde.

refutation [rəfyuwteyšən] *n.* salaare *(nde)*.

refute [rəfyuwt] *v.* salaade; filtinde.

regain [riygeyn] *v.* hébtude.

regard [rigɑd] *v.* Yeewde. *in ~ to* ko faati e.

regarding [rigɑdiŋ] *prep.* ko faati e.

regenerate [riyjənreyt] *v.* wuurtinde.

regent [rejənt] *n.* lomto *(o)*.

regicide [rəjəsayd] *n.* warngo laamɗo.

regime [rəjiym] *n.* laamu *(ngu)*.

region [riyjən] *n.* diiwaan *(o)*; nókku *(o)*.

regional [riyjənəl] *adj.* ko faati e nókku/diiwaan.

register [rejistə] *v.* windude; windaade; windeede.

regnant [regnənt] *n.* laamiiɗo *(o)*.

regress [riygres] *v.* tellaade; ruttaade.

regression [riygrešən] *n.* duttagól *(ngól)*; jahrugól caggal.

regret [riygret] *n.* nimsa *(o)*.

regret [riygret] *v.* nimsude.

regular [regilə] *adj.* ko haani.
rehearse [rihərs] *v.* reftaade.
rehoe [riyhow] *v.* remtaade.
reign [reyn] *n.* laamu *(ngu)*.
reimburse [riyimbərs] *v.* ruttude; yóɓtude.
reinforce [riyinfɔs] *v.* tiicɗtinde; tééɳtinde.
reinforcement [riyinfɔsmənt] *n.* tiicɗtingól *(ngól)*.
reiterate [riytret] *v.* reftaade e ko haalnoo; wacɗtude.
reject [rijekt] *v.* gukkude; ruttude; filtinde.
rejoice [riyjoys] *v.* weltaade.
rejoicing [riyjoysiɳ] *n.* weltaare *(nde)*.
relapse [riylaps] *v.* yantude; ruttaade. *have a ~* yantude.
relate [riyleyt] *v.* jaɳtaade **related** [riyleytəd] *adj.* ko jiidi; jiiduɓe; jiiducɗi. *be ~ jiidude. be ~ in an in-law relationship* ésondirde.
relation [riyleyšən] *n.* jiidigal *(ngal)*.
relationship [riyleyšənšip] *n.* bandiraagal *(ngal)*.
relative [rələtiv] *n.* bandiraacɗo *(o)*; hórééru *(ndu)*.
relator [riyleytə] *n.* jaɳtotoocɗo *(o)*.
relax [riylaks] *v.* weytaade.
relay [riylaks] *v.* jaɳtaade; habrude.
release [riliys] *v.* cɗaccitde. *~ from pressure* ñóⲅⲅitde.
relegate [rələgeyt] *v.* téllinde; lésdɗinde.
relevance [rələvəns] *n.* qiimaa *(o)*.
reliable [riylayəɓəl] *adj.* koolaacɗo.
reliance [riylayəns] *n.* hoolaare *(nde)*.
relieve [riyliyv] *v.* sóklitde; fóóftinde.
religion [rəliyjən] *n.* diine *(o)*.
religious [rəliyjəs] *adj.* ko faati e diine. *~ holiday* juulde taaske; juulde koorka. *~ teacher* ceerno *(o)*.
relinquish [relinkwiš] *v.* cɗaccude; yaafaade.
relucent [rəluwsənt] *adj.* ko jalbi; jalbucɗum.
rely [rilay] *v.* hoolaade; fawaade.
remain [rimeyn] *v.* heddaade. *~ long* duumde. *~ in a place* loppaade. *~ in a foreign country* luuttude. *~ for a long time* ɓóóytude. *It remains to be seen* Maa laaɓ.
remainder [rimeyndə] *n.* kedde *(cɗe)*; kó héddii.

remains [rimeynz] *n.* kedde *(cɗe)*.
remake [riymeyk] *v.* wacɗtude.
remark [riymɑk] *v.* wiide; teskaade.
remedy [remədi] *n.* safaara *(o)*.
remember [riymembə] *v.* siftorde; teskaade.
remembrance [rimembrəns] *n.* téskuya *(o)*.
remind [riymaynd] *v.* siftinde; saggitde.
reminisce [riyminis] *v.* siftorde.
remit [rimit] *v.* yoɓde; néldude njóɓdi.
remnant [remnənt] *n.* kedde *(cɗe)*.
remorse [riymɔs] *n.* nimsa *(o)*.
remorseful [riymɔsfəl] *adj.* nimsucɗo.
remorseless [riymɔsles] *adj.* mo alaa nimsa.
remote [riymowt] *adj.* kó wócɗcɗi.
removal [riymovəl] *n.* ittugol *(ngól)*. *~ of* hem hómbitande *(nde)*; kombitgol *(ngól)*. *~ of one's clothing* ɓoortagól *(ngól)*.
remove [riymuwv] *v.* ittude. *~ a pot from the stove* raattaade. *~ and set aside* héntude. *~ hair* huusde. *~ fish scales* baccude; warsude. *~ someone's clothing* ɓóórtude. *~ a person's sarong* tartude. *~ sewing* téppitde. *~ grains from stalks* duttude; lappude. *~ something that was glued* ɓakkitde; cɗakkitde. *~ a chief* fiiltude. *~ lice* ténnude. *~ from a leaning position* ɓaartude. *~ grains from ears* hoɓaade. *~ poison* sammitde. *~ from a hole* aaftaade. *~ couscous from a steaming utensil* nókitaade. *~ what was spread out to dry* liirtude. *~ grains* hiñaade.
removed [riymuwvd] *adj.* gittacɗum; ko ittaa.
remunerate [rəmyuwnəreyt] *v.* yoɓde.
remuneration [rəmyuwnəreyšən] *n.* njóɓdi *(ndi)*.
rename [riyneym] *v.* innitde.
rend [rend] *v.* feecde; seekde; taⲅde.
renew [rinyuw] *v.* héscɗitinde
renounce [rinawns] *v.* jébbilaade; cɗaccude.
renovate [riynowveyt] *v.* fééwnitde; héscɗitinde.
renown [rinawn] *adj.* gandaacɗo.
rent [rent] *n.* luwaas *(o)*.
repair [riper] *v.* feewnitde; wuggude.
reparation [repəreyšən] *n.* njóɓdi *(ndi)*.
repartition [repartiyšən] *n.* péccugól *(ngól)*.

epatriate [riypatreyt] v. nawtude to eyanoo; artirde

epeal [riypiyl] v. hébtude.

epeat [ripiyt] v. 1) reftaade 2) dimmitde. ~ *loudly after a speaker* nantinde.

epel [ripel] v. dóppude; ruttude; duuñtude.

epent [ripent] v. tuubde; imsinaade.

epentance [ripentəns] n. imsinaango (ngo).

epetition [repətiyšən] n. deftagól (ngól); dimmital (ngal).

epine [ripayn] v. woytaade.

eplace [riypleys] v. lomtaade; lómtinde.

eplacement [riypleysmənt] n. lomto (o); lomtagól (ngól).

eplenish [riypləniš] v. hébbitinde.

eplete [ripliyt] adj. kó hééwi; keewdo.

epletion [rəpliyšən] n. keewal (ngal).

eplication [rəpləkeyšən] n. jaabawól (ngól).

eply [rəplay] v. jaabtaade.

eport [rəport] v. jaᶇtaade.

epose [riypowz] v. foofaade.

epossess [riypowzes] v. hébtude; nangude.

epound [riypawnd] v. untaade.

eprehend [rəprihənd] v. felde.

eprehensible [reprihənsəbəl] adj. pelniido.

epresentative n. neddo gonando.

epress [ripres] v. ñóᒐᒐude.

eprimand [reprəmand] v. felde.

eprisal [reprayzəl] n. joftagól (ngól).

eproach [riyprowč] v. felde.

eproach [riyprowč] n. feloore (nde).

eproduce [riyprədyuws] v. waañjaade; waañjitaade.

eptile [reptayl] n. laadóóri (ndi); ndiwóóri (ndi).

epudiate [rəpyuwdyeyt] v. seerde; añtude.

epugnant [repʌgnənt] adj. kó néfnii; néfnidum.

epulse [ripʌls] v. nefde; ruttude.

epulsive [ripʌlsiv] adj. néfnidum.

eputable [repyuwtəbəl] adj. moᒐᒐo.

equest [rikwest] v. ñaagunde (nde).

equest [rikwest] v. ñaagaade. ~ *payment* yobnaade

equire [rikwayə] v. lamndaade.

requirement [rikwayəmənt] n. sardi (o).

rescind [riysind] v. haaytude; firtude.

rescue [reskyuw] n. faabaare (nde).

rescue [reskyuw] v. faabaade.

research [risərč] n. witto (ngo).

researcher [risərčə] n. bittoowo (o).

resell [riysel] v. yééytude.

resemble [rizembəl] v. nandude.

resent [rizent] v. nefde; añde.

resentment [rizentmənt] n. ngañgu (ngu); nefre (nde).

reserve [rizərv] v. joñde. ~ *a seat* jaggande palaas.

reserved [rizərvd] adj. nuggaro.

resh [reš] n. alkulal (ngal).

reside [rizayd] v. hodde.

residence [rəzidəns] n. hodorde (nde). hodorde (nde). *temporary* ~ jippunde (nde).

resident [rezidənt] n. koddo.

residual [rezijwəl] adj. ko faati e kedde.

residue [reziduw] n. kedde (de).

resign [rizayn] v. daccinde hooremum golle.

resist [rezist] v. jattinaade; biwaade.

resistance [rezistəns] n. biwaagol (ngól); jattinaagol (ngól); jattinande (nde).

resolute [rezəluwt] adj. bakkiliido.

resolution [rezəluwšən] n. wakkilaare (nde).

resorb [rizɔb] v. modde.

resourceful [rizɔsfəl] adj. tiidniido.

respect [rispekt] n. téddungal (ngal); fulla (o). *out of* ~ *to* sabu; sabaabu.

respectable [rispektəbəl] adj. téddudo.

respected [rispekted] adj. téddinaado.

respectful [rispektfəl] adj. téddudo.

respiration [respəreyšən] n. foofaango (ngo); poofaali (di).

respiratory [respərətəri] adj. ko faati e foofaango walla poofaali.

respite [respit] n. fooftere (nde).

resplendence [respləndəns] n. jalbugól (ngól).

respond [rispɑnd] v. jaabaade.

response [rispɑns] n. jaabawól (ngól).

responsibility n. defaare (nde).

responsible [rispɑnsəbəl] adj. défiido.

rest [rest] *n.* fooftere *(nde).*

rest [rest] *v.* fooftaade; yantinde. *I had a restless night* Mi ɗanaaki haa weeti; mi rendinaani yitere.

restaurant [restrənt] *n.* pasioŋ *(o).*

restful [restfəl] *adj.* póóftiiɗo.

restitution [restətyuwšən] *n.* njóɓdi *(ndi);* dókkital *(ngal).*

restlesness [reslesnes] *n.* 1) angere *(nde)* 2) piddugol *(ngól).*

restless [resles] *adj.* pidduɗo.

restoration [restəreyšən] *n.* pééwnitgól *(ngól);* pééwnital *(ngal).*

restore [ristowr] *v.* fééwnitde.

restrain [ristreyn] *v.* heytaade.

restraint [ristreynt] *n.* heytaare *(nde).*

restrict [restrikt] *v.* haaɗnude e; heertaade.

restroom [restrum] *n.* firlorde *(nde);* duus *(o);* taarorde *(nde).*

result [rizʌlt] *v.* jibinde.

resume [rezyuwm] *v.* ɓamtude.

resurface [riysərfis] *v.* suppitaade.

resurrect [rezyuwrekt] *v.* wuurtinde.

resurrection [rezyuwrekšən] *n.* ummital *(ngal).*

resurrectionist [rezərekšən] *n.* guurtinoowo *(o).*

resuscitate [resyuwsəteyt] *v.* wuurtinde.

resuscitator [resyuwsətyetə] *n.* guurtinoowo *(o).*

retail [riteyl] *n.* toŋo *(ngo).*

retailer [riteylə] *n.* toŋoowo *(o).*

retaining [riteyniŋ] *n.* suro *(ngo);* curgol *(ngól).*

retake [riyteyk] *v.* ɓamtude; heɓtude.

retaliate [riytəlyeyt] *v.* yoftaade.

retaliation [riytəlyeyšən] *n.* joftagól *(ngól).*

retard [ritɑd] *v.* lééltinde.

retardate [ritɑdeyt] *adj.* mo hakkille mum ustii.

retention [ritənšən] *n.* suro *(ngo).*

reticent [retisənt] *adj.* nuggaro.

retire [ritayə] *v.* lélóyaade.

retort [ritɔt] *v.* jaabaade; sontaade.

retortion [ritɔšən] *n.* jaabawól *(ngól).*

retrain [riytreyn] *v.* ééltude.

retreat [riytriyt] *v.* ruttaade; yahrude caggal.

retrieve [riytriyv] *v.* yiitude.

retrograde [riytrɔgreyd] *v.* yahtirde caggal; tellaade.

retrospect [ritrospekt] *n.* Ÿeewtagól *(ngól).*

return [ritərn] *v.* ruttaade; ruttude; iwtude; artirde; artude. *~ something* ruttude. *~ home* hootde. *~ greetings* salmitaade. *~ safely* jaaÿaade.

reunion [riyuwnyən] *n.* deental *(ngal).*

revamp [riyvamp] *v.* fééwnitde.

reveal [riyviyl] *v.* wééjnude; saaktude.

revel [revəl] *v.* weltaade.

revelation [revleyšən] *n.* caaktugól *(ngól).*

revelator [revleytə] *n.* caaktoowo *(o);* caaktuɗo *(o).*

revenge [rivenj] *v.* yoftaade.

reverberate [rivərbəreyt] *v.* oolde.

reverberation [rivərbəreyšən] *n.* óólél.

revere [riviyr] *v.* rewde.

reverence [revrəns] *n.* dewal *(ngal).*

reverse [rivərs] *v.* ruttaade; yahrude caggal.

revert [rivərt] *v.* ruttaade e.

review [rəvyuw] *v.* Ÿeewtaade.

reviewer [rəvyuwə] *n.* Ÿeewtotooɗo.

revile [riyvayl] *v.* Ÿettaade.

revise [rivayz] *v.* fééwnitde.

revival [rivayvəl] *n.* guurtingól *(ngól).*

revive [rivayv] *v.* wuurtude; wuurtinde.

revoke [rivowk] *v.* riiwde; niilnude.

revolt [rivolt] *v.* murtude.

revolt [rivolt] *n.* murtere *(nde);* murtugól *(ngól).*

revolve [rivolv] *v.* taaraade; yiilaade.

revolver [rivolvə] *n.* wolweere *(nde).*

reward [riwɔd] *n.* njeenaari *(ndi).*

reward [riwɔd] *v.* yeende.

rhematic [rematik] *adj.* ko faati e tafngo kelme.

rhetoric [retərik] *n.* jangde haala.

rheumatism [ruwmətizm] *n.* ñaw kééci.

rhinal [raynəl] *adj.* ko faati e hinere.

rhinocerous [raynəsərəs] *n.* buubu galagél.

rho [ro] *n.* alkulal *(ngal).*

riant [rayənt] *n.* jaloowo *(o);* kékitoowo *(o);* béltiiɗo *(o).*

rib [rib] *n.* beccal *(ngal);* wecco *(ngo).*

ribbon [ribən] *n.* léfól *(ngól).*

rice [rays] *n.* maaro *(ko)*; faro *(ko).* ~
seedlings jamba. ~ *farm* kamañaɗ.

rich [rič] *adj.* galo; nantiiɗo. ~ *man* galo
(o).

riches [ričiz] *n.* ngalu *(ngu).*

rick [rik] *n.* ñaayko *(ko)*; huɗo *(ko).*

rickle [rikəl] *n.* joowre huɗo.

rid [rid] *v.* ittude; laɓɓinde; séérndude. ~ *of
unwanted grains* wómbilaade.

riddle [ridəl] *n.* ciftól *(ngól)*; tindól *(ngól).*

ride [rayd] *v.* waɗɗaade.

rident [raydənt] *adj.* jaloowo; béltiiɗo.

rider [raydə] *n.* baɗɗiiɗo.

ridge [rij] *n.* ceɓtam *(ɗam)*; balól *(ngól).*

ridicule [ridəkyuwl] *v.* jalkitde.

ridicule [ridəkyuwl] *adj.* ko jalnii;
jalniɗum.

rife [rayf] *adj.* kééwɗum; ko heewi.

rifle [rayfəl] *n.* fétél.

rift [rift] *n.* céékól *(ngól).*

right [rayt] *n.* hakke *(o)*; tiindi *(ndi)*; hujja
(o). ~ *now* jóóni jóóni. *be* ~ haande;
feewde. ~ *hand* jungo ñaamo *(ngo). be* ~
haalde goonga; jeyde goonga.

righteous [rayčəs] *adj.* peewɗo.

righteousness [rayčəsnes] *n.* peewal *(ngal).*

rigid [rijid] *adj.* ko Ɣaggi; Ɣagguɗum.

rigidify [rijidəfay] *v.* Ɣagginde.

rile [rayl] *v.* séknude.

rim [rim] *n.* sara. *bicycle* ~ mbege *(o).*

rind [rind] *n.* kobjal *(ngal).*

ring [riŋ] *n.* feggere *(nde).*

ring [riŋ] *v.* seɲlude; siɲlinde.

ringer [riŋə] *n.* ciɲlinoowo *(o).*

rinse [rins] *v.* lallitde; lallude. ~ *one's
mouth* wufɁaade.

riot [rayət] *n.* murtugól *(ngól).*

riotous [rayətəs] *adj.* ko faati e murtugól.

rip [rip] *v.* taɁde; seekde.

ripe [rayp] *v.* ɓéndude; monginde.

ripen [raypən] *v.* ɓéndinde; monginde.

rise [rayz] *v.* haftaade; immaade; ummaade;
feerde. ~ *up suddenly* giddude. *make* ~
imminde; umminde. ~ *with the sun*
ummodaade e naange.

rising [rayziŋ] *n.* puɗal *(ngal)*; ummagól
(ngól).

rite [rayt] *n.* laawól *(ngól).*

rivage [rivaʒ] *n.* fongo *(ngo).*

rivalry [rayvəlri] *n.* póóɗóndiral *(ngal).*

rive [rayv] *v.* feecde; taɁde; séérndude.

river [rayvə] *n.* maayo *(ngo).*

riverine [rayvərayn] *adj.* ko faati e maayo;
ko takkii e maayo.

rivet [rivət] *n.* guurtól *(ngól).*

rivet [rivət] *v.* wuurtude (ñaaɁe).

riyal [riyal] *n.* kaalis *(o).*

roach [rowč] *n.* somre *(nde)*; mbóótu *(ngu).*

road [rowd] *n.* laawól *(ngól).* **main** ~ kallu
(o).

roam [rowm] *v.* lówwirde.

roar [rowr] *v.* hurɓude.

roar [rowr] *n.* hurɓaango *(ngo).*

roast [rowst] *v.* juɗde; sahde. ~ *for
someone* juɗande.

roast [rowst] *n.* juɗande *(nde).*

rob [rob] *v.* wujjude.

robber [robə] *n.* gujjo *(o).*

robbery [robri] *n.* nguyka *(ka).*

robust [robʌst] *adj.* ɓutto; tiiɗɗo;
cémbinɗo.

rock [rok] *n.* haayre *(nde).*

rocky [roki] *adj.* nókku keewɗo kaaɁe.

rod [rod] *n.* lóócól *(ngól)*

rogue [rowg] *n.* aawase *(o)*; tappale *(o)*;
borjoɗ *(o).*

roguery [rowgri] *n.* aawasaagal *(ngal).*

roguish [rogiš] *adj.* ko faati e aawasaagal.

roil [royl] *v.* irñitde.

role [rowl] *n.* liggééy *(o)*; gollal *(ngal).*

roll [rol] *v.* taggude; tallaade; tallude;
wergaade. ~ *one's clothing up* ñaafaade. ~
oneself up tiggaade. ~ *up a head pad*
tékkude.

roll [rol] *n.* tallande *(nde).*

roller [rolə] *n.* taggoowo *(o)*; morloowo
(o).

roof [ruwf] *n.* mbildi *(ndi)*; caali *(ki).*

roof [ruwf] *v.* bilde; hundude.

roofing [ruwfiŋ] *n.* bilngo *(ngo).*

room [rum] *n.* suudu. *little* ~ cuurél *(ngél).*

roommate [rumeyt] *n.* kóɗdiiɗo e nder
suudu.

roomy [ruwmi] *adj.* ko yaaji; ko lakkitii.

rooster [ruwstə] *n.* ngóri *(o).*

root [ruwt] *n.* ɗaɗól *(ngól)*

root [ruwt] *v.* wonande.

rootless [ruwtles] *adj.* ko alaa ɗaɗi.

rope [rowp] *n.* ɓóggól *(ngól)*

ropery [rowpri] *n.* nókku ɗo ɓóggi mottetee.

ropy [rowpi] *adj.* ko nandi e ɓóggól.

rosary [rozəri] *n.* kurus *(o)*.

rot [rot] *v.* ufde; ñolde.

rotate [rowteyt] *v.* yiilaade; yiilde.

rotation [rowteyšən] *n.* jiilagól *(ngól)*.

rotator [rowteytə] *n.* jiiloowo *(o)*.

rotten [rotən] *adj.* ñólɗum; koñoli.

rough [rʌf] *adj.* ko ñangi; ñanguɗo; ko ɗaataani.

round [rawnd] *adj.* murlo; murliɗɗo; ko murliɗi. **be** ~ murliɗde. **go** ~ taaraade; taartoyaade.

roundabout [rawndəbawt] *adj.* kó liilti.

roundish [rawndiš] *adj.* ko murliɗi.

rouse [rawz] *v.* findinde; umminde.

route [rawt] *n.* laawól *(ngól)*.

rove [rowv] *v.* lówwinde; lówwirde; huywude.

rover [rowvə] *n.* lówwinoowo *(o)*.

row [row] *v.* awʸude.

rowdy [rawdi] *adj.* pidduɗo.

rower [rower] *n.* awyoowo *(o)*.

royal [royəl] *adj.* ko faati e laamu.

royalty [royəlti] *n.* laamɓe *(ɓe)*

rub [rʌb] *v.* moomde; momlude; soccude; yiggude; nirkude; yirgude; oogde. ~ **on oneself** moomaade. ~ **one's eyes** tokñaade. ~ **dirt on someone** ɓaatde. ~ **something on oneself** momlaade. ~ **oil on oneself or on one's hair** wujaade. ~ **oneself** yiggaade. ~ **one's bottom on the ground** foflaade.

rubber [rʌbə] *n.* dalli.

rubbish rʌbiš] *n.* kurjuru *(o)*.

rubble [ruwbəl] *n.* kaalis *(o)*.

rubric [ruwbrik] *n.* inde *(nde)*.

ruby [ruwbi] *n.* haayre ñilkoore.

ruck [rʌk] *n.* ñórɓólól *(ngól)*.

ruddy [rʌdi] *adj.* bóɗéjum; kó wójji.

rude [ruwd] *adj.* neetaro.

rue [ru] *v.* sunaade; nimsude.

rug [rʌg] *n.* tappi *(o)*.

ruin [ruwin] *v.* boomde; bónnude.

ruin [ruwin] *n.* boomaare *(nde)*.

ruined [ruwind] *adj.* bonɗum; bonnaɗum.

rule [ruwl] *v.* laamaade)

rule [ruwl] *n.* laamu *(ngu)*.

ruler [ruwlə] *n.* laamɗo *(o)*; laamiiɗo *(o)*.

ruling [ruwliŋ] *n.* yamiroore *(nde)*.

rumba [rumba] *n.* ngamri *(ndi)*.

rumble [rʌmbəl] *v.* diirde.

ruminate [ruwməneyt] *v.* aactaade.

rumination [ruwməneyšən] *n.* aactere *(nde)*.

rummage [rʌmij] *v.* ʸeewde; sarde; likñitde.

rumor [ruwmə] *n.* nanalla *(o)*.

rumple [rʌmpəl] *v.* ñóngude; sowde.

run [rʌn] *v.* dogde. ~ **into accidentally** felmaade. **make** ~ dógnude. ~ **out** gasnude.

runner [rʌnə] *n.* dogoowo *(o)*.

running [rʌniŋ] *n.* dógdu *(ndu)*.

rupee [ruwpiy] *n.* kaalis *(o)*.

rupture [rʌpčə] *v.* fusde.

rural [ruwrəl] *adj.* ko faati e ladde/gese.

ruse [ruz] *n.* ʸoʸre *(nde)*.

rush [rʌš] *v.* heñaade.

rusher [rʌšə] *n.* kéñiiɗo *(o)*.

rust [rʌst] *n.* komaak *(o)*.

rustic [rʌstik] *adj.* kó ɓóóyi.

rustle [rʌsəl] *v.* sóññude.

ruth [ruwθ] *n.* sunaare.

ruthless [ruwθles] *adj.* mo yurmotaako.

S

sabbatical [səbatəkəl] *adj.* ko faati e fooftere.

saber [seybə] *n.* silaama *(ka)*; jaasi *(ki)*.

sabot [sabɔ] *n.* holngo *(ngo)*.

sabotage [sabɔtaʒ] *v.* bónnude.

saboteur [sabotər] *n.* bonnoowo *(o)*.

saccular [sakyuwlə] *adj.* annama sasa.

sachet [saše] *n.* sakkósél *(ngél)*.

sack [sak] *v.* teetde. he was sacked today o ittaama e liggeey makko hannde.

sack [sak] *n.* saak *(o)*; boot *(o)*; sasa *(o)*.

sacred [seykrəd] *adj.* ko reentaa; ko faati e diine.

sacrifice [sakrəfays] *n.* sadak *(o)*.

sacrifice [sakrəfays] *v.* layyaade.

sacrificial [sakrəfiyšəl] *adj.* ko faati e sadak.

sacule [səkyuwl] *n.* basél *(ngél)*.

sad [sad] *adj.* jurminiiɗo. *be ~ sunaade*; yurminaade.

saddle [sadəl] *n.* hirke *(o)*; waɗɗorde *(nde)*; jappeere *(nde)*.

sadness [sadnes] *n.* mettere *(nde)*; mette *(ɗe)*.

safe [seyf] *adj.* daɗɗo; kó hóólnii; koolniɗum. *It is not safe* ɗum hoolnaaki.

safety [seyfti] *n.* dandugol *(ngól)*. *~ pin* pingu *(o)*.

sag [sag] *v.* leefde; nooyde.

sagacious [səgeyšəs] *adj.* péértuɗo.

sagacity [səgasəti] *n.* péértugól *(ngól)*.

sage [seyj] *n.* gando *(o)*; peewɗo *(o)*.

sail [seyl] *v.* wiirde.

sail [seyl] *n.* wiir *(o)*.

sailor [seylə] *n.* jom laana; ɗannortooɗo laana; befoowo *(o)*.

saint [seynt] *n.* waliyyu *(o)*.

sake [seyk] *n.* sabu *(o)*; sabaabu *(o)*. *for the ~ of friendship* sabu cehilaagal.

salaam [səlam] *n.* kisal *(ngal)*.

salable [seyləbəl] *adj.* ko yeeyotoo.

salad [saləd] *n.* salaat *(o)*.

salamander [saləmandə] *n.* lugu *(o)*.

salaried [salərid] *adj.* joɓeteeɗo.

salary [saləri] *n.* njóɓdi *(ndi)*. *I received my salary* Mi yoɓaama.

sale [seyl] *n.* njééygu *(ngu)*.

salesman [seylzmən] *n.* jeeyoowo *(o)*.

saliva [səlayvə] *n.* jóódi *(ɗi)*; jóódól *(ngól)*.

salivate [sələveyt] *v.* joodde.

salon [salon] *n.* werandaa *(o)*; saal *(o)*.

salt [sɔlt] *n.* lamɗam *(ɗam)*. *little ~* lamkal *(kal)*. *piece of ~* urtulde *(nde)*.

salted [sɔltid] *adj.* lammuɗum; kaaɗɗum. *~ ground* lamolamongal *(ngal)*.

saltless [sɔltles] *adj.* tékum.

salubrious [saluwbrəs] *adj.* ko addata cellal.

salutary [salətəri] *adj.* ko addata cellal.

salute [salyuwt] *v.* maajde. *I salute you* Mi yettii ma.

salvable [salvəbəl] *adj.* ko dandotoo.

salvage [salvij] *v.* faabaade; dandude.

salvage [salvij] *n.* faabaare *(nde)*.

salvation [salveyšən] *n.* faabaare *(nde)*.

same [seym] *adj.* ko nandi; kó fóti. *It is the same thing* Ko gootum.

sameness [seymnes] *n.* nandugól *(ngól)*.

sample [sampəl] *n.* huunde *(nde)*; geɗal *(ngal)*; yéru *(o)*.

sanction [saŋkšən] *n.* kuugal *(ngal)*.

sanctuary [saŋkčəri] *n.* móólirde *(nde)*.

sand [sand] *n.* léydi *(ndi)*. *throw ~* ullude.

sandal [sandəl] *n.* faɗo féttuuwo.

sandy [sandi] *adj.* ko waɗi ceenal; seeno *(ngo)*.

sane [seyn] *adj.* célluɗo; YoYɗo.

sanginary [saŋginəri] *adj.* dufoowo YiiYam neegɗo.

sanitary [sənitəri] *adj.* ko faati e laaɓal.

sanitate [sənəteyt] *v.* laɓɓinde.

sanity [sanəti] *n.* cellal *(ngal)*.

sandal [sandəl] *n.* féttuuwo *(ngo)*.

sap [sap] *n.* ndiyam gawYal.

sapid [sapid] *adj.* bélɗum.

saporous [sapowrəs] *adj.* bélɗum.

sarcasm [sarkazm] *n.* jalkitgól *(ngól)*.

sarco [sarkow] *n.* tééw *(ngu)*.

sarong [saroŋ] *n.* wudere *(nde)*; haddaare *(nde)*. *tie a ~* haddaade wudere.

sash [saš] *n.* duhól *(ngól)*.

sass [sas] *n.* contagól *(ngól)*.

sass [sas] *v.* sontaade.

satan [seytən] *n.* ibliis *(o)*.

satanic [seytənik] *n.* ko faati e Ibliis. ~ *behavior* golle seytaane.

satchel [satčəl] *n.* gafakke *(o)*; saak *(o)*.

sate [seyt] *v.* haarnude; hébbinde.

satiable [seyčəbəl] *adj.* kaaroowo.

satiate [seyčeyt] *v.* haarnude.

satiated [seyčeytid] *adj.* kaarɗo; méytuɗo; jonaaɗo.

satirical [sətiyrəkəl] *adj.* jalniɗum; jalniiɗo; ko jalnii.

satisfaction [satəsfakšən] *n.* beltagól *(ngól)*.

satisfied [satəsfayd] *adj.* jonaaɗo.

satisfy [satəsfay] *v.* wéltinde.

Saturday [satədi] *n.* aset *(o)*. *It is Saturday* Hande ko aset.

sauce [sows] *n.* liyam *(ɗam)*; ñeekam *(ɗam)*.

saucer [sowsə] *n.* kóppu *(o)*.

saunter [sontə] *v.* daagaade.

savage [savij] *adj.* ko faati e golle jawdi.

savanna [səvana] *n.* nókku huɗo.

savant [savant] *n.* gando *(o)*.

save [seyv] *v.* hakkitde; dandude.

saver [seyvə] *n.* dandoowo *(o)*.

savior [seyvyə] *n.* dandoowo *(o)*; kakkitoowo *(o)*.

savory [seyvri] *adj.* bélɗum; uurɗum.

saw [sɔ] *n.* riis *(o)*.

say [sey] *v.* wiide. ~ *goodbye* waynaade. ~ *one's genealogy* innitaade. *They say so* Ko noon ɓe mbii.

sayable [seyəbəl] *adj.* ko ina wiyoo; ko haalotoo.

saying [seyiŋ] *n.* tindól *(ngól)*.

scab [skab] *n.* heɗɗere YiiYam.

scabies [skəbiz] *n.* gaaye *(ɗe)*; tiro *(ngo)*.

scaffolding [skəfowldiŋ] *n.* danki *(ki)*.

scald [skɔl] *n.* cumaram *(ɗam)*.

scald [skɔld] *v.* sumde.

scale [skeyl] *n.* waccere *(nde)*.

scale [skeyl] *v.* baccude.

scales [skeylz] *n.* péésirɗe *(ɗe)*; balayse *(ɗe)*.

scalp [skalp] *n.* nguru hoore.

scalpel [skalpəl] *n.* paakayél *(ngél)*.

scamp [skamp] *n.* mo nafataa.

scamper [skampə] *v.* dogde.

scan [skan] *v.* Yeewde.

scandal [skandəl] *n.* kersa *(o)*; gacce *(ɗe)*; koyeera *(o)*; bonande *(nde)*.

scandalize [skandəlayz] *v.* hersinde.

scanner [skanə] *n.* Yeewoowo *(o)*.

scant [skant] *adj.* seeɗa; ɓittuɗo.

scanty [skanti] *adj.* pamarum; ko heewaani; seeɗayal.

scapular [skapyuwlə] *adj.* ko faati e balabe.

scar [skɑr] *n.* ñaasal *(ngal)*; ñaasal battingal; ŋaatal battingal.

scarce [skeyrs] *adj.* ko heewaani; ŋakkuɗum.

scarcity [skeyrsəti] *n.* ŋakkere *(nde)*.

scare [skeyr] *v.* hulɓinde.

scarf [skɑf] *n.* kaala *(ka)*.

scart [skɑt] *v.* ŋaacde.

scary [skeyri] *adj.* kuulɓiniiɗum; ko hulɓinii.

scatter [skatə] *v.* fullude; sarde.

scattered [skatəd] *adj.* caakiɗum; cariɗum.

scavenge [skavenj] *v.* lawYude; fittude.

scavenger [skavenjə] *n.* pittoowo *(o)*.

scent [sent] *n.* uuratééri *(ndi)*.

scheme [skiym] *n.* feere *(nde)*.

schism [skizm] *n.* péccugól *(ngól)*.

scholar [skowlə] *n.* móódibo *(o)*; ganndo *(o)*.

scholastic [skowlastik] *adj.* ko faati e jangde.

school [skuwl] *n.* jangirde *(nde)*; lekkol; duɗal *(ngal)*.

sciatic [syatik] *adj.* ko faati e asangal/asaale.

science [sayəns] *n.* gandal *(ngal)*.

scintillate [sintəleyt] *v.* yaltinde peete; ñiilkude; jalbude.

scission [siyšən] *n.* taYóndiral *(ngal)*.

scissors [sizəz] *n.* siso *(o)*; mecekke *(ɗe)*.

scoff [skɑf] *v.* jalkitde; seknoraade.

scold [skowld] *v.* furaade.

scolopendra [skoləpendra] *n.* ligi *(o)*.

sconce [skɑns] *n.* haɗiinde *(nde)*.

scoop [skuwp] *n.* kuundal *(ngal)*.

scope [skowp] *n.* kééri *(ɗi)*.

scorch [skɑč] *v.* wurbude

orn [skorn] *n.* ngañgu *(ngu).*

orn [skorn] *v.* añde.

orpion [skorpyən] *n.* yahre *(nde).*

ot [skot] *n.* njóɓdi *(ndi).*

our [skawə] *v.* lawⱤude; heefde.

ourer [skawrə] *n.* lawⱤoowo *(o).*

owl [skowl] *v.* ñirɓinaade.

owler [skowlə] *n.* ñirɓiniiɗo *(o).*

rabble [skrabəl] *v.* Ŋaacde.

ram [skram] *v.* yaltude; yahde.

ramble [skrambəl] *v.* jilɓude; jilɓinde.

rap [skrap] *n.* taⱤatinde *(nde).*

rape [skreyp] *v.* heefde; haakde. ~ *off* ɓiirtude.

raper [skreypə] *n.* keefoowo *(o).*

ratch [skrač] *v.* Ŋaañaade; Ŋaacde; Ŋaañde. ~ *the ground* widaade. ~ *oneself* Ŋaañaade.

ratch [skrač] *n.* Ŋaacal *(ngal);* Ŋaacere *(nde).*

cream [skriym] *n.* haacande *(nde);* wulaango *(ngo).*

cream [skriym] *v.* haacde; iicaade; wullude; ilkinaade; oolaade; luukde.

creamer [skriymə] *n.* luukoowo *(o).*

creen [skriyn] *n.* heɗɗaawo *(ngo).*

crew [skruw] *n.* wiis *(o).*

crew [skruw] *v.* ɓiiⱤde.

cribe [skrayb] *n.* bindoowo *(o).*

crimp [skrimp] *adj.* daɓɓo; tokooso.

cript [skript] *n.* bindól *(ngól);* alkule *(ɗe).*

cripture [skripčə] *n.* deftere tellinaande.

crounge [skrawnj] *v.* réndinde.

crub [skrʌb] *v.* yiggude; lawⱤude; heefde.

cruff [skrʌf] *n.* hóⱤⱤudu *(ndu).*

crupulous [skruwpyələs] *adj.* gondaaɗo.

crutable [skruwtəbəl] *adj.* ko faamotoo.

crutator [skruwteytə] *n.* bittoowo *(o);* Ⱡeewoowo *(o).*

cuff [skʌf] *v.* daasde koyɗe.

cuffle [skʌfəl] *n.* hare *(nde).*

cull [skʌl] *n.* laana *(ka).*

culpt [skʌlp] *v.* sehde.

culpture [skʌlčə] *n.* céhgól *(ngól).*

cum [skʌm] *n.* tuundi *(ndi).*

cunner [skʌnə] *n.* ngañgu *(ngu).*

curry [skʌri] *v.* heñaade; yaawnaade.

cuttle [skʌtəl] *v.* ñékkude.

scythe [sayθ] *n.* wafdu *(ndu).*

sea [siy] *n.* gééc *(o).*

seal [siyl] *v.* muɓɓude.

seam [siym] *n.* ñóótól *(ngól).*

seam [siym] *v.* ñootde.

seaport [siypɔt] *n.* tééri.

sear [siyə] *v.* jelde.

search [sərč] *n.* njiilaw *(o).*

search [sərč] *v.* yiilaade.

searcher [sərčə] *n.* jiilotooɗo *(o).*

season [siyzən] *n.* céédu *(ngu);* ndungu *(ngu);* kawle *(ɗe);* demminaare *(nde).*

seat [siyt] *n.* jooɗorde *(nde);* siiraⱡ.

secede [səsiyd] *v.* taⱤaade; seerde.

secern [sisərn] *v.* séérndude.

secession [sisešən] *n.* céértugól *(ngól);* taⱤagol *(ngól).*

secessionist [siseyšən] *n.* taⱤotooɗo *(o).*

seclude [səkluwd] *v.* séérndude; taⱤde; heertaade; howde.

secluded [səkluwdəd] *adj.* ko heertaa; keertaɗum; keertaaɗo.

seclusion [səkluwʒən] *n.* keertagól *(ngól).*

second [sekənd] *ord.* ɗiɗaɓo *(o);* ɗimmo.

secondary [sekəndəri] *adj.* ɗiɗaɓo.

secondhand [sekənhand] *adj.* ko huutoraa; ko wonaa késum.

secrecy [siykrəsi] *n.* suuɗnde *(nde);* sirru *(o).*

secret [siykrət] *n.* sirru *(o);* suudnde *(nde).*

secrete [sikriyt] *v.* suuɗde; móóftude.

section [sekšən] *n.* taⱤre *(nde).*

sector [sektə] *v.* féccude.

sector [sektə] *n.* nókku *(o).*

secure [sekyuwr] *v.* dandude.

security [sekyuwrəti] *n.* kisal *(ngal);* dandugól *(ngól).*

sedate [sədeyt] *v.* déⱤⱤinde.

sedition [sədiyšən] *n.* fitina *(o).*

seduce [sədyuws] *v.* héɓtude hakkille neɗɗo; jarribaade; ɗehde.

seduction [sədʌkšən] *n.* ɗéhgól *(ngól).*

see [siy] *v.* yiide. ~ *someone out* duusde. ~ *someone off* duusde ɗannotooɗo.

seed [siyd] *n.* foɗɗere *(nde);* abbere *(nde).* *small* ~ gabbél *(ngél)*/poɗɗel *(ngél).*

seeing [siyiŋ] *n.* giile *(ɗe).*

seek   servant

seek [siyk] *v.* Yeewde; yiilaade; dabbude.
~charity yelaade; tooraade. *~ for someone*
dabbande. *~ protection* moolaade.
seeker [siykə] *n.* jiilotoodo *(o)*.
seem [siym] *v.* wayde.
seep [siyp] *v.* rewde; siyde.
seer [siyə] *n.* jiyoowo *(o)*; Yeewoowo *(o)*.
seesaw [siysɔ] *v.* sayyaade; yahrude yeeso e
caggal.
seethe [siyð] *v.* fasnude.
segment [segmənt] *v.* taYde; féccude.
segregate [səgrəgeyt] *v.* séérndude.
segregation [səgrəgeyšən] *n.* céérndugól
(ngól).
seismic [siyzmik] *adj.* ko faati e jérbugól
léydi.
seismograph [siyzməgraf] *n.* masiŋ
betoowo jérbugól léydi.
seize [siyz] *v.* sóngude; jaggude.
seizure [siyʒə] *n.* ciññel gujjo.
seldom [seldəm] *adj.* ko heewaani ko
wadata.
select [səlekt] *v.* subaade. *the ~ few*
subaabe.
selectee [səlektiy] *n.* cubaado *(o)*.
selection [səlekšən] *n.* cubagól *(ngól)*.
self [self] *n.* neddo; huunde. *~ respect* jom;
neddaagal *(ngal)*.
selfish [selfiš] *adj.* boroodo; kiidnitiido;
górdudo.
sell [sel] *v.* yeeyde. *~ one's belongings*
firlitde. *~ at a give away price* wantirde. *~
out* jarnude; jinditde.
seller [selə] *n.* jeeyoowo *(o)*.
sellout [selawt] *n.* jinditgól *(ngól)*.
semantic [semantik] *adj.* ko faati e maanaa.
semantics [semantiks] *n.* jangde maanaa.
semblable [sembləbəl] *adj.* ko nandi;
nandudi.
semen [siymən] *n.* kañtudi *(ndi)*.
semi [səmay] *n.* feccere *(nde)*; hakkunde.
semplice [semplicə] *adv.* beebdum.
send [send] *v.* néldude. *~ a person* nelde;
nulde. *~ back* ruttinde.
sender [sendə] *n.* neldoowo *(o)*; néldudo
(o).
senile [siynayl] *adj.* mo hakkille mum ustii /
dilli; kaangaado.
senior [siynyə] *n.* mawdo.

seniority [siynyɔrəti] *n.* mangu *(ngu)*.
sense [sens] *n.* hakkille *(o)*. he has good
sense omo moYYi miijo.
senseless [sensles] *adj.* mo/ko hakkilaani.
sensible [sensəbəl] *adj.* kakkildo.
sensory [sensəri] *adj.* ko faati e giile,
nande, meedgol walla memgol.
sentence [sentəns] *n.* 1) kongól timmungól
2) kuugal *(ngal)*; ñaawoore *(nde)*.
sentiment [sentəmənt] *n.* miijo *(ngo)*; gilli
(di).
sentimental [sentəməntəl] *adj.* ko faati e
gilli/miijo.
sentinel [sentinəl] *n.* deenoowo *(o)*.
sentry [sentri] *n.* soldaat *(o)*.
separate [sepəret] *v.* séérndude. *~ bran &
flour* sedde.
separation [sepreyšən] *n.* ceergal *(ngal)*.
separator [səpreytə] *n.* ceerndoowo *(o)*.
sept [sept] *num.* jéédidi.
septenary [septənəri] *adj.* ko faati e
jéédidi.
septentrional [septəntriynəl] *adj.* ko faati e
worgo.
septuagenarian *adj.* jom duubi capande
jeedidi pawdi.
sepulcher [sepʌlkə] *n.* yanaande *(nde)*;
ngaska *(ka)*.
sepulchral [sepʌlkrəl] *adj.* ko faati e
yanaande.
sequel [siykəl] *n.* jokkere *(nde)*; déwóndiral
(ngal).
sequence [siykwens] *n.* jókkóndiral *(ngal)*;
déwóndiral *(ngal)*.
sequester [səkwestə] *v.* sokde; heeraade;
séérndude.
sequestrate [sekwəstreyt] *v.* sokde;
heeraade.
serene [səriyn] *adj.* deeYdo; kó dééYi.
serenity [səriynəti] *n.* deeYre *(nde)*.
series [siyriyz] *n.* gede *(de)*; huundééji *(di)*.
serious [siyryəs] *adj.* tiidniido.
seriousness [siyryəsnes] *n.* tiidnaare *(nde)*.
sermon [sərmən] *n.* waajuya *(o)*; hudba
(o).
sermonize [sərmənayz] *v.* waajaade.
serpent [sərpənt] *n.* laadóóri *(ndi)*.
serry [seri] *v.* bittude.
servant [sərvənt] *n.* suufa *(o)*.

240

erve [sərv] *v.* nafde; sarwude. ~ *food* róttude.

server [sərvə] *n.* carwoowo *(o).*

service [sərvis] *n.* liggééy *(o)*; gollal *(ngal).*

serviceman [sərvismən] *n.* soldaat *(o).*

servile [sərvəl] *adj.* ɗówtiiɗo.

servitude [sərvityuwd] *n.* macungaagal *(ngal).*

session [sešən] *n.* jonde *(nde).*

set [set] *v.* mutde. ~ *milk* féndude. ~ *a child across one's legs* sataade. ~ *to work* yaalnude. ~ *aside* willude. ~ *down* jippinde. ~ *aside for someone* jubbande; nokkande; resande.

settee [setiy] *n.* jooɗorde *(nde)*; danki *(ki).*

settle [setəl] *v.* hawrude; hoɗde.

settlement [setəlmənt] *n.* kawral *(ngal)*; hoɗorde *(nde).*

seven [seven] *num.* jééɗiɗi.

sevenfold [sevenfowld] *adj.* laabi jééɗiɗi.

seventeen [seventiyn] *num.* sappo e jééɗiɗi.

seventy [səventi] *num.* capanɗe jééɗiɗi.

sever [sevə] *v.* éntude; séérndude.

several [sevrəl] *det.* kééwɗi; keewɗe; heewɓe.

severance [sevrəns] *n.* ceergal *(ngal).*

severe [səviyr] *adj.* ko saɗti.

severity [səviyrəti] *n.* caɗtugól *(ngól).*

sew [səw] *v.* ñootde; husde.

sewing [səwiŋ] *n.* nootgol *(ngól)*; ñootol *(ngól).* ~ *machine* masiŋ ñóótoowo.

sex [seks] *n.* kaake; njogoram *(ɗam).*

sexagenarian [seksəjəneyryən] *n.* jom duuɓi capanɗe jeegom.

sextuple [sekstyuwpəl] *v.* fiide laabi jeegom.

shabby [šabi] *adj.* ko furi.

shack [šak] *n.* barak *(o).*

shackle [šakəl] *n.* ceen *(o).*

shade [šeyd] *n.* ɓuuɓri *(ndi)*; béélól *(ngól).*

shadow [šadow] *n.* mbéélu *(ngu).*

shady [šeydi] *adj.* ko waɗi ɓuuɓri.

shaft [šaft] *n.* bamfaro.

shaggy [šagi] *adj.* guyɗo; ko wuyi. *be* ~ wuyeede; wuyde.

shake [šeyk] *v.* siññude; yeŕde; fiɗɗude; dillinde; dillude. ~ *off* fiɗɗude. ~ *off again* fiɗɗitde. ~ *milk* yónkude.

shaker [šeykə] *n.* dillinoowo *(o)*; dilloowo *(o).*

shaking [šeykiŋ] *n.* siññere *(nde)*; dillugól *(ngól).*

shaky [šeyki] *adj.* ko dillata.

shale [šeyl] *n.* ɓakkere *(nde).*

shallop [šaləp] *n.* laana *(ka).*

shallow [šaləw] *adj.* ko luggiɗaani. ~ *water* pokpokolam *(ɗam).*

shamble [šambəl] *v.* bónnude; daaldaalnude.

shame [šeym] *v.* hóynude; hérsinde; sémtinde.

shame [šeym] *n.* koyeera *(o)*; gacce *(ɗe).*

shamed [šeymd] *adj.* koyɗo.

shameful [šeymfəl] *adj.* kérsiniiɗum.

shameless [šeymles] *adj.* mo alaa gacce.

shank [šaŋk] *n.* korlal *(ngal).*

shanty [šanti] *n.* barak *(o).*

shape [šeyp] *n.* tagóódi *(ndi)*; mbaadi *(ndi).*

share [šer] *n.* geɗal *(ngal)*; feccere.

share [šer] *v.* féccude; réndude.

shark [šark] *v.* wujjude.

sharp [šap] *adj.* ɓelɗo; mbelka; ko weli. *be* ~ welde; wéémtude; seeɓde.

sharpen [šapən] *v.* laggaade; wélnude; woogde.

sharpening [šapniŋ] *n.* setto *(ngo).*

sharpie [šapi] *n.* laana *(ka).*

sharpness [šapnes] *n.* seeɓre *(nde).*

shatter [šatə] *v.* helde; bónnude.

shave [šeyv] *v.* fembude; laɓde; laɓaade. ~ *oneself* fembaade. *get* ~*ed* fembeede.

shaver [šeyvə] *n.* pemboowo *(o)*; ko fembata.

shawl [šɔl] *n.* mojaare *(nde).*

she [šiy] *pron.* omo; kañ; kanko; o; kam.

shear [šiyr] *v.* taŕde; hesde.

sheath [šiyθ] *n.* wana *(ka).*

sheathe [šiyð] *v.* naatnude e nder wana.

sheave [šiyv] *v.* réndinde.

shed [šed] *v.* werlaade. ~ *tears* ɓoñde. ~ *light* famminde.

sheen [šiyn] *n.* jalbugól *(ngól)*; ñilkugól *(ngól).*

sheep [šiyp] *n.* mbaalu *(ngu)*; baali *(ɗi).*

sheer [šiyr] *v.* selde.

sheet [šiyt] *n.* ɗéréwól *(ngól)*; darab *(o).*

sheet [šiyt] v. soomde.

shelf [šelf] n. kaggu *(ngu)*; yówirde *(nde)*.

shell [šel] n. wujo *(ngo)*; hodoore *(nde)*; hoɓre *(nde)*.

shell [šel] v. hoɓtude; hoɓde.

shelled [šeld] adj. koɓtaɗum. *a ~ corn ear* hormere *(nde)*.

shelter [šeltə] n. ɗuhorde *(nde)*.

shelter [šeltə] v. ɗuhaade

shelve [šelv] v. yowde.

shepherd [šefəd] n. gaynaako *(o)*.

shepherdless [šefədles] n. gaynaako debbo.

shield [šiyld] n. heɗɗaawo *(ngo)*.

shift [šift] v. ummaade; umminde.

shilling [šəliŋ] n. taransu.

shimmer [šimə] v. jalbude.

shin [šin] n. korlal *(ngal)*.

shine [šayn] v. jalbude; ñaarde; ɗélkude.

shiny [šayni] adj. jalboowo; ko jalbata; jalbuɗo; jalbuɗum.

ship [šip] n. laana *(ka)*

shipwreck [šiprek] v. yiwde laana.

shirk [šərk] v. wappaade.

shirt [šərt] n. turki *(o)*; simis *(o)*.

shirty [šərti] adj. cekɗo.

shit [šit] n. kuudi *(ndi)*; jaañe *(ɗe)*.

shit [šit] v. huwde; bónnitaade.

shiver [šivə] v. siññude.

shoe [šuw] n. faɗo *(ngo)*.

shoemaker [šuwmeykə] n. sakke *(o)*.

shog [šog] v. dillude; dillinde.

shoo [šuw] v. hulɓinde; riiwde.

shoot [šuwt] n. puɗdi *(ndi)*.

shoot [šuwt] v. féllude.

shop [šop] v. soodde; duggude. *~ for* duggande.

shop [šop] n. bitik *(o)*.

shopkeeper [šopkiypə] n. jom bitik.

shoplifter [šopliftə] n. gujjo *(o)*.

shopper [šopə] n. coodoowo *(o)*.

shore [šor] n. takko/daande maayo; fongo *(ngo)*.

short [šort] adj. daɓɓo; ŋappo. *be ~* toŋde; raɓɓiɗde; ŋakkude.

shortcut [šortkʌt] n. sodorde *(nde)*.

short-tempered [šortempəd] adj. looɓɗo.

shortage [šortij] n. ŋakkudi; ɓitteende; ŋakkere; ŋakke *(ɗe)*; sooño *(ngo)*.

shorten [šortən] v. raɓɓiɗinde.

shortly [šortli] adv. jóóni jóóni.

shortness [šortnes] n. raɓɓere *(nde)*.

shorty [šorti] n. daɓɓél.

shot [šot] n. fiyande *(nde)*.

shotgun [šotgʌn] n. fétél *(o)*.

should [šud] aux. fotde.

shoulder [šuldə] n. walabo *(ngo)*.

shout [šawt] n. wulaango *(ngo)*.

shout [šawt] v. wullude; haacde.

shouting [šawtiŋ] n. wowlaango *(ngo)*.

shove [šowv] v. duñde.

shovel [šavəl] v. peel.

show [šow] v. hóllude; hóllinde. *~ pity* yurmaade; yurmikinaade. *~ off* wasaade; baabaade. *~ an angry face* ñirɓinaade. *~ by drawing* aamnude.

shower [šawə] n. toɓo *(ngo)*; ɓuftagol *(ngól)*. *~ room* lootorde *(nde)*.

shower [šawə] v. ɓuftaade.

shred [šred] n. cééltól *(ngól)*.

shred [šred] v. sééltude.

shrew [šruw] n. debbo ñanguɗo.

shrewd [šruwd] adj. ƴoƴɗo; péértuɗo.

shriek [šriyk] v. wulaango *(ngo)*.

shrink [šriŋk] v. toŋde.

shrinkage [šriŋkij] n. tóngól *(ngól)*.

shrivel [šrivəl] v. ñongaade.

shroud [šrawd] n. kasanke *(o)*.

shroud [šrawt] v. hasnude; muurde.

shrub [šrʌb] n. lawñandi *(ki)*; manganace. *pile of dead ~* ñakkeere *(nde)*.

shrug [šrʌg] v. dillinde; fiɗɗude; ñeeɓaade.

shudder [šʌdə] v. siññude.

shuffle [šʌfəl] v. jiiɓde; baatirde; moylaade.

shuffler [šʌflə] n. baatiroowo.

shun [šʌn] v. nefde.

shut [šʌt] v. uddude.

shy [šay] adj. nuggaro. *be ~* nuggóriɗde.

sibling [sibliŋ] n. déwiraaɗo *(o)*.

sick [sik] adj. ñawɗo; dafaaɗo.

sicken [sikən] v. ñawnude.

sickening [sikniŋ] adj. ko ñawnata.

sickle [sikəl] n. wafdu *(ndu)*.

sickness [siknes] n. ñaw *(ngu)*.

side [sayd] n. baŋŋe *(o)*; wuttulo *(ngo)*; wecco *(ngo)*; sara *(o)*.

side [sayd] v. takkaade; sawndaade. ~ *with*
jingude; jingande; wuuranaade.
siege [siyj] v. taaraade.
siesta [syesta] n. muumnagól *(ngól)*.
sieve [siyv] n. tame *(o)*.
sieve [siyv] v. secɗe.
sift [sift] v. secɗe.
sigh [say] v. ŋuslude.
sigh [say] n. ŋuslaango *(ngo)*; maande.
sight [sayt] v. sooynaade; yiyde.
sight [sayt] n. giile *(ɗe)*.
sigma [sigmə] n. alkulal *(ngal)*.
sign [sayn] n. annama; maale *(ɗe)*.
significance [signəfikəns] n. maanaa *(o)*.
significant [signəfikənt] adj. ko nafata; ko
wacɗi maanaa.
signify [signəfay] v. amminde.
silence [sayləns] n. deŕŕere *(nde)*.
silencer [saylənsə] n. kó déŕŕinta;
déŕŕinoowo *(o)*.
silent [saylənt] adj. déŕŕucɗo.
silhouette [siluwet] n. mbéélu *(ngu)*.
silk [silk] n. sooye *(o)*.
silkworm [silkwɔm] n. ngilngu *(ngu)*.
silurid [siluwrid] n. andoonde *(nde)*.
silver [silvə] n. kaalis. ~ *coins* kodiije *(ɗe)*.
silvery [silvri] adj. ko nandi e kaalis.
similar [simələ] adj. nando; ko nandi;
nanduɓe.
similarity [simələrəti] n. nandugól *(ngól)*.
similitude [səmilətyuwd] n. nandugól
(ngól).
simmer [simə] v. defde.
simper [simpə] n. mooso *(ngo)*; móósóóli
(ɗi).
simple [simpəl] adj. bééɓcɗum; newicɗum.
simplicity [simpləsəti] n. bééɓgól *(ngól)*.
simplify [simpləfay] v. wééɓnude.
simulacrum [simyuwlakrəm] n. ñémbugól
(ngól).
simulate [simyuwleyt] v. ñémbude.
simulation [simələšən] n. ñémbugól *(ngól)*.
simultaneous [simʌltəneous] adj. ko yahdi;
ko wacɗi.
sin [sin] n. bakkaat *(o)*; haraam *(o)*.
sin [sin] v. bakkódinde; woofde.
since [sins] adv. ɓayde; gila; ɓayri. ~ *then*
gila ndeen.

sincere [sinsiyr] adj. koolaacɗo.
sincerity [sinsiyrəti] n. hoolaare *(nde)*.
sinew [sinyuw] n. ɗacɗól *(ngól)*.
sinful [sinfəl] adj. bakkódincɗo.
sing [siŋ] v. yimde. ~ *religious poems*
béytude.
singe [sinj] v. sumde; duppude.
singer [siŋə] n. jimoowo *(o)*. ~ *of religious*
poems beytoowo *(o)*.
single [siŋəl] adj. gooto; petto.
singular [siŋgilə] adj. gooto.
sinister [sinistə] n. bonande; moobaare
(nde).
sinistral [sənistrəl] adj. ko faati e bonande
walla moobaare.
sink [siŋk] v. mutde; mutnude; débbude;
yiwde. ~ *down* debbude.
sinkage [siŋkij] n. mutnugól *(ngól)*.
sinless [sinles] adj. mo bakkódinaani.
sinner [sinə] n. goofoowo *(o)*;
bakkódinoowo *(o)*.
sinuate [sinyuweyt] v. ooñde; kó óóñii.
sinuous [sinyuwəs] adj. kó óóñii; ko
fortaaki.
sip [sip] v. surɓaade; tuuɓde.
sipid [sipid] adj. bélcɗum.
siren [sayrən] n. debbo jom maayo.
sister [sistə] n. bandiraacɗo debbo.
sisterhood [sistəhud] n. miñiraagal *(ngal)*;
miñiraagu *(ngu)*; mawniraagal *(ngal)*.
sit [sit] v. joocɗaade. ~ *on one's knees*
hórfinaade. *throw* ~ *down abruptly*
dénkude. ~ *flat on one's bottom*
ɓarfinaade. ~ *on one's crossed legs*
ferlaade; hofaade. ~ *down abruptly*
denkaade. ~ *on eggs* woofaade.
site [sayt] n. nókku *(o)*.
sitter [sitə] n. joocɗotoocɗo *(o)*; jóócɗiicɗo
(o).
sitting [sitiŋ] n. jonde.
situate [sičweyt] v. héédnude.
situated [sičweytid] adj. keedcɗo.
six [siks] num. jeegom. ~*fold* piigol walla
cowgol laabi jeegom.
sixteen [sikstiyn] num. sappo e jeegom.
sixty [siksti] num. capancɗe jeegom.
sizeable [sayzəbəl] adj. ko yaaji; ko mawni.
size [sayz] v. fóndude; ɓetde.

size [sayz] *n.* juutééndi, njaajééndi e
tooweendi.

sizing [sayziŋ] *n.* póndugól *(ngól)*.

skeletal [skelətəl] *adj.* ko faati e Ỳiye.

skeleton [skelətən] *n.* Ỳiye ɓandu.

skellum [skelʌm] *n.* aawase *(o)*.

skelp [skelp] *n.* hello *(ngo)*.

skeptic [skeptik] *adj.* necɗo kóólkisiicɗo.

skepticism [skeptəsizm] *n.* hóólkisaare
(nde).

sketch [skeč] *v.* diidde.

sketchy [skeči] *adj.* ko timmaani.

skiff [skif] *n.* laana *(ka)*.

skill [skil] *n.* ñeeñal *(ngal)*; mbaawka *(ka)*.

skilled [skild] *adj.* ñeeñcɗo. *be* ~ ñeeñde.

skim [skim] *v.* mééwtude

skimmer [skimə] *n.* meewtoowo *(o)*.

skin [skin] *n.* nguru *(ngu)*. ~ *of a dead
animal* cawgu *(ngu)*.

skin [skin] *v.* huttude; ɓóóltude. ~ *fungus*
laamlaame *(cɗe)*. *little* ~ gurél *(ngél)*. *be
light ~ned* naawcɗude.

skinner [skinə] *n.* kuttoowo *(o)*.

skinny [skini] *adj.* cewcɗo; pooỲcɗo. *be* ~
sewde; cɗawsude; réétude; fooỲde. *a* ~
person kooñoor *(o)*; pooỲcɗo.

skip [skip] *v.* diwde.

skirmish [skwərmiš] *n.* hare *(nde)*.

skirt [skərt] *n.* sabba *(o)*; sippu *(o)*.

skive [skayv] *v.* seelde.

skiver [skayvə] *n.* ceeloowo *(o)*.

skulk [skʌlk] *v.* suucɗaade.

skull [skʌl] *n.* Ỳiye hoore.

sky [skay] *n.* kammu *(o)*; asamaan *(o)*.

slack [slak] *adj.* mo wondaaka.

slacken [slakən] *v.* lééltinde; yólbinde.

slake [sleyk] *v.* cɗómcɗitde; ɓuuɓnude.

slam [slam] *v.* buɓɓude; uddude.

slander [slandə] *v.* takkude.

slant [slant] *v.* wuuraade; wuuranaade.

slap [slap] *v.* héllude; suntude; maɓɓude.
He slapped his face O fii mo hello e
hakkille.

slap [slap] *n.* hello *(ngo)*

slash [slaš] *v.* taỲde; ñiɓde; yiwde; seekde.

slat [slat] *v.* werlaade.

slaughter [slɔtə] *v.* hirsude. ~ *house*
tóŊirde *(nde)*.

slave [sleyv] *n.* maccucɗo *(o)*; jiyaacɗo *(o)*.
real ~ macaacaa *(o)*. *big* ~ maccungal
(ngal). *behave like a* ~ macculinde.

slave [sleyv] *v.* maccinaade.

slavery [sleyvri] *n.* macungaagal *(ngal)*.

slay [slay] *v.* warde.

sleep [sliyp] *n.* cɗoyngol *(ngól)*.

sleep [sliyp] *v.* cɗaanaade. *make someone* ~
cɗanninde. *pretend to* ~ daankinaade. *I did
not sleep a wink all night* Hanki jamma
mi rendinaani yitere.

sleeper [sliypə] *n.* cɗaaniicɗo *(o)*;
cɗaanotoocɗo *(o)*.

sleepiness [sliypənes] *n.* ŊoŊcɗi *(cɗi)*;
ŊoŊgól *(ngól)*.

sleeping [sliypiŋ] *n.* cɗóyngól *(ngól)*.

sleepy [sliypi] *adj.* ŊoŊcɗo. *be* ~ ŊoŊde.

sleeve [sliyv] *n.* jungo cómcól.

sleeveless [sliyvles] *adj.* ko alaa juucɗe.

slender [slendə] *adj.* cewcɗo.

slenderize [slendərayz] *v.* séwnude.

slice [slays] *n.* eeɓre *(nde)*; ande *(nde)*.

slice [slays] *v.* eeɓre *(nde)*. ~ *a fish from
head to tail* eñde.

slide [slayd] *v.* moorde; taataade.

sliding [slaydiŋ] *n.* taatól *(ngól)*.

slight [slayt] *adj.* seecɗa; pamaro.

slim [slim] *adj.* cewcɗo.

sling [sliŋ] *n.* lóttundu *(ndu)*.

slinger [sliŋə] *n.* lottoowo *(o)*.

slip [slip] *v.* taataade; ɓoccitaade. ~ *away*
sortaade; leewtaade; ɓóccitaade. ~ *into a
hole* yólɓitaade. ~ *knot* wórsundu *(ndu)*.

slippery [slipri] *adj.* ɓoodcɗum; taatcɗum;
ɓorwucɗum. *be* ~ taatde; ɓoodde;
ɓórwude.

slit [slit] *v.* eeɓde; taỲde.

sliver [slivə] *v.* eeɓde.

slobber [slobə] *v.* joodde.

slobbery [slobri] *adj.* ko faati e
jóódi/jóódól.

slog [slog] *v.* góɓɓude; fiide.

slop [slop] *v.* wiccude; rufde.

slope [slowp] *n.* waho *(ngo)*.

sloth [slowθ] *n.* ngaameela *(ka)*.

slothful [slowθfəl] *adj.* gaamcɗo.

slow [slow] *adj.* leelcɗo; ko leeli. *be* ~ leelde.

slowly [slowli] *adv.* seese; jamjam.

slug [slʌg] *v.* fiide; goɓɓaade.

uggard [slʌgəd] adj. gaamɗo.

ugger [slʌgə] n. gooɓɓoowo (o); ʒoɓɓotooɗo (o).

umber [slʌmbə] v. ŋoŋde.

ump [slʌmp] v. yande.

ur [slər] n. Yettoore (nde).

ut [slʌt] n. debbo bonɗo; garbotooɗo.

y [slay] adj. YoYɗo.

nack [smak] n. hello.

nack [smak] v. fiide.

nall [smɔl] adj. tokooso (o); tókósél (ngél).

nall [smɔl] adj. pamaro; tokooso. be ~ famɗude; gallude; tójjude.

nart [smɑt] adj. YoYɗo. be ~ YoYde.

nash [smaš] v. helde; móññude.

nasher [smašə] n. keloowo (o); moññoowo (o).

near [smiyr] v. tunwinde.

nell [smel] v. uurnaade; banaade. ~ sweet ꞮꞮurde. ~ bad aamtude; sórɓude; siccude.

nile [smayl] v. moosde.

nile [smayl] n. móósóóli; moosol (ngól).

nirch [smərč] v. móddinde; tunwinde.

nirk [smərk] v. moosde.

nite [smayt] v. fiide.

nith [smiθ] n. baylo (o).

noke [smowk] v. suurkude; jawwinde; simmaade; urkinaade.

noke [smowk] n. cuurki (ki).

noker [smowkə] n. jawwinoowo (o).

nooth [smuwθ] adj. ɗaatɗum; ko ɗaati. be ~ ɗaatde.

nooth [smuwðən] v. bérkude; ɗaatnude.

nother [smoðə] v. warde; ñifde.

nudge [smʌj] v. móddinde.

nug [smʌg] adj. peewɗo.

nuggle [smʌgəl] v. naatnude é léydi jawdi cuuɗaandi; suuɗde.

nut [smʌt] v. móddude; móddinde; tunwinde.

naggle [snagəl] v. saafaade. ~ tooth ñiire saafiinde.

nail [sneyl] n. wujo (ngo).

nake [sneyk] n. laadoori (ndi); mbaroodi (ndi). big ~ billal (ngal).

nap [snap] v. ŋappude; buɓɓude.

nare [sner] n. wilde (nde).

snare [sner] v. tuufaade.

snarl [snɑrl] v. fúraade.

snatch [snatč] v. diftaade; biftaade; jaylaade.

sneak [sniyk] v. ɓittaade; sortaade; naatde.

sneer [sniyr] v. jalde; moosde.

sneeze [sniyz] n. islaango (ngo).

sneeze [sniyz] v. islude; iilde.

sniff [snif] v. susnaade; susde.

sniffer [snifə] n. cusnotooɗo (o).

sniggle [snigəl] v. saftaade; awde.

snip [snip] v. méccude.

snipe [snayp] n. suka (o); kurka (o).

snitch [snič] v. diftaade.

snivel [snivəl] v. Yusde.

snob [snob] n. ñémtinoowo (o).

snooze [snuwz] v. muumnaade.

snore [snowr] v. harde.

snoring [snowriŋ] n. haraango (ngo); kargol.

snort [snɔt] v. foofde.

snot [snot] n. ñitte (ɗe). draw ~ in nódditaade.

snow [snow] n. marmalle (ɗe).

snuff [snʌf] v. sumbaade; nodditaade.

snuffer [snʌfə] adj. cumbotooɗo.

snuggle [snʌgəl] v. takkaade e.

so [sow] conj. mbele; if.

soak [sowk] v. sóófnude.

soakage [sowkij] n. cóófnugól (ngól).

soaked [sowkt] adj. leppuɗum; ko leppi. be ~ léppude.

soap [sowp] n. saabunde (nde).

soar [sowr] v. weeyde.

sob [sob] v. Yusde.

soccer [sokə] n. fugu/fuku (o).

sociable [sowšəbəl] adj. jom yimɓe; jiɗɗo yimɓe; cakalo.

sock [sok] n. kawasal (ngal).

socket [soket] n. ngaska (ka).

sodbuster [sodbʌstə] n. demoowo (o).

sodden [sodən] adj. kó léppi.

sofa [sofə] n. leeso diwaa.

soft [soft] adj. ɗaatɗum; jaafɗum. be ~ leefɗe; ɗaatde; yaafde; nooyde.

soften [softən] v. ɗaatnude.

softener [softənə] n. huunde ɗaatnoore.

softly [softli] *adv.* seese.

softness [softnes] *n.* yaafngo *(ngo).*

soggy [sogi] *adj.* léppudo; léppudum.

soil [soyl] *n.* léydi *(ndi).*

sojourn [sojərn] *v.* yillaade.

solar [sowlə] *adj.* ko faati e naange.

soldier [soljə] *n.* soldaat *(o).*

sole [sowl] *adj.* gooto; petto; teppere.

solicit [soləsit] *v.* ñaagaade; dabbude.

solicitor [soləsitə] *n.* ñaagotoodo *(o);* dabboowo *(o).*

solid [solid] *adj.* ko heri; ko tiidi. *be ~* herde.

solidarity [solədarəti] *n.* nanóndiral *(ngal);* ballondiral *(ngal).*

solidarize [solədərayz] *v.* wallondirde; nangóndirde.

solidify [solədəfay] *v.* hérnude.

soliloquize [səliləkwayz] *v.* haaldude e hooremum.

solitary [solitəri] *adj.* gooto; petto.

solitude [solətyuwd] *n.* yeeweende *(nde);* teelre *(nde).*

soluble [solyuwbəl] *adj.* ko saayata.

solve [solv] *v.* yiitude.

somber [sombə] *adj.* ko nibbidi.

some [sʌm] *adj.* huunde.

somebody [sʌmbɑdi] *pron.* neddo *(o);* aadee *(o).*

someone [sʌmwan] *pron.* neddo *(o);* aadee *(o);* kaari. *~ else* neddo goddo. *~ else's* kaake janane.

something [sʌmθiŋ] *pron.* huunde.

sometimes [sʌmtaymz] *adv.* sahaa sahaa.

somnifacient [sʌmnəfeyšənt] *adj.* ko danninta.

somniferous [sʌmnəferəs] *adj.* ko danninta.

somnolence [sʌmnələns] *n.* ŋóŋdi.

somnolent [sʌmnələnt] *adj.* ŋoŋdo.

son [son] *n.* biddo gorko.

song [soŋ] *n.* yimre *(nde);* jimól *(ngól).*

Soninke [sowniŋke] *n.* Galambo *(o);* Sarkulle *(o);* alambe *(be);* sarkulleebe *(be).*

soon [suwn] *adv.* jóóni.

sooner [suwnə] *adj.* kó buri yaawde; ko adii. *~ or later* e ko fayi arde.

soot [suwt] *n.* tuundi cuurki.

soothe [suwð] *v.* dééΥnude.

sop [sop] *n.* taΥatinde.

soporiferous [soporəferəs] *adj.* kc danninta.

soppy [sopi] *adj.* kó léppi.

sorcerer [sorsərə] *n.* dabotoodo.

sorcerous [sorsərəs] *adj.* ko faati e dabare.

sorcery [sosəri] *n.* dabare *(de). perform ~* dabaade. *perform ~ for* dabanaade.

sordid [sordid] *adj.* tunwudo; tunwudum ko tunwi.

sore [sowr] *adj.* ko muusi.

sorghum [sorgəm] *n.* gawri *(ndi).*

sorrel [sorəl] *n.* follere *(nde).*

sorrow [sorow] *n.* sunaare *(nde);* mettere *(nde).*

sorrowful [sorowfəl] *adj.* cuniido.

sort [sot] *v.* séérndude.

sottish [sɑtiš] *adj.* jirwudo.

sough [səf] *v.* ñuumbaade; sóññude.

soul [sowl] *n.* fittaandu *(ndu).*

sound [sawnd] *v.* dillude; hóngude.

sound [sawnd] *n.* dillere *(nde).*

soup [sup] *n.* suppu *(o);* soos *(o).*

sour [sawə] *adj.* lammudum; kaaddum.

source [sos] *n.* iwdi *(ndi).*

souse [sows] *v.* léppinde.

south [sawθ] *n.* worgo *(ngo).*

southerner [sʌθənə] *n.* worganke *(o).*

southward [sawθwɔd] *adv.* bange rewo.

souvenir [suvəniyr] *n.* téskuya *(o).*

sovereign [sovrən] *n.* laamdo *(o).*

sow [sow] *v.* aawde; téppude. *~ before the rain* uulde.

sowing [sowiŋ] *n.* aawre *(nde); second ~* aawtere *(nde).*

space [speys] *n.* weeyo *(ngo);* ŋalde *(nde) ~ between teeth* yelde *(nde). open ~* lewr *(nde);* dingiral *(ngal).*

spacious [speyšəs] *adj.* ko yaaji.

spade [speyd] *n.* góppu *(o).*

spall [spol] *v.* helde.

span [span] *n.* sibre *(nde);* mudda *(o). shor ~ sahaa dabbo.*

spank [spaŋk] *v.* fiide cukalel e dote.

spar [spɑ] *n.* coorgal *(ngal).*

spare [sper] *v.* daccude; yaafaade.

sparge [spɑj] *v.* sarde.

ark [spɑk] *n.* feetere *(nde)*

arrow [sparəw] *n.* cólél *(ngél)*.

arse [spɑs] *adj.* ko sarii.

at [spat] *v.* dukde; haɓeede.

ate [speyt] *n.* ilam *(dam)*.

atial [speyšəl] *adj.* ko faati e weeyo.

eak [spiyk] *v.* haalde. ~ *loudly* bablude. ~ *with* haaldude.

eaker [spiykə] *n.* kaaloowo *(o)*.

ear [spiyr] *n.* mbaangu *(ngu)*; gaawal *(ngal)*; baawal *(ngal)*.

ecies [spiyčiyz] *n.* fedde *(nde)*.

ecify [spəsəfay] *v.* innude.

eck [spek] *v.* toɓɓere *(nde)*.

eckle [spekəl] *v.* tunwinde; gakkude.

ectacles [spektəkəlz] *n.* lone *(de)*.

ectator [spekteytə] *n.* jeeɓoowo *(o)*.

eculate [spekyuwleyšən] *v.* féfindaade; miijaade.

eech [spiyč] *n.* haala *(ka)*; bolle *(de)*.

eed [spiyd] *v.* yaawnaade; heñaade.

eed [spiyd] *n.* yaawre *(nde)*; heñaare *(nde)*.

eedy [spiydi] *adj.* jaawdo; ko yaawi.

eel [spiyl] *v.* ŋabbude; ŋaylude.

eer [spiyr] *v.* lamndaade.

ell [spel] *v.* hijjude.

elling [speliŋ] *n.* hijjo *(ngo)*; kijjugól *(ngól)*.

end [spend] *v.* feraade; wonde. ~ *the night* waalde. ~ *a day* ñallinde. ~ *the dry season* seedde. ~ *days in the farm* lulaade. ~ *wedding days* dammbaade. ~ *the rains* ruumde. ~ *the night with* waaldude. ~ *the day for* ñallannde. ~ *the day* ñallude **sperm** [spərm] *n.* kañtudi *(ndi)*.

ew [spyuw] *v.* ruttude; tuutde.

ice [spays] *v.* safnude.

icy [spaysi] *adj.* cafdum; kaaddum.

ider [spaydə] *n.* njamala.

ike [spayk] *v.* feŋde.

ill [spil] *v.* deelde; rufde; siimtude. ~ *over while boiling* wokde.

illed [spild] *adj.* dufdum; ciimtudum.

in [spin] *v.* móttude; yiilaade.

inal [spaynəl] *adj.* ko faati e nóóról kééci.

indle [spindəl] *n.* kardumbal *(ngal)*.

spine [spayn] *n.* nóóról kééci *(ngól)*.

spinner [spinə] *n.* mottoowo *(o)*; jiilotoodo *(o)*.

spinster [spinstə] *n.* lambudo *(o)*; cooydo *(o)*.

spire [spayə] *n.* jubudu tiba.

spirit [spirit] *n.* jinne *(o)*; wónki *(ki)*.

spiritual [spirəčəl] *adj.* ko faati e wónki.

spit [spit] *v.* tuutde; wukkitde. ~ *through the teeth* sirʏude. ~ *out* balʏude.

spite [spayt] *v.* tooñde.

spittle [spitəl] *n.* jóódól *(ngól)*.

splash [splaš] *v.* wiccude.

splay [spley] *v.* yaajnude.

spleen [spliyn] *n.* daamól *(ngól)*.

splendent [splendənt] *adj.* jalbudum.

splice [splays] *v.* jókkóndirde.

splinter [splintə] *v.* helde; móññude; sarfude.

split [split] *v.* feecde; éccitde; feeraade.

spoil [spoyl] *v.* bonnude; yakkude. ~ *again* bónnitde. ~ *a child* béwnude.

spoilage [spoylij] *n.* bonande *(nde)*.

spoiler [spoylə] *n.* bonnoowo *(o)*.

spoilt [spoylt] *adj.* bewdo; bonnaado; ko bonnaa.

spokesman [spowksmən] *n.* kaaloowo *(o)*.

spoliate [spowlyet] *v.* bónnude; wujjude.

spoliation [spowleyšən] *n.* nguyka *(ka)*; bonande *(nde)*.

sponge [sponj] *n.* tekkere lawʏirteende. *throw in the* ~ jebbilaade.

sponsor [sponsə] *n.* njaatige *(o)*.

spoon [spuwn] *n.* holfo *(ngo)*; kuddu *(o)*.

spoor [spuwr] *n.* laadól *(ngól)*; felo *(ngo)*; teppere *(nde)*.

sport [sport] *n.* coftal ɓalli; fijirde coftal ɓalli.

sportive [sportəv] *adj.* ko faati e coftal ɓalli.

spot [spot] *n.* toɓɓere *(nde)*.

spot [spot] *v.* yiide.

spouse [spaws] *n.* jom suudu; jom galle.

spout [spawt] *v.* juknude.

sprain [spreyn] *v.* fórñude.

sprained [spreynd] *adj.* pórñudo.

spray [sprey] *v.* fuufde; pompude.

spread [spred] v. layde; yaajnude; reɓde; weerde; wertude. ~ *a mat* daɗɗude; wertude. ~ *mud on a wall* laaltaade. ~ *out to dry* liirde. ~ *food to cool down* lañtude.

spreader [spredə] n. jaajnoowo (o).

spreading [sp__rediŋ] n. layo (ngo).

spring [spriŋ] n. sewnde (nde).

sprinkle [spriŋkəl] v. toɓde; roosde; wiccude.

sprinkler [spriŋklə] n. biccoowo (o).

sprint [sprint] v. dogde.

sprout [sprawt] v. fuɗde.

sprout [sprawt] n. puɗdi (ndi).

spur [spər] n. Yóɓɓirde (nde).

spurn [spərn] v. férgitaade e.

spy [spay] v. sunnaade; ñukkindaade.

spy [spay] n. ñukkindiiɗo (o); jaasuus (o).

squab [skwab] n. fóóndu (ndu); jooɗorde (nde).

squalid [skwaləd] adj. tunwuɗo.

squall [skwɔl] v. luukde; siikde.

squander [skwandə] v. bónnude; sarde.

square [skwer] v. yuɓɓude.

squash [skwaš] v. móññude.

squat [skwat] v. sóppinaade; Ŋómindaade; Ŋómsinde; ramde.

squat [skwat] n. sóppunde (nde).

squatter [skwatə] n. cóppiniiɗo (o).

squaw [skwɔ] n. debbo (o).

squawk [skwɔk] v. siikde; luukde.

squeak [skwiyk] v. siikde

squeak [skwiyk] n. siikaango (ngo).

squeal [skwiyl] n. siikaango (ngo); wulaango (ngo).

squeamish [skwiyməš] adj. nefɗo; nefoowo.

squeeze [skwiyz] v. hamYude; himYude; ɓiɗde; ɓittude; tamsindaade; hamde.

squeezed [skwiyzd] (adj) ɓittaaɗo; ɓiɗaaɗo.

squelch [skwelš] v. móññude.

squint [skwint] v. léttiɗde.

squint-eyed [skwintayd] adj. letto (o).

squirrel [skwərəl] n. jihre (nde); dóllundu (ndu).

squirt [skwərt] v. yuppude; yuppaade.

stab [stab] v. ñiɓde; yiwde.

stability [stəbiləti] n. deeYre (nde).

stabilize [steybəlayz] v. dééYnude.

stable [steybəl] adj. deeYɗo.

stack [stak] v. joowde.

stack [stak] n. wahre leɗɗe; tiggerⁱ ñoomre.

staff [stɑf] n. liggotooɓe (ɓe).

staff [stɑf] v. Yéttude gollotooɓe.

stagger [stɑgə] v. daaldaalnude (mandilɗo); daggude.

stagnate [stagneyt] v. daraade; deeYde.

stain [steyn] v. gakkude; gakkinde; toɓɓaade.

stain [steyn] n. fatere (nde); toɓɓere (nde).

stained [steynd] adj. módduɗum.

stairs [sterz] n. iskale.

stake [steyk] n. jaalal (ngal); peŊgal (ngal).

stale [steyl] adj. ko rappi.

stalk [stɑk] n. wasaango (ngo); gombaⁱ (ngal); gawYal (ngal); kuɗól (ngól).

stall [stɔl] v. faɓɓinde; lééltinde.

stallion [stɑlyən] n. puccu (ngu).

stamina [staminə] n. caasgól (ngól).

stammer [stamə] v. mehde

stammerer [stamərə] n. mehoowo (o).

stammering [staməriŋ] n. mehgól (ngól).

stamp [stamp] n. tembere (nde).

stampede [stampiyd] v. dogde.

stamper [stampə] n. unugal (ngal).

stance [stans] n. darnde (nde).

stand [stand] v. daraade. *make* ~ darnude. ~ *erect again* turtaade. ~ *over* tiimde.

standard [standəd] adj. kó wóni laawól.

standee [standiy] n. dariiɗo (o).

standing [standiŋ] n. darnde (nde); darngc (ngo).

staple [steypəl] v. réndinde.

stapler [steyplə] n. déndinoowo; kɗ réndinta.

star [stɑ] n. hoodere (nde).

stare [ster] v. laarde.

stare [ster] n. Yééwki (ki)

start [stɑt] v. fuɗɗaade; tuggude. ~ *over* fuɗɗitaade. ~ *a pregnancy* fewde. ~ *with* idoraade. ~ *cooking* sagginde.

starter [stɑtə] n. puɗɗoowo (o).

startle [stɑtəl] v. hulɓinde.

starvation [stɑveyšən] n. heege (nge).

starve [stɑv] v. heegeede.

h [staš] v. móóftude.

e [steyt] v. wiide; haalde.

e [steyt] n. tagóódi (ndi); léydi (ndi).

ement [steytmənt] n. haala (ka); kóngól ʒól).

ic [statik] adj. kó dééʕi.

ionary [steyšənri] adj. kó dééʕi.

tering [statəriŋ] n. mehgól (ngól).

ure [stačə] n. tóówééndi (ndi).

ute [stačuwt] n. yamiroore (nde); ʷól (ngól).

ʼ [stey] v. heddaade. ~ **home a lot** ade. ~ **long** duumde; ñiibde.

d [sted] n. nókku (o).

dy [stedi] adj. kó dééʕi.

k [steyk] n. hettere tééw.

l [stiyl] v. wujjude; beeynaade.

ler [stiylə] n. gujjo (o).

ling [stiyliŋ] n. nguyka (ka).

m [stiym] v. suurtinde.

m [stiym] n. cuurki (ki). **let off** ~ **tinde** ko woni e bernde mum.

mboat [stiym] n. laana cuurki.

med [stiymd] adj. cuurtinaadum; ko urtinaa. ~ **millet** dakkiri (ndi). **be** ~ urtude.

ming [stiymiŋ] n. cuurtingol (ngól). ~ t méltirde. ~ **utensil** yulnde (nde).

my [stiymi] adj. ko suurki.

d [stiyd] n. puccu (ngu).

k [stiyk] v. ñootde; réndinde.

l [stiyl] n. njamndi (ndi). ~proof ko tuli; do. be ~proof tulde.

p [stiyp] adj. ko tóówi/tiidi (cóggu).

plechase [stiypəlčeyz] n. dandu pucci.

r [stiyə] v. awʕude; kóndirde; dognude.

n [stem] v. hadde; dartinde.

p [step] n. teppere (nde). ~father **ppaaño** (o). ~brother keyniraado gorko. **sister** keyniraado debbo.

pladder [steplaadə] n. seel (o).

rile [stəril] adj. rimare; dimaro.

rnum [stərnʌm] n. domdomal (ngal).

rnutation [stərnəteyšən] n. islaango ʼgo).

w [stuw] v. defde.

ward [stuwəd] n. carwoowo e nder iiwoowa.

stick [stik] v. bakkude; takkude.

stick [stik] n. sawru (ndu); weduru (ndu); leggal (ngal). **little** ~ cawél (ngél); leggel (ngél). **big** ~ booldu (ndu); dókkééru (ndu); leggere (nde) **sticky** [stiki] adj. ko takkotoo; ko bakkotoo.

stiff [stif] adj. jaddudum; ko jaddi. **be** ~ jaddude.

stiffen [stifən] v. jaddinde.

stifle [stayfəl] v. warde (hadde foofaango).

still [stil] adj. deeʕdo.

sting [stiŋ] v. fidde.

stinger [stiŋə] n. huunde fidoore.

stingy [stinji] adj. tiiddo jungo.

stink [stiŋki] v. luubde. ~ing smell luuból (ngól); luubgol (ngól).

stipend [staypend] n. njóbdi (ndi).

stir [stər] v. iirtude. ~ milk wurwude.

stirk [stərk] n. gayél (ngél).

stirring [stəriŋ] n. iirtugól (ngól).

stirrup [stirʌp] n. alkabeere (nde).

stitch [stič] v. ñootde.

stitching [stičiŋ] n. ñóótgól (ngól); ñootol (ngól).

stock [stok] v. resde; joñde.

stocker [stokə] n. joñoowo (o).

stocking [stokiŋ] n. kawasal juutngal.

stodge [stoj] v. hébbinde.

stodge [stoj] n. ñamri (ndi).

stoke [stowk] v. hubbude; duñtude.

stoker [stowkə] n. duñtoowo (o).

stomach [stomak] n. fulkuru (ndu); réédu (ndu).

stone [stown] n. haayre (nde); aaludere (nde). **fruit** ~ ñewre (nde). **rubbing** ~ oogoore (nde).

stone [stown] v. werlaade kaaʕe.

stony [stowni] adj. kó hééwi kaaʕe; nokku kaaʕe.

stool [stuwl] n. addere (nde); kuudi (ndi).

stoop [stuwp] v. junaade.

stop [stop] v. surde; hadde; joofde; suraade; daraade. ~ by ʕaaɳde.

stoppage [stopij] n. daragól (ngól).

stopper [stopə] n. dartinoowo (o).

stopping [stopiŋ] n. darnde (nde).

storage [stowrij] n. jóñgól (ngól); móóftugól (ngól); water ~ mbalka (ka).

store [stowr] v. joñde; resde; móóftude; faggaade.

store [stowr] n. bitik (o).

stork [stɔk] n. ginal (ngal).

storm [stɔm] n. Ƴiiwoonde (nde).

stormy [stɔmi] adj. ko Ƴiiwi.

story [stori] n. mahól (ngól); tindól (ngól).

stound [stawnd] n. sahaa daɓɓo.

stour [stuwr] n. jilɓere (nde).

stout [stawt] adj. ɓutto. be ~ ɓuttiɗde; ɓalnude.

stove [stowv] n. fuurna (o); haatande (nde).

straddle [stradəl] v. waɗɗaade; sarde koyɗe.

straggle [stragəl] v. selde.

straight [streyt] adj. póóƳtiiɗo. be ~ feewde; fortaade; fooƳtaade. a ~ road laawol pooƳtingol.

straighten [streytən] v. fóóctude; fééwtinde; óóñtude; fórtude.

strain [streyn] v. siiwtude; siiwde; siimtinde; siimtude; tééɳnude.

strained [streynd] adj. ko siiwaa; ko siiwtaa.

strainer [streynə] n. yulnde (nde); siiwtirde (nde).

strait [streyt] adj. laawól paaɗngól; paaɗɗo; ko faaɗi.

stranded [strandəd] adj. toobɗo. be ~ toobde; laɳde; loggaade.

strange [streynj] adj. ko haawnii.

stranger [streynjə] n. koɗo (o).

strangle [straŋgəl] n. ɗéɗɗugól (ngól).

strangle [straŋgəl] v. ɗéɗɗude.

strap [strap] n. ɓóggól (ngól).

stratagem [stratəjəm] n. feere (nde).

strategic [stratiyjik] adj. ko faati e feere.

strategy [stratəji] n. feere (nde).

stratification n. pawóndiral (ngal).

stratify [stratəfay] v. fawóndirde.

stratocracy [stratəkrəsi] n. laamu soldateeɓe.

stratus [stratəs] n. duule (ɗe).

straw [strɔ] n. kuɗól (ngól)

stray [strey] v. majjude.

streak [striyk] n. majaango (ngo).

stream [striym] n. ilol (ngól); caaɗngól (ngól).

streek [striyk] v. fooƳtaade.

street [striyt] n. mbedda (o); laawól (ngól) strength [streŋθ] n. doole (ɗe); tiiɗg (ngól).

strengthen [streŋθən] v. tiiɗnude.

strenuous [strenyuwəs] adj. cémbinc caasɗo.

stress [stres] v. sembinde; tiiɗtinde.

stretch [streč] v. naaɗaade; jatde; sertaa fooƳtaade. ~ out fórtude. ~ ones naaɗaade; fooƳtaade.

stretcher [strečə] n. balankaar (o).

stretching [strečiŋ] n. naaɗagól (ngól).

strew [struw] v. sarde.

stricken [strikən] adj. barmuɗo; gaañiic gaañaaɗo.

strict [strikt] adj. póóƳtiiɗo.

strictly [striktli] adv. ko faati e pooƳtagól

stride [strayd] v. taaɓaade.

strife [strayf] n. hare (nde); luural (ngal).

strike [strayk] v. tappude; fiide. ~ with foot latde. ~ back fiitaade. ~ with lappir fiirude.

strike [strayk] n. géró (o).

string [striŋ] n. gaarawól (ngól). ~ of wa beads galól (ngól). ~ of beads góv (ngól).

strip [strip] v. sirde. ~ off sirde; ɓolde.

strip [strip] n. siro (ko). ~ of cloth lé (ngól). ~ of dried meat céélól (ng stripe [strayp] n. fantere (nde).

stripped [stript] adj. ɓolo; ɓólɗuɗo.

stripper [stripə] n.gamoowo (o); ciroo (o).

strive [strayv] v. tiiɗnaade.

stroam [strowm] v. yahnaade.

stroke [strowk] n. womre (nde).

stroll [strɔl] v. yahnaade.

strong [strɔŋ] adj. cembinɗo; tiiɗɗum. ~ tékkude; tiiɗde; sémmbinde; seɗɗaade

structural [strʌkčərəl] adj. ko faati tagóódi.

structure [strʌkčə] n. tagóódi (ndi); ma (ndi); mbaadi (ndi).

struggle [strʌgəl] v. hare (nde).

stub [stʌb] n. jullaare (nde).

stubble [stʌbəl] n. jullaare (nde).

stubborn [stʌbən] adj. ɳatɗo. be ~ ɳat sandóliɗde.

k [stʌk] *adj.* ɓakkiɗum; ko ɓakkii. *be ~* ɓkkaade; ɓakkaade. *be ~ in the mud* ɓaade.

‖ [stʌd] *n.* Yuulde *(nde).*

‖ent [styuwdənt] *n.* almuudo *(o)*; fósin

‖ious [styuwjəs] *adj.* tóppitiiɗo jangde.

‖y [stʌdi] *v.* jangude.

‖y [stʌfi] *adj.* ko urki. *be ~* urkude.

‖ble [stʌmbəl] *v.* allaade; fergitaade; fitde; felmaade.

‖p [stʌmp] *n.* jullaare *(nde).*

‖py [stʌmpi] *adj.* kó hééwi jullaaje.

‖ [stʌn] *v.* bómpilde.

‖t [stʌnt] *v.* haɗde; lééltinde.

‖efaction [styuwpəfakšən] *n.* kaawis

‖efy [stuwpəfay] *v.* haawde.

‖id [styuwpid] *adj.* ɗaayɗo. *be ~* ayde; weemde; muddiɗde; hawjude.

‖idity [styuwpiditi] *n.* ɗaayre *(nde)*; ‖ddiɗgól *(ngól).*

‖dy [stərdi] *adj.* cémbinɗo.

‖t [stərt] *v.* haɓde; dukde.

‖ter [stʌtə] *v.* mehde.

‖terer [stʌtərə] *n.* mehoowo *(o).*

‖e [stayl] *n.* mbaadi *(ndi).*

‖sion [sweyšən] *n.* waajuya *(o).*

‖ve [sweyv] *adj.* belɗo; belɗo YiiYam.

[sʌb] *pref.* les. *-Sahara* les Sahara.

‖altern [səbɔltərn] *adj.* jiimaaɗo.

‖divide [sʌbdəvayd] *v.* féccitaade.

‖division [sʌbdəviyʒən] *n.* péccitaagól ‖gól).

‖due [sʌbdyuw] *v.* foolde.

‖dued [sʌbdyuwd] *adj.* poolaaɗo.

‖ject [sʌbjekt] *v.* jiimde.

‖jugate [sʌbjəgeyt] *v.* foolde.

‖marine [sʌbmərin] *n.* laana *(ka).*

‖merge [sʌbmərj] *v.* mutnude.

‖mission [sʌbmiyšən] *n.* ɗowtaare *(nde).*

‖missive [sʌbmisiv] *adj.* ɗówtiiɗo.

‖mit [sʌbmit] *v.* hóllude; nawtude; ‖ttude.

‖ordinate [sʌbordənət] *v.* jiimde.

‖rogate [sʌbrəgeyt] *v.* lómtinde.

‖scription [sʌbskripčən] *n.* piye *(ɗe).*

subside [sʌbsayd] *v.* débbude; ɓappinaade; ustaade.

subsidy [sʌbzədi] *n.* ballal *(ngal).*

subsist [sʌbzist] *v.* wuurde; woorde.

subsistence [sʌbzistəns] *n.* nguura *(ka).*

substance [sʌbstəns] *n.* qiimaa *(o).*

substantial [sʌbstənšəl] *adj.* kééwɗum.

substantiate [sʌbstənšeyt] *v.* tééɭtinde.

substitute [sʌbstətyuwt] *v.* lómtinde; lomtaade.

substitute [sʌbstətyuwt] *n.* lomto *(o).*

subsume [sʌbsyuwm] *v.* naatnude e.

subtract [sʌbtrakt] *v.* ittude e; ustude.

subtraction [sʌbtrakšən] *n.* ustugól *(ngól).*

subvene [sʌbviyn] *v.* wallude.

subvention [sʌbvenšən] *n.* ballal *(ngal).*

subvert [sʌbvərt] *v.* yandinde; bónnude.

succeed [sʌksiyd] *v.* lomtaade; rewde; ɓamtaade; arwude.

success [sʌkses] *n.* ɓamtaare *(nde).* *We wish you success* Yo Alla newnu.

successful [sʌksesfəl] *adj.* arwuɗo. *be ~* ɓamtaade; yumtude.

succession [sʌksešən] *n.* déggóndiral *(ngal)*; déwóndiral *(ngal).*

successive [sʌksəsiv] *adj.* ko faati é déwóndiral walla déggóndiral.

successor [sʌksəsə] *n.* lomto *(o).*

succint [sʌksint] *adj.* juɓɓuɗum; ko yuɓɓi. *be ~* Yuɓɓude; raɓɓiɗinaade.

succor [sʌkə] *n.* ballal *(ngal).*

succulent [sʌkyuwlənt] *adj.* bélɗum.

succumb [sʌkʌm] *v.* fooleede; wareede.

suck [sʌk] *v.* muynude; ɓuucaade; murde. *make someone ~* muyninde. *~ before the cow is milked* hóóntude. *~ someone dry* fiɗɗinde neɗɗo.

sucker [sʌkə] *n.* ciiɓotooɗo; ɓuucotooɗo.

sucking [sʌkiŋ] *n.* muynugol *(ngól).* *prevent a calf from ~* daaYde.

suckle [sʌkəl] *v.* muyninde.

suction [sʌkšən] *n.* ciiɓagól *(ngól)*; ɓuucagól *(ngól).*

sudatory [suwdətəri] *adj.* ko faati e warñeende.

sudorific [suwdərəfik] *adj.* ko warñinta.

sue [suw] *v.* wullitaade.

suet [suwit] *n.* ɓellere *(nde).*

suffer [sʌfə] *v.* metteede; muuseede.

suffering [sʌfriŋ] *n.* muusééki *(ki)*; mettere *(nde).*

suffice [sʌfays] *v.* yonde.

sufficient [sʌfiyšənt] *adj.* kó yóni.

suffrage [sʌfrij] *n.* woote *(o).*

sugar [šugə] *n.* suukara *(o). lump of* ~ ɓoodde suukara

sugarcane [šugə] *n.* gawʸal suukara.

suggest [sʌjest] *v.* hóllude miijo mum.

suggestion [sʌješən] *n.* miijo.

suicidal [swiysaydəl] *adj.* ko faati e bartgól.

suicide [swiysayd] *v.* wartaade.

suicide [swiysayd] *n.* bartagól *(ngól).*

suit [suwt] *n.* cómci jahduɗi.

suit [suwt] *v.* hawrande.

suitable [swutəbəl] *adj.* kó fóti.

sulk [sʌlk] *v.* tikkude.

sulky [sʌlki] *adj.* nuggaro.

sullen [sʌlən] *adj.* tumminiiɗo.

sully [sʌli] *v.* móddinde.

sum [sʌm] *v.* réndinde.

summer [sʌmə] *n.* cééɗu *(ngu).*

summit [sʌmit] *n.* jubudu *(ndu)*; deental *(ngal).*

summon [sʌmən] *v.* yamirde; noddude.

sumo [suwmo] *n.* sippiro *(ngo).*

sun [sʌn] *n.* naange *(nge). The sun is high* Naange nge ñawlii. *The sun is up* Naange nge fuɗii. *The sun is down* Naange nge mutii.

sunbathe [sʌnbeyθ] *v.* saaɗnaade.

Sunday [sʌndi] *n.* dimaas *(o)*; alet *(o).*

sunder [sʌndə] *v.* séérndude.

sundown [sʌndawn] *n.* mutal naange.

sunray [sʌnrey] *n.* serééndu *(ndu).*

sunrise [sʌnrayz] *n.* puɗal naange.

sunset [sʌnset] *n.* mutal *(ngal).*

super [syuwpə] *adv.* dów.

superb [syuwpərb] *adj.* ko yuɓɓi; ko hawri.

superficial [syuwpəfiyšəl] *adj.* ko wóni dów; ko luggiɗaani.

superfluous [syuwpəfluwəs] *adj.* ɓurtuɗum.

superimpose [syuwpərimpowz] *v.* fawndirde.

superior *adj.* [suwpiyryə] ɓurɗo.

superiority [suwpiyryowrəti] *n.* ɓuɪ *(ngal).*

superlative [suwpərlətiv] *adj.* ɓurɗo fóf.

supernal [syuwpərnəl] *adj.* ko faati aljanna.

superpose [suwpəpowz] *v.* fawndirde.

supersede [suwpəsiyd] *v.* lomtaac ɓurtaade.

superstition [syuwpəstiyšən] *n.* woɗa *(o)*

superstitious [syuwpəstiyšəs] *adj.* ko fa e woɗa.

supervise [syuwpəvayz] *v.* reend wómbude.

supervisor [syuwpəvayzə] *n.* deenoo *(o)*; tóppitiiɗo *(o).*

supine [suwpayn] *adj.* gajjiiɗo.

supper [sʌpə] *n.* hiraande *(nde).*

supplant [sʌplant] *v.* lomtaade.

supplement [sʌpləmənt] *v.* ɓéydude.

supplicate [sʌpləkeyt] *v.* ñaagaade.

supplication [sʌpləkeyšən] *n.* ñaagun *(nde).*

supply [sʌplay] *v.* tóttude; rókkude.

support [sʌpɔt] *v.* tuggorde *(nde)*; wallu muñde.

supporter [sʌpɔtə] *n.* balloowo *(o).*

suppose [sʌpowz] *v.* sikkude.

supposition [sʌpowziyšən] *n.* sikke *(o).*

suppress [sʌpres] *v.* ñóʸʸude.

suppurate [sʌpəreyt] *v.* wórɗinde.

supreme [səpriym] *adj.* ɓurɗo fóf.

surcharge [sərčɔj] *v.* ɓurtinde.

sure [šuwr] *adj.* kó hóólnii; kóólniic koolaaɗo. *be* ~ *siirde*; hoolaa yananeede. *Are you sure* Aɗa yananaa?

surge [sərj] *v.* ummaade.

surgeon [sərjən] *n.* óppiroowo *(o).*

surgery [sərjri] *n.* oppeere *(o).*

surmise [sərmayz] *v.* sikkude.

surname [sərneym] *n.* sowoore *(nde)*; ir *(nde).*

surpass [sərpas] *v.* ɓurde. ~ *agɪ* ɓurtaade.

surplus [sərpləs] *n.* kó ɓurti.

surprise [sərprayz] *v.* béttude.

surprise [sərprayz] *n.* béttugól *(ngɪ* haawngo *(ngo).*

surrender [sʌrendə] *v.* jébbilaade.

rround [sərawnd] *v.* huurde; taaraade; taarnude; firlude.

rrounded [sərawndid] *adj.* ko taaraa.

rrounding [sərawndiŋ] *n.* sara.

rveillance [sərveyləns] *n.* déengól *(ngól)*.

rveillant [sərveylənt] *n.* deenoowo *(o)*.

rvive [sərvayv] *v.* wuurde.

rvivor [sərvayvə] *n.* guurɗo *(o)*.

spect [sʌspekt *v.* sikkitaade; hóólkisaade; jikkude; tuumde. ~ *one another* jikkóndirde.

spend [sʌspend] *v.* liggude.

spicion [sʌspiyšən] *n.* tuumre *(nde)*; tuumal *(ngal)*.

spicious [sʌspiyšəs] kóólkisiiɗo.

stain [sʌsteyn] *v.* ñamminde; wuurnude.

stenance [sʌstənəns] *n.* nguura.

surrant [suwsərənt] *n.* ñuumbiiɗo; ñuumbotooɗo.

surration [swusəreyšən] *n.* ñuumbagól.

uture [suwčə] *v.* réndinde; ñootde.

velte [svelt] *adj.* cewɗo.

waddle [swadəl] *v.* soomde.

wag [swag] *v.* wujjude; honde.

wagger [swagə] *v.* mawnikinaade.

wain [sweyn] *n.* suka *(o)*; gaynaako *(o)*.

wallow [swaləw] *v.* toɗɗaade; moɗde. ~ *without chewing* mookaade.

wallowing [swaləwiŋ] *n.* moɗgól *(ngól)*.

wamp [swamp] *v.* heewde.

wap [swap] *v.* wostaade.

wat [swat] *v.* fiide.

wathe [sweyθ] *v.* soomde.

way [swey] *v.* dillude.

wear [swer] *v.* waatde; woonde.

weat[swet] *v.* waaϒde; warñude; ówlude.

weat [swet] *n.* warñeende *(nde)*; waaϒo *(ngo)*; olowere *(nde)*.

weater [swetə] *n.* piliweer *(o)*.

weep [swiyp] *v.* fittude.

weeper [swiypə] *n.* pittoowo *(o)*.

weeping [swiypiŋ] *n.* pittugól *(ngól)*.

weet [swiyt] *adj.* belɗo; cafɗo. *be* ~ welde.

sweeten [swiytən] *v.* wélnude; safnude.

sweets [swiyts] *n.* tangal.

swell [swel] *v.* ɗuulnude; ɓuutde; ϒuufde. ~ *out* ɓuuteede.

swelling [sweliŋ] *n.* ɓuutdi *(ndi)*; ɗuulde.

swerve [swərv] *v.* selde.

swift [swift] *adj.* jaawɗo.

swig [swig] *n.* wooɓre *(nde)*.

swill [swil] *v.* lawϒude.

swim [swim] *v.* lummbaade; yinaade; wuulaade; yiraade; feeraade. ~ *fast* siirtaade. ~ *against the tide* roontaade waraango.

swimming [swimiŋ] *n.* lumbagól *(ngól)*; lumbayru *(ndu)*.

swindle [swindəl] *v.* wujjude.

swine [swayn] *n.* rawaandu *(ndu)*.

swing [swiŋ] *v.* sayyaade; jayde.

swirl [swərl] *n.* yiriinde *(nde)*.

swirl [swərl] *v.* yiileede; yiilde.

switch [swič] *v.* ñifde; huɓɓude. ~ *the light on* huɓɓude lampa. ~ *the light off* ñifde lampa.

swith [swið] *v.* yaawnaade; heñaade.

swizzle [swizəl] *v.* wurwude.

swollen [swolən] *adj.* ɓuutɗum; ko ɓuuti. ~ *testicles* wuuko *(ngo)*. ~ *glands below cheekbones* leeke *(ɗe)*.

swoon [swuwn] *v.* faɗɗaade.

sword [sɔd] *n.* silaama *(ka)*.

sympathize [simpəθayz] *v.* réndude.

symptom [simptəm] *n.* maale *(ɗe)*.

syncretize [sinkrətayz] *v.* etaade réndinde.

syndicate [sindəkeyt] *n.* fedde *(nde)*.

synonymous [sinownəməs] *adj.* ko nandi maanaa.

syntactic [sintaktik] *adj.* ko faati e célluka.

syntax [sintaks] *n.* célluka *(ka)*.

syrup [sirʌp] *n.* siro *(o)*.

system [systəm] *n.* feere *(nde)*.

systematic [systəmatik] *adj.* ko faati e feere.

T

tab [tab] *v.* ñikkude.

tabby [tabi] *n.* ullundu *(ndu)*.

table [teybəl] *n.* taabal *(ngal)*.

tableau [tablo] *n.* natal *(ngal)*.

tablet [tablet] *n.* foɗɗere *(nde). wooden ~* alluwal *(ngal)*.

taboo [tabu] *n.* woɗa *(o)*.

tabor [tabo] *n.* baggél *(ngél);* mbaggu *(ngu)*.

tabouret [tabure] *n.* jooɗorde *(nde)*.

tacit [tasit] *adj.* deeYɗo; kó dééYi.

taciturn [tasətərn] *adj.* nuggaro; deeYɗo.

tack [tak] *v.* béydude.

tackle [takəl] *v.* yandinde; naatóndirde.

tacky [taki] *adj.* ko bakólini.

tact [takt] *n.* teeyre *(nde)*.

tactful [taktfəl] *adj.* teeyɗo.

tactile [taktayl] *adj.* ko faati e mémgól.

taction [takšən] *n.* mémgól *(ngól)*.

taenia [tenya] *n.* saan *(o)*.

tail [teyl] *n.* laaci *(ki). reptile ~* dórlól *(ngól). turn ~* dogde.

tailor [teylə] *n.* jokkoowo *(o);* ñootoowo *(o);* tayoor *(o)*.

taint [teynt] *v.* ufde; bonde.

take [teyk] *v.* Ƴettude; bamde. *~ a large handful of* baaftude. *~ across the water* lumbinde. *~ one's foot off the ground* yabbitde. *~ out for* ittande. *~ out* sóórtude; lókkitde. *~ honey from a hive* jumde. *~ away by force* teetde. *~ the oath* woonde.

tale [teyl] *n.* tindól *(ngól);* taalól *(ngól). tell a ~* tindude.

talent [talənt] *n.* mbaawka *(ka)*.

talented [talənted] *adj.* baawɗo.

talebearer [teyltelə] *n.* tindoowo *(o)*.

talisman [taləsmən] *n.* ñawndogal; talkuru *(ndu)*.

talk [tɔk] *n.* kóngól *(ngól);* bolle *(ɗe). indirect ~* mallól *(ngól) She is all talk* O waawi tan ko haalde.

talk [tɔk] *v.* haalde; wiide. *~ back* sontaade. *~ indirectly about someone* mallude. *~ with* lébdude/haaldude e. *~ behind someone's back* ñohde. *~ too much* lebde.

talkative [tɔkətiv] *adj.* leboowo; keewɗo haala. *be ~* lémsude.

tall [tɔl] *adj.* juutɗo; toowɗo. *be ~* juutde; toowde.

tallow [taləw] *n.* bellere *(nde)*.

talon [talən] *n.* takkere *(nde)*.

tamarind [tamərind] *n.* yabbere *(nde);* jabbi *(ki)*.

tame [teym] *v.* ééltude

tameness [teymnes] *n.* ééltugól *(ngól)*.

tamer [teymə] *n.* eeltoowo *(o)*.

taming [teymiŋ] *n.* eelto *(ngo)*.

tamper [tampə] *v.* waylude.

tan [tan] *v.* ñóbbude; ɗatde

tandem [tandəm] *adj.* kó réggóndiri; ko réwóndiri.

tangent [tanjənt] *adj.* kó mémóndiri; ko mémóndirta.

tangerine [tanjərin] *n.* mandarin; soraas *(o)*.

tangible [tanjəbəl] *adj.* ko memotoo.

tangle [tangəl] *v.* jikde; jikóndirde.

tannage [tanij] *n.* ñóbbugól *(ngól)*.

tanner [tanə] *n.* ñoobboowo *(o)*.

tannery [tanri] *n.* ñóbbirde *(nde)*.

tanning [taniŋ] *n.* ɗatgól *(ngól)*.

tantamount [tantəmawnt] *adj.* kó fóti; ko wayi.

tap [tap] *v.* hóngude; feŋde.

tap [tap] *n.* róbiné *(o)*.

tape [teyp] *n.* banda *(o)*.

tape [teyp] *v.* nangude banda.

tar [tar] *n.* godoron *(o)*.

tardy [tɑdi] *adj.* leelɗo.

tare [ter] *n.* téddééndi *(ndi)*

target [tɑget] *n.* muuya *(o). hit the ~* fiɗde.

tariff [tarif] *n.* njóbdi duwaañ.

tarnish [tɑniš] *v.* móddinde; bónnude.

tarry [tari] *v.* heddaade.

tart [tɑt] *adj.* ko lammi; lammuɗum.

tartar [tɑtə] *n.* tuundi ñiiYe.

task [task] *v.* waawnude.

task [task] *n.* gollal *(ngal) It is your task* ɗum ko gollal maa.

tassel [tasəl] *n.* jombo *(ko);* kammonjawo *(o)*.

sel [tasəl] *n.* jómbinde

te [teyst] *v.* meeɗde; loɓɓaade.

te [teyst] *n.* meeɗgól *(ngól)* It has no **ste** Ina soofi.

teful [teystfəl] *adj.* kó wéli; ko dakmi.

teless [teystles] *adj.* tékum; ɔofɗum. *be* ~ soofde.

ter [teystə] *n.* meeɗoowo *(o).*

ty [teysti] *adj.* belɗum; cafɗum. *make* ~ **ɪfnude.** *be* ~ safde; dakmude; welde.

ter [tatə] *n.* cééltól *(ngól).*

tered [tatəd] *adj.* ceekiɗum. *be* ~ seerde; **ɛekaade.**

tle [tatəl] *v.* saaktude sirru.

tler [tatlə] *n.* caaktoowo sirru.

too [tatuw] *v.* finaade. ~ *someone's lips* **ɪppude.**

too [tatuw] *n.* fino *(ngo).*

tooer [tatuwə] *n.* tuppoowo *(o).*

ɪnt [tɔnt] *v.* jalkitde.

ɪrus [tɔrəs] *n.* ɓujiri *(ndi).*

ʋern [tavən] *n.* nókku ɗo sangara **ɛeyetee.**

ɪ [taks] *n.* kubbal *(ngal)*; alamaan *(o).*

ɪation [takseyšən] *n.* alamaan *(o);* kubbal *ŋgal).*

ɪi [taksi] *n.* taksi *(o)* Let us take a taxi ɪjolen e taksi.

ɪidermy [taksədermi] *n.* sókkiññe *(o).*

ɪ [tiy] *n.* ataaye *(o).* ~ *cup* taasa/kaas ttaye. ~ *kettle* satalla *(ka).*

ɪch [tiyč] *v.* janginde; andinde; ékkinde It *ʋill teach him a lesson* Ma ɗum wonan ɪo finnde.

ɪchable [tiyčəbəl] *adj.* ko jangintoo.

ɪcher [tiyčə] *n.* ceerno *(o);* janginoowo *ʻo).*

ɪching [tiyčiŋ] *n.* jangingól *(ngól).*

ɪk [tiyk] lékki *(ki)*; leggal *(ngal).*

ɪm [tiym] *n.* fedde *(nde).*

ɪpot [tiypot] *n.* berraada *(nde);* kurkur *ʻo).*

ɪr [ter] *v.* seekde.

ɪr [tiyə] *n.* góngól *(ngól). shed a* ~ *ʋoyde.*

ɪse [tiyz] *v.* yanaade; gaajaade.

ɪser [tiyzə] *n.* janotooɗo *(o).*

chnical [teknəkəl] *adj.* ko faati e ɪarallaagal.

technician [tekniyšən] *n.* karallo *(o).*

technique [tekniyk] *n.* feere *(nde).*

technological [teknəlowjəkəl] *adj.* ko faati e mbaylaandi.

technology [teknəloji] *n.* mbaylaandi *(ndi).*

tectonic [tektənik] *adj.* ko faati e mahdi.

tectonics [tektəniks] *n.* jangde mahdi.

ted [ted] *v.* yórnude.

tedious [tiyjəs] *adj.* ko tampini.

tedium [tiyjəm] *n.* tampere.

tee [tiy] *n.* alkulal *(ngal).*

teem [tiym] *v.* jibinde; heewde; ɗuuɗde.

teenager [tiyneyjə] *n.* surga *(o).*

teeth [tiyϴ] *n.* ñiiYe *(ɗe). remove one's* ~ solde ñiiYe mum.

teethe [tiyð] *v.* fuɗde ñiiYe.

teg [teg] *n.* mbórtu *(ngu).*

tegmen [tegmən] *n.* nguru *(ngu).*

tegument [tegyuwmənt] *n.* nguru *(ngu).*

telecast [teləkast] *v.* habrirde telewisoɭ.

telecommunication *n.* jangde kabróndiral.

telegram [teləgram] *n.* telegaraam *(o)* *Send him a telegram* Neldu mo telegaraam.

telephone [teləfown] *n.* telefoɭ *(o).*

telescope [teləskowp] *n.* longorɗe *(ɗe).*

telescopic [teləskowpik] *adj.* ko faati e longorɗe.

television [teləviyʒən] *n.* telewisoɭ(o). *watch the* ~ Yeewde televisoŋ.

tell [tel] *v.* wiide; haalande. ~ *lies* fende; riimde. ~ *a person's genealogy* askinde. ~ *stories* tindude; daarde. ~ *one's own genealogy* askitinaade.

teller [telə] *n.* kaaloowo *(o).*

temperament [tempərəmənt] *n.* jikku *(o).*

temperate [temprət] adj. ko hakindii.

temperature [tempəčə] *n.* ngulééki *(ki)*; ɓuuɓól *(ngól).*

tempest [tempəst] *n.* héndu mawndu dóólnundu.

temporal [tempərəl] *adj.* ko faati e mudda/sahaa.

temporary [tempərəri] *adj.* ko duumaaki.

tempt [tempt] *v.* jarribaade *I was tempted by the looks* Mi jarriba.

temptation [tempteyšən] *n.* jarabi *(o).*

ten [ten] sappo. ~ *books* defte sappo. ~ capanɗe *(ɗe).*

tenable [tənəbəl] *adj.* ko jaggotoo.

tenacious [təneyšəs] *adj.* ŋatɗo.

tenant [tenənt] *n.* koɗɗo e nókku janano.

tend [tend] *v.* móccude.

tender [tendə] *adj.* ko waggiɗi.

tenebrous [tenəbrəs] *adj.* ko nibbiɗi.

tenet [tenet] *n.* miijo *(ngo)*.

tense [tens] *adj.* kó ŋééri.

tent [tent] *n.* tilliisa *(o)*.

tentative [tentətiv] *adj.* ko faati e etagól.

tenth [tenθ] sappabo *(o)*.

tergiversate [tərjəvəseyt] *v.* waylude miijo mum.

term [tərm] *n.* mudda *(o)*; happu *(o)*; kónŋ ɔl *(ngól)*. *be in good ~ with* nano dirde; faamondirde.

terminate [tərməneyt] *v.* gasnude; haljitde.

termination [tərməneyšən] *n.* kaljitgól *(ngól,*.

terminology [tərmənowləji] *n.* kónguɗi.

terminus [tərmənəs] *n.* haaɗirde *(nde)*.

termite [tərmayt] *n.* móóyu *(ngu)*.

ternary [tərnəri] *adj.* ko faati e tati.

terrene [təriyn] *adj.* ko faati e aduna.

terrestrial [tərestryəl] *adj.* ko faati e leydi.

terrible [terəbəl] *adj.* kó hulbinii; kó bóni.

terrify [terəfay] *v.* hulbinde; wéftilde.

territory [terətəri] *n.* léydi *(ndi)*.

terror [terə] *n.* kulól *(ngól)*.

terrorize [terərayz] *v.* hulbinde; wéftilde.

tertiary [təršəri] *adj.* tatabo; ko faati e tati.

test [test] *v.* jarribaade *~ someone's patience* Yeewde ɗo muñal neɗɗo haaɗi.

testament [testəmənt] *n.* wasiya *(o)*; wasiya ndónu.

testicle [testəkəl] *n.* bottere *(nde)*.

testify [testəfay] *v.* jaŋtaade; seedaade

testimony [testəməni] *n.* jaŋtagól *(ngól)*.

testy [testi] *adj.* muñtóriɗɗo.

tetanus [tetənəs] *n.* tetaanoos.

tête-à-tête [tetatet] *adj.* hakkunde yimbe ɗiɗo.

tether [teðə] *v.* habbude; tongude.

tetra- [tetrə] *pref.* nay.

text [tekst] *n.* windande *(nde)*.

textile [tekstayl] *n.* bagi *(o)*.

textual [teksčəl] *adj.* ko faati e windande.

texture [teksčə] *n.* cañu *(ngu)*.

thank [θaŋk] *v.* jaarde. *~ you* a jaaraama; yettaama; albarka. *~ God* Alla jaaraama njetten Alla. *~s to him* Alla e makko.

thankful [θaŋkfəl] *adj.* jéttuɗo. *I an thankful to you* Mbeɗe yettu maa / M yettii ma.

that [ðat] *det.* oon; oya. *~ one* ooɗaa; oya

thatch [θatč] *v.* tibde; huurde; muurde.

thaw [θɔ] *v.* saayde.

the [ðə] *det.* ɗam; hoñ; ba; ɗi; ki; ɗe; ka ka; o; ba.

theater [θiyətə] *n.* tiyaataar *(o)*.

theatrical [θiyətrikəl] *adj.* ko faati tiyaataar.

theft [θeft] *n.* nguyka *(ka)*.

their [ðer] *pron.* mumen; mabbe; k mabbe.

theirs [ðerz] *pron.* mabbe; ko mabbe.

them [ðem] *pron.* kambe.

themselves [ðemselvz] *pron.* kamb koyemabbe.

then [ðen] *adv.* hanti; ndeen.

theoretical [θiytrəkəl] *adj.* ko faati miijo/miijóóji.

theory [θiyri] *n.* miijo *(ngo)*; miijóóji *(ɗi)*.

therapeutic [θerəpyuwtik] *adj.* ko faati safaara.

there [ðer] *adv.* to; ɗoon; toon; ɗaa.

therefore [ðerfowr] *adv.* ɗum noon.

thereupon [ðerʌpon] *adv.* ɗum noon.

thermal [θərməl] *adj.* ko faati e ngulééki.

thermos [θərməs] *n.* termos *(o)*.

thesaurus [θesərəs] *n.* saggitorde *(nde)*.

these [ðiyz] *det.* ɗii; koñ.

thesis [θiysiz] *n.* miijo *(ngo)*.

theta [θetə] *n.* alkulal *(ngal)*.

they [ðey] *pr.* be; kamen; kambe.

thick [θik] *adj.* tekkuɗum; modduɗum. *b ~ móddude*; tékkude.

thicken [θikən] *v.* móddinde. *~ sauce b adding flour* toorde.

thicket [θikət] *n.* dundu *(ndu)*.

thickness [θiknes] *n.* móddugól *(ngól)*.

thief [θiyf] *n.* gujjo *(o)* *You are a thief* Aa ko a gujjo.

thieve [θiyv] *v.* wujjude.

thigh [θay] *n.* buhal *(ngal)*; asangal *(ngal)*.

in [θin] *adj.* 1) cewɗo 2) ko wosii; ɠosiiɗo. *be ~* sewde; wosaade. *a ~ person* ɓewɗo *(o)*.

ing [θiŋ] *n.* huunde *(nde). some~* huunde *(nde).*

ink [θiŋk] *v.* miijaade; sikkude.

inkable [θiŋkəbəl] *adj.* ko ina miijee.

inker [θiŋkə] *n.* miijotooɗo *(o).*

ird [θərd] *ord.* tataɓo.

irl [θərl] *v.* yulde.

irst [θərst] *n.* ɗomka *(ka)*; ɗomɗugól *'ngól).*

irsty [θərsti] *adj.* ɗomɗuɗo. *be ~* ɟómɗude.

irteen [θərtiyn] *num.* sappo e tati.

irty [θərti] *num.* capanɗe tati.

is [ðis] *det.* oo; kii; ndii; baa.

ong [θoŋ] *n.* cééltól *(ngól).*

oracic [θorəsik] *adj.* ko faati e becce.

orax [θoraks] *n.* becce *(ɗe).*

orn [θorn] *n.* giyal *(ngal)*; hebbere *(nde);* ɟuppere *(nde).*

orough [θorə] *adj.* ko timmi; ko huɓtódini.

ose [ðowz] *det.* ɓeya; ɗiin; ɗiya.

ought [θɔt] *n.* miijo *(ngo)*; sikke *(o) a ɵenny for your ~s* hol ko miijoto ɗaa.

oughtful [θɔtfəl] *adj.* miijotooɗo.

oughtless [θɔtles] *adj.* mo heewaani miijo.

ousand [θawzənd] *n.* wuluure *(nde);* ujunere *(nde).*

rall [θrɔl] *n.* maccuɗo.

rash [θraš] *v.* lappude; foolde.

rasher [θraš] *n.* poolɗo.

read [θred] *v.* wuurtude.

read [θred] *n.* gaarawól *(ngól)*; motto *(ngo).*

reat [θret] *n.* baabagól *(ngól).*

reaten [θretən] *v.* gijaade; giddude; baabaade; ɓagde.

reatener [θretənə] *n.* gijotooɗo.

ree [θriy] *num.* tati.

reefold [θriyfowld] *adj.* laabi tati.

resh [θreš] *v.* sampaade; lappude gawri.

rift [θrift] *n.* ngañaari *(ndi).*

rill [θril] *v.* siññude.

riller [θrilə] *n.* ciññoowo *(o).*

thrive [θrayv] *v.* ɓamtaade; Yéllitaade.

throat [θrowt] *n.* góddól *(ngól)*; kondorobol *(ngól).*

throb [θrob] *v.* dillude (ɓernde); diwde.

throne [θrown] *n.* laamu *(ngu)* **throng** [θroŋ] *n.* deental yimɓe.

throttle [θrotəl] *v.* ɗéɗɗude.

through [θruw] *prep.* dów; nder.

throughout [θruwawt] *prep.* nókku kala.

throw [θrow] *v.* werlaade; weddaade. *~ off* tuuɗde. *~ down* yandinde; fukkude.

thrust [θrʌst] *v.* duñde; yiwde.

thud [θʌd] *n.* dille.

thug [θʌg] *n.* aawase *(o);* saaysaaye *(o);* banndi *(o).*

thumb [θʌm] *n.* féɗééndu wórdu.

thump [θʌmp] *v.* oYYude.

thunder [θʌndə] *v.* digaade

thunder [θʌndə] *n.* digaango *(ngo);* hartaango *(ngo).*

thunderbolt [θʌndərbolt] *n.* kaaYél manaango.

Thursday [θərsdi] *n.* alkamiisa *(o).*

thus [ðʌs] *adv.* noon.

thwart [θwɔt] *n.* luutndaade.

tibia [tibyə] *n.* Yiyal korlal.

tick [tik] *v.* dillude.

ticket [tiket] *n.* biyé *(o).*

tickle [tikəl] *v.* ñiklude. *~ be ~ish* weeɓeede jaleeɗe.

tickler [tiklə] *n.* ñikloowo *(o).*

tidy [taydi] *adj.* kó réggóndiri; kó fééwi.

tie [tay] *v.* haɓɓude; humde; sinndude. *~ in a bundle* saawde. *~ someone's belt* dadnude. *~ one's pants* duhaade. *~ around the waist* dadaade; délfinde. *~ one's sarong/skirt* haddaade. *~ around the head* fiilde. *~ legs up* tongude.

tiger [taygə] *n.* katamaawu *(ngu).*

tight [tayt] *adj.* ŋeerɗum; teeŊɗum. *be ~* faaɗeede. *be very ~* teeŊde; ŋeerde.

tighten [taytən] *v.* tééŊnude; Ŋéérnude; bukde.

till [til] *conj.* haa.

tilt [tilt] *v.* muurde.

timber [timbə] *n.* leggal *(ngal).*

time [taym] *n.* tuma *(o);* sahaa *(o);* mudda *(o). spend a long ~* ruumde. *a particular ~ ago* ñandeen. *another ~* góngól. *many*

~s laabi keewɗi. *What time is it* Hol waktu jonɗo?

timer [taymə] *n.* deenoowo waktu.

timid [timid] *adj.* nuggaro *(o); mo* wonaa cakalo.

timorous [timərəs] *adj.* béftilaaɗo; nuggaro.

tin [tin] *n.* boyet njamndi.

tine [tayn] *v.* majjude; majjireede; majjinde.

tingle [tiŋgəl] *v.* ŋatde.

tinker [tiŋkə] *n.* ɓasoowo *(o).*

tint [tint] *v.* bulde; noorde.

tiny [tayni] *adj.* pamarél; tókósél.

tip [tip] *n.* ceɓtam *(ɗam);* jóófirde *(nde).* ~ *top* ceɓtam. ~ *out* wancinde. *give a* ~ rokkude carwoowo kaalis.

tipple [tipəl] *v.* yarde sangara.

tipsy [tipsi] *adj.* cirwuɗo. *be* ~ sirwude.

tire [tayə] *v.* tampinde.

tired [tayəd] *adj.* tampuɗo. *be* ~ tampude. *be very* ~ tampude; hortaade; lohde.

tiredness [tayədnes] *n.* tampere *(nde).*

tiresome [tayəsʌm] *adj.* ko tampinta.

tithe [tayθ] *n.* asakal *(ngal);* usuru *(ndu).*

tithe [tayθ] *v.* askude.

tither [tiðə] *n.* askoowo *(o).*

titilate [titleyt] *v.* ñiklude.

title [taytəl] *n.* inde *(nde).* chief's ~ joom; bees *(o);* satigi *(o). fisherman's* ~ jaaltaaɓe *(o).*

titter [titə] *v.* jalde.

titubation [titəbeyšən] *n.* daaldaalnugól.

to [tuw] *prep.* to.

toad [towd] *n.* faaburu *(ndu).*

toast [towst] *v.* wulnude; wultinde.

tobacco [tobako] *n.* simme *(o).*

tocher [točə] *n.* teⁿɟe *(ɗe).*

tod [tod] *n.* ɓétirde *(nde).*

today [tudey] *n.* hande *(o).*

toddle [todəl] *v.* ruudde.

toe [tow] *n.* féɗééndu koyngal.

toenail [towneyl] *n.* segene féɗééndu koyngal.

tog [tog] *v.* yooɗnaade.

together [tugeðə] *adv.* kó wóndi.

toil [toyl] *n.* liggééy *(o);* gollal *(ngal);* liggaade.

toilet [toylet] *n.* firlorde *(nde).*

token [towkən] *n.* maale *(ɗe).*

tolerable [tolərəbəl] *adj.* ko muñotoo.

tolerance [tolərəns] *n.* muñal *(ngal).*

tolerant [tolərəns] *adj.* muñɗo.

tolerate [toləreyt] *v.* muñde.

toll [tol] *n.* njóɓdi *(ndi).*

toll [tol] *v.* séⁿɟlude.

tom [tom] wórdu.

tomahawk [toməhɔk] *n.* jambere *(nde).*

tomato [təmeytə] *n.* méntuⁿɟeere *(nde);* tamatere *(nde).*

tomb [tum] *n.* yanaande *(nde).*

tomcat [tomkat] *n.* baⁿɟbaⁿɟru *(ndu).*

tomfool [tomfuwl] *n.* beemɗo; puuYɗo.

tomorrow [tuwmərow] *adv.* jango.

tongue [tʌŋ] *n.* ɗemngal *(ngal). hold one's* ~ deYYude.

tonight [tuwnayt] *n.* hande jamma.

tonsil [tonsəl] *n.* ɗakañe *(o).*

tonsure [tonšə] *n.* pémbugól *(ngól).*

too [tuw] *adv.* kó ɓurti.

tool [tuwl] *n.* liggorgal *(ngal).* ~ *for digging* sombe *(o)* ~ *for mending* ɓasirgal *(ngal).* ~ *for leveling floors* meldugal *(ngal).*

toom [tuwm] *n.* meho.

tooth [tuwθ] *n.* ñiire *(nde).* ~*brush* coccorgal *(ngal).* ~ *ache* muusu ñiiYe. niire muusoore. *have a sweet* ~ yiɗde ko weli.

toothless [tuwθles] *adj.* colɗo.

top [top] *n.* dów.

tope [towp] *v.* yarde.

topi [towpi] *n.* lella *(ba).*

topography [topowgrəfi] *n.* sifaa *(o).*

topple [topəl] *v.* yandinde; fiiltude.

torch [tɔč] *n.* fooyre *(nde).*

torment [tɔmənt] *v.* haljinde.

tormentor [tɔməntə] *n.* kaljinoowo *(o).*

torn [tɔn] *adj.* ceekiiɗo; ceekiɗum; ko seekii. *be* ~ seekaade.

torrent [torənt] *n.* waraango *(ngo).*

torrential [torənšəl] *adj.* ko faati e waraango.

torrid [torid] *adj.* ko wuli.

torso [tɔso] *n.* becce *(ɗe).*

tort [tɔt] *n.* tooñange *(nge).*

tortoise [tɔtəs] *n.* heende *(nde).*

torts [tɔts] *n.* tooñange; hakke.

tortuous [tɔčuwəs] *adj.* kó óóñii.

torture [tɔčə] *v.* lébtude.

torture [tɔčə] *n.* lebte *(de).*

toss [tos] *v.* werlaade. ~ *and catch with the hand* tebbaade tot [tot] *n.* kurka *(o).*

total [towtəl] *n.* fóf.

tote [towt] *v.* wuundaade.

totem [totem] *n.* sanam *(o).*

touch [tʌč] *v.* memde. ~ *with* mémirde. ~ *again* mémtude. *be in* ~ jókkóndirde. *stay in* ~ jokkondirde.

touchy [tʌči] *n.* loobdo.

tough [tʌf] *adj.* tiiddo.

toughen [tʌfən] *v.* tiidnude.

tour [tuwr] *v.* dannaade; yiilaade.

tourist [tuwrist] *n.* danniido *(o);* jilliido *(o).*

tournament [tərnəmənt] *n.* kawgél *(ngél).*

tout [tawt] *n.* jaasuus *(o).*

tow [tow] *v.* sindude.

toward [tuwəd] *prep.* ko tiindii e.

towel [tawəl] *n.* sarbet *(o).*

tower [tawə] *n.* mahdi tóówndi.

town [tawn] *n.* saare *(nde). small* ~ gurél *(ngél).* ~ *crier* jeeynoowo *(o). Boghe is my home town* Njeyaami ko Boghe.

toxic [toksik] *adj.* ko faati e posone.

toy [toy] *n.* pijirgél *(ngél).*

trace [treys] *v.* yiitude.

trace [treys] *n.* diidol *(ngól).* ~ *left by a snake* laadól *(ngól).* ~ *left after hoing* paafal *(ngal).*

tracer [treysə] *n.* jiilotoodo *(o).*

trachea [trakiyə] *n.* kójómból *(ngól).*

track [trak] *n.* daasol; laawol. ~ *left by scraping* kééfól *(ngól).* ~ *of cattle* lappól *(ngól).*

traction [trakšən] *n.* póódgól *(ngól).*

tractor [traktə] *n.* sambatali *(o).*

trade [treyd] *v.* julaade.

trade [treyd] *n.* njeeygu *(ngu);* gostondiral *(ngal).* ~ *by barter* barja *(o)* haadi haada. ~ *season* teret *(o). everyone to his* ~ neddo fof ko mum.

trader [treydə] *n.* jeeyoowo *(o);* julanke *(o).*

tradesman [treydsmən] *n.* julanke *(o);* jula. *(o).*

trading [treydiŋ] *n.* julankaagal *(ngal).*

tradition [trədiyšən] *n.* aada *(o);* aadaaji *(di).*

traditional [trədiyšənəl] *adj.* ko faati e aada.

traduce [trədyuws] *v.* ñohde; janfaade; bónnitde.

traffic [trafik] *adj.* ótóóji/laade jahooje/ji.

tragedy [trajədi] *n.* bonande *(nde).*

tragic [trajik] *adj.* ko faati e bonande.

trail [treyl] *v.* rewde; abbaade.

train [treyn] *n.* laana njóórndi; otoraay *(o).*

train [treyn] *v.* nehde.

trainee [treyni] *n.* ekkotodo *(o).*

trainer [treynə] *n.* eékkinoowo *(o).*

training [treyniŋ] *n.* ekko *(ngo).*

trait [treyt] *n.* mbaadi *(ndi);* sifaa *(o).*

traitor [treytə] *n.* janfotoodo *(o).*

traitorous [treyčərəs] *adj.* ko faati e janfa.

trajectory [trəjektəri] *n.* laawól *(ngól).*

tramp [tramp] *v.* yahrude koyde; dénkude koyngal.

trample [trampəl] *v.* dénkude koyde.

tranquil [trənkwil] *adj.* deeYdo.

tranquility [trəŋkwiləti] *n.* deeYre *(nde).*

tranquilize [trəŋkwəlayz] *v.* deeYde; dééYnude.

transact [tranzəkt] *v.* haaldude; yééytóndirde; haaldeede; yééytóndireede.

transaction [tranzəkšən] *n.* kaaldigal *(ngal);* jééytóndiral *(ngal).*

transcend [transend] *v.* diwde; burde.

transcribe [transkrayb] *v.* windude.

transcription [trənskripšən] *n.* bindól *(ngól);* bindugól *(ngól).*

transfer [transfə] *v.* yahde nókku goddo; yuppude; éggude.

transfigure [transfigə] *v.* waylude mbaadi/tagoodi.

transform [transfɔm] *v.* waylude.

transformation [transfmeyšən] *n.* mbaylaandi *(ndi);* baylugól *(ngól).*

transgress [transgres] *v.* luutndaade; diwde laawól; bakkódinde; tooñde.

transgression [transgrəšən] *n.* luutndagól laawól.

transhumance [transhyuwməns] *n.* éggudu *(ndu).*

transient [transənt] *adj.* ko duumaaki; ko booyataa.

transit [tranzit] v. Yaaɳde; rewde.

translate [transleyt] v. firde; nantinde.

translation [transleyšən] n. firo *(ngo)*.

translator [transleytə] n. nantinoowo *(o)*; piroowo *(o)*

transmit [tranzmit] v. yéttinde nulal; raaɓde.

transpire [transpayə] v. warñude; waaYde.

transplant [transplənt] v. ñiɓtaade.

transport [transpɔt] v. nawde.

trap [trap] v. tuufaade.

trap [trap] n. wilde.

trash [traš] n. kurjuru *(o)*.

trashy [traši] *adj.* ko faati e kurjuru.

travail [trəvay] n. liggééy muusɗo.

travel [travəl] v. ɗanaade I am traveling today ko hande ɗannotoomi.

traveler [travələ] n. ɗanniiɗo *(o)*; ɗannotooɗo *(o)*.

traverse [travərs] v. taccude.

trawl [trɔl] n. gubból *(ngól)*.

trawl [trɔl] v. awde.

tray [trey] n. palaat *(o)*.

treacherous [triyčərəs] *adj.* ko faati e fuunti/janfa.

treachery [triyčəri] n. janfa *(o)*.

tread [tred] v. yaɓɓude.

treason [triyzən] n. janfa *(o)*.

treasure [treʒə] n. ngalu *(ngu)*.

treasury [treʒəri] n. móóftirde kaalis laamu.

treat [triyt] n. ɓagoore *(nde)*.

treat [triyt] v. safrude. ~ with respect téddinde. ~ *a guest* hóɗtude.

treatise [triytiz] n. tindól *(ngól)*; kawral *(ngal)*.

treatment [triytmənt] n. safaara *(o)*.

treaty [triyti] n. nanóndiral *(ngal)*; nandiral; ahdi *(o) sign a* ~ siifde nanondiral.

treble [trebəl] v. fiyde laabi tati.

tree [triy] n. lékki *(ki)*. ~ *trunk* foobre lekki.

tremble [trembəl] v. siññude. ~ *in every limb* siññude gerger.

tremendous [trəmendəs] *adj.* mawnuɗum; kééwɗum.

tremor [tremə] n. 1) ciññél gujjo 2) jerɓugol *(ngól)*.

trench [trenč] n. gaawól *(ngól)*

trespass [trespas] v. naattude e ; tooñde.

tress [tres] n. atturu *(ndu)*; móóról *(ngól)*; móóri *(ɗi)*.

trey [trey] n. tati.

triad [trayəd] n. fedde tato.

trial [trayəl] n. 1) ñaawoore *(nde)*. 2) ekko *(ngo)*; ekkagól *(ngól)*; etagól *(ngól)*.

tribal [traybəl] *adj.* ko faati e hinde/léñól.

tribe [trayb] n. hinde *(nde)*; léñól.

tribulation [trəbyuwleyšən] n. mettere.

tribunal [traybyuwnəl] n. ñaaworde *(nde)*; ñaawirde *(nde)*.

tributary [tribətəri] *adj.* jiimaaɗo.

tribute [tribyuwt] n. njóɓdi *(ndi)*.

trick [trik] v. fuuntude.

trickery [trikri] n. fuunti *(o)*.

trickle [trikəl] v. siimtude.

trickster [trikstə] n. puuntoowo *(o)*.

tricky [triki] *adj.* ko weeɓaani.

trier [trayə] n. etotooɗo.

trifle [trayfəl] v. gaajaare *(nde)*; meere *(nde)*; nufluɗum.

trigger [trigə] n. rawaandu fétél.

trilemma [trilemə] n. ngaanumma *(o)*.

trim [trim] v. méccude; ñaaltaade; hesde.

trimmer [trimə] n. kesoowo *(o)*.

trip [trip] v. taataade. ~ *along* ñékkude.

trip [trip] n. ɗangal *(ngal)*.

tripartite [traypərtayt] *adj.* geɗe walla pecce tati.

triple [tripəl] n. taɓɓitgal *(ngal)*.

triple [tripəl] v. taɓɓitde.

trisect [traysekt] v. féccude pecce tati.

triumph [trayəmf] v. foolde.

triumphant [trayəmfənt] *adj.* poolɗo.

triviality [trivyəlti] n. meere *(nde)*; maayka *(ka)*.

trivialize [trivyəlayz] v. sóófnude; fuuynude.

troll [trol] v. yimde.

troop [truwp] n. deental yimɓe.

trot [trot] v. ñékkude.

troth [troθ] n. ɗowtaare *(nde)*.

trouble [trʌbəl] n. tanaa *(o)*.

trouble [trʌbəl] v. ównude.

troublemaker [trʌbəlmeykə] n. tooñoowo *(o)*.

roublesome [trʌbəlsʌm] *adj.* tooñoowo.

rough [trɔf] *n.* waare ledde.

roupe [truwp] *n.* turup *(o).*

rousers [trawzəz] *n.* tuuba *(ba)* his wife wears the trousers ko o baawaado.

rousseau [truwsow] *n.* cómci walla cudaari jombaajo.

rout [trawt] *n.* liingu *(ngu).*

row [trow] *v.* sikkude.

ruant [truwənt] *n.* dogdo lekkol.

ruce [truws] *n.* daragól *(ngól)*; kawral *(ngal).*

ruck [trʌk] *n.* kamiyoŋ *(o)*

rucker [trʌkə] *n.* dognoowo kaniyoŋ.

ruculent [trəkyuwlənt] *adj.* ñangudo.

rudge [trʌj] *v.* yahde.

rue [truw] *adj.* kó wóni goonga.

ruism [truwizm] *n.* goonga.

rull [trʌl] *n.* garbotoodo.

rumpery [trʌmpəri] *n.* ko nafataa.

rumpet [trʌmpet] *n.* liital *(ngal).*

rumpeter [trʌmpətə] *n.* liitoowo *(o).*

runcate [trʌŋkeyt] *v.* rabbidinde.

runcation [trʌŋkeyšən] *n.* dabbidingól *(ngól).*

runcheon [trʌnčən] *n.* boloŋ *(o)*; bólóŋél *(ngél).*

runk [trʌŋk] n. 1) foobre *(nde)* 2) wakande *(nde).*

russ [trʌs] *v.* habbude.

russ [trʌs] *n.* wahre hudo.

rust [trʌst] *v.* hoolaade; góóŋdinde. ~ *with* halfinde

rust [trʌst] *n.* hoolaare *(nde).*

rustful [trʌstfəl] *adj.* kóóliido.

rustworthy [trʌstwɔði] *adj.* koolaado. *be* ~ hooleede.

ruth [truwθ] *n.* goonga *(o)* *tell the* ~ haalde goonga

ruthful [truwθfəl] *adj.* gooŋdudo. koolaado. *be* ~ góóŋdude.

ry *v.* etaade; énndude. ~ *hard* tiinnaade. ~ *on* fondaade.

tsetse [tsetse] *n.* mbuubu *(ngu).* *upland* ~ kayfal *(ngal)*

tub [tʌb] *v.* buftaade.

tuck [tʌk] *v.* naatnude.

Tuesday [čuwsdi] *n.* talaata *(o).*

tuft [tʌft] *n.* raYYere *(nde)*; raññeere *(nde)*; toggere *(nde).*

tug [tʌg] *v.* foodde; liggaade.

tuition [twiyšən] *n.* njóbdi jangde.

tum [tʌm] *v.* móttude.

tumble [tʌmbəl] *v.* yande; firlaade.

tumefaction [tuwməfakšən] *n.* buutdi *(ndi).*

tumefy [tuwməfay] *v.* buutde.

tumid [tyuwmid] *adj.* ko buuti.

tummy [tʌmi] *n.* réédu *(ndu).*

tumor tuwmə] *n.* buutdi *(ndi).*

tumult [tuwmʌlt] *n.* dille *(de).*

tun [tʌn] *n.* barigal *(ngal).*

tune [tyuwn] *n.* leebol *(ngól)*; baar *(o)* *get out of* ~ luurdeede.

tup [tʌp] *n.* njawdi *(ndi).*

turban [tərbən] *n.* méétélól *(ngól)*; kaala.

turbit [tərbit] *n.* uuga *(o).*

turbulence [tərbyələns] *n.* piddugól *(ngól).*

turbulent [tərbyələnt] *adj.* pidduďo.

turf [tərf] *n.* hudo siiwre.

turgent [tərjənt] *adj.* ko buuti.

turgid [tərjəd] *adj.* ko buuti.

turmoil [tərmoyl] *n.* jiibru *(ndu).*

turn [tərn] *v.* yiilaade; yiilnude. ~ *mature* yóntude. ~ *grey* furdude. ~ *one's back to* rumtaade. ~ *one's stomach* timde. ~ *around a place* wangaade. ~ *off* ñifde.

turnover [tərnowvə] *v.* hippude.

turret [tʌret] *n.* sóóróó *(o).*

turtle [tərtəl] *n.* amre *(nde).*

tusk [tʌsk] *n.* hoggo *(ngo).*

tussle [tʌsəl] *n.* hare *(nde)*; luurondiral *(ngal).*

tutor [tuwtə] *n.* caggitoowo *(o)*; janginoowo *(o).*

tutorage [tuwtərij] *n.* jangingól.

tweet [twiyt] *v.* Yiikde.

tweeze [twiyz] *v.* borde; doofde.

twelfth [twelfθ] *ord.* sappo e didabo.

twelve [twelv] *num.* sappo e didi.

twenty [twenti] *num.* noogaas

twice [tways] *adv.* laabi didi.

twig [twig] *n.* puddi *(ndi).*

twilight [twaylayt] *n.* futuro; weetndoogo *(ngo).*

twin [twin] *n.* funeere *(nde) He is my twin brother* Ko kanko woni funeere am gorko.

twink [twiŋk] *v.* majde.

twinkle [twiŋkəl] *v.* jalbude; léwñude.

twinkle [twiŋkəl] *n.* majaango *(ngo). in the ~ of an eye* e majaango yitere.

twirl [twərl] *v.* yiilde.

twist [twist] *v.* harlude; haaYde.

twitter [twitə] *v.* Yiikde.

two [tuw] *num.* ɗiɗi.

tycoon [taykuwn] galo.

type [tayp] *n.* mbaadi *(ndi).*

type [tayp] *v.* tappude.

typist [taypist] *n.* tappoowo *(o).*

tyrant [tayrənt] *n.* gownoowo bééli.

tyro [tayrow] *n.* ekkotooɗo *(o).*

U

biquitous [yubikwətəs] adj. kó wóni nókku kala.

gly [ʌgli] adj. coofɗo. ~ words haala coofka.

lcer [ʌlsə] n. ñaw (ngu); ñawannde (nde).

lema [uləma] n. gando (o); ceerno (o).

lterior [ʌltiyryə] adj. ko fayi arde.

ltima [ʌltəma] n. hijjande wattannde.

ltimate [ʌltəmet] adj. battano.

ltra [ʌltrə] adj. ko ɓurti.

lu [uwluw] n. paaka (ka); njuulaawi (ki).

lulate [yuwlyuwleyt] v. ŋuurde.

mbra [ʌmbrə] n. ɓuuɓri (ndi).

mbrage [ʌmbrij] n. tooñange (nge).

mbrella [ʌmbrəla] n. waado; paraseewal (ngal).

nabated [ənabeytid] adj. ko ustaaka; dóólnuɗo.

nable [əneybəl] adj. donkuɗo. be ~ rónkude. I am unable to meet with you today Mi waawaa hawrude e maa hande.

nabridged [ənabrijd] adj. ko dottaaka.

naccented [ənaksəntəd] adj. ko masaaka; kó tékkinaaka.

nacquired [ənəkwayəd] adj. ko heɓaaka.

nadjusted [ənəjəstəd] adj. ko fotaani.

nalterable [ənəltərəbəl] adj. ko waylaaka.

nanimity [yuwnənəmiti] n. yimɓe fóf.

napt [ənapt] adj. dónkuɗo.

narmed [ənɑmd] adj. mó jógitaaki.

nattainable [ənəteynəbəl] adj. ko heɓotaako.

nattended [ənətendəd] adj. mó tóppitaaka. Do not leave him unattended Hol to ɗaccu mo kanko gooto.

nattractive [ətraktiv] adj. ko/mo yooɗaani.

navailable [ənəveyləbəl] adj. ko/mo heɓotaako; mo heɓaaki. He is unavailable O heɓaaki.

nbend [ənbend] v. turtaade.

nbraiding [ənbreydiŋ] n. cañtugol (ngól).

ncertain [ənsərtən] adj. mo yananaaka. He is uncertain O yananaaka.

ncircumcised [ənsərkəmsayzd] adj. sólima (o); mo duhaaki.

uncle [ʌŋkəl] n. kaaw

unclean [ənkliyn] adj. tunwuɗo.

uncleanliness [ənklenlənes] n. tuundi (ndi).

unclose [ənklowz] v. udditde.

unconcerned [ənkənsərnd] adj. mo wondaaka.

uncooked [ənkukt] adj. ko defaaka; ko ɓendaani.

uncork [ənkɔk] v. sukkitde

uncover [ənkovə] v. hippitde; suurtaade.

under [ʌndə] prep. les. Go under the tree Sakko less lekki ki.

underline [ʌndəlayn] v. diidde les; tééɲtinde.

undermine [ʌndəmayn] v. bónnude; asde.

underneath [ʌndəniyθ] adv. les. be ~ sakkaade.

underpants [ʌndəpants] n. tuuba cakkiiba.

undersarong [ʌndəsaroŋ] n. péndél (ngél).

undersell [ʌndəsel] v. wantirde; ustude cóggu.

undershirt [ʌndəšərt] n. génsu (ngu).

understand [ʌndəstand] v. faamde; nande. I do not understand Mi faamaani.

understandable adj. ko faamnii.

understanding [ʌndəstandiŋ] n. faamaamuya (o). come to an ~ faamondirde.

undisciplined [əndəsəplind] adj. neetaro.

undo [əndu] v. firtude. ~ someone's hair sañtude. ~ one's braids sañtaade.

undress [əndres] v. ɓóórtude; ɓooraade; ɓoortaade. ~ someone ɓoorde.

undulate [ʌnjuwleyt] v. addude bempeYYe.

unearth [ənərθ] v. ubbitde.

uneven [əniyvən] adj. ko fotaani.

unexpected [ənekspektid] adj. ko tijjaaka.

unfaithful [ənfeyθfəl] adj. mo ɗowtaaki; pijoowo.

unfasten [ənfɑsən] v. habɓitde.

unfinished [ənfinišd] adj. ko gasaani.

unfold [ənfowld] v. sówtude.

unfortunate [ənfɔɔənət] adj. malkisaaɗo. be ~ jooteede; malkiseede. ~ person jootaaɗo (o); malkisaaɗo (o).

ungrateful [əngreytfəl] adj. mo rokkataa wune.

unhook [ənhuwk] v. lóggitde.

unification [yuwnəfikeyšən] n. dééntugól (ngól).

uniform [yuwnəfɔm] adj. kó fóti; kó nandi tagóódi; paltu; cómcól.

uniformity [yuwnəfɔməti] n. nandugól (ngól).

unify [yuwnəfay] v. rééntinde; réndinde.

unilateral [yuwnəlatərəl] adj. ko faati e bange gooto.

uninteresting [ənintərestiŋ] adj. tékum.

union [yuwnyən] n. deental (ngal).

unionize [yuwnyənayz] v. rééntude.

unique [yuniyk] adj. wootere; gooto; bajjo.

unitary [yuwnətəri] adj. kó réndinta.

unite [yunayt] v. rééntude; réndinde; réndude.

united [yunaytid] adj. ko réénti; rééntube.

unity [yunəti] n. deental (ngal).

universal [yunivərsəl] adj. ko hubtódini.

universe [yunivərs] n. windere (nde).

unjust [ənjʌst] adj. ooñiido. be ~ ooñaade.

unknown [ənnown] adj. ko andaaka; ko humpaa; kumpadum.

unlawful [ənlɔfəl] adj. ko rewaani laawól.

unleash [ənliyš] v. humtude.

unless [ənles] conj. so wonaa; illaa.

unload [ənlowd] v. rimtude. ~ from one's head rootaade.

unlock [ənlak] v. sóktude.

unlucky [ənlʌki] adj. malkisaado.

unpack [ənpak] v. habbitde kaake.

unpleasant [ənplezənt] adj. mettudo. be ~ méttude.

unpopular [ənpopulə] adj. mo darjaani.

unravel [ənravəl] v. jiktude.

unrest [ənrest] n. dillere (nde).

unripe [ənrayp] adj. kecco; baggo. be ~ waggidde; héccidde.

unroll [ənrol] v. taggitde.

unsatisfied [ənsatəsfayd] adj. jawdo; mo weltaaki. be ~ yawde.

unscrew [ənskruw] v. biiYtude.

unseal [ənsiyl] v. mubbitde.

unsold [ənsowld] adj. ko lambi; lambudum. be ~ lambude.

unstick [ənstick] v. takkitde; dakkitde.

untangle [əntaŋgəl] v. jiktude.

untie [əntay] v. fiiltude; habbitde; fibtude; humtude. ~ one's pants duhtude; duhtaade.

until [əntil] conj. haa. ~ now haa jooni.

untouchable [əntʌčəbəl] adj. ko memotaako.

unveil [əveyl] v. muurtude.

unwanted [ənwantid] adj. mo alaa jiddo.

unwariness [ənwerənes] n. hoomto (ngo).

unwary [ənweyri] adj. koomtaado. make ~ hóómtude.

unwed [ənwed] adj. cooydo. be ~ for a long time sooyde.

up [ʌp] prep. dów.

up-to-date [ʌptədeyt] adj. keso; késum.

upbringing [ʌpbriŋiŋ] n. néhdi (ndi).

update [ʌpdeyt] v. hésditinde.

upheaval [ʌphiyvəl] n. fitina (o).

uphold [ʌphold] v. heddaade e.

uplift [ʌplift] v. suutde; suutude.

upon [ʌpon] prep. dów; nde. once ~ a time Ina wona wonataa ko tindol.

upper [ʌpə] adj. gondo dów; burdo toowde.

uppermost [ʌpəmost] adv. burdo fóf toowde.

upright [ʌprayt] adj. kó fóóYtii; póóYtiido.

uprise [ʌprayz] v. ummaade.

uproar [ʌprowr] n. gulaali (di).

uproot [ʌpruwt] v. duggitde.

upset [ʌpset] v. séknude; laawde; haabnude. be ~ méttinde; sekde; laawaade; bérnude.

upside-down [ʌpsaydawn] adj. junnittidum. be ~ junnitaade.

upstairs [ʌpsters] adj. dów iskalé.

upward [ʌpwɔd] adj. ko fayi dów.

urge [ərj] v. waawnude.

urgency [ərjənsi] n. sokla keñoraado; ko heñoraa.

urinal [yurənəl] n. ko faati e sóófirde.

urinate [yuwrəneyt] v. diccaade; soofde; taaraade; bawlude; timpaade. ~ in one's clothing bónnitaade. have the urge to ~ buuYeede coofe.

urine [yuwrin] n. kaaye (de); taare (de); dicce (de).

us [ʌs] pron. enen.

able [yuwzəbəl] *adj.* ko huutortee; ko ina huutoree.

se [yuws] *n.* nafoore *(nde)*. *of no* ~ ko alaa nafoore. *of great* ~ ko heewi nafoore.

se [yuwz] *v.* naftoraade. ~ *as a pillow* aflaade.

sed [yuwzd] *adj.* kuutoraaɗum; ko huutoraa. *be* ~ *to* woowde.

seful [yuwzfəl] *adj.* nafojum; ko nafata. *be* ~ nafde.

selesness [yuwzləsnes] *n.* jaasre *(nde)*.

seless [yuwzles] *adj.* ko alaa nafoore. *be* ~ jaasde; lohde.

sual [yuwʒəl] *adj.* ko woowaa.

usually [yuwʒəli] *adv.* sahaa sahaa; sahaa kala.

usurer [yuwʒrə] *n.* ñamloowo *(o)*.

usurp [yuwʒərp] *v.* teetde.

usurpation [yuwʒərp] *n.* teetere *(nde)*.

utensil [yuwtənsəl] *n.* kaake défirteeɗe.

utility [yuwtələti] *n.* nafoore *(nde)*.

utilize [yuwtəlayz] *v.* huutoraade.

utmost [ʌtmowst] *adj.* ɓurɗo fóf.

utter [ʌtə] *v.* wówlude.

utterance [ʌtrəns] *n.* wowlaango *(ngo)*.

uvula [yuwvələ] *n.* ɗakañe *(o)*.

V

vacant [veykənt] *adj.* meho.

vacate [vəkeyt] *v.* éggude; iwde e nókku.

vacation [vəkeyšən] *n.* guurti *(ɗi)*.

vaccinate   [vaksəneyt] *v.* fesde.

vaccinated [vaksəneytəd] *adj.* pesaaɗo. *be* ~ fesaade.

vaccination   [vaksəneyšən]   *n.*   pesagól *(ngól)*. ~ *mark* fesande *(nde)*.

vaccinator [vaksəneytə] *n.* pesoowo *(o)*.

vacillant [vasələnt] *adj.* daaldaalnuɗo.

vacillate [vasəleyt] *v.* daaldaalnude.

vacuity [vakyuti] *n.* méhru *(ndu)*.

vacuous [vakyəs] *adj.* méhum.

vagabond [vagəbond] *n.* huywere *(nde);* mo alaa haaju/hammu.

vagabondage [vagəbondij] *n.* kuywaagu *(ngu)*.

vagina [vəjaynə] *n.* fii *(o);* sedere *(nde);* kóttu *(ngu);* melde *(nde)*.

vaginal [vəjaynəl] *adj.* ko faati e kaake debbo.

vagrant [veygrənt] *n.* huywere *(nde)*.

vague [veyg] *adj.* ko laaɓaani. *It is vague* ɗum laaɓaani.

vail [veyl] *v.* mutnude.

vain [veyn] *adj.* ko nafataa. *I waited in vain* Mi fadii mo kono o araani.

valediction   [valədikšən]   *n.*   baynagól *(ngól)*.

valet [vale] *n.* carwoowo *(o)*.

valiant [valyənt] *adj.* tiiɗɗo; tiiɗniiɗo; cuusɗo.

valid [valid] *adj.* kó góóŋɗini; kó móYYi. *It is not valid* ɗum moYYaani.

validate   [valədeyt]   *v.*   móYYinde; tééɭtinde.

valise [vəliyz] *n.* wólis *(o)*.

valor [valə] *n.* cuusal *(ngal)*.

valorous [valərəs] *adj.* cuusɗo.

valuable [valyəbəl] *adj.* ko nafata.

valuate [valyeyt] *v.* fiide cóggu.

value [valyuw] *n.* nafoore *(nde). set a ~ on* hiisaade.

van [van] *n.* oto *(o)*.

vandalize [vandəlayz] *v.* bónnude.

vanilla [vənilə] *n.* suukara wónni.

vanish [vaniš] *v.* wirnaade; majjude.

vanity [vanəti] *n.* nguttu *(ngu)*.

vanquish [vaŋkiš] *v.* foolde.

vapid [vapəd] *adj.* tékum.

vaporize [veypərayz] *v.* suyde.

variable [vəryəbəl] *adj.* ko waylotoo.

variance [vəryəns] *n.* baylagól *(ngól)*.

variation [vəryeyšən] *n.* baylagól *(ngól)*.

various [vəryəs] *adj.* kééwɗi; ko hééwi; heewɓe; céérɗi.

vary [veyri] *v.* waylude.

vasal [veysəl] *n.* neɗɗo luɓaaɗo léydi.

vase [veyz] *n.* lahal *(ngal)*.

vast [vast] *adj.* jaaYɗo; ko yaaji.

vaticinate [vatisəneyt] *v.* jéértinde.

vault [vɔlt] *v.* diwde; tuggaade e.

vaunt [vɔnt] *v.* wasaade.

veal [viyl] *n.* ñale *(nge)*.

veer [viyr] *v.* selde.

vegetable [vejətəbəl] *n.* lujum *(o)*.

vegetarian [vejəteryən] *adj.* mo ñaamataa tééw.

vegetation [vejəteyšən] *n.* huɗo e leɗɗe.

vehicle [vehikəl] *n.* oto *(o)*.

vehicular [vehiykilə] *adj.* ko faati e oto/móbél.

veil [veyl] *v.* muurde; suuɗde.

veil [veyl] *n.* ɓurtungal *(ngal)*; muurorde *(nde)*.

vein [veyn] *n.* fasawól *(ngól)*.

velocity [velowsəti] *n.* yaawre *(nde)*.

vend [vend] *v.* yeeyde.

vendor [vendə] *n.* jeeyoowo *(o)*.

venerate   [venəreyt]   *v.*   rewde;   hulde; téddinde.

vengeance [venjəns] *n.* joftagól *(ngól)*.

venom [venəm] *n.* tooke *(ɗe)*.

venomous [venənəs] *adj.* tookaaɗo; ko tookaa.

ventilate [ventəleyt] *v.* wifde; andinde.

ventilator [ventəleytə] *n.* bifoowo; ko wifata.

ventral [ventrəl] *adj.* ko faati e réédu.

venture [venčə] *v.* yillaade.

enue [venyuw] *n.* nókku deental; nókku.
What is the venue Hol to kawraten?

eracious [vəračəs] *adj.* goongante.

eracity [vərasəti] *n.* goonga *(o).*

eranda [vərandə] *n.* werandaa; jimbaꞇ.

erbal [vərbəl] *adj.* ko faati e haala.

erbatim [vərbeytəm] *adj.* ko faati e deftagól.

erdict [vərdikt] *n.* ñaawoore *(nde).* a *guilty* ~ ñaawoore kuugal.

erge [vərj] *n.* kééról *(ngól);* happu *(o).*

erify [verəfay] *v.* Yééwtindaade.

erity [verəti] *n.* goonga *(o).*

ermicide [vərməsayd] *n.* ko warata gilɗi.

ermin [vərmin] *n.* tooñoowo *(o);* kaaɓniiɗo *(o).*

erse [vərs] *n.* aaye *(o).*

erso [versow] *n.* hello ɗéréwól.

ertigo [vərdəgo] *n.* giilól *(ngól).*

ery [veri] *adv.* tigi. ~ *much* tigi tigi.

esicle [vezəkəl] *n.* basél *(ngél).*

essel [vesəl] *n.* laana *(ka).*

est [vest] *n.* gensu *(ngu).*

est [vest] *v.* ɓoornaade.

estiary [vesčəri] *adj.* ko faati e cómci/cómcól.

estibule [vestəbyuwl] *n.* bólééru *(ndu).*

estige [vestij] *n.* kedde *(ɗe).*

et [vet] *v.* safrude jawdi.

eteran [vetərən] *n.* nayeejo *(o).*

eterinary [vetərənəri] *adj.* ko faati e safaara jawdi.

eto [viytow] *v.* haɗde.

ex [veks] *v.* séknude.

exed [vekst] *adj.* cekɗo. *be easily* ~ looɓde.

ibrant [vaybrənt] *adj.* ko dillata; dilloowo.

ibrate [vaybreyt] *v.* dillude.

ice [vays] *v.* ayyiiba *(o);* ella *(o).*

icinity [visənəti] *n.* sara *(o).*

icious [višəs] *adj.* bonɗo.

ictim [viktim] *n.* tooñaaɗo *(o);* bonnanaaɗo *(o).*

ictor [viktə] *n.* poolɗo *(o).*

ictorious [viktowryəs] *adj.* poolɗo.

ictory [viktri] *n.* póólgól *(ngól).*

ictual [vikčəl] *n.* nguura.

viduity [vidyuwti] *n.* mudda mo debbo wóni diwo.

vie [vay] *v.* tiiɗnaade.

view [vyuw] *v.* yiide.

viewer [vyuwə] *n.* Yeewoowo *(o).*

vigilance [vijələns] *n.* pinal *(ngal);* deentagól *(ngól).*

vigilant [vijələnt] *adj.* pinɗo; dééntiiɗo.

vigor [vigə] *n.* sembe *(o).*

vigorous [vigrəs] *adj.* tékkuɗo; célluɗo; cémbinɗo; kó sémbini.

vilify [viləfay] *v.* bónnitde.

vilipend [viləpend] *v.* nuskude.

village [vilij] *n.* gurél *(ngél);* saare *(nde). newly built* ~ sincaan *(o).*

vincible [vinsəbəl] *adj.* mo ina foolee.

vindictive [vindəktiv] *adj.* muñtóriɗɗo; jiɗɗo yoftaade.

vinegar [vinəgə] *n.* bineegara *(o).*

violate [vayəleyt] *v.* tooñde.

violation [vayəleyšən] *n.* tooñange *(nge)*

violent [vayələnt] *adj.* kólliroowo doole.

violin [vayələn] *n.* ñaañóóru *(ndu).*

viper [vaypə] *n.* sohre *(nde).*

virgin [vərjin] *n.* mbóómri *(ndi).*

virginal [vərjənəl] *adj.* ko faati e mboombaagu.

virginity [vərjənəti] *n.* mboombaagu *(ngu).*

virile [virəl] *adj.* ko faati e ngoraagu.

virility [virələti] *n.* ngoraagu *(ngu).*

virtually [vərčəli] *adv.* ko buri heewde.

virtue [vərčuw] *n.* moYYere *(nde);* peewal *(ngal).*

virtuous [vərčəwəs] *adj.* peewɗo.

virulent [virələnt] *adj.* ko ñawnata.

vis-à-vis [vizəvi] yeeso; e yeeso.

visage [vizij] *n.* yeeso *(ngo).*

viscera [viskaryə] *n.* téktéki.

visceral [visərəl] *adj.* ko faati e téktéki.

visibility [vizəbiləti] *n.* giile *(ɗe).*

visible [vizibəl] *adj.* ko yiyotoo.

vision [vizən] *n.* giile. *be out of* ~ wirnaade. *come to* ~ wirnitaade.

visit [vizit] *v.* hófnude.

visitant [vizətənt] *n.* jilliiɗo *(o).*

visual [viʒwəl] *adj.* ko faati e giile.

visualize [viʒəlayz] *v.* Yééwrude hakkille.

vital [vaytəl] *adj.* ko faati e nguurndam.

vitiate [višeyt] v. bónnude.
vivace [viyvačə] adj. guurɗo.
vivid [vivid] adj. ko jalbi.
vivify [vivəfay] v. wélnude.
vocable [vowkəbəl] n. kóngól (ngól); inde (nde).
vocabulary [vowkəbyələri] n. kelme (ɗe).
vocal [vowkəl] adj. ko faati e daande/wowlaango.
vocalist [vowkəlist] n. liitoowo (o); guttoowo liital.
vocalize [vowkəlayz] v. wówlude.
vocation [vowkeyšən] n. liggééy (o).
vocational [vowkeyšənəl] adj. ko faati e liggééy.
vociferate [vowsəfəreyt] v. luukde; haacde.
vogue [vowg] n. kó jóli.
voice [voys] n. daande (nde). know by ~ heɓtinde daande neɗɗo.
void [voyd] v. niilnude. It is void ɗum niilii.
volume [volyuwm] n. tagande (nde); deftere (nde); njaajeendi (ndi).
voluminous [vəluwminəs] adj. ko yaaji; ko mawni.
voluntary [volʌntri] adj. Allah meho.

volunteer [volʌntiyə] v. ligganaade Alla meho.
voluptuary [volʌpčweri] adj. dewɗo aduna.
vomit [vomit] v. ruttude. make someone ~ tuutnude. ~ milk wolsude; tuutde vomit [vomit] n. tuure (nde).
voracious [voreyšəs] adj. gaybuɗo; ñaamgawiijo. be ~ saañde; aybude.
voracity [vorasəti] n. aybeende (nde).
vote [vowt] v. wootde.
voter [vowtə] n. gootoowo (o).
vouch [vawč] v. tééɭtinde.
vow [vaw] v. waatde.
vowel [vawəl] n. alkulal (ngal).
voyage [voyij] n. ɗangal laana.
vulnerable [vʌlnərəbəl] adj. mo ina gañee; gaañeteeɗo.
vulture [vʌlčə] n. dutal (ngal).
vulva [vəlvə] n. kaake debbo.

W

waddle [wadəl] v. ruudde.

wade [weyd] v. juuwde. ~ *in the mud* juuwde.

wader [weydə] n. juuwoowo *(o)*.

waft [waft] v. nawde.

waft [waft] n. kenal *(ngal)*.

wag [wag] v. dillinde. ~ *one's tail* dillinde laaci mum.

wage [weyj] v. waɗde. ~*s* njóɓdi *(ndi)*.

waggle [wagəl] v. dillinde.

wail [weyl] v. woyde; Ŷusde.

waist [weyst] n. dadorde *(nde)*; nadorde *(nde)*.

waistline [weystlayn] n. duhorde *(nde)*; duhórgól *(ngól)*; nadornde *(nde)*.

wait [weyt] v. fadde; tombaade. ~ *for water to flow* ɓulnaade. ~ *for food without invitation* ténkude. *Wait for me* Fadam.

waiter [weytə] n. carwoowo *(o)*.

waitress [weytres] n. debbo carwoowo.

waive [weyv] v. ɗaccude.

wake [weyk] v. findinde. ~ *up late* weetndorde.

waken [weykən] v. findinde.

walk [wɔk] n. yahdu *(ndu)*. *take a* ~ yahnaade.

walk [wɔk] v. yahde. ~ *hurriedly* jaylaade. ~ *slowly* ñaaYde. ~ *faster* móylude. ~ *everywhere* sooraade. ~ *carelessly* mafñaade.

walker [wɔkə] n. jahoowo *(o)*.

wall [wɔl] n. tata *(o)*; ɓalal *(ngal)*. *break a* ~ welditde.

wallet [walet] n. kalbe *(ɗe)*.

wallop [waləp] v. fiyde.

wallow [waləw] v. weytaade.

waltz [wɔltz] n. ngamri.

wamble [wambəl] v. yiiñeede.

wander [wandə] v. huywude; oorde. ~ *about* huywude.

wanderer [wandərə] n. kuywuɗo *(o)*.

wane [weyn] v. ustaade.

want [want] v. yiɗde; muuyde; leytude; faaleede.

wap [wap] v. soomde.

war [wɔ] n. kónu *(ngu)*

warble [wɔbəl] v. yimde.

ward [wɔd] v. reende.

warden [wɔdən] n. deenoowo *(o)*; kalfinaaɗo *(o)*.

warder [wɔdə] n. deenoowo *(o)*.

ware [wer] n. kaake *(ɗe)*.

warehouse [werhaws] n. sake *(o)*.

warfare [wɔfer] n. hare *(nde)*.

warm [wɔm] v. itde. ~ *oneself at the fire* itaade; iwlaade. *It is warm* ɗum jaangaani.

warn [wɔn] v. rééntinde; jéértinde *I warn you*. Mi reentinii ma.

warning [wɔniŋ] n. tintingól *(ngól)*.

warp [wɔp] v. ooñde.

warrant [wɔrənt] n. yamiroore *(nde)*.

warrantor [wɔrəntə] n. jamiroowo *(o)*.

warrior [wɔryə] n. kaɓeteeɗo *(o)*.

wary [weri] adj. dééntiiɗo.

wash [wɔš] v. loote; fukaade; wuppude; lawYude. ~ *one's feet* sembaade. ~ *oneself* lootaade; ɓuftaade. ~ *someone's face* sulmude. ~ *one's face* sulmaade. ~ *one's hands* sooɗaade.

washer [wɔšə] n. guppoowo *(o)*.

washing [wɔšə] n. guppol *(ngól)*; lawYugol *(ngól)* **waste** [weyst] n. bonande *(nde)*. ~ *of lambs and goats* bordooɗe *(ɗe)*.

waste [weyst] v. bónnude; tilfude; gókkude. *You are wasting your time* Aɗan tampina hoore maa tan.

waster [weystə] n. bonnoowo *(o)*.

watch [wɔč] n. montoor *(o)*.

watch [wɔč] v. Yeewde; laarde. ~ *over* Yeewtaade; aynude; reende. ~ *out* reento. *be on the* ~ reentaade.

water [wɔtə] n. ndiyam *(ɗam)*. ~ *already used to wash rice or millet* kalumbam *(ɗam)*. ~ *fall* waame *(o)*. ~ *fetching* Yóógól *(ngól)*. ~ *source* sewnde *(nde)*. ~ *storage instrument* mbandu *(o)*. *rinsing* ~ lallitam *(ɗam)*. ~ *holder* guttu *(o)*. *draw* ~ Yoogde.

water [wɔtə] v. wisde.

watermelon [wɔtəmelən] n. dende *(nde)*; wudduru *(ndu)*. *broken bits of* ~ laalakoñ.

waterproof [wɔtəpruwf] *adj.* ko tuɗi. *be ~* tuɗde

watery [wɔtri] *adj.* gaalɗuɗe. *Your eyes are watery* Gite maa ngaalɗii gonɗi.

wattle [watəl] *v.* sañde.

wave [weyv] *n.* wempeYere *(nde).*

waver [weyvə] *v.* sayyaade.

way [wey] *n.* feere *(nde);* bólól *(ngól);* laawol *(ngól).* *half ~* feccere laawol.

waylay [weyley] *v.* taYde; faddaade.

we [wiy] *pron.* min; enen.

weak [wiyk] *adj.* lohɗo; mo doolnaani/sémbinaani.

weaken [wiykən] *v.* lóhnude; ustude doole/sembe.

weakness [wiyknes] *n.* lóhgól *(ngól).*

weal [wiyl] *n.* jam *(o).*

wealth [welƟ] *n.* ngalu *(ngu).*

wealthy [welƟi] *adj.* galo. *be ~* alɗude. *~ person* dundariyanke *(o).*

wean [wiyn] *v.* éntude. *be ~ed* enteede.

weaning [wiyniŋ] *n.* éntugól *(ngól).* *act of ~* entere *(nde).*

weapon [wepon] *n.* kaɓirgal *(ngal);* njógitaari *(ndi).*

wear [wer] *v.* ɓoornaade. *~ inside out* hippude. *~ perfume* fuɗaade. *~ a veil* yómbinaade. *~ someone out* tampinde. *~ jewelery* suɗaade. *be worn out* hortaade.

weariness [weriness] *n.* tampere *(nde).*

wearisome [werəsəm] *adj.* ko tampinta.

weary [weyri] *adj.* tampuɗo.

weave [wiyv] *v.* sañde; wamde.

weaver [wiyvə] *n.* maabo *(o);* cañoowo *(o).* *He belongs to the weaver caste* Ko o cañoowo.

weaving [wiyviŋ] *n.* cañgól *(ngól).*

web [web] *v.* sañde.

wed [wed] *v.* resde. *be un~ for a long time* sooyde. *be ~* humaneede.

wedding [wediŋ] *n.* cuddungu *(ngu).*

wedlock [wedlok] *n.* dewgal *(ngal).* *bear out of ~* reedde.

Wednesday [wensdi] *n.* alaarba *(o).*

wee [wiy] *adj.* tókósél.

weed [wiyd] *v.* duulaade; remde. *~ around* duulaade.

week [wiyk] *n.* yontere *(nde).* *last ~* yontere ɓennunde *(nde)*

weekly [wiykli] *n.* yontere kala.

weep [wiyp] *v.* woyde.

weeper [wiypə] *n.* goyoowo *(o).*

weeping [wiypiŋ] *n.* bójji *(ɗi).*

weft [weft] *adj.* ko sañaa.

weigh [wey] *v.* peesde; yisɓude. *~ with* péésirde

weight [weyt] *n.* tedeendi *(ndi).* *~ measurement* muddo *(o);* mata *(o);* menkelde *(nde).*

weird [wiyd] *adj.* kaawniiɗo; kaawniɗum.

welcome [welkʌm] *v.* jaɓɓaade.

welcome [welkʌm] *n.* jaɓɓagól *(ngól).*

weld [weld] *v.* ɓasde; ɓasóndirde.

welfare [welfer] *n.* ɓamtaare *(nde);* kisal *(ngal).*

well [wel] *adj.* celluɗo. *be ~* hisde; séllude. *Get well soon* Yo Alla rokku jam ko neeɓaani.

well [wel] *n.* wóyndu *(ndu);* ɓunndu *(ndu).*

wend [wend] *v.* rewde.

were [wer] *v.* wonnoo; ngonnoo.

west [west] *n.* hirnaange *(nge);* gorgal *(ngal).*

wester [westə] *n.* héndu ummóriindu hirnaange.

Westerner [westənə] *n.* hirnanke *(o).*

wet [wet] *adj.* kecco. *be ~* hécciɗde; léppude.

whack [wak] *v.* fiide.

wharf [wɔrf] *n.* tufnde *(nde).*

what [wat] *pron.* huunde; hol. *What is it* Ko woni?

whatever [watevə] *adv.* kala.

wheat [wiyt] *n.* lorso *(ko).*

wheedle [wiydəl] *v.* jarribaade.

wheel [wiyl] *n.* njamndi pono.

wheeze [wiyz] *v.* lehde; siikde.

when [wen] *conj.* mande; nde. *When did you arrive* Mande ngarɗaa?

whenever [wenevə] *conj.* kala nde; mudda kala.

where [wer] *pron.* hol to; to.

wherever [werevə] *adv.* kala ɗo.

whet [wet] *v.* welnude; sééɓnude.

which [wič] *pron.* hol.

while [wayl] *n.* mudda *(o).* *once in a ~* sahaa sahaa kala.

whine [wayn] *v.* ŋuylude

hinny [wayni] v. hijde.

hip [wip] n. karwaas (o); lóócól (ngól).

hip [wip] v. fiide.

hirl [wərl] v. yiilaade.

hirlwind [wərlwind] n. dulééndu (ndu).

hirry [wəri] v. heñaade; yaawnaade.

hisk [wisk] v. fittude.

hisper [wispə] v. ñuumbaade; ñumptaade.

hisperer [wispərə] n. ñuumbotoodo (o).

histle [wisəl] n. wuudaango (ngo).

histle [wisəl] v. wuudde

histler [wislə] n. guudoowo (o).

hite [wayt] adj. daneejo; danejum; ko ranwi. ~ ants móóYi (di). ~ ant móóYu (ngu). be ~ ranwude; éérdude. very ~ tal. ~ person tuubaako (o).

hiten [waytən] v. ranwinde.

hitener [waytnə] n. danwinoowo (o).

hitewash [waytwɔš] n. laso (o).

hittle [witəl] v. sehde; séttude.

ho [huw] pron. neddo; hol. Who is it Holi aan?

hoever [huwevə] pron. kala.

hole [howl] adj. fóf. the ~ month lewru huurndu.

hom [hum] pron. hol.

homever [humevə] pron. kala.

hooping-cough [huwpiŋkʌf] n. teko (ngo).

hore [howr] n. garbotoodo (o).

hy [way] pron. ko wadi; hol ko tagi.

ick [wik] n. mees (o).

icked [wikid] adj. ñangudo.

ickedness [wikidnes] n. ñangere (nde).

ide [wayd] adj. ko yaaji; jaajdum. be ~ yaajde.

iden [waydən] v. yaajnude.

idow [widəw] n. késniido; mo jom galle mum maayi.

idowhood [widəwhud] n. edda (o).

idth [widθ] n. njaajééndi (ndi); tékkééndi (ndi).

ield [wiyld] v. huurde.

ife [wayf] n. jom suudu; debbo desaado. first ~ jeewo (o). second ~ lemmbél (o). third ~ lembeYél (ngél).

iggle [wigəl] v. dillinde.

wild [wayld] adj. ko faati e ladde. a ~ animal jawdi ladde.

wilderness [wildənes] n. ladde (nde); ladde tuulaa heelaa.

wile [wayl] n. fuunti (o).

wile [wayl] v. fuuntude.

willful [wilfəl] adj. gamdiido.

win [win] v. foolde. ~ a race dadde. ~ all opponent's possessions hoosde.

wind [wind] n. héndu (ndu). get ~ of nande; tinde.

wind [wind] v. yiilde. ~ into balls horwaade.

winding [wayndiŋ] adj. ko fortaaki.

window [windəw] n. falanteere (nde); henorde (nde).

wine [wayn] n. sangara (o).

wing [wiŋ] n. wibjo (ngo)

wink [wiŋk] n. majaango yitere. I did not sleep a wink Mi rendinaani yitere.

wink [wiŋk] v. majde.

winner [winə] n. pooldo (o); daddo (o). He is the winner Ko kanko fooli.

winning [winiŋ] n. póólgól (ngól).

winnow [winəw] n. Yaarngo (ngo); ñorgo (ngo).

winnow [winəw] v. weddaade; wesde; Yaaraade.

winter [wintə] n. dabbunde (nde). spend ~ dabbude.

wipe [wayp] v. fómpude. ~ oneself off momtaade. ~ off mómtude.

wiper [waypə] n. momtoowo (o).

wire [wayə] n. bóggól njamndi.

wire [wayə] v. néldude.

wisdom [wizdəm] n. gandal (ngal); peewal (ngal).

wise [wayz] adj. gando; peewdo.

wish [wiš] v. yidde; yidande. make a ~ wasiyaade.

wish [wiš] n. sago (o). have one's ~ hebde sago mum.

witch [wič] n. sukuña (o); ñamneejo (o).

witchcraft [wičkraft] n. dabare (de); dabotoodo (o).

withdraw [wiθdrɔ] v. sortaade; yaltude e. ~ one's word wultaade.

withdrawal [wiθdrɔl] n. jaltugól (ngól); jaltingól (ngól).

withdrawn [wiθdrɔn] *adj.* nuggaro.

withhold [wiθhold] *v.* waasde waɗɗe.

within [wiðin] *adv.* nder.

withstand [wiθstand] *v.* dartaade.

witness [witnes] *n.* seede *(o)*.

witness [witnes] *v.* seedaade.

wizard [wizəd] *n.* jinneyel *(ngél);* ñéngotooɗo *(o)*.

wobble [wobəl] *v.* yahrude bange.

woe [wɔ] *n.* moobaare *(nde);* bonande *(nde)*.

Wolof [wolof] jolfo *(o)*. ~ *language* jolfe *(ɗe)*.

woman [wumən] *n.* debbo *(o)*. *big* ~ dewal *(ngal)*. *little* ~ déwél *(ngél)*. ~ *with many pregnancies before marriage* réédunte *(o)*.

womanize [wumənayz] *v.* yomde.

womanly [wumənli] *adj.* ko nandi e/maale debbo.

womb [wum] *n.* éndu *(ndu)*.

women [wumen] *n.* rewɓe

wonder [wʌndə] *v.* miijaade.

wonder [wʌndə] *n.* kaawis *(o)*.

wonderful [wʌndəfəl] *adj.* moolanaande.

woo [wu] *v.* gerde; ɗabɓude.

wood [wud] *n.* leggal *(ngal);* leɗɗe *(ɗe)*. *piece of* ~ elo *(ngo);* tunnde *(nde)*. *trough of* ~ wahre *(nde)*.

woodcutter [wudkʌtə] *n.* peYYoowo *(o);* coppoowo *(o)*.

woodpecker [wudpekə] *n.* sam féYYóóru *(ndu)*.

woodwork [wudwərk] *n.* lawankaagal *(ngal)*. *caste specializing in* ~ labbo *(o);* gumbalaa.

woody [wudi] *adj.* cukkuɗo; ko sukki leɗɗe.

wool [wuwl] *n.* wiro *(ko);* leen *(o)*.

woolen [wulən] *adj.* kó fééwniraa wiro/leen; ko faati e wiro/leen.

word [wərd] *n.* helmere *(nde)*. *keep one's* ~ heddaade e haala mum.

word [wərd] *v.* lélnude kóngól.

wordly [wərdli] *adj.* ko faati e aduna.

work [wərk] *n.* gollal *(ngal)* liggeey *(o)*.

work [wərk] *v.* gollaade; liggaade.

worker [wərkə] *n.* liggotooɗo *(o);* gollotooɗo *(o)*.

world [wərld] *n.* aduna *(o);* windere *(nde)*.

worm [wərm] *n.* ngilngu *(ngu)*. *type of* ~ buɗɗu *(ngu);* buruuti *(ɗi);* mburuutu *(ngu)*.

worn-out [wɔnawt] *adj.* 1) kó wónti limsere 2) tampuɗo.

worried [wɔrid] *adj.* paayɗo *(o)*.

worry [wɔri] *v.* faayde. *Do not worry* Hol to faay.

worry [wɔri] *n.* faayoore *(nde)*.

worse [wərs] *adj.* ko ɓuri bonde.

worship [wɔšip] *v.* juulde; rewde Alla.

worst [wərst] *adj.* ko ɓuri/ɓurɗo fóf bonde.

worth [wɔθ] *n.* nafoore *(nde)*. *be* ~ jarde.

worthless [wɔθles] *adj.* ko alaa nafoore; ko nafataa; mo nafataa. *He is worthless* O alaa nafoore.

worthy [wɔði] *adj.* ko nafata.

wound [wund] *n.* ñawande; gaañande; yiwande; taalnande; barmande; fiire.

wound [wund] *v.* gaañde; taalnude.

wounded [wundid] *adj.* gaaniiɗo. *be* ~ barmude.

woven [wuvən] *adj.* cañaɗum; ko sañaa. ~ *reeds* mbiru *(ngu)*.

wrangle [raŋgəl] *v.* dukde.

wrangler [raŋglə] *n.* dukoowo *(o)*.

wrap [rap] *v.* soomde. ~ *oneself in* soomaade.

wrapper [rapə] *n.* coomoowo *(o)*.

wrath [raθ] *n.* mettere *(nde);* mette *(ɗe)*.

wreck [rek] *v.* yiwde.

wrestle [resəl] *v.* sippirde. ~ *someone down* liɓde.

wrestler [reslə] *n.* mbir *(o)*.

wrestling [resliŋ] *n.* sippiro *(ngo)*.

wretch [reč] *n.* cuniiɗo; mettaaɗo.

wriggle [rigəl] *v.* tallaade; ñongaade.

wright [rayt] *n.* gollotooɗo *(o)*.

wring [riŋ] *v.* hamde.

wrinkle [riŋkəl] *n.* ñórɓólól *(ngól)*.

wrist [rist] *n.* jokkorde *(nde)*.

write [rayt] *v.* windude.

writer [raytə] *n.* bindoowo *(o)*.

writhe [rayθ] *v.* haaYde.

wrong [roŋ] *n.* fenaande *(nde);* ko moYYaani. *be* ~ fende; waasde haalde goonga.

X

xebec [zebek] *n.* laana *(ka)*

xenophobe[zenəfowb] *n.*   neɗɗo kulɗo tumarankaagal

xenophobia   [zenəfowbya]   *n.*ngañgu tumarankaagal

xylography [zaylogrəfi] *n.* ñenkugol *(ngól)*

xylophone [zayləfown] *n.* balañji *(ɗi)*

Y

yacht [yat] *n.* laana *(ka)*.

yam [yam] *n.* pulóók *(o)*.

yammer [yamə] *v.* wullitaade

yank [yaŋk] *v.* fooɗde.

yap [yap] *v.* wofde.

yard [yɑd] *n.* dingiral *(ngal)*; diraa *(o)*. *How many yards is it* No diraaji ɗi poti?

yare [yar] *adj.* jaawɗo; ko yaawi.

yarn [yɑn] *n.* tindól *(ngól)*.

yatter [yatə] *v.* leɓde.

yaw [yɔ] *v.* selde.

yawn [yɔn] *v.* ŋaablude; yaalaade.

yawning [yɔniŋ] *n.* ŋaablere *(nde)*; ŋaablugól *(ngól)*.

yea [ye] *adv.* ééy.

yeah [yeya] *adv.* ééy.

year [yər] *n.* hitaande (nde). *last* ~ rawane. *this* ~ hikka *(o)* *three ~s ago* rawtitaane. *the* ~ *before last* rawane ndeya; rawtane.

yearling [yərliŋ] *n.* jom hitaande wootere.

yearly [yərli] *adj.* hitaande kala.

yearn [yərn] *v.* yiɗde.

yegg [yeg] *n.* gujjo *(o)*.

yell [yel] *v.* furaade; luukde. ~ *in a dispute* dukde.

yellow [yeləw] *adj.* oolo; ko oolɗi. *be* ~ óólɗude. *very* ~ buy.

yelp [yelp] *v.* wofde.

yerk [yərk] *v.* fiide.

yes [yes] *adv.* eey; éyyó.

yesterday [yestədi] *n.* hanki *(o)*.

yet [yet] *adv.* jóóni; sahaa jóóni o. *I have not seen him yet* Mi suwaa yiide mo tawo.

yield [yiyld] *v.* ɗaccude; ɗaccande; jibinde.

yip [yip] *v.* hawsude.

yirr [yər] *v.* ŋuurde.

yod [yod] *n.* alkulal *(ngal)*.

yogurt [yogət] *n.* yawuur *(o)*.

yoke [yowk] *n.* leggal déndinoowal gay/nay démóóji.

yolk [yɔk] *n.* óóldi ɓoccoonde.

you [yu] *pron.* a; aan; on. *If I were you I would go home* Sinno ko miin wonno maa mi hootanno.

young [yʌŋ] *adj.* sukaajo; suka *(o)*; surga *(o)*. *He is young* Ko o suka.

younger [yʌŋə] *adj.* keccaaɗo. ~ *sibling* miñiraaɗo *(o)*.

youngster [yʌŋstə] *n.* suka *(o)*.

your [yuwr] *det.* maa; maaɗa; mooɗon; mon.

yours [yuwz] *pron.* ko maa.

yourself [yuwsəlf] *pron.* aan hoore maa.

youth [yuwθ] *n.* kambaane; cukaagu.

youthful [yuwθfəl] *adj.* ko faati e cukaagu.

Z

zag [zag] n. celgol (ngól).

zag [zag] v. selde.

zap [zap] v. warde; bonnude.

zeal [ziyl] n. coftal. (ngal); caasgol (ngól)

zealous [ziyləs] adj. caasɗo; coftuɗo.

zebu [ziybu] n. nagge. (nge); holsere (nde).

zed [zed] n. alkulal (ngal).

zee [ziy] n. alkulal (ngal).

zephyr [zifər] n. kenal (kal).

zero [ziyrow] n. hay huunde; dara; meere.

zig [zig] n. celgol (ngól).

zig [zig] v. selde.

zigzag [zigzag] v. selde.

zing [ziŋ] n. njennoor (o).

zing [ziŋ] v. yennude.

zip [zip] n. hay huunde; dara.

zip [zip] v. mubbude.

zipper [zipə] n. koroos (o).

zone [zown] n. nokku (o).

zone [zown] v. howde.

zoo [zuw] n. nokku muumanton Alla.

zoology [zuwləji] n. jangde muumanton Alla.

zoom [zuwm] v. heñaade.

REFERENCES

Anderson, S.R. (1976). "On the Description of Consonant Gradation in Fula," *Studies in African Linguistics* VII, 1 pp. 93-136.

Ba Oumar(1968). *Glossaire des Mots Mandingues passes en Pulaar*.

------- (1972). *Glossaire des Mots Etrangers passes en Pulaar*.

------- (1980). *La terminologie geographique du Poular*, C.L.A.D., I.F.A.N., Dakar.

Gaden, Henri (1967). "Le Poular—Dialecte Peul du Fouta Senegalais," *Lexique Poular-Francais*,Tome second. Gregg Press Limited, England.

------- (1969). *Dictionnaire Peul-Français*. Fascicule I. Catalogues Institut Fondamental d'Afrique Noire, Dakar.

------- (1972). *Dictionnaire Peul-Français*. Fascicule II. Catalogues Institut Fondamental d'Afrique Noire, Dakar.

Gamble, David, P., and Mary Umah Baldeh (1981). *Gambian Fula-English Dictionary*, San Francisco, Gambian Studies no 12.

Ka, Fari Silate (1991). "Elements de Dialectologie Peule: Variations dialectales et problemes de standardization, In Isa Alkali Abba," Ibrahim Mukoshi and Gidaɗo Tahir (eds.) *Studies in Fulfulde Language, Literature and Culture*, Triumph Publishing Company Ltd., Nigeria.

Landau, Sidney I. (1993). *Dictionaries—The Art and Craft of Lexicography*. Cambridge University Press.

Niang, Mamadou (1995b). "Syllable 'Sonority' Hierarchy and Pulaar Stress—A Metrical Approach." *Kansas Working Papers in Linguistics*, V. 20.

Osborn, W. Donald, David Dwyer and Joseph I. Donoho, Jr. (1993). *A Fulfulde (Maasina)-English-French Lexicon*. Michigan State University Press, East Lansing

Sylla, Yero (1982). *Grammaire Moderne du Pulaar*. Les Nouvelles Editions Africaines, Dakar.

Other African languages from Hippocrene. . .

AMHARIC-ENGLISH/ENGLISH-AMHARIC DICTIONARY
ISBN: 0-7818-0115-X $40.00hc

FULANI-ENGLISH PRACTICAL DICTIONARY
ISBN: 0-7818-0404-3 $14.95pb

HAUSA-ENGLISH/ENGLISH-HAUSA PRACTICAL DICTIONARY
ISBN: 0-7818-0426-4 $16.95pb

LINGALA-ENGLISH/ENGLISH-LINGALA DICTIONARY AND PHRASEBOOK
ISBN: 0-7818-0456-6 $11.95pb

UNDERSTANDING EVERYDAY SESOTHO
ISBN: 0-7818-0305-5 $16.95pb

POPULAR NORTHERN SOTHO DICTIONARY: SOTHO-ENGLISH/ENGLISH-SOTHO
ISBN: 0-7818-0392-6 $14.95pb

SWAHILI PHRASEBOOK
ISBN: 0-87052-970-6 $8.95pb

BEGINNER'S SWAHILI
ISBN: 0-7818-0335-7 $9.95pb
2 audio cassettes: ISBN:0-7818-0336-5 $12.95

TWI BASIC COURSE
ISBN: 0-7818-0394-2 $16.95pb

VENDA DICTIONARY: VENDA-ENGLISH
ISBN: 0-6270-1625-1 $39.95hc

YORUBA-ENGLISH/ENGLISH-YORUBA CONCISE DICTIONARY
ISBN: 0-7818-0263-6 $14.95pb

ENGLISH-ZULU/ZULU-ENGLISH DICTIONARY
ISBN: 0-7818-0255-5 $29.50pb

Books of related interest. . .

PSYCHOLOGY OF BLACK LANGUAGE
ISBN: 0-7818-0086-2 $9.95pb

**CARIBBEAN CREOLE-ENGLISH/
ENGLISH-CARIBBEAN CREOLE CONCISE DICTIONARY**
ISBN: 0-7818-0455-8 $11.95pb

**HAITIAN CREOLE-ENGLISH/
ENGLISH-HAITIAN CREOLE CONCISE DICTIONARY**
ISBN: 0-7818-0275-X $11.95pb

**HAITIAN CREOLE-ENGLISH/
ENGLISH-HAITIAN CREOLE COMPACT DICTIONARY**
ISBN: 0-7818-0538-4 $8.95pb

TREASURY OF AFRICAN LOVE POEMS AND PROVERBS
ISBN: 0-7818-0483-3 $11.95hc

BEST OF REGIONAL AFRICAN COOKING
ISBN: 0-7818-0599-6 $11.95pb

All prices subject to change. TO PURCHASE HIPPOCRENE BOOKS contact your local bookstore, call (718) 454-2366, or write to: HIPPOCRENE BOOKS, 171 Madison Avenue, New York, NY 10016. Please enclose check or money order, adding $5.00 shipping (UPS) for the first book and $.50 for each additional book.